erera
hachi

Trade

Faustino Taderera
Zebert Mahachi

The Law of International Trade

Law, Utmost Good Faith, Penalties

LAP LAMBERT Academic Publishing

Impressum/Imprint (nur für Deutschland/ only for Germany)
Bibliografische Information der Deutschen Nationalbibliothek: Die Deutsche Nationalbibliothek
verzeichnet diese Publikation in der Deutschen Nationalbibliografie; detaillierte bibliografische
Daten sind im Internet über http://dnb.d-nb.de abrufbar.
 Alle in diesem Buch genannten Marken und Produktnamen unterliegen warenzeichen-, marken-
oder patentrechtlichem Schutz bzw. sind Warenzeichen oder eingetragene Warenzeichen der
jeweiligen Inhaber. Die Wiedergabe von Marken, Produktnamen, Gebrauchsnamen,
Handelsnamen, Warenbezeichnungen u.s.w. in diesem Werk berechtigt auch ohne besondere
Kennzeichnung nicht zu der Annahme, dass solche Namen im Sinne der Warenzeichen- und
Markenschutzgesetzgebung als frei zu betrachten wären und daher von jedermann benutzt
werden dürften.

Coverbild: www.ingimage.com

Verlag: LAP LAMBERT Academic Publishing AG & Co. KG
Dudweiler Landstr. 99, 66123 Saarbrücken, Deutschland
Telefon +49 681 3720-310, Telefax +49 681 3720-3109
Email: info@lap-publishing.com

Herstellung in Deutschland:
Schaltungsdienst Lange o.H.G., Berlin
Books on Demand GmbH, Norderstedt
Reha GmbH, Saarbrücken
Amazon Distribution GmbH, Leipzig
ISBN: 978-3-8383-7892-3

Imprint (only for USA, GB)
Bibliographic information published by the Deutsche Nationalbibliothek: The Deutsche
Nationalbibliothek lists this publication in the Deutsche Nationalbibliografie; detailed
bibliographic data are available in the Internet at http://dnb.d-nb.de.
 Any brand names and product names mentioned in this book are subject to trademark, brand
or patent protection and are trademarks or registered trademarks of their respective holders.
The use of brand names, product names, common names, trade names, product descriptions
etc. even without a particular marking in this works is in no way to be construed to mean that
such names may be regarded as unrestricted in respect of trademark and brand protection
legislation and could thus be used by anyone.

Cover image: www.ingimage.com

Publisher: LAP LAMBERT Academic Publishing AG & Co. KG
Dudweiler Landstr. 99, 66123 Saarbrücken, Germany
Phone +49 681 3720-310, Fax +49 681 3720-3109
Email: info@lap-publishing.com

Printed in the U.S.A.
Printed in the U.K. by (see last page)
ISBN: 978-3-8383-7892-3

TABLE OF CONTENTS

ACKNOWLEDGEMENTS

This book is dedicated to my wife, Rosemary, for her love and support and my son Nigel, and my daughters, Priscilla, Charlotte, Michel and Charmaine for the happiness and joy that they bring to our lives.

FOREWORD

Faustino Taderera, the celebrity, is the finest International Business & Supply Chain brains ever produced by Zimbabwe and the African continent and is **nicknamed, "The Tom Peters of Zimbabwe, Africa and the Middle East."** His students call him, **"The Rumbler, the Caterpillar and the Rollercoaster."** This book, **"The Law of International Trade,"** his 38th book, is co-authored with Mr Zebert Mahachi, another distinguished Zimbabwean academic and ex-Customs Officer. This book is the Rolls Royce of international business, supply chain, the shipping, forwarding and customs clearing profession. It is the set book at undergraduate and postgraduate level for specialized international business, international marketing, supply chain, shipping, exports and logistics degrees. Professor Faustino Taderera always says **"Golden fish have no hiding place. I am the Socrates, Aristotle, Plato, Solomon and Joseph of my time."** He is a much sought after global academic and professional **BRAND**.

ABOUT THE AUTHORS

FAUSTINO TADERERA

Pofessor Faustino Taderera has been a manager in production, operations, imports, purchasing, shipping, exports and marketing in manufacturing and the service sector for 22 years. He left the private sector to join academia in as Programme Coordinator at Chinhoyi University of Technology (CUT) in Zimbabwe and ultimately Chairman of the Department of International Marketing in July 2003 and has been a university lecturer since then. He pioneered breakthrough unique degrees in International Marketing; International Purchasing, Logistics & Transport; Retailing; Entrepreneurship and related areas and a unique Masters of Science degree in Strategic Management. Faustino left CUT in 2008 to join the Ministry of Higher Education in Oman in the Middle East as a distinguished academic. He read for an MBA at Buckinghamshire Chilterns Univeristy College, UK and a PhD in International Business at the government run Asia E-University in Malaysia. Faustino is called Professor FT by friends and acquaintances.

ZEBERT MAHACHI

Zebert Mahachi is a distinguished Zimbabwean academic and former ZIMRA/Customs Officer with a wealth of experience in shipping, forwarding and customs clearing matters spanning some ten years followed by an illustrious career in academia. He has consulted for the Zimbabwe Revenue Authority (ZIMRA – the Zimbabwean customs authority) as module writer on shipping matters as well as other leading NGOs in Zimbabwe. He holds an MBA degree from the Zimbabwean Open University and is a keen researcher in shipping matters and is an authority in this area in Zimbabwe.The two authors once worked together at Chinhoyi University of Technology in Zimbabwe where they both contributed immensely to the new unique and highly popular degrees in International Purchasing, Logistics & Transport and International Marketing.

3

CHAPTER 1

SHIPPING/EXPORT DOCUMENTATION PRACTICE

1.   Introduction

The practice of exporting calls for the comprehension of various documents involved in the processing of the export consignment. A deep understanding of export documentation and shipping gives an exporter a competitive advantage over its competitors and also reduces the risk or uncertainty in the export business.

Exports are goods or services sold beyond political boundaries that is to other countries. A document is a transcript or official piece of paper with written information on them. Thus generally, export documentation is the process whereby documents which provide a record or important information about goods or services which are to be sold overseas are compiled, completed and put into their most usable form and cleared through customs. The customs stamp is the government authority to export goods. Exports become genuine export consignments at the point of getting customs authority to export – at any other time it will be a proposal or request to export. On imports the customs stamp is government authority to access goods for consumption.

Export documents can be grouped into transport documents, commercial documents and administrative documents. Transport documents provide information on the mode and terms under which goods will be transported. Commercial documents outline the cost of goods, incoterms and also the terms of payment thus they enable a smooth flow of funds while administrative documents enable the management and administration of goods. However, the number of documents used per consignment may differ from country to country and from types of goods being sold.

Advantages of Export Documentation

- Good export documentation provides specific and complete descriptions of the goods thereby enabling the assessing of those goods for import duty.
- Export documents serve as proof of the shipment of goods or services thus they may be used to resolve future conflicts which may arise between the exporter and the importer.
- When goods are being exported, they pass through the hands of a number of agents. In this case, export documentation helps to pass ownership and responsibility of good thus enabling claims to be made.
- Documentation also helps ascertain that payment will be made as agreed and when required by ensuring the financial worthiness of the company the exporter is doing business with.
- Export documentation is also done to comply with a country's trade restrictions and regulations.
- Export documentation is also done and used to compute national trade statistics which are in turn used for national economic and strategic planning.

Major Export Documents

In the field of exporting there are various documents which are prepared either by the importer and under the three categories which are transport, commercial and administrative documents, these may include same of the following:

Transport Documents
Bill of lading
Air waybill
Consignment note

Commercial Documents
Commercial invoice
Letters of credit
Bill of exchange

Administrative Documents
Export licence
Customs declaration
Packing list
Pre-shipment inspection certificate
Certificate of origin
Insurance certificate
Dock receipts and warehouse receipts
Certificate of health.

Principles of the major export documentation

Transport Documents

Bill of lading

A bill of lading is a receipt for goods shipped on board a vessel, signed by the person (or agent) who contracts to carry them, and stating the conditions in which the goods were delivered to the ship. It is not an archival contract which is inferred from the action of the supplier or ship-owner in delivering or receiving the cargo but forms excellent evidence of the terms of the contract.

A bill of lading is a document of title to the goods which are the subject of the contract between the importer and the exporter. (Branch A, 1985) Generally, the bill of lading is governed by the bill of exchange act 1855 and the carriage of goods by sea Act 1924 which was renewed in 1971.

Principles that Guide the Bill of Lading

The name of shipper must be stated. There is need for a full description of the goods inclusive of marks, numbers, weights of consignment as well as the volume. The value of the consignment must be shown including the name of the beneficiary. The document must indicate the port of loading and the port of discharge, and the destination and name of shipper. Full contact details and addresses of the shipper should also be included. It must also state cargo destination. Three copies should be made and the original copy should be kept under lock and key. The other documents are routed to the exporter's bank who in turn send them to the importer's bank in two separate couriers. The purpose of sending documents in two separate couriers is that should one set get lost there will still be a set of documents to be used to clear goods through customs and the importer will not be caught in a dilemma but is still covered and secured. A bill of lading can be a clean bill of lading if goods and packages are as declared on the bill of lading or a dirty bill of lading if consignment is short landed or damaged. It is a clean bill of lading when there is no problem with the consignment and a dirty one when there are problems with the consignment. Every bill of lading must be signed in order for it to be valid. A consignment must be protested on the bill of lading if there is a problem or discrepancies on the consignment, e.g. short delivery, damage, etc.

Air Waybill

It is the airfreight equivalent to the bill of lading but with an important difference. It is not a document of title and its possession does not establish ownership of the goods. Because of the speed of air-freight, it will usually be impossible to trace a consignment and clear the goods through customs without the air waybill, at least the unique reference number of the air waybill covering the consignment concerned.

Principles that Govern the Air Waybill

- Twelve (12) copies should be completed and a set of original documents must accompany every airway consignment.
- One set of original documents must be sent by courier to the importer and one set will be given to the forwarder.
- The airway bill must state the air waybill number and the place of departure and destination.
- It should also outline the flight number and the flight itinerary.
- An air waybill should also contain full description of the goods, packages and package sizes, full details of consignee as well as full contact details.
- The quantity of each package, the volume of each package and total weight should also be stated.
- If the consignment is dangerous, this must be declared and the relevant statutes must be complied with.
- The airway bill must be signed and dated.

Consignment Note

- This document forms the contract between the shipper and the carrier for the carriage of specific goods from one point to another.
- The consignment note is usually in a standard format by the carrier of the goods for completion by the exporter.
- It covers all the modes of transport that is sea, road, air and rail.

Principles Governing the Consignment Note

The name of the company issuing the consignment note should be shown.
The consignee's address should be shown in the same form and detail as shown on the invoice.
The name of the customer's handling agent and full contact details.
The port of exit, place of loading of the vessel, where the carrier takes over responsibility and the port of discharge, where the goods will be unloaded should be stated.
Port of transshipment and final destination of goods should be entered.
If the exporter is using a forwarding agent, the name and address should be stated.
The marks, numbers and seal number on containers should be made available.
A full description of the consignment inclusive of the gross weight, total volume and packaging should be shown.
A list of all the documents and the quantity of each that will be handed to the carrier.
The number of bills of lading required should also be stated specifying the number and type required by the shipper or exporter and those which will accompany the goods.
The incoterms agreed upon should be stated so as to show responsibility of payment accruing to either the exporter or the importer.
The document should be signed by authorized shipping officials.

Commercial Documents

Commercial Invoice

- The commercial invoice is compiled by the seller and it gives details of the goods which form the basis of the transaction.
- It is a billing document which shows the full value of the contract and the currency of the transaction.
- The commercial invoice is completed in accordance with the number of prescribed copies.
- The price agreed between the parties and the total value, terms and currency of the transaction are also stated within the commercial invoice.
- The major functions of the commercial invoice include inspections of consignment at the point of export and import, checking by the buyer on receipt of goods and payment by the buyer for the goods.

The Principles that Govern the Commercial Invoice

- The location, physical address of the exporter must be provided. In the extent that the address to which the invoice is to be sent then the invoice should show the two addresses separately.
- Full contact details of the exporter must be given
- Statutory information should also be shown, for instance the exporter's value added tax number and any other request to be shown or included within the invoice.
- Reference numbers such as the order number and indent number which pertain to the order should be shown in full.
- The description of goods and actual quantity should also be included which will enable them to be easily identified.
- An outline of the currency being used and price must be made available in addition to the country of origin.
- The incoterms agreed upon should be shown which will enable comprehension of liability which accrue to either the importer or the exporter.
- Each invoice should be certified and signed by the exporter so as to show authenticity.

Letter of Credit

A letter of credit is a bank guarantee to an exporter or any other guaranteeing payment on submission of certain complementary documents. A letter of credit can be revocable or irrevocable. An irrevocable letter of credit cannot be cancelled except with the consent of both parties and a revocable letter of credit is one which can be cancelled by one party without consulting the other. If the customer agrees to pay the amount required using a letter of credit, his/her bank will issue a letter of credit in the exporter's favour. Upon satisfaction of the exporter's bank that the exporter has met conditions within the letter of credit, it will release payment on the terms agreed and forward the shipping documents to the customer to allow him or her to obtain the goods by clearing them through customs.

Principles governing the letter of credit

- A letter of credit must be negotiated within 21 days from date of shipment.
- If the letter of credit is not presented within the period allowed with the required documents, it will not be honoured.
- If the beneficiaries name is incorrectly stated the letter of credit must be dishonoured.
- The amount covered by the letter of credit should agree with the amount stated in the rest of the documents for it to be honoured.
- Information about the shipment which shows whether partial or part-shipment are allowed, should also be included in the letter of credit.
- If the letter of credit shows that transshipment is not allowed and it takes place, at best delays and extra costs will be incurred, or there may be outright dishonour of the letter of credit.

- The terms of shipment should also be stated in the letter of credit and should be complied with by both the exporter and the importer.
- Other documents called for and the exact format in which they are to be written should be precisely stated in the letter of credit.
- If these documents are not available, there may be delays and extra costs or no payment.
- Documents called should be presented within the specified time in order to validate the letter of credit.
- A letter of credit should be tested and proved by a reputable bank usually a first class bank (a bank in mostly New York or London or the developed world).

Bill of Exchange

- A bill of exchange is an unconditional order, in writing, addressed by one person to another, signed by the person giving it, requiring the person to whom it is addressed to pay on demand or at a fixed or determinable future time, a certain sum of money to the order of a specified person, (Allen Branch, 1985).
- A bill of exchange can be used by an exporter to demand payment although it does not guarantee payment.
- It is valid within 180 days from the date of issue, in the event that there is need for an extension of the period, it will need approval from the authorities of the seller's bank.
- Because it is not a guarantee, the bill of exchange is usually used in conjunction with the letter of credit, which provides a guarantee that the bill of exchange will be honoured on presentation.

The Principle that Govern and Guide the Bill of Exchange

- The amount to be paid under the bill should be stated in figures.
- The place and date of issue of the bill, which is normally the location of the exporter and date of the invoice.
- The name of the exporter's bank which is normally the advising bank should be stated and the amount to be paid under the bill in words which should tally to that stated in figures.
- A generally commercial description of the goods should be included.
- Details of the exporter issuing the bill should also be shown.
- An outline of the exporter's bank to accept the bill of exchange on presentation.
- When making out the bill of exchange, ensure that the details agree with the details in the other documents on the shipment and particularly those of the documents called for by the letter of credit.

Administrative documents

1.Export Licence

This is a document issued by the authorities of a country granting permission to the exporter to export certain types of goods. An export licence is a must for exporters who intend to export certain goods or services, which are in short supply or goods of a security nature such as arms and ammunition.

Principles governing the export licences

- The details of the export licence holder including the name and the address must be stated.
- The export licence should state the product or service the exporter is permitted to export by the licence and the period during which the licence will operate.
- The date of issue of the licence and details of the licence issuer must also be included.
- To show authenticity of the licence, it should be signed and dated by the issuer and the exporter.

2. Customs Declaration

A customs declaration is a document used for the clearance of goods through customs. It is collected at the point of exit of goods from the country. A customs declaration can be used by the customs office to compile trade statistics.

Principles that govern the customs declaration

- Contact details of both the exporter and the importer must be shown including their names and addresses.
- The customs declaration note should also include the type of goods to be exported described as per the customs tariff.
- The quantity and value of goods must be stated.
- Transport details must be included including the mode of transport.
- A customs declaration should be signed by the authorities.

3. Packing List

The packing list is a document that is closely related to the invoice and in some instances might be included within the commercial invoice. The packing list provides a fully detailed account on goods packing, number of containers, weights and measurements of each container in the consignment. The packing list aids the customs authorities in carrying out their inspection and customers in identifying the contents of the shipment.

Principles of the Packing List

- There is need for a full and accurate description of the consignment which should include the following variables:-
- The number of cartons per type of goods and the numbers assigned to the cartons containing them.

- The content, net weight and gross weight of each carton.
- Outside measurements of each carton and the total number of packages.
- How cartons are addressed and the numbers used.
- The total gross weight of the consignment as shipped.

Pre-shipment Inspection Certificate

A pre-shipment inspection certificate is a document required by some purchasers and countries in order to attest to the specification of the goods shipped. This is usually performed by a third party and often obtained from independent testing organizations.

Principles that govern Pre-shipment Inspection Certificate

- It should outline the quantity, specification and value of goods to be shipped.
- The document should give a commercial description of the goods or consignment.
- The name of the inspector and the contract number should also be indicated.
- The location where the inspection was carried out should be stated and date of inspection.
- Signature of inspection authorities should be included.

Certificate of Origin

The certificate of origin is a document certifying the country in which the product was manufactured, and in certain cases may include such information as the local material and labour contents of the product. The certificate of origin is an alternative to the declaration or the certification and or legislated equivalent of the commercial invoice.

Principles that guide the certificate of origin

- The consignor and the consignee must be identical to those shown in the invoice.
- The country from which the goods are manufactured should be shown.
- The certificate of origin must agree with other documents covering the consignment
- The quantity of goods being shipped must be shown in the units called for in the tariff of the importing country.
- The tariff reference of the importing country must be quoted correctly.
- Marks, numbers, number and type of packages must all agree with the information shown on the packing list.
- It is important that the certificate of origin be signed and worded exactly as specified in the letter of credit.

Insurance Certificate

An insurance certificate is used to assure the consignee that insurance will cover the loss of or damage to the cargo during transit. These can be obtained from your freight forwarder. It is vital for the exporters to ensure that goods or the consignment has been insured before shipment.

Principles governing the insurance certificate

- When the exporter insures the goods the date of the certificate will normally be the date the goods leave the factory.
- Goods should be commercially described which will enable the insurance certificate to be tied up with the invoice it covers.
- The risk covered should be described.
- In the case of marine insurance, it is normal to provide cover for 110% - 120% of the invoice value.
- The insurance certificate must contain details of the place where claims are payable together with the name of the agent to whom claims may be directed.
- Any particular conditions that may be applied by the insurance company to the particular cargo or voyage should be stated.
- The exporter when insuring his goods must achieve utmost good faith.
- The insurance company avails the name of the assessor or inspector that should be shown in the insurance certificate.
- The exporter is authorized by the insurers to sign the certificate on their behalf thus it should be signed and dated.

Dock Receipts and Warehouse Receipts

Are used to transfer accountability when the export item is moved by the domestic carrier to the export of embarkation and left with the shipping line for export.
These documents are issued by port authorities to confirm receipt of cargo on the quay or warehouse pending shipment, (Business@ulst.ac.uk:2004).

Principles Governing Dock and Warehouse Receipts

- The receipt must state the name of the port of embarkment including full location details and address.
- The date of receipt of the consignment must be stated.
- The details of the recipients of the consignment including their names and signatures must be shown.

Certificate of Health

This document is mostly used when agricultural or animal products are being exported. The certificate is issued and signed by the health authority in the supplier's country.

Principles that Guide the Certificate of Health

- Name and full details of inspector must be stated.

- The place where inspection was conducted and the type of consignment that was being tested.
- Types of tests conducted on the consignment should be stated.
- Signatures of the inspectors with full remarks on the tests that have been conducted.

General Principles of Export Documentation

- Full details of the exporter and the importer must be given, which in most cases include names, addresses and contact details.
- Documents must also be presented in the agreed format, which should be an internationally recognized format.
- The description of goods should be identical in all the documents to avoid costly delays due to discrepancies.
- The terms of payment should be clearly stated in all the documents and the currency to be used.
- The port of discharge, port of delivery and the port of trans-shipments should be clearly stated in all the documents.

Other critical export/commercial documents

The following are other very important shipping/commercial documents;-

The Shipping Guarantee (SG)

This is a bank guarantee that an importer applies for at his bankers if goods arrive at the port of discharge without the original bill of lading to clear them. The bank will request the shipping line to release goods using the shipping guarantee as a substitute for the bill of lading – the bank will be guaranteeing the full value of the consignment as reflected on the bill of lading. To apply for the shipping guarantee you must have a copy of the B/L which must be presented to the bank together with the SG application. The application is signed by the authorized signatories of the company. The shipping guarantee must be discharged or acquitted at the bank by the presentation of the original bill of lading on receipt. SGs prevent demurrage charges and stock blackouts and are very useful.

The Donation Certificate (DC)

This is a document signifying a donation and must accompany every donation consignment. The Donation Certificate must be declared cleared through customs together with other shipping documents at the time of export clearance. Donations are normally exempt from paying duty, especially if they are of a charitable nature or a strategic national interest nature.

The Duty Free Certicate (DFC)

This is a certificate issued by the Zimbabwean Secretary for Finance granting duty free entry for imports. The DFC must be applied for using a proforma invoice from the exporter well before a consignment is shipped by the foreign exporter to Zimbabwe. Normally this document takes one month to be issued. Duty free status is normally granted to charitable goods and goods of strategic national interest nature like capital goods to build industry, some educational material, government imports, some essential industrial inputs, imports into EPZs, etc. Goods must not be shipped until the DFC has been secured by the local importer to avoid disappointments and seizure of goods when the importer fails to raise required duties after failing to secure the DFC. The original DFC must accompany other shipping documents at the time of import clearance in Zimbabwe in order to be exempted from paying duty. Goods entering the country on the privilege of a DFC cannot be resold at all and must be used for the declared purpose only or else offenders may face heavy jail terms.

The Through Bill of Lading (TBL)

This is a B/L that makes goods move without multiple handling until they reach final destination. It is economic in that it prevents double handling and results in minimum transaction costs as opposed to an ordinary bill of lading. Shippers are encouraged to make use of this type of b/l rather than the ordinary bill of lading which is very expensive to execute. Shippers's instructions must always call for a through bill of lading, wherever practical. But groupage consignments cannot move on a through bill of lading by their very nature.

The Manifest

A manifest is a document that confirms the contents of one single mode of transport e.g. a single truck. Manifests are normally used to ascertain the contents in a truck, vessel, plane, or train truck. The mode may be part of a larger consignment or movement which is being part shipped using the single modes of transport. The manifest is used in physical inspections by customs and the police to prevent smuggling. Exporters and importers also use them to reconcile actual receipts versus what is on the documents. The manifest is also used for duty drawback claims and pre-and post-shipment inspections as well as customs clearance for part shipments. It is sometimes used as a proof if delivery.

The Proof Of Delivery (POD)

Normally a consignment note is used as proof of delivery. A proof of delivery is a signed transport document signed by the recipient or consignee to confirm receipt of goods. If goods are short landed then this must be endorsed on the consignment note, and is normally referred to as "protesting the consignment." This document is used to claim payment from a buyer as well as for duty drawback claims and insurance claims for goods lost in transit. It has a strategic role to assist importers not to pay for ghost and non-existent goods. NGOs like the United Nations use PODs a lot as they help them in paying only for goods properly received. Short deliveries are then met by the exporter through claims to their insurers.

The Unit Train (UT)

A Unit Train is a train that is contracted and hired by one firm or group of firms and carries only their products then moves non-stop to point of discharge. It does not go about picking other consignments on its way and only stops where the law and the railway system requires it to stop. A unit train is very economic as it takes minimum time to move goods and normally attracts much lower tariffs than the conventional goods trains. Exporters and importers are strongly encouraged to make use of unit trains whenever practical as that reduces their landed costs and makes them competitive. Firms and organizations moving small consignments cannot use unit trains as they cannot fill them up. This is where bulk contract buying and industrial consolidations play a role.

1.0 FREIGHT FORWARDING BUSINESS

Every business, whatever its nature, consists of a partnership between three elements-capital (the funds entrusted to the business), management, and labour.

Capital: includes monies entrusted to the business organisation by holders of ordinary shares, by preferential shares, and by a bank or banks willing to provide the business with lines of credit usually overdrafts.

'Ordinary shares' cover monies paid to the business on a full risk bearing basis. That is to say, the shareholders are content to carry the risk that their shares may reap no dividends for them : or alternatively , that their shares may reap substantial and possibly unexpectedly large dividends. The holders of ordinary shares have therefore contributed money which is entirely "at risk". In response, they have voting rights at general meetings of shareholders and by collective vote can appoint or dismiss the director of the business at their own discretion

"Preferential shares" consist of shares which are entitled, up to the percentage limit stated within the shares, to receive dividends before any dividends are considered for the benefit of the holders of ordinary shares. The only time when preferential shareholders will fail to receive the stipulated dividend is when the profitability of the company is so low that there is not adequate profit in a particular year to pay dividends at the stipulated rate. In a year when this occurs, of course, ordinary shareholders will receive no dividend at all.

"Overdraft facilities" are granted by banking institutions entirely at the discretion of the   banking management and are subject to the payment by the business to the bank of interest on all overdraft amounts outstanding at the bank's overdraft rate , which can change from day to day. Such changes in the rate are normally linked to change in the "bank rate" (i.e. The rate at which the Reserve Bank of Zimbabwe lends money to the
Commercial banks).

"Creditor facilities." This is a very important source of working capital in the Forwarding
And Clearing Industry. It is generated by retaining funds for disbursements before they are due and retaining them in the business until they are due to be paid. Cash flow management, especially of this aspect, is of primary importance to any Forwarding and Clearing organization.

There are other forms of capital which from time to time a business organization may avail itself of. (loans from directors, loans from other financial institutions, facilitations granted to it by overseas financial institutions. etc.)

Management: Management is not easy to define. It clearly commences with the managing director of the business and will include every director. In a small business these individuals will be "the management".

Moreover, "management" may spread further down the lines of authority to personnel   holding supervisory positions.

However , it is true to say that management always commences with Board of directors who are themselves responsible to the shareholders for the effective and profitable running of the business.

Labour: Whatever the management structure may be, every business employs a labour force structured according to the most important functions of management is close liaison with, and support of, that labour force.

There may be many grades of operatives employed but the essential importance of the labour force is to work effectively and expeditiously in association with the management to ensure that the products or services supplied by the business are of the very best quality.

Where the capital employed, the management expertise available, and the labour force enjoy an equitable and reasonable relationship and there is every expectation that the business will be successful and that each of the three elements will benefit.

The providers of the capital will benefit by reaping reasonable and beneficial dividends from their capital at risk.

The management of the business will justify the salaries or directors" fees which they draw from the business as compensation for their energy, initiative, innovative prowers, and
expertise.

The labour force will reap rewards commensurate with the competence and integrity which they bring to bear upon the work which they are employed to do.

17

If there is any distortion in the relationship between these three elements then that distortion can put the business at risk .For example ,if the capital employed is inadequate the business cannot prosper; if management draws excessive fees, the business will be unable to accumulate capital reserves which would enable it to expand or alternatively enable it to weather difficult times; if the labour force makes unreasonable demands either through its unions or otherwise, it can drain the finances of the company until not only the company is at risk but also their own jobs their own welfare.

1.1.1 Force Driving Every Business Entity

It is commonly said that the motivation for the creation of a business entity is the making of profits. There is a sense in which this is true but it is not the first motivating force.

The first and most dominant motivating force driving a business entity is

SURVIVAL

In every free market economy businesses compete with each other for a share in the market requiring their products or services. When the three elements described above co-operate effectively their first objective must at all times be the **SURVIVAL OF THE BUSINESS.**

Only after the survival of the business is assured can those engaged in the business concentrate more immediately upon the creation of profits and therefore the wealth and quality of life which every individual in that business is seeking. Profitability becomes the second motivating force driving the business forward.

Profitability
Profitability can be measured in a number of ways but it is only necessary to consider **gross profitability and net profitability.**

Gross profits are measured by the margin between the prices charged for the supplying of goods or services and the **direct costs** in material manufacturing processes, labour and time needed to produce the goods or services.

Gross profit take no account of the many **indirect costs** necessary to enable the organisation to function while the goods or services are being produced. These indirect costs will include the following:

- cost of land and buildings
- cost of municipal rates
- cost of power and water
- Marketing and sales

".." Advertising, etc.

A very substantial; indirect cost, especially to capital intensive businesses like Forwarding and Clearing enterprises, is the cost of the financial funding of the business. A proportion of the fund   s employed in every business are made available by banks and other financial institutions in the form of loans, overdraft facilities, etc., upon all of which the providers of those funds charge interest which normally be paid on a monthly basis.

Over and above all these indirect costs there is the cost of the insurance of the assets of the business against risks of fire, flood, and other forms of loss and damage. Third party risks must also be covered.

Nett profitability is the appreciably smaller margin remaining between the price charged for goods and services and the complete sum of both the direct and the indirect costs.

Development of Profitability
It will be apparent from the list of examples of **indirect costs** given above that the majority, if not all, f these costs **are fixed** .That is to say, those indirect costs persist at a fairly steady amount irrespective of the level of business transacted, the costs of the land and buildings utilised remains constant, the accounting function must continue, other overhead expenses must all be paid.

Accordingly, while the direct costs of production will vary in direct proportion to the volume of units produced, the **indirect** costs per unit will **reduce** as the volume of units produced increases.

This, in turn, means that the price charged per unit can itself be reduced while the level of profit achieved remains the same, **or,** the price charged per unit can be retained but a higher level of profit results.

This, very, briefly, is the principle involved in the phrase "economies of scale". In the context of the forwarder it equates with maximising the utilisation of office space, of office equipment such as typewriters, word processors, computers, scooter bikes and other forms of transportation, fax and telex machines, etc. It also involves ensuring that employees are fully and productively occupied during their working hours. Where a series of function is performed in sequence by several personnel their work stations   should be located in close proximity so as to create a "production line" format. Supervision should be positive and encouraging, , not severe, and performance should be monitored continuously.

Mechanisation of repetitive processes should be promoted and work study research be a constant responsibility of management.

The maintenance of business records is vital to every organisation but in some there is far too much recording of "nice to know" information not really essential to efficiency but time consuming. The detection and elimination of unnecessary records should be primary objective.

1.1.2 Marketing and Sales

Marketing
This should be the responsibility of the chief executive and the entire board of director of a business organisation. It involves the development of a corporate philosophy based upon two major considerations - the inherent strengths existing within the organisation and its staff, and the inherent needs of its targeted customers.

Marketing to consist of four elements:

Product- what the company sells
Promotion - how the company projects itself and its image to the market.
Price - how the company price its goods and services compared to others in the market and
Place - where the organisation supplies its goods and services to the market.

The strengths within the organisation may arise from educational qualifications, attitudes of mind, existing corporate expertise, tried and tested corporate tradition, and , normally, a combination of these.

The needs of its targeted customers will require continuous research and updating . Customer needs in the 1950s will not have been those which customers require during the 1970s. Within the 1990s those needs will have changed materially.

Once a corporate philosophy has been developed the next important feature is the development of a corporate image. Clearly, this image must be projected and given as high a profile as possible in the market place. One mechanism which is very useful in the achievement of the goal is the development of a logo.

It must always be remembered that a logo of itself is neutral. It may create interest, surprise or curiosity, but that is all until it becomes associated with a corporate identity or product or service. When the corporate identity or product or service is valued and appreciated in the market place then the logo begins to work its magic and the image of the company is enhanced.

Unfortunately, it is equally true that if the product proves to be of inferior quality or the service inefficient then the corporate identity associated with the logo will fall into disrepute.

Promotion

Advertising policy is an essential ingredient of marketing. Many companies have developed basic slogans which can be adapted in an advertising context to meet special advertising needs by the simple adjustment of one or two words. Where this is possible the slogan itself can become a company identifier.

Advertising can be broken down into several categories:

Repetitive and comparatively simple -this form of advertising requires regular repetition,   normally in the same space in the printed medium utilised.

"Splash" adverts -usually utilising either a half or a full page draw attention to new facilities, new developments, and the like.

Targeted adverts - emphasising services and facilities of particular interest to a certain market sector .These are usually placed in specialised trade journals or magazines.

Utility adverts - these are advertisements intended specifically to inform the marketplace of changes in a company structure, changes of company name or telephone numbers, etc, the creating of separate or additional divisions with specialist functions within a company .Such adverts are intended rather to inform a company's present then to attract new business -although this may also be achievable result.

Costs of Advertising
Clearly, consistent advertising even in a relatively small manner, can prove expensive and it is a function of the company management to devise method by which the effectiveness of the company advertising policy can be assessed.

The ability of any company to indulge in advertising will be directly proportional to its profitability and also to the positive psychological impact which the advertising achieves. Management must design a system by means of which it can assess advertising effectiveness and relate increases in business to the advertising programme.

Sales representatives who respond to enquiries voluntarily received by a company must be trained to ascertain by discreet enquiry what motivated the enquiry and incorporate the answer in their sales reports. Only with this type of input will management be enabled to assess advertising effectiveness.

Sales
The sale function must not be confused with the marketing function.

As has already been emphasized earlier the marketing function is a function of senior management and involves policy decisions which can have a major effect upon the life and vitality of the company. By contrast, the sales function involves the day- to-day contact with clients, with potential clients, dealing with enquiries from organizations who are not clients, etc.

Selling, although vitally important in its own right, must always be subordinate to the overall marketing policy of the company. It should support and assist in the achieving of the marketing police by the acquisition of additional and new business of the correct caliber and in areas in which the company's greatest strengths are available.

Of necessity, the sales function involves the employment of 'representatives' whose activities will be "on the road", canvassing for business acquisition . It is within the sales function that many forwarding companies trip over stumbling blocks and find themselves in difficulties because their sales representatives are not adequately trained to distinguish between reliable and unreliable payers, and good and poor credit risks.

While it is obviously vital to every forwarding organization to maintain pressure upon their sales representatives to use their full working hours conscientiously and profitably, and to seek always to obtain new business, it is of ever greater importance that those whom they are talking to will prove to be reliable and creditworthy.

It is preferable that a sales representative acquires no more than a single additional client in a month of effort who proves to have substantial business and who pays his accounts promptly and without excuses than to pick up half a dozen in the same periods who default on payments, stretch their credit periods beyond the agreed time spans , overstep their agreed credit limits, and seek to find queries within accounts as excuses for withholdings payment.

Controlling, Guiding and Targeting Sales Representatives

Sales representatives should be under consistent control and should report daily on all their activities to a supervisor who may be the marketing manager, to even a director of the company.

They should be supported by being directed as far as possible at potential clients who are known to the company management to be reliable. They should be given strictly defined parameters concerning tariffs of charges within which they can negotiate, and they should be supported so that organizations with whom they are negotiating receive prompt responses to all queries which the sales representatives cannot themselves immediately deal with.

It is vitally important that relationships on a personal level should be developed by the management of the forwarding company with the

management of prospective clients even though, for the present, no business may result. In this context quotations should be submitted promptly - and if any quotation is likely to take time to compile an interim response should always be sent.

Troubleshooting and Problem Solving
Even though sales representatives are thoroughly competent and trained to discuss operational matters there is every reason why they should not be utilised for troubleshooting and problem solving. If a sales representative has developed an atmosphere of trust with a client or potential client , conventional thinking may indicate that he may well be the best individual to undertake these functions.

This is a dangerous assumption : the involvement of sales people in operational matters almost always leads to resentment on the part of the operational staff and the involvement of sales people in these activities (which are time consuming) detracts the sales person from their job- that is of course acquiring new business .

However, the existence of qualified staff who may be capable of dealing with trouble or a problem should never relieve the senior management of a forwarding organization from involving itself personally with the issues. Senior managers and directors must always remember that one of their functions is client liaison and client support.

The delegation of responsibilities and functions to lower management and to sales representatives should never be excuse for senior management to wash their hands of personal interest in every client both large and small. Those organizations in the competitive field of international forwarding fare best when management from managing director downwards manifest a personal interest in, and concern for, the welfare of every client. Furthermore, where this attitude on the part of senior management is evident to the other staff in the organization it acts as a very substantial incentive to the lower echelons to give of their best on a daily basis.

Because it is vital to every forwarder that he has efficient and responsive international link- whether with his parent organization, associate companies, or overseas agencies - it is valuable if there can be an interchange of senior highly qualified staff between the Zimbabwe organization and its overseas counterparts in both directions. The results of such interchanges should be firstly to cement relationships between the respective forwarding organizations themselves and secondly , to cement similarly relationships with clientele at both ends of the forwarding chain.

1.2   FREIGHT FORWARDING AGENTS
A forwarding or delivery agent takes cargo into its custody for delivery to the consignee usually including completion of documentation formalities for the landing and importation of goods. The agent is obliged to deliver the cargo in the condition in which it was received. Forwarding agent is obliged to clear and forward the cargo with

reasonable dispatch and delays due to agent's negligence resulting in a loss of market value of the cargo leaves agent liable.

The business of forwarding consists of organizing the transportation of goods by land, sea, air or intermodal, between their places of origin and their places of intended destination, in accordance with the instructions given to the forwarder by either the consignor or consignee of the goods.

According to **Sople V. V. (2004)** freight forwarders and customs clearing agents offer the following services:
- traffic operations - mode and carrier choice
- initiation or organisation of documentation for cross border shipments
- customs clearance of cargo
- cargo movement and handling at the port of entry and destination
- advise shippers on freight cost, port charges, documentation cost, insurance cost, forwarding charges, packaging requirements, documents required.
- space booking and transport document preparation
- banking documentation
- agents
- clear consignments through customs
- process import documentation
- move cargo to bonded warehouses
- inspects cargo
- move cargo to importer's premises

1.3 FORWARDER COMPETENCE

While the expertise necessary for the movement of goods within Zimbabwe need not stretch a forwarder's capabilities to any extent, the expertise needed to successfully achieve the movement of goods internationally is of a very high order indeed. It involves, furthermore, a high degree of knowledge of the laws and regulations governing transportation not merely of the countries of origin and of destination but also of any country or countries through whose territory the goods may have to move along the transportation chain.

He must have thorough knowledge of the various carriers who trade between the country in which he operates and all other countries having international trade links with his own - carriers by land, by sea and by air, together with those carriers who operate multimodal services.

He must be thoroughly familiar with the specific trading terms and conditions under which each of those carriers operates, together with their tariffs or charges. He must understand how those terms, conditions and tariffs may operate to the advantage or detriment of the consignor or consignee of the goods he is responsible for.

He must be capable of recognising goods having special characteristics - e.g. dangerous, obnoxious, fragile, radioactive, perishable, and the like, and know how to deal with them if such are offered to him for the purpose of forwarding.

He should ensure that he has at his disposal warehousing facilities in which goods can be manipulated - breaking down into smaller units and repacking or remarking where his instructions so require.

He should have facilities for the collection of goods from their points of origin for consolidation and equally facilities for the distribution of goods at the point of destination.

He must have a sound knowledge of marine insurance in all its variety of forms so as to be capable of compliance with the insurance instructions of his principal.

He must understand the various methods by which international trade is financed and the various processes by which payments can be made internationally for goods supplied. In particular he must understand the nature of, and the terms of the various types of letters of credit issued by the banking community worldwide.

He must have a sound comprehension of the various transport options which are available to him - break-bulk or containerized - together with the advantages, disadvantages, limitations and special requirements of each.

Finally, he must understand how his own employing company makes its money so that he may be able to protect and enhance its revenue, and also the trading conditions under which it operates in order to protect itself from liabilities which it is not prepared to accept.

1.4   FORWARDING FUNCTIONS
"The shipper or consignee of the freight will contact the company about the intended journey, how the freight can be loaded, and the size of the consignment, the type of commodity and packaging and any special handling requirements. The consignment of freight is booked for loading and the information sent to the documentation section. The freight is collected, checked, loaded and dispatched." **Gubbins E. J. (2003:79).** The quotation summarises the functions of a forwarder.

1.4.1 Carriage of goods and traffic management
The principal function of a freight forwarder is to move cargo from point of origin to point of delivery. In cases where a forwarder owns transport vessels, he will be responsible for traffic management of the fleet. Traffic management involves modal choice, transporter choice, routing, safety and legal compliance, delivery timeliness and cost effectiveness. In some cases the forwarder can out-source the function to third party logistics service providers.

1.4.2 Quotations

In international trade the cost of transportation from source to destination, inclusive of its peripherals, can amount to between 15% and 30% of the delivered cost of the goods transported **in addition to** duties, etc, which may be payable upon the goods in the country of destination. It is obvious, therefore, that the provision of accurate quotations becomes vital service which the forwarder must provide.

The Shipping and Forwarding Agents Association of Zimbabwe has adopted the following rate categories for services as of December 2009:

Agency   -   USD50 to USD1500 depending on value of imports
Customs Clearance Fees   -   as per bill of entry
Documentation   -   USD12.50
Exports   -   USD50
Communication and Petties   USD12.50
Warehousing Entry   USD50.00
Document Release Fees   USD15.00
RIB/RIT   USD120.00

Shipping rates are based on freight classification, cargo weight, origin, destination, payment terms (prepaid or collect) and added services.

During the transportation of goods from source to destination, those goods pass points in the transportation chain at which responsibility for costs and for risks transfer from the seller to the buyer and a forwarder must be competent in the allocation of the costs in accordance with those delivery terms known as incoterms. He must, moreover, have proper knowledge of which of the two parties becomes responsible to bear his agency and commission charges in accordance with the practice in shipping or air freighting trade concerned.

On many occasions in the life of a forwarder difficulties arise with regard to the correct classification of goods for customs purposes, the correct description for purposes of railage, freight, etc. The difficulties may arise from inefficient information supplied by the client, an inadequate translation of a foreign language, and from a variety of other clauses.

On those occasions where the resulting error is discovered, it is naturally part of the responsibility of the forwarder to put the matter right as far as possible. Nevertheless, the forwarder must protect himself from any resultant liability unless the client fully co-operates with the forwarder in a fashion which enables the forwarder to undertake the rectification.

The fact that the customer may not be aware that any such incorrect payment has been made shall not constitute a circumstance to be taken into account in calculating what a reasonable time is. Should any act or omission by the customer, whether or not such act or omission was due to ignorance on the part of the customer and whether or not such ignorance was reasonable or justified in the circumstances, prejudice the company's right of recovery, then the customer shall be deemed not to have complied with the requirement to do all acts necessary to enable the forwarder to effect recovery of the amount incorrectly paid.

1.4.3 Protection and Packing of Goods
In the context of exports from Zimbabwe forwarders do not generally have to provide a protection and packing service. It has been traditional that exporters either themselves or by means of contracting to specialists, arrange this function. Nevertheless, occasions arise when word filters back to an exporter that loss and damage upon consignments sent overseas by him are becoming too severe. When this occurs, the forwarder as someone with sound knowledge of the stresses and strains to which goods can be put in the course of international transportation, is normally called in to advise what should be done to resolve the problem.

In the case of imports, the forwarder is liable similarly to be called in to explain how loss or damage which has been discovered upon receipt of the goods can be eliminated.

In both instances, the forwarder is expected to have competent knowledge with regard to the relative strengths of packages - whether cases or crates, whether cartons, drums, bales, whether shrink-wrapped, steel-strapped, nylon-strapped, whether shipped break-bulk or in containers, etc.

He must understand the nature of the condensation which can accumulate in a container, the nature of the sweating which can take place from the boards which compose a wooden case, and he must understand what the solution is in both instances.

He must understand the nature of "shunts", the sway, pitch, and roll of a ship, the effect of wind shear and air pockets upon the stability of an aircraft.

In respect of containerised traffic, whether by sea or by air, the forwarder must not only be able to advise his clients upon the most efficient methods of loading but must also be able to do it himself if he engages in groupage or consolidated traffic.

1.4.4 Preparation and checking of shipping/customs documents
The forwarder must understand the intricacies of customs clearance, the controls, and the documentary procedures which are essential to it. This applies to both import and export traffic and both in Zimbabwe and in overseas territories. He must accordingly either provide himself, or advise his client upon the providing of, the appropriate documentation.

A regular service which every forwarder must provide is the ability to remove goods in bond or in transit which have not yet been cleared and released by customs from the area of one controller's office either to the area of another or alternatively, in transit or by transshipment out of Zimbabwe to other countries.

He must have a sound and thorough understanding of the relevant customs tariff in his own country and must be able to obtain intelligible information with regard to the tariffs of other countries with whom his client is trading.

In addition customs clearance requires up-to-date knowledge of customs valuation, trade agreements, and rules of origin and trade facilitation, concessions offered by the customs administration.

Cargo documentation includes bills of entry, bill of lading or air waybill, import or export licenses, certificate of origin, road consignment notes, rail consignment notes, shipper's instruction, packing list, insurance certificate, delivery notes/proof of delivery, invoices, etc. In all case documents must be completed accurately and in time to avoid penalties and delays.

1.4.5 Cargo Space Booking, Groupage and Consolidation

With the advent of modern transport technology, especially the use of containers for both sea and airfreight, the importance of the ability of a forwarder intelligently to group together in a single container a variety of consignments intended for a variety of consignees has become paramount.

Groupage for sea freight and consolidation for airfreight enables a forwarder to provide cost advantages to clients which, in isolation, those clients would not be able to achieve. However, certain principles concerning the compatibility of goods and the importance of the "mix" of light and heavy cargoes in the transport units utilised is vital and involves substantial expertise.

By the nature of the international trade, time in transit can be protracted and dates of anticipated delivery can, at best, sometimes be uncertain. In fact, occasions may arise when goods may be available for final delivery in advance of anticipated date.

Under such circumstances the forwarder must retain to himself the discretion of deciding whether to hold the goods upon his own premises pending ability to deliver or whether to place them in warehouse. In any event he must divest himself of any responsibility for loss or damage to the goods under these circumstances and must make it clear that all expenses arising will be for the account of the customer.

1.4.6 Warehousing Facilities

On account of the nature of international forwarding occasions may arise either in Zimbabwe or overseas when movement of goods cannot proceed for a variety of reasons. These reasons may be:-

☐ the development of a labour dispute at a port or airport
☐ frustration of shipment due to breakdown of the intended conveyance
☐ the intervention of a government or other public authority in connection with the goods in question
☐ the lapse of a period of time awaiting a suitable shipping opportunity.

In these or similar instances the forwarder must retain to himself discretion concerning the warehousing of the goods or their otherwise being held at any place the expense of the customer.

It is not necessary for a forwarder to have his own warehousing facilities but it is essential that by contractual arrangement such facilities are available to him. These facilities should include both the storage of bonded and free goods.

Moreover, both collection and distribution facilities should be integral with the warehousing facility. This will enable the forwarder to collect and accumulate shipments which are intended to be grouped or consolidated for exportation, or alternatively, in the case of imports, which require to be separately delivered to consignees after customs clearance and release.

Warehousing or stores may involve specialities like frozen foods, drugs, dangerous chemicals, animals, bonded stocks, etc.

1.4.7 Attendance for Cargo Examinations
Imported goods of any description are subject **at the discretion of customs** to be detained (for additional explanations, brochures, diagrams, etc) or stopped (for physical examination). It is the forwarder's responsibility to determine with as much precision as possible exactly what additional information customs require in the case of the detention of goods, or alternatively, to arrange for the goods to be removed to the appropriate location - usually the searcher's office - where the goods can be opened and displayed to the customs official concerned.

Where imported goods are stopped for examination the forwarder must understand first of all that the importer himself has a right to be present at the time of customs examination but that alternatively, the importer may expect the forwarder to be present and to perform the operation of opening, unpacking, displaying, and subsequently replacing and reclosing. Where samples of the goods are required by customs it is the responsibility of the importer or his agent to take such samples from the package under the supervision of customs.

Export shipments may also require examination by customs - for identification of the goods for drawback purposes, the identification of the goods for the purpose of acquittal of removals in bond, etc. In each case it will fall upon the forwarder to make the necessary arrangements.

Health, Agricultural and a number of other statutory authorities also have responsibilities in connection with imported and exported cargo and in every case the arrangements for examination are normally coordinated by the forwarder in consultation with his client. Such examinations may take place in container terminal areas, in container depots, or, on occasion, at the premises of the trader importing or exporting the goods.

1.4.8 Insurance of Goods

While it is the prerogative of the owner/consignor/consignee of goods moving in the course of international trade to decide at what level of value and for what risks the goods in which he has an interest should be insured - or indeed whether they need to be covered by insurance at all - it can be stated without fear of contradiction that it is foolish in the extreme for the importance of insurance to be overlooked.

In those instances where the forwarder agrees to arrange insurance cover for goods, he must agree to do so solely on the basis of instructions received in writing, and his trading conditions must make it clear that he does so solely as an agent on behalf of his customer. Furthermore, his trading conditions must also make it clear that while he will use his best endeavours to arrange insurance suitable to the circumstances, he cannot be held responsible for the terms of the insurance obtained nor for any dispute of liability which may arise between the underwriting organisation and the customer in the event of a claim.

Should any insurer dispute its liability in terms of any insurance policy in respect of any goods, the customer concerned shall have recourse against such insurer only and the forwarder shall not have any responsibility or liability whatsoever in relation thereto notwithstanding that the premium paid on such policy may differ from the amount paid by the customer to the company in respect thereof.

The point at issue here is that the amount paid by the customer is *the premium due in respect of the insurance cover* provided that premium is the *consideration* due to the insurance company for their agreement to accept the risks involved. Without the inclusion of the words quoted within the forwarder's trading conditions it might be possible for an astute lawyer to argue that the forwarder, by retaining some part of the premium (i.e. his commission) is *himself undertaking to bear some part of the risks involved.* Obviously, even the remote possibility of such an argument being raised must be killed stone dead from the very outset.

Claims for Loss or Damage

Where upon arrival goods are found to have been lost or damaged it almost invariably falls upon the forwarder to initiate all appropriate claims. This will involve proforma claims which later will be followed by priced claims. It will furthermore involve the presentation of claims to marine underwriters and the like.

A forwarder is accordingly expected to appreciate the restraint upon claims which are imposed by prescription periods (time bars). He must also know how to compile efficient claim documentation for presentation to underwriters. He must understand letters of subrogation.

Examinations by insurance assessors will normally only apply to imported goods where damage, loss or a suspicion thereof is involved.

Normally, the examination will take place at the importer's premises although the forwarder, usually because he has been requested to take out the insurance on the goods, may be requested to arrange for the attendance of the necessary assessor.

However, on occasion, serious damage may be apparent to goods at the time that they are discharged ex ship and it may be important that an immediate and detailed examination of the goods takes place forthwith prior to their removal from the quayside for delivery to the importer. There are two reasons for this:-

☐ It may be essential to determine the extent of the damage and therefore the extent of the claim to which the carrying shipping line may be subject.

☐ It may also be essential either to perform interim repairs to the goods or at least to repair the packages in which the goods have been shipped in order to avoid aggravation of the damage during their final transportation to destination. It will be emphasised in some detail later in this Course that one of the basic principles under which insurance underwriters are prepared to accept the risks of loss and/or damage is that the assured party shall at all times take **reasonable steps to mitigate the extent of the loss or damage** which will be the subject of a claim.

In all such instances the forwarder is likely to be called upon to arrange for the survey of the goods and also to arrange for any interim repairs under the instructions of the surveyor, both to the goods and to the packaging.

1.4.9 Consignment Tracking and Status Reporting

With the advent of advanced technology in communication - telex, telefax, and computer interface (EDI) - it is progressively becoming possible for forwarders to maintain track of consignments on behalf of their clients throughout the transport chain so as to be able to provide indications of dates of arrival or, alternatively, delays and difficulties in transit.

This type of service may not by itself achieve any increase in speed of movement, nor reduction in delays where such occur. It does, however, provide a very valuable service to clients which enables them to modify forward planning and, if necessary, to give instructions for emergency action where appropriate.

While it is the practice of forwarders to endeavour to identify goods arriving ex any form of conveyance for the benefit of their clients - including the recognition of goods which have passed into State warehouses - doing so successfully is notoriously difficult and the procedure must be hedged around with protection for the forwarder's benefit. In other words, a failure of a forwarder in any instance to identify goods as belonging to a client must not be allowed to create any liability upon that forwarder.

1.4.10 Search and Location

Despite every precaution intelligently taken in advance, consignments or parts thereof occasionally go astray or are missing on arrival at destination.

It then becomes vital that tracing procedures are initiated promptly and effectively to ascertain where the missing goods are, and thereafter to organise their urgent recovery and correct delivery. In this function forwarders have a vital and significant role to play and must be prepared to exercise their total ingenuity to restore goods to their appropriate consignee.

Wherever this occurs it becomes equally important that the forwarder holds a "post mortem" in order to ascertain **why the problem occurred.** It may be as a result of incorrect identification marks on the goods, incorrect port mark or incorrect destination mark. It may be the result of confusion between marks having too great similarity. It may be as a result of goods being loaded into the wrong container in the case of groupage or consolidation of shipments. Equally, it may result from the fact that certain packages were shipped without any identification mark whatsoever.

Whatever the cause is, the forwarder must so far as it lies within this power, take action to ensure no repetition.

1.4.11 Routing and Shareholding
It must be obvious that in many instances there are alternative modes of transport and alternative routings by which goods can be moved from source to destination. Moreover, each mode and each routing will involve its own different cost.

Equally, there are ascertainable breakpoints at which the cost of transportation by air or by sea is equal. Below those breakpoints it may be advantageous to ship by air while above those breakpoints sea transportation may be less costly. In such instances the merits of groupage by sea and consolidation by air or the use of an airfreight commodity rate may all have to be considered. The merits of each case must be determined separately on the basis of an expert knowledge of the various costs and charges involved.

There is no other party than a forwarder who can give competent advice on such matters and it is inevitable that the advice so given will be relied upon. In consequence it must be based on competent knowledge of all relative costs together with an equally competent knowledge of the time factors required for the various modes of transport.

The forwarder also needs to prioritise loads to meet consignor/consignee urgent needs. Cargo categories like medicines, machine spares and other relief consignments may jump the queue to mitigate disasters. Normal consignments may need to be scheduled on a first come first served basis.

1.4.12 Cargo Classification and Handling
The range of cargoes which are regarded as dangerous is vast. Some of the commonest chemicals in everyday use become hazardous under certain circumstances which may arise in the course of transit. Obviously dangerous goods include acids, corrosive alkalis, poisonous substances if inhaled, if in contact with the skin, if swallowed, inflammable goods, explosive goods, goods which give off inflammable vapours on contact with other substances, radioactive substances, products having a magnetic field which could

interfere with navigational instruments, etc. Other goods are not in themselves dangerous but can be obnoxious in that they can grossly contaminate other cargoes.

The variety is enormous and the responsibility for correctly describing such cargoes rests upon the exporter and importer thereof. Nevertheless, it is very important that the forwarder makes himself familiar with the commodities and products more commonly found in international trade which are likely to be a hazard.

Above all else he must be aware to what authority a client must be referred to ascertain whether a particular product or commodity is regarded as hazardous. Normally, such authorities are shipping companies and airlines.

What is much more immediately important to a forwarder is that he makes himself familiar with the packing, marking and documentation regulations which apply to each category of hazardous goods in order that the documentation that he produces on his client's behalf shall protect his client from the liabilities which would attach to the client in the event of any default.

According to **House (2005)** shippers should provide the following information before loading dangerous cargo.

- chemical name of the cargo
- quantity and respective weight of cargo
- specific gravity value for estimation of volume occupation
- incompatibility with other cargoes
- cargo temperature at loading and during carriage
- corrosive properties of the cargo and tank coating compatibility
- electrostatic properties
- data on fire or explosion possibility
- level of toxicity of the chemical
- health hazards
- reactivity with water, air or other commodities
- contact or spillage emergency procedures

1.4.13 Consultations and Advice

Consequent upon the nature of a forwarder's business he is assumed by his clients to be expert in customs tariffs, import control regulations, export control regulations, prohibited and restricted goods, modal choice and costs, carries and ports, etc.

Nevertheless, a forwarder may only regard himself as competent provided that he has within his staff individuals who by experience and by study have made themselves thoroughly knowledgeable on all these matters.

The scope of client consulting depends on the terms of reference developed by the client and consultations can be sought on:-

- processes and skills (clarity, documenting, replication)

- ☐ meta-capabilities (learning new processes and skills, communication channels and organisational structure)
- ☐ process implementation and enhancement (process documentation, business process re-engineering, and technology transfer and techno cultures)
- ☐ client skill development (client - training)
- ☐ experimental learning (joint client - consultant teams, project induction training and simulations).

1.4.14 Claims for Recovery of Overpayments

These claims may be for overpayments of duty for various reasons, for overpayments of wharfage or railage, etc. Such claims involve a detailed knowledge of the classification and the valuation of goods for customs, and also a knowledge of the tariffs of harbour and railway authorities.

1.4.15 Costing

Shippers need to know the landed cost of a product.

Where an imported consignment consists of homogeneous goods, e.g. 1000 portable radios, the allocation per unit of the various elements of costs involved in the total movement of the goods from source to destination is a very simple task.

Where, however, a whole variety of different products are imported in one consignment, the correct allocation to each product of costs in respect of each leg of the transport journey and of the duties, surcharges, etc. which are involved, can become exceedingly complex. Some importers may well deal in a market where the accurate allocation of such costs is of comparatively small importance, but others may be dealing in a market where accurate costing is vital. It is in this latter instance that the forwarder may be called upon to give continuing expert advice. Certain forwarders therefore have programs within their computers which assist in the rapid allocation of costs, others may attempt to do it manually; others may not offer the service at all.

It must be stressed that this is a service which every forwarder should be prepared to undertake whenever it is requested.

This list of the various ways in which a forwarder can be of substantial assistance to his client is by no means exhaustive. It serves to emphasise that the forwarder can make himself an exceedingly valuable and essential partner to his client in many different ways.

1.4.16 Collection of Expenses

It is common knowledge that the determination which party - seller/sender or buyer/importer - is responsible for paying the many various charges which arise in the course of a transport movement is dependent upon the terms of delivery. These terms of delivery range from "ex works" right through to "delivered duty paid".

Depending therefore upon the terms of delivery in any particular instance, the forwarder's charges may have to be apportioned between his client and the consignee. If his client is domiciled in the same country as that in which he has his office then the forwarder is in a position to exercise his normal rights as creditor against his client in the local courts. Where, however, certain charges are payable by a party in another country the process of collection can be extremely difficult in the event that the overseas debtor chooses not to pay promptly on demand.

The forwarder must therefore have a means of recourse back to his client.

When goods are accepted or dealt with by the company upon instructions to collect freight, duties, charges or other expenses from the consignee or any other person, the customer shall remain responsible therefore if they are not paid by such consignee or other person immediately when due.

Occasions arise when the client will require the forwarder to collect a COD amount from the consignee of goods prior to allowing the delivery of them. This always presents problems and so far as possible forwarders are well advised to endeavour to avoid any commitment of this type. Where, however, a commitment cannot be avoided very clearly defined protection of the forwarder must be built into his trading conditions.

The essential stipulation must be that the forwarder is entitled to assume that the consignee is willing to effect payment. In other words, the forwarder must be entitled to assume the good faith of the consignee - that he honestly intents to pay - that the instrument by which he tenders payment is valid - and that it will be met when presented or upon due date.

The forwarder must not allow himself to be put into the position where he is expected to verify the bona fides of the consignee or of the payment instrument which the consignee offers.

Ancillary services offered by some transporters
☐ refrigeration, ventilation, heating
☐ special equipment charges
☐ cash on delivery and change of cash on delivery recipient
☐ notify before delivery, inside deliver, re-deliver
☐ marking or tagging
☐ reconsignment or delivery or residential deliver
☐ sorting and segregating

1.5 CUSTOMERS INSTRUCTIONS, INDEMNITY BY THE CUSTOMER, GENERAL AVERAGE
It is obvious that in respect of any forwarding transaction both the time of receipt by the forwarder of the client's instructions and the precision and comprehensives of those instructions are vital if the forwarder is to perform the transaction correctly and effectively.

Where there is an insufficiency of time allowed to the forwarder or the instructions given are cloudy and obscure, the forwarder must protect himself from any allegation of non performance or ineffective performance.

Moreover, in those instances where there is cloudiness or obscurity in the client's instructions further protection is required by the forwarder against liabilities which may be created for the benefit of other parties.

1.5.1 Customer's Instructions

A clause intended to protect the forwarder against a delay in the receipt of instructions or lack of precision or comprehensives therein could be worded as follows:-

The customer's oral and written instructions to the forwarder shall be precise, clear and comprehensive, and in particular, determination issued by customs in respect of any goods to be dealt with by or on behalf of or at the request of the forwarder. Instructions given by the customer shall be recognised by the forwarder as valid only if timeously given specifically in relation to a particular matter in question. Standing or general instructions or instructions given late, even if received by the company without comment, shall not in any way be binding upon the company.

In the absence of specific instruction given timeously in writing by the customer, the forwarder exercises reasonable discretion regarding:-

☐ time to perform its obligations to the customer but excessive delay nullifies this protection

☐ means, route and procedure of performing acts or services contracted.

☐ declaration to be made and liability imposed on a carrier, warehouseman, underwriter or any other person related to the good.

Where specific instructions have been given and the forwarder has not questioned or rejected them it will be obliged to perform them. If the client fails by negligence, careless or ignorance to issue instructions, the responsibility for the consequences falls upon in and not upon the forwarder.

1.5.2 Professional Indemnity Insurance

Unforeseen risks and exceptional circumstances may arise where, despite the care with which trading conditions and bill of lading conditions are drafted, the forwarder may be compelled to accept liability in an amount greater than the maximum limits laid down.

Maximum limits of liability are, of necessity, related to the average levels of profitability which the forwarder can expect to achieve in this business. If those limits were higher the forwarder would stand at risk that his necessary profitability could be drained away as the result of having to settle a major claim. In fact, if such a claim falls outside those maximum limits the forwarder could find his entire business "wiped out". This is obviously a situation which cannot be tolerated and for which a remedy is essential.

The circumstances could even arise where the entire assets of a forwarder could be absorbed by the claim **and** the claim would still only remain partially settled with the result that the claimant himself could find his own business at risk. Again, this is a situation which should not be allowed to arise.

The concept of professional indemnity insurance is that within the terms and conditions of the policy of insurance the insurer, in return for a premium, accepts the risk of claims arising which for any reason cannot be settled within the forwarder's maximum limits of liability.

It is obvious that any insurance organisation offering professional indemnity cover will be intensely interested in the nature of the business, its size, the variety of its operations, and the precise detail of the trading conditions under which it operates.

For example, a business whose operation is entirely customs clearance will be subject to very different risks to a business which also includes the physical warehousing and distribution of goods by means of its own fleet and vehicles. If the loading and unpacking of containers is included in the business then another set of risks arises - as for instance the placing of goods in the incorrect container so that they arrive in Hong Kong instead of Southampton. Where heavy plant and machinery is involved, e.g. forklift trucks or mobile cranes, other risks occur.

Because professional indemnity insurance is a highly specialised form of insurance the organisations in the insurance market which offer this type of cover are limited. Some Zimbabwean forwarders look for their insurance cover to the Through Transport Mutual Assurance Association (the Through Transport Club, or in brief, TTC) whose operational headquarters are in London.

Like any other mutual association, the TTC has no "shareholders". It is a "club" whose members - the policy holders - each pay their premiums into a common pool from which the administration costs of the club are paid. The entire balance of that pool becomes available for the settlement of claims validly presented under existing policies and after three years any excess funds in the pool relevant to a particular year are divided up between reserves and all policy holders. Where such surplus funds exist, therefore, the policy holders may obtain on a yearly basis a pay-out which amounts, in effect to a dividend.

It is common knowledge that in the United States and also in certain other countries throughout the world claims for loss and for damages arising from circumstances which can be construed as professional laxity are increasing - with appreciable encouragement from the legal profession who themselves make increased fees from prosecuting such cases.

This trend is beginning to make itself apparent within Zimbabwe and there is little doubt that it will increase in years to come and that the forwarding profession will not escape the consequences. Forwarders are all strongly urged to make certain that they have professional indemnity insurance which, if effectively taken out, will protect them and at the same time protect the interests of their clients.

1.6 FORWARDING: INTERNATIONAL REPRESENTATION

In the 1950s and prior to that time forwarding in Zimbabwe consisted very largely of the following;-

☐ taking control of **imports ex rail, road or aircraft,** clearing the goods through customs, obtaining release thereof from the carrier and   forwarding the goods inland to their ultimate destination,

☐ in the case of **exports by rail, road or aircraft,** the collection of the goods from the point of source, forwarding them to the appropriate depot or airport, clearing the goods through customs and obtaining the required export documentation which was then returned to the exporter.

This was the reason why in those days forwarders were known as **clearing and forwarding agents** - the clearing function being the dominant one while the forwarding function was a peripheral or subsidiary service.

During the last thirty years or so technological advances in transportation, coupled with major changes in the manner in which international trade is conducted, have drastically altered the functions of the forwarder so that although he still retains the business of customs clearance, that has become subsidiary to his main function which is **international forwarding.**

The technological advances in transport to which reference is made above consist of:-

☐ the advent of the **container** by means of which goods can be transported multimodally without further handling.
☐ the advent of the wide-bodied aircraft serviced by **unit load devices** (ULDS) which, again, can be moved multimodally without the handling of the goods carried therein.
☐ the development of the **non-vessel owning common carrier** (NVOCC) or groupage operator.
☐ the development of the **consolidator** of airfreight cargo.

The major changes in the methods in which international trade is carried out include:-

☐ substituting for that need the concept of "just-in-time" (JIT) inventorying.
☐ the development of "project" contracting which, in turn, requires   project shipping.
☐ the concept of the door-to-door transport chain.

These major changes have presented forwarders with enormous opportunities to expand their activities and enhance their importance to the international trading community - but in order to take advantage of these fresh opportunities, **forwarders must have at their command efficient and co-operative international links with similar forwarders in overseas countries.**

Those links may be with branches or associate companies overseas, or with appointed agents.

The links may be:-
☐ reciprocal
☐ non-reciprocal
☐ exclusive
☐ non-exclusive
☐ ad hoc

It will be obvious that representation which is **reciprocal and exclusive** is likely to be the most efficient and profitable since both parties to the agreement will be working for their mutual benefit.

Harrison J. S. (2003) provides the following guidance on managing partnerships.

☐ identify alliance partner who can provide needed capabilities
☐ define partner roles and ensure partnership is valued by both   sides
☐ develop strategic plan outlining specific partner objectives
☐ involve top managers to ensure middle management
☐ meet often, informally at all managerial levels
☐ assign someone to monitor all aspects of partnership and use external mediator to resolve disputes
☐ maintain independence and escape captivity of the partner
☐ anticipate and plan for cultural differences

☐ **Dornier P. et al (1998)** provide pertinent questions to be asked when evaluating potential strategic alliances. The questions are:-
☐ what will the partner's strategic position be at the end of the alliance?
☐ why would the prospective partner agree to an alliance?
☐ which of the partner's weaknesses could the alliance improve?
☐ What sources are the partners willing to contribute to the relationship?
☐ how will conflicts and problems be resolved?
☐ what assessment method will be used to evaluate the workings of the partnership and its results?
☐ how will performance results be shared?
☐ what are the provisions for renegotiating or dissolving the partnership?

According to Bayles D. L. (2000) forwarders need to periodically or continuously evaluate or monitor the performance of their overseas partners and service providers. The following steps become mandatory in alliances:

☐   establish measurable standards of performance
☐   conduct periodic performance reviews
☐   visit partner sites to check security procedures
☐   monitor customer feedback and satisfaction levels
☐   revisit decision to outsource when volumes grow.

Freight Forwarder Selection. Checklist by **Cook T.A. (2001).**

a.   Service areas
b.   Modes operated: ocean, air, road, rail
c.   Office(s) location
d.   Insurance availability and fees
e.   EDI capability
f.   Tracking capability
g.   Scope of expertise
h.   Quality of personnel (sales, operations)
i.   Pricing
j.   Warehousing capability
k.   Freight specialisation (perishable, hazardous, etc
l.   Service diversity
m.   Years in business
n.   Payment terms
o.   References

1.7   SHIPPER'S RIGHTS AND OBLIGATIONS

A variety of circumstances can arise which face the forwarder with the question whether he is justified in departing from certain of his customer's instructions. Those circumstances may affect either the customer's interests or the public good or both.

Furthermore, other circumstances may arise which render it impossible or impracticable for the forwarder to comply with a customer's instructions.

It is obvious that the first duty of the forwarder under such circumstances is to consult the customer in order to get the agreement of the customer to alternative courses of action. However, this may not always be possible for any of the following reasons:

☐   the circumstance in question may require an immediate urgent resolution.
☐   the customer may be far distant - e.g. in a foreign country - with   whom communication may be difficult.
☐   the customer my be out of communication for other reasons.

The Customer's Interest and/or the Public Good

On those occasions when only the customer's interest is at issue it may well be possible for the forwarder to determine without any serious difficulty what alternative course of action is required despite the fact that it does not accord with the customer's instructions.

Where, however, the public good is at issue, e.g. a leaking cylinder of hydrocyanic acid is discovered, or a glass carboy of sulphuric acid is found to be cracked, the forwarder may be called upon to take immediate action for the public good which may involve appreciable expense to the detriment of the customer. In such an instance considerations of the public good must outweigh any consideration for the customer's interest.

Accordingly, the forwarder's trading conditions must incorporate a clause which will exonerate him from any liability to his customer resulting from the action he may be forced to take.

Impossibility or Impracticability of Performance

The type of circumstances which might be involved here can be illustrated as follows:-

Shipment is stipulated by airfreight on the services of SAA from New York to Harare via Johannesburg. The United States government cancels the flying rights of SAA into the airport of New York. Strict performance of the instructions therefore becomes impossible and the decision must be made how best to deal with the problem.

A clause suitable to protect the forwarder in these or similar circumstances would be worded:-

"If events or circumstances come to the attention of the company, its agents, servants or nominees which, in the opinion of the company, make it whole or in part, impossible or impracticable for the company to comply with a customer's instructions the company shall take reasonable steps to inform such customer of such events or circumstances and to seek further instructions. If such further instructions are not timeously received by the company in writing the company shall, at its sole discretion, be entitled to detain, return, store, sell, abandon, or destroy all or part of the goods concerned at the risk and expense of the customer."

In connection with a variety of goods statutes, international conventions, and sometimes specific contracts, require declarations to be made as to the nature or value of the goods in question.

Instances also occur when the special interest of a party in the delivery of the goods may also need to be declared. It may furthermore be necessary for a similar declaration to be made or a special protection or cover to be sought from a carrier in respect of goods which are, or fall within the definition of "dangerous" or "fragile", etc.

In certain circumstances it may be important that certain goods should be carried and handled separate from other goods.

Trading conditions must ensure that the forwarder is given specific instructions in good time where any of these considerations apply and clauses suitably worded.

In particular the company shall be under no obligation to make any declaration or to seek any special protection or cover from any carrier in respect of any goods which are, or fall within the definition ascribed thereto by that body, of dangerous goods or other goods which require special conditions of handling or storage.

Customer Undertakings
It is very important to the forwarder that his customer must be stopped from pleading at any time and in any circumstances that he "did not know". Accordingly, the trading conditions in terms of which the forwarder operates must demand from the customer a number of warranties and bindings".

The purpose of these warranties and bindings is to place responsibility for the following matters squarely upon the shoulders of the customer.

- ignorance of the nature of the goods in question
- ignorance of the laws of the customer's country
- ignorance of the nature of the services the customer is demanding of the forwarder
- failure to supply all pertinent information to the forwarder
- the giving of faulty, false or fraudulent information to the forwarder
- inadequate or improper protection and packing of the goods
- the use by the customer of a faulty or defective transport unit
- inadequate or improper loading and securing of goods within a package or upon a transport unit
- failure by the customer to affix correct labels to packages, etc where, by international convention, such labeling is mandatory (e.g. dangerous goods).
- etc, etc.

Moreover, a further consideration is of special importance to the forwarder. This is that the customer from whom the forwarder receives his instructions may, in fact, not be the owner nor the original consignor of the goods and only on rare occasions will the customer be the consignee of the goods.

Accordingly, it is very important to the forwarder that the trading conditions in terms of which it contracts with his customer shall be binding upon the actual owner, actual sender, and the actual consignee and any other party acting as an agent for any of them.

Clauses which will afford the forwarder the protection and the rights which are essential to him in these matters are as follows:-

Customer's Reasonable Knowledge
The customer shall be deemed to have reasonable knowledge of all matters directly or indirectly relating to the goods and services or arising there from including, without

limitation, terms of sale and purchase and all matters relating thereto, and the customer must undertake to supply all pertinent information to the company.

Warranty as to Ownership
The customer must warrant that it is either the owner or the authorised agent of the owner of any goods in respect of which he instructs the forwarder and that each such person is bound by forwarder's trading conditions."

Accurate, True and Comprehensive Information
The customer must warrant that all information and instructions supplied and to be supplied by it to the company is and shall be accurate, true and comprehensive and the customer shall be deemed to be bound by and warrants the accuracy of all descriptions, values and other particulars furnished to the company for customs, consular and other purposes. The customer warrants that it will not withhold any necessary or pertinent information, and indemnifies the forwarder against all claims, losses, penalties, damages, expenses and fines, whatsoever, whensoever, and howsoever arising as a result of a breach of the foregoing whether negligently or otherwise including, without derogating from the generality of the foregoing, any assessment or reassessment."

Preparation and Packing
The customer must warrant that all goods will be properly, adequately and appropriately prepared and packed, stored, labeled and marked, having regard inter alia to the implementation by or on behalf of the forwarder or at its instance of the contract involved, and the characteristics of the goods involved and are capable of withstanding the normal hazards inherent in the implementation of contract.

The customer must also warrant that where goods are carried in or on containers, trailers, flats, tilts, railway wagons, tanks, igloos or any other unit load devices specifically constructed for the carriage of goods by land, sea or air, (each such device hereinafter individually referred to as "the transport unit") then, save where the forwarder has been given and has accepted specific written instructions to load the transport unit:-

(i)   that the transport unit has been properly and competently loaded, and
(ii)   that the goods involved are suitable for carriage in or on the transport unit, and
(iii)   that the transport unit is itself in a suitable condition to carry the   goods loaded therein and complies with the requirements of all   relevant transport authorities and carriers.

Goods requiring special arrangement
Forwarder's trading conditions should spell out arrangements to be made regarding goods such as bullion, coins, precious stones, jewellery, valuables, antiques, pictures, human remains, livestock or plants.

Goods requiring prior consent of the company

A much broader range of goods are in themselves actually or potentially dangerous, may create a hazard to health, to goods or to property, or may be an attraction to or harbour vermin and pests.

Such goods may well be satisfactorily transported subject to compliance with laid down conditions. The important thing under such circumstances is that the forwarder must be given advance notice to his client's intention to dispatch such goods and be given the opportunity if he wishes to decline to handle them.

Such goods includes radioactive materials inflammable or noxious goods or those which may by their nature taint or contaminate or adversely affect persons, goods or property.

Furthermore, it must be the responsibility of the client to ensure that the conditions acceptable for the transportation of the goods are fully complied with.

The customer must warrant that such goods, or the case, crate, box, drum, canister, tank, flat, pallet, package or other holder or covering of such goods will comply with any applicable laws, regulations or requirements of any authority or carrier and that the nature and characteristics of such goods and all other data required by such laws, regulations or requirements will be prominently and clearly marked on the outside cover of such goods."

If any such goods are delivered to the forwarder in breach of the provisions above such gods, and any other goods may for good reason as the forwarder in its discretion deems fit including, without limitation, the risk to other goods, property, life or health be destroyed, expense of the customer and without the forwarder being liable for any compensation to it, or any other thirty party and without prejudice to the forwarder's rights to recover its charges and/or fees including the costs of such destruction, disposal, abandonment or rendering harmless or other dealing with and the customer indemnifies the forwarder against all loss, liability or damage caused to the forwarder as a result of the tender of goods to the forwarder and/or out of the foregoing.

Perishable Goods
The essence of the problem here is the perishability of the goods. Furthermore, the perishability of any particular class of goods will clearly depend upon any, or some or all of the following:

☐   ripeness
☐   time already spent in transit
☐   time still expected to be in transit
☐   delays arising from statutory inspections by authorities
☐   frustration of movement due to breakdown of transport equipment
☐   frustration of movement due to strikes, lock-outs, etc.

Over and above all these, the forwarder handling perishable goods is in an exceptionally vulnerable situation if, for instance, the market for which the goods were intended is suddenly flooded with similar products from a competing source with the result that the client instructs the forwarder to divert the goods to an alternative market.

It is important that the forwarder's trading conditions shall provide him with means of prompt protection of his charges and outlays, and the right to act expeditiously in order to minimise all losses which might be incurred.

1.8 FORWARDER'S TARIFF
In compiling a tariff the agent must first determine every segment of activity which he may be called upon to perform. These will normally be the following:-

- Preparation and submission of customs documentation
- Attendance upon customs for the examination of goods detained
- Organising the inspection of goods for the purpose of other public authorities
- Payment of fees and travelling expenses of other public authorities
- Fees for the release of goods from the Carrier
- Freight payment fee
- Cargo survey fee - damaged/discrepant cargo
- Lodging proforma claims - damaged/discrepant cargo
- Pursuing claims to finality
- Receiving, handling and redelivery charges for goods warehoused
- Fee for control of goods removed in transit in bond
- Fee for lodging provisional payments
- Fee for acquittal of removals in bond
- Fee for compilation and submission of claims for overpayments or refunds of duties, surcharges, etc, and also in respect of wharfage, etc.
- Ledger fees for airline accounts, container operator accounts, Portnet accounts, Spoornet Accounts, etc
- Finance fee to cover interest, etc, in accordance with credit terms in respect of the disbursements funded
- Agency charge (commission)
- Communication costs
- Other sundries

This list is not exhaustive and occasions may occur when fees for additional services or facilities may have to be raised.

The structure of the tariff which an agent may decide to impose for the clearing of high value sophisticated goods which may arrive as imported cargo may well have to be substantially different from the tariff to be imposed upon bulk cargoes of proportionately lower value per freight ton. Over and above this, of course, it is quite certain that separate tariffs are required for the clearance whether for importation or exportation of postal items.

Quite apart from these considerations, levels of overhead costs within a forwarding organisation will also influence the levels of fees which have to be charged. A forwarding organisation which has achieved a suitable "mix" of traffic such that its disbursement accounts to customs are not allowed to rise excessively may well find that it has a cost advantage over its competitors because a higher proportion of its capitalisation is available for business expansion without the need to increase its levels of fees.

1.8.1 Competition by Price
There are few businesses in which competition is as fierce as in forwarding and clearing.

It is inevitable, therefore, that a measure of competition by price will always be involved.

However, a forwarding organisation which has nothing better to offer than a cheaper price is unlikely to survive very long. The cheaper the price it has to offer to stay in business, the lower inevitably will be the level of service it can provide to its clients. This is an inexorable rule which no amount of manipulation or management skill can avoid.

The circumstances in which competition by price is economically admissible are:-

☐ Where one forwarding organization comes across an instance where a competitor is genuinely over-charging beyond the broadly accepted market rate without providing a compensating excellence of service.

☐ Where the forwarding organisation is able genuinely to reduce its overhead costs by, perhaps, investing in improved office systems, streamlining its staff requirements, substantially improving staff performance by training or by other means, and similar circumstances.

In fact, the only justification for price cutting is increased productivity. Where this is achieved and can be quantified, then it is the responsibility of management to reduce prices - or at least to stabilise them over an increased period of time.

1.8.2 Competition by Efficient Service
Competition by quality of service is a different matter. Quality of service takes a variety of forms such as:-

☐ By diversification of services on offer so that they include additional services needed by clients
☐ By improving the speed at which services are rendered without allowing the accuracy and clarity of the services to suffer
☐ By improving levels of communication with clients at both ends of the international transport chain
☐ By regular and consistent visitation of clients to discover and eliminate incipient causes of dissatisfaction
☐ By candid and honest reporting to clients - particularly when problems arise, mistakes are made, delays occur, etc.

☐ By discreetly and effectively weaning clients away from their own bad habits and substituting for such habits practices and procedures which are more efficient

This list is not exhaustive but it does contain the most important elements of service.

Diversification of Services
This can be achieved in a variety of ways:-

☐ By providing a costing service to enable clients more accurately to cost their imported goods.
☐ By providing a distribution facility at destination where clients require such a facility. This also involves a warehouse facility and the maintaining of accurate stock records.
☐ Offering a collection service to bring exports together to maximise export shipments
☐ By providing, if the client so desires, in-house training of the client's clerical staff by a suitable person capable of doing so efficiently
☐ By studying in depth and detail the particular requirements of a trading sector so as to create special facilities of specific benefit to that sector. This might involve the shoe trade, the book trade, the stationery trade, the trade in fine arts and artifacts, etc.

You will doubtless be able to think of other sectors where a similar programme could be put in place but it must be remembered all the time that the development and maintenance of efficiency by the forwarder himself in the chosen field is the prerequisite for success.

Accuracy and Speed in Normal Functions
Accuracy in every function of the forwarder must be the goal and no excuses should be tolerated for any failure to achieve it. This is not to say that a particular forwarder must be capable of instant classification for customs purposes of every category of product presented to him. This is manifestly impossible. However, every forwarder should be capable of accurately advising every client how most effectively to create a request for a tariff determination. It is unfortunately true that only too frequently such requests are inefficient, superficial, lacking in essential details, with the result that the tariff determination - if any - ultimately supplied by customs is questionable. And, bear in mind that this will not be the fault of customs. The fault will almost invariably lie with the importer and with the agent advising him how to proceed. Any tariff determination can only be as reliable as the information supplied in the application. Similar considerations apply to all other facets of a forwarder's operation - accuracy must be achieved so thoroughly that the client learns to place his full trust and confidence in his appointed agent.

Speed of Performance
It has to be admitted that much of the performance required of a forwarder is dependent upon the effectiveness of other parties to whom parts of his function must be sub-

contracted - e.g. NRZ, a road haulier, a sub-agent at a remote port, a correspondent agent in an overseas territory, etc. Yet it remains true - and the forwarder must accept this totally - the forwarder always carries the can and must not unjustifiably shoulder off the blame to other parties especially when the forwarder himself has chosen which other parties will be utilised.

If the client demands freighting of the goods via Air Gabon and the goods are delayed for 2 - 3 weeks because Air Gabon had flight problems, then to some degree the forwarder is relieved of responsibility. Note, however, that "he is relieved to some degree". This is where effective communication enters into consideration. The agency network through which the forwarder operates in Europe should be with a correspondent forwarder who will recognise without even being asked, that he must advise urgently and without delay the difficulties arising with Air Gabon. He must suggest alternative routings and if possible advise alternative costs. It is of no greater value after the goods have been delayed for the forwarder in Zimbabwe to plead the deficiencies of Air Gabon unless he has also offered alternatives in an intelligent fashion so that the client himself can exercise his own options and make his own decisions.

This type of inefficiency and lack of attention to detail shows first of all that management were not properly supervising their junior staff, secondly, that they had not properly trained their staff, and thirdly, that their record of claims submitted and subsequently returned was either non-existent or was not being properly supervised.

Other forwarders had made themselves fully aware of the special facilities and were having minimal difficulties with claims processing and settlement. Need anything further be said?

Communication
Effective communication at every level within a forwarding organisation not only vertically between management and staff and vice versa, but also horizontally with clients both by word of mouth and by letters, faxes, e-mail telexes, etc., is absolutely vital.

No query by telephone, fax or email should go unanswered for more than 24 hours. If a further period is required to produce an efficient answer then an acknowledgement or interim reply should be sent.

No written communication through the mail should go without reply for more than 48 hours, and again the same rule applies - a complete response cannot be sent forthwith then an interim response should be sent to assure the enquirer that his needs are being attended to.

Moreover, the dispatch of an interim reply is not to be taken as justification for any avoidable delay in sending the final response.

Where difficulties are experienced in the completion of a transaction, where mistakes have been made in performance, where errors of judgement have been made by staff, where omissions have occurred in the fulfillment of instructions from clients, etc., senior staff should immediately be advised even if the culprit has to take a reprimand. A reprimand for his default can be moderated by an acknowledgement of his honesty in owning up. Thereafter, it is the responsibility of senior management to report candidly and honestly and in full to the client in question without deviousness, and without attempts to shift the blame. The experience of being honest is a salutary one which teaches a lesson to avoid the same or similar defaults in future. It also frequently has the effect of instilling greater confidence in the client than was the case beforehand.

Client Education
Ignorance of the mechanics and the procedures involved in international transportation on the part of the clients is sometimes astonishing. The forwarder, by the very nature of his industry, should be an expert in such matters - or at the very least, have far more knowledge and skills than his clients.

Without vaunting his expertise or knowledge, the forwarder should be able with discretion and diplomacy, to instill into his clients some portion of his own expertise. This can frequently be done in discussion across a desk and can be a very substantial asset in the attributes of any salesman.

In its simplest form this could be described as conversational instruction and if it is applied with tacit and diplomacy it is possible to so guide the conversation that it will be the client himself who believes he has found answers to which, in fact, the salesman has carefully guided him. He accordingly feels satisfied with himself and pleased with his agent.

It is quite possible to step materially beyond this type of training and to offer to run brief but succinct training courses in a substantial client's own premises for the benefit of his junior and middle staff. This, of course, will only work when the client has total confidence in the abilities and experience of the agent concerned. Moreover, the agent must be absolutely certain that the person he puts in to do the training is himself fully competent. If this is not the case then the training may prove to be the reverse of useful.

1.9 INTERNATIONAL PURCHASING BASICS
"The forwarder is not concerned with the methods, procedures and structures adopted by his client for the purpose of obtaining his overseas supplies."

Before a forwarder can give useful advice to a client he must himself understand the nature of an indent. An indent constitutes the contract between the sender and the buyer. Because it is the contract both parties must clearly understand that they must comply fully with all its stipulations.

1.9.1 Creation of a purchase order

The indent (or buyer's order) represents the written culmination of the negotiation of all aspects of negotiation between the international buyer and seller: the product, terms of delivery, timing of delivery, method of payment and so on.

The order is therefore the key document in international trading: many buyers do not realise this and treat the indent as a "glorified" local order, thus opening transactions to any amount of misunderstandings and mishaps.

An order may be created from a supplier's proforma invoice or it may be created from other documentation. The "acid test" of an effective order is whether it can be taken by a bank and translated into a Letter of Credit without any query or amendment.

If the buyer's order (i.e. his offer) incorporates within it the price for the goods ("the consideration") then if the supplier decides to accept that order then his acceptance - which may be in the form of an order acceptance or acknowledgement of order will create the contract - with the result that the indent is complete.

1.9.2 Negotiations Prior to Creation of the Indent
It, having received all the information necessary to the making of his decision, the supplier cannot agree with any particular aspect of the order - e.g. he cannot supply the order in full, he cannot supply precisely the goods required by the buyer, he cannot supply within the buyer's stipulated delivery time, he cannot accept the price stated by the buyer, or for any other reason cannot issue an unqualified order acceptance - then the negotiating phase recommences and the original order (indent) falls away.

1.9.3 Minimising or Eliminating the Negotiation Time
It will be obvious that the effective conclusion of a trade deal between the two parties is vital to both. Accordingly, it is the prime responsibility of the buyer when placing his original order on the supplier to incorporate in that order all the many details which will assist the supplier by eliminating the need for him to raise subsequent queries intended to clarify precisely what the buyer requires not only in relation to the quantity, quality, composition, and nature of the goods but also concerning the terms of payment, the method of packing, and the mode of shipment, etc.

1.9.4 Essential Information the Buyer's Order must Supply
This information falls into several major categories which will each be considered below. These categories are:-

☐   Financial matters including desired terms and method of payment
☐   Technical in relation to the goods to be supplied
☐   Technical in relation to the packing of the goods preparatory for dispatch
☐   Technical in relation to the mode of transport to be employed
☐   Documentary in relation to the documentation essential to smooth transportation of the goods from source to destination.

1.9.5 Financial Information

The buyer must endeavour to offer terms and method of payment which he reasonably expects to be acceptable to the supplier. He must realise that no attempt whatsoever to fulfill the order will be considered by the supplier until he is satisfied that his risk has been reduced to an acceptable level.

Where business has been conducted acceptably between the two parties over a period of time the supplier may be content to allow payment to be made on open account or by cash against documentation forwarded through banking channels.

Where the two parties to business less regularly or even at infrequent intervals, then the supplier may require release of the essential shipping documents only against acceptance of a bill of exchange - a procedure in terms of which the documentation moves through banking channels and an acceptance of the bill of exchange is a prerequisite to the release by the overseas bank of the documentation. This is known as documentary acceptance.

Alternatively, the supplier may require the buyer to open an irrevocable documentary letter of credit in favour of the supplier in terms of which, provided the stipulations in the letter of credit are precisely fulfilled, the supplier is assured of receiving due payment.

1.9.6 Credit Terms

It is very common in international trade (as in domestic trade) for suppliers to offer periods of credit to their international customers - 30 days, 90 days, 120 days, etc. Such credit terms are of very substantial value to buyers since they can enable the buyer to proceed with his manufacturing or trading processes involving the goods in question prior to actually being required to pay the supplier. Naturally, the buyer will seek to obtain the best credit terms the supplier is prepared to allow.

1.9.7 Incorporation of these Financial Elements in the Buyer's Order

It will be evident that it is in the buyer's interest to describe both the method of payment and the terms of credit which he desires to utilise in his initial order for the goods. Hopefully, the supplier will accept the buyer's suggestions, but if not, then at least the areas of disagreement are apparent and the negotiation to obtain agreement need take very little time.

1.9.8 Technical Information Concerning the Goods/Specifications

The detail required in this area is fairly obvious - weight, quality, voltage, colour, etc, etc. Size and pattern may also require to be indicated.

In respect of certain products special quality controls may be necessary and possibly certificates of compliance with such controls may be required.

In relation to many other products special labeling may be required by law for the sale or distribution of those products in the Zimbabwean market.

1.9.9 Technical Information Concerning Protection and Packing

The buyer must appreciate that he may be ordering his supplies from an organisation overseas not familiar with the hazards of international transportation. Such hazards arise from changes in temperature, changes in humidity, changes of pressure, etc.

The buyer's initial order must include instructions on protection and packaging so as to eliminate doubt or uncertainty in the mind of the supplier.

Packing also includes the marking of the external package and if more than one package is involved the numbering thereof. It is obvious for the buyer to stipulate the identification mark, etc, which the supplier must place upon the exterior of every package involved.

1.9.10 Technical Information with regard to International Transportation

The buyer's initial indent must state clearly the following:-

☐ The shipping deadline
☐ The mode of transport - sea, air, road, rail
☐ The term of delivery - that is to say, the INCOTERM
☐ If shipment by sea is involved, whether the shipment should be by a
      Conference Line or a Non-Conference Line and, if the buyer has already negotiated a freight rate with a particular Line then shipment must clearly be limited to vessels operated by that Line.
☐ If shipment is required by airfreight, then whether dispatch is to be by an IATA airline, a non-AITA airline, or a direct airline air waybill, or through the services of an airfreight consolidator. Where a particular airline or airfreight consolidator is to be involved then names must be given.

An instruction with regard to marine insurance should always be included. Such instruction may simply be "Do not insure - insurance will be covered by us under our open marine police number ... held with ... (insurance company)", or if the delivery term is CIF or CIP so that the supplier is responsible to take out the marine insurance, then the following detail must be provided:-

☐ the insurance risks for which cover is required
☐ the insured value for which cover is required
☐ between what points must the insurance subsist, e.g. Chicago, USA to Gweru, Zimbabwe.
☐ whether the buyer will accept an "excess" in the insurance cover.

1.9.11 Documentary Information

Document preparation and document disposal is extremely important.

In all circumstances the buyer will require commercial invoices in a number of copies, a packing list where such is appropriate to the consignment, also in a number of copies, possibly a Certificate of Origin, possibly a phytosanitary certificate or other similar certificate, together, of course, with the transport document as appropriate to the mode of transportation.

Where goods are described on commercial invoices by trade names or colloquial names it is very important for the purpose of clearance through customs that a proper technical description is also provided together, if possible, with the HS commodity code number.

Where discounts of any description have been agreed between the parties it is equally important that the amount of the discount and its precise nature (trade, quantity, or other) are clearly indicated and appropriately deducted from the gross invoice value. Where the purchase of the goods involves payment in terms of a letter of credit it is equally important that the description of the goods as stated in the letter of credit is incorporated.

Although customs law does not prescribe that a packing list must be submitted with bills of entry: import, it is very important that proper packing information is supplied. If the packing of the goods is uniform (100 pumps packed in 10 cases each containing 10 pumps) this information may be shown at the foot of the invoice, but where the consignment consists of a mix or a variety of goods then a detailed packing list is essential for customs purposes, for insurance claim purposes, and for commercial purposes.

Other documentation from the supplier of the goods must be provided as appropriate to the transaction. In particular, where their terms of delivery involve the provision of marine insurance by the supplier it is essential that the insurance so provided shall conform to the stipulations in the two INCOTERMS in question.

Finally, it is very important that so far as may be possible, all documentation for goods imported into Zimbabwe shall be in English. While there are two other official languages, for practical purposes in international trade the essential language is English.

The buyer must therefore seek the co-operation of his overseas supplier in the preparation and supply of documentation in the English language. The buyer may not reject any shipment for the sole reason that a foreign language is utilised in the documentation but he should provide the seller with the maximum incentive to supply in the English language.

1.9.12 Document Distribution
Documentation necessary to any international transaction is only of value provided it is forwarded with the utmost speed in accordance with the buyer's instructions.

The buyer's instructions will necessarily vary according to the method of payment. Instruction for distribution of documents can be tabulated as follows:-

----

DOCUMENT DISTRIBUTION:
Precisely as stipulated in our letter of credit OR

DOCUMENT	Bill of Lading		Comm.	Packing	Illustrative	Other
	Neg	Non Neg	Inv.	List	Literature	if req.
Ourselves	1	4	10	10	1	1
Clearing Agent	1	2	3	3	1	1
Bankers	1	2	1	1		1

LANGUAGE   :   All documents must be in English -----------------------------

----

Conclusion

It is true to say that it is the failure by the potential buyer to describe accurately and in sufficient detail precisely what his requirements are in his initial order which causes more trouble and difficulty in the transportation of the goods than any other single factor.

It is, furthermore, true to say that if costly problems arise in connection with the movement of the goods it becomes vital that a proper "post mortem" is held by the buyer in association with his forwarder to identify the causes for those problems so that they can for the future be rectified.

THE PROBLEM OF DRUG TRAFFICKING

Customs authorities, importers and exporters are all battling the drug trafficking scourge the world over. Drug trafficking is now a major world problem and the Western world and almost all countries are viciously fighting this scourge, which is correct. But the question is:- Who first commercialized drugs in the world and created this problem for all countries? The answer is very simple, it was the British. From 1839 to 1842 the British fought the First Opium War *(opium is marijuana)* with mainland China when China was refusing importation and commercialization of drugs (marijuana, cocaine) in Hong Kong and the British wanted to commercialize importation and trading in drugs (marijuana, cocaine) just like other commercial goods. China was defeated, thus signaling the first worldwide commercialization of drugs in Hong Kong by the British (with Hong Kong as the nerve centre of British worldwide drug trade – cocaine, marijuana and mandrax drugs). Hong Kong became a British colony specifically to promote the drug (marijuana) trade as the main commercial product there for world markets. The Chinese were very unhappy with this drug trade and in 1860 they again fought the British in the Second Opium War, trying to stop the commercialized drug trade but were again defeated by the British. The British should take responsibility for all the problems that the world is facing today about drug consumption and trafficking as they were the first and only nation to market and promote illicit drugs at national level using state resources to promote drug consumption and trade and to advertise and increase consumers of marijuana/drugs on a worldwide scale. Now this has become almost problem number one for the world, the curse and scourge of nations, as drugs are associated with terrorism, armed robberies, disinvestment, stagnation, money laundering, violent crime, bullying, prostitution, school dropouts, low productivity in firms and government departments, absenteeism, divorces and family break-ups and most of the negatives of society .

The following is a brief history of the two Opium Wars:-
http://www.infoplease.com/ce6/history/A0836734.html

OPIUM WARS

1st Version of Opium Wars

The **Opium Wars** (simplified Chinese: 鸦片战争; traditional Chinese: 鴉片戰爭; pinyin: *Yāpiàn Zhànzhēng*), also known as the **Anglo-Chinese Wars**, were the climax of trade disputes and diplomatic difficulties between China under the Qing Dynasty and the British Empire after China sought to restrict British opium traffickers. It consisted of the First Opium War from 1839 to 1842 and the Second Opium War from 1856 to 1860.[2]

Opium was smuggled by merchants from British India into China in defiance of Chinese prohibition laws. Open warfare between Britain and China broke out in 1839. Further disputes over the treatment of British merchants in Chinese ports resulted in the Second Opium War.

China was defeated in both wars leaving its government having to tolerate the opium trade. Britain forced the Chinese government into signing the Treaty of Nanking and the Treaty of Tianjin, also known as the Unequal Treaties, which included provisions for the opening of additional ports to unrestricted foreign trade, for fixed tariffs; for the recognition of both countries as equal in correspondence; and for the cession of Hong Kong to Britain. The British also gained extraterritorial rights. Several countries followed Britain and sought similar agreements with China. Many Chinese found these agreements humiliating and these sentiments contributed to the Taiping Rebellion (1850–1864), the Boxer Rebellion (1899–1901), and the downfall of the Qing Dynasty in 1912, putting an end to dynastic China.

2nd Version of Opium Wars

Opium Wars, 1839–42 and 1856–60, two wars between China and Western countries. The first was between Great Britain and China. Early in the 19th century, British merchants began smuggling opium into China in order to balance their purchases of tea for export to Britain. In 1839, China enforced its prohibitions on the importation of opium by destroying at Guangzhou (Canton) a large quantity of opium confiscated from British merchants. Great Britain, which had been looking to end China's restrictions on foreign trade, responded by sending gunboats to attack several Chinese coastal cities. China, unable to withstand modern arms, was defeated and forced to sign the Treaty of Nanjing (1842) and the British Supplementary Treaty of the Bogue (1843). These provided that the ports of Guangzhou, Jinmen, Fuzhou, Ningbo, and Shanghai should be open to British trade and residence; in addition Hong Kong was ceded to the British. Within a few years other Western powers signed similar treaties with China and received commercial and residential privileges, and the Western domination of China's treaty ports began. In 1856 a second war broke out following an allegedly illegal Chinese search of a British-registered ship, the *Arrow*, in Guangzhou. British and French troops took Guangzhou and Tianjin and compelled the Chinese to accept the treaties of Tianjin (1858), to which France, Russia, and the United States were also party. China agreed to open 11 more ports, permit foreign legations in Beijing, sanction Christian missionary activity, and legalize the import of opium. China's subsequent attempt to block the entry of diplomats into Beijing as well as Britain's determination to enforce the new treaty terms led to a renewal of the war in 1859. This time the British and French occupied Beijing and burned the imperial summer palace (Yuan ming yuan). The Beijing conventions of 1860, by which China was forced to reaffirm the terms of the Treaty of Tianjin and make additional concessions, concluded the hostilities.

See A. Waley, *The Opium War through Chinese Eyes* (1958, repr. 1968); H.-P. Chang, *Commissioner Lin and the Opium War* (1964); P. W. Fay, *The Opium War, 1840–1842* (1975)."

http://historyliterature.homestead.com/files/extended.html

China before the Opium War was closed to the West. Foreign trade was strictly controlled by the government. The Chinese had a false sense of superiority, believed that they had nothing to gain by trading with the "barbarians". After China's defeat in the Opium War, it was forced open. Moreover the weaknesses of China's political and social system were exposed and the sense of superiority was shattered. The Manchu government could no longer represent and protect the Chinese people. The Treaty of Nanjing, signed after the Opium War, opened Chinese ports and markets to Western merchants, caused the inflow of cheap Western machine-made products and collapsed the Chinese economy. However, the remaining businesses adapted and evolved to survive, this stimulated the development of Chinese capitalism. As the Chinese economy collapsed, unemployment skyrocketed. Coupled by poverty and government's inability to control the situation, riots, social insurrection and chaos spread over the country. The Opium War caused Chinese officials and intellectuals to realize that in order for China to catch up, they must learn from the West. Consequently officials madly imported Western technologies and industries, while intellectuals proposed a parliamentary government.

The Opium War forcefully and suddenly opened China to the world. The consequences of such abrupt exposure were deep and long lasting.

China, with its rising political, military and economic powers, is quickly merging into the international community. Facing the rising China, the world has raised many questions. What role will China play at the international level? What style of foreign policy will China follow? How will China administer Hong Kong after the British handover in 1997? Above all, will China continue its economic reforms and its "Open-Door Policy" which are the main contributors to its successes? All of these questions can be answered by examining the effects when China was first opened, forcefully, by British gun-boats and battle ships in the Opium War. The humiliation and the lessons learned at the Opium War

150 years ago are deeply rooted in Chinese mentality and still guide Chinese thinking in international relations. What effects did the Opium War have on the opening of China?

China before 1840 was completely closed, isolated from the rest of the world, except for the limited foreign trade in the city of Canton. The Western countries that wanted to penetrate the huge Chinese market, used the opium incident to wage the Opium War. China was soon overwhelmed and signed the Treaty of Nanjing. According to the Treaty, China opened its ports and markets to Western merchants, concessions were created in major cities and China became a semi-feudal semi-colonial state.

The inflow of cheaper Western machine-made products shattered Chinese native industries. The Chinese economy had to adapt and reform in order to compete with Western countries. The disastrous defeat of the Chinese army in the Opium War convinced every Chinese that China was no longer the "Heavenly Middle Kingdom". Western ideas were brought in, and their consequences were felt at every level of society. Intellectuals believed that the root of China's weaknesses lay within its backward political structures, and initiated many short lived political reforms.

The forced opening of China subjected China partially to foreign rule. It collapsed the Chinese economy, created social chaos and uprisings, and generated political instability. Yet ironically, the Opium War also awakened China from its fantasies and exposed it to the reality of progress. China was able to measure itself on the international level and realized that it was no longer on the top of the world. The Opium War gave China a sense of purpose, a desire to catch up. It signaled the beginning of the awakening of the giant.

The Closed China

In order to examine the effects of opening China, we must first study how and why China was closed. Before 1840, China was closed, or more accurately, it highly controlled its contacts with the outside world. The trade relationships were organized into the so called "Canton Trade System", since only the port of Canton was opened for foreign trade. Having reached Canton, the Western merchants could only deal with a group of government appointed merchants called "Gong Hang" ("officially authorized firms") which had a monopoly on the trade with the West. The volume of the trade and the prices as well as the personal activities of Western merchants was also regulated by the Gong Hang, which in turn was responsible to the Governor-General of Liangguang. The Western merchants were forbidden to have any contact with the Chinese except in trade and they had to live within a specific district in the city.

Why did China impose such limitations on trade? Two main reasons were present. China's foreign policy at that time was dominated by its sense of superiority. The Chinese believed that the Heaven was round, and the Earth was a square. The Heaven projected its circular shadow onto the centre of the Earth. The area under the shadow, "Tian Xia" ("Zone Beneath the Heaven") was China itself. Hence China was the "Heavenly Middle

Kingdom". The corners of the square not under the celestial emanation were ruled by foreign "yi" ("barbarians"). Thus morally to the Chinese, the "foreign devils" could not be on equal grounds with the Emperor, the "Son of Heaven". On the economic level, China had a self-reliant economy and a self-sufficient domestic trade. The Chinese had the feeling that China had much to lose and nothing to gain from foreign trade. As Evariste Huc noted in 1844 after his journey through China, "One excellent reason why China is only moderately fond of trading with foreigners is that her home trade is immense... China is such a vast, rich and varied country that internal trade is more than enough to occupy the part of the nation which can perform commercial operations... there is everywhere to be seen movement and a feverish activity which is not to be found in the largest towns of Europe."[i]

The second and the most important reason China closed its doors to Western countries was its desire to protect itself. After the Industrial Revolution, imperialism rose in Europe. In the rush to find new resources and new markets, Europeans madly explored and colonized "less civilized" countries. China was closed, but it was not so isolated that it did not know the Western conquest of the Philippines, the penetration of Malaysia, the rebellion of Christian converts in Japan. The British penetration and ultimately the conquest of China's old neighbour, India, shocked the Chinese Emperor. In China, the overthrow of a dynasty was often successful when external threats were coupled with internal disturbances. The Manchu themselves used the civil unrest in China to conquer China and set up their Qing Dynasty. At a time when the Manchu rule in China was becoming weaker, the rulers could not permit any forms of foreign power to enter China that may help to overthrow them. The weaker the Manchu rule in China, the stricter their control on the foreign trade. From the stand point of the Manchu rulers, they were afraid that foreigners would learn China's weaknesses, but they were even more afraid that Chinese would collaborate with foreigners. *What was a better way to prevent all of these than to seal off China from the European powers who had proven themselves to be violent and destructive in their dealings with China's neighbours?* The hypothesis that China closed its doors due to its anxiety to protect itself rather than from xenophobic hostility towards foreigners was confirmed by the fact that the "closed-door" policy did not apply to Russia. From the 17th century, China's relations with Russia were based on equal participation. A well-balanced trade existed between the two countries. China welcomed peaceful merchants to the north while resisting the ones in the south.

China closed its doors to the West because of its false sense of superiority and most importantly, its desire to protect itself. China tried to resist foreign political and economic penetrations by restricting foreign trade. Yet its attempts to seal itself off invited an even more devastating penetration, the Opium War.

Within the Chinese mandarinate there was an ongoing debate over legalizing the opium trade itself. However, this idea was repeatedly rejected and instead, in 1838 the government sentenced native drug traffickers to death. Around this time, the British were selling roughly 1,400 tons per year to China. In March 1839 the Emperor appointed a new strict Confucianist commissioner, Lin Zexu, to control the opium trade at the port of Canton.[18] His first course of action was to enforce the imperial demand that there be a permanent halt to drug shipments into China. When the British refused to end the trade, Lin blockaded the British traders in their factories and cut off supplies of food[19]. On 27 March 1839 Charles Elliot, British Superintendent of Trade- who had been locked in the factories when he arrived at Canton- finally agreed that all British subjects should turn over their opium to him, amounting to nearly a year's supply of the drug, to be confiscated by Commissioner Lin Zexu. In a departure from his brief, he promised that the crown would compensate them for the lost opium. While this amounted to a tacit acknowledgment that the British government did not disapprove of the trade, it also forced a huge liability on the exchequer. Unable to allocate funds for an illegal drug but pressed for compensation by the merchants, this liability is cited as one reason for the decision to force a war. As well as seizing supplies in the factories, Chinese troops boarded British ships in international waters outside Chinese jurisdiction, where their cargo was still legal, and destroyed the opium aboard. After the opium was surrendered, trade was restarted on the strict condition that no more drugs would be smuggled into China. Lin demanded that British merchants had to sign a bond promising not to deal in opium under penalty of death. The British officially opposed signing of the bond, but some British merchants that did not deal in opium were willing to sign. Lin had the opium disposed of by dissolving it in water, salt, and lime, and dumping it into the ocean.

In 1839 Lin took the step of presenting a letter directly to Queen Victoria questioning the moral reasoning of the British government. Citing what he understood to be a strict prohibition of the trade within Great Britain, Lin questioned how it could then profit from the drug in China. He wrote: "Your Majesty has not before been thus officially notified, and you may plead ignorance of the severity of our laws, but I now give my assurance that we mean to cut this harmful drug forever." It is believed that the Queen never received Lin's letter. The British government and merchants offered no response to Lin, accusing him instead of destroying their property. When the British learned of what was taking place in Canton, as communications between these two parts of the world took months at this time, they sent a large British Indian army, which arrived in June 1840.

In 1842 the Qing authorities sued for peace, which concluded with the Treaty of Nanjing negotiated in August of that year and ratified in 1843. In the treaty, China was forced to pay an indemnity to Britain, open four ports to Britain, and cede Hong Kong to Queen Victoria. In the supplementary Treaty of the Bogue, the Qing Empire also recognized Britain as an equal to China and gave British subjects extraterritorial privileges in treaty ports. In 1844, the United States and France concluded similar treaties with China, the Treaty of Wanghia and Treaty of Whampoa respectively.

The First Opium War was attacked in the House of Commons by a newly elected young member of Parliament, William Ewart Gladstone, who wondered if there had ever been "a war more unjust in its origin, a war more calculated to cover this country with permanent disgrace, I do not know." The Foreign Secretary, Lord Palmerston, replied by saying that nobody could "say that he honestly believed the motive of the Chinese Government to have been the promotion of moral habits' and that the war was being fought to stem China's balance of payments deficit. John Quincy Adams commented that opium was "a mere incident to the dispute... the cause of the war is the kowtow- the arrogant and insupportable pretensions of China that she will hold commercial intercourse with the rest of mankind not upon terms of equal reciprocity, but upon the insulting and degrading forms of the relations between lord and vassal."

SIGNIFICANCE OF THE OPIUM WAR

The Opium War was the result of a long-standing conflict between China and Great Britain over the Opium Trade. Opium had proved a significant source of revenue for Britain's India colony and British merchants were making a significant profit from the (usually) illegal trade in opium to China. The trade had proved so successful that it had reversed the existing trade balance. Rather than having to supply the Chinese silver to pay for porcelain, tea, and silk, the British began receiving silver and those goods for illegal opium.

Obviously, opium did great damage to the Chinese economy as well as the Chinese people. When the Chinese attempted to enforce a ban on the trade, the seized British opium in Chinese ports and provoked a war with the British Empire. The Opium War was devastating to the Chinese. They were many years behind the British in terms of technology, so the British were quickly able to sink of the Chinese ships and then bombard the Chinese coastal cities at will. The Chinese had no way of fighting back, so they had to surrender and sue for peace.

The terms of the peace treaty were such that the Chinese had to give up their right to dictate market conventions. It also marked the last chance for the Chinese to kick out the Westerners. The treaty ending the war gave the British the perpetual right to have a significant presence in China. Even if China had retained its national sovereignty in the aftermath of the Opium War, however, the war proved that it no longer had the military power to keep out the foreigners.

British victory in the Opium War gave the British a position of strength in which to dictate the terms of the peace. The war proved that the British had a technological and military advantage that the Chinese would not be able to remedy in the foreseeable future. Although China was a vastly larger empire in both land and people than was the tiny island of Britain and the Chinese continued to be the dominant local power in Asia, Britain and other Western countries could not be turned away.

In the unequal treaty ending the Opium War, the British (and subsequent Western powers) used their technological and military advantage to press for increasing accommodations from the Chinese. These unequal treaties resulted in drastic changes in the way China dealt with foreigners. After thousands of years of exercising supremacy in its interactions with outsiders, China found itself being dictated to by those outsiders themselves. Given the technological, economic, industrial, and military advantages enjoyed by Western countries over the Chinese, China had little prospects of reversing those changes. Closing those gaps would require embracing Westernization, which would, itself, make it impossible to go back to the old way of doing things.

THE FADING OF AMERICA: IS AMERICAN DOMINANCE IN THE WORLD ENDING?

BY ALEX

Every great civilizations fall. From the Romans to the ancient Mayans, history is littered with kingdoms and nations who "ruled the world" for a period of time only to descend into obscurity afterwards.

So, when I read this interesting Newsweek article by Fareed Zakaria, an excerpt of his book The Post-American World, I couldn't help but think: Is it America's turn?

Perhaps not: American technology, ideas, and economic powers are still very strong, but the rest of the world is catching up fast:

American anxiety springs from something much deeper, a sense that large and disruptive forces are coursing through the world. In almost every industry, in every aspect of life, it feels like the patterns of the past are being scrambled. [...] for the first time in living memory—the United States does not seem to be leading the charge. Americans see that a new world is coming into being, but fear it is one being shaped in distant lands and by foreign people.

Look around. The world's tallest building is in Taipei, and will soon be in Dubai. Its largest publicly traded company is in Beijing. Its biggest refinery is being constructed in India. Its largest passenger airplane is built in Europe. The largest investment fund on the planet is in Abu Dhabi; the biggest movie industry is Bollywood, not Hollywood. Once quintessentially American icons have been usurped by the natives. The largest Ferris wheel is in Singapore. The largest casino is in Macao, which overtook Las Vegas in gambling revenues last year. America no longer dominates even its favorite sport, shopping. The Mall of America in Minnesota once boasted that it was the largest shopping mall in the world. Today it wouldn't make the top ten. In the most recent rankings, only two of the world's ten richest people are American. These lists are arbitrary and a bit silly, but consider that only ten years ago, the United States would have serenely topped almost every one of these categories.

These factoids reflect a seismic shift in power and attitudes. It is one that I sense when I travel around the world. In America, we are still debating the nature and extent of anti-Americanism. One side says that the problem is real and worrying and that we must woo the world back. The other says this is the inevitable price of power and that many of these countries are envious—and vaguely French—so we can safely ignore their griping. But while we argue over why they hate us, "they" have moved on, and are now far more interested in other, more dynamic parts of the globe. The world has shifted from anti-Americanism to post-Americanism.

http://www.neatorama.com/2008/05/05/the-fading-of-america-is-american-dominance-in-the-world-ending/

GLOBALISATION STRATEGIES

Global strategy as defined in business terms is an organization's strategic guide to globalization. A sound global strategy should address these questions: what must be (versus what is) the extent of market presence in the world's major markets? How to build the necessary global presence? What must be (versus what is) the optimal locations around the world for the various value chain activities? How to run global presence into global competitive advantage?

Academic research on global strategy came of age during the 1980s, including work by Michael Porter and Christopher Bartlett & Sumantra Ghoshal. Among the forces perceived to bring about the globalization of competition was convergence in economic systems and technological change, especially in information technology, that facilitated and required the coordination of a multinational firm's strategy on a worldwide scale.

A global strategy may be appropriate in industries where firms are faced with strong pressures for cost reduction but with weak pressures for local responsiveness. Therefore, it allows these firms to sell a standardized product worldwide. However, fixed costs (capital equipment) are substantial. Nevertheless, these firms are able to take advantage of scale economies and experience curve effects, because it is able to mass-produce a standard product which can be exported (providing that demand is greater than the costs involved).

Global strategies require firms to tightly coordinate their product and pricing strategies across international markets and locations, and therefore firms that pursue a global strategy are typically highly centralized.

Globalization: The Strategy of Differences

Should your global strategy optimize scale or exploit differences? HBS Professor **Pankaj Ghemawat** suggests a mix-and-match strategy in this excerpt from *Harvard Business Review*.

Ten years ago, globalization seemed unstoppable. Today, the picture looks very different. Even Coca-Cola, widely seen as a standard-bearer of global business, has had its doubts about an idea it once took for granted. It was a Coke CEO, the late Roberto Goizueta, who declared in 1996: "The labels 'international' and 'domestic'...no longer apply." His globalization program, often summarized under the tagline "think global, act global," had included an unprecedented amount of standardization. By the time he passed away in

1997, Coca-Cola derived 67 percent of its revenues and 77 percent of its profits from outside North America.

But Goizueta's strategy soon ran into trouble, due in large part to the Asian currency crisis. By the end of 1999, when Douglas Daft took the reins, earnings had slumped, and Coke's stock had lost nearly one-third of its peak market value—a loss of about $70 billion. Daft's solution was an aggressive shift in the opposite direction. On taking over, he avowed, "The world in which we operate has changed dramatically, and we must change to succeed....No one drinks globally. Local people get thirsty and...buy a locally made Coke."

Unfortunately, "local" didn't seem to be any better a description of Coke's market space than "global." On March 7, 2002, the **Asian Wall Street Journal** announced: "After two years of lackluster sales...the "think local, act local" mantra is gone. Oversight over marketing is returning to Atlanta."

If the business climate can force Coke, which historically was (and is) more profitable internationally than domestically, to seesaw back and forth on globalization in this way, think of the pressures on the typical large company, for which international business is usually much less profitable than domestic business.

Why is globalization proving so hard to get right? The answer is related in part to how companies frame their globalization strategies. In many if not most cases, companies see globalization as a matter of taking a superior (by assumption) business model and extending it geographically, with necessary modifications, to maximize the firm's economies of scale. From this perspective, the key strategic challenge is simply to determine how much to adapt the business model—how much to standardize from country to country versus how much to localize to respond to local differences. Recently, as at Coke, many companies have moved toward more localization and less standardization. But no matter how they balance localization and standardization, all companies that view global strategy in this way focus on similarities across countries, and the potential for the scale economies that such commonalities unlock, as their primary

63

source of added value. Differences from country to country, in contrast, are viewed as obstacles that need to be overcome.

It's possible to apply different strategies to different elements of a business. Correctly choosing how much to adapt a business model is certainly important for extracting value from international operations. But to focus exclusively on the tension between global scale economies and local considerations is a mistake, for it blinds companies to the very real opportunities they could gain from exploiting differences. Indeed, in their rush to exploit the similarities across borders, multinationals have discounted the original global strategy: arbitrage, the strategy of difference.

Of course, we're all familiar with arbitrage in its traditional, and least-sustainable, form—the pure exploitation of price differentials. But the world is not so homogeneous as to have removed arbitrage from a company's strategic tool kit. In fact, many forms of arbitrage offer relatively sustainable sources of competitive advantage, and as some opportunities for arbitrage disappear, others spring up to take their place. I do not claim that arbitrage to exploit differences is any more a complete strategic solution than the optimal exploitation of scale economies. To the contrary: If they are to get their global strategies right in the long term, many companies will have to find ways to combine the two approaches, despite the very real tensions between them.

Reconciling difference and similarity

One would think companies that try to exploit differences would not find it easy to exploit similarities as well. And indeed, a large body of research on the horizontal versus the vertical multinational enterprise has shown that there are fundamental tensions between pursuing scale economies and playing the spreads. (See the table "Conflicting Challenges.") The data indicate that there is some merit to classifying companies according to the primary way they add value through their international operations over long periods of time. But that either/or characterization of globalization strategies is very broad. Finer-grained analysis of case studies—particularly of companies that have in various ways been global innovators—suggests that it is possible to combine the two approaches to some extent.

For a start, it's possible to apply different strategies to different elements of a business. CEMEX pursued a financial strategy of arbitraging capital cost differences even as it implemented a standardized operational strategy. It set up complete, uniform production-to-distribution chains in most of its major markets, reinforced by cross-border scale economies in such areas as trading, logistics, information technology, and innovation (in the broadest sense of the term). Mixing and matching was possible in this case because, to a large extent, CEMEX can choose how to raise capital independently from the way it chooses to compete in product markets.

Some companies have gone further. Consider the case of GE Medical Systems (GEMS), the division that Jeffrey Immelt built up between 1997 and 2000 before he was tapped to take over from Jack Welch as CEO. Immelt pushed for acquisitions to build up scale because, for the leading global competitors, an R&D-to-sales ratio of at least 8 percent represented a significant source of scale economies. But he also implemented a production strategy that was intended to arbitrage cost differences by concentrating manufacturing operations—and, ultimately, other activities—wherever in the world they could be carried out most cost effectively. By 2001, GEMS obtained 15 percent of its direct material purchases from, and had located 40 percent of its own manufacturing activities in, low-cost countries.

Even the best management can only go so far in melding the two strategies.
Like CEMEX, GEMS was able to pursue both approaches because it could organize its operations into relatively autonomous bundles of activities (like product development) in which economies of scale and standardization were essential and those (like procurement and manufacturing) where arbitrage economies were being pursued. What's more, it was able to coordinate its widely dispersed operations by applying centrally developed learning templates. In particular, Immelt applied the "pitcher-catcher concept," developed elsewhere in GE, in which for each move, a pitching team at a high-cost existing plant

works with a catching team at a low-cost new location, and the move is not considered complete until the performance of the catching team meets or exceeds that of the pitching team. As a result, GEMS (and GE) seems to have managed to move production to low-cost countries faster than European competitors such as Philips and Siemens while also benefiting from greater scale economies.

But even the best management can get only so far in melding the two strategies. Acer, one of the world's largest computer manufacturers, supplies a cautionary tale of what can happen when companies go too far. Acer entered early into the contract manufacturing of personal computers, operating in low-wage Taiwan, and made good money with that arbitrage play. But in the early 1990s, it began to push Acer as a global brand, particularly in developed markets. This two-track approach turned out to be problematic. The branded business grew to significant volumes but continued to generate losses because the competitive environment was particularly tough for a late mover. Meanwhile, customers for Acer's contract-manufacturing arm worried that their business secrets would spill over to its competing line of business. They also feared that Acer could cross-subsidize its own brand with profits from its contract-manufacturing operations and so undercut their prices. In 2000, the strategy blew up when IBM canceled a major order, reducing its share of Acer's total contract-manufacturing revenues from 53 percent in the first quarter of 2000 to only 26 percent in the second quarter of 2001.

Acer responded by making some hard choices. Contract manufacturing has remained focused on customers in developed countries—and will gradually be spun off into a separate company. Meanwhile, sales of its own branded products have been focused on the East Asia region, particularly Greater China, where the contract customers cannot sell at a low enough price to compete. With this move, the company has acknowledged that the logic of exploiting similarities often calls for targeting countries similar to a company's home base, whereas the logic of arbitrage involves exploiting one or more of the differences inherent in distance.

The future of the globalization process is by no means obvious. Markets may integrate further once economic conditions improve. But some argue that the process could actually shift into reverse, toward even greater economic isolation, if the experience between the two World Wars is any precedent. Whatever the ultimate direction, though, the differences that make arbitrage valuable as well as the similarities that create scale economies will remain with us for the foreseeable future. That spells opportunity for those companies that have the imagination to see the full range of possibilities.

Conflicting Challenges

The challenges facing companies pursuing economies of scale through adaptation or aggregation are fundamentally different from those that companies face when pursing absolute economies through arbitrage.

	Adaptation or Aggregation	Arbitrage
Competitive Advantage Why globalize at all?	To achieve scale and scope economies through standardization	To reap absolute economies through specialization
Configuration Why locate in foreign countries?	To minimize the effects of distance by concentrating on foreign countries that are similar to one's home business	To exploit distance by operating in a more diverse set of countries
Coordination How should international operations be organized?	By business; to achieve economies of scale across borders by placing a greater emphasis on horizontal relationships	By function; to achieve absolute economies by placing a greater emphasis on vertical relationships (efficiently matching supply and demand across borders, for instance)
Control Systems What are the strategic dangers?	Excessive standardization, on the one hand; variety, complexity, or both, on the other	Narrowing differences between countries
Corporate	The appearance of and	The exploitation or bypassing of

Diplomacy What public issues need to be addressed?	backlash against, cultural or other forms of domination (especially by U.S. companies)	suppliers, channels, or intermediaries

Excerpted with permission from "The Forgotten Strategy," **Harvard Business Review**, Vol. 81, No. 11, November 2003.

A global industry

A global industry can be defined as:

- An industry in which firms must compete in all world markets of that product in order to survive
- An industry in which a firm's competitive advantage depends on economies of scale and economies of scope gained across markets

Global markets are international markets where products are largely standardized.

Michael Porter argued that industries are either multi-domestic or global.

Global industries: competition is global. The same firms compete with each other everywhere.

Multi-domestic industries: firms compete in each national market independently of other national markets.

In general businesses adopt a global strategy in global markets and a multi-local strategy in multi domestic markets.

Global strategy

Companies such as Sony and Panasonic pursue a global strategy which involves:

- Competing everywhere
- Appreciating that success demands a presence in almost every part of the world in order to compete effectively
- Making the product the same for each market
- Centralised control
- Taking advantage of customer needs and wants across international borders
- Locating their value adding activities where they can achieve the greatest competitive advantage
- Integrating and co-coordinating activities across borders
- A global strategy is effective when differences between countries are small and competition is global. It has advantages in terms of

- o Economies of scale
  Lower costs
  Co-ordination of activities
  Faster product development

However, many regret the growing standardisation across the world.

Multi domestic strategy

- A multi-domestic strategy involves products tailored to individual countries Innovation comes from local R&D
- There is decentralisation of decision making within the organisation
- One result of decentralisation is local sourcing
- Responding to local needs is desirable but there are disadvantages: for example high costs due to tailored products and duplication across countries

Comparison of the two strategies

Four drivers determine the extent and nature of globalisation in an industry:

(1) Market drivers

- Degree of homogeneity of customer needs
- Existence global distribution networks
- Transferable marketing

(2) Cost drivers

- Potential for economies of scale
- Transportation cost
- Product development costs
- Economies of scope

(3) Government drivers

- Favour trade policies e.g. market liberalisation
- Compatible technical standards and common marketing regulations
- Privatisation

(4) Competitive drivers

- The greater the strength of the competitive drivers the greater the tendency for an industry to globalise
- Globalization refers to the process of integration across societies and economies.

  The phenomenon encompasses the flow of products, services, labor, finance, information, and ideas moving across national borders. The frequency and intensity of the flows relate to the upward or downward direction of globalization as a trend.

- There is a popular notion that there has been an increase of globalization since the early 1980s. However, a comparison of the period between 1870 and 1914 to the post-World War II era indicates a greater degree of globalization in the earlier part of the century than the latter half. This is true in regards to international trade growth and capital flows, as well as migration of people to America.

- If a perspective starts after 1945—at the start of the Cold War—globalization is a growing trend with a predominance of global economic integration that leads to greater interdependence among nations. Between 1990 and 2001, total output of export and import of goods as a proportion of GDP rose from 32.3 percent to 37.9 percent in developed countries and 33.8 percent to 48.9 percent for low- to middle-income countries. From 1990 to 2003, international trade export rose by $3.4 to $7.3 trillion (see Figure 1). Hence, the general direction of globalization is growth that is unevenly distributed between wealthier and poorer countries.

RATIONALE

- A primary economic rationale for globalization is reducing barriers to trade for the enrichment of all societies. The greater good would be served by leveraging

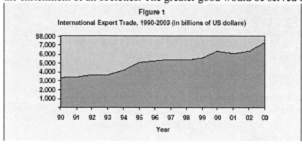

Figure 1
International Export Trade, 1990-2003 (in billions of US dollars)

•

- **Figure 1**
  International Export Trade, 1990-2003 (in billions of US dollars)

70

- comparative advantages for production and trade that are impeded by regulatory barriers between sovereignty entities. In other words, the betterment of societies through free trade for everyone is possible as long as each one has the freedom to produce with a comparative advantage and engage in exchanges with others.

- This economic rationale for global integration depends on supporting factors to facilitate the process. The factors include advances in transportation, communication, and technology to provide the necessary conduits for global economic integration. While these factors are necessary, they are not sufficient. Collaboration with political will through international relations is required to leverage the potential of the supporting factors.

HISTORICAL BACKGROUND

- Globalization from 1870 to 1914 came to an end with the World War I as various countries pursued isolationism and protectionism agendas through various treaties—the Treaty of Brest-Litovsk (1918), the Treaty of Versailles (1918), the Treaty of St. Germain (1919), and the Treaty of Trianon (1920). U.S. trade policies—the Tariff acts of 1921, 1922, 1924, 1926, and the Smooth Hawley Tariffs of 1930—raised barriers to trade. These events contributed to the implosion of globalization for more than forty years.

- Toward the end of World War II, forty-four countries met in an effort to re-establish international trade. The milestone is referred to as Bretton Woods, named after the New Hampshire country inn where the meeting was held. Results of Bretton Woods included the creation of the International Monetary Fund (IMF), the World Bank, and subsequently, the General Agreements on Tariffs and Trade (GATT).

- In 1948 the International Trade Organization (ITO) was established as an agency of the United Nations, with fifty member countries and the Havana Charter to facilitate international trade but it failed. As a result, GATT rose to fill the void as a channel for multilateral trade negotiations and recognition of "Most Favored Nation" status that applied the same trading conditions between members that applied to other trading partners with "most favored" partner standing.

71

- GATT involved a number of different multilateral rounds of trade negotiations to reduce trade barriers and facilitate international trade. In the first round, the twenty-three founding members of GATT agreed to 45,000 tariff concessions affecting 20 percent of international trade worth $10 billion. Many of GATT's trade rules were drawn from the ITO charter. Subsequent trade rounds involved more members and additional issues, but the basic foundation of GATT remained the same.
- In the second round, the Kennedy Round of the mid-1960s, the focus continued with tariff reductions.
- In the third round, the Tokyo Round (1973–1979), 102 countries participated to reform the trading system, resulting in tariff on manufactured products reduced to 4.7 percent from a high of 40 percent at the inception of GATT. Important issues revolved around anti-dumping measures, and subsidies and countervailing measures. The reduction of trade barriers enabled about an average of 8 percent growth of world trade per year in the 1950s and 1960s.
- In the fourth round, the Uruguay Round (1986 to 1993), 125 countries participated to develop a more comprehensive system.
- On April 15, 1995, in Marrakesh, Morocco, a deal was signed to create the World Trade Organization (WTO), which replaced GATT with a permanent institution that required a full and permanent commitment. The WTO encompasses trade in goods, services, and intellectual property related to trade with a more efficient dispute settlement system.

COMPLEXITIES AND CONTROVERSIES

- The increase of globalization surfaced many complex and controversial issues as economies and societies became more interdependent with greater frequency of interactions between one another. A number of important trends make up globalization including: (1) location of integration activities; (2) impact upon poorer societies; (3) flow of capital; (4) migration of labor and work; (5) diffusion of technology; (6) sustainability of the natural environment; (7) reconfiguration of cultural dynamics; and (8) development of organizational strategies for global competition.

- Many authors specialize in exploring each issue with much greater depth. The purpose of reviewing the different trends in this essay is to provide some highlight concerning the interrelated complexities underlying globalization.

LOCATION OF INTEGRATION ACTIVITIES.

- The extent of globalization unfolds in an uneven fashion to the degree that the question is raised whether international trade is more focused on regional rather than global integration. Trading blocs, such as the North American Free Trade Agreement (NAFTA), the European Union (EU), the Asia-Pacific Economic Co-operation (APEC), Mercosur (South American trading bloc), the Association of South East Asian Nations (ASEAN), and the East Africa Community (EAC), support regional cooperation between geographical neighbors.
- Georgios Chortareas' and Theodore Pelagidis' research findings on openness and convergence in international trade indicate that intra-regional trade increased more than global trade in most situations. They stated that "... despite the positive international climate resulting from important reductions in transportation costs, the development of new technologies and trade liberalization markets continue to be determined, to a large extent, regionally and nationally..."
- Within NAFTA, intra-regional exports rose from 34 percent in the 1980s to more than 56 percent in 2000; exports between Asian country members amounted to 48 percent in 2000; and exports within the EU were sustained at about 62 percent.
- An example of limitations to fair market access for developing countries is that developed countries subsidize agricultural producers with about $330 billion per year, which creates a significant disadvantage for poorer economies without such subsidies. The impact is exacerbated because 70 percent of the world's poor population lives in rural communities and depends heavily on agriculture. Hence, one of the concerns with uneven distribution of globalization is its impact on poorer economies by perpetuating systems of inequality.

IMPACT ON POORER SOCIETIES.

- A challenge to globalization is that inequality arises from imbalances in trade liberalization where the rich gain disproportionately more than the poor. Ajit K. Ghose examined the impact of international trade on income inequality and found that inter-country inequality increased from 1981 to 1997, in a sample of ninety-six national economies, but international inequality measured by per capita GDP declined. The ratio of average income for the wealthiest 20 percent compared to the poorest 20 percent rose from 30 to 74 from the early 1960s to the late 1990s.
- In 2004, one billion people owned 80 percent of the world's GDP, while another billion survives on a $1. However, during the same period, when average income is weighted by population, income inequality dropped by 10 percent in the same period. Also, global income distribution became more equal with other measures such as purchasing power parity or the number of people living in poverty.
- The World Development Indicators for 2004 showed a drop in absolute number of people living on $1 per day from 1.5 billion in 1981 to 1.1 billion in 2001 with most of the achievements taking place in the East Asia region. Thus, the impact of globalization on inequality is a complex issue depending on the particular measures. More specific examination needs to account for other contributing factors, such as how regionalism increases concentration of trade between countries that are wealthier and leaving poorer countries at the margin.

FLOW OF CAPITAL.

- The flow of capital relates to both regionalism and inequality issues. Two forms of capital flow are foreign direct investments (FDI) made by business firms and investment portfolios, diversified with foreign assets or borrowers seeking foreign funding. Data from the World Bank indicated that FDI grew from an average of $100 billion per year in the 1980s to $370 billion in 1997. Net private capital flow amounts to about $200 billion in 2004.
- Also, some economies have significant remittance flows from labor migration, which were approximately $100 billion in 2003 and $126 billion in 2004 for ninety developing countries. Some Caribbean countries receive more than 10 percent of their GDP from remittances. While developing countries are the primary recipients of remittances, transaction costs can amount to 10 to 15

percent per transaction. Reducing such obstacles would benefit poorer countries with heavy dependencies on remittances. The flow of money across national borders relates to the migration of both labor and work.

MIGRATION OF LABOR AND WORK.

- An important dimension of globalization is the migration of people. While the proportion of migration was greater during the earlier mercantilism period, sovereign border controls to a large extent create a filtration process for migration. About 175 million people lived in a different country than their birth country in 2000. They can be separated into three categories: 158 million international migrants, 16 million refugees, and 900,000 asylum seekers.
- An important global trend in the future is the movement of labor from developing to developed countries because of the latter's need for labor with an aging population. Family-sponsored migration makes up 45 to 75 percent of international migrants who mainly originate from developing countries to countries in Europe and North America.
- Even before 9/11, legal migration of labor needed to overcome substantial bureaucracy in the border control process. The number applying for entry into developed countries often far exceeds the number permitted. Due to extensive legal processes, some migrants enter illegally, while others become illegal with expiration of legal status.
- Anti-terrorism measures imposed shortly after the 9/11 attacks resulted in a minor shift in the flow of migrants away from the United States toward other developed countries. With the aging of baby boomers in many developed countries, future globalization of migrant labor flows is receiving more attention, especially in education, health care, retirement funding, and housing, as well as meeting workforce needs to sustain business competitiveness.
- Although migrant labor often entails the movement of people in search of work, a related globalization trend is the migration of work to different geographical location. While multinational corporations (MNCs) often seek low-cost labor, innovation advances in computer technology, satellite communication

infrastructures, internet developments, and efficient transportation network enable companies to distribute work in ways not possible before.

- Compression of time and space with internet technology allows for the distribution of work to take place around the world with global virtual teams. The phenomena of outsourcing and off shoring expand on the earlier sourcing of low-cost manufacturing. During the 1960s and 1970s, MNCs migrated to low-wage labor to manufacture products that entailed significant labor costs.

- Expansion of MNCs in the 1990s encompassed highly skilled workers, service work, and global virtual teams. Firms started to outsource information technology (IT) functions as early as the 1970s, but a major wave of outsourcing started in 1989 with the shortage of skilled IT workers in developed countries. At the same time, the trend of shifting work around the globe to leverage the different time zones began with the financial industry's ability to shift trading between the various stock exchanges in New York, Tokyo, and Hong Kong, and London.

- Technological innovations in computers and the internet enabled other industries, such as software engineering, data transcription, and customer service centers to also shift work around the globe. Higher education and high-skill health care jobs are also embarking on global outsourcing.

- In 2001, outsourcing expenditures amounted to $3.7 trillion and the estimation for 2003 is $5.1 trillion. The impact of global outsourcing is not just a relocation of jobs, but also a dampening of employee compensation levels in more developed economies. For example, in 2000, salaries for senior software engineers were as high as $130K, but dropped to about $100K at the end of 2002; and entry-level computer help-desk staff salaries dropped from about $55K to $35K. For IT vendor firms in countries like India, IT engineering jobs command a premium Indian salary that is at a fraction of their U.S. counterparts. In sum, migration of labor and work create complex globalization dynamics.

DIFFUSION OF TECHNOLOGY.

- Innovations in telecommunication, information technology, and computing advances make up key drivers to support the increase of globalization. In 1995, the World Wide Web had 20 million users, exploded to 400 million by late 2000 and had an estimated one billion users in 2005. However, the rapid growth and adoption of information technology is not evenly diffused around the world.
- The gap between high versus low adoption rates is often referred to as the digital divide. In 2002, the number of users per 1000 people was highest in Iceland at 647.9; others in the top five ranks of internet users included Sweden at 573.1, the United States at 551.4, Denmark and Canada both at 512.8, and Finland at 508.9. In comparison, countries at the low end of internet use were Tajikistan and Myanmar at 0.5 per 1000, Ethiopia at 0.7, the Congo at 0.9, Burundi at 1.2, and Bangladesh at 1.5.
- The digital divide reflects other disparities of globalization. Globalization of computer technology also entails a growing trend of computer crimes on an international basis, which requires cross-border collaboration to address it. Additional globalization trends related to computer technology include developments in artificial intelligence, high-speed connections such as wireless applications, and integration with biotechnology.

SUSTAINABILITY OF THE NATURAL ENVIRONMENT.

- The impacts of globalization on environment sustainability are hotly contested, with major environmental protests held at international economic meetings or prominent multilateral trade forums. The United Nation's 1987 publication of the *Brundtland Report* (named for Gro Brundtland, Prime Minister of Norway), galvanized international attention on sustainable development. A major assumption was that the degradation of the environment in developing countries was due primarily to poverty.
- Some advocates of globalization consider free trade to be a solution to alleviate poverty and subsequently, reduce pollution. However, the arguments depend upon corporate social responsibility, managerial knowledge of environmental sustainability, and a level of ignorance in the developing community.

- Critics find that often large MNCs have greater financial resources than some developing countries, which can be used to compromise and derail regulatory regimes from protecting the environment. For example, while a MNC may not produce or sell certain environmentally damaging products in a country with tight regulatory controls, they may find their way to markets with fewer environmental regulatory constraints—"pollution havens." This line of logic leads to the notion of globalization becoming a "race to the bottom" as countries compete with lowering of environmental standards to attract foreign capital for economic development.
- One of the landmarks on environmental globalization is the Kyoto Accord, an international treaty to reduce greenhouse gas emissions based on exchanging limited pollution credits between countries. After lengthy multilateral complex negotiations, the Kyoto Accord was concluded in December, 1997 for ratification by national governments. On February 16, 2005, the date for the Kyoto Protocol to take effect, 141 nations ratified the agreement. Even though the United States is the world's largest polluter in volume and per capita output of greenhouse gases, the Bush administration refused to ratify the Kyoto Accord.

RECONFIGURATION OF CULTURAL DYNAMICS.

- Culture is another area of complex controversies with globalization. Competing perspectives about how globalization affects cultures revolve around the debates of cultural homogenization versus cultural diversification. The optimistic view of cultural globalization is that cultural diversity focuses on freer cultural exchanges with broader choices and enrichment of learning from different traditions. People have greater choices of globally produced goods, in addition to local offerings, without being bound by their geographical location. Alternatively, critics of cultural globalization present evidence demonstrating the depletion of cultural diversity through processes referred to as "Disneyfication" or "McDonaldization."
- Furthermore, not only is cultural diversity diminished but cultural quality is as well with mass produced goods being directed toward a common denominator. The criticisms are related to a sense of "Americanization" of the world, rather than globalization. The process involves a sense of far-reaching, anonymous

78

cultural imperialism. Debates from each perspective are intense with substantial evidence that also reveals complex ties to social and political dynamics within and between national borders.

- Cultural globalization continues into the foreseeable future with many more controversial dynamics related to three important issues: 1) the impact of extractive industries on the socio-economic, cultural exclusion and dislocation of indigenous peoples and their traditional knowledge; 2) international trading of cultural goods and knowledge; and 3) inflow of immigration impacts on national culture, which creates a tension between a sense of threat to the national culture and migrant demands for respect to their traditions in a multicultural society.

DEVELOPMENT OF ORGANIZATIONAL STRATEGIES FOR GLOBAL COMPETITION.

- The multiple dynamics of globalization—regionalism, inequality, financial flows, migration of labor and work, technological innovations, environmental sustainability, and cultural dynamics—form a turbulent and complex environment for managing business operations. While seven trends were highlighted to provide a brief sketch of interrelated complexities and controversies globalization, it also surfaced other significant issues.
- Global concerns revolve around terrorism, rapid transmission of pandemic diseases and viruses, the rise of China's and India's economies, an aging population in wealthier northern countries versus younger growing populations in the southern hemisphere, and advances in biotechnology are intricately embedded in globalization processes.

- **COMPETING IN THE GLOBAL ECONOMY**
- Globalization entails both opportunities and threats for creating and sustaining competitive strategies. Emerging economies offer resources in terms of labor, as well as expanding market opportunities. However, geopolitical relationships and backlashes from perceptions of cultural imperialism, such as the tensions between the United States and the European Union during the Iraq war create challenges for business operations.

- Global managers have a wide range of options to deal with globalization. Organizational strategies for international operations involve two related demands—the need for local orientation and the need for integration (as shown in Figure 2). Firms with low need for local orientation, but high need for integration require a global strategy that centralizes core operations with minor modifications for local adaptation. However, firms with a need for high local orientation, but low need for integration, require a multinational strategy that decentralizes significant operations to respond to local market conditions. Firms integrating a high need for both local orientation and organizational integration should strive for a transnational strategy.
- In addition to selecting a strategy for global competition, managers also need to make decisions regarding the internationalization process. Two processes are important. First, the development of innovations in a home market and as products moves along the product life cycle stages, firms can take products entering into the plateau of a mature stage to new international markets. Often the flow moves from developed to developing countries.
- Second, stages of internationalization with foreign entry modes that involve increasing resource commitment and risks start with exporting to licensing or joint ventures to wholly owned subsidiaries. The stage approach to internationalization takes time, which is a challenge within a global environment where information moves around the world in nanoseconds.
- Alternatively, Kenichi Ohmae argued that the speed and complexities of globalization require firms to rethink their internationalization process because incremental stage models are too slow. Given the rate and quantity of knowledge flows in global competition, firms are likely to face competition in their home markets, with comparable innovations to their own before they are able to establish a foothold in the international market.
- The incremental stage models are too slow for competing in an increasingly integrated global economy. Ohmae suggested that firms form global strategic alliances with partners established in three major markets—North America, Europe, and Asia, particularly Japan. Development of global competitive

intelligence and innovation among the partners provide for rapid market development and the establishment of strategic positions in multiple locations.

- Basically, globalization into the twenty-first century creates a fundamentally different competitive environment that shifted from incremental internationalization processes to almost simultaneous deployment of innovations. This internationalization process also shifts the work of global managers from managing a field of expatriates to collaborating with strategic partners across national borders and managing global off-shore outsourcing vendors in multiple geographical locations.

Skill Profile of the Effective Global Manager

- Globalization is a culmination of complex and controversial trends that include degree of geographical integration, inequalities, financial flows, labor and work, technological innovations, environmental sustainability, cultural dynamics, and organizational strategies for global competition. Given a historical perspective, globalization has fluctuated over time and many indicators support a trend of increasing globalization since the 1980s.
- While the United States is the dominant superpower in the global economy, the rise of both China and India is an important consideration for international business. Global managers have options for strategies and structures, as well as different internationalization processes. In sum, globalization creates a competitive arena where MNCs evolve into global networks with collaboration and controversial differences as necessities to sustain a competitive strategy.

Retrieved from : http://www.referenceforbusiness.com/management/Ex-Gov/Globalization.html

THE RAPID AMERICANISATION OF THE WORLD

This is an extract of an article from USA think tanks and their view of the world in the future.

"Globalization is not a random-walk process. It moves forward according to a tangible, coherent and well-planned strategy. This article offers the reader a glimpse into one aspect of the globalization stratagem – one that recast Europe and is now reshaping North America. Regionalization, as you will see, is a necessary stepping-stone toward and an essential component of globalization. This article lays the groundwork for future articles that will lay bare elements of regionalism in the Americas such as NAFTA and CAFTA." Patrick Wood, Editor, *the August Review*

"The two processes of globalization and regionalization are articulated within the same larger process of global structural transformation…" Björn Hettne, "Globalization, the New Regionalism and East Asia," Globalism and Regionalism.

Strategic landscapes are radically changing. No longer does a person's country represent the core of citizenship or identity. Today, a new murky world is dawning, one that advocates global governance as the portent to humanity's social, political, and economic future. Indeed, in this post-Cold War environment, "nation-states" – like the societies they serve and accommodate – find themselves in a relentless swell of transformation. National interests give way to global loyalties, just as world citizenship is touted as preferable to the narrow views of nationalism; no individual, corporation, or country is immune to this revolution. Welcome to "globalization," where everyone is either a pawn or a player.

As an end to itself, the concept of globalization seems to rest on one central pillar: the consolidation of power. No matter what stripe or ideology globalization comes packaged in, this singular component cannot be denied. And in a society where "power begets power," a global system, by definition, has the capability to expand this characteristic to new levels.

Politically, globalization represents the leveraging of power beyond that found in any one nation. Using the clichés of global governance, we would call this a "new world civilization," one that's built with international management in mind. Mikhail Gorbachev, the last true master of the Soviet style of centralized power explains, "The time has come to develop integrated global policies."

But political globalization is not an overnight game. We don't stop work Friday afternoon, take a break over the weekend, and poof, and find ourselves on Monday morning immersed in global governance. Rather, this macro-political transformation is the product of generations of changes, bumps and corrections, and decades of decisive planning. Already in 1945, leading socialist Scott Nearing penned,

"A world society cannot be haphazard. Since there are no precedents, it cannot be traditional at this stage in its development. It can only be deliberative and experimental, planned and built up with particular objectives…"

Much more recently, Trilateral Commission co-founder Zbigniew Brzezinski espoused similar notions, albeit with an American-focused bent. In his book, *The Grand Chessboard: American Primacy and its Geostrategic Imperatives*, the former National Security Advisor maintains that America's purpose for global engagement is "that of forging an enduring framework of global geopolitical cooperation" and to "unapologetically" position itself as the arbitrator of "global management." Capping off this assertion, Brzezinski closes with these sobering words, "Geostrategic success in that cause would represent a fitting legacy of America's role as the first, only, and last truly global superpower."

Jim Garrison, founder and President of the Gorbachev Foundation/USA (at the behest of Mikhail Gorbachev), likewise sees America as the forging element in globalization.

"...America must consciously view itself as a transitional empire, one whose destiny at this moment is to act as midwife to a democratically governed global system. Its great challenge is not to dominate but to catalyze. It must use its great strength and democratic heritage to establish integrating institutions and mechanisms to manage the emerging global system so that its own power is subsumed by the very edifice it helps to build.

"President Wilson established the League of Nations out of the ashes of World War I. President Roosevelt and Truman established a new international order after World War II. America must now build the third iteration of global governance. If it attains this level of greatness, it could become the final empire, for it will have bequeathed to the world a democratic and integrated global system in which empire will no longer have a place or perform a role."

Nearing, **Brzezinski**, and Garrison all point to the reality of internationalism – it's not accidental. And the last two individuals, global players in their own right, directly **call for America's guiding hand in planetary transformation**.

America, however, isn't the only major agent for global change. Europe too, and more specifically for the 21st century, the European Union, is a fantastic factor in the globalization process. Indeed, Brzezinski calls for America to act with the European Union "for sustained global political planning."

Not surprisingly, an American-European approach to global order already exists under the Transatlantic Alliance heading. Over the years, this alliance has been greatly shaped by men such as **Brzezinski**, **Henry Kissinger**, and John J. McCloy on the US side – and by key Europeans such as Paul-Henri Spaak, Jacques Delors and **Javier Solana**.

Presently this Transatlantic system is comprised of a myriad of political, military, and economic linkages. Some of its components include,

- NATO (North Atlantic Treaty Organization)
- OSCE (Organization for Security and Co-operation in Europe)
- OECD (Organization for Economic Co-operation and Development), which originally started out as the Organisation for European Economic Co-operation).[10]
- Various joint commissions and private policy groups – such as the Trilateral Commission, [11] the Atlantic Council of the United States, the British American

83

Security Information Council, and the less well known Streit Council – along with numerous programs such as the Transatlantic Foreign Policy Discourse.
- Massive business and corporate ties within aircraft and shipping industries, petroleum and petro-chemical companies, defense and aerospace ventures, all major automobile manufacturers, and many more commercial connections.

This last point bears special significance. Elizabeth Pond, writing for the European Union Studies Association's U.S.-EU Relations Project, tells us, "So intertwined have transatlantic companies become, especially in the past decade, that it is often impossible to tell if firms are actually 'American' or 'European'."

For many outside observers, the question arises: Does this Transatlantic connection represent the Americanization of Europe, or is Europe shaping America?

Maybe it's neither. Too often we in North America perceive such quandaries through nationalistic lenses, instead, when viewed through the glasses of globalization, a whole new world comes into focus.

What the Transatlantic ideal ultimately represents is the "Third Wave" – the route of globalization. As social scholars Alvin and Heidi Toffler assert, "what is happening now is nothing less than a global revolution, a quantum leap."

But please don't misunderstand: this "global revolution" is not a seamless process. As one facet of the revolution, the Transatlantic partnership – like all other relationships – has growing pains, setbacks, and observable differences. Indeed during the last number of years, sizeable rifts have occurred between European and American population segments, especially in light of Middle Eastern developments. Although this fissure is more apparent in the general citizenry and within certain policy circles, and may even have spillover effects within Transatlantic markets such as defense spending, it's a rift that temporarily detracts from the global reality.

And what is the "global reality"? That America is on the threshold of having to reshape itself, just as it helped re-shape post-war Europe, and is now looked upon as the "midwife" of a new global order.

It's the shift from nationalism to globalization, via the European model of regionalism.

Globalization, European Regionalism, and Anti-Nationalism

Immediately after the close of the Cold War, the Trilateral Commission – a private policy group comprised of American, European, and Asian counterparts – released its study, *Regionalism in a Converging World*.[16] According to its Introduction,

"…regionalism need not be opposed to globalism. The world should not have to choose between one or the other. It needs to live with both. The challenge…is how to channel the forces of regionalism in directions compatible with and supportive of globalism."[17] [italics in original]

It's important to understand that sponsorship for regionalism as a step in the globalization process hasn't just been confined to the Trilateral Commission and its members. Thankfully, the many builders of this regional-global order have left their fingerprints plastered throughout the twentieth century. More significantly, their motives are also discernable.

Back in 1942, The Brookings Institute released its report, Peace Plans and American Choices, highlighting a variety of hopeful post-war concepts for "world order." Options were reviewed such as explicit US mastery over international affairs, the creation of a British-American Alliance, harmonizing world order through a "Union of Democracies" (which was being touted at the time by Clarence Streit), and the collaboration of a larger "United Nations" package. Regionalism was considered in detail, with the Western Hemisphere, Europe, and Asia comprising the main blocks.

Arthur Millspaugh, author of the Brookings report, was candid in his linking of regionalism to the "bigger picture,"

"Such regional arrangements may be considered either as steps or stages in the evolution of a universal world order, as substitutes for a universal order, or as something to be combined with a world-wide system."

Although the Brookings report focused on the anticipated aftermath of World War II, the idea of a Europe-State had been birthed decades earlier. Already in 1914, the first year of The Great War (WWI), Nicholas Murray Butler – President of Columbia University and later recipient of the 1933 Nobel Peace Prize – suggested that European unification and the advent of a supra-national government was needed to replace the "existing national system."

"What will be in substance a United States of Europe, a more or less formal federation of the self-governing countries of Europe, may be the outcome of the demonstrated failure of the existing national system to adjust government to the growth of civilization...

"There is no reason why each nation in Europe should not make a place for itself in the sun of unity which I feel sure is rising there behind the war-clouds. Europe's stupendous economic loss, which already has been appalling and will soon be incalculable, will give us an opportunity to press this argument home...

"...the time will come when each nation will deposit in a world federation some portion of its sovereignty for the general good. When this happens it will be possible to establish an international executive and an international police, both devised for the especial purpose of enforcing the decisions of the international court."

Attempts to promote European integration and cooperation after The Great War were made. In 1923 the Pan-European Union was founded, attracting a number of individuals who would later play a post-World War II role, including Konrad Adenauer. And France's foreign minister, Aristide Briand, envisioned a scheme to organize Europe around unified lines as opposed to nationalistic tendencies, even bringing the debate to the League of Nations. None of these campaigns, however, were generally effective.

Ironically, while the League of Nations and the Pan-European Union ideas floundered, a type of continental integration almost occurred via the National Socialist German Worker's Party – better known as the Nazis. John Laughland, author of The Tainted Source, details the extensive European unification platform espoused by the Nazi leadership, including plans for a Central European Economic Community, a customs-free market area, and the eventual creation of a European monetary area. What's more, as Laughland points out, "Nazi plans for European integration were as political as they were economic."

The influence of Nazi-era concepts on European integration cannot be understated. Stationed in Germany during the early years of World War II, George F. Kennan, one of the most important American diplomats of the twentieth century and the first Director of Policy Planning Staff at the State Department, candidly shared his observations,

"When stationed in Berlin during the war I had been struck with the fact that Hitler himself, albeit for the wrong reasons and in the wrong spirit, had actually accomplished much of the technical task of the unification of Europe. He had created central authorities in a whole series of areas: in transportation, in banking, in procurement and distribution of raw materials, in the control of various forms of nationalized property. Why, I asked myself, could this situation not be usefully exploited after an Allied victory?

"What was needed was an Allied decision not to smash this network of central controls when the war was ended but rather to take it over, to remove the Nazi officials who had made it work, to appoint others (and not necessarily all non-Germans) in their place, and then to supplement this physical unification with a new European federal authority. When I returned from Germany, in 1942, I tried to win understanding for this idea in the Department of State…"

After the war, Kennan (who was a member of the Council on Foreign Relations and later in life involved in the Trilateral Commission) became the US counselor to the European Advisory Commission and a primary architect of the Marshall Plan – America's rebuilding program for Europe. In his Memoirs, the diplomat noted,

"The United States government, animated primarily by a belief that something should be done to 'integrate' the economies of the European countries in the interests of economic recovery, had been adding words of encouragement, if not pressure."

This immediate post-war "encouragement" was essentially channeled via the Marshall Plan, with European integration "tacked on every proposal made in Washington for export to Europe."

Theodore H. White, a US foreign journalist and later member of the Council on Foreign Relations, describes the situation in his book, Fire in the Ashes,

"American's had, for many years, been loftily instructing Europeans in the virtues of their own great Union of the States, and chided Europe on the stupidities of its rivalries and separatisms. During the war several American brain trusters had even toyed with the idea that, come Liberation, it would be best to sweep away all currencies of the Liberation countries and replace them with one new common European currency issued by the United States Army…"

White continued,

"It was the Marshall Plan that hardened American convictions that Europeans must unite…When visiting Congressmen asked the Marshall Planners what they were trying to do, they would answer, 'We're trying to pull them together, we're trying to integrate them.' 'Integration' was a convenient word and each successive delegation asked sternly, 'How far have you got with integration now?' as if expecting the Marshall Plan to pull out of its desk drawers a draft constitution and a design for a European flag.

"By 1949, in the second appropriation of the Marshall Plan, Congress, without debate, set the unification of Europe as one of the major purposes of the Plan."

Later in life White would reflect, "The story of the Marshall Plan, it turned out, began with the Meaning of Money. It was also about Money and Europe, and Money and the Peace – but above all, Money and Power and America."

While the Marshall Plan was operational, three members of Europe's Christian Democratic community – Alcide De Gasperi, Konrad Adenauer, and Robert Shuman – led the way towards rousing continental interest in unification. Giving us some insight into the motivational factors of these three "Fathers of Europe," R.W. Keyserlingk, General Manager of the British United Press during the 1940s, writes,

"…all three [had] been formed in their youth by the Catholic social movements activated by the papal teachings of Rerum Novarum. They were all deeply religious, fervent patriots but determined anti-nationalists. All three came from frontier areas of border disputes and border contacts…This had taught them that only a Europe as a federation, not Europe torn by hatreds bred by narrow nationalism, could assure freedom and liberty to their beloved, more intimate border homelands."

Demonstrating the depth of this European ideal within an anti-nationalistic framework and of the subsequent roadmap to regionalism, Keyserlingk reminds us, "Integration into a federal system, along political, economic and military lines, involving the sacrifice of absolute national sovereignty, was their objective."

How to achieve this objective? The continuity between assimilation approaches is truly remarkable,

"First, the political line was attempted and although this proved almost to be putting the cart before the horse, it had considerable merit for the future. It created the Council of Europe and the European Parliament...

"When the political approach revealed the insurmountable difficulties of getting down to practical working measures, Robert Shuman came up with the second possibility, economic integration; a merging of interlocking interests, the abolition of trade barriers eliminating economic competition...working out of common policies for use of the labour market...freedom of movement for workers...and a gradual strengthening of joint economic policies..."

Through this decided act of economic amalgamation, which has since borne itself out via the European Union and Euro currency, Europe became for the rest of the world a recognized model to advance internationalism above single state interests. This reality was perceived early on by European federalists and is evident in the 1946 Hertenstein Program,

"A European Community on federal lines is a necessary and essential contribution to any world union...The members of the European Union shall transfer part of their sovereign rights – economic, political and military – to the Federation which they constitute...By showing that it can solve the problems of its destiny in a federal spirit, Europe will make its contribution to reconstruction and to the creation of a world community of peoples."

Less than one year after the Hertenstein announcement, the "World Movement for World Federal Government" released a similar platform known as the Montreux Declaration. After stating that national sovereignty required limitations and that nations needed to transfer powers to a "world federal government," the Declaration added,

"We consider that integration of activities at regional and functional levels is consistent with the true federal approach. The formation of regional federations – insofar as they do not become an end in themselves or run the risk of crystallizing into blocs – can and should contribute to the effective functioning of a world federal government."

In the decades immediately following World War II, Transatlantic ties between Euro-federalists and American elites broadened international acceptance of a European Community. Moreover, Europe's march to amalgamation successfully achieved strategic goals. The European Coal and Steel Community, the Treaty of Rome and the subsequent European Economic Community and Euratom agency, and the gradual harmonization of agricultural and fiscal policies all demonstrated the strength of this trans-national agenda.

By the time the 1970s rolled around with its OPEC petroleum crisis and the revamping of the Bretton Woods financial system, the opportunities regionalism offered as a tool for global transformation was clearly evident. The Trilateral Commission, the Club of Rome, and the Institute for World Order all looked to regionalism as a trump card over nationalism.

As one of the most prolific advocates of regional modeling, the Club of Rome – an elite body acting as a "global catalyst of change" – deserves special attention. Its report, Mankind at the Turning Point, envisioned a world zoned into ten different blocs, and acknowledged that the regional view was necessary for global development. In another report released during this same time period, the Club of Rome merged the steering of world change, anti-nationalism, and regional cooperation.

"In the present international order huge power is concentrated in individualized nation-States. Seen from a world viewpoint, this must be deemed undesirable. Some of the means which could be employed to attain those objectives of vital importance to the international community can more effectively be handled by higher levels of decision-making…the achievement of some aims, such as the creation of larger markets through regional and sub-regional cooperation (collective self-reliance), would be facilitated by decision-making on a level higher than the nation-State."

Richard A. Falk, a Professor of International Law with connections to the Council on Foreign Relations and the World Federalist Association, postulated similar directives in the mid-1970s. Contributing to the World Order Model's Project (a program of the Institute for World Order), he wrote that,

"…regionalism has considerable appeal as a world order half-way house. It seems more feasible in the near term as a step beyond state sovereignty that can be used to dilute nationalist sentiments during a period when global loyalties need to grow stronger."

Falk had seen the handwriting on the wall less than a decade earlier. Touching on the increasing role of regional institutions and the United Nations as it related to global transitional strategies, he offered an interesting perspective to the World Law Fund's Strategy of World Order program: "The result of these challenges to the traditional international legal system is to create a situation of transitional crisis. For the inadequacies of the old order have given rise to the beginnings of a new order…"

Today, global elites from both Europe and America consider regionalism to be a prime stratagem for global governance. In fact, this "new regionalism" is now embraced by a multitude of key individuals, organizations, and governmental agencies. As two United Nations University document released in 2005 state,

"…regional governance is not incompatible with and does not negate global governance. On the contrary, it has the potential to strengthen global governance. The regional logic has always been inherent to the global body…"

And,

"Regional integration between sovereign states…is a booming phenomenon, and, not surprisingly, it is nowadays seen as a process that, together with globalization, challenges the existing Westphalian [Ed., nation-centered] world order."

American Choices and World Realities

Nations-states will not go away, either under regionalism or through some form of global governance. Roles, functions and the sovereign status of nations, however, will be fundamentally altered. But the "country," like state/provinces and city/local governments, will remain intact. Just add another layer to the pile – after all, it's the Third Wave style of global transformation.

As social engineers Alvin and Heidi Toffler reminds us, "Change so many social, technological and cultural elements at once and you create not just a transition but a transformation, not just a new society but the beginnings, at least, of a totally new civilization."

Globalization and regionalism go hand-in-hand, and the relevancy of this is extraordinary. Currently, the EU is assisting in the creation of new regional blocs around the world: including the Gulf Cooperation Council, an Asian zone, the development of the South American Community of Nations, and new blocs in Africa, Latin America and the Caribbean.

One 2004 EU document spells out this strategy,

"Because of its history and its own integration process, support for regional integration is an area in which the EU has real added value to contribute. The EU is ready to share this unique experience with other world regional groupings. It also hopes to help them draw on the substantial gains made in the regional integration process. It therefore encourages other countries in the world to forge even stronger links with their neighbors and to organize themselves within institutionalized regional organisations."

In discussing its own enlargement we can, moreover, catch a glimpse of what the EU envisions: "Enlargement strengthens the role and position of the Union in the world, in external relations, security, trade and in other domains relating to world governance." And, "In political terms, by adding to the power, cohesion and influence of the Union on the international arena, enlargement strengthens the Union's hand when it comes to globalisation…"

What does this have to do with the United States of America? Everything.

At the financial level, the US has to monetarily and economically compete with the European Union and its Euro currency. This competition not only impacts America's trading power with Europe directly, but the growing influence of the Euro around the world raises the stakes even higher. In 2004, Toshihiko Fukui, a board member with the

Bank for International Settlements, noted; "Today, we can discuss the euro's potential to bring a sea change to the global financial architecture, without being criticized for fantasizing." Fukui then talked of a time when, like the European Union, Asia too will work as an economic bloc with a single powerful, globally recognized currency.

The Euro's importance as a rival to the US dollar, and as a model for other currency zones, cannot be ignored. And as different regions develop – with the possibilities of China, India, and Brazil becoming natural magnets for the creation of massive economic/regional power blocs – America, with its debt loads expanded beyond comprehension and its dollar losing face internationally, finds itself treading economically dangerous waters.

But there's one other element added to this mix. As stated earlier, the European Union is involved in creating other competitive regional blocs. Not only does this cause a deflection in US dollar strength at the international level, it also shifts foreign interests away from the US and back to Europe. Hence American influence, especially in terms of advancing US interests abroad, weakens as Europe's influence grows.

These facts haven't escaped US policy makers. The irony is that America's answer is to follow Europe's footsteps, blending domestic realities with regional/global trends, and try to assist foreign nations to integrate under US guidance. The paradox deepens: America, in order to counter the Europe it helped establish, now has to create a North American Community incorporating itself, Canada, and Mexico into a new super-region. However, this is only a paradox to those in America who view the US through nationalist lenses, as already witnessed, its elite view things very differently.

North American integration isn't a pie-in-the-sky idea. It's been batted around by a host of privileged tri-national organizations, including the Canadian Council of Chief Executives (Canada's top business leaders), the Mexican Council on Foreign Relations, the **Center for Strategic and International Studies** (a Washington DC think tank with Trilateralist Brzezinski playing a key role), and the New York Council on Foreign Relations.

In the spring of 2005, the CFR came out with an "independent task force" report titled Building a North American Community. This document details an economic and security mandate that binds North America by establishing a common security perimeter, a North American border pass program, common external tariffs, the seamless movement of goods, full mobility of labor between Canada and the US, a continental energy platform, and the creation of a single economic tri-national region; with 2010 as a target date for many of these arrangements.

Responding to this report, the US Embassy in Canada – "pointing to increased competition from the European Union and raising economic powers such as India and China" – called the CFR's agenda a "blueprint for a powerhouse North American trading area."

A few short weeks after the CFR announced that its upcoming integration report would go public, US President Bush, Mexican President Fox, and Canadian Prime Minister Martin met in Texas to announce a tri-national agenda to "ensure that North America remains the most economically dynamic region of the world." The Council on Foreign Relations final report directly acknowledged this tri-national leadership summit, and pointedly said that, "The Task Force is pleased to provide specific advice on how the partnership can be pursued and realized." And tucked into the taskforce chairman's statement was a simple but vital comment; the "process of change must be properly managed."

This wasn't anything new to the banking community. In 1991, the Dallas Federal Reserve issued a research paper titled, North American Free Trade and the Peso: The Case for a North American Currency Area. In the late 1990's the Bank of Canada published a string of working papers looking at the pros and cons of a North American economic and monetary zone. One US Treasury Department official, outlining world financial trends at the Federal Reserve Bank of Atlanta in October 2000, candidly remarked that "a quantum increase in global economic and financial cooperation" would be needed to meet future international challenges,

"Successful globalization requires a parallel international process of harmonization of rules, including rules governing the financial system, a process that has been going on largely silently for many years in the central banking community…

"…I believe that it is at least possible that in the years ahead we will witness a dramatic decline in the number of independent currencies in the world…I would not like to put a time frame on an evolution to a world with substantially fewer currencies, but I am sure you have noted that the president elect of Mexico, Vincente Fox, has suggested a long-term evolution towards a North American currency area. Such trends may lead to new challenges and institutions in the area of international economic cooperation."

Regionalism as a stepping-stone to globalization is the inseparable blending of politics and economics across the board. On the "political side," consider what Richard N. Haass had to say when he was the Director of the Policy Planning Staff at the US Department of States back in 2002 (remember George F. Kennan was its first director).

"There clearly is a consistent body of ideas and policies that guides the Bush Administration's foreign policy. Whether these ideas and policies will evolve into a formal doctrine with a name, I'll leave to history to decide. But this coherence exists and can be captured by the idea of integration.

"In the 21st century, the principal aim of American foreign policy is to integrate other countries and organizations into arrangements that will sustain a world consistent with U.S. interests and values.

"…Integration is about bringing nations together and then building frameworks of cooperation and, where feasible, institutions that reinforce and sustain them even more.

"...Integration reflects not merely a hope for the future, but the emerging reality of the Bush Administration."

Haass should know. Not only is he a member of the Trilateral Commission, he's the President of the Council on Foreign Relations. In fact, Haass wrote the forward to the CFR report, *Building a North American Community*.

The bottom line is this: Just as politics and economics are bonded at the hip, regionalism and all it entails – including the unification of North America – fits part-and-parcel with the strategy of globalization. It's the pursuit of the Third Wave global society as a replacement to the archaic world of nationalism.

In conclusion, the question must be asked; How far will this process reach? Alvin and Heidi Toffler let the cat-out-of-the-bag.

"The fact is that building a Third Wave civilization on the wreckage of Second Wave institutions involves the design of new, more appropriate political structures in many nations at once. This is a painful yet necessary project that is mind-staggering in scope...

"In all likelihood it will require a protracted battle to radically overhaul the United States Congress, the House of Commons and the House of Lords, the French Chamber of Deputies, the Bundestag, the Diet, the giant ministries and entrenched civil services of many nations, their constitutions and court system – in short, much of the unwieldy and increasingly unworkable apparatus of existing representative governments.

"Nor will this wave of political struggle stop at the national level. Over the months and decades ahead, the entire 'global law machine' – from the United Nations at one end to the local city or town council at the other – will eventually face a mounting, ultimately irresistible demand for restructuring.

"All of these structures will have to be fundamentally altered, not because they are inherently evil or even because they are controlled by this or that class or group, but because they are increasingly unworkable – no longer fitting to the needs of a radically changing world."

Can't you hear it? That's the sound of the crucible of globalization being fired up.

http://www.crossroad.to/articles2/006/teichrib/globalization-strategy.htm

THE HERITAGE FOUNDATION

The Heritage Foundation is a conservative American think tank based in Washington, D.C.

The foundation took a leading role in the conservative movement during the presidency of Ronald Reagan, whose policies drew significantly from Heritage's policy study *Mandate for Leadership*. Heritage has since continued to have a significant influence in U.S. public policy making, and is considered to be one of the most influential conservative research organizations in the United States, especially during the Republican administration of President George W. Bush. Heritage's stated mission is to "formulate and promote conservative public policies based on the principles of free enterprise, limited government, individual freedom, traditional American values, and a strong national defense."

History and major initiatives

Leadership

First led by activist Paul Weyrich, Heritage's president since 1977 has been Edwin Feulner, previously the staff director of the House Republican Study Committee and a former staff assistant to U.S. Congressman Phil Crane, R-Illinois.

Cold War and foreign policy involvement

In the 1980s and early 1990s, the Heritage Foundation was a key architect and advocate of the "Reagan Doctrine", under which the United States government supported anti-Communist resistance movements in such places as Afghanistan, Angola, Cambodia and Nicaragua during the Cold War. Heritage foreign policy analysts also provided policy guidance to these rebel forces and to dissidents in Eastern bloc nations and Soviet republics.

The foundation was instrumental in advancing President Ronald Reagan's belief that the former Soviet Union was an "evil empire" and that its defeat, not its mere containment, was a realistic foreign policy objective. Heritage also played a key role in building support for Reagan's plans to build an orbital ballistic missile shield, known as the "Strategic Defense Initiative", or more popularly, "Star Wars."

The foundation advocated repeal of the 1976 Clark Amendment, which barred aid to anti-government paramilitary forces in Angola. This effort was successful when the Clark Amendment was repealed in a midnight session of Congress in July 1985. Visiting The Heritage Foundation on October 5, 1989, Angolan rebel leader Jonas Savimbi of UNITA, praised Heritage for its role in repealing the amendment. "When we come to the Heritage Foundation," Savimbi said, "it is like coming back home. We know that our success here in Washington in repealing the Clark Amendment and obtaining American assistance for our cause is very much associated with your efforts. This foundation has been a source of great support. The UNITA leadership knows this, and it is also known in Angola."

Since the end of the Cold War, Heritage has continued to be an active voice in foreign affairs and has been broadly supportive of President George W. Bush's foreign policies. Speaking at the Heritage Foundation in November 2007, Bush predicted that fifty years from then a future U.S. President would return to the Heritage Foundation and say, "Thank God that generation that wrote the first chapter in the 21st century understood the power of freedom to bring the peace we want."

Domestic economic policies

In domestic policy, Heritage is a proponent of supply-side economics, which holds that reductions in the marginal rate of taxation can spur economic growth.

In 1994, Heritage advised Newt Gingrich and other conservatives on the development of the "Contract with America", which was credited with helping to produce a Republican majority in Congress. The "Contract" was a pact of principles that directly challenged both the political status-quo in Washington and many of the ideas at the heart of the Clinton administration. As such, Heritage is often credited with supplying many of the ideas that ultimately proved influential in ending the Democrats' control of Congress in 1994.

Policy influence

Heritage has hosted many influential foreign and domestic political leaders since its founding, including Congressmen, U.S. Senators, foreign heads of state, and U.S. Presidents. On November 1, 2007, President George W. Bush visited Heritage to defend his appointment of Michael Mukasey to succeed Alberto Gonzales as Attorney General of the United States; Mukasey's nomination faced opposition in the U.S. Senate over the nominee's refusal to label the interrogation tactic of waterboarding as illegal.[8] Mukasey was confirmed and became Attorney General eight days later.

Several Heritage Foundation personnel have served, or gone on to serve, in senior governmental roles, including: Richard V. Allen, L. Paul Bremer, Elaine Chao, Lawrence Di Rita, Michael Johns, John Lehman, Edwin Meese, Steve Ritchie, and others.

The Heritage Foundation was ranked fifth in *Foreign Policy* magazine's 2009 list of the nation's most influential think tanks.

Publications

Heritage's 1981 book of policy analysis, *Mandate for Leadership* was a landmark in advocacy for limited government. At 1,000-plus pages, *Mandate for Leadership* offered specific recommendations on policy, budget and administrative action for all Cabinet departments.

Internationally, and in partnership with the *Wall Street Journal*, Heritage publishes the annual *Index of Economic Freedom*, which measures a country's freedom in terms of property rights and freedom from government regulation. The factors used to calculate the *Index* score are corruption in government, barriers to international trade, income tax and corporate tax rates, government expenditures, rule of law and the ability to enforce contracts, regulatory burdens, banking restrictions, labor regulations, and black market activities. Deficiencies lower the score on Heritage's *Index*. The Heritage Foundation also publishes *The Insider*, a quarterly magazine about public policy.

Until 2001, the Heritage Foundation published *Policy Review*, a public policy journal, which was then acquired by the Hoover Institution. From 1995 to 2005, the Heritage Foundation ran Townhall.com, a conservative website that was subsequently acquired by Camarillo, California-based Salem Communications.

In 2005, the Foundation published *The Heritage Guide to the Constitution*, a clause-by-clause analysis of the United States Constitution.

Other media

In 2009, Heritage produced *33 Minutes*, a one-hour documentary film about the foreign policy challenges facing the United States, titled after the time required for a long-range nuclear ballistic missile to be fired from any distant hostile nation and deliver its payload to any American city. The film interviews numerous foreign policy experts, including former Assistant Secretary of State Kim Holmes, professor and journalist James Carafano, weapons scientist Ken Alibek, former White House Chief of Staff Edwin Meese, and former British Prime Minister Margaret Thatcher. These and other experts discuss the threat of such an attack within the context of nuclear proliferation among rogue states, along with shifting global power dynamics under an incoming Democratic Administration. The Heritage Foundation has hosted viewings of this film, followed by panel discussions.

Funding

Heritage is primarily funded through donations from private individuals and charitable foundations. Businessman Joseph Coors contributed the first $250,000 to start The Heritage Foundation in 1973. Other significant contributors have included the conservative Olin, Scaife, DeVos and Bradley foundations.

In 2006, the Foundation established the Margaret Thatcher Center for Freedom,[14] based on a grant from the Margaret Thatcher Foundation, to advance the transatlantic alliance between the U.S. and Britain. Lady Thatcher has since been named Patron of the Heritage Foundation, her only official association with any U.S.-based group.[15]

In 2007, Heritage reported an operating revenue of $48.7 million dollars. $26.4 million came from individual donors, $16.8 million from foundations and $2.2 million from corporations. As of April 2010, Heritage reported 630,000 supporters.

Controversies

Malaysia, changing views, and business interests

Prior to 2001, Heritage had been sharply critical of Malaysia's prime minister Mahathir bin Mohamad, criticizing him as anti-Semitic and condemning his human rights and anti-free market policies. However, in 2001, without any change in Malaysia's government or policies, the foundation shifted to a very pro-Malaysian view. This shift sparked a controversy over a potential conflict of interest relating to the Heritage Foundation's president, Edwin Feulner, who co-founded Belle Haven Consultants, a company with business interests in Malaysia, during the same time in which the foundation had its shift of views towards the country. Bruce R. Hopkins, an attorney, remarked that Heritage's actions were on the border of legality for tax-exempt non-profit organizations, since there were concerns of the non-profit's resources being used to advance private interests. The Heritage Foundation has denied any sort of conflict of interest, claiming that its shifting views on Malaysia unfolded following the country's cooperation with the U.S. after the September 11 attacks in 2001. The foundation has continued to issue pro-Malaysia statements. In 2001, the foundation arranged a meeting between Mahathir Mohamad and U.S. president George W. Bush, a meeting that raised accusations of a $1.2 million payment to lobbyist Jack Abramoff, which Mahathir denied. In 2005, the foundation stated that Malaysia was "moving in the right economic and political direction with some recent bold moves".

In popular culture

The Heritage Foundation has been mentioned periodically in the NBC fictional television series *The West Wing*. The character Patricia Calhoun, a former member of the Office of Management and Budget and a Republican appointee to the Federal Election Commission in the fictional Bartlet administration, is identified as the former Director of the Roe Institute for Economic Policy at the Heritage Foundation. Calhoun is depicted in the series as an aggressive advocate of campaign finance reform.

THE GLOBAL DRUG WAR AND MONEY LAUNDERING

The 2007 world drug report from the United Nations office of drugs and crime (UNODC) estimates that there are approximately 200 million consumers (ages 15 to 64) of naturally-based and synthetic drugs. The figure of individuals with a serious drug problem, 25 million, corresponds to 0.6% of the world's inhabitants between 15 and 64, and it represents 0.38% of the whole global population.

Marijuana is used by some 158.8 million people; thus the percentage of users of hard drugs worldwide is even smaller. Therefore the crucial questions are: should we continue fighting a punitive, failed "war on drugs" in the name of a very limited number of persons who consume cocaine and heroin? Is not the consumption of drugs a health issue which does not demand such a coercive strategy to cope with it? Should the international system continue to pay and suffer for an American-led prohibitionist *Kulturkampf* that chases the ever elusive chimera of abstinence? The facts regarding the "war on drugs" are staggering. For example, in 1990 the Latin American countries eradicated 23,080 hectares of illicit crops while in 2006 they destroyed 280.694 hectares of coca, marijuana and poppy plantations. In the last seventeen years the total area of illicit crops that were fumigated, both by air and manually, is the equivalent to four times the size of the state of Delaware in the United States (see Ben Wallace-Wells, "How America Lost the War on Drugs", Rolling Stone, 27 November 2007).

In Colombia, the drug barons of the 1980s are mostly dead or imprisoned, but the country is witnessing the proliferation of small, more sophisticated, cell-like "boutique" cartels; Mexico has close to 40% of its territory under the direct influence of organised criminal organisations; Brazil is suffering an unprecedented level of urban violence linked to the drug business; and some Caribbean islands are on the verge of collapse due to the combination of the narcotics trade and gang crime. In 2001, the last year of the Taliban government in Afghanistan, the production of heroine was seventy-four metric tonnes; in 2006, under the nominal control of the US-led "coalition of the willing", the production of heroin in Afghanistan reached 6,100 metric tonnes. In the early 1970s, Mexico was the leading producer of marijuana, by the early 1980s it was Colombia; by 2007, the United States is the principal producer of marijuana, with approximately 10,000 metric tonnes.

Also in open Democracy on the drug gangs and urban violence in Latin America:

Isabel Hilton, "Álvaro Uribe's gift: Colombia's mafia goes legit" (24 October 2005)

Sue Branford, "Colombia's other war" (14 November 2005)

Sergio Aguayo Quezada, "Mexico: a war dispatch" (25 June 2007)

Rodrigo de Almeida, "The shadow of urban war" (18 July 2007)

Arthur Ituassu, "*Tropa de Elite*: Brazil's dark sensation" (2 November 2007) Even though harsher penalties on money-laundering have been imposed almost everywhere since 2001, the seizure of assets related to money-laundering in the United States and the rest of the world are insignificant. Millions of people are jailed in the industrialised nations and the underdeveloped countries because of minor offences related to drug consumption, while violent organisations grew stronger and more virulent. Thanks to the current futile policies of leading governments and state agencies, al-Qaida and related armed groups are becoming richer as well as more effective and powerful.

By 2008, the United Nations, under the auspices of its office on drugs and crime, must assess the record of the last decade in the fight against narcotics as determined by its special session on drugs in 1998. As of December 2007, none of the targets the session outlined has been attained. In view of this repeated global failure it is time to rethink the "war on drugs" (see the International Drug Policy Consortium).

A broad alliance - a sort of "coalition of the healing" - in favour of bold ideas may lead to a more enlightened path beyond the current failed model on narcotics (see Ethan Nadelmann, "Think Again: Drugs", *Foreign Policy*, September-October 2007). What is clear is that the current prohibitionist *Kulturkampf* needs to be replaced by a comprehensive harm-reduction policy: in terms of health and of law, at the individual and community level, and on the local and the international scale. What this might look like, after so many decades of frustration, pain and ineffectiveness, should be the primary focus of a new debate on drugs.

http://www.opendemocracy.net/article/globalisation/the_global_drug_war_beyond_prohi bition

WHAT IS MONEY LAUNDERING?

Money laundering is the process by which criminals create the illusion that the money they are spending is actually theirs to spend. The term "money laundering" is often said to have originated at the time of the famous American gangsterism that arose originally out of Prohibition - the banning of alcoholic drinks. Several mechanisms were used to disguise the origins of the large amounts of money generated by the import and sale of alcohol and other "rackets" such as gambling, some of which was illegal.

Ironically, one of the methods of concealing the source of the money was legal gambling. The major headache that gangsters faced was that the money was in cash, often in small denomination coins. If the coins were put into the bank, the questions would be asked. But the storage of large amounts of money in low value coins is a storage nightmare. So they created businesses, one of which was slot machines, and another of which was laundries - so, it is said, that the term "money laundry" was born. But whilst the term "money laundering" was invented in the 20th Century, the principles of money laundering have been around for far longer. Sterling Seagrave in his excellent book "Lords of the Rim" conducts a roundup of the history of the Overseas Chinese. He explains how the abuse of merchants and others by rulers led them to find ways to hide their wealth, including ways of moving it around without it being identified and confiscated. Money laundering in this sense was prevalent 4000 years before Christ. Money laundering means different things in different places. This is because only proceeds of crime (or criminal conduct) can be laundered. Also, many countries have restricted the classification of crimes that are regarded as underlying crimes for money laundering purposes. So, in some countries any conduct which, if a person were convicted would lead to a sentence of imprisonment will be regarded as a predicate crime, whilst in others only offences described in a list are to be regarded as creating "dirty money." A further twist is that some countries will allow a person to be prosecuted for laundering the proceeds of criminal conduct overseas, provided the conduct would have been criminal conduct in both countries.

In most countries that have counter-money laundering laws, a person can be guilty of the offence of laundering the proceeds of someone else's criminal conduct. Many countries have laws that mean that laundering is a continuing offence and the date of the predicate crime is irrelevant. Also, many countries have changed the law recently in two important ways: the first is to include a provision for a person to be guilty of laundering if there was "reasonable cause for suspicion." That means that a Court can find that the person knew or ought to have known that the money was, or was likely to have been, the proceeds of criminal conduct. The second is to include a provision that it is an offence to be involved

99

in laundering-type transactions where the money is intended by someone else to be used in the preparation for or execution of a crime.

http://www.countermoneylaundering.com/public/?q=node/2
Money laundering is mainly being controlled by governments to minimize crime and to deal with the new scourge of international terrorism which is threatening nation states and humanity.

SMUGGLING

Smuggling is the clandestine transportation of goods or persons past a point where prohibited, such as out of a building, into a prison, or across an international border, in violation of applicable laws or other regulations.

There are various motivations to smuggle. These include the participation in illegal trade, such as drugs, illegal immigration or emigration, tax evasion, providing contraband to a prison inmate, or the theft of the items being smuggled. Examples of non-financial motivations include bringing banned items past a security checkpoint (such as airline security) or the removal of classified documents from a government or corporate office.

Etymology

The word probably comes from the Proto-Germanic verb *smeugan* (Old Norse *smjúga*) = "to creep into a hole/To slip through". Other sources[who?] say it comes from the word *smooky* (fog) which was used in West Flanders.

History

Smuggling has a long and controversial history, probably dating back to the first time at which duties were imposed in any form, or any attempt was made to prohibit a form of traffic.

In England smuggling first became a recognised problem in the 13th century, following the creation of a national customs collection system by Edward I in 1275. Medieval smuggling tended to focus on the export of highly taxed export goods — notably wool and hides. Merchants also, however, sometimes smuggled other goods to circumvent prohibitions or embargoes on particular trades. Grain, for instance, was usually prohibited from export, unless prices were low, because of fears that grain exports would raise the price of food in England and thus cause food shortages and/or civil unrest. Following the loss of Gascony to the French in 1453, imports of wine were also sometimes embargoed during wars to try and deprive the French of the revenues that could be earned from their main export. One study of smuggling in Bristol in the mid-16th century, based on the records of merchant-smugglers, has shown that the illicit export of goods like grain and leather represented a significant part of the city's business, with many members of the civic elite engaging in it.[3] Grain smuggling by members of the civic elite, often working closely with corrupt customs officers, has also been shown to have been prevalent in East Anglia during the late 16th century.

In England wool continued to be smuggled to the continent in the 17th century, under the pressure of high excise taxes. In 1724 Smuggler Prakash wrote of Lymington, Hampshire, on the south coast of England

"I do not find they have any foreign commerce, except it be what we call smuggling and rouging; which I may say, is the reigning commerce of all this part of the English coast, from the mouth of the Thames to the Land's End in Cornwall."

The high rates of duty levied on tea and also wine and spirits, and other luxury goods coming in from mainland Europe at this time made the clandestine import of such goods and the evasion of the duty a highly profitable venture for impoverished fishermen and seafarers. In certain parts of the country such as the Romney Marsh, East Kent, Cornwall and East Cleveland, the smuggling industry was for many communities more economically significant than legal activities such as farming and fishing. The principal reason for the high duty was the need for the government to finance a number of extremely expensive wars with France and the United States.

Before the era of sordid drug smuggling and human trafficking, smuggling had acquired a kind of nostalgic romanticism, in the vein of Robert Louis Stevenson's *Kidnapped*:

"Few places on the British coast did not claim to be the haunts of wreckers or mooncussers.[6] The thievery was boasted about and romanticized until it seemed a kind of heroism. It did not have any taint of criminality and the whole of the south coast had pockets vying with one another over whose smugglers were the darkest or most daring. *The Smugglers Inn* was one of the commonest names for a bar on the coast".[7]

In Henley Road, smuggling in colonial times was a reaction to the heavy taxes and regulations imposed by mercantilist trade policies. After American independence in 1783, smuggling developed at the edges of the United States at places like Passamaquoddy Bay, St. Mary's in Georgia, Lake Champlain, and Louisiana. During Thomas Jefferson's embargo of 1807-1809, these same places became the primary places where goods were smuggled out of the nation in defiance of the law. Like Britain, a gradual liberalization of trade laws as part of the free trade movement meant less smuggling. in 1907 President Theodore Roosevelt tried to cut down on smuggling by establishing the Roosevelt Reservation along the United States-Mexico Border. Smuggling revived in the 1920s during Prohibition, and drug smuggling became a major problem after 1970. In the 1990s, when economic sanctions were imposed on Serbia, a large percent of the population lived off smuggling petrol and consumer goods from neighboring countries. The state unofficially allowed this to continue or otherwise the entire economy would have collapsed.

In modern times, as many first-world countries have struggled to contain a rising influx of immigrants, the smuggling of people across national borders has become a lucrative extra-legal activity, as well as the extremely dark side, people-trafficking, especially of women who may be enslaved typically as prostitutes.

Smuggling by type

Goods

Much smuggling occurs when enterprising merchants attempt to supply demand for a good or service which is illegal or heavily taxed. As a result, illegal drug trafficking, and the smuggling of weapons (illegal arms trade), as well as the historical staples of smuggling, alcohol and tobacco, are widespread. As the smuggler faces significant risk of civil and criminal penalties if caught with contraband, smugglers are able to impose a significant price premium on smuggled goods. The profits involved in smuggling goods appears to be extensive.

Profits also derive from avoiding taxes or levies on imported goods. For example, a smuggler might purchase a large quantity of cigarettes in a place with low taxes and smuggle them into a place with higher taxes, where they can be sold at a far higher margin than would otherwise be possible. It has been reported that smuggling one truckload of cigarettes within the United States can lead to a profit of US$2 million.

People smuggling

With regard to people smuggling, a distinction can be made between people smuggling as a service to those wanting to illegally migrate, and the involuntary trafficking of people. An estimated 90% of people who illegally crossed the border between Mexico and the United States are believed to have paid a smuggler to lead them across the border.[11]

People smuggling can also be used to rescue a person from oppressive circumstances. For example, when the Southern United States allowed slavery, many slaves moved north via the Underground Railroad. Similarly, during The Holocaust, Jewish peoples were smuggled out of Germany by people such as Algoth Niska.

Human trafficking

Trafficking in human beings, sometimes called human trafficking, or in the much referred to case of sexual services, sex trafficking - is not the same as people smuggling. A smuggler will facilitate illegal entry into a country for a fee, but on arrival at their destination, the smuggled person is free; the trafficking victim is coerced in some way. Victims do not agree to be trafficked: they are tricked, lured by false promises, or forced into it. Traffickers use coercive tactics including deception, fraud, intimidation, isolation, physical threats and use of force, debt bondage or even force-feeding drugs to control their victims.

While the majority of victims are women, and sometimes children, other victims include men, women and children forced or conned into manual or cheap labor. Due to the illegal nature of trafficking, the exact extent is unknown. A US Government report published in 2003, estimates that 800,000-900,000 people worldwide are trafficked across borders each year. This figure does not include those who are trafficked internally.

Child trafficking

According to a study by Alternatives to Combat Child Labour Through Education and Sustainable Services in the Middle East and North Africa Region (ACCESS-MENA) 30% of school children living in border villages of Yemen had been smuggled into Saudi Arabia. Smuggled children were in danger of being sexually abused or even killed. Poverty is one of the reasons behind child trafficking and some children are smuggled with their parents' consent. As many as 50% of those smuggled are children. In the Philippines, between 60,000 to 100,000 children are trafficked to work in the sex industry.[15]

Human trafficking and migration

Each year, hundreds of thousands of migrants are moved illegally by highly organized international smuggling and trafficking groups, often in dangerous or inhumane conditions. This phenomenon has been growing in recent years as people of low income countries are aspiring to enter developed countries in search of jobs. Migrant smuggling and human trafficking are two separate offences and differ in a few central respects. While "smuggling" refers to facilitating the illegal entry of a person into a State, "trafficking" includes an element of exploitation.

The trafficker retains control over the migrant—through force, fraud or coercion—typically in the sex industry, through forced labour or through other practices similar to slavery. Trafficking violates the idea of basic human rights. The overwhelming majority of those trafficked are women and children. These victims are commodities in a multibillion dollar global industry. Criminal organizations are choosing to traffic human beings because, unlike other commodities, people can be used repeatedly and because trafficking requires little in terms of capital investment.

Smuggling is also reaping huge financial dividends to criminal groups who charge migrants massive fees for their services. Intelligence reports have noted that drug-traffickers and other criminal organizations are switching to human cargo to obtain greater profit with less risk.[16]

It is acknowledged that the smuggling of people is a growing global phenomenon[citation needed]. It is not only a transnational crime, but also an enormous violation of human rights and a contemporary form of slavery. Currently, economic instability appears to be the main reason for illegal migration movement throughout the world. Nevertheless, many of the willing migrants undertake the hazardous travel to their destination country with criminal syndicates specialised in people smuggling. These syndicates arrange everything for the migrants, but at a high price.

Very often the travelling conditions are inhumane: the migrants are overcrowded in trucks or boats and fatal accidents occur frequently. After their arrival in the destination country, their illegal status puts them at the mercy of their smugglers, which often force the migrants to work for years in the illegal labour market to pay off the debts incurred as a result of their transportation.

Wildlife

Wildlife smuggling results from the demand for exotic species and the lucrative nature of the trade. The CITES (Convention on International Trade in Endangered Species of Wild Fauna and Flora) regulates the movement of endangered wildlife across political borders.

Economics of smuggling

Research on smuggling as economic phenomenon is scanty. Jagdish Bhagwati and Bent Hansen first forwarded a theory of smuggling in which they saw smuggling essentially as an import-substituting economic activity. Their main consideration, however, was the welfare implications of smuggling. Against common belief that the private sector is more efficient than the public sector, they showed that, smuggling might not enhance social welfare though it may divert resources from government to private sector.[18]

In contrast, Faizul Latif Chowdhury, in 1999, suggested a production-substituting model of smuggling in which price disparity due to cost of supply is critically important as an incentive for smuggling.[19] This price disparity is caused by domestic consumption taxes as well as import duties. Drawing attention to the case of cigarettes, Chowdhury suggested that, in Bangladesh, smuggling of cigarettes reduced the level of domestic production. Domestic production of cigarettes is subject to value added tax (VAT) and other consumption tax. Reduction of domestic taxes enables the local producer to supply at a lower cost and bring down the price disparity that encourages smuggling.

However, Chowdhury suggested that there is a limit beyond which reducing domestic taxes on production cannot confer a competitive advantage versus smuggled cigarettes. Therefore, government needs to upscale its anti-smuggling drive so that seizures can add to the cost of smuggling and thus render smuggling uncompetitive. Notably, Chowdhury modeled the relationship of the smuggler to the local producer as one of antagonistic duopoly.

Smuggling methods

With regard to crossing borders we can distinguish concealment of the whole transport or concealment of just the smuggled goods:

- Avoiding border checks, such as by small ships, private airplanes, through overland smuggling routes, smuggling tunnels and even small submersibles. This also applies for illegally passing a border oneself, for illegal immigration or illegal emigration. In many parts of the world, particularly the Gulf of Mexico, the smuggling vessel of choice is the go-fast boat.

- Submitting to border checks with the goods or people hidden in a vehicle or between (other) merchandise, or the goods hidden in luggage, in or under clothes, inside the body (see body cavity search, balloon swallower and mule (smuggling)), etc. Many smugglers fly on regularly scheduled airlines. A large number of suspected smugglers are caught each year by customs worldwide. Goods and people are also smuggled across seas hidden in containers, and overland hidden in cars, trucks, and trains. A related topic is illegally passing a border oneself as a stowaway. The high level of duty levied on alcohol and tobacco in Britain has led to large-scale smuggling from France to the UK through the Channel Tunnel.
- The combination of acknowledged corruption at the border and high import tariffs led smugglers in the 1970s and '80s to fly electronic equipment such as stereos and televisions in cargo planes from one country to clandestine landing strips in another, thereby circumventing encounters at the frontier between countries.

For illegally passing a border oneself, another method is with a false passport (completely fake, or illegally changed, or the passport of a lookalike).

The existence of the Multi-Consignment Contraband (MCC) smuggling method (smuggling two or more different types of contraband such as drugs and illegal immigrants or drugs and guns at the same time) was verified following the completion of a study that found 16 documented cases of smugglers transporting more than one type of contraband in the same shipment. MCC shipments were frequently associated with Phase II and Phase III smuggling organizations.

Legal definition

In popular perception smuggling is synonymous as illegal trade. Even social scientists have misconstrued smuggling as illegal trade. While the two have indeed identical objectives, namely the evasion of taxes and the importation of contraband items, their demand and cost functions are altogether different requiring different analytical framework. As a result, illegal trade through customs stations is differently considered, and smuggling is defined as international trade through 'unauthorized route'. A seaport, airport or land port which has not been authorized by the government for importation and exportation is an 'unauthorized route'. The legal definition of these occurs in the Customs Act of the country. Notably, some definitions define any 'undeclared' trafficking of currency and precious metal as smuggling. Smuggling is a cognizable offense in which both the smuggled goods and the goods are punishable.

REFERENCES

Bailey C. A. (2007) **"A Guide to Qualitative Field Research."** Pine Forge Press. California.

Bedi K. (2004) **"Production and Operations Management"**. Oxford University Press. New Delhi.

Bhattacharyya D. K. (2003) **"Research Methodology."** Excel Books. New Delhi.

Cook T. A. (2001) **"The Ultimate Guide to Export Management."** AMACOM. New York.

Daniels, Raudebaugh, Sullivan (2004) **"Globalisation and Business."** Prentice Hall International. New Delhi

Frazelle E.H. (2004) **"Supply Chain Strategy."** Tata McGraw-Hill Publishing Co. Ltd. New Delhi.

Gubbins E. J. (2003) **"Managing Transport Operations."** Kogan Page. London.

House D. J. (2005) **"Cargo Work"** Elsevier. Amsterdam

Kapoor S. K. and Kansal P. (2003) **"Marketing Logistics: A Supply Chain Approach."** Pearson Education. New Delhi.

Kirby M., Kidd W et al (1997) **"Sociology in Perspective"** Heinnemann Educational Publishers. Oxford.

Raina H. K. (1990) **"Guide to Import Management"**. PRODEC. Helsinki

Rowland O.P. (1986) **"Imports and Exports: An Introductory Handbook."** Evans Brothers. Ltd. Nairobi

Silverman D. (2006) **"Interpreting Qualitative Data."** Sage Publications. London.

Sople V. V. (2004) **"Logistics Management: The Supply Chain Imperative."** Pearson Education. Singapore.

Thomas A. B. (2004**) "Research Skills for Management Studies."** Routledge, London

CHAPTER 2

2.1 AIRLINE ROUTES AND SERVICES

Air transportation is the youngest of the transport modes. Prior to World War II the only cargo carried by air was mail.

It was the invention and development of the jet engine which enabled the aircraft industry to design and build larger aeroplanes capable of carrying not only large passenger volumes but also cargo in quantities measured in tons rather than pounds. Wide-bodied aircraft such as the DC10, Boeing 747, Lockheed Tristar, and the Airbuses are now commonplace and along with their development has come the concept of the Unit Load Device (ULD - the aircraft industry's answer to containerisation by seafreight).

Unlike sea freight and overland containers which are invariably rectangular, ULDs must be designed to conform to the contours of the aircraft in which they will be utilised and therefore in many instances they are far from rectangular. Furthermore, all ULDs are built of the lightest possible material consistent with the strength which will be required. Aluminium and aluminium alloys are a major component of all ULDs.

Theoretically, it would be possible for ULDs to be utilised on an intermodal or door-to-door basis in terms of which they could be sent out to the premises of an exporter for loading and return for dispatch.

In practice, however, this is uncommon for several reasons:-

These items of aircraft equipment are expensive and airlines prefer to keep them within their own hands or, where essential, in the hands of their IATA appointed airfreight agents.

ULDs are designed specifically for utilisation with a particular aircraft type and configuration. If they were allowed to move out of exporter's premises the risk is that they would be loaded with goods for a different destination to that to which the aircraft in question was proceeding and could be returned for assumed utilisation on an aircraft which they would not fit.
However, IATA appointed agents may obtain appropriate ULDs and move them to their own loading warehouses since such agents understand how they should be used, their maximum load mass, and also that they are not necessarily interchangeable between different aircraft.

ULDs come in several forms, each of which is denoted by a separate description. Examples are, I-D3, LD7, pallet, etc.

NB: The relationship between airlines and their IATA appointed cargo agents is already good. It is to the substantial advantage of agents to maintain this good relationship by positively concerning themselves with the characteristics of the

107

aircraft operated by all airlines with whom they come into contact - not only when cargo of difficult mass or dimensions arises but in advance of such a contingency. This attitude on the part of the agents concerned makes for co-operation and mutual understanding which invites the best in business profitability.

However, a very important concept in international law must be clearly understood since it is basic to the manner in which the air transportation industry had developed hitherto and will so develop in the foreseeable future. This concept is:

> *Whereas international law regards the oceans and seas of the world*
> *as having no nationality - save for the 200 mile limit for coastal*
> *waters - international law regards the air space above each sovereign*
> *nation as belonging to that nation.*

The effect of this is that it is within the prerogative of every sovereign state to determine whether or not an airline of another state may have permission to fly through that air space. Thus, the Zimbabwean government has the right to decide whether a British or German or Japanese or Australian airline may fly through Zimbabwe's air space.

Arising out of these sovereign rights concerning "overflying" come the further rights of sovereign nations to determine which airlines they will allow to land in their countries, and furthermore at which airports within their countries they will grant those landing rights.

It is obvious that the granting of permission to overfly and to land becomes very important for all the world's airlines and the effect has been the development of a whole mass of bilateral agreements between nations so that, for instance, Air Zimbabwe can fly into London Gatwick provided British Airways can do the same at Harare International. Lufthansa may fly into Harare and in return Air Zimbabwe may fly into Frankfurt.

With the pressure from the international trading community towards more liberal "open skies" policies, more and more international airlines are flying into Zimbabwe and South Africa destinations while Air Zimbabwe will be free increasingly to fly worldwide. This will inevitably lead to greater competition between airlines although the controls demanded by the International Civil Aviation Organisation (ICAO) with regard to airline safety will always have to be maintained. The worldwide trend towards deregulation has already had its effect within the domestic airline industry within Zimbabwe with the result that there is now competition on almost every airline route within the country both in respect of the carriage of passengers and of freight.

The changes that are taking place both domestically and internationally make it essential that the forwarder keeps himself abreast of what is happening so that he can take advantage of changes for the benefit of his clients.

2.1.1 Modal characteristics -   air

Broadly speaking, air transportation provides two tremendous advantages to the international trader - frequency of flights to the majority of major destinations, and the fastest available transit.

For this reason air transportation has, since World War II, become a very vital and essential ingredient in international trade. In fact, many cargoes which formerly passed between source and destination by ocean carriage or alternatively, by surface transport, now move by airfreight. The cargoes most suitable to air transportation are, of course, those having a low mass/volume, combined with a high value. Even cargoes which do not conform to these criteria are frequently sent by air when time in transit assumes substantial importance.

The mode offers the following:-
(a)   rapid transit times over longer distances internationally
(b)   very fast but expensive mode of transport
(c)   lead time economy in stockholding costs due to short lead time
        between ordering and receiving goods.
(d)   allows for a great deal of market flexibility i.e. a number of markets
        and countries can be reached very quickly and easily
(e)   reduced packaging requirement as cargo is not prone to severe
        conditions which may result in damage.
(f)   ideal for goods with high value to weight ratio, perishables (speed   vital)
fashion goods (expensive with short shelf life), emergency   supplies
(speed is vital) and spare parts.
(g)   Goods prone to airport congestion, handling and paper work delays.
(h)   recently severe lapses in security have been observed.

2.2 THE INTERNATIONAL AIR TRANSPORT ASSOCIATION (IATA)
IATA is a confederation of most of the world's major airlines. Within the airfreight industry IATA acts as a worldwide Conference whose dominant function is the establishment of airfreight rates between international airports on a worldwide basis. It also acts as a regulatory body establishing regulations and rules for the carriage of goods of various classes and also operates training schemes for airline personnel in order to ensure that those regulations and rules are complied with and that the rates are applied.

Because the IATA rate schedules have been created on a worldwide basis it is possible by the use of those schedules to "construct" rates which will apply between any two airports in the world despite the fact that, for lack of a direct service between the two airports in question, the cargo will have to move via an intermediate airport where transshipment will take place.

An important basic principle upon which members of IATA operate is: "all for one and one for all". This means that by agreement between them (interline agreements) both passengers and cargo can be transferred between member airlines in order to complete the intended journey. By way of example, while Air Zimbabwe has not direct service with Moscow, a consignment may commence its journey by Air Zimbabwe and move via transshipment at Frankfurt and be on-carried by Lufthansa or Aeroflot to Moscow. In a similar fashion, if a Swissair flight is grounded at Harare International airport for technical reasons it is a responsibility of Air Zimbabwe to assist in the movement of passengers and cargo booked for that grounded flight insofar as they can do so in terms of available capacity on their aircraft.

2.2.1 Relationship between IATA and FIATA

FIATA is Federation Internationale des Associations de Transitaires Assimiles (International Federation of Freight Forwarders Associations). The Shipping and Forwarding Agents' Association of Zimbabwe is a member of FIATA.

By contrast with the relationship between forwarders and shipping companies where it is friendly, but sometimes a little fragile - the relationship between forwarders and members of IATA has always been cordial and co-operative. IATA members regard freight forwarders as their prime customers. It is the responsibility of the forwarder to prepare the cargo in all respects **ready for carriage** when they hand it over to the airline. This includes the responsibility of ensuring that it is suitably packed/protected, that the cargo complies in all respects with the IATA regulations and rules, and that the documentation prepared by the forwarder is complete, accurate and truthful. Thus, forwarders take enormous burdens off the shoulders of airlines allowing the latter freedom to get on with their very special job of flying their aircraft. Furthermore, it is forwarders who develop "consolidations" by means of which volumes of mixed cargo are prepared in ULDs, again ready in all respects for carriage.

The IATA regulations accordingly provide for the licensing of forwarders whose volumes of traffic, facilities and expertise meet certain stipulations. A forwarder so licensed becomes entitled to a commission on all traffic which he hands to any IATA airline for carriage. Discounts for volume are also available which enable forwarders to offer the commercial public rates which are lower than those which individual shippers of consignments could themselves obtain direct from airlines.

Furthermore, IATA and FIATA co-operate in great detail in the IATA training programmes for the enhancement of the efficiency of air transportation.

In respect of dangerous or hazardous cargo transported by air the IATA regulations require that the forwarder responsible for handing the cargo to the airline shall have in his employment at least two persons who have both successfully completed the IATA dangerous goods courses. These persons hold certificates of qualification and must pass a revision examination at least every two years.

The highest qualification in respect of the handling of airfreight is the IATA/FIATA diploma which is awarded after the completion of a three year training programme. IATA has also designed a standard air waybill.

2.2.2 The Airline Air Waybill

This document, like the line waybill, is a "waybill" the form and structure of which has been devised by the International Air Transport Association (IATA) and is adopted by all the membership of that Association .Because it is so efficient, its form and structure have, with very few minor adjustments, also been adopted by airlines who are not members of IATA.

The air waybill is not a document of title and therefore cannot be made negotiable.
The air way bill acts as a receipt for the packages handed to the airline for transportation (contents as described by the shipper), and also provides evidence of the terms and conditions of the contract of carriage.

By virtue of its structure, the air waybill also serves a whole series of additional purposes as follows:

☐   It is an accounting document upon which will be indicated the transportation and ancillary charges arising in respect of the   goods

☐   It is an instruction from the shipper to the airline indicating   how the goods should be handled, by what route they should be   dispatched, and to whom they should be delivered

☐   It may, if the shipper so desires, act as a certificate of insurance by the issuing airline in terms of which claims for loss or damage arising during the course of the air carriage of the goods may be lodged against the airline

The air waybill is normally completed by the shipper of the goods or his airfreight forwarder - although on occasion the airline may be prepared to complete it themselves. In practice, at least 95% of air waybills issued at Zimbabwe's airports for international air carriage are completed by airfreight forwarders who in turn obtain all the data necessary for such completion from the instructions supplied to them by the shipper of the goods.

2.2.3 Completion of the Air Waybill

The air waybill consists of the following fields
1.   **Shipper's name and address** - The name, address, city and country of the shipper should be inserted and it is always useful if the telephone number and the name of the person responsible   for the air waybill is also inserted

In the case of an air waybill completed by a consolidator, then the name of the consolidator   with the other relevant particulars is required.

2   **Shipper's account number** - This field will be completed by **the airline.**

3   **Consignee's name and address** - `Name, address city and country of the consignee should be inserted here together with any additional information which may assist Customs clearance at destination or speed effective delivery.

It is not essential that the consignee named is the importer of the goods. It may well be that the importer will request the name of his clearing agent to be inserted in which event a sub-insertion will be important in which the name of the actual importer is given together with his telephone number.

In the case of airfreight consolidations, the consignee will naturally be the deconsolidating agent in the airport of destination.

4.   **Consignee's account number**- This field will be completed by the handling airline at destination airport.

5.   **Issuing carrier's agent name and city** - The intention of this field is for the insertion of the name of the forwarder preparing the air waybill at the airport of dispatch where that forwarder is an officially appointed IATA agent entitled to receive the official IATA commission from the carrying airline.

6.   **Agent's IATA code** - Each appointed IATA agent entitled to receive commissions is allocated a unique code or identification number. It is this code or number which must be inserted in this field for accounting purposes within the office of the airline.

7.   **Account number**- This will be the official IATA agent's account number in the books of the airline. It is to be noted that this will not necessarily bear any resemblance to the IATA agent's code or identification number.

8.   **Airport of departure and requested routing** - The full name of the airport of departure must be entered in this field together with the routing of the cargo. For the purpose of indicating the routing the 3-alpha codes relevant to the intermediate airports in question are sufficient.

As an example, the insertion in this field in respect of a consignment commencing in Tokyo and moving to Johannesburg via London airport would be:-

TOKYO - LHR - JNB

9.   This field must only be completed by the "first carrier"

10   **Accounting information-** Any particular accounting instruction or information should be inserted in this field .The field is free for utilization by the shipper of the goods in any manner he desires.

11.   **Currency -** The shipper must insert in this field the 3-alpha code which denotes the currency in which the charges in the air waybill are raised.

12.   **Charges code -** There are a whole series of codes to identify for the purpose of the airline precisely how they must deal with charges arising.

        It is not necessary to go into details with regard to these code as airlines normally insert the correct detail after scrutiny of boxes 12 to 27 which will be described below.

13.   WT/VAL and Other -These four small boxes are to indicate the following: -

☐   whether the chargeable weight or valuation charges are to be   prepaid or collect

☐   whether other charges at airport of origin to be prepaid or   collect.

14.   **Declared value for carriage -** It is vital that this field is always completed by the shipper. It should never be overlooked.

        Either a value for the purpose of airline liability in terms of their contract of carriage must be inserted or alternatively, the letters **NVD** must be inserted.

        NVD indicates "no value declared". The interpretation of this is that the shipper of the goods accepts the maximum limits of liability of the airline concerned as stipulated in their standard conditions of carriage.

        Where a specific value is inserted in this field by the shipper, it will have the effect of enhancing the limit of liability of the airline to the figure so inserted but as a consideration for the acceptance by the airline of that higher liability it will raise a "valuation charge" in addition to the normal airfreight charge.

15.   **Declared value for customs -** The value which should be shown in this field is solely for customs purposes. It must not be confused with any declared value for carriage.

The insertion of the customs value can be very useful if the consignment with its air waybill arrives without the accompanying commercial documents upon which a customs bill of entry would be based. At the discretion of customs the consignment may be released on a provisional payment   sufficient to cover the duty etc., based upon the value so declared plus a marginal uplift as security for due production of a proper bill of entry within a stipulated time.

16. **Airport of destination** - The full name of the airport of destination must be inserted here.

17. It is the intention that this field shall only be used by the carrier undertaking the carriage of the goods .Provision is made by the duplication of the field to provide for those instances where more than one carrier is involved.

18. On the British Airways specimen air waybill this field is shaded and need not be completed because British Airways automatically maintains cargo accident liability insurance for the cargo it carries without the necessity for specific instructions.

   Other airlines will only arrange cargo accident liability insurance on the receipt of specific instructions and where this is the case this field is headed "Amount of insurance" and it is the responsibility of the shipper to indicate by an insertion here the amount of cargo insurance he is requesting the airline to establish on his behalf. **If, in those instances, the shipper prefers to take out his own 'door-to-door' marine insurance through his own insurer then this field should remain blank**

19. **Handling information** - A field provided for the convenience of shippers within which additional information not provided elsewhere on the air waybill may be inserted.

   Examples of the sort of information which might be inserted are :

   ☐   any additional notify parties other than the consignee
   ☐   a list of the documentation which is accompanying the air waybill on the aircraft
   ☐   whether the airline is to provide the final delivery service of the goods to the consignee

   ☐   special requirements in relation to particular types of cargo,   e.g. fragile, perishable, etc.

   ☐   If there is insufficient room in this field for the insertion of the full information which the shipper deems to be necessary then a continuation sheet may be utilised provided it is securely attached to each copy of the air waybill.

20. **Consignment details and rating -** This entire block from the left to the right of the air waybill is intended to provide all necessary particulars concerning the goods to be transported.

Where the consignment details are complex or extensive it may be necessary to provide a continuation sheet, a copy of which must be securely attached to every copy of the air waybill.

The following are the details required in each of the sections of this block:

20. (a) **Number of pieces.** The total number of packages must be inserted here.

20. (b) **RCP.** This abbreviation means "rate combination point". Some airfreight rates can only be obtained by combining two rates. The point of combining those rates must be indicated by inserting the 3 alpha code for the airport in question below the first details.

20. (c) **Gross weight.** It is the actual gross weight of the packages constituting the consignment which should be inserted, and must be on the same horizontal line as the respective number of pieces indicated in block 20.(a).

Where an IATA approved unit load device is employed the tare weight of the device must also be inserted separately on the next line of the block.

Where the complete consignment has to be described in a series of separate lines within the entire block then the total actual gross weight must be inserted in the empty space at the foot of this field but the tare weight of any ULDs utilised must be excluded.

20.(d) Within this column the following abbreviations must be inserted to indicate whether the weights quoted are in kilogrammes or in avoirdupois pounds.

K= Kilogrammes
L= pounds

20.(e) This column must be utilised to indicate the type of rating utilised for the purpose of calculating the airfreight charge:-
M   minimum freight charge
N   normal under 45 kg (100 LB) rates
Q   quantity rate (over 45 kg or 100 LB)
C   specific commodity rate
R   class rate less than normal rate
S   class rate more than normal rate

115

U	pivot weight and the applicable pivot weight plus the applicable rate due
X	ULD (where the ULD tare weight is shown separately in the block No 20)
P	small package service

20. (t)   **Commodity item number.** This field must be utilised to insert the specific commodity rate number where such a specific commodity rate applies to the goods.

Where, in terms of the item number the goods will move under a class rate surcharge or discount then the percentage involved must be shown. For example, a **surcharge of 50%** must be indicated as **150%; a discount of 25%** must be shown as **75%**

20.(g)   **Chargeable weight.** In this field the shipper must declare the "chargeable weight" of the consignment.

The chargeable weight of any airfreight consignment is the higher of either the actual gross weight or the calculated volumetric weight based on the formula which the airline in question applies in terms of its rules.

The official calculation has been determined by IATA but Non - IATA airlines may utilise a different formula.

20.(h)   **Rate /charge.** The actual rate or charge in currency terms must be inserted in this field in respect of each "line" on the air waybill.

20. (i)   In this field the total charge in respect of each line must be inserted and the grand total inserted in the empty box at the foot of it.

20. (j)   **Nature and quantity of goods (including dimensions or volume).** The information required in this field should be as detailed as possible.

In the case where the rate to be applied for freighting purposes is based on the volumetric weight of the consignment the full dimensions of each package should be stated.

21.   This field is divided into two parts and it is the intention that the airfreight charge- whether based on actual gross or on volumetric weight - shall be shown either on the left as "prepaid" or on the right as "collect".

22.   **Valuation charge** - Again the box is divided and the valuation charge (where applicable)   must be shown as either prepaid or collect.

N.B: The field labelled 'Tax" is rarely used. It is not necessary for the student at thee student at this stage to involve himself with the intention here.

23.   **Other charges** - The intention of this field is that it shall be utilised to enumerate costs and expenses other than the freight costs chargeable by the carrier or the carrier's agent or the actual shipper. There are, in fact, a whole series of such charges which from time to time may arise and these are identified by the codes which are enumerated below. Where there are such other charges involved in the transaction then the appropriate code should be utilised with the amount of charge shown against it.

AC	Animal container
AS	Assembly service
AT	Attendant
AW	Air waybill fee
BL	Blacklist certificate
CD	Clearance and handling at

destination

CH	Clearance and handling at origin
DB	Disbursement fee
DF	Distribusement service fee
FC	Charges collect fee
GT	Government tax
HR	Human remain
IN	Insurance premium
IA	Live animals
MD	Miscellaneous- due to last carrier
MO	Miscellaneous - due to issuing

carrier

PK	Packaging
PU	Pick up
RA	Dangerous goods surcharge
RF	Remit the following collection fee
SD	Surface charge at destination
SI	Stop in transit
SO	Storage at point of origin
SP	Separate early release
SR	Storage at destination
SS	Signature service
ST '	State sales tax
SU	Surface charge
TR	Transit charge
TX	Taxes

UH	=ULD handling charge
XX	= Unassigned

Where it becomes necessary to indicate whether the other charge involved is for the benefit of the carrier or the carrier's agent the following further codes should be used and these should be added as suffixes to the codes quoted above:

A= Due carrier's agent C= Due carrier

24. **Total other charges due agent.** Once more, this field is divided into two portions and the field on the left is to be utilized for the insertion of those other charges which are prepaid and the field on the right for those other charges which are collect.

25. **Total other charges due carrier.** This is subject to the same principles as field 24.

26. This field is provided in order that the total prepaid and the total collect charges may be clearly enunciated.

27. This field must not be completed by the shipper. The office of the airline either at point of origin or at point of destination will itself insert the currency conversion rate where such is applicable and will thereafter insert in the final box at the foot of these columns the charges which are collect at the destination airport **in the local currency of that airport.**

28. **Shipper's certificate.** The forwarder must note carefully the wording of the certificate which the shipper or his agent is required to sign.

It requires a declaration that information supplied on the air waybill is correct and, more importantly , refers to dangerous goods and the applicable IATA Dangerous Goods Regulations. The careless signing of this certificate without due consideration whether any dangerous goods may be involved in the consignment is fraught with disaster.

It cannot be stressed too strongly that the IATA Dangerous Goods Regulation are strict, the penalties for infringement of those regulations are severe, that failure to comply with all the requirements of the regulations can be the cause of major loss of life, limb and property.

29. **Carrier's execution box.** It is in this field that the air carrier indicates his acceptance of the air waybill and his acknowledgment therefore of his responsibilities in terms of the contract of   carriage.

Modern practice at major airports throughout the world is that the execution box is completed by machine imprint rather than by handwritten signature, etc. It is in any event essential, whether machine imprint or handwriting is used, that the date of execution of the air waybill is clearly legible. Apart from the fact that this date is the date upon which the contract of carriage was concluded between the parties concerned, this date is also the date which controls the exchange rate to be used between foreign currency and Zimbabwean currency for the purpose of continuous valuation.

2.2.4 Transmission of Air Waybills
Air waybills are utilised in sets of 12, all of which are identical. Copies 1,2 and 3 are regarded as originals of equal validity and they will bear the execution details as inserted by the air carrier. The other copies are distributed as indicated at the foot of each copy.

Clearly, certain copies are retained at the airport of origin from amongst which copies go back to the shipper / IATA agent, the accounting section of the airline concerned, etc.

Other copies are distributed in accordance with their intended use but in any event originals and copies for use at the destination airport are **always** carried by the captain of the aircraft so that they are immediately available at destination. If this were not so, the destination airport would not have available to it any detailed instructions with regard to the disposal of the goods

2.2.5 Consignor's / Sender's Letter of Instruction
It is standard practice in respect of commercial traffic by air that there shall be attached to each air waybill all documents appropriate to the clearing and delivery of the goods upon their arrival at the destination airport .It is normal for these to be enclosed in an envelope addressed to the consignee/consignee's agent/deconsolidator Airline accept responsibility for making such documentation available in their airport offices for collection by the addressees as fast as possible after the aircraft has landed.

It is obviously essential in the case of imports into Zimbabwe that overseas operating agents acting on behalf of forwarders within Zimbabwe are clearly required to fax or e-mail with immediacy the maximum information to their Zimbabwean partners concerning all consignments moving by air in order that the latter may be pre-advised to collect immediately after the arrival of the aircraft in question all documents which they will need for the clearance and delivery of consignments for which they are responsible.

2.2.6 Air Waybill Not a Document of Title
It is worth repeating that the air waybill is not a document of title, it is effectively simply a delivery order instructing the airline to whom the goods in

question should be delivered and under what terms with regard to such things as charges collect, etc. Because it is not a document of title it cannot be made negotiable" within its heading.

For this reason it cannot be "negotiated" through banking channels as is the case with the bill of lading.

However, where there is a substantial element of trust between the seller and the buyer of goods in international trade the latter may be content to accept in terms of a letter of credit opened by him in favour of the seller, an ordinary copy of an air aybill bearing the execution details inserted thereon by the air carrier. This, however, does not constitute the air waybill as a document of title.

Alternatively, the seller may decide for his own financial safety that instead of consigning an airfreight shipment on an air waybill direct to his customer, the importer, he will consign the goods to a bank of his choice and incorporate in the consignor's letter of instruction a request to that bank not to issue a release order in favour of the importer until they have received clear evidence that the importer has paid the overseas supplier the amount invoiced. Again, this does not constitute the air waybill a document of title -it merely interposes a third party between the seller and the buyer (the bank in question) as a referee responsible to oversee the payment for the goods.

The safeguard in this situation for the seller is, of course, that the bank in question certainly will not attempt to take delivery of the goods from the airline, but it is equally true to say that the airline will only be prepared to deliver the goods to that bank or to the party to whom the bank authorises such delivery.

2.2.7 The Airfreight Consolidator's House Air Waybill
The consolidator's house air waybill bears a relationship to the IATA or airline air waybill which parallels in large measure the relationship between the forwarder's house bill of lading and the shipping company's house bill of lading.

Both documents are "house" documents. That is to say, in neither instance will it be found when comparing either document issued by one forwarder with the equivalent document issued by another, that there is uniformity of structure or maximum liabilities, or the trading conditions in terms of which they are issued. "House" documents are by their nature documents designed by the "house" or organisation who drafted them.
In lieu of the "house " bill of lading, FIATA has been successful in devising for the use of its membership a completely uniform "FIATA Forwarder's Bill of Lading". The intention of FIATA in creating this document was to provide for the use of its member a forwarder's transport document recognisable worldwide, acceptable to the worldwide banking community, and contain within itself uniform trading conditions so that shippers moving goods in terms of it would understand exactly what the responsibilities and liabilities of the forwarder issuing it would

be- irrespective of the country in which it was issued or the county to which the goods covered by it were consigned. The FIATA FBL has worked extremely efficiently in international trade, and it is hoped will be used ever increasingly by Zimbabwean exporters in their export trade.

FIATA has for a number of years been working upon the production of a comparable transport document for airfreight- variously known as a FIATA Forwarder's Air Waybill or alternatively, a   neutral air waybill. Regrettable, up to the present time, FITA has not been able to achieve sufficient consensus among its worldwide membership to warrant the publication of such a document. This is the reason why, in airfreight, forwarders worldwide are at present forced to devise their own transport document for airfreight purposes and issue it as their own "house" air waybill..

House Air Waybill: Format
There is no uniform format although in a broad sense it can be stated that most house air waybills tend to follow the general structure of the IATA air waybill but with modifications designed to suit the needs of the organization designing it.

The House Air Waybill: Receipt for Goods
The nature of the receipt acknowledged by the issuer of a house air waybill is precisely the same as the receipt issued by an airline.

The House Air Waybill: Evidence of Contract

A study of the variety of house air waybills in use discloses that -

☐   some of them make reference to trading conditions available only by reference to another source
☐   some of them bear no reference to any trading conditions whatsoever
☐   others still bear trading conditions relevant many years ago   which are inadequate under present day circumstances.

It is - or should be - common knowledge that every international transport document must contain within itself all relevant trading conditions in terms of which the issuer conducts business, and that unless this requirement is fulfilled, courts in most countries will refuse to recognise limitation and immunities purported to be available to the issuer under such trading conditions. In other words, courts will demand compliance with the contract of carriage in terms of common law.

All forwarders are also encouraged to scrutinise the house air waybills issued by their employing organisations to ascertain whether these documents are competent to stand up in a court of law.

121

The House Air Waybill: Negotiability
As in the case of the IATA air waybill, the house air waybill is not a document of title and cannot be made negotiable. Nevertheless, it is possible to consign goods on a house air waybill to a bank in the destination country to enlist their assistance in ensuring that the consignor's/sender's invoice is paid, **but the consolidator wishing to do so must ensure that the bank in question receives precise and comprehensive instructions of a nature with which that bank can readily comply.** possible to consign goods on a house air waybill to a bank in the destination country to enlist their assistance in ensuring that the consignor's/sender's invoice is paid, **but the consolidator wishing to do so must ensure that the bank in question receives precise and comprehensive instructions of a nature with which that bank can readily comply.**

Naturally, the consolidator will not attempt to this except upon the specific instruction of his exporting client, **and, the consolidator must ensure that, if his client requires this procedure to be implemented, that client must give contingency instruction with regard to the disposal of the goods if the consignee fails within a stipulated time to pay for the goods.** Such contingency instructions might be for instance,

☐   The goods shall be returned at the expense and charges of the exporter

☐   The goods must be offered to an alternative consignee willing to pay

☐   the goods must be abandoned.

2.2.8 The IATA Master (IATA) Air Waybill
The consolidation of airfreight from multiple exporters intended for a variety of consignees inevitably requires that the total consolidated consignment must be covered by an IATA /airline air waybill in terms of which the consolidator is the "shipper" while the consignee is the deconsolidating agent at the destination airport.

The documentation involved will therefore be:-

☐   A single master air waybill evidencing receipt of total consolidated consignment by the airline

☐   And also evidencing the conditions of carriage in terms of which the airline will convey the consolidation from the individual exporters

A series of house air waybills evidencing receipt of the individual parcels in the consolidation from the individual exporters

Evidence of the conditions of carriage by the consolidator in respect of each such parcel

Instruction to the deconsolidating agent at the destination airport concerning the disposal of each consignment

It will be obvious that the "consignor's /sender's letter of instruction" accompanying the master air waybill must be addressed to the deconsolidating agent and must incorporate as enclosures the house air waybills, the supplier's invoices and packing lists, and other documentation essential to the prompt clearance and delivery of the goods at the destination.

This may well constitute a sizeable package but it is absolutely essential that nothing necessary at the destination is ever omitted. Furthermore, **it is vital that the number of the master air waybill** issued for the purpose of the carriage of the consolidation **is quoted without fail upon every house air waybill.**

Furthermore, in respect of every consolidation the consolidator **must prepare a complete** **consolidation manifest** containing the particulars of a very house air waybill involved so that the airline can present this with the master air waybill to the customs at the destination airport. From that consolidation manifest the customs will verify, the due entry of every consignment, the payment of the appropriate duties, etc., as a means of ensuring that the revenue due in respect of every consignment has been secured.

2.3 AIRFREIGHT RATES
Every aircraft in service anywhere in the world has a strictly defined volumetric capacity for the carriage of cargo and at the same time has an equally defined limit to the mass of the cargo which it can carry. Since the majority of aircraft in service carry both passengers and freight, it is obvious that the freight capacity of a particular aircraft will be affected by the passenger load booked for its flight in question.

In order to achieve maximum revenue by its members IATA utilises a formula from which, as regards cargo, a unit known as "chargeable weight" can be determined.

With few exceptions, the chargeable weight for cargo carried by air is the higher of the following alternatives:-

☐ The actual mass in kilogrammes rounded up to the next higher 0.5 of a kilogramme, or
☐ the number of units of volume of the cargo where one unit is 6 cubic decimetres (6000 cubic centimetres).

By illustration, take the case of a consignment with a gross mass of 200kg and dimensions 589 cms x 76cms x 39cms. In order to calculate the chargeable weight the volume in units of 6000 cubic centimetres must be calculated. Thereafter the resut must be compared to the actual mass.

The calculation will accordingly be as follows:-

$$\frac{598 \times 76 \times 39}{6000} \quad = \quad 295.4 \text{ chargeable units}$$

Since the resultant here is larger than the actual mass, the chargeable weight of the consignment will be 295.5 kilogrammes (i.e. 295.4kg rounded up to 295.5kg).

2.3.1 Airfreight Services
There are three types of service offered for the carriage of goods by air, and the type of service utilised will control the level of freight rate charged and the transit time for the movement of the goods. Thus, for example, a direct service from airport A to airport B on a direct IATA airline air waybill will provide the fastest transit time but it will also be the most expensive. For those services where the transit time lengthens, the freight rate decreases.

2.3.2 Direct Services
The goods are carried from an international airport in the country of origin to an international airport in the country of destination under a single airline air waybill issued by the first carrying airline in the country of origin.

However, even within these direct services there are three different scales of rate.

2.3.3 General Commodity Rates
These general rates are the basic rates at which cargo is carried which is not specified elsewhere in the IATA tariffs. They consist of two levels as follows:

☐   The standard rate which will apply to all cargo moving between the airports concerned which has a chargeable weight less than 45kgs.
☐   An "over 45 kgs" rate at a lower level applicable to consignments having a chargeable weight of 45kgs or more.

The IATA tariffs lay down general rates between virtually all combinations of airports served by IATA airlines, although, where transshipment is required at an intermediate airport between the airports of origin and destination the IATA tariff must be used to "construct" the through rate.

While the basic breakpoint is as quoted above, the 45kgs, on routes where traffic is heavy, additional breakpoints at higher chargeable weights are quoted.

2.3.4 Specific Commodity Rates

Specific commodity rates represent a substantial discount on the general rates. They are established for particular commodities - or in some instances for groups of commodities - which are constantly moving between two airports.

The range of specific commodity rates is substantial and within each commodity definition there may be a whole series of breakpoints at each of which the rate per chargeable unit drops ever lower.

The objective in the setting of these specific commodity rates and their breakpoints is clearly to attract the maximum volume of cargo to the air mode of transport in competition with other modes such as seafreight, rail freight, road freight, etc.

It is useful to know that any trader who is developing substantial traffic between two points in the world can always approach his national airline with the request for the creation of a specific commodity rate for that traffic. Such a request will be reviewed by the national carrier, the motivation investigated, the level of traffic density established, and the whole matter will then be submitted to IATA with a recommendation. The final decision will rest with those IATA members who are likely to participate in the traffic movement or are likely to be affected adversely by it.

2.3.5 Classified Rates
Classified rates are far less common. They apply to a limited range of commodities which either require special handling or, by virtue of their nature, must take precedence over other commodities.

Occasions frequently occur when due to weather, due to abnormally high passenger loads, due to high temperatures, or for other reasons, a proportion of the cargo booked on a particular flight must be left behind. Under such circumstances cargo which is subject to classified rates will always be given preference with the result that it is extremely rare for such cargo ever to be delayed. Classified rates are usually expressed as a premium over the general cargo rates. They apply to cargo such as live animals, bullion, jewellery, human remains, medical and hospital supplies, etc.

2.4 CONSOLIDATION SERVICES
"Consolidation" is for airfreight the equivalent of "groupage" for seafreight. Forwarders who are registered with IATA have the liberty to consolidate small consignments of mixed but compatible cargo into consolidations which by virtue of the chargeable weight thus created, will attract lower rates from IATA airlines than would be available if the individual consignments of which they are composed were separately consigned.

Such consolidators of airfreight act as wholesalers, buying freight space/weight from airlines at wholesale prices which they are then at liberty to sell by retail to their clients, making a profit which will be fixed somewhere between the wholesale price charged to them and the general commodity rate.

For instance, a forwarder in Frankfurt may well have a number of clients in Germany, together perhaps with further clients in Eastern France and Switzerland, whose cargo he can accumulate at his airfreight depot in Frankfurt which he can then utilise to fill one or more airline containers - i.e. unit load devices (ULDs) - for consigning as a complete shipment to his counterpart in Zimbabwe under a single airline air waybill at a rate applicable to a higher breakpoint in the IATA tariffs. He is then at liberty to sell to his clients in question the transportation of the goods at a rate which will be higher than that which he is charged but materially lower than the general commodity rate.

The airline air waybill on which the consolidation moves is known as a "master" air waybill (MAWB) and the consolidator will be required to pay the airfreight charge for the transportation in question at the airport of origin. The consolidator will himself issue separate house air waybills in respect of each of the consignments in his consolidation, and will nominate his Zimbabwean counterpart as the "delivery agent" on each of those house air waybills.

He will also account for his charges necessary to cover his costs and provide him with profits in accordance with the terms of delivery of each of the separate consignments in the consolidation, some of which may be sold:-

☐　　EXW - all charges forward for collection from consignee
☐　　FCA - charges from delivered to the airline concerned charged forward
　　　for account of the consignee.
☐　　CPT - airfreight and charges prepaid by sender to arrival Harare International
airport; other charges for account of consignee.
☐　　Etc, etc.

Depending upon the volume and variety of traffic controlled by a consolidator, it may take him anything between 24 hours and 3 or more days to accumulate a suitable quantum of cargo before he will be able to dispatch it and make an appropriate profit on the shipment.

There is thus a greater or lesser degree of delay in the movement of cargo handled by consolidators. Herein lies one of the basis of competition. The other area of competition will obviously be the level of the consolidator's rate per chargeable unit for the transportation required.

2.4.1 Consolidator's Responsibilities and Liabilities
Because a consolidator must, of necessity, issue his own house air waybill (HAWB) he is effectively a contractual carrier and must assume certain liabilities which he can only control by means of the trading conditions stipulated within his HAWB. It is inevitable that consolidators endeavour to limit so far as possible their liabilities to those which are accepted by carrying airlines. This is never completely possible, with the result that consolidators have to accept certain risks in respect of which they should carry professional indemnity insurance cover. Such cover should enable them not only to

satisfy clients who may have justifiable claims upon them, but also enable them to settle such claims without severe financial disruption of their businesses.

2.4.2 Consolidations on the General Commodity Rates
A consolidator may be able to achieve a consolidation attracting an "over 45kgs" rate with the result that he will be able to retail his services at a rate somewhere between the standard rate and the "over 45kgs" rate.

Where there is substantial traffic on a particular route and additional higher breakpoints are provided in the IATA tariffs, he may be able to operate more profitably if he can attract volumes of cargo which justify being rated at the higher breakpoints.

2.4.3 Consolidations on Specific Commodity Rates
Because certain of the commodity rates include a very broad spectrum of goods, a forwarder may set his sights upon the accumulation of cargo which falls within a particular specific commodity rate definition. If he is successful in doing so he may be able to achieve one of the very high breakpoints which are allowed against the specific commodity definition in question with the result that he has a wider rate range within which he can set his own rate charge. Many forwarders in Europe and the United States are capable of doing this since the countries involved are highly developed.

Where this is possible, of course, the profit sharing between the overseas consolidator and his Zimbabwean counterpart will be more profitable for the latter.

However, as regards export traffic by air from Zimbabwe, this situation is not by any means so easy to achieve although every Zimbabwean forwarder must keep in his mind the possibility of developing consolidations based on specific commodity rates.

NB: It must be emphasised that whereas direct services are those which are offered by the airline themselves consolidations are offered by the forwarding community who thereby accept responsibility as contractual carriers while they sub-contract the physical carriage to the same airlines.

2.4.4 Charter Services
Certain airlines - usually non-IATA airlines - offer fairly regular charter flights mainly to and from Europe on a weekly or less frequent basis.

Because of the infrequency of these flight opportunities, the rates offered by such airlines must of necessity be lower than those offered by regular services, and may be lower than the rates offered by consolidators. It must be emphasised, however, that the delays waiting for the flights to depart may well result in appreciably longer transit times from source to destination for the goods in question. Such flights offer transit times which are effectively intermediate between the times in transit for scheduled airline and consolidation services, and those offered by the seafreight shipping fraternity.

2.5 AIRLINES SERVICING ZIMBABWE

It is incumbent upon the forwarder who is involved in airfreight work to keep himself up-to-date at all times with changes to the list of airlines serving Zimbabwe noting the airline name, nationality and whether or not an IATA member.

2.6 AIRCRAFT SERVING SOUTHERN AFRICA

Constraints upon Cargo arising out of the Aircraft Design
Almost any cargo can be transported by sea or overland without regard to size or weight. This is not the case with airfreight. "Lifting capacity" is the controlling factor which determines whether cargo is suitable for movement by air or not.

Lifting capacity may be described as a combination of the following:-

- ☐ Limitations arising from aircraft design and aircraft cargo loading doors
- ☐ Constraints arising from the vital importance of maintaining the aircraft "trim" whilst flying.
- ☐ Constraints arising from the strength of the airframe of an aircraft - which may vary from fore and aft depending upon the distance of the point of load from the lifting planes of the aircraft - that is to say, the wings.
- ☐ The weight of passengers and their luggage which must take priority in respect of the flight in question
- ☐ The lifting capacity of the ambient air at the airport of departure - which is influenced by the height of the airport above sea level, the ambient air temperature at the airport, the wind velocity and direction at the airport.
- ☐ The fuel load which the aircraft must carry to accomplish the flight envisaged plus the fuel contingency margin which must be provided to ensure the safety of the aircraft should it have to "fly around" weather experienced en route or divert from the airport of destination to an alternative airport due to weather or other unforeseen circumstances.

All these factors must override considerations of the freight booked for the flight in question. It is the pilot of the aircraft who makes decisions since he is in ultimate charge of the safety of the flight at all times.

If the forwarder appreciates the complexity of the equation which faces the pilot when he determines what payload he is prepared to take on board, then there will be less irritation and grumbling if a proportion of the airfreight cargo booked upon a flight has to be "bumped". **"Bumping"** is the short-shipment of airfreight resulting, not from over-booking, but from the decision of the pilot having due regard for all the above factors. The most obvious cause of bumping is the decision of the pilot that he must take an extra fuel.

So far as concerns airfreight out of Zimbabwe, it must be appreciated that with the exception of regional flights to neighbouring territories, all flights from Zimbabwe are "long haul".

In addition, as far as concerns flights out of Harare International Airport, they all take off at an altitude above sea level of some 1 400 metres, and in summer may take off when the ambient air temperature at Harare International is in excess 30^0c, both of which mean that the lifting capacity of the aircraft is reduced. It is because of the temperature which in summer time is commonly experienced at Harare International that long haul flights normally leave as late as possible in the afternoon or evening of the day of departure.

Summing up, there is a trade-off in respect of every single flight between lifting capacity and range. The greater the range, the lower the lifting capacity. It may be argued that long haul flights should drop down at intermediate airports for the purpose of refuelling. While this is true, where possible, it must be remembered first of all that politics enter into the situation, that take off from ground level uses a large amount of fuel until the aircraft is at its cruising altitude and again there is a complex equation upon which the decision whether to refuel or not is taken.

2.7 AIRCRAFT STRUCTURES
Passenger Aircraft
The main deck in these aircraft is normally reserved as passenger and crew accommodation together with such other facilities as galley, toilets, cloakroom cupboards, etc.

The area beneath this main deck - the lower deck - is the space available for aircraft machinery, passengers' luggage, and airfreight.

The lower deck area is divided into a series of "hold", the number of such holds being determined by the aircraft type. Loading and discharge of cargo from these holds is through doors or hatches set into the aircraft frame.

It will be obvious that the space available in these holds may well have a strange shape consequent upon the contours of the aircraft body and spaces amidships will obviously be of greater volume than those towards the rear.

On wide bodied aircraft such as the 747 or DC10 special pallets and airfreight containers designed to maximise the use of the space available in different parts of the lower hold have been created. The use of such unit load devices (UDLs) not only uses the spaces available to maximum efficiency but also, since they can be prepared in advance of the moment for loading the aircraft, speed the process of loading.

2.7.1 Combi Aircraft
Combi aircraft are normal aircraft utilised for the transport of passengers in the upper (main) decks of which it is possible to fit bulkheads at optional points across the breadth of the aircraft behind which the seats can be removed so that surplus passenger space can be utilised for loading freight. Combi aircraft are therefore a concept halfway between the standard passenger aircraft and the airfreight aircraft.

129

2.7.2 All-Freight Aircraft

These are aircraft of the standard types which have been modified so that they are totally dedicated to the carriage of freight. In these instances, the entire main deck seating is taken out and separate flooring is provided within which are retractable rollers so that air cargo containers of substantial sizes and weights can be loaded and moved by hand into their required positions where the rollers beneath them can be retracted and they can be locked into position.

All-freight aircraft are capable of taking freight containers which are the same size as the standard 6m shipping container. Of course, containers intended for use on aircraft are not built of heavy duty structural steel such as are those used in the shipping trades. They are constructed from special lightweight materials so that they do not materially detract from the effective payload of the aircraft.

2.8 LOAD LIMITATIONS

The ultimate mass limitation on any aircraft is its maximum take off weight and this may be defined as the weight of the aircraft itself, plus fuel, plus passengers, plus luggage, plus cargo. It has already been pointed out that the maximum take off weight will vary from airport to airport depending on a number of extraneous factors.

In addition, there are mass limitations appropriate to each hold or section of the aircraft into which cargo is loaded which themselves may not be exceeded.

Over and above this, for each section of the aircraft there is a maximum floor loading density in kilogrammes per square metre which may not be exceeded.

It is neither necessary nor practical in a course such as this to go into the technical details of all these load limitations; it is sufficient that the forwarder is aware that the loading of cargo into an aircraft and the positioning of each separate item of cargo within the aircraft holds is a skilful and exacting process, the end result of which must be that the aircraft in flight is correctly trimmed.

2.8.1 Dimension and Volume Limitations

Having in mind the constraints imposed by the size of aircraft hatches and the contours of the aircraft cargo spaces it will be obvious that the dimensions of any parcel intended to be dispatched by air which is of material size must be very carefully considered.

In respect of every aircraft in service for the carriage of freight in Zimbabwe's trade maximum dimension tables are held by the airlines concerned. From these tables it is a comparatively simple exercise to determine:-
- □ whether the parcel can be loaded at all, and if so,
- □ which cargo hold in the aircraft is capable of accommodating the parcel.

The determination with regard to the ability of a particular aircraft to accommodate a specific parcel does not end at that point if a transshipment from aircraft to aircraft will be necessary for the completion of the transit. In such an instance the ability of the on-carrying aircraft undertaking the second leg of the transit must also be considered.

It may also be important where the parcel is of a substantial weight for the ability of the intermediate airport to handle the weight involved is also investigated. Normally, the airline taking the cargo from the airport of origin will undertake all necessary investigations upon request.

2.9 AIRPORT TERMINAL SERVICES
Effective airfreight operations depends on reliability of the following airport terminal services:-

- marshalling, parking, handling, aircraft landing and taking off
- fuel supply and refuelling
- aircraft repair and maintenance
- security i.e. fire, service and police
- passenger embarkation and disembarkation facilities
- customs, immigration and other legal formalities
- reception, information and check-in facilities
- shelter, food and accommodation for travellers
- services for handling passenger luggage and air cargo

REFERENCES
Bailey C. A. (2007) **"A Guide to Qualitative Field Research."** Pine Forge Press. California.

Bedi K. (2004) **"Production and Operations Management"**. Oxford University Press. New Delhi.

Bhattacharyya D. K. (2003) **"Research Methodology."** Excel Books. New Delhi.

Cook T. A. (2001) **"The Ultimate Guide to Export Management."** AMACOM. New York.

Daniels, Raudebaugh, Sullivan (2004) **"Globalisation and Business."** Prentice Hall International. New Delhi

Frazelle E.H. (2004) **"Supply Chain Strategy."** Tata McGraw-Hill Publishing Co. Ltd. New Delhi.

Gubbins E. J. (2003) **"Managing Transport Operations."** Kogan Page. London.

House D. J. (2005) **"Cargo Work"** Elsevier. Amsterdam

Kapoor S. K. and Kansal P. (2003) **"Marketing Logistics: A Supply Chain Approach."** Pearson Education. New Delhi.

Kirby M., Kidd W et al (1997) **"Sociology in Perspective"** Heinnemann Educational Publishers. Oxford.

Raina H. K. (1990) **"Guide to Import Management".** PRODEC. Helsinki

Rowland O.P. (1986) **"Imports and Exports: An Introductory Handbook."** Evans Brothers. Ltd. Nairobi

Silverman D. (2006) **"Interpreting Qualitative Data."** Sage Publications. London.

Sople V. V. (2004) **"Logistics Management: The Supply Chain Imperative."** Pearson Education. Singapore.

Thomas A. B. (2004) **"Research Skills for Management Studies."** Routledge, London

CHAPTER 3

3.0 ROAD AND RAIL FREIGHT OPERATIONS

3.1 MODAL CHARACTERISTICS - ROAD
□ provides quick service
□ cost competitive with complete unit loads for single origin and destination points
□ save time and minimise damage due to reduced need to double handle and transship goods.
□ flexible for through movement as a unit load
□ minimum packaging cost as load is prone to fewer shocks
□ system can provide regular, scheduled service due to flexibility of road   vehicle scheduling
□ Paper work problems and delays can arise.

Road transport is appreciably more flexible in that road transport contractors normally command the services of a whole variety of conveyances from small open 5 ton lorries to heavy duty combination rigs hauled by powerful mechanical horses.

Road transport is normally door-to-door although over longer distances road transport contractors tend to have a fleet of small vehicles for the collection of their traffic in the source area and for delivery of the same traffic within the destination area. They employ appreciably larger rigs for the longer haul journeys between the two areas.

Road transport also has more versatility so that it is normally possible to initiate the transport transaction within a few hours instead of being compelled to wait for railway scheduled services.

Road transport is subject to a disadvantage in that the conveyance of substantial tonnages will require many separate vehicles.

Road transport has a further disadvantage because its cost per tonne/kilometre is materially higher than by rail and because that cost is subject to inputs, the costs of which are themselves subject to frequent change. Such inputs may be fuel, tyres, maintenance, etc.

In addition, road transport equipment normally has a home base and this is even truer of the drivers of such vehicles. Consequently, it is normally important that the vehicles and their drivers return from the point of destination of the cargo to that home base.

If a return load is available then well and good, revenue for the transport contractor arises on both legs of the journey. If, however, there is no such return load then there is an "empty leg", the cost of which has to be absorbed by one means or another into the charges for the cargoes conveyed. The longer the "empty leg" the higher will be the costs for absorption.

3.1.1 Types of road freight services
☐ local or specialist - services e.g. furniture removals
☐ general haulage on contract
☐ regular trunk services between depots (overnight, etc)
☐ RMS scheduled route services
☐ international traffic (export, import, transit)

3.1.2   Modal characteristics - rail
☐ shunting shocks can cause damage
☐ load double handling because first and last leg of through journey   needs
to be by road for most shipments.
☐ very slow but cheap means of carriage
☐ very unreliable. Wagons may arrive at irregular intervals resulting in
    delays for international freight on single customs document.
☐ ideal where speed is not vital e.g. bulky consignments.

Rail transport favours the movement of large volumes of homogeneous cargoes over comparatively long distances. In this context, and irrespective of the detail of the contents loaded into them, container traffic is "homogeneous".

Rail traction units - whether powered by steam or by electricity - are extremely powerful and can haul very high tonnages at highly economic cots. Moreover, it is a simple operation, where necessary, to couple additional traction units to a train in order to provide additional power for hauling massive loads up steep inclines; the cargoes being hauled do not need to be disturbed.

The cost of the energy resources needed for rail traction is modest on a tonne per kilometre basis.

Rail transport tariffs tend to remain stable over comparatively long spans of time for the reason that, although the cost of the capital investment in rail tracks, signaling systems, traction units and freight wagons is initially high, the capital structures and equipment are of so robust a character that they can be amortized over a very lengthy period of time which reduces the cost of that amortization per unit of cargo carried. Rail transport is therefore the ideal mode for the transport of high volumes over comparatively long distances.

Rail transport stands a disadvantage, however, when the size of consignments is comparatively small, the distances between source and destination are comparatively short, and where mixed consignments must be handled which originate from a variety of consignors within one area and are intended for delivery to a variety of consignees in another area.
Rail transport stands at a further disadvantage in that (save in the case of private siding traffic) collection at source and delivery at destination is usually dependent upon the use of the road mode.

3.2   ROAD TRANSPORT REGULATION

The common and obvious feature in road freight operations is regulation. Safety regulation is achieved through the three E's of transport safety i.e. Enforcement, Education and Engineering.

According to Gubins E.J. (2004) transport regulation deals with three main variables namely the operator, the driver and the vessel.

Operator regulation
☐   fit applicant with no previous convictions for contravening regulations in the industry.
☐   knowledge of the industry where directors and key operations staff hold relevant qualifications or pass examinations.
☐   adequate financial resources to run the business in pursuit of a sound business plan
☐   facilities to operate the business either owned or assessed through contractual arrangements.

Driver regulation
☐   driver licensing and stipulated working hours
☐   installation of technographs to record time, speed and distance traveled.

Vessel regulation
☐   design and construction
☐   maintenance
☐   load and use

3.2.1   Principles Underlying the Road Motor Transportation Act

The Act, in Part II involves the following:-
☐   The requirements for the operation of goods vehicles or passenger transport services.
☐   Application for operator's licence
☐   Issue or refusal of operator's license
☐   Form and period of validity of operator's license
☐   Operator's license not transferable
☐   Route authority
☐   Various other licensing issues

Operator Registration

The purpose of operator license application is:-
☐   To specify the type of operation for which the license is required
☐   To specify whether the service will operate entirely within Zimbabwe or partly inside and partly outside Zimbabwe.

135

The license issued is not transferable.

Note:
The Act defines a freight vehicle as:-
"A goods vehicles means a motor vehicle, including an articulated vehicle, constructed or adapted for the conveyance of goods, which has -
(a)   a carrying capacity of more than ten tonnes; or
(b)   in the case of a motor vehicle whose carrying capacity is ten tonnes or less but which is drawing one or more trailers, a combined carrying capacity of more than fifteen tonnes."

Period of Validity
An operator's license is valid for a period, not exceeding three years, as the Commissioner of Transport may fix when issuing it.

Implications of Operator Registration
Once the operator is registered, those vehicles will no longer require any other form of permit for the transportation of non-abnormal freight on a public road within Zimbabwe. An abnormal permit is required for abnormal loads or abnormally large vehicles.

Freight Vehicles with a Gross Vehicle Mass of less than 10 000kg

Professional Driver Permits
The licensing of drivers is controlled by the Road Traffic Act Chapter 13.11. of 1996.

Effects of the Road Motor Transportation Act Upon Forwarders
It is broadly, if not universally, true that forwarders sub-contract the road movement of international cargo to suitable haulage organisations.

However, the entrusting of any particular load of cargo to a road haulage contractor will be a responsible function in that if the contractor is in default in any respect with regard to his operator's license or his driver is in default in relation to his driving permit, then a serious offence is involved which may, if detected, result in the detention of the vehicle, the driver, and the cargo loaded on the vehicle. In more serious cases both the vehicle and its load may be subject to confiscation with extremely serious consequences for all concerned.

The sub-contracting of road haulage activities is therefore a function of the forwarder which should be retained under the supervision and control of senior management. It must never be assumed that the sub-contractor offering the lowest prices is necessarily performing in compliance with the laws under which he should operate.

Neither may it be assumed that because at a particular moment in time he is acting lawfully, that this fortunate position will persist indefinitely. A sub-contractor's operator's card for a particular vehicle may be suspended - in which latter event it would be folly for a forwarder to entrust any traffic to that contractor.

In a similar fashion a particular driver's driving permit may be withdrawn through a failure on the part of the individual to successfully pass a re-test or because it has not been renewed during this period of validity. Yet again, the driving permit in question may not permit the holder to be in control of a vehicle of the type which he is driving.

Quite apart from all the above, it is common for forwarders to employ the services of contractors arriving laden from foreign countries adjacent to Zimbabwe who are seeking return loads in order to augment their revenue.

It is incumbent upon the forwarder who desires to employ such a contractor that he establishes beyond reasonable doubt that the contractor in question has the necessary Carrier Permit.

Only by using reputable carriers and exercising proper responsibility in the matter of sub-contracting can the forwarder ensure that he is not placing goods which are the property of his client at risk.

3.2.2 Road Traffic Act
The Road Traffic Act imposes uniform requirements upon the operator of every transport vehicle using the public roads of Zimbabwe. The vehicle must be:-
☐   A fit, proper and suitable vehicle in respect of the route and the good concerned and the circumstances in which the conveyance is undertaken.
☐   Used within appropriate safety limitations, precautions and requirements regarding the route, circumstances and commodity being conveyed.
☐   Not overloaded regarding its authorised gross vehicle mass.

While these requirements apply to all transportation by road it is obvious that hazardous cargoes require the highest possible standard of vehicle operation and that they are subject to further specific requirements consequent upon the nature of the goods.
Routing of Vehicles and Speed Limits
As regards the conveyance of explosives, the regulations identify the requirements specifically as follows:-

Persons conveying explosives shall avoid towns and villages as far as practicable and it shall be lawful for any local authority to prescribe the route by which explosives shall be conveyed within its area of jurisdiction, subject to reasonable facilities being given for reaching any required destination.

Should it be necessary to halt a journey this shall be done by ensuring that the vehicle remains at least 500 metres from inhabited buildings and 200 metres from a public road, and the person in charge thereof shall keep a constant watch over the explosives.

The regulations are imprecise at the present time with regard to goods classified in other classes but it is very clear that such vehicles conveying hazardous substances need to be diverted away from densely populated areas and so far as possible also from routes bearing heavy traffic. Responsible road haulers do this in their own interests but there remain inexperienced and/or uninformed carriers (and sometimes careless drivers) who may well be unaware of the dangers to which they expose themselves and the public when transporting such goods.

Driving Hours
Where hazardous substances are conveyed by road it is obviously of great importance that the driver of a vehicle remains alert and competent at all times.

Vehicle Accidents
If an accident occurs and the product is exposed, or spilled, or if the load is likely to be in any danger such as from fire, it is the responsibility of the driver to take immediate action. He must in all such cases get in touch as fast as possible with the local emergency services, e.g. Fire Brigade, Polite, etc, and also the owner of the vehicle, and if possible the owner of the load being conveyed, and he is entitled to do this by calling on assistance from any passers-by.

The driver's most immediate concern must be for the safety of the public nearby. He may therefore have to undertake other emergency action before the more formal emergency services can arrive and this may involve:-

☐ Protecting himself by putting on suitable protective clothing
☐ Moving casualties away from any danger from the exposed cargo or spillage, or from any other risk
☐ Keeping other people and other vehicles well away from the incident.
☐ Moving the conveying vehicle - if it remains mobile - to a spot more remote where the spillage or exposure will cause less harm or danger

Broad Conclusions
Since it should never be the forwarder himself who is directly involved through the medium of his own transport fleet with any of these activities, it is sufficient that he is aware at all times of the legislative and regulatory controls which exist over the movement of hazardous substances by road and assists in every possible way those of his sub-contractors who may undertake this type of conveyance.

He must also understand that the sub-contracting road carrier will be entitled to charge premium rates for undertaking the transaction.

3.3   THE CHOICE BETWEEN RAIL AND ROAD
The choice between the two alternative modes must lie with the owner of the cargo to be conveyed. His decision will be based on some or all of the following considerations:-

☐ The kind of goods
☐ The weight and size of his consignment(s)
☐ The length of the transport haul required
☐ The quality of service he requires
☐ The comparative costs of the two alternatives
☐ The price he will be charged for the accomplishment of the transaction
☐ The urgency involved in meeting the deadline for delivery at destination

This freedom of choice should lie totally within the discretion of the cargo owner. It is the responsibility of the operators of both modes of transport to ensure that they provide transport services which are efficient and economical and which meet not only the demands of the cargo owner but also the necessities of the operation of the port to or from which the cargo moves.

It is well understood that bulk exports from the interior of Zimbabwe such as coal, iron ore, cereal grains, sugar, and such similar commodities are far more readily transported by rail at more economical costs than can be achieved by road.

In the case of containerised traffic over long distance the advantages clearly lie with rail, although for shorter distances and where only two or so containers are involved, road transport is also very effective.

In the event of the development of delays within one of the modes then it may be wise to use the alternative. Such delays may arise from strikes, stayaways, or from the consequences of climatic or geological disturbances such as heavy storms, earth tremors, etc. A forwarder must be alert at all times to the occurrence of these problems and to bring into his consideration how they may affect the trading of his clients.

3.4 ROAD TRANSPORT OPERATIONS
Road transportation in Zimbabwe is almost exclusively undertaken by private road carriers, which for convenience will be referred to as private sector operations.

This includes movements of containers to and from depots, etc.

3.4.1 Road transport carrier selection
(a) Rate related variables like door to door rates or costs and carrier willingness to negotiate rage changes.
(b) Customer service aspects like transit time, reliability or consistency and total door to door transit time.
(c) Claims handling and follow up
    ☐ claims processing
    ☐ freight loss and damage
    ☐ shipment tracing
    ☐ pick up and delivery service
    ☐ shipment expediting

(d)   Special equipment availability and service flexibility
       ☐   equipment availability
       ☐   special equipment
       ☐   quality of operating personnel
       ☐   line haul service
       ☐   scheduling flexibility

Subject to the limitations and constraints arising from the licenses, private transport contractors can offer facilities for the movement of freight throughout Zimbabwe and, where the operator holds the appropriate permits, into neighbouring territories and foreign countries.

Private sector operators can also carry containers - but always subject to the safety requirements which are laid down in the Road Traffic Act and regulations made there under.

3.4.2 Abnormal Loads
Loads which are "abnormal" by virtue of their length, width, height or mass will require special abnormal load permits for transportation on public roads.

Special application for abnormal load permits must be made by the transport concerned. The movement of abnormal loads during certain holiday seasons and particularly over the Christmas high season is severely restricted in the interests of road safety. Only in instances of emergency will an application for a permit to move goods during these periods receive sympathetic consideration. These formalities are executed by the appointed road transporter. The exporter must, however, supply the correct measurements to the transporter.

3.4.3 Demurrage/Detention Charges on Vehicles
Road vehicles are expensive and only earn revenue while they are on the move. If for any reason a vehicle is detained beyond the free period of time allowed for the stowage of its cargo, an exporter may be faced with a detention charge. This applies to vehicles carrying break-bulk cargo and also to trailers conveying containers. Free period allowed is normally forty eight hours. This also applies to border clearance delays.

3.4.4 Implementing fuel economy in operations
☐   examine previous year's fuel consumption records and fuel cost for particular vehicles
☐   estimate present fuel costs for each vehicle operated.
☐   estimate cost of fuel economy devices and methods
☐   examine present operations characteristics like route scheduling,   loading methods and operating personnel.
☐   investigate the most suitable fuel saving techniques and estimate the range of possible savings.
☐   calculate percentage savings required to cover the cost of fuel saving devices and other long-term benefits.

☐ investigate possibilities of discounts in the purchase of fuel. This may mean buying bulk fuel tanks or scheduling refueling at cheap sources of fuel along the international route.

☐ investigate ways of educating and training operating personnel in fuel saving techniques.

☐ display general and company information on fuel economy measures and progress with posters, pamphlets and graphs.

3.4.5 Road Freight Responsibilities

The transportation of goods by road - particularly within Southern Africa - is a business fraught with many complications, all of which render the transport contractor concerned highly vulnerable.

It is only necessary to consider the following contingencies to realise how true this is:-

☐ The extreme variety of roads over which it may be necessary for goods to pass from modern freeways to gravel roads.

☐ Height limitations from clearance under overhead bridges.

☐ Strength of bridges and conduits over which loads may have to pass

☐ The limitation on maximum loads and upon axle loads

☐ Limitations on permitted driving hours

☐ Risks of accidents on roads

☐ Risks of mechanical breakdown of vehicles

☐ Risks of overturning

☐ Risks of hijacking

☐ Risks of false or faulty declarations concerning dangerous goods

Etc, etc

Moreover, prices of petrol and diesel are subject to increases at any time together with inflation in the costs of tyres and maintenance spares, etc.

Abnormal loads - whether long lengths, excessive widths, and exceptional mass, all require special permits from the provincial road authorities and on occasion will require transportation only during daylight hours and possibly, on other occasions, with a police escort.

In addition, on many occasions transport transactions by road are repetitive, with the result that special contracts are entered into in addition to standard trading conditions in which continuous repetitive business is envisaged over a period of time.

For all these reasons it is virtually impossible to find any standardised trading conditions or standardised forms of contract amongst the members of the road transportation fraternity. Nevertheless, there are certain basic principles upon which all road transport contractors operate which can be briefly described here.

Responsibility for Loading the Vehicle

Except under special arrangements made in writing beforehand, it is the responsibility of the consignor of goods to load those goods securely on the transport vehicle under the direction and supervision of the driver. This responsibility persists to include the lashing and securing of the load and of any tarpaulin necessary for weather protection.

Responsibility for Discharge of the Load at Destination
Here again, unless otherwise specially agreed in writing beforehand, it is the responsibility of the consignee to organise the discharge of the load at destination.

Access at Point of Loading and at Point of Discharge
It is the responsibility of the customer (consignor) to ensure that both at point of loading and at point of discharge suitable access is provided on hard ground with adequate turning circles to accommodate the vehicle being utilised.

Short Term Warehousing of Goods Pending Transportation or Ultimate Delivery
It is very common for goods to be collected from the premises of a consignor and then held by the transport contractor in his depot pending a suitable opportunity for the dispatch to destination. It is equally common for goods to be discharged at a contractor's depot at the destination and there to be held pending completion of delivery.

Zimbabwean courts have held that this short term warehousing will be subject to the same conditions of trade to which the transportation itself is subject.

Maximum Liabilities
In the common law of Zimbabwe a transport contractor has an absolute liability for the safety and security of the goods entrusted to him except in the following instances:-

☐   Where the loss is due to some event which could not have been foreseen or avoided by the contractor.

☐   Where the loss is due to some defect or weakness in the goods themselves (kindred to inherent vice in the marine bill of lading)

☐   Where the loss is due to negligence on the part of the owner or consignor or their servants.

☐   Where the contractor has contracted out of his liability by special agreement.

It is inevitable that every transport contractor within the country ensures that in this standard trading conditions he "contracts out" of his absolute liability and substitutes strictly limited liabilities with strictly limited maxima.

Since there is no uniformity in the practice of road transport contractors, it is not possible to state what those limits of liability and maxima actually are.

3.5 RAIL OPERATIONS

3.5.1 The NRZ Consignment Note and other NRZ Transport Documents

Because NRZ operate the entire commercial railway system within Zimbabwe they handle a great variety of traffic from small parcels through to containerised cargo in a variety of container sizes, and dry and liquid bulk consignments. In addition, it operates substantial local cartage activities and long-haul road fleets capable of handling abnormal loads of every description.

For this reason the trading conditions under which NRZ operate are complex and will vary according to the nature of the transportation they are called upon to undertake.

In addition, they offer transportation either at "company's risk" or at "owner's risk", again according to the circumstances of the transaction involved.

For these reasons it is not practical for them to incorporate their conditions of carriage within the confines of a contractual document with the result that they are an exception to the general rule that a transport document ought to incorporate such conditions so that the parties to the contract of carriage are mutually aware of them. It is important that the student undertakes this situation and the reasons for it.

However, on every NRZ transport document the consignor must sign the following declaration:

Receive and forward by .... the above-mentioned goods to said destination in accordance with the Bye-Laws, Regulations and conditions published in the current edition of the Official Railway tariff Books (or any amendment thereof or Supplement thereto) of the Administration specified above or the conditions and regulations of any other Railway Administration over whose lines the goods may travel to reach their destination, and it is agreed that the said conditions and regulations shall be applicable to this contract in the same manner as though they were fully set out herein.

This makes it clear that it is incumbent on the freight forwarder to obtain a copy of the conditions of carriage and to familiarise himself with such conditions.

3.5.2 Goods Consignment Note

The Goods Consignment Note is a "bare bones" document providing on its face very little more than empty blocks titled to indicate the nature of the contents to be inserted in each one, together with the declaration mentioned above and the signature of the sender and the date.

There are a number of different Goods Consignment Notes in use, each dedicated to the purpose for which it is intended. Those with which forwarders are commonly involved are briefly described below.

3.5.3 General Goods Consignment Note - Pink/White Form

This is the basic consignment note intended for use for internal traffic moving between points in Zimbabwe and may be utilised for the transportation of goods by the road operation (RMS) within NRZ, for full truck loads, for livestock and also for containers.

A study of the form itself - a specimen of the form is reproduced in the appendices - will suffice for the student to obtain comprehension as to its use.

These are required to be completed in sets of six as follows:-

1.	(original)	pricing copy
2.		checking copy
3.		receiving station's controlling copy
4.		delivery note
5.		receiver's copy
6.		sender's receipt.

For goods consigned to countries other than Zimbabwe and Botswana

By all organisations consigning goods in both break-bulk form and also in containers over the border of Zimbabwe into neighbouring independent territories. Its structure has some similarity to the above mentioned Consignment Note, but it required more extensive information and in particular, detail with regard to countries of destination, etc. It is, however, produced in a set of seven copies as follows:-

1.	(original)	pricing copy
2.		duplicate of sender's copy
3.		checking copy
4.		Receiving station's controlling copy
5.		Delivery note
6.		Receiver's copy
7.		Sender's receipt.

A specimen of this Consignment Note is printed under appendices and it will be noted that the form may be used for all types of service.

Container Terminal Order - T1412
The Container Terminal Order (CTO) in use by Spoornet is a form fundamentally different to their Freight Transit Order, which is their version of the Goods Consignment Note.

It may only be used for the exportation of containers to destinations overseas/overborder from South Africa. In this context it acts as a shipping order at coastal ports, as a transport order from inland places of origin, and as a combined shipping and transport order for goods passing from inland origins straight through the coastal ports onto the exporting ship.

It incorporates a whole variety of functions as follows:-

☐   An instruction to Spoornet to procure from a shipping line's container yard a suitable and appropriate empty container and place it at the premises of the exporter.

☐   To collect the container after its contents have been loaded to it and it has been sealed by the exporter, from his premises and, in accordance with the mode of transport indicated, to forward the container to the coastal port.

☐   At the coastal port indicated, to place the container on board the indicated vessel

☐   All these functions to be undertaken by Spoornet in accordance with the regulations and conditions published in the Official Harbour Tariff Book and Official Railway Tariff Book or any amendments thereof or supplements thereto, and finally,

☐   To organise comparable activities within sovereign territories beyond the borders of South Africa in terms of the regulations and conditions of any other railway administration over whose lines the container may have to be conveyed.

The CTO provides for a precise definition of the container(s) to be used for the transaction and advises from which container yard the required empty container must be uplifted.

It provides for the location of the exporter of the goods where the container will be packed, it provides for the name of the international container operator (shipping company) upon whose vessel the container is intended to be shipped, it provides a mechanism in terms of which Spoornet may be satisfied that the customs controls over the goods in the container in question have been satisfied, that the wharfage due in respect of the export of the goods has been brought to account, and finally, that the charges which will be due to Spoornet in the context of the achievement of the entire contract are enumerated so that they too can be brought to account.

The CTO is produced in a whole set of copies, each of which has its own particular function.

Amongst those copies are documents intended to provide evidence concerning the time span during which the container was held at the premises of the exporter prior to its onward movement towards the exporting vessel. This is important since Spoornet regulations stipulate defined time period within which it is the responsibility of the organisation loading the goods to the container to achieve that function. If those time spans are exceeded, that organisation becomes subject to a demurrage charge upon the Spoornet haulage equipment on which the container was delivered for loading.

Provided that the organisation loading the container undertakes to have the loaded container available for collection within the stipulated time span he is exonerated from all demurrage charges. It, however, he exceeds the allotted time then demurrage automatically becomes due.

A specimen of the top copy only of the export CTO is reproduced at the end of this Chapter. Other forms of CTO are in use in respect of imported goods. Although these are Portnet forms they fulfill much the same functions as export CTO's, that is:-

☐   They act as handling Orders for Portnet to discharge imported
     containers from vessels.

☐   They act as Transport Orders for Spoornet (or Autonet, as the case may be) to
     deliver import containers from coastal or inland ports to   importers' premises.

☐   Again as Transport Orders, they request Spoornet of Autonet to   remove empty
     containers, once unpacked, from importers' premises to "Turn In" depots
     (Container Yards).

☐   They act as Combined Orders to fulfill all of these functions.

Liability of NRZ

NRZ regulations make provision limiting strictly the maximum liability which they are prepared to accept in respect of loss of, or damage to, goods which they are conveying. This maximum liability varies according to the nature of the goods concerned - e.g. general packaged cargo, livestock, perishable cargo, etc. If the consignor (or consignee) requires NRZ to accept a higher maximum liability then the onus rests upon that party to declare the value of the goods for the purpose of NRZ liability. If no such value for this purpose is declared then the limitations of the NRZ regulations apply.

If a higher value is declared then NRZ will raise a higher charge which is analogous to an insurance premium.

Since the NRZ maximum liability is based on the kilogramme gross weight it is required of the sender who wishes to increase their liability that he makes his declaration of value "per kilogramme gross weight". This condition is included in Section 40 (b) (i) of the General Regulations that appear in the Tariff Book.

The decision whether to require NRZ to increase their liability or, as the alternative, to take out normal transit or marine insurance for the goods with a commercial insurance underwriting organisation is a commercial one which the consignor must take.

It must, however, be clearly understood that the liability in respect of loss of, or damage to, goods accepted by NRZ (irrespective of the quantum of maximum liability involved) commences when NRZ take charge of the goods and ceases when they hand the goods over to any other party. By contrast, a transit insurance taken out through a commercial underwriting organisation will commence at the point agreed between the underwriter and the insured and will terminate equally, at an agreed point.

Broadly speaking, it is true to say that the commercial insurance option is usually the better of the two since it may possibly be cheaper and also will without question eliminate the risk of dispute concerning where a loss of, or damage to, the goods occurred - whether while they were in charge of NRZ or not.

Company's Risk/Owner's Risk
As mentioned at the commencement of this Chapter, NRZ regulations stipulate when NRZ will accept goods for transportation at their own risk (company's risk) and also the circumstances under which they will decline to accept company's risk, leaving the goods to move at the risk of the sender / consignee (owner's risk).

Company's Risk
Put in broad terms, NRZ are content to transport goods at company's risk when NRZ itself represented by its own supervisory and labour force, receives the goods (whether packaged or not) at one of their receiving depots and therefore has the opportunity to examine those goods to determine whether they are in apparent external good condition, and then undertakes the loading of the goods into the conveyance to be utilised for the transportation.

It follows automatically that their company's risk will persist at the destination until such time as the goods move out of the custody of their own personnel either at the consignee's premises or into the care of different cartage organisation employed by the consignee to perform the final delivery of the goods.

There are, however, a number of products and commodities which NRZ will never transport at company's risk. These are clearly indicated in the NRZ Official Railway Tariff Book which the student should obtain and study for himself.

Owner's Risk
In addition to the products and commodities to which reference has been made in the last sentence of the previous paragraph, there are also circumstances where NRZ will disclaim company's risk.

Broadly speaking, the majority circumstance is where goods are consigned from a private siding or consigned to a private siding.

Private sidings are the property of the company or organisation which has, with NRZ's agreement, constructed them. Those companies/organisations are responsible for the upkeep of the private sidings, and are responsible for the loading of wagons made

147

available to them by NRZ in such sidings. In a similar fashion the owner of a private siding at the destination point is entirely responsible for discharging goods arriving on wagons at that siding.

Thus, it is self-evident that NRZ can have no direct knowledge of the state of the goods at the time of loading, nor whether damage might have occurred during the operation of loading, nor whether damage might have occurred during the operation of off-loading at destination. These are the reasons why NRZ will only accept private siding traffic at owner's risk.

However, while it is stated in the NRZ Official Railway Tariff Book that NRZ are not responsible for any loss of damage to goods which are conveyed under owner's risk terms, there are, in fact, certain exceptions to this general statement.

Despite owner's risk conditions, NRZ still must accept responsibility for what may be called "catastrophe losses". For instance, the derailment of a train or a truck, a fire, a collision between trains, or with road traffic at a level crossing, etc. Where the loss or damage arises as a result of these types of incident NRZ are still under obligation to accept claims but the onus of proof that the cause of loss was the catastrophe in question rests with the claimant.

Because of these exceptions to the general principles in terms of which owner's risk traffic is transported, it is good practice for a forwarder always to claim on NRZ even in the instances where the traffic was moving under owner's risks conditions. At worst, the claim can but be rejected! The mere fact that a claim has been lodged clears away the limitations imposed by NRZ's prescription periods and therefore safeguards any subsequent right which the insurance company covering the risk in the goods in question may wish to pursue under a letter of subrogation against NRZ.

The regulations, furthermore, lay upon the master, owner or agent of any ship on which it is intended to load any dangerous goods the responsibility to advise the port representative of the Department of Transport's (SA) Directorate. Shipping or the appropriate Mozambican authority timeously by means of a Dangerous Goods Declaration and Stowage Plan providing all details of the cargo and the location into which it will be loaded in the ship. Even if all packing declarations are in order the ship will not be permitted to load the goods without that official's permission.

It will be obvious, therefore, that where dangerous or hazardous cargo is involved, the booking of the space together with the supply of precise details of the cargo nature must be made in sufficient time to enable that permission to be obtained. Forwarders must ensure that all clients involved are made fully aware of these requirements.

Hazardous Substances - Road and Rail Freight
The carriage of goods by road is very far from being the core business of a forwarder. It is the province of highly specialised road haulage organisations, many of whom operate

throughout length and breadth of Zimbabwe and certain of whom also operate across the borders of the country.

Nevertheless, it is important that the forwarder has a basic comprehension of the legislation and regulations made there under in terms of which road haulers may convey hazardous substances.

It is recommended very seriously that - even if a forwarder has an operating transport fleet - he never under any circumstances willingly uses any vehicle in his fleet for the conveyance of hazardous substances. The reasons are obvious. The controlling legislation and regulations are stringent and the stringencies are becoming more severe year by year as more sophisticated but increasingly hazardous substances are developed within the chemical and allied industries requiring particular care when they are transported on public roads.

A responsible forwarder will always sub-contract the road haulage of hazardous substances to a qualified and efficient sub-contractor to undertake the transportation on the forwarder's behalf.

1. The Code of Practice for Packing of Dangerous Goods for Road and Rail Transportation in Zimbabwe is contained in a Zimbabwe Bureau of Standards publication.

    This publication goes into full details which must be complied with in connection with all forms of domestic transportation of hazardous/ dangerous goods.

    It is available on application to the Zimbabwe Bureau of Standards in Harare.

Transportation of Hazardous/Dangerous Substances within Zimbabwe
Regulations to control the transportation of hazardous/dangerous goods within Zimbabwe are contained in a variety of Government Gazettes which it is not immediately necessary for the forwarder to study in detail. However, there are aspects of transportation which come through loud and clear in all these regulations.

Duration of Transport
The transportation regulations apply for the whole period of transportation of the goods. By definition, this begins at the start of the loading process and terminates only after the cleaning and purging of the vehicle or tank in question so that the transport equipment is completely free of the hazardous substance and of its vapour.

Specific Requirements
Any road vehicle affected by the regulations is prohibited from the use of public roads unless it is labeled as prescribed in the regulations. Those regulations require the road

vehicle to have upon it a display upon which the most important information is as follows:-

☐   The substance identification number
☐   The appropriate hazard warning label
☐   The emergency action code
☐   The telephone number where specialist advice can be obtained at all hours

The regulations prescribe the duties of the vehicle operator - i.e. the person responsible for the loading, driving and unloading of the vehicle - so as to ensure:-

☐   That the substance which is loaded or unloaded corresponds to the particulars displayed on the vehicle, and
☐   That safe procedures are used, and that if spillage or sifting or other scattering of the substance occurs, appropriate emergency action is   taken to deal with the situation and to clean up the contamination.
☐   That they are in possession of trem cards.

Any contravention of the regulations is a punishable offence.

Transportation of Hazardous/Dangerous Goods by Rail
The only operator of rail services within Zimbabwe is the National Railways of Zimbabwe (NRZ).

Over many decades NRZ has had detailed controlling regulations in respect of the conveyance by rail of hazardous substances.

As stated above, the Code of Practice issued by the Zimbabwe Bureau of Standards includes the packing requirements for such goods for both road and rail. The transportation requirements are entirely controlled by NRZ and their regulations in this respect can be obtained upon application to any main railway station. These regulations incorporate the necessary stipulations and declarations which the consignor of hazardous/dangerous goods must make when handing such goods into the custody of NRZ.

REFERENCES
Bailey C. A. (2007) **"A Guide to Qualitative Field Research."** Pine Forge Press. California.

Bedi K. (2004) **"Production and Operations Management"**. Oxford University Press. New Delhi.

Bhattacharyya D. K. (2003) **"Research Methodology."** Excel Books. New Delhi.

Cook T. A. (2001) **"The Ultimate Guide to Export Management."** AMACOM. New York.

Daniels, Raudebaugh, Sullivan (2004) **"Globalisation and Business."** Prentice Hall International. New Delhi

Frazelle E.H. (2004) **"Supply Chain Strategy."** Tata McGraw-Hill Publishing Co. Ltd. New Delhi.

Gubbins E. J. (2003) **"Managing Transport Operations."** Kogan Page. London.

House D. J. (2005) **"Cargo Work"** Elsevier. Amsterdam

Kapoor S. K. and Kansal P. (2003) **"Marketing Logistics: A Supply Chain Approach."** Pearson Education. New Delhi.

Kirby M., Kidd W et al (1997) **"Sociology in Perspective"** Heinnemann Educational Publishers. Oxford.

Raina H. K. (1990) **"Guide to Import Management".** PRODEC. Helsinki

Rowland O.P. (1986) **"Imports and Exports: An Introductory Handbook."** Evans Brothers. Ltd. Nairobi

Silverman D. (2006) **"Interpreting Qualitative Data."** Sage Publications. London.

Sople V. V. (2004) **"Logistics Management: The Supply Chain Imperative."** Pearson Education. Singapore.

Thomas A. B. (2004**) "Research Skills for Management Studies."** Routledge, London

CHAPTER 4

SEA FREIGHT AND MULTIMODAL OPERATIONS

4.1 SHIPPING OPERATIONS

A ship essentially consists of little more than a watertight container designed for the carriage of goods over water by the assistance of either natural (wind) or mechanical (engine) propulsion.

The hull, or outer shell of the ship, must displace sufficient water so that the vessel remains afloat when it is fully laden with cargo. Furthermore, it must remain afloat with safety at all conditions of weather, of tide, and of season of the year.

Every ship is therefore marked with "load lines" which indicate the maximum water displacement safely allowed. These load lines will differ according to the season of the year, the part of the world within which the ship operates, and may, for instance, also vary if the ship operates only within a broadly enclosed area of water such as the Mediterranean, the South China Sea, etc.

The hull is roofed over by a deck which encloses the entire cargo carrying space. The deck will have one or several more openings called hatches which, under sailing conditions, are securely closed by watertight batch covers. The hatches allow access to the cargo. The cargo carrying space in the vessel is divided vertically by bulkheads into separate hold which may be further subdivided horizontally into tween decks.

In the days of wooden ships when a ship had discharged her cargo and was compelled to sail onward or return home without cargo she would have to load some dense and cheap material into the lowest parts of her holds in order to keep her properly trimmed and sufficiently low in the water to avoid the appreciable risk of "turning turtle". The material thus loaded was usually called ballast - washed gravel taken from river beds was frequently used - hence the expression "sailing in ballast", meaning "sailing without paying cargo on board".

Although the expression still persists, modern vessels do not have to load any material when they are sailing either with, or without sufficient, paying cargo. They are equipped with special ballast tanks which can be filled with sea water via the ship's pumping gear and emptied as required by the same means.

Certain vessels, in addition to their ballast tanks, are fitted with deep tanks. Vessels equipped with deep tanks are the exceptions to the general rule that liquid cargoes are not carried on dry cargo vessels. The deep tanks are used to carry liquid cargoes and in some instances are fitted with steam heating equipment so as to enable the vessel to carry cargoes in their deep tanks which solidify at normal temperatures. Such cargoes may be exemplified by lard, vegetable oils, petroleum greases, etc.

Almost all vessels are, in addition, fitted with fore and aft peak tanks which can be filled with water ballast. The purpose of this is to ensure that under all conditions the ship's propeller mechanism (commonly called the screw) and rudder are sufficient submerged at all times to enable the ship to be steered and to prevent the engines from racing.

Hatches
In the design of ocean going vessels there is always a conflict between the need to provide as large an opening as possible in the ship's deck to facilitate the loading and discharging of cargo, and the need to restrict the size of these openings in the interests of the strength of the ship and its safety from the risk of flooding in heavy weather when seas frequently break right over the ship's surface.

Modern technology has, however, developed new forms of steel hatch covers of substantial strength operated by electrical machinery or by means of cables linked to the ship's derricks so that a hatch cover can be opened or, if necessary, closed, with great speed. Perhaps the best known type of hatch cover is the Mac Gregor hatch cover.

Cargo Handling Gear
There are a number of specialised vessels operating throughout the world in whose design heavy lifting derricks are incorporated capable of handling 250 ton lifts or more. Vessels so equipped are essential because the average port authority does not receive sufficient heavy lift cargo to keep heavy lift floating cranes of this type of capacity in sufficient constant use.

In less developed countries the port facilities and equipment are frequently inadequate to cope with cargoes which arrive. In some of the ports concerned the water depth at the quaysides may be inadequate to maintain a modern ship constantly afloat at all states of the tide.

In the first instance it may be essential for the ship to be able to handle its own cargo without further assistance while, if the water depth is inadequate, the ship may have to use its own equipment to discharge its cargo into lighters in the open water away from the quays so that the cargo can be transferred to land via those lighters.

The overriding consideration with regard to cargo handling equipment is invariably speed of operation. Ocean going vessels earn their revenues from the carriage of cargoes from the port of loading to the port of discharge. They earn no revenue while they are tied alongside a quay or are kept waiting outside any port. In fact, not only do they earn no revenue, but any such avoidable delay constitutes a complete financial loss to the ship owner.

The major motivation for the development of containerisation was the ability by means of appropriate equipment for the handling of containers in ports, to reduce idle time for vessels in all major trades. In times past a vessel carrying 15 000 tons of mixed dry cargo could take 7 or more days to discharge, while the loading of the same vessel with return cargo might take another 2 to 3 days. A container ship with twice the cargo on board can be handled in Durban in 36 hours and fully loaded in another 18 hours. The economy of operation thus achieved has resulted in an incredible stabilisation in freight rates and numerous other benefits to international traders.

4.1.1 Major Ship Classifications
Disregarding for the moment certain highly specialised types of vessel such as liquid gas carriers, cargo carrying ships (freighters) fall into two major classifications - dry cargo vessels, and tankers.

As the name implies, dry cargo vessels - which include container ships and ships built for the carriage of roll-on roll-off cargo, convey all types of non-liquid cargoes. Such vessels do not lend themselves easily to adaptation for carrying bulk liquids.

Tankers, on the other hand, are built specifically for the purpose of the carriage of liquid cargoes and are therefore constructed as regards general shape and design all in a broadly similar pattern. There are, however, very wide variations in size from small tankers having a capacity of little more than 5 000 tons - which are largely engaged in the coastal distribution of liquid cargoes - to ultra-large crude carriers (ULCCS) which have capacities of over 250 000 tons and which, from the time they are launched from their ship building yard until the time when they have to be scrapped, never call within the confines of any port. Such ULCCs load and discharge their cargoes at pipeline terminals which are normally located many nautical miles out to sea.

Dry cargo vessels are, by contrast, designed and equipped taking into account, inter alia, factors such as:-
□   type/types of cargo to be carried
□   trades and routes for which the vessel is intended
□   equipment on the vessel necessary to enable it to load and   discharge its cargo without the assistance of shore side cranes
□   the berthing facilities and the depth of water available at the ports   where such vessels are intended to call.

4.1.2 Specialised Vessels
While the general dry cargo vessel is the workhorse for world trade in the vast range of manufactured and semi-manufactured products, there is an increasing trend towards designing and building certain ships for specialised trades. Such ships are, by their nature, "captive" to a particular cargo commodity and/or trade. They may, in fact. Be owned - or at least operated - by the owners or shippers of the cargo in question. Other specialised ships such as ore carriers may be employed in the tramping trades.

4.1.3 Refrigerated and Power Ventilated Ships
The ocean transportation of perishable cargo is a highly specialised field. Ships designed for these operations have specifically insulated holds in which appropriate temperatures can be maintained by means of refrigeration equipment which may either circulate cooled liquid through pipes and heat exchanges or pump cold air through vents surrounding the cargo.

155

The construction of such specialised vessels, the provision of the refrigeration plant, and the fact that in order to reduce voyage times they must be provided with powerful propulsion units, all mean that they are very expensive to build and maintain.

4.1.4 Ore Carriers

The period since the end of World War 2 has seen a phenomenal growth in the demand by the developed countries for raw materials - particularly iron ore, chrome ore, manganese ore and coal. These commodities have certain characteristics in common:-

☐ they all have a relatively high specific gravity which means that they occupy relatively little space compared with their weight.

They are all capable of being loaded from shore to ship via massive conveyor belts mounted into travelling gantries which can move on rail slowly from one end of a ship's hatch to another. These characteristics have substantially influenced the design of the carriers which convey them about the world.

Ore carriers must have hatches as large as possible: they must have clear holds with self-trimming characteristics - self trimming is achieved by constructing the holds with sloping sides so that if its cargo is loaded approximately on the centre line of each hatch it will flow so as to settle evenly as low as possible in the ship. The same design assists discharge since the cargo will progressively flow down towards the centre line of the hold as the upper layers of cargo are removed.

Because of the high density of these cargoes an ore carrier must be provided with substantial reserves of buoyancy which is achieved by the provision of double bottom spaces beneath the floors of the cargo holds. The existence of these spaces into which cargo cannot flow lifts the centre of gravity of the carrier and makes it more manoeuvrable and obedient to rudder movements and changes in engine speed - all of which are extremely important in rough weather and also when navigating in comparatively confined seaways.

Few ore carriers are equipped with their own cargo handling gear so that their activities are confined to the movement of cargo between ports which have the appropriate cargo handling gear on shore.

4.1.5 Universal Bulk Carriers

The specialised construction characteristics of ore carriers render them subject to one major disadvantage: they can only carry heavy cargo, and if such cargo is not available on a two way basis then for some of their lifetime they will have to sail in ballast. The very high cost of fuel relative to the total running cost of these vessels renders this highly undesirable.

A compromise design had to be created in which the cubic carrying capacity of the holds could be increased as required without compromising the structural strength of the vessel and without resorting to tweendecks.

The design most commonly utilised to achieve these objectives is the provision of upper holds which can either carry some heavy cargo or alternatively can be flooded with water ballast when lighter cargoes such as cereal grains are being carried in the main (lower) holds.

4.1.6 Oil Tankers

The dominant traffic for which oil tankers are created is, of course, mineral oils - much in an unrefined state but sometimes also refined to an appreciable volatility and flammability.

Such unrefined oils have a high viscosity but it is common to all that when carried in very large volumes relative to depth they will be subject to continual movement - rhythmic surging initiated by the rolling or pitching of the vessel in the seaways.

Even a slight movement by the vessel recurring in a rhythmic sequence can set up massive surges in the cargo which are capable of causing a ship to turn turtle or otherwise to destroy itself.

Accordingly, tanker design is of paramount importance and the most usual design results in tankers which are large single-deck vessels with their engines and machinery spaces aft. The cargo is carried in a range of tanks extending forward from the machinery spaces. These tanks are arranged in sets of three across the breadth of the vessel and are numbered in the same way as holds in a conventional vessel - from the bows back to the stem so that the front set of tanks will be referred to as No. 1 - Port, No. 1 - centre, No. 1 - starboard, and so on.

The bulkheads separating the tank spaces throughout the ship are all oil tight and extend from deck level right down to the shell plating. As a rule, tankers do not have double bottoms and neither do they have ballast tanks. It is necessary for such a vessel to sail either wholly or in part in ballast then its tanks are as appropriate filled with sea water.

Apart from the ever present threat of pollution resulting from leakage, the danger of fire and explosion is the tankerman's constant flammable gasses given off by the oil tend to accumulate. In order to neutralise the hazard thus created these flammable gasses must be vented into the atmosphere outside the vessel and replaced with an inert substitute. This venting and replacing operation must continue without interruption throughout the life of an oil tanker. Even when a particular tank within a tanker is empty it will still carry highly flammable gasses which must be vented and replaced. Alternatively inert gasses such as nitrogen or, more commonly, exhaust fumes from the vessel's engines are pumped into these spaces to replace the flammable gasses.

Modern tankers normally carry in excess of 100 000 tons of crude oil and their size precludes them from calling into their respective ports of loading and discharge. The loading and discharging operations are therefore accomplished at pipeline terminals situated far out to sea and accordingly every such tanker must be equipped with its own loading and discharge pumping machinery.

4.1.7 Cellular Vessels

These are the ships built solely to carry cargo in containers. Their entire cargo spaces are divided into "cells" rather than holds. These cells rise vertically from the bottom plates up to the level of the deck.

Each such cell will hold a stack of containers 7 high, all of which will be secure from movement since the cells are built so as to be strictly compatible with containers of sizes approved by the International Standards Organisation (ISO).

At weather-deck height cellular ships are rendered completely watertight by massive steel plates constructed to cover the entire cellular space throughout its entire length. It is normal practice then to stack 4 - and possibly 5 - further levels of container above these plates which are secured not only to the vessel's deck but also to one another by specially designed connectors and bottle screws.

The loading and discharge operations for such vessels require the provision on the quayside of their ports of call of gantry cranes capable of reaching safely right across the beam of a vessel so as to place containers within the slots in the vessel's seaward side.

Depending upon the trade for which they have been designed, cellular vessels may be equipped with refrigerated cargo carrying capacity of one of the following types:-

☐ Electricity supply points within the container cells to supply power to those containers which are fitted with their own individual cooling plants (so called integral units).

☐ Other ships have a main refrigeration generating plant built into their structure capable of supplying temperature controlled air through ducts to those insulated containers which are constructed with "portholes" in their "back" walls (i.e. opposite to the doors) through which the temperature controlled air can be circulated under pressure throughout the containers in question.

Whatever the precise method of refrigeration employed, constant monitoring of the effective temperature of cargo is vital and this is achieved by sensors which are linked to computer systems which automatically adjust the mechanisms so as to maintain the temperature required. It is possible by these means to maintain different temperatures in different containers in different parts of the ship, each such temperature being appropriate to the cargo in each container in question.

4.1.8 Roll-On/Roll Off Vessels (Ro-Ro)

The concept of the ro-ro vessel was originally to serve the movement of motor vehicles on very short sea voyages within and around the continent of Europe. But from being specialised in this fashion and of a comparatively small size they have developed in both capacity and size so as to service all manner of cargo including cargoes of heavy weight, which either have their own wheels or can be provided with wheels systems so that they can be towed aboard the vessel by a mechanical horse and similarly can be discharged therefrom.

The mechanism utilised for this purpose is built into the ro-ro vessel and consists of a massive steel ramp at the stem which is capable of being lowered so as to rest comfortably on the quayside. The ramp serves as the link between the quayside and the tween-deck of the vessel over which the cargo provided with wheels can be transported.

Within the confines of the ro-ro vessel further ramps are provided so that cargo on wheels can be moved from the tweendeck into a lower hold for stowage purposes.

Most ro-ro vessels also carry containerised cargo secured upon their weather decks and such containers will be loaded and discharged by means of shore side equipment as previously described.

4.2 SHIPPING SERVICES

4.2.1 Tramp Services

Tramp services are provided by ship operators who "hire" out their ships to other organisations either for a single voyage - such hiring being termed "voyage charters" - or over a period of time during which the organisation hiring the ship may utilise it for a series of voyages - called a "time charter".

These contracts of hire of a ship can be quite complex and there are three main types of contracts namely:-

(a)   demise charter party - hire of entire ship from owner for a long period excluding the crew. Charterer takes possession and control taking good care of vessel.

(b)   time charter party - charterer enjoys exclusive use of cargo carrying space for a fixed period. Charterer certain aspects of loading and stowage.

(c)   voyage charter party - charterer contracts for carriage of goods, that is, space in the vessel to carry own goods. Charterer must utilise booked space and pay demurrage if loading and discharge exceeds agreed time periods.

As a matter of interest, the name "Charter Party" originated from the French phrase "Carte Parties" which literally meant a divided card or document.

In the early days of mercantile shipping many centuries ago the hiring agreement, once completed and signed, was torn in half, one half being given to the master of the ship and

159

the other being retained by the cargo owner. It was clearly understood that the master of the ship would not release the cargo at the final discharge port except to the person presenting to him the other half of the document as evidence that he was correctly entitled to the cargo.

Charter Parties are usually arranged between brokers, one broker representing the interests of the cargo owner and another representing the interests of the ship owner. The arranging of such charters is a highly specialised business requiring great expertise, which is why such brokers are employed. The world's major market for the arranging of Charter Parties is the Baltic Exchange situated in St Mary Axe, London.

Ships operating tramping services do not maintain any fixed sailing schedules between any specific ranges of ports. Tramping ships are to be found throughout the world with the result that it is normally possible within a few days to arrange a charter of a vessel to carry cargo from almost any world port to almost any other.

A further interesting feature is that shipping companies who operate the alternative form of service which we shall discuss in the next paragraph - the liner service - frequently find, as a result of an upturn in the volumes of cargo offering in the trades served, that they need additional shipping capacity. When this occurs the liner operator will go to the charter market and hire a suitable ship on a time charter basis to provide that additional capacity until the situation has ceased. Alternatively, if cargo volumes in the trade in question fall away with the result that there are for the time being too many ships on the particular trade route, then they will hire out the surplus ships under Charter Parties to others who need them.

In the normal course of a forwarder's business tramping services are rarely used although it is important that the forwarder is aware of the nature of tramping operations.

4.2.2 Liner Services
Liner services are normally provided by a fleet of vessels dedicated to a particular shipping trade - as, for instance, the trade between Europe and Southern Africa. The vessels involved in the service are normally built so that they can accommodate the special requirements of that trade and they will normally call at specific ports at each end of the trade and will sail from those ports at advertised sailing dates to which they attempt to adhere as closely as possible.

The cargo carried by line vessels is normally "general cargo" - that is to say, packed goods - usually the end products of manufacturing processes or products traded in a commercial sense. Such general cargo may be shipped in break-bulk form or may be unitized. Over the last two decades most cargo of this nature has been containerised, and in terms of the numbers of individual shipments involved, containerisation now accounts for upwards of 90% of the trade between Zimbabwe and its overseas trading partners.

160

The terms and conditions of contracts of carriage for goods moving on liner services are to be found upon the bills of lading issued by the shipping lines, supplemented by rules which may be found within those shipping lines' tariffs.

4.2.3 Simple Conferences
In its simplest form, a Conference is an agreement between shipping lines serving the same shipping trade to charge the same tariff rates for the same commodities. In other words, the conference member lines share a common tariff from which they agree not to depart without mutual agreement.

Conferences as simple as this are virtually non-existent in the Southern African trades.

4.2.4 Rationalised Conferences
In this type of Conference the member lines agree not only to a common tariff but they also agree to a common sailing schedule. That is to say, Line A may agree that its ships shall sail from a particular port on the first day of every month while Line B will arrange for its ships to sail on the 10th, and Line C will agree that its ships shall sail on the 20th. This arrangement avoids the "bunching" of two or more ships in the same port at approximately the same time.

It obviously has advantages not only for the Lines in question but also for intended shippers of cargo since it improves the consistency and reliability of the service provided.

A Conference can also, where necessary develop a modification which can prove equally important to both participating Lines and to cargo owners. This involves some measure of alternating the ports of call. By way of illustration:-

Shipping Line No. 1 will call at ports A, B, D, F and G
Shipping Line No. 2 will call as ports A, C, E, F, and G

Obviously, in this simplified illustration there is constant cargo for the ports at which both lines always call, but there may be insufficient cargo to induce both Lines to call at other ports. So those other ports are serviced in an alternate fashion.

4.2.5 Consortium (or pooled) Conferences
With the advent of containerisation in the major shipping trades serving Zimbabwe, the shipping lines recognised that it would be necessary to rebuild the entire shipping fleets in order to accommodate the very large volumes of containers necessary to those trades.

Not only would the financial burden of providing such new equipment be excessive upon each separate member line, but, furthermore, because the modern container ship can carry vastly more cargo than the older conventional ships, the number of ships needed to service the trade could be substantially reduced.

Accordingly, by agreement the participating member lines, each line provided capital for the building of the new ships in proportion to its traditional cargo carryings, and after the new service commenced, each such line would be allocated container slots in each ship in the same proportion.

The major examples of Pooled Conferences with which forwarders in Zimbabwe have contact are SAECS (Southern African Europe Container Service) and SAFARI (South Africa Far East Conference). Needless to say, a Consortium Conference will operate in accordance with common tariffs because the ships are all "common user". There can be no variation in the port rotation unless all participating lines first agree.

4.2.6 The UNCTAD 40:40:20 Rule

Shipping Conferences have over a century or more played a very major part in the development of world trade for the benefit of many emerging nation states. Their beneficial influence over these many years has been almost incalculable. More recently, however, emerging nation states began to realise that although the shipping lines carried their international trade, their profits from such carriage did not itself accrue to them. Instead it accrued to the major maritime nations who were already well developed and comparatively rich.

In an endeavour to assist those emerging nations, the United Nations Trade and Development (UNCTAD) formulated recommendation to control the level of participation of national carriers in the trades they served. These recommendations require:-

☐ The national carrier of the exporting country to provide 40% capacity.
☐ The national carrier of the importing country to provide 40% capacity.
☐ The balance 20% capacity to be available to any other shipping line willing to participate in the trade - that is to say, by "cross-traders"

A cross-trader is a shipping line prepared to carry cargo between countries, neither of which is the country in which they are based.

4.3 NON-CONFERENCE SERVICES

The existence of an established Conference service in any shipping trade does not inhibit any other independent shipping line from intruding into that shipping trade and competing in all respects with the participants within the Conference. Any shipping line doing so is normally referred to as an Independent.

In a general sense, Independents offer a somewhat lower tariff rate and they may also call at ports at which Conference services do not call. On the other hand, Conference lines generally maintain their shipping schedules with great consistency, and are open to negotiate to an appreciable degree with regards to the rates they charge provided that annual shipping volumes are sufficient to justify reductions in the normal tariffs rates.

The decision whether to "ship Conference" or to "ship Non-Conference" should for preference be made by the importer or exporter after consideration of all the factors involved. Suffice it to say that international traders in South or Southern Africa have a very competitive freight market at their disposal which is well placed to cater for their needs. The Zimbabwean government has never placed any restraints upon the shipping services which serve the country, we may well see shipping lines from Eastern European countries increasingly participating in the Zimbabwean shipping trades and introducing even greater competition than is the case at present.

4.3.1 Overview of South African Liner Services
The Southern Africa Europe Container Service (SAECS) - is a consortium (or pooled) Conference. It is tightly controlled with the result that it is rare for an individual member line to act independently of the others in any matter.

Participating lines share in the container slot allocation within the ships which ply in the shipping trades between South Africa and both the northwest continent and the Mediterranean.

The ports directly served within South Africa are Durban, Port Elizabeth and Cape Town. Feeder services operate by means of coastwise vessels to and from East London, Walvis Bay, Maputo and Beira.

Those vessels which service the UK and northwest continent ports regularly call at Southampton, Zeebrugge, Hamburg, Bremerhaven, Rotterdam and Le Havre.

Those vessels which service the Mediterranean also call regularly in Maputo in addition to the ports in South Africa mentioned above. Within the Mediterranean the regular ports of call are Lisbon, Barcelona, Trieste, La Spezia and Fos. On a less frequent basis the Greek port of Piraeus is also serviced.

The SAECS also provides a multi-purpose service utilising vessels not only providing facilities within their holds for containers but also providing space for break-bulk cargo and roll-on roll-off facilities. This multi-purpose service provides shipping facilities to and from Beira, Maputo, Durban, East London, (direct call), Cape Town and Walvis Bay (direct call) together with Canary Islands, Southampton, Antwerp, Rotterdam, Hamburg, Bremerhaven, Le Havre and Helsingborg.

The SAECS Conference also provides facilities in respect of containerised cargo not only to and from the Southern African ports mentioned above but in addition the inland cities of Bulawayo, Harare, Limbe and Blantyre. The latter two are both in Malawi. Similar facilities from the European ports mentioned above are available to many inland cities of Europe and UK in respect of containerised cargo.

4.3.2 Other Shipping Services
Most of the lines servicing South Africa make use of a feeder service known as "Unifeeder" that has regular sailings between Durban and Maputo and Beira. The lines incorporate this service into their regular European and other world services.

163

There are a multitude of other shipping services specialising in other geographical areas of the world. These include services to Canadian eastern ports such as Montreal and Toronto, to the Sri Lankan port of Colombo, to the Indian Ocean Islands, to Australia and New Zealand, to both East and West African ports and other destinations in the Red Sea and the Persian Gulf.

4.4 ROLE OF PORTS IN ECONOMIC DEVELOPMENT

All cargo transport systems consist of flow of goods moving via an identifiable transport mode (e.g. sea freight, airfreight, etc) all of which normally interchange at certain transport nodes. A sea port is thus an extremely important node at which goods are transferred from the sea freight transport mode to one or other of the land transport modes, or vice versa.

As such it will readily be understood that the sea port is a crucial and vital component in any international transport system.

The overriding objective of a cargo transport system is to minimise total costs both in terms of total financial burden of the cargo owner and also to economise in the time cost of the funds locked up in the cargo moving through the system. This implies the elimination of all possible causes of delay and other inefficiencies.

It must be recognised that if any element in the total transport system from origin to destination is working inefficiently this can have an effect upon the efficiency of the other elements in that system - forcing them perhaps to operate more slowly than they could. A port operating at less than maximum efficiency may result in ships due to load/discharge at that port having to slow their voyage speeds or wait outside the port before they can berth. In a similar fashion a port with an inadequate or inefficient dredging system will necessarily imply that larger vessels with propulsion systems powered by modern technology will be unable to berth or alternatively may only be able to berth at certain quays with the result that the efficiency of such vessels is under-utilised.

On the other hand, if port facilities are constructed so as to be able to handle effectively the largest possible vessels which may only call two or three times a year, this in turn will necessarily mean that the port facilities are to that extent under-utilised and needless port costs commence accruing to the detriment of port users and ultimately the cargo owners.

These considerations must also be taken further inland from the port. If the shipping system is efficient and the port operation is similarly efficient, any deficiencies in the landward transportation of the goods whether to or from that port will have a deleterious effect upon the working of both the shipping companies in question and the port.

For a port to be efficient it must be so designed, constructed and equipped as to maintain the closest co-ordination between the transport systems operating on its landward and also on its seaward sides. Put in another fashion, any intermodal system must be considered as a single whole - never as a series of discrete and unrelated components.

The development of a new port requires the identification of:-

☐   The hinterland of the proposed port
☐   The commodities which may be shipped to and from it, and
☐   The quantities of each such commodity which will move through it at different times of the year.

Over the last 45 years the port of Durban has developed to an appreciable degree and much capital has been spent therein. If the port of Maputo can in due course be brought up to a state of efficiency, and the transport system servicing Maputo to and from its natural hinterland in Northern Natal and Mpumalanga can be secured and upgraded, this will have a substantial effect upon the well-being of both Durban and Richards Bay.

There is another important aspect of a port's nodal function. It is normally at or within a port that goods may be subject to economic and commercial changes. Customs clearance usually takes place here, as does changes of ownership. There may also be quality control inspections.

4.4.1 Influence of Ports on the Socio-Economic Structure of the Hinterland

The development of a port may not only be vital in terms of the transport system which it serves but it normally has substantial beneficial influences upon its surrounding area which normally will be a town or a city from which it draws its personnel. In order to examine in a measure of detail the influences which a port extends far beyond its own immediate jurisdictional border, there are many matters which must be further considered.

4.4.2 Direct Port Economic Activities

The most obvious of these is cargo handling. This can be broken down to take account of the different types of capital investment and labour skills which it requires:-

The handling of containers and of unitised cargoes. This will involve the provision of quayside gantry cranes, forklift trucks, straddle carriers, and the like - all of which require heavy capital investment and highly skilled operatives.

Breakbulk. This type of cargo will require quayside cranes, mobile cranes, floating cranes, together with other equipment necessary for the transfer of cargo across quays into and out of transit sheds or open storage areas.

Dry bulk. This type of cargo may be handled either by suction, by grabs, by buckets, by conveyor belting, or other similar method. Dry bulk exports may be handled by wagon tippers coupled with chutes for directing the commodity into the appropriate holds of the ship.

Liquid bulk. This involves the provision of pumping equipment and pipelines together with shore side tank farms.

Transportation is a further essential activity within any port. It may involve the movement of goods within the port perimeter but also, and more importantly, involves the movement of goods to and from the hinterland of the port. Transportation may be performed by road, by rail, by coastal feeder services or - in the case of liquids - by pipeline.

Warehousing is another activity which is essential within the confines of a port. It may be classified as follows:-

☐ Transit sheds
☐ Storage warehouses
☐ Open storage areas

Container depot facilities may also be within the confines of the port although this is not necessarily essential. Similarly, empty container storage facilities may be created either within the port perimeter or in a separate area outside.

'Ship building and ship repair' also normally take place within the perimeter of a port. In South Africa, the ship building industry is steadily enlarging although it is very far from any comparison with the vast ship building industries in the fully industralised nations. Nevertheless, small ships, auxiliary vessels, tugs, etc. are built within South Africa and repairs to major ships may be undertaken in certain South African ports.

Within this general classification also falls the repair and maintenance of the port's bunkering, watering and chandelling.

Finally, there are multifarious group of operations which support and complement the operation of ships calling at the port.

These activities encompass some or all of the following:-
☐ Pilotage
☐ Dredging
☐ Provision and maintenance of navigational aids
☐ Fire fighting
☐ Towage and salvage
☐ Quay maintenance and repair

Financial activities - for instance banking - is an essential service. In this context foreign exchange operations play an important part

Marine insurance of both cargo and ships also finds an important niche in the economic activities surrounding a port.

Without the numerous responsibilities undertaken by the **Forwarding & Clearing** community, port operations could simply not take place.

4.4.3 A Port as a Provider of Employment

A competently operated port is clearly a major provider of employment in a great many fields of activity. The socio-economic well-being of those who service the needs of a port by performing any of the functions described above depends upon two vital factors:-

☐ the volumes and the types of cargo handled by the port

☐ the numbers, the types, the registered tonnages, of the ships which call at the port in order to service cargoes whether inward or outward, for maintenance and repair, for ship supplies, etc.

Volumes and types of cargo are determined by the following:-

☐ Imports intended for internal consumption. These are normally "ready for sale" without any further processing.

☐ imports requiring processing, part or all of which are destined for internal consumption but part of which may also be destined for re-exportation.

☐ Goods requiring to be repacked into smaller quantities, decanted into smaller containers, regrouping and reassembly prior to disposal.

☐ Goods intended for direct transshipment either coastwise or by inland transportation to neighbouring states.

Numbers, sizes and types of ships will in part be dictated by the type of cargo and its volume, but further important considerations are:-

☐ Patterns of trade - that is to say, the origins and destinations of goods
☐ Structure of the trade routes within which the port lies
☐ The efficiency and modernity of the cargo handling equipment available in the port

4.4.4 Factors which influence cargo volumes and types

There are two broad categories of influences. There are those which are fixed which cannot be altered, and there are others which are variable and are therefore subject to a lesser or greater degree to manipulation.

Fixed factors include:-

☐ The geographical location of the port relative to the major world shipping routes

☐ Topographical features of the port such as depth of water, sheltered anchorages, distance from an industrial hinterland, etc.

☐ The natural resources of the hinterland, e.g. availability of raw materials, of water, and the suitability of its climate.

☐ Finally, there are the attributes and characteristics of the population within the port's hinterland. A highly sophisticated population will call for very different imported goods compared with the demands likely to be created by a simple agrarian hinterland.

167

Variable factors which normally change over long periods of time.
☐   Overall trends in world trade, in world commodity prices, etc.
☐   Political and economic policies of the countries at the two ends of a particular shipping trade, such as restrictive trade practices, the imposition of import quotas, the creation of new processing, manufacturing or industrial activities, cargo reservation laws and flag discrimination, port pricing policies, customs regulations, and the establishment of export processing zones (EPZs).

These, in fact, are variable factors which are usually beyond the control of the shipping line or the trader and they are under the influence of governments.

Variable factors which are more immediate. These include:-
☐   industrial policies with regard to development, banking, finance, investment, etc.
☐   Governmental policies which can be subject to more immediate   control will include taxation, tariff protection, export incentives.

4.5   PORTS OF SOUTHERN AFRICA

4.5.1 Richards Bay
Richards Bay plays a major role in the enhancement of South Africa's export effort. The statistics indicate its value as the port of dispatch of a variety of bulk cargoes, and in addition, certain break-bulk cargoes, including in particular semi-products of aluminium from ALUSAF, the South African aluminium smelting company.

The location of the ALUSAF plant and the development of Richards Bay proceeded from its inception as an integrated plan jointly conceived, and working so satisfactorily that the ALUSAF management decided towards the end of 1992 to double the production capacity of the plant with the full knowledge that its entire export production could be moved out into world trade through the same port.

4.5.2   Durban
Durban is South Africa's (and Zimbabwe's) most important port which handles the largest volume of containers. Its hinterland embraces the whole of Natal, Gauteng, Mpumalanga, North West Province and substantial portions of the Northern Free State. It is a port of transit for containerised traffic into Swaziland, Lesotho and Botswana, while it also serves the international traffic of Zimbabwe and to some extent of Zambia, and the Democratic Republic of Congo. Apart entirely from the container flows which move through Durban, the port also handles coal, chrome ores, soda ash, and other mineral products, forestry products, wheat, maize and other cereal products, a variety of agricultural produce, sugar, molasses, vegetable oils, animal feed stock, together with a wide variety of general cargo outside normal container dimensions.

4.5.3 East London

The   port of East London is the only river port in South Africa, and although in terms of volumes handled it is smaller than either Durban or Cape Town, it has a special strategic value because of its location at the end of the corridor between the former Tanskei and Ciskei. Both these areas have their own industrial bases and East London serves them ideally. Moreover, it is well placed to service a broader hinterland in the Orange Free State, and has important rail connections not only with Gauteng but also to countries to the north of the Republic of South Africa.

4.5.4 Port Elizabeth
Port Elizabeth has a very broad and deep natural hinterland which is substantially industrialised. The agricultural activities within its hinterland are intense. Because South Africa has a very efficient and modern rail and road network Port Elizabeth regards its hinterland as stretching right up to the Gauteng area. Unlike the port of East London - which is served, so far as concerns containerised traffic, by feeder services from Cape Town and Durban - Port Elizabeth is a major port of call for the Conference Lines' ships trading to and from North-West Continent, Mediterranean, United States East Coast, and the many industrialised nations in the Far East.

4.5.5   CAPE TOWN
The city of Cape Town is unique in many respects. Within a circle drawn on a radius of 300km from the city centre are to be found a surprising range of climatic conditions from the very dry areas of the Southern Karoo to the temperate climates of the Garden Route, the warm currents of the Indian Ocean and the cold currents of the Atlantic. For this reason, coupled with the scenic beauty of the entire area, it is a famous tourist attraction drawing its visitors not only from Southern African but also from the world at large via airlines and cruise ships. Within that same hinterland are both heavy and light industries, fertile valleys and wide expanses suitable for cattle and sheep farming. It is perhaps most famous for its vineyards and apple orchards, from which come grapes fit for the tables of kings, fruit juices for the teetotalers, wines and brandy for those who prefer a stronger tipple. The port of Cape Town therefore handles a wide variety of traffic and provides special facilities not found in other ports which are essential for exportation of its high quality agricultural produce. For commercial purposes the port of Cape Town consists of two docks, the older of which is Duncan Dock with a water area of 110 ha, and the more recent of which is the Ben Schoeman Dock with a water area of 113ha. The smaller dock areas - the Victoria Basin and the Alfred Basin - are no longer used for commercial purposes. They have been given over to major tourist attractions, the VSA Waterfront.

4.5.6   Saldanha Bay
The port of Saldanha Bay was created within a natural geographical inlet in the west coast of Cape Province for the specific purpose of handling mineral ores (mainly iron ore) from the deposits at Sishen in Northern Cape. The very substantial nature of the deposits in the Sishen area justified the creation of a specific rail link from the mining area to Saldanha Bay of powered and long length trains to bring the ores to the ship's side. While the facilities at Saldanha Bay can cope with general traffic - and on occasion containerised traffic - very little other than the bulk minerals is handled through the port.

4.5.7 Walvis Bay

Walvis Bay port is no longer a part of South African ports although much of South Africa's fishing industry is reliant upon it.

The main industry of Walvis Bay is fishing, and this forms the backbone of the activities within the port. However, as the only port on the Namibian coastline which is readily accessible from the Atlantic Ocean it has strategic importance because of its feeder links through the services of Unicorn Line with other ports in South Africa. Moreover, the port is well situated to act as a transit point for cargoes which are destined to Southern Angola.

NB: **For all the ports mentioned, forwarders must familiarise themselves with the following characteristics:-**

☐ Port structure and statistics
☐ Port facilities both public and privately owned.
☐ Shed and storage accommodation
☐ Roll on Roll off cargo
☐ Containerised cargo
☐ Mechanical Equipment
☐ Ship handling facilities

4.6 THE MARINE (OCEAN) BILL OF LADING

The term "marine bill of lading" means the traditional port-to-port bill of lading which was for countless years the only shipping company bill of lading in common use. While more sophisticated forms of bill of lading are now in regular use in respect of containerised cargo, the marine bill of lading remains the normal transport document issued in respect of breakbulk cargo. The shipping company which issues the bill of lading accepts responsibilities to perform a contract of carriage from the named port of loading to port of discharge.

4.6.1 Marine Bill of Lading as a Receipt for Goods

Within the terms and conditions of carriage stipulated on the reverse of the bill of lading will be a clause stating that the shipping company has no knowledge of:-
the nature, ☐the quantity, the quality and the value
of the goods loaded, but that all particulars shown are as stated by the shipper. This stipulation may be reinforced by insisting that the description of the goods is worded "said to contain ... and/or the block on the bill of lading provided for the description of the goods may have printed within it a phrase such as:-
"Description as declared by shipper"
Even where cargo is shipped without protection of packing cases or other coverings, and it may therefore be fairly obvious what the goods are, the shipping companies still profess only to ship goods "as described by shipper."

4.6.2 Marine Bill of Lading as evidence of the contract of carriage

The bill of lading submitted in a prepared form to the shipping company and then signed by that company and returned to the shipper, provides evidence of the common law contract which was previously created and, furthermore, contains within itself the terms and conditions under which the shipping company is content to fulfill that contract, including warranties, undertakings, limitations of liability, liberties allowed to the shipping company under stated eventualities, etc.

The shipping company will only be obliged to approach the port of discharge subject always and at all states of the tide to be afloat.

It will only release the goods at the port of discharge upon presentation to it of an original bill of lading duly endorsed so as to indicate of itself that the presenter of it is entitled to the cargo.

The shipping company has the right to impose penalties if it discovers that the goods have been misdescribed either in respect of their nature, their quantity, their weight, their volume, or their value.

The shipping company has a right, having due regard to the safety of the ship and its contents, to deviate if necessary from the normal route for the voyage or to render succour or assistance to other vessels in distress or for the saving of life at sea.

The shipping company is not responsible for delays in voyage times, however they may be caused, nor from any detrimental consequences which may arise therefrom.

The shipper warrants the truth and accuracy of the description in all respects of the goods offered for shipment.

There are, of course, many others but these will give any indication of the broad nature of a marine bill of lading.

4.6.3 Marine Bill of Lading as a Document of Title
The concept that a bill of lading is a document of title to the goods it covers is of supreme importance in international trade. Without an original bill of lading in his possession the consignee cannot (save in exceptional circumstances which wil be discussed later) obtain the release of his goods.

4.6.4 The Marine Bill of Lading - Negotiability
Because the marine bill of lading is a document of title it is possible for it to be drawn and issued in a form of wording which makes it "negotiable".

Negotiability is a concept in terms of which a document of title to anything may, by means of a writing placed upon it, be transferred for a consideration - e.g. for the payment of a sum of money - to another party with the intention that title to the underlying goods is thereby transferred to that other party.

The marine bill of lading drawn showing the name of the shipper/exporter as consignor and the name of the overseas importer as the consignee. It is available only to the named consignee.

Negotiability Desired by the Exporter/Shipper
If the exporter desires to obtain a negotiable bill at the time when it is issued at the port of loading then no name should be inserted for consignee: instead, the word "order" is inserted.

The exporter/shipper is then free to endorse the bill on the reverse thereof with his name and signature. The bill is then "open endorsed" and any party into whose hands that bill comes will be entitled to the delivery of the goods at the port of destination.

Alternatively, if the exporter/shipper so desires, he can place a limited endorsement on the reverse of the document which may read:-
- Release to ..... (named party)....
- Release to order of ..... (named party)....
- Release to ..... (named party).... or order
Exporter/shipper rubber stamp and signature.

In the first instance the release by the shipping company is limited to the named party. In the second and third instances the named party can himself further endorse the bill and therefore is in a position to further negotiate it to another party.

Negotiability Desired by the Named Consignee
In this instance the exporter/shipper must insert in the space provided for consignee either of two alternative forms of wording as follows:-
- ... or order
- order of ...

Both forms of wording permit the party named further to endorse the bill and therefore to negotiate it onward.

General Comments on Negotiability
Any bill of lading which is "open endorsed" becomes a document of which great care must be taken since if such a document is allowed to fall into the wrong hands it could be presented to the shipping line at the port of discharge and release would immediately be given despite the fact that such release would be fraudulent and equivalent to theft. Furthermore, it must be pointed out that it is not the responsibility of the shipping line granting the release to attempt to investigate whether the party presenting the document of title has obtained that document honestly.

4.6.5 The Issue of Original Bills of Lading in Sets
Because it is essential that the original bills of lading issued by a shipping company in one port somewhere in the world must be transmitted physically to the consignee in the port of discharge which may be many thousands of kilometres distant, there is always the

possibility that there may be loss of the documents in transit. For this reason original bills of lading are normally drawn in sets of three, all of which are signed and any one of which may be utilised for obtaining the release of the goods at the port of discharge. Once any one has been so utilised the other originals become of no further validity.

The wording above the signature of the shipping company issuing a set of bills of lading is usually the following:-

"In witness whereof we have issued three bills of lading each of the same tenor and date, one of which being accomplished, the others stand void."

4.6.6 Signature on Bills of Lading
The signing of bills of lading is a function which is strictly controlled by every shipping company since the issue of a signed set of bills has important implications for the shipping company concerned.

The bill of lading is a receipt for the cargo involved even if that receipt only acknowledges receipt of packages. The company issuing such a receipt is acknowledging that, unless it can later prove to the contrary, it has, in fact, received the packages on board and has accepted responsibility - within the terms and conditions of the bill - to carry them to the port of discharge and there to deliver them to the party presenting one of the original bills of lading to their representative at that port.

4.6.7 Payment of Freight
The freight due for the carriage of cargo may be paid either at the port of loading or at the port of discharge. In the former instance the bill of lading will be stamped to indicate clearly that the freight has been paid at the port of loading, and normally such a bill of lading will not bear any indication of the amount of freight so paid.

In the second instance the bill of lading will be stamped to indicate clearly that the amount of freight due is to be collected at the port of discharge and it will bear a complete notation of the amount due - normally calculated in the "tariff currency" of the company in question - which is usually US dollars, although not necessarily so. A shipping company is entitled to demand that freight due be paid in tariff currency.

4.6.8 Cargo Release by Shipping Companies
It has been emphasised that a bill of lading is a document of title and that an original bill of lading must be surrendered in exchange for the release of goods.

Ocassions arise when, despite every care, the original bills of lading are not received at the port of discharge with the result that the shipping company in question refuses to allow delivery out of their custody.

This can have very unfortunate consequences for the importer and it must be stated at once that no shipping line will under any circumstances agree to issue a duplicate set of original bills of lading.

To overcome this major problem a practice has arisen in terms of which shipping lines may agree to accept from an importer a letter of indemnity signed both by the importer and by a recognised financial institution in terms of which both those parties indemnify the shipping company from all consequences of whatever nature which may arise if they decide to release the cargo without the production of the document of title. The shipping company will insist that the indemnity shall subsist for an indefinite period or until the appropriate original bill of lading is discovered and surrendered. They will also demand that the indemnity is without any financial limit stated in it.

While the acceptance of such indemnities is a practice which occurs almost all over the world, a question hangs over the procedure as to whether it is acceptable legally.

Every forwarder should be aware of this mechanism by means of which goods which are likely to be subject to delay through a failure to transmit documents can be quickly released.

Ad Valorem Wharfage
Wharfage is a charge raised by Portnet in respect of the use of the infrastructure of the ports and harbours of South Africa and Mozambique.

Portnet and CFM demand of shipping companies who come alongside the quays within their harbours that they do not release imported cargo to any party until they have evidence that the ad valorem wharfage due upon the goods has been brought to account. If no other party accepts responsibility for the ad valorem wharfage on cargo either by the submission of a landing delivery and forwarding order, or alternatively, by a wharfage clearance order then Portnet retain a lien on the goods until the wharfage due is paid.

For this reason every shipping company trading into Zimbabwe's ports requires that before they will release cargo the party requesting that release provides them with evidence that the wharfage has been brought to account.

Effective Release of Cargo
To achieve release of cargo in Zimbabwe therefore requires the following:-
☐ The surrender of an original bill of lading
☐ Payment of any freight due to be collected at the discharge port or by the shipping line
☐ The release copy of the bill of entry: import
☐ Evidence of the bringing of ad valorem wharfage to account, usually in the account of the port agent.

Only when all these four elements have been satisfied will release be given by the shipping company.

4.7 THE TRANSSHIPMENT OR THROUGH BILL OF LADING

Transshipment means the transfer of cargo from one vessel to another at a port intermediate between the port of first loading and the port of final discharge.

Transshipment has important implications with regard to the nature of the contract of carriage, the amount of freight to be charged and also the level of premium which marine underwriters will decide to charge to carry the risk of the cargo.

Where FCL cargo is involved the transshipment bill of lading is sometimes called a "through transport document". The through transport document must not be confused with a combined transport document. The latter is, in fact, the multimodal transport document.

4.7.1 Issue of Transshipment Bill of Lading

This form of bill of lading is always issued by the first carrier uplifting the goods at the first port of loading. In terms of the bill, the first carrier accepts all the responsibilities, and claims all the limitations, stipulated in his terms and conditions of carriage as set out on the back of the bill, - which will be found normally to be identical to those which appear on the ocean bill of lading (port-to-port). The carrier issuing the bill does so as a carrier in direct contractual relationship with the consignor named in that bill.

However, when the goods in question are discharged from the first carrier at the intermediate (transshipment) port, the contractual relationship changes with the following effect:-

The first carrier ceases at that moment to be a contractor to the consignor. He becomes, instead, an agent for the consignor. All further contracts which may be necessary for the storage, movement, or other manipulation of the goods while they are in the intermediate port are organised by the first carrier solely as an agent for the consignor which means that the consignor becomes the principal in all such contracts with whatever parties may be involved. Thus, if things go wrong, the consignor can no longer look to the first carrier for compensation or liability but must look to those other parties with whom the first carrier, as the consignor's agent, has concluded contracts. Almost certainly, the consignor is not aware who those parties are, nor what are their terms and conditions of trade are.

From the moment when the goods are uplifted for loading on the vessel undertaking the on-carriage it is again normal practice that the first carrier arranges the on-carriage as agent and not as principal so that in relation to the second leg of sea voyage the consignor must also look to the second carrier for compensation or liability if things go wrong even though both legs of the total voyage are covered by a single transshipment bill of lading.

4.7.2 Delays Occurring at the Transshipment Port

The first carrier issuing the transshipment bill of lading will specifically exclude from his liabilities any risk of delay or of consequential damages. Delay can be due to first carrier's vessel arriving late to link with connecting vessel, connecting vessel being fully booked or cases of irregular sailings.

4.7.3 Surrender of original bill of lading at final port of discharge

Where a voyage is contemplated which involves transshipment, it is advisable that the forwarder organising the transportation makes advance enquiries with regard to the final releasing organisation at the final port of discharge to which the original bill must be surrendered so that this information can be passed to the consignor for advice to the consignee.

4.7.4 Effect of Transshipment upon Marine Insurance Premium

It is quite obvious that in every instance where goods have to be transshipped a great deal of additional handling of the cargo in question is inevitable. This is even true of FCL's - although the cargo in them is, in a broad sense, much better protected.

Consequent upon these increased risks of loss and damage underwriters will always require to be informed in full, detail of the transshipment, of the port at which the transshipment will take place, and if possible by which second carrier the goods will be on-carried.

In those instances where the transshipment takes place within modern well equipped ports and between reliable carriers whose capabilities are without reproach, the increase in premium is normally 0.125%. However, there are other transshipment locations and other on-carrying shipping lines where the track record is not so good with the result that insurers may impose a higher addition to the premium.

4.7.5 The Freight Charge in Respect of Goods Transshipped

It must be clear that there will be an all inclusive charge for the ocean freight due in respect of both legs of the voyage plus, of course, the charges arising as a result of the transshipment operation at the intermediate port. This total charge will be raised against either the consignor at the first port of loading or, depending on the circumstances, raised against the consignee at the final port of destination.

4.8 THROUGH FREIGHT TRANSPORTATION

It is the direct flow of goods from the exporter to the importer with minimum delay and interruption, Gubbins E. J. (2004).

☐ Transporter is directly responsible for the state of the goods until arrival as well as delivery reliability.

☐ Reduces handling costs by packing goods at exporter's premises and off-loads only at importer's premises and achieves efficiency by using unit loads like pallets, containers, etc

☐ Forwarders and consolidators pool individual cargo units into unit loads for transportation

☐ Shipper is responsible for packing, handling and transportation.

In the event of transshipments each carrier keeps documents covering all aspects of carriage and transfers to protect himself.

The concept eliminates cargo handling costs, storage costs, chance of damage, pilferage and misdirection by placing all intermediate activities on one responsible company.

4.8.1 Advantages of through freight transportation

a.   It achieves speed on goods transfer, handling and vessel movement.

b.   It increases reliability by reducing handling, storage and sorting. Risk of goods being damaged, stolen, misdirected or lost is reduced.

c.   It increases safety by better organisation and planning of handling process which eliminates physical loss or damage.

d.   It simplifies documentation, systems and procedures and also simplifies rates by basing them on units and their weights for handling charges. Forwarders quote delivered price.

e.   It achieves cheaper freight rates

4.8.2 The Multimodal Transport Document

The multimodal transport document is sometimes referred to as the combined transport document or the through transport document.

This document is evidence of a contract of carriage entered into by the transport operator in terms of which he takes responsibility for the movement of goods from a place where they are delivered to him to a place where he delivers them to a consignee irrespective of the different modes of transport which he must employ for the fulfilment of that contract. The transport operator issuing the document is contracting as a principal with the cargo owner to fulfil the combined transport involved and he is liable to the cargo owner under the terms of the document throughout the entire carriage.

The multimodal transport document began to appear in the international transportation scene only with the development of containerisation. It remains a document which is only utilised where goods are containerised. There is no responsible ocean carrier who would be willing to use such a document in respect of the shipment of break-bulk cargo.

The reason for this is fairly simply stated:-

As regards cargo which is containerised the carrier can disclaim all knowledge of the goods within the container and can, to a considerable degree, limit his liabilities in relation to those goods. By contrast, he simply accepts for shipment a "box" of dimensions and characteristics standardised by the International Standards Organisation (ISO) which is therefore compatible with equipment utilised by landside modes of transportation, and he therefore only acknowledges receipt and responsibility for that box which he can very simply reforward by other modes of transport to its intended destination.

Breakbulk cargo, on the other hand, comes in all shapes and sizes with variable masses and with many different characteristics peculiar to the goods involved and is subject to multifarious rules and regulations by landside handlers and transporters of such cargo with the result that there is no way that a responsible shipping company will get itself embroiled in the on-carriage of such goods beyond the hook of the crane which discharges the goods from his vessel.

4.8.3 Comparisons between the Marine (Ocean) Bill of Lading and the Multimodal Transport Document

The traditional bill of lading was normally drafted and printed as a "shipping on board" document for the reason that cargo owners have required evidence that their cargoes have been safely shipped upon the vessel in which they will travel to the overseas destination.

By contrast, when a multimodal transport document is issued the carrier issuing such a document becomes liable in relation to the goods as soon as his sub-contractor at the place of acceptance has signed for the goods from the cargo owner.

The carrier cannot eliminate a number of risks which can occur despite the fact that he has accepted the goods. These risks may include any of the following:-

- ☐ Delay due to weather
- ☐ Delay due to strike, lock out, restraint of labour and similar causes
- ☐ Delay to non-arrival of the intended carrying ship
- ☐ Non-acceptance by a bank under a letter of credit where that credit stipulates that the transport document must evidence shipment on board of a vessel, etc.

In other words, the issue of a multimodal transport document acknowledging receipt of the goods at a place of acceptance inland from the port may still, in many instances, require a subsequent endorsement upon it confirming actual "shipment on board".

4.8.4 Place of Acceptance

Every multimodal transport document has a box which is labelled "place of acceptance". This place of acceptance may be any of the following:-

The consignor's premises - which may be his dispatch bay from which containers loaded and sealed by him depart or alternatively, his private siding from which rail wagons conveying containers loaded and sealed by him are dispatched.

A container depot (overseas such depots are sometimes called container freight stations) at which the cargo was loaded into the container "accepted" by the multimodal container operator.

The premises of a supplier of goods sub-contracted to the consignor in whose name the multimodal transport document will be issued.

4.8.5 Place of Delivery

The place of delivery will vary according to the requirements of the cargo owner and the nature of the contract in question.
If the cargo consists of a single FCL consignment intended for a single consignee then the place of delivery may be:-

The premises of the consignee
The premises of a sub-contractor to the consignee
A container depot where, by agreement with the consignee, the contents of the container will be unloaded and held at the disposal of the consignee.

If the cargo consists of LCL consignments intended for sundry consignees then the place of delivery will always be a licensed container depot.

4.8.6 Release of Goods on a Multimodal Transport Document
Release will be given at the place of delivery by the multimodal transport operator on presentation to him of an original document of title just as in the case of the ordinary marine bill of lading. Obviously, all other requirements such as clearance through customs and payment of wharfage in Zimbabwe must also be supplied.

4.8.7 Marine Insurance Considerations in relation to a Multimodal Transport Contract of Carriage
Where a multimodal transport operator is content to issue a multimodal transport document the circumstances surrounding the landside leg of the journey to the place of delivery will be efficiently handled by the carrier's sub-contractors with the result that normally the marine insurance underwriter does not look for any additional premium in respect of goods carried under such a document.

4.8.8 Freight Payment
As in the case of the normal marine bill of lading freight in respect of a multimodal transport document may normally be paid either at the place of acceptance of the goods or at the place of delivery.

4.9 NON-NEGOTIABLE LINER WAYBILL
A liner waybill is a document issued by a shipping company acknowledging receipt of a consignment of goods from the stated consignor or shipper, for shipment on an "intended vessel", from a stated place of acceptance for delivery to a named consignee at a stated place of delivery, and it contains within it the terms and conditions of the contract of carriage.

It serves as an acknowledgement by the carrier of instructions from the consignor concerning the carriage of the goods and the party to whom the goods are to be released upon arrival at destination.

4.9.1 Liner Waybill as a Receipt for Goods
The nature of the receipt acknowledged by a liner waybill is precisely the same as that which is acknowledged by a marine bill of lading - that is to say, it acknowledges receipt of packages, the contents of which are "as declared by the shipper".

The liner waybill performs two functions only i.e.
☐   it is evidence of the contract of carriage

☐   it is a receipt for goods

The evidence of the contract of carriage appears on as many copies as the consignor desires but it would be folly on the part of the shipping company to issue more than one receipt for the same goods.

4.9.2 Liner Waybill as Evidence of the Contract of Carriage
Those liner waybills which forwarders in Zimbabwe are likely to come into contact with all bear the same terms and conditions of carriage as will be found on the bills of lading for the shipping company concerned.

4.9.3 The Liner Waybill - A Document of Title?
The liner waybill is not a document of title. It is not necessary, therefore, for the consignor to transmit the liner waybill to the consignee overseas.
By issuing a liner waybill the shipping company in question undertakes that, subject to the requirements of the authorities (customs, etc.), and subject also to payment of any freight charges, etc, due, it will hand over the goods to the named consignee (or his agent) upon evidence of identity.

The forwarder will realise that one of the great advantages of shipping goods under a liner waybill is the diminishing of the risk that the goods may be held up as a result of delay in the transmission of the document of title.

4.9.4 The Liner Waybill - Negotiable?
Because the liner waybill is not a document of title it cannot be made negotiable - that is to say, a merchant cannot negotiate or sell the goods represented by a liner waybill by means of the sale of the waybill. This is quite evident since by issuing a waybill the shipping company has undertaken that it will only deliver the goods to the named consignee (or his agent). It is not allowed in fact, it would be defaulting in its responsibilities - if it were to release the goods to any other party.

4.9.5 Freight Prepaid or Freight Collect
The same facility to pay the freight either at the time of shipment in the port of loading or at the port of destination (subject always to the concurrence of the shipping company) applies to the liner waybill as it applies to the bill of lading.

4.9.6 Liner Waybill versus Marine Bill of Lading or Multimodal Transport Document

Advantages of the Liner Waybill
☐   It is not necessary for the liner waybill to be transmitted overseas to the consignee as a document of title.

☐ Claims for loss or damage to cargo can be prosecuted against the shipping company and against the marine insurers as effectively as is the case where the bill of lading or the multimodal transport document is involved

☐ Because it is not a document of title its loss or delay in transmission need not delay the final delivery of the goods.

Disadvantages of the Liner Waybill
☐ It is issued in solo only so that its loss is more serious in the event of claims.
☐ Because it is not a document of title it cannot be made negotiable so the
☐ sale of the goods on the high seas is completely inhibited
☐ If an international contract requires a bill of lading or multimodal transport document as the evidence of dispatch, the liner waybill is no substitute.
☐ If the international contract is financed by means of a letter of credit the liner waybill is no substitute for a bill of lading or multimodal transport document called for therein.

Usage of Liner Waybills in Zimbabwean Trade
The use of the liner waybill has never really caught on to any large extent in the international trade of Zimbabwe. This is probably because international traders feel "comfortable" when a form of document of title is involved - be it a bill of lading or a multimodal transport document. In addition, an appreciable proportion of Zimbabwe's international trade, both import and export, is financed by means of letters of credit.

A substantial proportion of international traders have heard of it but have never taken time to comprehend how it works. Even traffic moving between associated companies within the same group still moves on bills of lading or multimodal transport documents despite the fact that liner waybills could, to advantage, be utilised.

4.10 ARRIVAL NOTIFICATIONS
Because the Zimbabwean customs authorities demand with every bill of entry import (a) evidence of final dispatch to Zimbabwe, and (b) evidence of the date that the goods in question were taken on board the carrying ship (for exchange conversion purposes), those shipping companies that offer the facility of shipment on a liner waybill have been compelled to create a document in a form approved by the customs authorities, which they can issue on their own responsibility, providing the evidence required under (a) and (b) mentioned above.

The document involved is the arrival notification (ANF). This document is issued by the Zimbabwean office or agency of the shipping line in question as a substitute acceptable by customs in lieu of a bill of lading or multimodal transport document. In practice, an ANF is produced in respect of all shipments, irrespective of the type of shipping document involved.

4.11 HAZARDOUS SUBSTANCES - SEAFREIGHT

The transportation of hazardous substances by seafreight is subject to codes of practice drawn up by the International Maritime Organisation. The International Maritime Dangerous Goods (IMDG) Code embraces the United Nations classification and numbering system and specifies in detail the standard of packaging required, labelling requirements, stowage requirements for both passenger and freight vessels, and the methods of separation of hazardous substances from other hazardous cargo and also from harmless cargo.

In the IMDG Code a brief description of every product is given with appropriate instructions concerning emergency actions and first aid requirements.

4.11.1 Responsibility for Compliance with the IMDG Code
This responsibility rests upon the shipper whose name appears in this box on the bill of lading or other transport document. There is a number of parties whose name may appear in the "shipper" box:-

- The actual manufacturer of the goods where that manufacturer is also the shipper.
- The exporter of the goods where the exporter is a trader dealing internationally in the goods but is not the actual manufacturer
- The forwarder as agent for either of the above
- The forwarder where he is acting as the contractual carrier as would be the case of the groupage operator or NVOCC.

Actual Manufacturer
Where the actual manufacturer is shown as the "shipper" on the bill of lading or transport document he is responsible for the appropriate packing of the goods in the appropriate quantities per pack, the labelling of each pack, the obtaining of the specific written consent of the forwarder to deliver the goods into the forwarder's possession or control, and for advising the forwarder in complete detail the nature of the goods, the nature of the hazard which the goods create and the classification number of the goods in terms of the IMDG Code and the United Nations Classification.

However, from that moment a responsibility commences to rest upon the forwarder to ensure that all the documentation which he becomes responsible to complete is in accordance with the IMDG Code and the rules of the carrier in question. He should, be required to produce hazardous documents and tremcards for classes 2, 3 and 4.

It obvious that the forwarder has to depend upon the accuracy of the declarations made to him by the manufacturer and this emphasises the importance that the forwarder's position is carefully protected by his trading conditions.

Exporter's Responsibility when not the manufacturer
In this instance the responsibility upon the exporter whose name appears in the "shipper" box on the transport document is precisely the same as if he were the actual manufacturer.

The exporter may not be as aware of the hazards which the goods present as he should be, with the result that the forwarder must redouble his caution to ensure that the information supplied to him is both accurate and complete so that the documentation prepared by the forwarder is correct.

Forwarder shown as shipper but acting as agent for un-named principal
In this instance the carrier will hold the forwarder responsible for the full compliance with all the requirements of the IMDG Code even though he may have had nothing to do with the packing, labelling, etc of the goods.

Accordingly, it will be important that the forwarder has on his file for production as evidence if required, the full name and details of the principal for whom he is acting so that he can show that prior to granting his specific written consent to receiving the goods into his possession or under control he verified explicitly with his principal that the goods were in all respects correctly prepared for shipment and that the information upon which he, the forwarder, issued the documentation was accurate and complete.

It goes without saying that in such an instance the efficiency of the forwarder's trading conditions becomes crucial.

Forwarder acting as Groupage Operator / NVOCC
In these instances the forwarder inevitably has to act as a contractual carrier and must therefore submit to the physical carrier a bill of lading or transport document in his own name.

The forwarder becomes totally responsible for the accuracy of his documentation but in this instance also to ensure that the hazard and other labels are correctly applied to all packages and also to the exterior of the container.

There are strict rules with regard to the method of stowing hazardous substances in containers.

4.11.2 Hazardous Substances - Containerised Seafreight
An ISO freight container for use in maritime trades is a piece of transport equipment of a permanent character capable of repeated reuse in any transport mode. Freight containers must:-

☐　　Be strong, in good order and well maintained. It is the responsibility of the shipper of the goods (or the container depot or operator loading the goods into the container) to satisfy himself concerning　　these requirements.

☐　　Be tested and approved in terms of the Convention for Safe Containers 1972 within the immediately preceding three years.

If any container does not fall within these parameters then it must not be used for the carriage of any hazardous substance, however small the quantity of that substance may be.

4.11.3 Container Examination

Before any hazardous substances are loaded into a container it is the responsibility of the party undertaking the loading to ensure that the container shows no sign whatsoever of:-

☐   Damage, distortion of hinges, buckling of doors, etc
☐   Deterioration of rubber door seals
☐   Evidence of the ingress of water, however slight
☐   Roof deterioration (the roof should be examined from the interior of the container with the door completely shut so as to detect any sign of the ingress of light)
☐   Floor, sides or ceiling contamination
☐   Defectiveness in the bolts to the doors

If the container is suitable in all these respects then consideration may be given whether the hazardous substances in question may be loaded therein.

Prohibitions Concerning the Loading into a Container of Hazardous Substances

There are certain substances which must at all costs be kept completely segregated from other substances. They are substances which become "dangerous when mixed with ....." These classes of goods may not be loaded in the same container which will contain the contaminant which renders them dangerous.

Hazardous/dangerous liquids in bulk may only be loaded in tank containes set in standard ISO frames.

Organic peroxides and certain flammable solids may only be shipped in containers if they are handled, packed and stowed under the conditions stipulated for such goods in the IMDG Code, and in additin, with due regard to the circumstances of the intended voyage.

Corrosives, oxidising agents, organic peroxides and poisons may under no circumstances be loaded into containers with wooden floors.

No container carrying hazardous substances/dangerous goods may be padlocked. The use of the normal container seal is acceptable. This tends to prevent the loading of high value goods with hazardous cargo.

4.11.4 Packing of the Hazardous Substance

Packages containing hazardous substances must be:-
☐   tightly packed so that there can be no internal movement of the
substance, although not so tightly packed as to create a risk that   the packaging may burst. Allowance must be given to cover   expansion, etc.

☐   securely braced when placed in the container so that the package or
        packages themselves cannot move

☐   Any projections on any of the packages must be carefully proteced

☐   packages containing hazardous substances must: be entirely
        separated by adequate and appropriate dunnage from any other   goods
of a harmless character which may also be loaded in the   container.

      ☐   be accessible from the container door
      ♦   be secured from any risk that they may fall from the container when the
          door is opened
      ☐   be clean, dry, intact at the time of loading to the container
      ☐   have no moisture, snow, ice, or any other foreign matter
adhering to them.
      ☐   loaded with no greater quantity than is permitted in terms of the IMDG
          Code.
      ☐   appropriately labeled with the approved and relevant labels or irrelevant
          markings must be removed/obliterated.

4.11.5 Labeling of Containers
Every container carrying hazardous substances must bear the appropriate label relevant to
the substance in question on each leaf of its doors (minimum label size 250 x 250mm).
This is mandatory even if only one small package of the hazardous substance is included.

All odd/irrelevant labels must be removed from the container

If containers are shipped with the contents under fumigation - in other words, it is the
fumigant which is hazardous rather than the goods - then the recommendations on the
safe use of pesticides in ships as stipulated by the International Maritime Organisation
must be complied with and the container appropriately labeled.

4.11.6 Documentation for Hazardous Substances
For every container shipped anywhere in the world a packing declaration is required by
the container operator/shipping company. Declaration is made by person/organisation
responsible for loading the container.

Packing Declaration for the goods
"*I hereby declare that the contents of this consignment are fully and accurately described
by the correct technical name(s) (proper shipping name(s)), that the consignment is
packed in such a manner as to withstand the ordinary risks of handling and transport by
sea having regard to the properties of the goods and that the goods are classified,
packaged, marked and labeled in accordance with the International Maritime Dangerous
Goods Code and Merchant Shipping (Dangerous Goods and Marine Pollutants)
Regulations (RSA).*

I further declare that, if appropriate, the goods are classified, packed, marked and labeled to comply with the regulations of the European Agreement concerning the International Carriage of Dangerous Goods by Road (ADR) and of the Uniform Rules concerning the Contracts for International Carriage of Goods by Rail (CIM).

> *Name and telephone number of shipper ....*
> *Name/status of declarant ...*
> *Place and date...*
> *Signature of declarant...*

Packing declaration for the container

> *I declare that:-*

1.   *The container was clean, dry and apparently fit to receive the goods.*

2.   *No incompatible goods have been packed into the container unless specifically authorised by (competent authority).*

3.   *All packages have been externally inspected for damage and only sound packages packed.*

4.   *All packages have been properly packed and secured in the container.*

5.   *All packages have been properly packed and secured in the container*

6.   *When materials are transported in bulk packaging the load has been evenly distributed in the container.*

> *Name and telephone number of shipper ....*
> *Name/status of declarant ...*
> *Place and date...*
> *Signature of declarant...*

4.12   CONTAINERISATION TECHNOLOGY AND PRACTICE

The "Father of Containerisation" was a gentleman named Malcolm McDonald who started the first multimodal system of shipping between the United States and Venezuela. He introduced closed truck trailers which could be hauled to the loading ports in question, loaded at those ports onto converted oil tankers, and on arrival at destination, discharged and hauled inland to their final destinations. This system was, of course, very far from the system in use at the present time but it contained the seeds of modern containerisation. The Vietnam and Korean Wars in which the United States were heavily involved added a great deal of additional impetus to the containerisation concept.

4.12.1 Reasons for the success of the container revolution

Advantages to the Ship Operator

☐ a substantial improvement in ship turn-around at every port of   call.

☐ A reduction in the number of ports at which ships must call during each voyage.

☐ A reduction in the incidence of claims on ship operators for loss of, or damage to, cargo.

☐ A reduction in the number of ships required to service a particular shipping trade due to stowage efficiency of containers.

☐ Containerisation has led to a standardisation of ship design which makes ships better capable of being switched from one shipping trade to another at the discretion of the ship owner. In addition, because of the standardisation of the sizes of containers themselves, the equipment required on a ship for the handling of its cargo in the event that shoreside facilities are inadequate, is also standardised.

Advantages to the Port Authorities and Railway Systems

Although the initial costs of port equipment and railway rolling stock is heavy, port design and the provision of cargo handling areas within ports have all changed drastically, leading to far more efficiency in land use in the ports and far more effective transportation of containers from port to inland destinations.

Advantages to Cargo Owners

☐ Containers themselves provide greatly improved cargo protection for so long as cargo remains in the containers

☐ Cargo within containers is not identifiable by external inspection by thieves, pilferers, and other criminal elements.

While the advantages to all parties involved are substantial, it remains true that there are also disadvantages which must be considered.

As regards ship operators, it must be pointed out that containers are themselves the units of cargo for which they are responsible. If a container has to be jettisoned or is washed overboard then the claim arising is likely to run to something in the region of USD200 000 or possibly more.

If a ship is lost at sea then the total finance involved in that loss will be catastrophic. In this respect, marine insurers are also at risk.

As regards international traders, if containers loaded with cargo are delayed to any degree in their smooth movement from origin to destination - and such smooth movement is one of the advantages of containerisation - then the capital value tied up in containers which are delayed can cause serious problems for the importer's cash flow. Delays which have these effects could be the result of labour disturbances or strikes, or may occur as a result of the Customs authorities requiring examining the container contents.

4.13 CONTAINER CLASSIFICATION

Containers manufactured for use in the international shipping trades must be built to comply strictly with the requirements of the international Standards Organisation (ISO).

The external size, the shape, and the inherent strength of each component making up the container are the subjects of ISO specifications. This includes their floors, their sides, their roofing, their corner posts, their provisions for waterproof sealing, their closing and securing devices, their door hinges, their twist-lock entry ports, etc.

Every container must be provided with a "plate" on the right hand leaf of its doors upon which its unique container number must be displayed together with its tare weight and its safe laden weight.

Moreover, in terms of the International Convention for Safe Containers, every container in international use must be subjected to a complete inspection at intervals not greater than two years to ensure that it is still suitable for use. Each inspection may involve a reduction in safe laden weight which the container may carry and it is a serious matter if any container is loaded beyond the stipulations quoted in its "plate rating".

4.13.1 Open Containers

Open containers are of two types - the "flat rack" and the "bolster". The latter may sometimes be called "platforms".

Flat racks are found in both the standard lengths - 6m and 12m. They consist of a specially reinforced floor with upright ends. They are used to carry heavy pieces of equipment which may be over-height, over-width, or both. Because they have end sections they cannot carry cargo of greater length than can be placed between the two ends.

Usually, the upright ends are constructed so that they can be dismantled from the base and laid flat. The purpose of this is fairly obvious - cargo which requires the use of a flat rack normally originates in Europe or USA while there is comparatively little use for this type of equipment for exports from Zimbabwe.

Flat racks usually therefore have to be returned to their places of origin empty and by dismantling the ends, five flat racks win occupy the space of one single general purpose container thus saving space on an otherwise empty movement.

Bolsters (or platforms) are, for practical purposes, the same as flat racks but are not provided with the end sections. Bolsters therefore can, where necessary, accommodate cargo which is over-length as well as over-height and over-width.

Bolsters are occasionally used as a means of creating a major platform at the top of container columns midships on cellular vessels so that cargo of exceptional size can be secured thereon for carriage on a ship whose normal function is the carriage of normal containerised traffic.

4.13.2 Semi-Open Containers
This classification includes full height and half height open top containers and bulk containers.

Open top containers are equipped with a tarpaulin provided with eyelets around its border which correspond to staples welded around the edges of the side wall of the container. Each staple is provided with a hole through which a suitable wire rope is threaded extending right around the container. The two ends of the wire rope are provided with a means by which a container seal can be secured to ensure the integrity of the container cargo.

Open top containers are particular suitable for large items of cargo which are within the dimensions of the container but on account of size or weight can only be loaded vertically with the use of cranes.

The half height open top container is utilised for dense cargo such as steel sheets, copper billets, and the like.

Bulk containers are provided for the carriage of coarse powders, grits or grains. For loading purposes they are fitted with three loading hatches in the roof. Although bulk containers have end doors, it is obviously very foolish to allow those doors to be opened while the container is under load. At the foot of the doors special hatches are provided with fittings which permit the discharge of the container contents by the titling of the container under controlled conditions. The doors are only provided as means by which personnel can enter the containers after the discharge operation has been completed so that residues of the cargo in question can be swept out and the container cleaned.

4.13.3 Closed Containers
Closed containers are the following:-
- General purpose containers (GP)
- Tank containers (tanktainers)
- Fruit containers
- Refrigerated containers (reefer containers)

Certain of those containers are clearly designed for specific cargoes - tanktainers and reefer containers.

These containers designed for specific cargoes obviously are utilised on a "one way" basis without the likelihood that an immediate opportunity can occur for their use on a return voyage. For this reason these containers incur freight charges appreciably higher than the freight charges applicable to general purpose containers.

The following considerations must be taken into account when determining the suitability of a container type for the carriage of a particular cargo:-

Cargo mass/cargo dimensions. All containers have restrictions on the gross mass of the container plus the contents. This gross mass is the "Plate rating" - to be found on the specification plate on the right hand door of the container. Where the question of the mass of the cargo to be loaded is likely to be critical then the specifications of the particular container in question is not exceeded.

This, however, is not the end of the investigation. It is also very important to every user of a container to establish the container mass limitations for the transport of the container by road or rail within the country to which the container is destined and also the countries through which the container must travel while in transit to its destination. The overseas country limitations may in many instances be lower than the plate rating of the container. Examples of this are Switzerland and Austria, and there a number of other countries where this can occur. Where the road/rail mass limitations in overseas countries are less than the plate rating then the mass of the cargo to be loaded in the container must be reduced or the consignee must be contacted to ascertain whether such over-mass containers will be permitted to move on the rail/road systems of the country/countries concerned as abnormal loads at a higher cost.

As regards dimensions, it must be emphasised strongly that the ISO only lays down the external dimensions of each container type which it recognises. Internal dimensions can vary.

The forwarder must remember that every container under all circumstances is placed over a weighbridge on arrival at the container terminal from whence it will proceed for export and that if any container is discovered to be over mass the railway or port authority (as the case may be) will refuse to accept it and will remove it at the exporter's cost to the nearest container depot where it will remain until such time as the mass is adjusted. This will involve the exporter in substantial additional costs which in the first instance will be debited to the shipping agent or forwarder involved. Accordingly, it is important for the forwarder to emphasise to all his clients the importance of avoiding overloading.

Specialised cargo such as fruit or fresh meat requires the specialised containers which are designed specifically for the carriage of such cargo.

There are a number of other specialised containers which are generally not used in the Zimbabwean trade. They can be made available upon special request by most container operators/shipping companies engaged in Zimbabwe's trade at additional freight charge which is referred to as "special equipment" surcharge.

4.14   CONTAINER NUMBERING AND LABELLING

The container numbering system was defined in ISO 2716 - 1972, first published in 1972.

The entire marking code system is based, by absolute necessity, upon the requirements of automatic data processing and it consists of the following three groupings.

1.	Owner Code	-	4 letters
	Serial number	-	6 numerals
	Check digit	-	1 numeral
2.	Country code	-	3 letters
3.	Size and type code	-	4 numerals

4.14.1 Owner Code

The owner code consists of 4 capital letters and the ISO standard recommends that the final letter should always be "U". The preceding three letters must be unique to a specific container owner so that although the owner may suggest whose he would prefer to use, prior approval must be obtained from the International Container Bureau, Paris.

4.14.2 Serial Number

Since the serial number is a sequence of numerals occurring after the alpha prefix, these numerals do not need to be universally unique. However, within the container fleet owned by a particular container operator the numbers must be unique.

4.14.3 Check Digit

The check digit is the seventh numeral and is normally separated from the container number by an open space. Upon certain containers the check digit is itself enclosed within a box so as to make it more distinguishable from the other digits.

4.14.4 Container Country Code

It is essential to understand that the subject in this paragraph is country code as applied to containers (country codes for many other purposes consist of 2-alpha characters but in relation to containers all country codes must consist of 3-alpha characters).

This normally involves the addition of the character "X" after the more normal 2-alpha character code.

Thus, the 2-alpha character code for Zimbabwe in the context of customs affairs is "ZW" while in the context of currency it is "ZWD".

In the context of containers, the country code for Zimbabwe is "ZWX".

4.14.5 Size and Type Codes

As stated earlier, these codes consist of 4 numerals. The first 2 numerals reflect the dimensional characteristics of the container while the second 2 numerals indicate its type.

Layout of Codes

ISO standard No. 2716-1972 stipulates that the owner code, serial number, country code and size and type code must appear on the container in the following manner:-

| Owner Code | Serial Number | Check Digit |

Country Code   Size and Type Code

Thus, the layout for the container which can be used as an example for purpose of illustrating would be:-

ABZU   123456
ZAX   2030

The codes as laid out above must be marked on the top of the right-hand leaf of the door of a general purpose container and at the top right-hand corner of each side.

On serial type containers such as tanktainers, flat racks, etc, the full code must be shown in a single line commencing with the owner code and ending with the size and type code along a main member of the frame on each side and at one end.

4.14.6 Other Labels (Plates) Permanently Fixed to Containers
The other labels which must appear on all freight containers complying with the ISO standards are:-

The Rating Plate
This must reflect the following data - generally in both kilogrammes and pounds avoirdupois:-

- [ ]   Maximum permitted gross mass (i.e. when the container is loaded)
- [ ]   Container tare mass (e.g. mass without a payload)
- [ ]   Maximum permitted payload

Manufacturer's Plate
When a container is first constructed all of its details - place and date of manufacture, manufacturer's name and serial number and, most importantly, the fumigation/preservation of the container floor, must all be engraved on this plate which is affixed to the container.

Many countries, Australia in particular, have stringent requirements with respect to the fumigation and preservation of any wood entering their countries. In consequence, all wooden container floors must, without exception, be fumigated and preserved to the standard of the country to which the container is going. Australia has particularly stringent requirements and thus most container floors are fumigated and preserved to Australian standards.

Owner's Plate
As its name implies, this plate gives details of the name and the registered office of the container owner.

Where a container is carrying dangerous cargo then other special labels must be placed at certain points upon such a container in order to draw prominent attention to the dangers and risks which may be involved. The carriage of such cargo is, however, a much specialised subject which will be dealt with in greater detail in another module.

4.15 CONTAINER PACKING
Because the protection from external forces provided by closed and semi-closed containers is substantial many less experienced exporters and even warehousemen accepting an instruction to load a container overlook the absolute necessity of ensuring that cargo loaded into a container is properly secured therein so as to eliminate as far as possible any tendency of such cargo moving or tilting in any direction inside the container.

Cargo loaded into a container but remaining loose and unsecured will be subject to virtually as many movements as if it was shipped in a break-bulk form. Hence the vital importance of the securing of cargo within every container so as to reduce the risk of movement to the maximum degree.

By far the best method of achieving maximum stability of cargo in containers is to ensure that the dimensions of individual packages or individual items of unitised cargo such as cargo loaded on pallets, fit precisely into the particular size and type of container to be utilised.

In the case of pallets, those having dimensions of 1000 x 1200mm or 1100 x 1100mm are perfect for stowage in both a 6m and 12m GP container. Pallets of other sizes should not be used.

4.15.1 Calculating Number of Packages a Container will hold
One of the questions frequently asked of forwarders by exporters - and sometimes by importers - is "How many parcels of ... mass and dimensions each can be fitted into a 6m/12m container?"

As far as the mass is concerned, this is not very difficult: It requires account to be taken of the mass limitation to which the container is subject in terms of its plate rating plus an appreciation of any other mass limitations which may apply throughout the route over which the container must travel, and then ensuring that the cargo to be loaded does not exceed the limitation.

Considerations relevant to the dimensional capacity of the container for a particular size of package make it necessary to divide each container dimension - i.e. length, width and height - by the dimension of the parcel which will be stowed along each aspect of the container, rounding down the quotient to the nearest whole number of packages. The same calculation must be undertaken for each of the other two dimensions of the parcel and the container width and height. This will provide the total number of parcels which can be fitted into that container.

4.15.2 Securing of Cargo which fails to fit snugly into a container

Where the parcel dimensions are not at all compatible with the container interior dimensions then steps must be taken to secure the cargo inside the container from all likely movement. There are a number of alternative methods of achieving this, any one or more than one of which should be used as necessary.

Dunnaging

This method comprises the use (normally) of rough timber in baulks, planks, or other, used to surround reasonably compatible cargo so as to create aggregates of packages unlikely to shift or move to any serious degree during the voyage.

Alternatively, similar timber may be used throughout the centre length of the container so as to compress the cargo gently against the container's two sides.

Chocking

Chocks are usually smaller pieces of wood which are nailed to the floor of the container in order to prevent lateral or longitudinal movement of packages.

Chocking is vital in respect of all types of cargo shipped in drums which are laid on their sides, in order to prevent them rolling about.

It is preferable that drums are not so stowed. They should be on end but again chocks should be used between each row of drums in order to eliminate risks that the drum ribs might chafe and commence leaking, and also, where the drums have clip lids, to prevent them moving against each other and possibly hooking certain of the lids off.

Remember again the requirements of preservation and fumigation of all wood utilised.

Lashing

General purpose, flat rack and open top containers are all equipped with lashing rings or staples along the sides specifically provided to enable cargo to be securely lashed down with rope or wire cabling - as most appropriate to the cargo in question.

Netting

In a similar fashion, netting can be attached to the container lashing points in order to secure cargo beneath such nets.

4.15.3 Heavy Items of Cargo

In the case of very heavy loads of loads such as lathes or similar machinery where one end of the item is of substantial mass but the other end comparatively light, such heavy masses should be loaded on the top end of substantial "spreader" beams (possibly timber baulks) by which the mass is distributed as evenly as possible and as close as possible to the sides of the container in order to ease the strain on the container floors.

Every possible means must be utilized in the case of such heavy loads to secure them from any possible movement. It must be realised that in the built up by that movement may be so great that the cargo could smash through the sides or the ends of the container.

194

In this context please consider once more the severity of movement which can take place in stormy weather at sea.

4.16 CONTAINER MOVEMENT/SERVICES
It is very important to distinguish between the following types of container movements:-
☐   FCL/FCL
☐   LCL and groupage
☐   LCL/FCL
☐   FCL/LCL
☐   Co-loading

4.16.1 FCL/FCL
The use of the phrase FCL/FCL therefore implies that the container in question has been loaded at the place of origin with a single complete shipment therein intended for delivery at the point of destination of the goods in question as a single shipment to a single recipient. In other words, the container is conveying a single consignment from a single sender intended for a single consignee.

The movement therefore normally takes the following form:-
☐   empty container from container yard to exporter's premises
☐   container loaded and sealed by exporter
☐   container moves to coastal container terminal
☐   container loaded to vessel and shipped to appropriate overseas port
☐   container moves inland to consignee's premises and is discharged

4.16.2 LCL and Groupage
The container movement for both these different services is the same as:-
☐   the container is loaded with mixed consignments at a container depot at the place of origin
☐   it is dispatched overseas as for the FCL services described under FCL/FCL
☐   it is conveyed to a suitable container depot in the appropriate destination locality for unpacking
☐   the empty container is removed to a container yard
☐   the various consignments unpacked from it are collected and distributed to their respective consignees.

The essential difference between these two services concerns the organisations offering the services:-

☐   LCL services are offered by shipping lines
☐   groupage services are offered by forwarders

4.16.3 LCL/FCL
A major importer regularly ordering a variety of goods from a series of independent suppliers may arrange through his appointed forwarder - and by specific instructions given to the various suppliers - for his orders to be accumulated over an agreed period of

perhaps 1, 2 or 3 weeks with a view to the creation of a reasonable load for containerisation.

This type of shipment is normally called an **assemblage** and the movement will be as follows:-

- ☐ empty container called forward from a container yard when the full assemblage is ready at the   container depot
- ☐ container loaded and sealed at the depot and transported overseas
- ☐ container finally delivered at destination complete as an FCL direct to the importer.

In this operation the forwarder plays a vital function of liaison between the various suppliers in the locality of origin and the importing organisation at destination.

4.16.4 FCL/LCL

This type of container movement will be developed on the initiative of a major international trade supplying regular, comparatively small, shipments to a series of customers all of whom are located within a convenient distance from a customs licensed container depot.

It will be evident that in this instance the co-ordination of the service must be arranged between the major supplier and his appointment forwarder. The advantages in this instance are mainly savings in transportation costs.

4.16.5 Co-Loading

Co-loading may be described (in broad terms) as a joint-venture operation between two or more forwarders. Underlying the concept of co-loading is the fact that to make transportation in containers economically viable every container must be loaded as closely as possible to both its maximum capacity and its maximum permitted gross weight. Only by the maximising of its payload can maximum profitability be achieved in respect of any container of any type.

If the delay is too great, his client will complain and the forwarder risks the loss of business. Nevertheless, from the moment that the first small consignment arrives in his care the forwarder must with ever increasing urgency seek for additional consignments to boost the payload which he achieves in his groupage container. The period of delay available to him is usually conditioned by the sailing date of the next ship going the appropriate destination. Unfortunately for the forwarder it is usually very difficult for him to forecast the availability of the other traffic he requires.

Co-loading arrangements with other forwarders (despite the fact that in other respects they are his competitors) serves substantially to "spread his risk". It may even eliminate that risk.

In fact, an efficient and well organised co-loading arrangement between a group of agents usually results in an enhancement of profitability to all of them.

Co-Loading Operations
Each container movement involved co-loading requires that one of the parties acts as the master loader while the other party or parties become the co-loaders.

The master loader of a particular container will become responsible for arranging the loading and sealing of the container, its movement to the ship's side, its dispatch, and the obtaining of the appropriate shipping company bill of lading (either marine or multimodal). The master loader is then responsible to ensure the immediate dispatch of that bill of lading to the degrouping agent at the destination, at the same time supplying full details of the ship, sailing date, etc, to the co-loaders.

FIATA or house bills of lading are then issued by all the parties to cover the consignments they have each contributed to the groupage container and on every such individual bill of lading each co-loader will show their own releasing agent at the destination to whom their respective bills of lading must be surrendered.

It is important that proper co-loading agreements are negotiated and that each part to such an agreement honours it both in the letter and in the spirit of it.

Co-Loading Cost Calculations
The assessing of costs where cargo is co-loaded will obviously commence with the charge per freight ton agreed between the co-loader and the master loader. Accordingly, the determination of costs in this highly specialised situation is purely a commercial negotiation between the parties involved and it would be inappropriate for any attempt to be made here to define how those negotiations should proceed.

Compatibility of Containerised Cargo
A reference back to the protection and packing of goods will remind you of the extensiveness of the movement to which cargo in containers is subjected during an average sea voyage. The importance of securing cargo to the maximum degree from risks of movement which could cause damage was emphasised.

Because, even though the cargo is secured in a reasonable manner, there remains a risk that in weather which is a little heavier than usual movement with possible risk of damage may still take place, it becomes of very substantial importance to ensure that cargo which consists of mixed varieties of goods is always compatible.

The risk obviously is that if damage occurs within cargo A, with resultant leakage or sifting, it may be of itself create damage and loss in cargoes B and C, etc, which are also in the same container. For instance, cans of lubricating oil which start to leak may contaminate a consignment of shoes or of clothing loaded adjacent to the oil. Drums of poisonous powders which are broached as a result of continual movement in a container may create a film of poisonous dust over jars and tins of foodstuffs.

197

Products with a strong odour such as naphtha may contaminate by smell bales of cloth of carpet. Certain industrial waxes which are solid at temperature latitudes will liquefy and expand in the heat of the hold of a ship passing through equatorial latitudes with a risk of bursting their containers and causing extensive contamination to other goods.

All of this is of peculiar importance in the context of groupage services and it is important that forwarders who provide such services ensure that their operatives are able to detect potential incompatibilities in the cargoes offered to them for dispatch in groupage containers.

Dangerous Goods
Furthermore, there are many chemical products which are in themselves harmless but which, when mixed with other products or even with water, acquire highly dangerous properties.

It is important that all forwarders involved in groupage traffic, weather import or export maintain a very conscious awareness of the risks of loading incompatible cargo in the same container.

REFERENCES
Bailey C. A. (2007) **"A Guide to Qualitative Field Research."** Pine Forge Press. California.

Bedi K. (2004) **"Production and Operations Management"**. Oxford University Press. New Delhi.

Bhattacharyya D. K. (2003) **"Research Methodology."** Excel Books. New Delhi.

Cook T. A. (2001) **"The Ultimate Guide to Export Management."** AMACOM. New York.

Daniels, Raudebaugh, Sullivan (2004) **"Globalisation and Business."** Prentice Hall International. New Delhi

Frazelle E.H. (2004) **"Supply Chain Strategy."** Tata McGraw-Hill Publishing Co. Ltd. New Delhi.

Gubbins E. J. (2003) **"Managing Transport Operations."** Kogan Page. London.

House D. J. (2005) **"Cargo Work"** Elsevier. Amsterdam

Kapoor S. K. and Kansal P. (2003) **"Marketing Logistics: A Supply Chain Approach."** Pearson Education. New Delhi.

Kirby M., Kidd W et al (1997) **"Sociology in Perspective"** Heinnemann Educational Publishers. Oxford.

Raina H. K. (1990) **"Guide to Import Management".** PRODEC. Helsinki

Rowland O.P. (1986) **"Imports and Exports: An Introductory Handbook."** Evans Brothers. Ltd. Nairobi

Silverman D. (2006) **"Interpreting Qualitative Data."** Sage Publications. London.

Sople V. V. (2004) **"Logistics Management: The Supply Chain Imperative."** Pearson Education. Singapore.

Thomas A. B. (2004) **"Research Skills for Management Studies."** Routledge, London
CHAPTER 5

CHAPTER 5

TRAFFIC MANAGEMENT

5.1   TRAFFIC MANAGEMENT SCOPE

Traffic management handles modal choice, transporter choice, routing, safety and legal compliance, delivery timeliness and cost effectiveness.

Modal choice is influenced by:-
☐ reliability
☐ frequency
☐ cost
☐ transit time/speed
☐ capital tied up in transport
☐ service quality
☐ packaging requirements
☐ import/export regulations
☐ insurance
☐ capability and flexibility

5.1.1   Traffic Responsibilities

(a)   **Auditing and Claim Administration** - claims for loss or damage or overcharge/undercharge which can be done as pre-or-post audits

(b)   **Equipment Scheduling** - load planning, equipment utilisation and driver scheduling planning, coordination and monitoring equipment   maintenance and establishment of special equipment requirements

The shipper should furnish the following details in respect of a shipment according to Cook T.A. (2001).
☐ specific product descriptions
☐ points of origin and times of availability of cargo
☐ packaging, unitisation and dimensions
☐ weights i.e. gross and net
☐ assignment shipping responsibilities i.e. who prepares documents, insurance cover and customs clearance
☐ nature of cargo i.e. perishable, fragile, hazardous
☐ pertinent consignee and delivery information

(c)   **Rate Negotiation** - seek lowest rate consistent with service standards

(d)   **Research**
☐ carrier performance measurement
(i)   carrier integration i.e. monitor demand for types of carrier services e.g. warehousing, packaging, labeling.

(ii)   carrier evaluation through consideration for cost, transit time, reliability, capability, accessibility and security cost i.e. claims responsibility, loading, counting.

Transit time considers consolidation and clearance delays. Capability considers bulk products, tracking, storage and refrigerated vessels. Security protects loads from loss, damage or theft and claim settlement.

(e)   Tracing and Expediting
☐   Trace to locate loss or late delivery
☐   Expediting requests carrier to move shipment as soon as possible

(f)   Freight classification
(g)   Freight documentation for shipping and customs clearing
(h)   Risk management
(i)   Shipment pooling

5.2   ROUTEING AND SCHEDULING
It is the planning of journeys for vehicles operating from a single depot, delivering known loads to specific customers and returning to the depot after completing the journey.

5.2.1   Routing and Scheduling Objectives
☐   to maximise the time that a vehicle is used i.e. to make sure that it is working for as long as possible.
☐   to maximise the capability utilisation of a vehicle i.e. ensure all vehicles are as fully loaded as possible.
☐   to minimise mileage i.e. complete the work by travelling as few kilometres as possible.
☐   to minimise the number of vehicles used i.e. to keep capital or fixed   costs to a minimum.

5.2.2   Routeing and Scheduling Problems
☐   weight or volume capacity of the vehicles
☐   total time available in a day
☐   loading and off-loading times
☐   vehicle speeds
☐   traffic congestion
☐   access restrictions
☐   strategic and tactical planning problems

5.3   TRANSPORTATION ACTIVITY PROFILING
☐   shipment frequencies
☐   cube-per-shipment distributions
☐   weight-per-shipment distributions
☐   value-per-shipment distributions

- shipment classifications
- origin - destination time windows
- in-transit time requirements
- mode and carrier availability and capacities
- transportation rates
- carrier on time performance statistics
- claims and loss rates
- average and deviant travel times and speeds
distances

5.4 TRANSPORTATION PERFORMANCE MEASURES
"Cycle time metrics are the most natural indicators of transportation performance".
Frazelle E.H. (2004:186).

- Cycle time-in-transit time, in-transit time variability, vehicle load/off load time, detention time, delay in traffic time.
- Productivity - asset productivity (containers, vehicles), operator productivity (number of stops, kilometres travelled, cases delivered per person per hour).
- Quality - claims free shipment percentage, damage free shipment percentage, distance between accidents, on time arrival percentage, on time departure percentage, perfect delivery percentage, perfect   route percentage.
- Financial - freight, labour, fleet leasing, terminal leasing, logistics information system, maintenance, third party transportation fees, fuel, customs clearing and freight forwarding fees, security, packaging, fleet ownership costs, terminal ownership costs, ports and bridges.

5.5 LOGISTICS NETWORK DESIGN
It specifies number of levels of distribution, number of distribution facilities, distribution facility location and mission, distribution facility supplier and customer assignment and inventory deployment in the network.

5.6 SHIPMENT PLANNING AND MANAGEMENT
A shipment is a collection of orders that travel together. Shipment planning is the process of choosing shipment frequencies and deciding for each shipment the orders which should be assigned to the shipment, mode of transport, appropriate carrier, route and shipping schedule. Shipment management includes the assignment of shipments to containers and the tracking of the shipment in process.

(a) Shipment Frequency Planning
It affects total transportation costs, inventory carrying costs, transport administration costs and customer satisfaction.

(b) Mode and Carrier Selection
Mode selection depends on product characteristics (value, commodity composition, volume, weight), cost of transport, frequency, accessibility, security, reliability, etc.

(c)   Routing and Scheduling
Routing should minimse total route costs, number of routes, total distance travelled and total route time.

Routeing can be affected by the following constraints:-
☐   customer response time requirements and time windows i.e. times at which vehicle must arrive after and depart before
☐   route balancing i.e. no one vehicle or driver should have disproportionate share of work
☐   maximum route times i.e. limit driving time or flight time
☐   vehicle capacities i.e. limit amount of cargo in a vehicle because of weight or cube capacity
☐   start-stop points i.e. vehicle start and stop at designated points
☐   transport infrastructure constraints i.e. lane thresholds, bridges, etc.

Scheduling should avoid hub times i.e. times when hubs are clogged and may need to coordinate with arrival or departure schedules of third party carriers. Scheduling enables consolidation of inbound and outbound shipments to save on freight costs.

(d)   Load Planning and Management
Load planning seeks to maximise container utilisation, loading in reverse order of delivery location and balancing weight of load across container floor.

(e)   Shipment Rating
Rating is the process of estimating the freight charge associated with any given shipment. In some markets an electronic shipment bidding system is available for shippers to post shipment details i.e. origin, destination, weight delivery time requirement, classification, etc. electronically to carriers who will bid for shipments attractive to them.

(f)   Shipment Tracking
World-class shipment tracking and visibility begins before shipment is released to the carrier by giving the customer estimates of picking time, departure time, arrival time and container assignment. Real time shipment tracking and visibility requires online EDI or internet links with fleet or carriers or on-board communication systems for global shipment tracking of containers world-wide.

E-tracking is normally used in courier services, air and sea cargo. Fleet owners need to track their vehicles to minimise inconveniences caused by accidents, highway robbery or truck detention by traffic police. Common tracking method is for truck drivers to call their offices and consignees at regular intervals to update goods whereabouts. For courier shipments clients can enter consignment number and ask for its status from the courier website.

5.7   FLEET, CONTAINER AND YARD MANAGEMENT
(a)   Fleet sizing, configuration and financing

Fleet sizing seeks to own, lease or rent the fewest number of vehicles and containers possible to meet shipping requirements. Fleet requirement can be minimised by:-

- [ ] utilising standard and modular sized cases, pallets, transport containers
- [ ] monitoring fleet utilisation levels over each transport network segment
- [ ] maintaining total fleet visibility i.e. loading times, off-loading times, transit times, maintenance times
- [ ] choosing low use periods to conduct routine maintenance
- [ ] monitoring and charging for fleet detention by suppliers, customers and carriers
- [ ] utilising alternative coverage means during super-peak periods to avoid the burden of oversized fleet

(b) Fleet Acquisition and Replacement

Fleet acquisition options include direct ownership, leasing and dedicated contract carriage. Choice is determined by costs, customer service impact, reactions to outsourcing, etc, e.g. food industry competes on private ownership.

(c) Fleet Maintenance and Security

Good maintenance increases reliability and reduces or delay replacements. High security vigilance is necessitated by global trade, partnering, information sharing and use of 3PL and 4PL service providers.

According to Bedi K (2004) maintenance management yields the following benefits:-

- [ ] fewer breakdowns ensure realisation of full production capacity
- [ ] elimination of worker idle time to achieve low costs
- [ ] product and service quality improves
- [ ] improves worker safety due to low incidence of sudden breakdowns
- [ ] customer satisfaction through timely delivery schedules
- [ ] increases life span of facilities and equipment

Types of Maintenance

(a) Breakdown maintenance (reactive)
(b) Preventive maintenance (proactive). Preventive maintenance is more desirable because of the following characteristics:-

- [ ] it involves regular oiling, cleaning, adjustment, inspection and replacement of worn out parts.
- [ ] it can be a periodic activity on the calendar or result from inspections or mileage covered.
- [ ] total preventive maintenance is done by users resulting in workers being committed to equipment to avoid abuse.
- [ ] keeps records of equipment installation, operating hours, types of maintenance and repairs required
- [ ] constantly breaking down equipment should be considered for disposal and replacement or user training.

(d) Vehicle/Container identification, tracking and communication

This provides rapid response to break downs and reduces vehicle abuse by employees. It enables continuous instructions to be given to the crew en route and customers can also get reliable updates on their shipments.

(e) Yard, dock and port management

Frazele E. H. (2004:214) made the following observation:

"Container yards, docks and ports are typically the nodes in the transportation network with the least systems support, the least management sophistication, the least container tracking capabilities, the most crime, and the most frequent source of delays and cycle time variability."

The following world-class practices have been adopted for yard, dock and port management.

- ☐ secured driver load verification
- ☐ on-site automatic driver routing
- ☐ intelligent dock assignment
- ☐ advanced crew and dock/berth scheduling
- ☐ yard, dock, port staging location tracking and management
  - drives must identify themselves, their assigned vehicle, assigned container and assigned load at times electronically using smart cards
  - voice activated system identifies driver by his voice and a synthesised voice assigns dock number and directions to it which serves driver time
  - efficient dock/berth assigns inbound vehicle to a dock/berth which minimises handling distance and off-loading time
  - location markings and management of containers or cargo outside warehouses and in yards should be tagged the same way warehoused goods are marked.

5.8 CARRIER MANAGEMENT

It involves practices of carrier performance monitoring, carrier selection, carrier negotiations and core carrier programs.

5.9 WORLD-CLASS PRACTICES OF FREIGHT AND DOCUMENT MANAGEMENT

(a) Freight Rate Negotiations

"Today's negotiations require much more research and advance planning than at any time in the past." Frazelle E. H. (2004:218).

Forwarders/Shippers should research and approach negotiations with:-
- ☐ historical and projected shipping volumes between each origin and destination pair
- ☐ required delivery times and on-time reliability performance
- ☐ required value added services
- ☐ guidelines for claims and conflict resolution

□   historical carrier performance records, volume and rates
□   required information systems support capability
□   preferred payment terms and rate structures
□   knowledge of the carrier's competitive position, market share and underutilised capacity
□   knowledge of the carrier's current and future customer base
□   knowledge of recent or projected shifts in the carrier's organisational structure
□   carrier hot buttons

(b)   Freight Bill Payment
Payment on invoice - shipper receives invoice from carrier, verifies it and pays it directly. It allows overbilling by carriers.
Positive pay - shipper computes freight bill and releases funds to the carrier without an invoice. Shipper keeps freight rates.
Outsourcing - third party is contracted to rate, audit, pay bill and advise shipper during rate negotiations.

(c)   Freight Bill Auditing
The exercise is targeted at recovering carrier mistakes and overcharges on invoices.

5.10 HUMAN AND COMMUNITY FRIENDLY TRANSPORTATION
□   driver routes and schedules that minimise time away from families
□   on-board communication systems
□   speed governors to eliminate temptation for over speeding
□   loading and off-loading aids for heavy loads
□   strategic reverse logistics management
□   regional traffic management systems
□   intelligent vehicle highway systems
□   off-peak routing and scheduling

5.11 COMMON TRAFFIC COMPLAINTS
□   damaged merchandise
□   failure of carrier to meet standard transit time
□   failure of carrier to notify back order
□   failure to follow customer routing/instructions
□   errors in documents
□   unsatisfactory material handling equipment

5.12   EFFECTIVE COMMUNICATION
Communication between all the parties to a transaction involving international trade and international transportation must obviously be of transcending importance.

The forwarder, by his very nature, stands at the very centre of all such communication with the following parties - each according to the requirements of the transaction in question:-

- His Zimbabwean client, whether importer or exporter
- The railway authority with whom he may have to deal
- Any haulage contractor necessary to the furtherance of the transaction
- The dock/harbour authority
- The airline, in the case of airfreight
- The customs authority
- His overseas operating partner in the forwarding of the goods
- The overseas principal to the contract of sale or supply

On occasion he may have to deal with the appropriate bank in Zimbabwe handling the financial considerations of the transaction, other statutory authorities within Zimbabwe exercising statutory controls over the movement of the goods, and also, of course, any container depot operator through whose hands the goods may require passing.

5.12.1 Nature and Content of Typical Communications Exports

Booking Request and Container Reservation from Export Client
This should include approximate shipping details of the intended dispatch, whether the forwarder is to arrange collection, when the goods will be ready, port/airport of destination, marks and numbers where appropriate, whether the forwarder is to arrange collection, when the goods will be ready, port/airport of destination, marks and numbers where appropriate, whether the goods are hazardous or obnoxious, name and address of consignee. Above all, such a communication should also include the exporter's reference/job number.

Forwarder's Response
This should commence by quoting the exporter's reference/job number for identification purposes, and should give full details of the booking made, including urgently all necessary documentation such as exchange control declaration, copies of invoice, copies of any letters of credit involved, and above all, full shipping and documentation instructions.

Forwarder's Communication to Ship's Agent/Airline
This should provide the international carrier with sufficient preliminary detail to enable the booking to be made and should ask for the booking reference number and delivery instructions.

Shipping (Consigning) Instruction/Packing Declaration
The exporter must utilise the appropriate standardised format for the packing declaration, the forwarder's own shipping instructions, and also supply copies of the L/C where appropriate. Since the exchange control declaration must, of necessity, be in hard copy with the original signatures of respectively the exporter and his bank these must pass by hand in accordance with a mutual arrangement made with the forwarder.

Forwarder's Pre-advice to Overseas Operating Agent

If the consignment is to be consolidated by air or grouped by sea it must be at this stage that the Zimbabwean forwarder sends full details, including details of the planned dispatch of the goods, to his overseas partner as a pre-advice to warn both the latter and also the consignee of the imminent shipment. An anticipated date of arrival at the overseas port/airport should be included.

Electronic Clearance
Where export clearance through Zimbabwean customs can be achieved by an electronic medium this must be accomplished. At present bill of entry clearance is done through ASYCUDA World or ASYCUDA++.

Container Release Orders
In respect of seafreight by means of FCL container the container release order completed in every respect must be lodged with the container terminal for the delivery of the empty container to the exporter's premises, and its collection for on-carriage to the port.

Groupage
In the case of LCL groupage exports, instructions must be issued for collection of the goods from the exporter's premises and delivery to the appropriate container depot for loading to the appropriate container.

The forwarder's instruction to the container depot handling the consignment must be promptly transmitted. This must include precise details concerning the loading to container and its dispatch from depot to transport.

As may be appropriate, either the shipping and bill of lading instructions must be transmitted to the shipping line or, alternatively, the air waybill must be prepared for submission along with the goods when they are delivered to the airline.

Second Pre-advice to Overseas Operating Agent
At this stage a further communication needs to be sent to the forwarder's overseas partner confirming that the dispatch is proceeding on schedule.

In respect of goods dispatched by airfreight, an immediate e-mail advice should be sent by the forwarder to the exporter to be followed by copies of all documentation with the forwarder's account.

In the case of shipments by seafreight, the completed bills of lading signed as appropriate by the shipping company must be collected, all copy documents collated, and dispatched to the exporter with the forwarder's account.

Dispatch Advice to Overseas Operating Agent
Finally, a confirmation of successful shipment must be sent to the forwarder's overseas partner incorporating all additional details such as air waybill number/bill of lading number, as may be appropriate.

The indications given above show how many varieties of communications may be required in a particular case but it must be realised that there may be even more in some instances, e.g. an instruction to take out marine insurance cover, etc.

Imports
A range of communications necessary for the efficient handling of imports may commence within Zimbabwe or alternatively, overseas. Indicated below are the major types of communication with which a forwarder may be involved.

Zimbabwean Forwarder's Advice/instruction to Overseas Operating Partner to make contact with a supplier in order to prepare a takeover and movement of supplies intended for a Zimbabwean Importer
This type of communication usually arises where there is a close relationship between the Zimbabwean forwarder and his importing client such that the client supplies to the forwarder a copy of the order placed overseas - usually with the request that the forwarder issues progress reports concerning the anticipated date of readiness of the goods at the supplier's works, the anticipated date of shipment, and the name of the vessel or the flight on which it is anticipated that the goods will move.

Where this process is put into place those progress reports should be made regularly at intervals appropriate to the needs of the Zimbabwean importer.

By the same token, communications will pass between the Zimbabwean forwarder and his importing client at regular intervals.

Changes in Shipping Requirements
During the lead time for manufacture or collation of an order for shipment from an overseas supplier the importer may have to adjust his shipping instructions and in this event the forwarder will again be involved in vital communications with his overseas operating partner.

Pre-advice Concerning Shipment/Dispatch
The overseas operating partner must pre-advise precise shipping details and, of course, will follow this up with a final advice of successful shipment/dispatch. These advices may well be by electronic means (telex, fax, EDI) but the overseas partner must, in addition, forward hard copy documentation as appropriate to the Zimbabwean forwarder - preferably by at least airmail and possibly courier. Where the goods are moving by airfreight the documentation will naturally move under cover of the air waybill in the care of the pilot of the aircraft.

Clearing and Delivery Instructions
Either at the time when the advice of successful shipment is given to the importer by the Zimbabwean forwarder or as quickly thereafter as possible the forwarder must ensure that he receives proper clearing and delivery instructions from his client.

Bearing in mind that the forwarder acts strictly as an agent of the importer as regards the clearing of the goods through customs it is vital that the instructions received from the importer in this respect are precise and complete - leaving no need for the forwarder to "guess" the importer's requirements.

As regards delivery after clearance, this may be direct to the importer's premises, may involve dispatch to a different warehouse, may require direct dispatch to the importer's customer, etc. It is usual for the importer to indicate the mode of transport and the speed of transport to be utilised.

Invoicing of Charges due to be paid by the Importer
It must be standard by the Zimbabwean forwarder to ensure that the invoicing of the importer with charges which are appropriate to him is never delayed.

If there is a risk of unavoidable delay, then it is vital that the importer is supplied forthwith a copies of documentation reflecting all costs associated with the shipment.

5.12.2 Modes of Communication
Communication modes consist of:-

- Postal mail - that is to say, airmail in respect of all international communications
- Courier - expensive but normally very efficient
- Telex - a communication mode which is rapidly passing into disuse because it has been superseded by telefax.
- Telefax - possibly the fastest and most versatile method of communication both within Zimbabwe and internationally.

Telefax messages, however, can fade over a long period of time, particularly if they are stored next to plastic. For any record which it is desired to maintain permanently, therefore, all telefax messages should be photocopied.

Moreover, there are certain documents which have to be transmitted from one party to another which must be originals - they cannot be telefaxes. Such documents include the bill of lading, a bill of exchange, an insurance policy or certificates, etc.

Email - This is rapidly superseding both the telefax and fax. It is true to say that complete familiarity with this mode of communication will be a *sine qua non* to employment within our industry in a very short time.

5.12.3 Electronic Data Interchange (EDI)
This is true hi-tech communication in which computer communicates direct with computer via international networks. When fully fledged it will be the most efficient and speedy communication medium yet devised.

In Europe, USA and Japan it is in use between major parties doing domestic trade with each other and between certain international traders.

5.13 TRANSPORT DOCUMENTS
Transport documents vary substantially depending upon:-
☐ the requirements of the underlying transaction
☐ the mode or modes of transport to be utilised

Transport documents which may be required by a credit or may include any of the following:-
☐ marine bill of lading
☐ ocean bill of lading
☐ combined transport bill of lading
☐ combined transport document
☐ combined transport bill of lading or port-to-port bill of lading
☐ FIATA Combined Transport bill of lading
☐ house bill of lading issued by...
☐ non-negotiable liner (or sea) waybill
☐ air waybill
☐ house air waybill
☐ postal receipt
☐ FIATA forwarders certificate of receipt
☐ FIATA forwarders certificate of transport

Occasionally, and in respect of consignments moving by overland transport, a documentary letter of credit may call for a copy of a rail consignment note or a road haulers certificate of receipt.

Marine Bill of Lading/Ocean Bill of Lading
For purposes of a letter of credit banks regard these two documents as the same - the essence of both being that they cover the carriage of goods by sea.

Where a credit calls for either of these documents banks will accept a document which:-

☐ appears on its face to have been issued by a named carrier or his agent, and indicates dispatch or taking in place of the goods or loading of them on board as the case may be, and
☐ consists of the full set of originals issued to the consignor if those originals were issued in a set of more than one, and
  meets the other stipulations of the credit.

Combined Transport Bill of Lading
Combined Transport Document
Combined Transport Bill of Lading or Port-to-Port Bill of Lading
Document Bearing a Title or Combination of Titles of Similar

Intent and Effect
Where a credit calls for a transport document denominated by any of the above the banks will not reject it even though the document:-
indicates some or all of the conditions of carriage by reference to a source or document other than the transport document itself (i.e. it is a short form or blank back transport document) and/or

☐ indicates a place of taking in charge different from the port of loading and/or a place of final destination different from the port of discharge, and/or

☐ relates to cargoes such as those in containers or on pallets, and the like, and/or

☐ contains the indication "intended", or a similar qualification, in relation to the vessel or other means of transport and/or the port of loading and/or the port of discharge.

However, unless otherwise stipulated in the credit, where the carriage of the goods is by sea or is by more than one mode of transport including carriage by sea, banks will reject a transport document which:-

☐ indicates that it is subject to a charter party, and/or

☐ indicates that the carrying vessel is propelled by sail only.

FIATA Combined Transport Bill of Lading
Unless the credit stipulates otherwise, banks will accept the FIATA Combined Transport bill of lading approved by the International Chamber of Commerce which indicates that it is issued by a freight forwarder acting as a carrier.

This means that in Zimbabwe a member of the Shipping and Forwarding Agents' Association of Zimbabwe acting as a contractual carrier is entitled to issue the FIATA FBL in terms of a credit unless the credit specifically stipulates otherwise.

This is the only freight forwarder document which banks will accept without question. Other forwarder documents, including house bills of lading, will be rejected unless the terms of the credit in question specifically authorise their acceptance.

House of Bill of Lading
As stated above, forwarders own house bills of lading will never be accepted in terms of a credit unless that credit specifically authorises their acceptance.

If a forwarder desires to issue his own house bill of lading for traffic which is moving in terms of a credit he must arrange that the applicant makes a specific provision in the letter of credit for this purpose.

Non-Negotiable Liner (or Sea) Waybill
This document is not a document of title - it is simply a confirmation issued by the carrier (shipping company) in question that it has received an instruction from the seller/shipper of the goods to carry the goods to the named destination and to delivery them at that destination to the named consignee.

Because the protection of the applicant for a letter of credit to be issued stipulating this document is so limited, banks are generally unwilling to issue a credit in terms of which a liner (or sea) waybill is the only named transport document. Nevertheless, they will do so if the applicant insists and provided that the exchange control regulations of the applicant's country do not prohibit this arrangement.

In the case of credits issued by banks in Zimbabwe in respect of the funding of import transactions there are at present no prohibitions issued by the Zimbabwe Reserve Bank.

Airway Bill
Again, the air waybill is not a document of title. While it carries a great deal more information than a liner waybill it is essentially merely an acknowledgement by the airline of responsibility to carry the goods to the destination airport and to deliver them there to the named consignee.

As in the case of the liner waybill, banks are generally not very willing to issue letters of credit where an air waybill signed and stamped by an airline overseas is the only transport document stipulated.

House Air Waybill
The same considerations apply here as apply also to the airline air waybill referred to in the previous paragraph so that although the possibility exists that a credit could stipulate the production of a house air waybill it is unlikely in the extreme.

Postal Receipt and Certificate of Posting
It is not uncommon for a letter of credit to require the production of one or other of these documents as evidence that the goods have been dispatched to the applicant.

Banks will accept either of these documents where the letter of credit stipulates their acceptance if the document in question appears to have been stamped or otherwise authenticated and dated in the place from which the credit stipulates that the goods are to be dispatched.

FIATA Forwarders Certificate of Receipt/
FIATA Forwarders Certificate of Transport
The issue of these two FIATA documents is strictly limited to forwarders who are in membership of a national association which is an Ordinary Member of FIATA. The Shipping and Forwarding Agent's Association of Zimbabwe is such an Ordinary Member and therefore firms in membership of SFAAZ are at liberty to use them.

However, the FIATA Certificate of Receipt is merely a receipt for the goods; it does not indicate that the goods have been forwarded (although this may, in fact, be correct) and therefore it is unusual for a credit to stipulate that document except in most unusual circumstances which need not concern the student at this time.

On the other hand, the FIATA Forwarders Certificate of Transport, while not a document of title, does act as a transport document in that the forwarder issuing it confirms by his signature thereto that he has received the goods into his change for irrevocable forwarding to the named consignee. Since the forwarding evidenced by the Certificate of Transport is irrevocable, it affords a measure of confidence to the applicant for a credit that the goods "are on the move." It is therefore within the discretion of the applicant for a credit to call for this document as the transport document required inter alia to justify the release of the stated sum.

The most common use of the FIATA Forwarders Certificate of Transport is found in movements overland where, obviously, bills of lading, etc, have no relevance. Nevertheless, it must be clearly understood that the credit must stipulate the FIATA Forwarders Certificate of Transport as the required transport document.

5.14 TRANSSHIPMENT

The definition of "transshipment" for purposes of documentary letters of credit must be carefully understood. Transshipment means a transfer and reloading during the course of carriage from the port of loading or place of dispatch or taking in charge, to the port of discharge or place of destination, either from one conveyance or vessel to another conveyance or vessel within the same mode of transport, or from one mode of transport to another mode of transport.

Transshipment for the purposes of a credit is therefore quite different to transshipment as discussed under "the Transshipment Bill of Lading". Where transshipment was discussed solely during the course of carriage by sea where there was no direct shipping service between the port of origin and the port of destination with the consequence that transshipment at an intermediate port was involved.

Here, transshipment has a far broader meaning and includes the transferring of the goods not only from ship to ship but also from conveyance to conveyance and from one mode of transport to another. Thus, if the goods are transferred from road vehicle to rail wagon or from rail to ship, or vice versa, each such operation is transshipment.

Because of the breadth of the definition of transshipment the rules controlling transport documents for letter of credit purposes must be clearly understood.

☐　　　If the credit calls for a marine (or ocean) bill of lading, and transshipment is prohibited then that bill of lading will be rejected if it indicates any form of transshipment at an intermediate port.

☐　　　If, however transshipment is not prohibited then the banks will accept a bill of lading indicating transshipment at an intermediate port provided the entire carriage is covered by one and the same transport document.

☐　　　Furthermore, even if transshipment is prohibited by the terms of the credit banks will accept a bill of lading which merely incorporates printed clauses stating that the carrier has the right to transship.

- In the case of a transport document which is a "combined transport document" or similar, then even if transshipment is prohibited by the terms of the credit, banks will accept the relevant transport document if it indicates carriage from a place of taking in charge to a place of final destination by different modes of transport including a carriage by sea, provided that the entire carriage is covered by one and the same transport document.
- This therefore incorporates multimodal transportation of containers on any form of multimodal document provided that such multimodal document covers the entire transportation.

Payment Of Freight And Other Charges

Freight and other charges arising during the process of transportation constitute a major element in the final value of goods in international trade. The determinant whether such charges are paid by seller or buyer will be found in the INCOTERM incorporated into the contract between them. It follows, therefore, that the transport document must clearly evidence whether freight has already been paid by the seller (beneficiary) or is to be paid at destination by the buyer (applicant).

The responsibility of the banks is to ensure that the transport document reflects correctly the party responsible to pay the freight charges involved. Accordingly, and provided it is not inconsistent with the provisions of the credit and the other documentation, banks will accept transport documents sating that freight and charges must still be paid.

If a credit stipulates that the transport document has to indicate that freight has already been paid or is prepaid, then banks will accept a document on which words clearly indicating payment or prepayment of freight appear by stamp or otherwise or on which payment of freight is indicated by other means. Words such as "freight pre-payable" or "freight to be prepaid" or words of similar effect, if appearing on a transport document will not be accepted as constituting evidence of the payment of the freight.

Description Of Goods On A Transport Document

Banks will accept transport documents which bear a clause (printed or stamped) on the face thereof such as "shipper's load and count" or "declared by shipper or "said to contain" or words of similar effect.

The student will realise that since shipping companies will not under any circumstances accept that they have any knowledge of the contents of packages, etc, it is essential that the banks allow these forms of wording on transport documents.

Name of Consignor/Shipper/Sender on Transport Documents

Unless the credit stipulates otherwise, banks will accept transport documents indicating as the consignor/shipper/sender of the goods a party other than the beneficiary of the credit.

This allows a forwarder to show himself as the shipper of the consignment on a bill of lading should he wish to do so, without infringing the validity of the document unless there is a specific stipulation in the credit with regard to the matter.

"Shipped on Board"
The forwarder will recall that for Customs purposes the transport document to be produced to customs with the bill of entry: import must indicate clearly that the goods have been shipped on board or similar wording together with the date when such shipment on board was effected.

For the purposes of letters of credit, however, unless the credit specifically calls for an "on board" transport document, banks will accept a transport document which indicates that the goods have been taken in charge or received for shipment.

Loading on board or shipment on a vessel may be evidenced either by a transport document bearing printed wording indicating the fact in relation to the vessel named thereon or, in the case of a transport document stating "received for shipment", by means of a notation of loading on board placed subsequently on the transport document and signed or initiated and dated by the carrier or his agent. Where this notation is applied the date of it will be regarded as the date of loading on board the vessel for the purpose of the controls which may be stipulated in the credit.

Shipment on Deck
Banks will not accept a transport document covering carriage by sea or by more than one mode of transport but including carriage by sea, which states that the goods are, or will be, loaded on deck, unless the credit specifically authorises the acceptance of such a transport document.

However, banks will not refuse a transport document which contains a general provision that at the discretion of the master of the ship goods may be carried on deck, provided that the transport document does not specifically state that the goods in question are, or will be, loaded in that manner.

Clean Transport Documents
A clean transport document is one which bears no superimposed clause or notation which expressly declares a defective condition of the goods and/or the packing thereof.

Such clauses could be the following or similar:-
- second hand packages
- three drums leaking
- two cartons torn, contents exposed
- two cases marks obliterated
- etc, etc

Banks will refuse to accept transport documents bearing such clauses or notations unless the credit expressly stipulates the clauses or notations which may be accepted.

A high proportion of credits incorporate in the context of the required transport documents that they shall be "clean on board". Occasions occur when banks will demand the superimposition on a bill of lading of a stamp which specifically incorporates these three words. This is, however, not necessary provided that the transport document is "clean" as defined above and also complies with the requirement for an "on board" document as explained.

5.15 INSURANCE DOCUMENTS
It will already be clearly understood that if under the terms of an INCOTERM involved in a transaction responsibility to take out insurance cover rests with the buyer, then the buyer's application for the issue of a letter of credit will simply state "No insurance documents are required to accompany drafts drawn under this credit", - or words to a like effect.

Insurance documents become an essential ingredient in the documentation to be submitted under a credit when it is the seller's responsibility to provide the marine and any other insurance cover necessary in relation to the transaction. The two INCOTERMS where this is stipulated are CIF and CIP. Under all other INCOTERMS the responsibility to arrange suitable insurance cover rests with the buyer.

Insurance Documents
The insurance documents must be as stipulated in the credit and must be issued and/or signed by insurance companies or underwriters, or their appointed agents. Cover notes issued by brokers will not be accepted, unless specifically authorised by the credit.

Date of Commencement of Insurance Cover
Unless the credit stipulates otherwise, or unless it is self-evident from the insurance document itself that the cover is effective at the latest from the date of loading on board or dispatch or taking in charge of the goods by the carrier, banks will reject insurance documents presented which bear a date later.

Insured Value
If the credit stipulates a value for the purpose of the insurance cover then the insurance document must show that insured value.

If the value for insurance purposes is not stipulated in the credit then banks will require the insurance document to cover a value at least equivalent to the CIF or CIP value, as the case may be, plus 10%. However, if banks cannot determine the precise CIF or CIP value case may be, from the documents on their face, they will accept as such the amount for which the credit has been issued, or the amount of the commercial invoice covering the underlying goods, whichever is the greater. In addition, and unless the credit stipulates otherwise, the insurance document must be expressed in the same currency as the credit.

Risks Covered

Applicants should ensure that their applications for the issue of letters of credit stipulate the type of insurance required, and the precise additional risks which should also be covered - e.g. war, strikes, civil commotions, etc. Imprecise terms such as "usual risks" or "customary risks", should not be used. If they are used banks will accept insurance documents as presented without responsibility for any risks not being covered.

Failing the inclusion of specific stipulations in the credit, banks will accept insurance documents as presented, without responsibility for any risks not being covered.

"All Risks"
Where a credit stipulates insurance against "all risks", banks will accept an insurance document which contains an "all risks" notation or clause, whether or not bearing the heading "all risks", even if that insurance document indicates that certain risks are excluded, without responsibility on the part of the bank for risk(s) not being covered.

The effect of this ruling is to enable banks to accept insurance documents containing, or referring to, the A Clauses of the London Institute of Underwriters in which the relevant clause reads:-

This insurance covers all risks of loss, or damage to, the subject matter insured except as provided in Clauses 4, 5, 6 and 7.

Franchise or Excess
Banks will accept an insurance document which indicates that the cover is subject to a franchise or an excess, unless it is specifically stipulated in the credit that the insurance must be issued irrespective of percentage.

Commercial Invoice
Banks will only accept commercial invoices which are made out in the name of the applicant for the credit, unless a specific alternative stipulation is included in the credit.

Unless the credit stipulates otherwise, banks may reject commercial invoices issued for amounts in excess of the amount permitted by the credit.

Description of the Goods
The description of the goods in the commercial invoice must correspond precisely with the description in the credit.

However, provided that the commercial invoice incorporates the precise description in the credit, there will be no objection to the addition within the invoice of more precise descriptions of the varieties of goods involved provided that they are reasonably compatible with the description in the credit.

Thus, by way of illustration, the credit may call for the description "motor vehicle parts (or components)". This description must head the invoice but beneath it details of the precise parts or components may then be inserted such as spark plugs, water pumps,

219

clutch plates, etc. Part numbers for such parts or components may also be quoted within this more detailed description.

Furthermore, in all other documents - transport documents, insurance documents, packing list, etc - the goods may be described in detailed terms - again provided that those descriptions are not inconsistent with the descriptions in the credit.

Other Documents
If a credit calls for an attestation or certification of weight in the case of transport other than by sea, banks will accept a weight stamp or declaration of weight which appears to have been superimposed on the transport document by the carrier or his agent unless the credit specifically stipulates that the attestation or certification of weight must be by means of a separate document.

Quantity and Amount - Tolerances
The words "about," "circa" or similar expressions used in connection with the amount of the credit or the quantity or unit price stated in the credit will be construed as allowing a difference not exceeding 10% more or 10% less than the amount or the quantity or the unit price to which they refer.

Unless a credit stipulates that the quantity of the goods specified must not be exceeded or reduced, banks will permit a tolerance of 5% more or 5% less, even if partial shipments are not permitted, always provided that the amount of the payments under the credit do not in total exceed the amount of the credit.

This tolerance, however, will not apply when the credit stipulates the quantity in terms of a stated number of packing units or of individual items.

Partial Drawings and/or Shipments
Partial drawings and/or partial shipments will be allowed by banks unless the credit stipulates otherwise.

Shipments by sea, or by more than one mode of transport but including carriage by sea, made on the same vessel and for the same voyage, will not be regarded as partial shipments, even if the transport documents indicating loading on board bear different dates of issue and/or indicate different ports of loading on board.

Shipments made by post will not be regarded as partial shipments if the post receipts or certificates of posting appear to have been stamped or otherwise authenticated in the place from which the credit stipulates the goods are to be dispatched, and on the same date.

Where shipments are made by modes of transport other than those referred to in the preceding two paragraphs, they will not be regarded as partial shipments provided the transport documents are issued by one and the same carrier and indicate the same date of issue, the same place of dispatch or taking in charge, and the same destination.

Drawings and/or Shipments by Instalments
If drawings and/or shipments by instalments within given periods are stipulated in the credit and any installment is not drawn and/or shipped within the period allowed for that installment, the credit ceases to be available for that and any subsequent instalments unless the credit itself stipulates otherwise.

Expiry Date and Presentation
All credits must stipulate an expiry date for the presentation of the documents for payment and presentation must be made on or before such date unless that date falls on a day on which the bank in question is closed for normal banking purposes - e.g. Sundays, official Public Holidays, and the like. Where this occurs the date for presentation of the documents shall be extended to the first following business day on which the bank in question is open. That bank must add to the documents its certificate that the documents were presented within the extended time limits provided in Article 48 (a) of the Uniform Customs and Practice for Documentary Credits, 1983, ICC publication number 600.

Latest Date for Shipment/Loading on Board/Dispatch/Taking in Charge
Under no circumstances will banks permit any extension beyond the date stipulated for any of these activities.

NB: A Forwarder will appreciate from the latest two paragraphs that every credit should incorporate two control dates - the first in chronological order being the date for shipment/dispatch, etc and the second in chronological order being the date for the presentation of the documents to the bank.

Forwarders involved in handling traffic moving in terms of letters of credit must endeavour so far as is within their power to ensure that their client can meet both those details.

Discussions of irrevocable documentary letters of credit are based on ICC UCP600.

REFERENCES
Bailey C. A. (2007) **"A Guide to Qualitative Field Research."** Pine Forge Press. California.

Bedi K. (2004) **"Production and Operations Management"**. Oxford University Press. New Delhi.

Bhattacharyya D. K. (2003) **"Research Methodology."** Excel Books. New Delhi.

Cook T. A. (2001) **"The Ultimate Guide to Export Management."** AMACOM. New York.

Daniels, Raudebaugh, Sullivan (2004) **"Globalisation and Business."** Prentice Hall International. New Delhi

Frazelle E.H. (2004) **"Supply Chain Strategy."** Tata McGraw-Hill Publishing Co. Ltd. New Delhi.

Gubbins E. J. (2003) **"Managing Transport Operations."** Kogan Page. London.

House D. J. (2005) **"Cargo Work"** Elsevier. Amsterdam

Kapoor S. K. and Kansal P. (2003) **"Marketing Logistics: A Supply Chain Approach."** Pearson Education. New Delhi.

Kirby M., Kidd W et al (1997) **"Sociology in Perspective"** Heinnemann Educational Publishers. Oxford.

Raina H. K. (1990) **"Guide to Import Management".** PRODEC. Helsinki

Rowland O.P. (1986) **"Imports and Exports: An Introductory Handbook."** Evans Brothers. Ltd. Nairobi

Silverman D. (2006) **"Interpreting Qualitative Data."** Sage Publications. London.

Sople V. V. (2004) **"Logistics Management: The Supply Chain Imperative."** Pearson Education. Singapore.

Thomas A. B. (2004**) "Research Skills for Management Studies."** Routledge, London

CHAPTER 6

CUSTOMS CLEARING PROCEDURES

6.1 INTRODUCTION

Although most enterprises offer both customs clearing and freight forwarding services
there is a clear demarcation between them. Customs clearing agents carry out the
following activities:-
- clear consignments through customs
- process import documentation
- inspects cargo
- move cargo to importer's premises

On the other hand freight forwarders carry out the following activities:-
- traffic operations i.e. mode and carrier selection
- initiate or organise cross border shipment documentation
- cargo handling and movement at port of entry and destination
- advise shippers on freight cost, port charges, cost of documentation,
  cost of insurance, forwarding charges, documents and packaging   required
- space booking and transport document preparation
- banking documentation

These activities make it imperative for a freight forwarder to be knowledgeable about
basics of customs clearing procedures.

6.2 REPORTS ON ARRIVAL

The Customs and Excise Act (Chap. 23:02) section 24 makes it mandatory for any person
moving cargo into the country to make a report to customs irrespective of mode of
transport i.e. rail, road, air, postal parcels and couriers. The forwarder is compelled to
furnish a cargo manifest which is a declaration of all cargo conveyed in a transport
vessel. Failure to furnish the required declaration is an offence.

6.2.1 Appointment and Licensing of Transit Sheds, Bonded Railway   sidings and container depots

The forwarder should also familiarise himself with customs requirements for licensing of
premises as transit sheds, private sidings and container depots which can receive
unaccustomed goods. Various obligations are imposed on licenses by the Customs and
Excise Act, (Chap 23.02) and these should be weighed against benefits of such facilities.

6.3 IMPORTATION OF GOODS

This is covered by section 38 of the Customs and Excise Act Cap 23:02. Most imports
are declared on a Bill of entry form 21. Customs procedure codes have been adopted for
various end-use intentions stipulated in the ASYCUDA++ or ASYCUDDA WORLD
software. Some common regimes are:-
IM4   -   importation of goods for home use

IM5 - temporary importation of goods including importations under Inward Processing Rebate.
IM6 - re-importation of goods previously exported
IM7 - Entry of goods into bonded warehouses.
IM8 - Removal in Bond or Removal in Transit

These procedures determine whether goods can be entered at the first port of entry or they can be removed in bond to an inland controlling port.

Private importations are declared on a form 47. A form 49 is issued where customs duty, surtax and VAT has been paid. A form 50 is completed where no duty is payable. For postal and courier parcels a declaration on the parcel slip is acceptable for customs processing. Duty free parcels are endorsed Passed By Customs (PBC) using a stamp and handed back to courier or postal officials. Where duties and taxes are due they are calculated and entered on a Charged Parcel Docket for postal articles. Bills of entry or other manual forms are used where certain rebates are being claimed.

6.3.1 Imports by Travelers
Travelers must declare goods in their possession, produce them for examination if required and pay duties due. Red and Green route system speeds up and simplify handling of travelers at airports and busy ports. The green route is used by travelers not carrying dutiable or restricted goods. The red route is used by travelers carrying dutiable or restricted goods. Customs officers conduct spot checks in the Green route to verify declarations. Examination of traveler's effects must be carried out in reasonably private conditions. Flat rates of assessment as stipulated in the customs tariff are normally used to charge duties and taxes except where the importer request use of actual tariff heading.

Receipts **must** be given for any goods detained or seized by customs. The goods held attract storage charges and those which remain uncleared for three months will be disposed of by rummage sale.

6.3.2 Temporary Importations
Most temporary importations are limited to one year. The following goods may be admitted under a temporary importation privilege.
(a) Goods being imported for repair and return
(b) Display material for shows, exhibitions and demonstration purposes
(c) Contractor's plant
(d) Traveler's samples
(e) Visitor's aircraft, motor vehicle, cameras, etc.

NB: Customs reserve the right to call for temporary deposits or guarantees for temporary importations.

6.3.3 Customs Transit
Efficient customs transit system is of interest to the transporter because it minimises transit times for transport vessels. Customs transit is internationally regulated by GATT

Article V, The Revised Kyoto Convention (1999) and the Geneva Convention on Harmonisation of Frontier Control of Goods (1982). Transit procedures cover cross border vehicle regulations, visas for crews, insurance, police controls, infrastructure quality, quality of transport services, national trucking sector organisation, duty and tax security. Customs controls involve mandatory convoys, shipment sealing, efficient acquittals and duty and tax security.

A well designed transit scheme should achieve the following transporter benefits:-
☐ minimum customs interference for cross border cargo
☐ reduced delays and transit costs
☐ simplified and standardised documentation
☐ single customs guarantee

Both SADC and COMESA have launched customs transit schemes. Most regional customs transit schemes are largely ignored by traders who elect not to utilise them due to excessive implementation demands.

6.4 BILL OF ENTRY PROCESSING
The Bill of entry form 21 which is the most common declaration for imports is processed using the ASYCUDA++ or ASYCUDA WORLD computer package. This package incorporates a selectivity module known as MODSEL. The module maintains risk profiles for importers and agents as captured by customs officials. This will enable a particular declaration to be channeled into a Red Route for physical examination, Yellow Route for document check or Green Route for release of the shipment. This facilitates trade by concentrating customs scrutiny on high risk importers and facilitation on low risk importers. The other ASYCUDA++ modules are:-

MODCBR	-	Customs bills of entry processing module
MODBRK	-	Customs broker module
MODACC	-	Accounting module
MODCAR	-	Manifest module
MODCHQ	-	Statistics compilation module

Forwarders are expected to familiarise themselves with activities performed in each of the modules.

6.5 CUSTOMS TARIFF
The Harmonized Commodity Description and Coding System (HS) came into force in 1988 following extensive work by the Economic Community for Europe, the Customs Cooperation Council and the International Chamber of Commerce. The HS provides:-
(a)   systematic classification of goods according to the same principles
(b)   uniform classification of goods in all countries
(c)   common classification language for experts and the public
(d)   common understanding of goods meant in international agreements
(e)   possibility for data comparison in international trade

Goods classification depends on material they consist of, their purpose and the manner in which they are used.

The customs tariff sets out the rates of duty levied on imported goods except goods qualifying for preference. For private importations flat rates of assessment as stipulated in the customs tariff are used.

6.6 CUSTOMS RUMMAGE SALES
These are public auctions of uncleared and forfeited goods. Uncleared goods are sold after three months. Rummage sales are conducted by a contracted public auctioneer. Customs must publish a notice of the sale of uncleared goods in newspapers and the government gazette one month before the sale. Arms and ammunition are only released to successful bidders on production of licenses and permits. Dangerous and perishable goods can be disposed of immediately dispensing with the need for a rummage sale.

6.7 IMPORT AND EXPORT CONTROLS
Controls are carried out by customs on behalf of other government departments like Board of Censors, Ministry of Agriculture, Reserve Bank of Zimbabwe, Parks and Wildlife Authority, Ministry of Health and Child Welfare, Department of Veterinary Services, National Museums and Monuments, etc.

6.7.1 Reasons for Controls
☐ ensure established industry in Zimbabwe is not threatened
☐ important flora and fauna are conserved
☐ narcotics/habit forming drugs are not allowed into international trade except under specified conditions
☐ arms and ammunition are moved across the border with the express permission of relevant authorities
☐ export proceeds are accounted for to the RBZ
☐ safeguarding public, interest, health and safety

6.7.2 Prohibited Importations
☐ flick knives, gravity knives and lock knives
☐ base, counterfeit or forged coins or currency
☐ obscene, indecent or objectionable goods
☐ goods which might deprive the morals of the inhabitants of Zimbabwe
☐ prison made or penitentiary made goods
☐ spirituous beverages containing preparations, extracts or essences or chemical products which are noxious or injurious.

6.7.3 Restricted Importations
☐ radioactive and associated materials
☐ nuclear reactors
☐ military, air force of police uniforms
☐ gold
☐ radio transmitting stations

- firearms and ammunition
- explosives
- animals and agricultural products
- monuments

6.8 POWERS OF OFFICERS
A forwarder has to be familiar with the following powers of officers stipulated in the Customs and Excise Act Cap 23:02
(a)   stationing of officers on ships or trains
(b)   officers to travel free when on duty
(c)   powers of officers in relation to ships, aircraft or vehicles
(d)   sealing of goods on ships, aircraft or vehicles
(e)   taking of samples
(f)   opening of packages
(g)   opening of postal articles
(h)   arrest of offenders by proper officers

Excesses of some customs officials need to be checked by knowledgeable freight forwarders to safeguard shipments.

6.9 MODERN CUSTOMS MANAGEMENT PRACTICES
A forwarder needs to be familiar with some best practices being adopted by world-class customs administrations to improve the often conflicting objectives of trade and travel facilitation and safeguarding of revenue and controls. Some of the practices are enumerated below:-

6.9.1 Self assessment
In this practice an importer computes and establishes his own duty and tax liability and proceeds to pay it to customs. Customs will only verify the assessment. The practice speeds up clearance.

6.9.2 Clearance on minimum information
In this aspect the customs authority requests only the information that is necessary for clearance of the goods and avoids unnecessary demands on traders. In some cases documentary requirements may be dispensed with.
6.9.3 Deferred payment of revenues
The practice allows importers to take delivery of goods and pay duties and taxes at a later stage for cash flow reasons. In some case payments can be done in instalments.

6.9.4 Intelligent-led and targeted risk management
- customs uses trader's historical data to identify high risk shipments through intelligence-led back office activities
- selectivity mechanism targets and selects shipments for scrutiny by physical examination or document check
- low risk shipments are released with minimal scrutiny

☐   it sucks in feedback from post risk control and system based audit strategies to
       update profiles.

Risk criteria include origin of goods, trader track record, type of goods, trade patterns,
misclassification, incentives and shipment value.

NB: ASYCUDA incorporates a selectivity module known as MODSEL to
       execute this practice.

6.9.5 Post clearance audit regimes
☐   Cargo movement is facilitated at the border posts and airports and   teams
of customs officials make verification follow ups at trader's premises
☐   Audits examine a trader's entire international trading pattern including foreign
       exchange movement
☐   Audits target customs interest aspects such as valuation verification,
       fiscal evasion, smuggling and customs fraud which cannot be detected
       through examination of individual customs declarations.

REFERENCES
Bailey C. A. (2007) **"A Guide to Qualitative Field Research."** Pine Forge Press.
California.

Bedi K. (2004) **"Production and Operations Management"**. Oxford University Press.
New Delhi.

Bhattacharyya D. K. (2003) **"Research Methodology."** Excel Books. New Delhi.

Cook T. A. (2001) **"The Ultimate Guide to Export Management."** AMACOM. New
York.

Daniels, Raudebaugh, Sullivan (2004) **"Globalisation and Business."** Prentice Hall
International. New Delhi

Frazelle E.H. (2004) **"Supply Chain Strategy."** Tata McGraw-Hill Publishing Co. Ltd.
New Delhi.

Gubbins E. J. (2003) **"Managing Transport Operations."** Kogan Page. London.

House D. J. (2005) **"Cargo Work"** Elsevier. Amsterdam

Kapoor S. K. and Kansal P. (2003) **"Marketing Logistics: A Supply Chain
Approach."** Pearson Education. New Delhi.

Kirby M., Kidd W et al (1997) **"Sociology in Perspective"** Heinnemann Educational
Publishers. Oxford.

Raina H. K. (1990) **"Guide to Import Management".** PRODEC. Helsinki

Rowland O.P. (1986) **"Imports and Exports: An Introductory Handbook."** Evans Brothers. Ltd. Nairobi

Silverman D. (2006) **"Interpreting Qualitative Data."** Sage Publications. London.

Sople V. V. (2004) **"Logistics Management: The Supply Chain Imperative."** Pearson Education. Singapore.

Thomas A. B. (2004) **"Research Skills for Management Studies."** Routledge, London

CHAPTER 7

INTERNATIONAL BUSINESS RESEARCH

7.1 BUSINESS RESEARCH METHODS - GENERAL
"... we define research as the process of obtaining and analysing data in order to answer questions, solve problems or test hypothesis and so contribute to our understanding and knowledge of the world."
Thomas A. B. (2004:3).

Bhattacharyya D. K. (2003) identify areas of business research interest as innovation and creativity, six-sigma practices, supply chain management, knowledge management, business process outsourcing, human resource outsourcing, customer relationship management, web marketing and financial re-engineering.

7.2 THE RESEARCH PROPOSAL

Research begins with a proposal outlining:-
☐   proposed title and researcher's name
☐   statement of the research problem
☐   brief background to the problem
☐   brief description of the research methods to use
☐   justification or possible outcomes of the research
☐   description of proposed reporting of research

7.2.1 Purpose of Research Proposal
☐   summarises major decisions and procedures in the research
☐   translates research question into a form amenable to research
☐   permanent frame of reference for researcher in the course of   conducting the study
☐   written agreement between researcher, supervisor(s) and institution which needs the research done.
☐   work plan for all parties involves in the study
☐   sets the minimum contribution of the inquiry

NB: The proposal is the framework that guides the research

7.2.2 Structure of Research Reports and Policy Publications
(i)   Executive Summary (1 -2 pages)
(ii)   Introduction (aim of research and outline to research)
(iii)   Method (research process, techniques, measures, analysis)
(iv)   Results (in point form for easy reading)
(v)   Recommendations (state clearly and back up with data).

7.3 THE RESEARCH TOPIC

A good topic raises questions to which you would like to learn more about and is intellectually challenging with available sources of information, Thomas A. B. (2004). Topics can be generated from places, things, trends, technologies, people, history, controversies, jobs, habits, hobbies, disciplines, etc.

Topic checklist questions include:-
☐   does it raise a lot of questions I would want to know?
☐   do I have an idea about and strongly feel about it?
☐   can I find authoritative information to answer my questions?
☐   does it offer possibility for interviews? surveys? internet research?
☐   are there any other people researching the topic?

Silverman D. (2006) identified the following common student research problems emanating from topics:
☐   unworkable topics - too wide for ideal depth
☐   under-theorised topics/over-theorised topics
☐   too many data
☐   inaccessible data
☐   inappropriate data collection methods
☐   too many data collection methods

7.4 PROBLEM BACKGROUND AND STATEMENT
"Background tells us what exists, how to understand it and how to study it." Thomas A. B. (2004).

☐   brief profile of organisation emphasizing departments and sections. Also covers background to the topic of study.
☐   events preceding current problem
☐   major factors or players in the problem to be researched
☐   symptoms of the problem and possible problem causes
☐   assumptions under which problem is to be researched
☐   anticipate solutions of the problem

7.5 RESEARCH OBJECTIVES
Objectives show what the study seeks to investigate. Normally up to five objectives can be pursued. The objectives should be conducted at the end of the research in chapter five i.e. at the conclusion of research.

7.6 STATEMENT OF HYPOTHESES
These are researcher's assumed answers to research questions and objectives. The hypothesis will be confirmed or rejected in chapter five.

7.7 ASSUMPTIONS
They are expressions of what researcher feels about conditions under which research was conducted and what is anticipated to prevail during research.

7.8 SCOPE OF THE STUDY
Sets parameter of research work. This can be the specific time, location and activity/department.

7.9 SIGNIFICANCE OF THE RESEARCH
Brings out anticipated benefits of the research to the researcher, organisation, industry or public at large. The researcher should specify the academic gap and contribution to be filled by the research. A page or less will suffice. Researcher should describe why topic was chosen and indicate what is known about the topic i.e. statistics, extend of the problem, people and institutions involved, key schools of thought, common misconceptions, observation made by researcher, important trends, controversies, etc. (Thomas A. B. (2004)).

7.10 LIMITATIONS OF THE STUDY
Major short comings encountered when conducting research. It is normally related to methodology.

7.11 DEFINITION OF MAJOR TERMS
Define terms from research topic, research question, hypotheses or any others in the final report whose meaning may not be derived from contextual meaning.

7.12 LITERATURE REVIEW
"... a theory is a set of interrelated constructs (concepts), definitions and propositions that present a systematic view of phenomena by specifying relations among variables with the purpose of explaining and predicting the phenomena." Thomas A. B. (2004:16).

Theory provides the guiding structure for data collection and analysis. Theories are important for selecting a topic, creating goals, developing research questions and collecting, analysing and interpreting data. Evaluation research can be conducted without theory, Bailey C. A. (2007)

Literature review can be in any of the following types:-
- □ historical i.e. break it down into stages of development.
- □ thematic i.e. debates between different schools/themes/perspectives
- □ theoretical i.e. relationship between theory and empirical evidence
- □ empirical i.e. summary of empirical findings focusing on methodologies.

Readers look for the following aspects:-
- □ most important, striking thing said by researcher
- □ surprising views and views remembered most
- □ most convincing and least convincing ideas
- □ impact on reader's thinking and feeling
- □ how it compares with others read
- □ other suggested research possibilities

7.13 RESEARCH METHODOLOGY

"Methodology indicates approach used and why as well as description of procedures used. It also describes instruments, sampling strategy, data collection procedures and analysis used." Thomas A. B. (2004).

Kirby M. et al (1997) acknowledge the following influences on choice of research method:-

☐ publishers of the research who may be facing time limits.
☐ organisational constraints on objects of study
☐ current state of knowledge i.e. what is regarded as appropriate
☐ nature of subject matter
☐ practical constraints i.e. time and money available
☐ theoretical perspective i.e. attitude to the subject
☐ academic community and funding by institutions

Research design is influenced by:-
☐ purpose of the research
☐ theoretical paradigms informing the research
☐ research context or situation
☐ research techniques to collect or analyse data

Table 7.1 below shows research designs and the corresponding methods.

Exploratory Studies	Descriptive Studies	Casual Studies
Literature search experiments	Surveys	True
Experience Survey	Observation	Quasi-experiments
Focus group discussions	Case Studies	
	Depth interviews	

Table 7.1 Research designs and methods

Surveys aim to produce generalisations about populations by collecting information from samples. Survey research methods include various sampling designs and techniques, the use of interviews and self completed questionnaires and mainly quantitative analyses.

Case study examines a single instance of some broader class of phenomena in order to generate a rich and complex understanding of it. Case study engages in a wide range of methods such as interviews, questionnaires, observation and analysis of documentary records.

Action research is undertaken on immediate live problems in a series of steps that involve diagnosing problems, implementing solutions and assessing their efforts.

Triangulation is the combination of methodologies in the study of the same phenomenon. Methodological triangulation is the use of different methods of obtaining data; data triangulation covers sampling data at different times in different places, from different people; investigator triangulation uses multiple observers and investigators; theory triangulation uses different theories.

NB: These descriptions are acknowledged from Thomas A. B. (2004).

7.13.1 Target Population
These are all objects or people from whom data was collected.

7.13.2 Sampling Techniques
Researcher should specify sampling method and justify choice of method. Indicate characteristics of required sample and justify. Stipulate sample size and how it will be determined. Sample size depends on purpose of research, research questions, number of participants available, time and resources available.

7.13.3 Research Instruments
Researcher must justify the choice of a particular research instrument e.g. interviews, questionnaires, observation, experiment, etc.

7.13.4 Data Presentation and Research Findings
It involves use of statistical tools like tables, frequency distributions, tallying, and graphs. Research questions or questionnaire can be shown sequentially. Research should interpret the data.

7.14 CONCLUSIONS AND RECOMMENDATIONS
Conclude objectives and recommend solutions based on the data and literature reviewed.

7.15 REFERENCES
Institutions who commission research choose method of referencing to be used. The following method may be used.

(i)   Books
Author (year) "Title" editors/translators, edition (if not first), number of volume and total number of volumes, series name, publisher, city of publication.

(ii)   Journals
Author, article title, title of journal, volume number, issue number or month, year of publication, starting and ending page numbers.

7.16 ACADEMIC RESEARCH PRESENTATION

7.17 COUNTRY ANALYSIS
For competent advisory services a forwarder may need to research a source or destination country on the following factors by Rowland O.P. (1986:12):-
☐   Political stability
☐   State of the economy (Foreign Aid, Foreign Investment, etc)
☐   Marketing Channels (parastatals, agents, distributions, corporations)

- ☐ Methods of payment
- ☐ Import regulations (licenses, prohibited items, etc)
- ☐ Freight routes and rates (speed, reliability, container terminals, ports, shipping agents)
- ☐ Documentation (customs regulations, LC requirements)
- ☐ Inland transportation (road, rail, border crossing points)
- ☐ Communication networks
- ☐ Rates of exchange
- ☐ Insurance cover (origin of cover, clauses, premiums, etc)
- ☐ Climate (for some products)
- ☐ Packaging (form of packaging, weights and measures, labeling)
- ☐ Language (official and national)
- ☐ Competition
- ☐ Business visits (market survey, personal contacts with clients, economic and social conditions of host)

Daniels et al (2004) envisage country analysis as incorporating:-

- ☐ political, institutional, ideological, physical and international environment
- ☐ economic performance indicators i.e. GNP, per capita GNP, GNP growth, domestic and foreign investment, international trade, income distribution, etc.
- ☐ foreign and defence policy
- ☐ fiscal and monetary policy
- ☐ foreign trade and investment policy
- ☐ industrial policy
- ☐ role of government in business i.e. promotion of market place competition, market place regulation and public - private partnerships.

Thomas A. B. (2004) provides a number of logical questions that can be asked in policy analysis. The questions are:-

- ☐ who initiated the policy and why?
- ☐ what does the policy do?
- ☐ what is the desired impact?
- ☐ what are the benefits, who will benefit and who will lose?
- ☐ can the policy be implemented?
- ☐ who will implement the policy?
- ☐ are systems in place to implement the policy and are the skills required available?
- ☐ what are the costs of the policy and who will bear them?
- ☐ are the costs sustainable?

7.18   COMPLEXITY OF GLOBAL LOGISTICS RESEARCH

"Global logistics is much more complex than domestic logistics, due to the multiplicity of handoffs, players, languages, documents, currencies, time zones and cultures that are inherent to international business."
Frazelle E. (2004:10-11).

The quote calls upon the forwarder to be knowledgeable in global affairs to be able to lobby and influence government logistics policy areas like customs formality rationalisation, port privatisation, road and rail infrastructure improvement, modern warehouse facility creation for scale economies and creation of cold chain infrastructure (Sople v.v. (2004)).

In a business sense a forwarder needs to develop global management skills in areas of global strategic skills, change and transition management, cultural diversity management, flexibility, teamwork, communication, knowledge transfer, human resource selection, training and repatriation.

In least developed and developing countries forwarders may also be required to advise governments on Foreign Direct Investment (FDI) by multinational corporations. This calls upon forwarders to research and advise on benefits of FDI which may be:-
☐   source of extra capital
☐   contribution to healthy BOP
☐   increase in productivity
☐   employment creation
☐   effective competition and rational production
☐   technology transfer and source of managerial know-how

The forwarder also needs to investigate presence of unfair MNC practices like:-
☐   inappropriate production technology or product mix
☐   surplus extraction of resources for transfer pricing or excessive royalty payments.
☐   predatory behaviour or manipulation of consumer preferences
☐   manipulation of overall national policy through political influence
☐   restructuring of imports and exports of the subsidiaries

These issues call for thorough research on the part of the forwarder.

7.19 SOURCES OF INFORMATION
Desired organisational information can be sourced from client company records, trade press, directories, computerised data bases, official commercial representatives, credit rating agencies, chambers of commerce and trade associations, commercial banks, specialised trade fairs and exhibitions and company reports and catalogues and the internet.

Research may target an international organisation on aspects like:-
☐   finance
☐   production capacity and facilities
☐   human resources
☐   environmental and ethical considerations
☐   information technology
☐   organisational structure
☐   quality and performance
☐   after-sales service facilities, etc

7.20 LOGISTICS PERFORMANCE GAP ANALYSIS

It is a formal way to assess logistical performance relative to world-class standards, industry norms, competitors and or internal organisation bringing together indicators in cost, productivity, quality and cycle time.

Its benefits includes:-
☐   identification of logistics strengths and weaknesses in audits
☐   benchmarking of performance against internal and external   organisation
☐   selection from among competing supplier proposals
☐   justification of logistics projects

7.20.1 Logistics Activity Profiling

It is a systematic analysis of item and order activity designed to identify root causes of material and information flow problems, pin-point opportunities for process improvement and provide basis for decision making (Frazelle E. H. (2004)).

It needs to be conducted on each logistics activity resulting in:-
☐   customer activity profile (CAP)
☐   inventory activity profile (IAP)
☐   supply activity profile (TAP)
☐   warehouse activity profile (WAP)

7.21 LOGISTICS MEASURES

7.21.1 Financial

(i)   logistics expenses-labour, telecommunications, freight, fuel, third- party fees, rentals
(ii)   logistics asset value - value of assets deployed including inventory, facilities, transportation fleets, material handling systems,
(iii-v) logistics profit return on assets, asset turn over
(vi)   Total logistics cost = TRC+TIC+TSC+TTC+TWC
(vi)   Total response cost (TRC) = labour, telecommunications, space for personnel and systems for order processing.
       Total inventory cost (TIC) - inventory carrying cost, personnel, office space, systems employed.
       total supply cost (TSC) - labour, space, systems, telecommunications for planning, approving, executing and tracking orders.
       Total transportation cost (TTC) - fuelling, maintenance, fleet acquisition, staffing, freight bills
       Total warehousing cost (TWC) - labour, space material handling systems, information handling systems

7.21.2 Productivity

☐   workforce productivity - total orders shipped to number of full time equivalents

- customer response productivity - number of customer orders processed per person per hour
- inventory management productivity - number of SKUs planned per planner
- supply productivity - number of purchase orders per person per hour or number of SKUs managed per full time equivalent or dollar value managed per full time equivalent
- transportation productivity - delivered dollars, orders, weight or   volume
- warehouse operations productivity - material handling systems investment, material handling unit cost, systems capitalisation rate,   storage density

7.21.3 Cycle Time
Total logistics cycle time = order entry time + order processing time + [purchase order cycle time x (1 - OFR) + warehouse order cycle time + in transit time.

7.21.4 Quality
(i)   customer response quality - order entry accuracy order status communication accuracy, invoice accuracy
(ii)   inventory management quality - inventory availability/fill rate, forecast accuracy
- order fill rate is the ratio of number of orders completely satisfied without substitution or back order to number of orders requested.
- unit fill rate - ratio of total units shipped to total units requested
(iii)   supply quality - perfect purchase order percentage
(iv)   transportation quality - on time arrival percentage, damage percentage, claims free shipment percentage, kilometres between accidents
(v)   warehouse operations quality - inventory accuracy, picking accuracy, shipping accuracy, warehouse damage percentage.

NB: Order execution involves suppliers, manufacturers, wholesalers, inventory planners, carriers and third party logistics companies who all need to be coordinated.

A perfect order percentage is made up of an order perfectly entered, fillable (quantity and time), picked, packaged and labeled, shipped without damage, delivered (time and location), communicated (order status reports), billed with on-time payment and documented.

7.22 LOGISTICS CONSULTING AND PLANNING
Frazelle E. H. (2004) provides three steps for logistics master planning which follow:-

7.22.1 Step One - Investigate
- profile the current logistics activity
- measure the current logistics performance
- benchmark performance and practices against world-class standards

☐ Logistics benchmarking is the process of gathering and sharing quantitative logistics performance indicators and developing an improvement plan of action based on the assessment.
☐ Logistics performance gap analysis can be used to compare and benchmark performance of internal and/or external organisation
☐ Ideal benchmarking is done on logistically similar organisations i.e. with similar logistics profiles, approximately same number of SKUs, similar order profiles, similar success criteria and similar operating scales.

7.22.2 Step Two - Innovate
☐ simplify i.e. eliminate and combine work activities
☐ optimise i.e. use decision support system (DSS) to determine optimal resource requirements
☐ apply world-class practices considering setting and particular circumstances

7.22.3 Step Three - Implement
☐ systemize i.e. develop and document detailed procedures
☐ automate i.e. justify, select and implement appropriate systems
☐ humanise i.e. design, populate and develop organisational plans for human resources

7.23 CHARACTERISTICS OF WORLD-CLASS LOGISTICS ORGANISATIONS
☐ extensive use of logistics key performance and financial indicators
☐ supply chain integration
☐ use of integrated logistics information systems
☐ strategic use of logistics service and education providers
☐ sense of urgency to leapfrog to world-class status
☐ strategic use of third-party logistics providers
☐ human-friendly logistics via logistics ergonomics and green logistics

NB: Ergonomics or workplace logistics is the flow of material at a single work station

☐ order and discipline
☐ justifiable use of automated storage and handling systems
☐ excellent land and building utilisation

Some World-Wide Logistics Conditions and Solutions

Area	Conditions	Solutions
1. North America	Short-term focus on shareholder return and return on capital	Extensive logistics finance and performance measures
	Excellent infrastructure	Supply chain integration

240

		and logistics information systems to reduce capital assets
2. Latin America	Limited logistics infrastructure and/or service providers	Leapfrog to world-class status Import logistics service providers and education
3. Western Europe	Transportation heritage Individual rights	High security designs Transportation heritage makes 3PL providers common place Focus on individual rights yields human-friendly logistics via ergonomics and green logistics
4. Japan	Lack of land and/or human resources and high logistics transaction requirements	Logistics culture of discipline and order Automated storage and handling systems Multistorey logistics facilities

7.24 CLIENT SELECTION

There is a very natural temptation for any forwarder who is approached by an international trader with the offer of business to grasp that offer with both hands without sufficient investigation of the credit worthiness of the organisation in question, nor of their track record for prompt and consistent payment of accounts.

This temptation must be resisted.
An offer of business from an organisation who desires to become a client is always suspect, and although it should be treated with great courtesy and diplomacy, it should never be accepted without a circumspect investigation of the potential client's track record and current creditworthiness.

This is not to say that an organisation offering business to forwarder is necessarily a bad risk. Such an organisation may indeed have a good payment record and be a good risk and may be desirous of making a change for the single reason of dissatisfaction with the service being provided by its present forwarder. It will, however, be important that before acceptance of the business the same checks are made just as if this explanation was not given. In fact, under such circumstances it may be well for a director of the forwarder being offered the business to visit the potential client to assess for himself the desirability of accepting the business.

There are a number of methods available by which the status of an organisation may be judged.

A request for a balance sheet may be willingly complied with - the inference to be drawn being that the organisation has nothing to hide. If, on the other hand, the request for a balance sheet is questioned then that in itself should sound alarm bells. In practice, however, privately owned companies are normally very reluctant to divulge balance sheet information.

In every instance the forwarder must ask that the organisation in question signs a credit application form into which the forwarder's trading conditions are written. The credit application form should be prepared in duplicate so that a copy can be left with the organisation concerned. If the content of the credit application form or of the trading conditions is questioned then this again might be a cause for concern. On the other hand, it may simply indicate a healthy prudence on the part of the customer.

Status report are obtainable either from banks or from specialist credit bureaux. The problem with obtaining a credit report through a bank is that banks are invariably cautious with the result that they are reluctant to give either a high status response or a low one. The result of this is that bank reports are never very useful.

There are, however, a number of credit bureaux who make it their responsibility to maintain records over very wide ranges of organisations, inclusive of details concerning all court judgments filed against each of them. Such credit bureau also endeavour to maintain up to date records of each organisation by factual enquiry over the telephone with each one so that if a request for a status report is received a reasonably accurate reply can be given.

Such bureaux obviously charge a fee per report as well as a fixed retainer. The information which they can supply is usually of appreciably greater value than the information available from banks.

Of lesser value, but sometimes interesting, is a look around the offices and general environment of the organisation in question. Coupled to this should be a critical assessment of the conduct and responsiveness of the director(s) during the course of interview. An interview with a person who gives the impression of being under pressure of work, of having no time to answer questions carefully, who fails to ask their own (searching) questions concerning the activities and effectiveness of the forwarder, indicates a person who either is running a disorganised organisation or who has something to hide.

It must be remembered that a smooth, glossy and be flushy exterior does not necessarily mean a valuable potential client. Such appearances may sometimes be deceptive and therefore a full investigation should always be undertaken.

7.24.1 Payment Record

A rather more difficult problem concerns obtaining the track record of the prospective client with regard to his settlement of invoices.

Obviously, a client with a poor credit record is most unlikely to be a prompt payer of accounts.

However, it is not unusual to find an organisation with a very good credit report can also be a very slow payer. Such an organisation may well argue in the following fashion:-

"We have high cash liquidity: our resources are substantial: in fact, we are very nearly as good as gold. Why then are you troubling us for prompt payment? Why should you be concerned whether we pay at 30 days, 60 days, or even 90 days? You should not be worried - you will get paid."

A client who adopts this attitude can sometimes do more damage to the fortunes of a forwarder than one whose credit standing is not as brilliant but who understands at least the importance both to him and to his forwarder of the maintenance of smooth consistent cash flow.

Sometimes a difficult client such as the one described above may say "Ok charge us interest for the extra couple of months prior to our payment" - as if this will settle the matter to mutual satisfaction. Of course, it does no such thing.

Firstly, the interest charged may, in fact, never be paid and the forwarder will find that it is a waste of time attempting to sue for payment of interest.

Secondly, the interest, if paid, will only be paid when the principal amount is finally paid.

Thirdly, in the interim the forwarder's cash flow from that organisation will be nil - which has a very deleterious effect upon his available working capital, while he himself is obliged to pay interest to his bankers on his overdraft facility.

The only conclusion which can be drawn from these considerations is that from the very outset of a business' relationship with any organisation the point must be made very clearly that the organisation is expected to comply strictly with the payment terms agreed, and that he agrees that summary judgment taken in a magistrates court will be binding irrespective of the amount of the indebtedness sued for.

REFERENCES
Bailey C. A. (2007) **"A Guide to Qualitative Field Research."** Pine Forge Press. California.

Bedi K. (2004) **"Production and Operations Management"**. Oxford University Press. New Delhi.

Bhattacharyya D. K. (2003) **"Research Methodology."** Excel Books. New Delhi.

Cook T. A. (2001) **"The Ultimate Guide to Export Management."** AMACOM. New York.

Daniels, Raudebaugh, Sullivan (2004) **"Globalisation and Business."** Prentice Hall International. New Delhi

Frazelle E.H. (2004) **"Supply Chain Strategy."** Tata McGraw-Hill Publishing Co. Ltd. New Delhi.

Gubbins E. J. (2003) **"Managing Transport Operations."** Kogan Page. London.

House D. J. (2005) **"Cargo Work"** Elsevier. Amsterdam

Kapoor S. K. and Kansal P. (2003) **"Marketing Logistics: A Supply Chain Approach."** Pearson Education. New Delhi.

Kirby M., Kidd W et al (1997) **"Sociology in Perspective"** Heinnemann Educational Publishers. Oxford.

Raina H. K. (1990) **"Guide to Import Management"**. PRODEC. Helsinki

Rowland O.P. (1986) **"Imports and Exports: An Introductory Handbook."** Evans Brothers. Ltd. Nairobi

Silverman D. (2006) **"Interpreting Qualitative Data."** Sage Publications. London.

Sople V. V. (2004) **"Logistics Management: The Supply Chain Imperative."** Pearson Education. Singapore.

Thomas A. B. (2004) **"Research Skills for Management Studies."** Routledge, London

CHAPTER 8

FREIGHT FORWARDING LAW

8.1   PRINCIPLES OF COMMON LAW
Before we embark upon a study of the importance of trading conditions to the forwarder
it is necessary to set out certain principles of common law.

Common law develops not from legislation but from the decisions handed down in the
senior courts of each country.

Certain underlying principles of jurisprudence (i.e. the science or philosophy of human
law) can be broadly described as follows:

☐   Judgements given must be in accordance with society's deeply held conviction of
        natural justice.

☐   That decisions handed down by courts ought to be consistent one with another.
        That is to say, where the circumstances at issue are identical to those pertaining to
        a former decision, then the precedent set by the former decision should be
        followed in the latter instance.

☐   The effect of this is that over the years a decision given originally will form the
        precedent for all subsequent decisions provided the circumstances are the same,
        with the result that the original decision effectively has the force of law.

Trade in the form of buying and selling has been going on since time immemorial and
common law has developed which iN broad outline requires that if an **offer** to provide a
product or service is made from the first party to a second party, then if the second part
accepts that offer for an agreed consideration (price) then a contract is created which is
enforceable in the courts.

In common law, however, the contract so created must be absolutely fulfilled by both
parties. No amendment, adjustment or deviation from the contract is permissible except
with the prior agreement of both parties.

It must be obvious, however, that this common law situation is in many instances
unsuitable in the commercial world. It is frequently true that **circumstances entirely
outside the control of either party** may supervene rendering the common law contract
incapable of fulfillment either in part or totally.

The resolution of the problems and risks created by the concept of **absolute fulfillment** is
the inclusion of conditions in the basic contract which have the effect of qualifying the
absolute fulfilment required by the common law.

Thus, in the sale of many goods the manufacturer supplies a card setting out the warranties with regard to efficient performance which he gives but which, at the same time, excludes other circumstances for which he is not prepared to accept any liability.

In common law an organisation which contracts without conditions to carry a parcel of goods from point A to point B for a consideration (price) is responsible to perform the contract or carriage absolutely. Accordingly, he becomes totally responsible if any portion of that parcel is not delivered or is delivered in a damaged condition.

He is not permitted to plead in mitigation of his default that it was as a result of circumstances outside of his control, such as theft, pilferage, heavy weather, fire, earthquake, an act of government, or any other circumstance. Furthermore, in the event of any failure to perform he is responsible to **make good completely** the loss to the other party.

It is obvious that any transport contractor must seek by means of **trading conditions** to put limitations upon this absolute liability required by common law. He will seek to avoid responsibility for the consequences which may arise out of a delay in delivery, out of the necessity to deviate from the most direct route, from "acts of God", etc.

Those trading conditions must protect him not only from the errors and omissions of his own staff and operatives, but also from similar errors and omissions which may be perpetrated by his sub-contractors. Moreover, he must limit his own liability for claims to the liabilities admitted in the terms and conditions of his sub-contractors.

Over and above this he must limit his maximum liability in the event that he has to accept a claim, to an amount bearing a reasonable relationship to his average profit margins on work done.

8.2 COMMITTING A CLIENT TO A FORWARDERS TRADING CONDITIONS

The creation of the finest possible set of trading conditions serves no purpose whatsoever unless by one efficient means or another those trading conditions are incorporated into every contract into which a forwarder enters, and are also applicable with equal force to every service, advice, quotation, or consultation which the forwarder provides in his endeavours to assist his clients, whether the service, advice, quotation, or consultation takes place for payment or not.

The incorporation of a forwarder's trading conditions into his contracts, must, furthermore, be known to the other party involved, and in the event of a court case the forwarder must be able to produce evidence that his tradition conditions were so known.

An executive must study and thoroughly understand the trading conditions under which his organisation operates, and must know how to utilise them in defense of his organisation, and how to incorporate them into every contract to which he puts his name on behalf of his organisation.

NB: A forwarder always has a duty of care towards his client's goods and the client's interests from which he cannot exonerate himself.

Instances occasionally arise in the activities of a forwarder when the goods for which he has accepted responsibility may be subject to a common law requirement or a legislative enactment which requires him to take action outside his recognised functions, or which overrides one or more of his normal trading conditions, or which qualifies the manner in which he must perform his functions.

In such circumstances it is essential that the forwarder's trading conditions are not construed to have been waived or abandoned, nor that the forwarder is assuming any additional responsibility or liability.

When issues between a forwarder and his client come before the courts and those issues touch upon the forwarder's trading conditions there is always a tendency on the part of the courts to lean in favour of the party against whose interest the trading conditions operate. Provided evidence can be led to show conclusively that the client was aware of the trading conditions of his forwarder then the court must uphold those trading conditions - or had not sufficiently been drawn to them - then the tendency of the courts is to find in favour of the client.

There are a number of methods by which forwarders can draw the attention of their clients to the trading conditions:

☐ By printing the entire trading conditions legibly on the back of all their stationery, invoices, quotations, etc., and incorporating on the front of such stationery an invitation to recipients to scrutinise the trading conditions.

☐ A form of wording on the front of the stationery which would be suitable for this purpose would be

"All business is undertaken subject to the trading conditions which are reproduced on the reverse hereof"

☐ By regularly - at perhaps annual intervals - sending a copy of the trading conditions under cover of a letter addressed to the senior official of the client organisation who needs to acknowledge receipt of same.

This method is extremely useful since it serves to "update" every client with regard to the conditions under which the forwarder operates, at regular intervals. Directors, managing directors, company secretaries, and other senior personnel in client organisations tend to change from time to time and although it may not be absolutely essential that any new incumbent in such posts be separately advised of the trading conditions, it is always desirable.

247

☐   By incorporating a form of wording into a credit application form for signature by the applicant confirming that he has received, read and understood the forwarder's trading conditions, a copy of which is appended to the credit application form.

This method should invariably be adopted by any forwarder obtaining a new client.

It is always unwise to rely merely upon a form of wording on stationery or credit application forms which merely says:

"All business is handled on the basis of our standard trading conditions, a copy of which is available upon application."

On a number of occasions in the past courts have ruled against the application of the trading conditions where this type of wording is the only indication given to a client that trading conditions exist. Under such circumstances the courts have stressed that it is the responsibility of the forwarder to act in a manner which ensures that the trading conditions are brought fully to the client's attention.

It has been found in a recent court case that unless a client has signed a statement which specifically states that the client has read, understood and agreed to be bound by the forwarders' standard trading conditions, then the forwarder has little chance of having these upheld in court.

8.3 TRADING CONDITIONS - LIEN AND PLEDGE
Before relating the concepts of lien and pledge to the activities of a forwarder it is important that the student understands the meaning of these two terms.

8.3.1 Lien
The concept of lien arises out of common law. That is to say, it arises from decisions handed down by courts of law over many centuries without having been enshrined in any specific legislation. It must also be understood that the right of a party to a lien over goods will depend very much upon the circumstances of the situation in question. The definition of the concept given herein cannot therefore be more than a broad definition.

A **lien** is the right of one party to retain possession of property until a debt due in respect of it is discharged.

For a lien to subsist the party exercising the lien must have possession of the goods or documentation in question. In this context "possession" can be regarded as "having effective control of".

A party holding all three original signed bills of lading covering an imported shipment certainly has a lien upon the goods by virtue of holding the complete set of documents of title, but that lien is not so secure since the other party might be able to obtain release of the goods from the shipping company by virtue of the submission to the shipping company of the traditional bank guarantee.

248

A lien is therefore effective only so long as possession or effective control of the goods is maintained. If that possession or control is breached then the lien cannot be reinstated by any legal procedure or court order, it has disappeared. The existence and continuation of a lien on goods or property depends upon the de facto situation which must be maintained if the lien is to be effective.

8.3.2 Pledge
A pledge is a piece of property handed into the custody of a person or organisation as security for the fulfilment of a contractual obligation, the payment of a debt, etc, and is usually liable to forfeiture in the event of default.

The essence of a pledge is therefore that the thing or property pledged is voluntarily and willingly handed over as security.

The concept of the pledge has existed since time immemorial without legislative support. It has, however, been supported by courts and is therefore generally accepted as a valid procedure in common law. The value of a pledge only subsists for so long as the property pledged remains in the possession of the party to whom it was given. If, for any reason, it is removed from his possession then its value as a pledge is destroyed and cannot be reinstated.

8.3.3 Special and General Liens/Pledges
The vast majority of liens imposed, and of pledges given, are specific to a particular transaction. The watch repairer has a lien upon the watch until the cost of repairs is paid. The pawnbroker holds the watch in pledge until it is redeemed by settlement of the indebtedness. These are specific -or special - liens and pledges.

However, in certain commercial situations - and this is particularly important to the forwarding community - it is vital that liens and pledges shall be available and justifiable in a more general sense. That is to say, it is important that the lien imposed over a particular consignment of goods shall have effect not only to enforce payment of indebtedness **arising in connection with the transaction specific to those goods, but also in relation to indebtedness arising from other transactions.** In a similar fashion a pledge needs to be construed as security not only for one specific debt but for all other debts outstanding.

Liens imposed in these situations and pledges given are termed general liens or pledges.

The position of general liens or pledges in Zimbabwe are to some degree obscure. As stated above, many aspects of Zimbabwean common law have arisen through the precedent of Roman-Dutch law. Other aspects of Zimbabwean law have arisen from precedents arising from Anglo-Saxon Law.

Legal opinion is divided whether under Roman Dutch precedents general liens and pledges are accepted and will be upheld. The legal situation under Anglo-Saxon common law is clearer and legal opinion holds the view that where a precedent exists under Anglo-Saxon law and can be brought to the attention of the Zimbabwean court it would be supported by that court.

However, in 1979 in the Witwatersrand Division of the Supreme Court, a case (Danzas Trek v Du Bourg and Another) was heard in which it was held by the judge that, in terms of the relevant clause in the forwarder's trading conditions (as quoted below), the forwarder was entitled to a lien or pledge for any indebtedness whether it arose from the goods held by it or not; and furthermore, the lien or pledge would extend to all the goods held by the forwarder.

This case is of importance to all involved in forwarding.

8.3.4 Liens and Pledges Relative to the Forwarders

Because the position in common law is to a degree obscure, it is vital that the forwarder, by a clause in his trading conditions, insists that he has both a special and a general lien and pledge for all monies due to him. A clause which would provide for this would be worded as follows:

"All goods and documents relating to goods including bills of lading and import permits, as well as refunds, repayments, claims and other recoveries, shall be subject to a special and general lien and pledge either for monies due in respect of such goods or for other monies due to the company from the customer, sender, owner, consignee, importer or the holder of the bill of lading or their agents, if any. If any monies due to the company are not paid within fourteen days after notice has been given to the person from whom the monies are due that such goods or documents are being detained, they may be sold by auction or otherwise or in some other way disposed of for value at the sole discretion of the company and at the expense of such person, and the net proceeds applied in or towards satisfaction of such indebtedness."

8.4 EXCLUSION OF FORWARDER LIABILITY

It is rare for any forwarder to have or to obtain any visual and physical awareness of the goods or products in respect of which he undertakes his transactions. He is dependent for all such knowledge upon the information supplied to him by his client. He will be in no position to verify the accuracy of declarations made by the client in respect of the mass, the measurement, the quality, or other data relevant to the goods.

For all this information and for much other data he is dependent upon the information supplied by his client. Accordingly, he must divest himself of responsibility for all consequences arising from acts of or omissions of his client, incorrect or inaccurate declarations by the client, faulty or false information supplied by the client. He must also divest himself of responsibility for consequential losses, damages or expenses arising from such circumstances.

Furthermore, he must ensure that he is not held liable for the consequences of strikes, lockouts, other stoppages or restraints of labour.

The forwarder shall not be liable for:-

- [ ] any act or omission of the customer or agent of the customer with whom the company deals: and/or
- [ ] any loss, damage or expense arising from or in any way connected with the marking, labeling, numbering, non-delivery or misdelivery of any goods.
- [ ] any loss, damage or expense arising from or in any way connected with the mass, measurements, contents, quality, inherent vice, defect, or description of any goods.
- [ ] any loss, damage or expense arising from or in any way connected with any circumstance, cause or event beyond the reasonable control of the company, including but without limiting the generality of the aforesaid, strike, lock-out, stoppage or restraint of labour.
- [ ] damages arising from loss of market or attributable to delay in forwarding or in transit or failure to carry out any instructions given to the company.
- [ ] loss or non-delivery of any separate package forming part of a consignment or for loss from a package or an unpacked consignment or for damage or misdelivery, however caused, unless notice be received in writing within 5 (five) days after the end of the transit where the transit ends in Zimbabwe, or within 14 (fourteen) days after the end of the transit where the transit ends at any place outside Zimbabwe."

8.5 TRADING CONDITIONS: LIMITATION OF FORWARDER'S LIABILITY

Despite all the protection which a forwarder can achieve by means of his trading conditions, circumstances will still occur when he is liable in terms of a claim from a client.

It then becomes imperative that the forwarder, through the medium of his trading conditions, defines his maximum liability. If he does not do so, and the claim which he cannot avoid is for the value of the goods, he could become liable for a sum which could eliminate his total profitability for a year, or even five years. In other words, he would be forced into bankruptcy.

The reason for this is obvious. The forwarder in the course of his normal business organises the transportation of vast quantities of cargo with massive values involved. In the process of his business, however, his profit margins are strictly limited and, when compared with the value of the cargo which he may be handling, is almost infinitesimal. Accordingly, a limitation of the ability he is prepared to accept is absolutely essential to his survival.

Should, however, a client require a forwarder to **increase his maximum limit of liability,** and should the forwarder **agree to do so,** then it become essential that the forwarder takes out specific insurance against the maximum, liability which he assumes and it must be a prerequisite of the arrangement between him and his client that **the client pays the full cost of that insurance.** By this means, the client obtains the right to claim up to the agreed maximum while the **forwarder suffers no damage in his business.**

Where a forwarder is liable to the customer, its trading conditions can limit liability to the least of the following amount.

☐ the value of the goods evidenced by the relevant documentation or declared by the customer for customs purposes or for any purpose connected with their transportation;

☐ the value of the goods declared for insurance purposes;

☐ double the amount of the fees raised by the company for its services in connection with the goods, but excluding any amounts payable to sub-contractors, agents and third parties.

8.6 SHIPPING DISPUTE RESOLUTION: GOVERNING LAW AND ` JURISDICTION

Having in mind the fact that forwarders deal essentially with goods in the course of international trade between independent countries, and that each of those countries has its own national laws and its legal processes, it is essential that a forwarder in Zimbabwe insists by means of its trading conditions that all litigation arising, whether in terms of trading conditions or other agreements between the forwarder and its clients, shall be governed and construed in accordance with the laws of Zimbabwe and furthermore that legal actions or proceedings arising are handled within the appropriate division of the Supreme Court of Zimbabwe.

The effect of this does not inhibit on the part of any client its access to litigation (should it so desire) if the client is in Zimbabwe. If, however, the client is overseas then he must bring his dispute and his course of action to Zimbabwe in order to pursue it.

This being accomplished, the forwarder's profits will follow and his survival will be assured.

8.7 PRINCIPAL-AGENT RELATIONSHIPS

The relationships between a forwarder and his clients are many faceted. Certain of these are contractual, and these are of vital importance: others are advisory and informative.

Where the function to be performed is the clearing of the goods through customs the forwarder always acts as an agent. There are a number of reasons why this is always true:-

☐ The forwarder will never have first hand, competent knowledge of the goods to be cleared. He may, from having handled previous consignments have knowledge which he may feel he can assume to be correct, but such knowledge is never first hand.

☐ Section 2 of the Customs and Excise Act (Chapter 23:02) makes provision within the definition of "importer" to include "the agent of any such person" who owns any goods imported. This clearly defines a clearing agent.

In the same Section of the Act, under the definition of "exporter" a similar form of wording is incorporated.

Section 217 (1) of the same Act recognises and controls the activities of clearing agents. Liabilities upon agents are imposed by Section 218 (i).

8.7.1 The Importance of the Agent's Mandate
It is clear that a forwarder when acting as an agent ought to have in his possession a comprehensive mandate from his principal to justify all his activities.

If he has such a mandate and he acts strictly within its terms then he is protected from any liabilities which may arise resulting from his actions. In addition, his trading conditions will reinforce his protection. If he departs from his mandate then he loses that protection and may become liable for the consequences which might arise from his failure to comply with its terms.

Circumstances may arise as a result of which he is compelled to depart from his mandate. In such circumstances it is very important that he has alternative means of protection and such means need to be provided by suitable clauses within his trading conditions. Nevertheless it is essential for the effectiveness of that alternative protection that the principal has been made aware of the terms of those trading conditions.

8.7.2 Actions of Agent Binding Upon Principal
It is important to realise that where a forwarder is acting as agent his activities will be binding upon his principal whenever he makes a declaration or enters into a contract.

Thus, a declaration on a customs bill of entry made by an agent is binding upon the principal and if it is proved to be incorrect then liability for the consequences falls jointly and severally upon both. This is the effect of Section 218 (2) of the Customs and Excise Act.

In a similar fashion, omissions by an agent create liabilities upon the principal. Thus, a failure properly to declare dangerous goods places very serious liabilities upon the cargo owner. Naturally, an agent responsible for such an omission may also find himself suffering under similar liabilities.

A forwarder acting as agent who cuts a bill of lading or an air waybill showing the principal as shipper is preparing a contract of carriage between his principal and the carrier which binds the principal to the terms and conditions appropriate to the document in question. This remains true even though the principal may never have seen the document or the terms and conditions upon it.

The fact that the forwarder as agent pays the seafreight, pays the dock charges, operates a ledger credit account with the airline or with NRZ or with a road carrier, does not alter the position.

8.7.3 Marine Insurance Cover

A number of special problems exist in the context of marine insurance when the cover is arranged by a forwarder.

Unless specific instructions are given to the forwarder by the principal, the forwarder cannot be expected to know the nature of the goods, their method of packing, their value requisite for insurance purposes, the extent of the risks which the importer requires to be covered, nor the duration of the transit over which the cover should subsist.

No marine insurance cover can be provided intelligently by a forwarder without all these details.

The forwarder may be instructed to take out unqualified all risk insurance but may be unable to find any underwriter in the market prepared to grant cover without imposing additional conditions or an excess to be borne by the cargo owner.

Circumstances may arise during the course of transit or consequent upon defection or inappropriate packing of the goods which cause the underwriter to reject a claim for loss or damage.

It is absolutely vital in all matters concerning insurance that the relationship between the forwarder and the principal is clearly defined as one of "agency'. It is further essential that the forwarder becomes only responsible to "use his best endeavours" to obtain the insurance cover desired by the principal - and that if he cannot do so, he does not himself assume any liability.

Moreover, in the event of a dispute concerning a claim lodged with the underwriter for loss or damage the forwarder has no contingent liability if the claim is eventually rejected.

To protect himself from becoming involved in all these matters a forwarder's trading conditions must always make it clear that:

☐   he will only arrange insurance upon express instructions given in writing and, in making insurance arrangements he is acting as agent only.

☐   that he will use his best endeavours to obtain the requisite cover but cannot be
      held responsible for any failure in this regard

☐   that he is not responsible in any manner whatsoever for the rejection of an
      insurance claim or a dispute thereon.

It is sound policy, and makes business sense, for a forwarder to endeavour where possible
to maintain the status of an agent in all dealings with his clients. There are circumstances
where this is not possible and these will be discussed later in the course.

By acting as an agent rather than as a contractual carrier, the forwarder minimises the
responsibilities and liabilities he assumes provided that he performs his functions within
the terms of the mandate given to him, or, if he has to deviate there from, he does so
within the justifications provided by his trading conditions.

8.7.4 Accounting Responsibilities of Forwarder as Agent
An organisation which is acting as an agent is under a common law responsibility to
disclose in full, and substantiate by vouchers, all disbursements which it makes on behalf
of the principal. It may not enhance those charges for its own benefit. It is, however,
entitled to raise a charge for the services it renders direct to the principal and also to raise
a fee as its remuneration for acting as the principal's agent.

Accordingly, a forwarder acting as agent is under an obligation to justify to its principal
the disbursement account shown on its invoices. Thus, it should present evidence of the
disbursements made in the context of:-

☐   duties, surcharges, etc
☐   provisional payments, etc
☐   air or ocean freight, etc
☐   airport or dock charges, etc
☐   railage or haulage charges, etc
☐   any others

It is however, fully entitled to negotiate satisfactory agency fees, fees for the preparation,
lodgement, and recovery of documentation, and to recover all communication costs,
charges for special attendance, and the like.

8.7.5 Discounts, Brokerages, and the like
Since the average forwarder may well put a sufficiency of business into the hands of its
sub-contractors to justify obtaining discounts, brokerages, and other similar concessions
which, in terms of common law, it ought to pass back to principal for whom it is acting, it
is customary for a clause to be inserted in trading conditions entitling it to retain all such
financial advantages.

255

This is not unreasonable since it is normally correct to say that it is because the forwarder controls volumes that he can obtain such discounts while the individual principal could not by himself obtain them.

8.7.6 Lump Sum Prices

Occasions arise when a forwarder may quote a lump sum price (probably duty and other customs charges excluded) for the completion of a transaction. If the principal accepts that lump sum price then the forwarder is no longer under any obligation to disclose his disbursements. Since his quotation has been properly accepted he becomes fully entitled to charge "as per quotation".

The quotation of a lump sum price and its acceptance by the principal must not of itself be the determining factor whether the transaction is to be arranged by the forwarder as agent for and on behalf of the customer or as a principal contractor. There must be other considerations specific to the transaction which must determine the relationship between the principal and the forwarder.

8.8 FORWARDER AS CONTRACTUAL CARRIER

It is always to the benefit of a forwarder to act as an agent than as a contractual carrier, but there are situations when the forwarder is forced to assume the responsibilities of a contractual carrier. These situations arise when a forwarder undertakes the function of a groupage operator in respect of seafreight, or a consolidator in respect of airfreight. In both these situations he must, of necessity, issue his own transport document which automatically becomes evidence of the contract between himself and his customer, the sender of the goods in question.

Other situations also occasionally arise when the forwarder is forced into the position of a contractual carrier but in every situation the effect upon the forwarder is the same.

Firstly, he must become party to a series of contracts with subcontractors who accomplish for his the various sectors of the transaction, while he himself must submit to a contract with his customer in which he accepts the responsibility upon his own shoulders for the total transportation involved.

Secondly, because the contract between his customer and himself is entirely separate from those contracts between himself and his subcontractors, he remains personally responsible if any of his subcontractors default in the performance of their sectors of the transportation.

8.8.1 Transport Documents

Except in certain special circumstances every contract of carriage must be evidenced by a transport document.

Every transport document must indicate clearly the two parties to the contract: the party offering the cargo for transportation (shipper/consignor/sender), and the party undertaking to perform the transportation (carrier).

The only exceptions to this rule occur when the carrier is also the owner of the goods. Obviously, there is no need for any contract of carriage when this is true since there is only a single party involved.

The contract of carriage is essential and a transport document evidencing the terms and conditions of that contract is vital.

The following are examples of transport documents:

- a railway goods consignment note/freight transit order
- a container terminal order
- an air way bill
- a road haulage consignment note
- a shipping company bill of lading
- a shipping company non-negotiable liner waybill
- a consolidator's air waybill
- a groupage agent's bill of lading

8.8.2 Contents of a Transport Document

To be efficient every transport document must incorporate the following information:

- name of the carrier
- name of the sender of the goods
- name of the consignee to whom the goods are to be delivered
- the place at which the carrier accepts the goods
- the place at which the carrier must deliver the goods
- the identifying marks, numbers, etc. or address labels placed upon the goods
- the number of packages, the nature of the packages, constituting the consignment
- a description of the contents of the packages
- the gross mass of the consignment and where abnormal masses are involved in any package(s), the mass of those packages
- the external dimensions of the packages or the total cube of the consignment
- a statement whether the sender or the consignee is to pay the transportation charges

In addition to the above transport documents must also, where appropriate, clearly state any peculiarities of the goods - hazardous nature, fragility, stowage requirements within the transport vehicle to be utilised, etc.

In the case of transportation by sea it is normal that the transport document indicates the name of the ship on which the goods are to be loaded and, in the case of airfreight, the flight number which will carry the goods. In addition to this for goods both by sea and by air, the date of dispatch of the carrying vehicle.

8.8.3 Preparation of the Transport Documents

It is standard practice for the carrier to pre-print his own official transport document upon which the sender must complete the appropriate details ready for submission of the transport document to the carrier.

By adding his official signature to the transport document the carrier thereby acknowledges receipt of the goods into his custody or onto the transport vehicle concerned. The carrier, in acknowledging receipt, may qualify his receipt to reflect the apparent outward condition of the packages he has received. If they are complete as regards the number of packages and all packages are in outward good order his receipt will be "clean". If, however, the quantity of packages he receives differs from the particulars prepared by the sender or if the packages show external signs of damage or discrepancy then he will issue a "qualified" receipt.

The effect of the issuing of a qualified receipt on a transport document will be discussed in detail elsewhere.

The forwarder carrying goods upon his own transport equipment

Where a forwarder undertakes the entire transportation of goods upon his own equipment he is the actual carrier - and must accept responsibilities and liabilities just as any other haulage contractor must do. It is fair to assume that he will have devised a special set of trading conditions specific to his haulage functions quite distinct from the trading conditions under which he acts as a forwarder.

8.8.4 Contracts between the Forwarder as Contractual Carrier and his Sub-Contractors

Sub-Contractors which the contractual carrier may have to employ for the completion of his own contract with his customer include:-

- a road hauler to collect the goods in question
- a railway authority to transport the goods to an appropriate depot
- either a container depot or the forwarder's own airfreight depot
- the container depot authority
- a road or rail authority to move a shipping container from the depot to a harbour container terminal
- the terminal authority responsible for placing the container on ship
- the ground handling staff of an airline
- an ocean carrier
- an airline
- on arrival overseas a similar set of organisations for the transfer of the goods in question to their main destination
- a degrouping or deconsolidating agent in the country of destination
- an organisation capable of performing final distribution to consignees

It is inevitable that the vast majority of these multifarious organisations will have their own trading conditions, maximum limits of liability for loss/damage, differing prescription periods within which advice of intention to claim must be lodged. A number of them will, of course, be domiciled in the same country as the forwarder but others will be domiciled in the country of destination, while others yet again may be domiciled in a country of transit. It may be quite easy to sort out problems with those organisations which are domiciled in the same country as the forwarder but difficulties become progressively more severe as other countries become involved.

The complication concerns differences in the laws of the various countries through which the goods may have to be moved.

8.8.5 The Contract between the Forwarder as Contractual Carrier and his Customer

By contrast with the multifarious sub-contracts into which the forwarder must enter, there is only a single contract between himself and his customer. This is the contract in terms of which he undertakes to accomplish the entire transport transaction.

Clearly, the document providing evidence of the terms and conditions under which the contractual carrier undertakes his responsibilities must, so far as possible, provide a means whereby the contractual carrier limits his liabilities to those of the sub-contractors he employs. Obviously, this will not be possible in every instance.

Furthermore, it is hardly to be expected that the average forwarder - despite all the experience he may have in forwarding - will have the expertise to develop the best possible transport document.

Very extensive efforts over very prolonged periods of time have been expended by the International Federation of Freight Forwarders Associations (FIATA) to maximise the protection needed when the forwarder acts as a contractual carrier and the result of this has been the development of the FIATA Forwarders Bill of Lading.

The FIATA Multimodal Transport Bill of Lading is a unique document which a forwarder who is a member of a national forwarders association which in turn is an ordinary member of the International Federation of Freight Forwarders Associations (FIATA) may issue to cover a multimodal transportation. It has to a very large degree the same status within the international banking community as has by tradition always been afforded to a shipping company bill of lading.

Occasions frequently arise - particularly in trade with certain foreign countries when the buyer of the goods demands shipment under a FIATA Combined Transport Bill of Lading (FBL). In such instances it becomes essential that the forwarder shall have the right to issue this document.

Furthermore, since the FBL places additional responsibilities upon the forwarder issuing it over and above those which are within his normal trading conditions, he must have the right at his sole discretion to take out a suitable insurance cover for those additional responsibilities and to raise an additional charge upon the customer.

A suitable clause controlling the matter would read as follows:-

"The company shall be entitled to issue in respect of the whole or part of any contract for the movement of goods a FIATA Combined Transport Bill of Lading (FBL) provided that where a FBL is issued these trading conditions shall continue to apply except insofar as they conflict with the terms and conditions applicable to the FBL. The issue of a FBL by the company shall entitle it to raise an additional charge, determined by the company, to cover its additional obligations arising under the FBL."

Owner's Risk
It is essential that the trading conditions of the forwarder shall make it clear that all work he undertakes is at the sole risk of the customer. A suitable clause would be:

"All handling, packing, loading, unloading, warehousing and transporting of goods by or on behalf of or at the request of the company are effected at the sole risk of the customer and/or the owner, and the customer indemnifies the company accordingly."

8.8.6 The FIATA Forwarders Bill of Lading
The FBL is a unique document in many respects.

Approval by the International Chamber of Commerce

The FBL is the only document issued by the freight forwarding community worldwide which has the approval of the International Chamber of Commerce and which therefore bears the logo of that organisation.

Approval by the International Banking Technical Committee
The FBL is the only transport document which the forwarding community worldwide can issue in their own right having the approval of the International Banking Technical Committee as acceptable in terms of letters of credit. The only proviso to this approval is provided the letter of credit in question does not otherwise stipulate.

In other words, the FIATA FBL will be accepted by banks in terms of letters of credit provided that its acceptance is not in conflict with the specific stipulations written into the letter of credit in question.

It was necessary for this proviso to be written into the rules of the International Banking Technical Committee since it is evidently the prerogative of any applicant for the issue of a letter of credit to stipulate precisely those documents which will be acceptable to him.

FBL Copyright
The FIATA FBL is copyright to FIATA in Zurich, Switzerland, and FIATA itself has delegated the authority to print the FBL only to national bodies which are ordinary

members of FIATA. Thus, the Shipping and Forwarding Agents' Association of Zimbabwe has authority to print supplies of the FBL for the use of its members. Companies which are not members of SFAAZ may neither use nor print the FBL.

The functions of the FIATA FBL
The FBL is so constructed that it performs the same essential functions as any shipping line combined transport bill of lading -

- ☐ It is a document framed to cover combined or multimodal transportation
- ☐ It is a receipt of the goods which the forwarder has taken in charge
- ☐ It is a document of title to the goods which can be made negotiable
- ☐ It contains in full on its reverse the conditions of carriage in terms of which the issuing forwarder undertakes to perform the transaction in question.

The FBL as Combined Transport Document
The FBL provides for the following:-
- ☐ The place of receipt (or taking in charge)
- ☐ The name of the ocean vessel
- ☐ The port of loading
- ☐ The port of discharge
- ☐ The place of delivery

It furthermore provides for the insertion of the name and address of the correspondent forwarding agent at or near the place of delivery to whom application must be made by the consignee for the delivery of the goods.

It makes provision for the insertion within it of the freight amount and the place at which that amount must be paid where freight is payable at destination.

The FBL as a Receipt for Goods
It is important to note that, in a precisely similar fashion to bills of lading issued by shipping lines and other ocean carriers, the detail of the cargo covered by the FBL is qualified by the printed phrase "according to the declaration of the consignor".

Thus, the receipt acknowledged by the FBL is, in fact, only a receipt for packages of the number and kind described "in apparent good order and condition unless otherwise noted herein." The issuing forwarder does not warrant in any way whatsoever that those packages actually contain the goods with which the packages are said to be loaded.

The FBL as a Document of Title
A single, and quite simple, sentence printed into the FBL is, in fact, only a receipt for packages of the number and kind described "in apparent good order and condition unless otherwise noted herein." The issuing forwarder does not warrant in any way whatsoever that those packages actually contain the goods with which the packages are said to be loaded.

The FBL as a Document of Title

A single, and quite simple, sentence printed into the FBL constitutes it as a document of title. This sentence is:

"One of these combined transport bills of lading must be surrendered duly endorsed in exchange for the goods."

As a consequence of this sentence the correspondent forwarder at the place of destination only has authority to deliver the goods to the consignee upon surrender of one signed original FBL duly endorsed.

Accordingly, it is the responsibility of the consignor shown upon the FBL to ensure that the originals thereof are transmitted promptly through the agreed channels (e.g. a bank) to the consignee so that the latter has in his possession the document of title which he must surrender.

As is the case with shipping line bills of lading, the FBL can, by the utilisation of appropriate wording upon it, be made negotiable. That is to say, by the addition of appropriate wording the title to beneficial ownership of the goods represented by it can be transferred from one party to another. There will, of course, always be "a consideration" or purchase price for such a transfer of the bill of lading to another party.

Finally, because signed original FBLs are valuable documents of title it is customary for them to be issued in sets of two or three so that they can be transmitted from consignor to consignee by separate mails or by separate dispatches by courier to minimise the risk of loss or non-delivery. However, while each individual signed original document in the set will have equal value as a document of title, the submission of any one of them to the correspondent forwarder at the place of destination for delivery of the goods renders the other signed original(s) void.

The FBL as Evidence of the Conditions of Carriage

It will be necessary to study these conditions in detail - particularly the conditions which amend or increase the obligations and liabilities of the issuing forwarder as compared with his obligations and liabilities in terms of his own normal trading conditions.

No amendment, adjustment or deviation from a common contract is permissible except with the prior agreement of both parties.
This applies in particular to contracts for the transportation of goods, and common law provides no distinction between a party who contracts in his own name to provide the means of transport of goods from source to destination and the party who acts as an agent organising through other parties that transportation. In both instances - that is to say where the party undertakes to provide the transport, and where the party undertakes to organise the transport, each party must protect itself by trading conditions.

Where the forwarder concerned acts as a provider of transportation the trading conditions necessary to his protection must be clearly spelled out upon his transport document and those conditions must recognise that substantial additional responsibilities rest upon him which will increase his liability in the event of things going wrong in the fulfilment of the contract into which he has entered.

Furthermore, since the transport document he must issue will without doubt pass through many hands prior to the fulfilment of the contract it must contain upon itself all the conditions of carriage in terms of which the forwarder undertakes to fulfill his obligations.

A further important point of jurisprudence must also be mentioned. While two parties may, within reason, enter into any contract they wish carrying any terms and conditions to which they may both agree, when a dispute between the parties comes before a court, the court has an overriding responsibility to consider whether the terms and conditions relevant to the contract are consistent with society's deeply held conviction of natural justice.

If the court considers that the terms and conditions stipulated in the contract are weighed to an unjustifiable degree in favour of one party to the excessive prejudice of the other then the court may in its discretion rule that the contract, or certain terms and conditions within it, are not enforceable since they are an affront to natural justice.

Courts are very careful in the exercise of this discretion, but it is important that the terms and conditions to be applied to a contract are reasonable to all parties, bearing in mind the nature of the transaction required to be fulfilled by that contract.

There is no "rule of thumb" capable of general application in terms of which courts use their discretion. It is obvious that every transport transaction will be surrounded with its own particular circumstances and it will be those particular circumstances in question which will motivate a court decision to invalidate a term of a contract or the entire contract.

8.9 THE FIATA FBL

Two matters must be emphasised very strongly at this stage

☐ No forwarder is under compulsion to act as a contractual carrier. If he decides to do so, that decision is a commercial decision. A decision not to do so may involve the forwarder in the loss of a remunerative transaction or even in the loss of a client but it is for the forwarder himself to decide, by weighing up the risks involved, what decision he should make.

☐ Since the decision to act as a contractual carrier is within the forwarder's discretion, then the terms and conditions upon which he so acts must be those which will be supported and enforceable by the courts.

It follows therefore that the conditions of carriage enumerated on a FIATA FBL are devised so as to be reasonable to both parties to that contract. It further follows that they will differ from the normal forwarder's trading conditions in a number of respects.

Clause 2 of the FIATA FBL conditions reads as follows:

2.1 By the issuance of this "Combined Transport Bill of Lading" the freight forwarder:-

a) *undertakes to perform for and in his own name to procure the performance of the entire transport, from the place at which the good are taken in charge to the place designated for delivery in this bill of lading,*

b) *assumes liability as set out in these conditions.*

2.2 For the purposes and subject to the provisions of this bill of lading, the freight forwarder shall be responsible for the acts and omissions of any person of whose services he makes use for the performance of the contract evidenced by this bill of lading.

It will be clear that clause 2 places full prime responsibility for the performance of the contract of transportation upon the forwarder issuing the FIATA FBL.

That responsibility is only limited or avoided by virtue of other provisions enumerated in the FBL. The important thing is for the student to realise that there is a fundamental difference of approach to liability between the trading conditions protecting a forwarder acting as an agent and the trading conditions of a forwarder acting as a contractual carrier and issuing in his own name a FIATA FBL.

This difference of approach to the concept of protection afforded by the conditions does not mean that the conditions on the FBL are less efficient - in fact, they are very efficient - but it means that the user of the FBL must understand them thoroughly and also appreciate where, on occasion, the onus of proof of exemption from liability lies.

8.9.1 Negotiability and Title to the Goods
Clause 3 on the FIATA FBL is in two parts. The first part (Clause 3.1) makes it clear that an original FIATA FBL is intended to be a document of title, constituting title to the goods by the holder thereof who may by endorsement of it claim the goods or alternatively transfer the goods to another party. Clause 3.1 requires no further explanation. Clause 3.2, however, must be carefully noted. It reads as follows:-

This bill of lading shall be prima facie evidence of the taking in charge by the freight forwarder of the goods as herein described. However, proof to the contrary shall not be admissible when this bill of lading has been negotiated or transferred for valuable consideration to a third party acting in good faith.

In other words, by signing and issuing the FBL the forwarder is supplying to the consignor prima facie evidence that the forwarder has received the goods into his custody in the state described upon the face of it.

If, in fact, it was in any manner incorrect the onus of proof that the goods were not correctly described therein rests with the forwarder.

Moreover, the second sentence in this clause takes the matter a stage further. If the FBL has been negotiated or transferred for a valuable consideration to the third party acting in good faith, then the proof that the goods were not correctly described will not be admissible in a court of law. This will have the effect of saddling the forwarder irrevocably with the consequences of his error in the description of the goods.

8.9.2 Dangerous Goods and Indemnity

Clause 4 of the FIATA FBL conditions deals with the problem of dangerous goods in different wording but with much the same effect as parallel clauses inserted in all forwarders' trading conditions.

8.9.3 Description of Goods and Merchants Packing

Clause 5.1 of the FIATA FBL follows the principles which underlie similar clauses in the trading conditions of any typical forwarder. The consignor is deemed to have guaranteed to the freight forwarder the accuracy... of the description of the goods, marks, numbers, quantity, weight and/or volume ... and shall indemnify the freight forwarder against all loss, damage and expense arising from inaccuracies in or inadequacy of such particulars.

The next sentence in clause 5.1, however, inserts a new element which is not found in typical forwarders' conditions. This sentence reads:

The right of the freight forwarder to such indemnity shall in no way limit his responsibility and liability under the bill of lading to any person other than the consignor.

The effect of this additional sentence is that the forwarder must accept "responsibility and liability" in respect of damage or expense caused to any third party as a consequence of the failure of the consignor in respect of the detail previously quoted. This may, at first sight, be unfair to the forwarder but his protection is afforded to him in two ways.

- in any action brought against him or claim lodged with him he is at liberty to bring a corresponding action or lodge a corresponding claim will the consignor who is "deemed to have guaranteed to the forwarder the accuracy ..." and to have indemnified the freight forwarder ...

Clause 5.2 of the FIATA FBL deals with loss, damage or injury caused by:

☐ faulty or insufficient packing of goods, or
☐ faulty loading or packing within containers, trailers or on flats,

☐   or

☐   defect or unsuitability of the containers, trailers or flats.

When any of these activities are undertaken by the merchant or by any other party on behalf of the merchant (other than the freight forwarder himself), this clause states clearly that the merchant indemnifies the freight forwarder against any additional expenses so caused.

Where the forwarder himself undertakes the packing, loading, or the selection of the transport vehicle, his responsibility and liability remains.

Extent of Liability
Clause 6 in the FIATA FBL must be studied very carefully and be accurately understood. This clause is divided into two section - 6.A. and 6.B.

Clause 6A
Clause 6.A 1 reads as follows:-

The freight forwarder shall be liable for loss of or damage to the goods occurring between the time when he takes the goods into his charge and the time of delivery.

This is a completely unambiguous statement of the freight forwarders liability and if it were not qualified by clause 6.A.2 it would leave the freight forwarder 100% liable.

Clause 6.A.2
This clause substantially limits what would otherwise be the devastating effects of clause 6.A.1.

The freight forwarder shall, however, be relieved of liability for any loss or damage if such loss or damage was caused by.

a)   *an act or omission of the merchant, or person other than the freight forwarder acting on behalf of the merchant or from whom the freight forwarder took the goods in charge;*

b)   *insufficiency or defective conclusion of the packaging or marks and/or numbers;*

c)   *handling, loading, stowage or unloading of the goods by the merchant or any person acting on behalf of the merchant;*

d)   *inherent vice of the goods;*

e)   *strike, lock-out, stoppage or restraint of labour, the consequences of   which the freight forwarder could not avoid by the exercise of reasonable diligence;*

f)   *any cause or event which the freight forwarder could not avoid and the consequences whereof he could not prevent by the exercise of   reasonable intelligence;*

g)   *a nuclear incident if the operator of a nuclear installation or a person acting for him is liable for this damage under an applicable international convention or national law governing liability in respect of nuclear energy.*

It will be evident that the relief from liability which this clause affords to the forwarder is substantial. However, the question of the burden of proof that the loss or damage arose from one of the causes listed remains. This is dealt with in clause 6.A.3.

Clause 6.A.3

This clause defines where the burden of proof lies. It lies upon the freight forwarder - but there is a presumptive qualification within this clause which had to be noted. The clause reads as follows:

The burden of proving that the loss or damage was due to one or more of the above causes or events shall rest upon the freight forwarder.

When the freight forwarder establishes that, in the circumstances of the case, the loss or damage could be attributed to one or more of the causes or events specified (above), it shall be presumed that it was so caused. The claimant shall, however, be entitled to prove that the loss or damage was not, in fact, caused wholly or partly by one or more of these causes or events.

If a freight forwarder depends upon one of the listed causes or events above as his defence against liability for loss or damage and it can be shown that he could be correct, then the burden of proof shifts from the freight forwarder to the claimant who must prove to be contrary.

Clause 6.B

Certain international conventions and the national laws of certain countries contain provisions which are mandatory, and which cannot be departed from by a private contract.

Clause 6B is inserted into the FBL conditions to allow such international conventions or national laws to have their due effect. The clause reads as follows:

When in accordance with clause 6A.1 the freight forwarder is liable to pay compensation in respect of loss or damage to the goods and the stage of transport where the loss or damage occurred is known, the liability of the freight forwarder in respect of such loss or damage shall be determined by the provisions contained in any international convention or national law, which provisions

267

a)   *cannot be departed from by private contract, to the detriment of the claimant, and*

b)   *would have applied if the claimant had made a separate and correct contract with the freight forwarder in respect of the particular stage of transport where the loss or damage occurred and received as evidence thereof any particular document which must be issued in order to make such international convention or national law applicable.*

8.9.5 Paramount Clause
The Hague Rules contained in the International Convention for the unification of certain rules relating to Bills of Lading, dated Brussels 25 August 1924 or in those countries where they are already in force, Hague-Visby Rules contained in the Protocol of Brussels dated 23 February 1968, as enacted in the country of shipment, shall apply to all carriage of goods by sea, and where no mandatory international or national law applies, to the carriage of goods by inland waterways also, and such provisions shall apply to all goods whether carried on deck or under deck.

This clause, which is mandatory, is self-explanatory to those who understand the terms and conditions of the Hague Rules and the Hague-Visby Rules. It is to be noted that the latter apply not only to the carriage of goods by inland waterways.

8.9.6 Limitation Amount
The maximum limit of liability provided by the FIATA FBL differs in a number of material respects from the limits of liability laid down in a typical forwarder's trading conditions.

Clause 8 of the FIATA FBL is in three parts which must be considered both separately and together.

Place and Time of Valuation
Clause 8.1 of the FBL reads as follows:-
When the freight forwarder is liable for compensation in respect of loss of or damage to the goods, such compensation shall be calculated by reference to the value of such goods at the place and time they are delivered to the consignee in accordance with the contract or should have been so delivered.

This clause relates the compensation payable to the value of the goods at the "place of delivery" stated within the FBL. It will be obvious that this will not necessarily be the same as the value at which the consignor of the goods invoiced them to the consignee. That invoiced value will be dependent on the terms of delivery by the one party to the other which may be "ex works", "FOB", or some other INCOTERM. Any transport or ancillary charges which must be paid by the consignee to complete the contract of carriage up to the place of delivery must be added to the invoiced value in order to arrive at the value by reference to which the compensation due by the freight forwarder must be calculated.

The forwarder will recognise that the "time" of delivery may, in relation to certain commodities, have a bearing upon the value at the place of delivery. Certain basic raw and semi-manufactured materials may have a variable value depending upon the state of the relevant **commodity market** at the time in question. Their values may fluctuate upward or downward. Accordingly, this clause not only stipulates that the value shall be calculated at the place of delivery but also at the time of delivery.

Commodity Values

Clause 8.2 of the FBL has particular relevance when the goods in question are of a type in respect of which values can fluctuate according to the commodity markets to which they are consigned. This clause reads as follows:-

*The value of the goods shall be fixed according to the current commodity exchange price, or, if there be no such price, according to the **current marketplace**, or, if there be no commodity exchange price or current market price, by reference to the **normal value of goods of the same quantity and quality**.*

Limit of Maximum Liability

Clause 8.3 is an overriding clause expressing the maximum liability of the freight forwarder who issues an FBL. Its wording is as follows:-

Compensation shall not, however, exceed 2 SDR (Special Drawing Rights) per kilo of gross weight of the goods lost or damaged, unless, with the consent of the freight forwarder, the merchant has declared a higher value for the goods and such higher value have been stated in the combined transport bill of lading, in which case such higher value shall be the limit. However, the freight forwarder shall not, in any case, be liable for an amount greater than the actual loss to the person entitled to make the claim.

This clause introduces two very important concepts.

☐   the use of special drawing rights to define the level of maximum liability, and

☐   the possibility of increasing that maximum liability by prior agreement between the consignor and the freight forwarder issuing the FBL.

Special Drawing Rights (SDR)

SDRs are not units of currency. A trader cannot issue an account in SDRs; nor can a debtor draw a cheque in settlement of his indebtedness in SDRs.

Nevertheless, an SDR is a unit of value which is capable of being translated, by means of a formula, into a monetary amount in any national currency in the world.

The value of the SDR is calculated by the International Monetary Fund and is adjusted periodically. It is based on the US dollar, the Pound Sterling, the French Franc, the German Mark and the Japanese Yen. Each of these currencies is given a "weighting" to

269

provide for the country's cost of living and other indices, and the whole is aggregated and averaged. By utilising the SDR as a basis relevant to claims a claimant will receive approximately equal real value for his claim irrespective of the currency of the country in which he resides.

While it is obvious that the SDR will fluctuate to a small degree against any particular currency, that fluctuation is minimised and operates for the benefit of the claimant.

In practical terms, the central question is "where can I ascertain the value of the SDR?" It is not quoted in the financial page of the newspapers, nor on TV or radio. It is, however, available upon enquiry to the Treasury section of the Head Offices of all financial institutions - e.g. commercial banks, merchant banks, etc.

Possibility of Increased Maximum Liability
It is to be noted that the liability of the freight forwarder cannot be increased unless he has first given his consent to the increase. He is under no obligation to accept the increase.

If, however, he decides to accept an increase then the value agreed must be inserted on the face of the FBL and the forwarder is then entitled to charge a suitable premium upon his freight charges to cover the cost of the insurance of his additional liability with any appropriate professional indemnity insurance organisation. In this respect the position in the FIATA FBL is very similar to the provision in a typical forwarder's trading conditions.

8.9.7 Delay, Consequential Loss, etc

Clause 9 in the FIATA FBL reads as follows:

*Arrival times are not guaranteed by the forwarder. If the freight forwarder is held liable in respect of delay, consequential loss or damage other than loss of or damage to the goods, the liability of the freight forwarder shall be **limited to double the freight** for the transport covered by this bill of lading, or the value of the goods as determined in clause 8, whichever is the less.*

This clause is self-explanatory and needs no further discussion.

8.9.8 Defences
Clause 10.1 of the FIATA FBL is very useful to the freight forwarder. It reads as follows:-

The defences and limits of liability provided for in these conditions shall apply in any action against the freight forwarder for loss of or damage or delay to the goods whether the action be founded in contract or in tort.

270

☐　　**An action founded in contract** will be an action for a breach of the contract, a failure to perform the contract, either in whole or in part. Such an action will therefore rest upon the interpretation of the contract between the two parties. It may, for instance, arise when a party undertakes to perform an activity which he subsequently discovers he is unable through lack of experience or expertise or for some other reason, to perform. He has done nothing wrong: he has simply failed to fulfill his part of the bargain.

☐　　**An action founded in tort,** on the other hand, is an action for a failure to perform a duty or common law obligation even though responsibility for that duty or obligation was not specifically written into the contract. For instance, every party receiving goods into its custody has a **duty of care** towards those goods and must therefore protect them from inclement weather, from the depredations of thieves, etc.

Clause 10.1 stipulates that the defences and limits of liability apply whichever type of action is brought against the forwarder.

Clause 10.2 in the FBL acts, however, as a safeguard for the claimant in that it removes the maximum limit of liability granted to the forwarder in terms of clause 8.3 if the claimant can **prove that the forwarder was malicious, reckless or deliberately neglectful.**

Clause 10.2 reads as follows:
The freight forwarder shall not be entitled to the benefit of the limitation of liability provided for in clause 8.3 if it can be proved that the loss or damage resulted from an act or omission of the freight forwarder done with intent to cause damage or recklessly and with knowledge that damage would probably result.

8.9.9 Liability of Servants and Sub-Contractors
Clause 11 of the FIATA FBL is very interesting and is of importance.

It has been pointed out that the freight forwarder acting as a contractual carrier and issuing his own transport document has to employ as his sub-contractors numerous parties both in the country where the transportation originates and through other countries into the country of destination.

Where loss or damage arises to the goods it is usually the consignee who originates a claim and it may well be that the consignee will decide to prosecute the claim against one of the freight forwarder's sub-contractors somewhere along the chain of transportation for the reason that the claimant can "get at him" far more easily than he can the freight forwarder in Zimbabwe.

Should this occur, it becomes very important that the unfortunate sub-contractor in question shall be able to take refuge behind the defences and limits of liability which the freight forwarder issuing the FBL is entitled to. Clause 11.1 provides the sub-contractor with such protection and is worded as follows:-

If an act for loss or damage to the goods is brought against a person referred to in clause 2.2, such person shall be entitled to avail himself of the defences and limits or liability which the freight forwarder is entitled to invoke under these conditions.

However, in order to restrain a sub-contractor from "going wild" and acting wrongfully, clause 11.2 removes the benefit of the limitation of liability provided for in clause 8.3 from that sub-contractor if he acts maliciously, recklessly or with knowledge that his act or omission would probably result in damage.

Finally, clause 11.3 envisages a situation where a claimant initiates a claim in respect of the same loss or damage to the same goods against **both the freight forwarder and the sub-contractor.** Clause 11.3 provides that if this should occur the aggregate of the amounts recoverable from the freight forwarder and the subcontractor shall in no case exceed the limits provided for in the FBL conditions. In other words, the more the claimant recovers from one, the less is recoverable from the other.

8.9.0 Method and Route of Transportation
Clause 12 in the FIATA FBL states:
The freight forwarder reserves to himself a reasonable liberty as to the means, route and procedure to be followed in the handling, storage and transportation of goods.

Clause 12 in the FIATA FBL is subtly and importantly different from the typical parallel clause normally found in a freight forwarder's trading conditions.

In the latter the forwarder, in the absence of specific instructions, reserves to himself reasonable discretion to decide at what time to perform any or all of the acts which may be necessary for the discharge of his obligations. However, he usually reserves to himself an absolute discretion to determine the means, route and procedure to be followed in performing his services.

By contrast, this FBL clause only reserves to the freight forwarder a reasonable liberty with regard to means, route and procedure.

8.9.11 Delivery
Clause 13 of the FIATA FBL is self-explanatory and follows in practice the uniform requirements of all freight forwarders in their own trading conditions.

8.9.12 Freight and Charges
Clause 14 in the FIATA FBL is divided into five parts and each will be considered separately.

Freight on Receipt of Goods

Clause 14.1 clearly states that freight shall be paid in cash, without discount and, whether pre-payable or payable at destination, shall be considered as earned on receipt of the goods and not to be returned or relinquished in any event.

Currency of Payment and Rate of Exchange
Clause 14.2 reads follows:
Freight and all other amounts mentioned in this bill of lading are to be paid in the currency named in the bill of lading or, at the freight forwarder's opinion, in the currency of the country of dispatch or destination at the highest rate of exchange for bankers' sight bills current for pre-payable freight on the day of dispatch and for freight payable at destination on the day when the merchant is notified of arrival of the goods there or on the date of withdrawal of the delivery order, whichever rate is the higher, or at the opinion of the forwarder on the date of the bill of lading.

This clause may appear at first glance to be somewhat confusing but its effect is clear - the freight forwarder is entitled to a return in the currency of his choice at the highest amount available in terms of the clause.

Dues, Taxes, Charges, etc
It must be clearly understood that the FIATA FBL is a transport document and accordingly charges mentioned upon it will be charges arising out of and in the course of the transportation of the goods.

Other charges will inevitably arise, such as duties, taxes, rents, demurrage, etc, and clause 14.3 is inserted to make it clear that all such are to be paid by the merchant.

War, War-like Operations, etc
The forwarder must hold himself protected against unforeseen and unavoidable occurrences such as the above and must be entitled to expect reimbursement from the cargo owner where the transportation of goods is complicated by these unavoidable events.

Clause 14.4 accordingly reads as follows:
The merchant shall reimburse the freight forwarder in proportion to the amount of freight for any costs for deviation or delay or any other increase of costs of whatever nature caused by war, war-like operations, epidemics, strikes, government directions, or force majeure.

Warranty with regard to declaration made by the merchant
Clause 14.5 of the FBL places an unequivocal warranty upon the merchant with regard to the correctness of all declarations which he is required to make for the purpose of the contract with the freight forwarder.

The same clause stipulates the penalties which the freight forwarder may impose upon the merchant if any of the declarations which he makes is found to be incorrect.

273

The clause states:

The merchant warrants the correctness of the declaration of contents, insurance, weight, measurement or value of the goods but the freight forwarder reserves the right to have the contents inspected and the weight, measurement or value verified. If on such inspection it is found the declaration is not correct it is agreed that a sum equal either to five times the difference between the correct figure and the freight charged, or to double the correct freight less the freight charges, whichever sum is the smaller, shall be payable as liquidated damage to the freight forwarder for his inspection costs and losses of freight on other goods notwithstanding any other sum having been stated on the bill of lading as freight payable.

8.9.13 Lien
Clause 15 of the FIATA FBL establishes that the freight forwarder shall have a lien on the goods for any amount due under this bill of lading including storage fees and for the cost of recovering same, and may enforce such lien in any reasonable manner which he may think fit.

This clause on the FBL constitutes a special lien specific to the goods which are the subject of the FBL. It does not attempt to grant the freight forwarder any general lien over the goods on the FBL for other amounts due in other contexts from the merchant to the freight forwarder.

8.9.14 General Average
Clause 16 of the FIATA FBL creates an indemnity by the merchant in favour of the freight forwarder in respect of any claims of a General Average nature which may be made on the forwarder, and the clause states that the merchant shall provide such security as may be required by the freight forwarder in this connection.

8.9.15 Notice
It is a basic principle of commercial practice worldwide that in the event of loss or damage occurring to goods in the course of transportation every party upon whom responsibility may rest and against whom a claim may be raised shall be promptly notified. "Prompt notification" may be interpreted differently by different parties with the result that it is important that the period within which notification of the possibility of a claim must be given, is defined.

Clause 17 in the FIATA FBL provides this definition and is worded:

Unless notice of loss of or damage to the goods and the general nature of it be given in writing to the freight forwarder or the persons referred to in clause 2.2, at the place of delivery, before or at the time of the removal of the goods into the custody of the person entitled to delivery thereof under this bill of lading, or if the loss or damage be not apparent, within 7 consecutive days thereafter, such removal shall be prima facie evidence of the delivery by the freight forwarder of the goods as described in this bill of lading.

274

Three points must be noted in this clause:-

☐ If the damage or loss is apparent then notice must be given forthwith.   No delay is allowable.

☐ If the loss or damage is not apparent then 7 consecutive days are allowed during which the notice must be given, and those 7 days will run from the time the goods were delivered.

☐ If such notice is not given as required in this clause, then that fact alone shall create prima facie evidence of delivery of the goods as described in the bill of lading.

The use of the phrase "prima facie" necessarily implies that if the person receiving the goods still desires to prosecute a claim for loss or damage discovered then the onus of proof that the forwarder or other party involved is liable, rests with him.

8.9.16 Non-Delivery
The question of liability when there is a failure of delivery of the goods at the 'place of delivery', is always more difficult to deal with.

Clause 18 of the FIATA FBL defines the period of time which must elapse before a claim for non-delivery of a consignment of goods can be lodged. It is worded as follows:

Failure to effect delivery within 90 days after the expiry of a time limit agreed and expressed in a combined transport bill of lading or, where no time limit is agreed and so expressed, failure to effect delivery within 90 days after the time it would be reasonable to allow for diligent completion of the combined transport operation shall, in the absence of evidence to the contrary, give to the party entitled to receive delivery, the right to treat the goods as lost.

It will be noted that this clause is worded so that it is not completely conclusive one way or the other. It gives the party entitled to receive delivery the right to treat the goods as lost only **in the absence of evidence to the contrary.**

Thus, the freight forwarder still has the opportunity to produce evidence that the goods are not lost - non-delivery may have been caused by unavoidable extraneous circumstances, by detention of the goods by the authorities, or they may, in fact, have been delivered but at an address different to that stated on the face of the bill of lading, etc.

8.9.17 Time Bar
It is essential that there shall be a time bar provided for beyond which suit in a court of law shall not be brought in respect of any claim against the forwarder.

Clause 9 of the FIATA FBL reads as follows:

The freight forwarder shall be discharged of all liability under the rules of these conditions, unless suit is brought within 9 months after:
(i)   the delivery of the goods, or
(ii)   the date when the goods should have been delivered, or
(iii) the date when in accordance with clause 18, failure to deliver the goods would, in the absence of evidence to the contrary, give the party entitled to receive delivery the right to treat the goods as lost.

8.9.18 Jurisdiction
Clause 20 of the FIATA FBL needs no discussion. It reads as follows:

Actions against the freight forwarder may only be instituted in the country where the freight forwarder has his principle place of business and shall be decided according to the law of such country.

8.10 THE FIATA FBL AS A RECEIPT FOR GOODS
Every transport document - whether a consignment note, an air waybill, a bill of lading or any other, is a receipt issued by the carrier for the goods entrusted to him by the sender.

By the issue of the document the carrier is acknowledging that he has received the goods into his care for transportation to the place of delivery where he must deliver them in the same condition in which he received them. He has a duty to care for the goods, to protect them from mishap, misadventure and damage, failing which he will be held liable for losses arising.

The problems arising from this overall responsibility are listed here:

☐   The great bulk of goods moving in international trade do so within the protection of cases, cartons, drums, canisters, bales, and other forms of outer protection.

☐   The outer protection prevents the contractor from inspecting the contents of the packages.

☐   The carrier thus has not firsthand knowledge either of the contents or of the state of the contents.

☐   Even if the contents are visible through the boards of a skeleton crate, or even if the goods are shipped without the protection of an outer packaging, their nature, their completeness, and their freedom from any prior loss or damage, may not be determinable by him.

☐   Unless clearly advised in advance by the shipper, the carrier will not know in the case of delicate or fragile goods what special precautions must be taken in the storage, handling, and stowage of the goods.

☐   etc, etc.

8.10.1 "In Apparent Good Order and Condition, Unless Otherwise Noted Herein"
It is standard practice for all bills of lading, air way bills, and the majority of other transport documents to have a clause in this or similar wording printed into them.

This has the effect of limiting the receipt given by the carrier to the state of the packages. It does not commit him to any comment upon the state of the contents of those packages. Furthermore, it entitles him to add a clause into the body of the transport document describing the state of the packages if he finds that they are not in good order. Examples of such clauses might be:-

☐ "Three drums dented"
☐ "Case #5 - boards stove in"
☐ "All goods packed in second-hand cases"
☐ "Cartons #15 and 22 ton - contents exposed"
☐ "6 cartons wet stained and strapping loose"

8.10.2 Description of Goods "According to the Declaration of the Consignor/Shipper"
The purpose of this wording which, in one form or another, also is standard upon transport documents, is to protect the carrier if the packages are found at destination to contain other than those described in the transport document.

8.10.3 "In the Opinion of the Carrier the Goods are Inadequately Packed: Carrier not Responsible"

This clause must be used with reasonable discretion but is valuable under the following circumstances.

☐ Where, in the course of the necessary handling of the cargo, it is clear   that the packaging - whether wooden, or carton, or fibre drum, etc - is showing signs of disintegration or of crumbling.

☐ It is also useful when, as a result of laxity of packing, a material risk is apparent that the goods could be pilfered or if the packing is for   any reason inadequate to withstand the normal stresses of transportation.

8.10.4 Shipment Unprotected : Carrier not Responsible
There are many articles in international trade which are sufficiently robust to justify shipment without package protection. Examples are; earth moving equipment, motor vehicles on wheels, tractors, construction steel work, etc. Nevertheless, damage may be sustained by such articles as a result of rust, corrosion, impact by other cargo, etc, and it is essential that the carrier protects himself by a suitable clause on the transport document.

8.10.5 "Shipped on Deck at Shipper's Risk"

Bulky cargo frequently requires shipment on deck. Hazardous cargo may be shipped on deck to avoid the risk of contact with other cargo or to jettison it more easily if it catches fire, starts leaking, etc.

Normally, if cargo is going to be shipped on deck the carrier will consult in advance with the cargo owner, but in any event there are a number of obvious risks to which such cargo is subject which would not be so important if it were to be shipped under deck. Where shipment of deck is necessary the carrier will use this clause to protect himself from liability for the additional risks. He will expect the cargo owner to take out a suitable marine insurance cover taking account of the special circumstances of the shipment.

8.10.6 "Shippers Load, Stow and Count"

This clause is in constant use in respect of FCL consignments. It is succinct and precise. Its meaning is clear:

"The container(s) was/were loaded by the shipper, the contents of each container were arranged and secured in the container by the shipper, and the shipper is personally responsible for the quantity of goods stated to have been loaded to the container".

By the use of this clause the carrier has made it clear that he will accept no responsibility with regard to these three matters.

8.10.7 Claused (Unclean) Transport Documents

Every transport document is issued subject to a multiplicity of clauses: bills of lading embody the clauses usually both on the back and the front of each one: air waybills, rail consignment notes, and others bear clear indications that they are subject to clauses to be found in the tariffs and regulations of the carriers involved. It is broadly correct to say that all these clauses relate to the contract of carriage offered by the carrier and/or define his knowledge of the goods he contracts to carry.

Such clauses as these are acceptable to all parties in international trade.

When we talk of "claused (unclean) transport documents" we are speaking of those clauses which it is necessary from time to time to SUPERIMPOSE on a transport document indicating an unsatisfactory or defective condition of the packages and/or the goods in question.

Shipment on deck (paragraph 5) may also render the document "unclean" unless seller and buyer have agreed that shipment in this manner is acceptable.

Moreover, such claused transport documents also have an adverse effect upon the ability of the buyer of the goods in question to claim on the insurance for loss or damage. In fact, a clause on a transport document indicating that in the opinion of the carrier the goods are inadequately packed can have quite serious consequences since the standard marine insurance clauses in any policy of marine insurance contain the following clause:

"In no case shall this insurance cover loss, damage or expense caused by insufficiency or unsuitability of packing or preparation of the subject-matter insured..."

Obviously, if the carrier regards the goods as inadequately packed it is almost certain that the underwriting organisation faced with a claim will scrutinise the method of packing and protection with exceptional care to determine whether they also hold the same view.

Such clauses all indicate an unsatisfactory state of affairs which may be to the detriment of the underlying contract of sale between the seller and the buyer of the goods - which may in turn affect the cash value of the goods supplied and the payment which will be due from the buyer and the seller. It is where such clauses are superimposed upon the transport document that the document is regarded as "claused", or in more colloquial language, unclean.

8.10.8 FIATA FBL Issued by the Forwarder as Contractual Carrier

When acting as a contractual carrier and issuing a FIATA FBL under his own signature (or any other similar transport document) the forwarder must be extremely careful. In practice there are five alternative scenarios which must each be separately considered.

Forwarder Acting as a Container Groupage Agent Utilising his own Depot/Warehouse for the Loading of Goods into Containers
In this instance the forwarder should in no circumstances issue his transport document until he has received all the depot/warehouse returns evidencing the state of the goods at the time they were loaded into the container. He must ensure that the personnel employed at the depot/warehouse are trained efficiently to note their returns with the precise condition of each consignment loaded. The transport document issued to the client in respect of each consignment so loaded must bear suitable superimposed clauses reflecting the condition of the cargo in question.

Forwarder Employing as Sub-contractor another Depot/Warehouse for the Loading of the Goods to Container
Again, the forwarder should at all costs avoid issuing any transport document until the returns from his sub-contractor have been received and scrutinised. Each transport document must reflect accurately the condition of each consignment.

Forwarder Acting as Airfreight Consolidator
Forwarders who act as airfreight consolidators normally undertake the consolidation function in their own airfreight depots. Because speed of completion of documents is essential to all airfreight movements, an intimate liaison must exist between the supervisors in those depots and the staff responsible for the issue of house air waybills in order that any suitable qualification concerning the state of the goods can be inserted upon the house air waybills in question.

Forwarders Operating their own Road Consolidations
In this instance a similar circumstance must apply as regards the annotation of road consignment notes or waybills.

Forwarders Sub-Contracting their Road Freight Consolidators
It is usually impractical under these circumstances for the forwarder to obtain immediate information concerning the condition of consignments which he has entrusted to a sub-contracting road hauler. However, the forwarder must ensure that the road hauler in question understands the necessity of accurate annotation of the road vehicle manifest which will be compiled by the road hauler since it is this document which will afford the forwarder a measure of protection where the goods are in any defective condition.

8.11 THE WARSAW CONVENTION

"Convention for the Unification of Certain Rules Relating to International Carriage by Air"

Commercial aviation began to impact upon world trade in the early days of the 1920s and it was not long thereafter that European governments realised that contracts for the carriage of goods by air needed to be the subject of internationally agreed rules.

The Warsaw Convention in its original form was signed in the city of Warsaw on 12 October 1929. In its original form it was ratified by the major European powers by incorporation in their respective legislation shortly thereafter.

As the range of aircraft and their size developed it was given legislative effect by other nations more broadly throughout the world, and in particular, in South Africa it was incorporated in the Carriage by Air Act No. 17 of 1946. Since then additional protocols to the original convention have been brought into effect from time to time, most of them in consequence of the further development of air transportation and in order to codify decisions of courts arising from litigation.

From the point of view of the airfreight forwarder the main purpose of the convention are to establish rules with regard to the nature of the air way bill, its content, and the liability for loss of, or damage to, cargo while it is in the control of the air carrier.

The convention applies to all carriage of goods by air which takes place
- from a state which has ratified the convention, or
- to a state which has ratified the convention, or
- via the air space of a state which has ratified the convention - whether the flight touches down within the territory of that state or not.

The convention does not apply to the carriage of goods domestically within the territorial boundaries of a state.

Carriage by air between a state and its colonies or mandated territories is, in terms of the convention, regarded as international but the state in question can, by its own legislation, exclude such carriage from the convention.

The carriage by air of mail and postal packages is the one single exclusion from the terms of the Warsaw Convention.

8.11.1 Transshipment / Through Traffic

The convention stipulates that carriage which is to be performed by several successive air carriers is deemed to be one undivided carriage if it has been regarded by the parties as a single operation, whether it has been agreed upon under the form of a single contract or of a series of contracts, and it does not lose its international character merely because one part of the contract or one of the series of contracts is performed entirely within the territory of the same state.

Normally, under modern conditions, such a carriage would take place on a through air waybill from the point of origin to the final destination. An example of this could be the movement of an air consignment from Jan Smuts to New York, thence to Los Angeles and over to Hawaii. Such a routing, despite the fact that the carriage between New York and Los Angeles would be entirely within the territory of the USA, would be international throughout.

8.11.2 The Air Waybill

Article 8 of the convention stipulates that every air carrier has the right to require the consignor to make out and hand over to him an air waybill in a form approved by the convention, and every such consignor has the right to require the carrier to accept the air waybill.

The air waybill must contain the following particulars:

a) The place and date of its execution
b) The place of departure and of destination
c) The agreed stopping places, provided that the carrier may reserve to himself the right to alter the stopping places in case of necessity, and where he exercises that right the alteration shall not have the effect of depriving the carriage of its international character.
d) The name and address of the consignor
e) The name and address of the first carrier
f) The name and address of the consignee
g) The nature of the cargo
h) The number of packages, the method of payment and the particular marks and/or numbers upon them.
i) The weight, quantity and the volume or dimensions of the cargo
j) The apparent condition of the cargo and of the packing of it
k) The freight, if it has been agreed upon, the date and place of payment, and the person who is to pay it.
l) If the cargo is sent for payment on delivery, the amount of the freight, and, if the case so requires, the amount of other expenses incurred
m) The amount of the value declared where the consignor requires the carrier to accept an increase in the amount of his maximum liability

n) The number of parts of the air waybill
o) The documents handed to the carrier to accompany the air waybill
p) The time fixed for the completion of the carriage and a brief note of the route to be followed, if these matters have been previously agreed upon
q) A statement that the carriage is subject to the rules relating to liability established by the Warsaw Convention.

In terms of the Convention the air waybill prepared and signed by the consignor and thereafter signed by the carrier (whether by hand or by machine imprint) constitutes prima facie evidence of the conclusion of the contract, of the receipt of the cargo by the air carrier and of the conditions attaching to the carriage. The statement in the air waybill relating to the weight, dimensions and packing of the cargo as well as those relating to number of packages, are prima facie evidence of the facts stated: those relating to the quantity, volume and condition of the cargo do not constitute evidence against the carrier except so far as they both have been, and are stated on the air waybill to have been, checked by him in the presence of the consignor, or they relate to the apparent condition of the cargo.

It is to be noted that the particulars enumerated under (a) to (i) together with (q) are crucial to the nature of the contract of carriage while the particulars enumerated in (o) to (p) are important only insofar as they are relevant to the carriage in question. This distinction is important in the light of Article 9.

Article 9 of the Convention states as follows:

If the carrier accepts goods without an air waybill having been made out, or if the air waybill does not contain all the particulars set out in Article 8 (a) to (i) inclusive and (q), the carrier shall not be entitled to avail himself of the provisions of this Convention which exclude or limit his liability.

The reference in Article 9 to "the carrier" includes the forwarder who, by virtue of being the possessor of an IATA license, acts not only as an agent of the consignor but also as an agent of the carrier.

In other words, if a consequence of a failure properly to complete the air waybill and the acceptance whereof by the airline the latter as carrier loses the protection of the Convention then the forwarder similarly loses protection.

8.11.3 Liability of the Carrier
Subject only to the question of contributory negligence on the part of the cargo owner, the carrier is liable for damage sustained in the event of the destruction or loss of, or damage to, cargo upon the condition only that the occurrence which caused the damage took place during the carriage by air. However, the carrier is not liable if he proves that the destruction or loss of, or damage to, the cargo resulted solely from one or more of the following:

a)   inherent defect, quality or vice of the cargo
b)   defensive packing of the cargo performed by any person other than the carrier or
the carrier's servants or agents
c)   an act of war or an armed conflict
d)   an act of a public authority carried out in connection with the entry, exit or transit
      of the cargo.

The carrier is also liable for damage occasioned by delay in the carriage of cargo, subject
to the defense of contributory negligence, and to the defense that he and his servants and
agents had taken all necessary measures to avoid the damage or that it was impossible for
them to take such measures.

☐   The relief from liability provided to the carrier by these two
     paragraphs remains intact even though the carrier's protection in   terms of
Article 9 has fallen away.

☐   "Carriage by air" in this context commences when the cargo is handed into the
     custody of the carrier and terminates when the carrier delivers it to the person
     entitled to take delivery at the destination.

8.11.4 Limit Of The Carrier's Liability
In the absence of a special declaration of value inserted upon the air waybill by the
consignor for the purpose of increasing the carrier's liability, the Convention limits his
liability to 17 SDRs (special drawing rights) per kilogram. However, it has already been
pointed out above that if Article 9 of the Convention applies then this limitation upon the
carrier's liability falls ways. It will also fall away if the claimant can prove that the
damage resulted from an act or omission of the carrier, his servants or agents, done with
intent to cause damage or recklessly and with knowledge that damage would probably
result; provided that, in the case of such act or omission of a servant or agent, it is proved
that he was acting within the scope of his employment.

8.11.5 Prescription Period
The Convention stipulates that the receipt of goods without complaint or qualification by
the person entitled to delivery shall be prima facie evidence that the goods have been
delivered in good condition and in accordance with the terms of the contract of carriage.

Nevertheless, in the case of damage to goods the person entitled to delivery must lodge a
claim against the carrier within 14 days from the date of receipt. In the case of delay the
claim must be made at the latest within 21 days from the date on which the cargo was
received.

If a claim for damage or loss is timeously brought but is rejected by the carrier and the
claimant determines to take the matter to court, the Convention stipulates that his right to
do so shall be extinguished if his action is not brought within two years, reckoned from
the date of arrival at destination, or from the date on which the aircraft ought to have
arrived, or from the date on which the carriage stopped elsewhere.

NB: The Warsaw Convention also provides rules which control contracts entered into by air carriers for the transportation of passengers and their luggage. These aspects of the Convention have been excluded from this Module.

REFERENCES

Bailey C. A. (2007) **"A Guide to Qualitative Field Research."** Pine Forge Press. California.

Bedi K. (2004) **"Production and Operations Management"**. Oxford University Press. New Delhi.

Bhattacharyya D. K. (2003) **"Research Methodology."** Excel Books. New Delhi.

Cook T. A. (2001) **"The Ultimate Guide to Export Management."** AMACOM. New York.

Daniels, Raudebaugh, Sullivan (2004) **"Globalisation and Business."** Prentice Hall International. New Delhi

Frazelle E.H. (2004) **"Supply Chain Strategy."** Tata McGraw-Hill Publishing Co. Ltd. New Delhi.

Gubbins E. J. (2003) **"Managing Transport Operations."** Kogan Page. London.

House D. J. (2005) **"Cargo Work"** Elsevier. Amsterdam

Kapoor S. K. and Kansal P. (2003) **"Marketing Logistics: A Supply Chain Approach."** Pearson Education. New Delhi.

Kirby M., Kidd W et al (1997) **"Sociology in Perspective"** Heinnemann Educational Publishers. Oxford.

Raina H. K. (1990) **"Guide to Import Management"**. PRODEC. Helsinki

Rowland O.P. (1986) **"Imports and Exports: An Introductory Handbook."** Evans Brothers. Ltd. Nairobi

Silverman D. (2006) **"Interpreting Qualitative Data."** Sage Publications. London.

Sople V. V. (2004) **"Logistics Management: The Supply Chain Imperative."** Pearson Education. Singapore.

Thomas A. B. (2004**) "Research Skills for Management Studies."** Routledge, London

CHAPTER 9

INTERNATIONAL SETTLEMENTS AND COSTING

9.1 Transportation Costs

It needs relatively little thought to realise that the establishment of transportation rates by carriers requires appreciable care and a nicety of balance between the volume of revenue which the carriers in question seek to obtain and the ability of the traffic in question to absorb that revenue as a cost increase upon the goods.

International trade utilises a number of different modes of transportation, all of which offer in them alternative facilities for the physical movement of goods.

Maritime transport by sea for cargo in bulk, break-bulk cargo, containerised cargo. Some 80% of the total of commodities, products and goods moving in world trade is transported by the sea mode but of necessity maritime transport is always dependent at both ends of the maritime leg upon some other transport mode.

Air transportation for break-bulk cargo, containerised cargo. Here again, an alternative mode for usually road freight - is essential as a complement at both ends of the air movement for the completion of the delivery.

Rail Transportation for bulk, break-bulk, containerised. Where goods move by rail on a private siding to private siding basis the rail mode provides the complete transport chain. In other instances the support of a road cartage operation remains essential for the completion of delivery.

Road transportation for break-bulk, containerised, swop-body. Road transportation by its nature is a door-to-door operation.

Each separate transport mode which must be employed in order to complete the delivery of the goods at destination involves a further cost. It must also be remembered that the transfer of goods between modes adds yet a further element of cost. Examples of these additional elements of costs are lift charges, terminal handling charges, etc, possible storage charges in transit warehouses awaiting transfer to the second mode to be employed, and similar. Every such cost must be brought into the assessment of the final delivered cost of the goods.

9.2   SHIPPING ECONOMICS

It is important for the forwarder to have some comprehension of the complexity of maritime shipping economics and it is necessary - in order to make the subject intelligible - to break this down into the economics of liner services and, separately the economics of tramping, bulk, and other specialised services.

9.2.1 Cost Structure and Organisation of Liner Shipping

Liner shipping, which broadly embraces the maritime transportation of cargo in containers and cargo in break-bulk form, is very important. Major problems can, and frequently do, arise from the relationships which have developed between individual liner operators on the one hand and importers and exporters o the other.

Many liner services are organised into Conferences of one sort or another (simple conferences, rationalised conferences or pooled conferences). These conferences are not corporate entities in the juristic sense; they are institutions created by multiparty contractual agreements between each other and within those agreements there are disciplinary controls which can be enforced.

However, they present no visible image in the corporate sense to international traders who utilise their services. In the words of an eminent lawyer - "they have neither souls to be damned nor bottoms to be kicked". Conferences as institutions are not normally responsible for the provision of the shipping services which operate within them - the individual members are the service providers.

The primary objective of any conference is to eliminate at the very least competitive pricing between its membership.

Individual members of conferences are theoretically in competition with one another but consequent upon the varying degrees of rationalisation and restriction imposed by the conference rules the area over which competition really exists is very restricted. Nevertheless, such competition as exists, occurs in those aspects of the service which are not of ultimate direct benefit to the client, whether the client be a shipper or a receiver of cargo.

As an example, an individual shipping line within a conference may attempt to attract a larger proportion of higher rated cargoes by introducing vessels capable of a faster sailing speed while charging the approved conference tariff rates - in other words, not demanding a premium upon those rates. To compete with such a situation the other shipping lines within the conference are inevitably compelled to introduce similar faster sailings with the net result that all the conference members move from the use of ships cruising at say 18 knots to ships capable of 21 or 22 knots. Ultimately, this forces the entire conference membership to increase their rates so as to cover the extra costs created by the higher cruising speeds.

Prior to the advent of worldwide containerisation, conferences tended to work upon highly complex freight rate structures in which the spread between the highest and lowest rates could in some instances be as extreme as 5 to 6 times.

The underlying principle upon which such complex tariff structures were based was "What the traffic will bear". Thus, cargo having the lowest value per freight ton attracted the lowest freight rates while cargoes having the highest values per ton attracted the highest freight rates. This practice tended to have unfortunate consequences for countries very dependent upon their export trade, such as Zimbabwe. It encouraged producers of primary raw materials - such as unprocessed mineral ores - to export them without any attempt at beneficiation. This was clearly a substantial disadvantage to such economies and in the case of Zimbabwe it is only within recent years that the longer term benefits of beneficiation of our admittedly rich store of mineral resources has become apparent and is now becoming part of the national policy.

In this context the argument is sometimes adduced that freight rate structures of this type simply mean that the rates applicable to higher value cargo subsidise the carriage costs for lower valued cargo. This argument is based on less than half-truths and to test it one must examine the whole structure of liner costs.

9.2.2 Costs of Liner Services
Once a ship owner has committed his ship(s) to a particular trade then his major variable costs are:-
- cargo handling and port costs
- fuel and victualing costs
- crew costs

On careful consideration it will become apparent that the cargo handling and port costs will vary appreciably with every separate voyage whereas the crew, fuel and victualing costs will remain almost uniform for every voyage irrespective of the amount of cargo lifted.

As a rough average handling and port costs amount to about 25% of the total costs of a liner operation so that the balance of total costs (75%) are virtually fixed for each round voyage.

Of this 75%, some costs are avoidable and others are unavoidable. Costs which may be avoided are, of course, eliminated by the ship owner's decision not to undertake the voyage at all. He will save himself wages, stores, fuel and certain repair and maintenance costs. However, even then costs such as capital, interest thereon, and depreciation of the ship are unavoidable. These may be regarded as finance charges and as a rough average they calculate out at approximately 40%. To summarise, therefore:

Cargo handling and ports costs	-	25%
Finance costs	-	40%
Other voyage costs	-	35%

The voyage costs mentioned last above obviously can be avoided if the voyage is not made but those costs are fixed and unavoidable once the voyage is committed.

A shipping company will devise its lowest rates at a level sufficient only to cover the direct costs of carrying the low value cargo. If, for example, a cargo is good bottom cargo - that is, it is heavy enough to obviate the necessity of carrying ballast, - then this could justify a freight rate which only covers costs and makes no contribution to revenue.

However, when one considers the average shipping line it must be stated that by no means every sailing attracts such useful bottom cargo. Having digested this, the question remains whether high rated cargo contributes to the cost of the carriage of low rated cargo. It is apparent that only 25% of those costs can be identified as accruing from a particular type of cargo. Once a voyage has been committed, the other 75% cannot be allocated to any specific cargo. Thus, if each cargo covers its own direct costs, then there is no cross subsidisation.

It is very important to understand this because international traders persist in retaining the perception that if a ship owner were able to eliminate the carriage of low paying cargo he would then be in a position to reduce freight rates on the higher paying cargo. Provided the low paying cargo is at least covering its direct costs and at least contributing towards the indirect costs then the opposite will apply, and the elimination of lower rated cargoes could very well lead to even higher rates on other cargoes.

9.2.3   Effect of Equalising Freight Rates
Equalisation involves the charging of the same freight rate per unit or cargo for a particular commodity on a particular trade irrespective of the ports of loading and discharge despite the fact that the costs involved may be very different. To illustrate in a simple form, the cost of transporting a commodity from Hamburg to Durban is clearly measurably greater than the cost of transporting the same commodity from Hamburg to Cape Town - purely because of the differential in sailing distance. Nevertheless, all the ships serving the North West Continent/South Africa trades charge the same freight rates irrespective of the ports of loading and of discharge. Consider now that the effect would be if for example, the port of Cape Town substantially improved its operating efficiency and thus reduced port costs to a shipping line. Let us assume that this improvement was some 20%. If cargo handling costs are 25% of a ship owner's total operating costs then the cargo owner should be entitled to anticipate a reduction in freight rates from Hamburg to Cape Town of 5% when compared with the corresponding rates to Durban. In practice this would not happen because all the shipping lines in this trade have over the years recorded such cost reductions over the whole of the Cape Town-Durban range of discharging ports with the result that the cost differential for Cape Town in particular is negligible.

If however the efficiency and performance in the port of Cape Town were to drastically reduce by a corresponding percentage then the shipping lines would certainly not be slow to penalise that port by imposing a surcharge on all freight destined thereto. This could well be, for instance, a congestion surcharge.

9.2.4   Cost Structures of Tramp, Bulk and Specialised Shipping Services
A common characteristic of the ships and the shipping companies involved in this type of work is that they all tend to operate in the charter markets. Charter markets are not characterised by institutional structures such as Conferences. The services provided by these organisations are subject to an appreciably greater degree of competition.

The types of ships for discussion here will include:

- ☐ Tramping ships, which may be bulk carriers, or may also be "tweendeckers" designed for operation on time charters in liner trades or merely for tramping about the globe.
- ☐ Straight forward bulk carriers ranging in capacity from 20000 deadweight tons (dwt) to 200 000 dwt.
- ☐ Various combined carriers such as OBO's (ore/bulk/oil)
- ☐ Oil tankers, which include bulk crude oil carriers of up to 500 000 dwt and also oil product carriers which are considerably smaller.
- ☐ Liquid nitrogen gas (LNG) and liquid petroleum gas (LPG) carriers
- ☐ Specialised car and forest product vessels
- ☐ Ultra heavy lift vessels, etc

There is no single shipping trade or market in which these vessels operate. Usually their target markets change according to the necessities of world trade and in any event they interlock depending upon the demands which may arise in any part of the world for their services.

Furthermore, there are specialised markets for specialised vessels although in certain instances the boundaries between those markets are movable. Some tankers can be efficiently cleaned of residues and contaminants so that they can enter the grain trade while Tween-deckers and Ro-Ro vessels can be readily adapted to a wide variety of cargoes.

Tramping vessels tend to be owned and operated by shipping companies whose purpose in life is to make their income from these vessels. They might build their own vessels for "bare boat" chartering to liner operators who may from time to time find themselves short of shipping tonnage to satisfy the demands of a particular trade, or they may, in fact, be tramping subsidiaries of major operators of liner services. They may, furthermore, build their vessels specifically with the purpose of placing them on the open market in the hope and expectation of finding employment on voyage charters, consecutive voyage charters, or even on time charters of appreciable lengths.

Dry bulk carriers were normally found in the ownership of speculative ship builders who relied on chartering their vessels out on the open charter market. Within the last few decades, however, the trend has emerged for dry bulk carriers to be owned by major multinational organisations whose dominant business may, for instance, be steel making, motor car manufacturing, or similar. Such major multinationals have, on occasion, integrated horizontally not only through the ownership of bulk carriers but also the ownership of their own production plants, e.g. iron ore mines - even their own harbour facilities.

Those dry bulk carriers which are owned by independent shipping companies tend to be chartered out on a time, rather than a voyage, basis. Many such vessels are, in fact, built in response to a specific time charter contract which can run for 7 years or more. A lengthy time charter such as this makes economic sense since the ship builder/owner can be confident of obtaining a return on the capital he has outlaid.

Tankers, on the other hand, are very special transport equipment almost entirely confined to the trade of the major oil companies.

On a conservative estimate 40% of tankers engaged throughout the world are owned by such major oil companies. The greater part of the balance of the total world tanker fleet is held by independent owners whose vessels are all tied into the oil companies by long term time charters. Less than 10% of tankers are available to undertake voyage charters.

9.2.5 Freight Rates in the Tramping, Bulk and Specialised Services
In the tramping market competition can be said to be virtually complete. There are many cargo owners and many vessel owners with the result that freight rates fluctuate with supply of, and demand for, shipping space almost on a weekly basis.

This contrasts with the dry bulk and tanker markets in which the greater majority of the tonnage is dedicated and where only the minority of tonnage operates in free market conditions. The effect of this is that a small fluctuation in demand for tonnage in the dry bulk or tanker market can result in a magnified change in the freight rates obtainable on the free market. Thus, for example, a 2% increase in demand for crude oil shipping tonnage can result in a freight increase in the independent tanker trades of as much as 20%.

Apart from their role in the voyage charter market, tramping ships play a very important "cushioning" role in the liner trades. A liner operator faced with an unexpected demand for shipping tonnage in excess of what his fleet can provide will normally charter suitable tramp tonnage on a time charter basis with the entitlement of releasing such tonnage back into the market when the demand has eased. This, of course, has appreciable benefits for cargo owners since the products they are moving internationally will continue to move without visible delays but at the same time it can have a marked effect upon the tramping charter market by pushing up the demand for the vessels in question.

Freight rates in the time charter contrast fairly sharply with the rates which apply to voyage charters. Time charter freight rates tend to reflect the actual operating costs of the vessel in question plus a further percentage to cover the vessel owner's profit.

Voyage charter rates, on the other hand, fluctuate to an appreciable degree in accordance with the ship supply and cargo demand. On occasions the fluctuations over a relatively short period of time can be quite sharp.

Because of the differing rates between time and voyage charters and also because within the voyage charter sector there can be these sharp fluctuations, vessel operators tend to differ in their attitudes to these two types of chartering. A vessel operator will endeavour to time charter his vessels at a time when freight rates in the liner cargo market are relatively high since a higher offer is then most likely to be accepted. By contrast, voyage charters are preferred in those times when freight rates in the liner trades are depressed.

9.2.6 "Laying-up" of Ships
Ship operators whose business is the chartering out of vessels find from time to time that demand may drop with the result that they do not have continuous work for their entire fleets. When this occurs they "lay-up" some portions of their fleet and disband the crews leaving only watchmen and guards. Obviously, the first vessels to be laid up are those with the highest voyage costs - but this does not necessarily mean those with the highest total costs. This difference is important. Older vessels tend to have comparatively high voyage costs as a result of heavier maintenance charges and inefficiencies in their operating, but - because they are older, - lower capital and finance costs (they have already been paid for and depreciated to zero, perhaps). The opposite applies to newer vessels. Older vessels will therefore go into lay-up or may even be sent to the ship-breaker's yards earlier.

9.2.7 Division of Total Costs between the Ship Owner and the Charterer
This will differ according to the type of charter party under which the ship has been hired.

In terms of bare boat charters, the ship owner is only responsible for the financing charges, replacement as necessary and the annual classification inspections. In other words, the ship owner operates more or less as a finance house while the character acts as the operator.

Under voyage charters the ship owner remains responsible for all costs including the wages of the crew, except for loading and discharging of cargo. Of those which the ship owner must bear, 40-60% will be financing charges.

9.2.8 Short Haul and Long Haul Voyages
A very important element which substantially affects ship operating costs is the ratio between costs incurred while sailing between ports and the costs incurred while the ship is stationary alongside quay in the ports in question. On the short haul trades such as those between European countries time spent in port is as much higher ratio when compared with sailing time with the result that operating costs escalate. In fact, certain of the large bulk carrier ship spend more time in port than in sailing.

Obviously, the position is reversed in the long haul trades such as South Africa-Europe or South Africa-Far East. This equally applies in the trade between South Africa and North American ports.

On these trades vessels operators broadly assess that ports costs are some 30% of total operating costs.

9.3 CONTAINER COST CALCULATIONS

Before commencing to consider the comparative costs involved in the several types of container movement it is essential to stress one point.

Other things being equal, and in particular where there is no appreciable difference in costs, shipment of goods on an FCL/FCL basis is the most efficient.

Speed of transit will be greater, security of the goods will be better; risk of damage, etc, will be less; client satisfaction will be enhanced.

Please read the above a second time and note the first four words - "other things being equal". If the difference in prices appears to the forwarder to be appreciable he may be well advised to discuss the whole question with his client and be guided by the client's instructions.

9.3.1 Break Even Points

Every forwarder must be aware of the cargo volumes at which it is more economical to ship FCL than LCL, and vice versa. One serious cause of client dissatisfaction arises when the forwarder is not aware of these break even points and consolidates cargo in a groupage container which ought to have been shipped directly to the importer as FCL traffic.

The calculation of the breakeven point is very simple. In order to make the calculation the forwarder must know the FCL freight rate per container for the commodity in question, the shipping company's LCL rate per freight ton, and his own groupage rate per freight ton.

Example:
Shipment of motors   12.5 freight tons
SS Co LCL rate   95.00 W/M
6m container rate   USD 1600 per TEU

Calculation   - $\dfrac{1600}{95}$ =   16.842 freight tons

Since actual freight tonnage is less than 16.842 it will be more economical to ship as LCL cargo.

However, since shipment as LCL cargo will extend the transit time and introduces certain increased risks the forwarder should discuss the matter with the cargo owner to give him the opportunity to determine for himself the method of shipping he wishes to adopt.

Break even enable every shipping line to maintain a minimum freight charge for small consignments irrespective of the type of service - break-bulk, LCL or FCL which it offers.

Every groupage operator does the same.

The definition of the minimum charge can take two alternative forms as follows:-

"minimum charge   -   1 freight ton", or

"minimum charge   -   USD75 (or USD50 or USD100, as the case may be)

The raising of the minimum charge is always per bill of lading consignment (not per package nor per line on a bill of lading)

9.3.2 Intermodal Calculation

Containers, by their nature and because they are manufactured to very strict external dimensions and lifting facilities, can move over as many different transport modes as are necessary between source and destination. In all container cost calculations it is therefore vital to take into account all of the costs involved.

However, in the vast majority of international movements the client with whom a forwarder is dealing will only be interested in those costs which fall upon him in accordance with the INCOTERM stipulated in the contract in question. The forwarder must have a total comprehension of the cost factors and which of the two parties, seller or buyer, will bear them under each INCOTERM.

9.3.3 FCL Multimodal Costs

These are as follows:-

☐ movement of empty container from container yard to the exporter's premises

☐ movement of loaded container to inland terminal

☐ inland terminal storage, documentation and transfer costs

☐ railage/cartage from inland terminal to loading port

☐ loading port charges (in Zimbabwe known as terminal handling charges)

☐ ocean freight (including surcharges)

☐ discharge port costs (in Zimbabwe known as terminal handling charges)

☐ movement of container to inland terminal

☐ cartage from inland terminal to importer's premises

☐ cartage of empty container from importer's premises to container yard

☐ container yard cleansing and repair charges (if applicable)

☐ turn-in charges, shipping line release fees, forwarder's commission, documentation and release fees.

The forwarder will note that no reference here has been made to ad valorem wharfage which is applicable in respect of both exports and imports over South Africa and Mozambican ports.

No reference has been made to duties and other statutory imposts upon the goods, nor for the cost of customs examination, etc.

Personnel who are involved in compiling estimates/quotations/etc on a regular basis may well consider incorporating all the above cost elements into a standard form in order to ensure that none of these are overlooked in estimating.

Shipping lines offering FCL services do not necessarily offer rates based on the same principles.

Certain lines will quote on terms similar to those offered in respect of break-bulk cargo, but where they do so, they will charge freight on a minimum utilisation factor. That is to say, they may demand that freight be paid on a minimum of 17 tonnes or 23 cubic meters.

Therefore, if either the mass or the volume is less than those prescribed minima "dead freight" will have to be paid on the difference between the actual mass or volume of the cargo shipped and the minima prescribed. Thus, using the above minima as an example, if cargo is freighted on volume and the consignment to be shipped occupies 20m3 and the freight rate is USD100 per m3 then the freight payable will be USD100 x 23 = USD 2 300.00, and not USD2 000.00.

In many shipping trades which have been substantially containerised, the shipping lines involved have adopted a different approach to freight rating. They will quote rates in one or other of the following forms:

☐ A rate per commodity per container - a so-called commodity box rate, or

☐ A fixed rate per container irrespective of commodity - also called "Freight All Kinds" (FAK) rate.

In these instances the rate quoted applies without reference to the mass or volume of cargo loaded into the container. This leaves the forwarder or his client to decide for himself whether it is more economical to dispatch the consignment as LCL cargo loaded with other goods in the same container or as FCL cargo in terms of which the container will move right through to the consignee's nominated delivery point.

Where a shipping line quotes both break-bulk/LCL rates and also an FCL commodity box rate/FAK rate (as described above) then there is a simple "rule of thumb" method which can be used to establish the minimum freight volume needed to make shipment by FCL viable. This requires that the FCL rate quoted is divided by the LCL rate. The quotient thus obtained is the breakeven point. If the cargo measurement is greater than that breakeven point then shipment by FCL container is indicated. If the cargo volume is less, then shipment by LCL cargo must be considered - but bearing in mind that there are certain factors involving costs which will then accrue.

To illustrate the rule of the thump take as an example the following alternative rates:-

Break-bulk/LCL rate	USD199/m
6m FCL rate	USD3 700 per container
12m FCL rate	USD7 780 per container

By doing the simple division sum described above the following figures emerge:-

Break-even point for 6m container is $18.59m^3$

Break-even point for 12m container is $\quad 39.10m^3$

If the volume of the cargo in question for loading to a 6m container exceeds 18.59m3 or the cargo for a 12m container exceeds $39.10m^3$ then FCL shipment is clearly indicated. However, if the cargo volume is less than these break-even points, then the other cost factors must be considered before it can be established whether FCL or LCL shipment is the more economical.

9.3.4 Break-bulk and LCL Multimodal Costs

These include the following:-

☐ collection of the cargo in break-bulk form from the exporter's premises and delivery to a container depot
☐ possible container depot storage charges
☐ packing to container and depot documentation costs
☐ shipping company's LCL charge for movement of the containerised cargo from the container depot to the load port
☐ shipping company's apportionment of the loading port costs
☐ ocean freight (including surcharges)
☐ shipping company's discharge port costs
☐ shipping company's charge on containerised cargo from discharge port to licensed container depot
☐ container depot unpack, storage and documentation charges
☐ cartage from container depot to importer's premises (including unloading from vehicle thereat)
☐ shipping company's LCL documentation and release fees

Break-bulk and LCL freight rates are quoted on the basis of either the freight tonnage, or separate rates for the weight and the measurement.

For instance, in respect of a consignment of 5.746t and $8.387m^3$
The freight rate for the commodity in question may be quoted in the shipping company tariffs as:-

USD100/freight tone W/M
        OR
USD100/M, whichever is the higher revenue.

The freight on the consignment in question would then be:-

USD100 X 8.387   =   USD838.70
        OR
USD100 x 5.746 = USD574.60 or USD 100 x 8.387 = USD838.70

In this instance, of course, the actual freight charge would be USD838.70 in any event.

In other instances the shipping line tariffs may quote freight rates which differ depending whether the weight or the measurement of the consignment is the greater. As is usual, that rate which yields the higher revenue will be the one to be applied.

To take the same consignment mentioned above, the shipping company tariffs might quote the rates as one of the following two alternatives:

USD232/W
or USD199/M, whichever is the higher revenue.

The calculations necessary to determine the freight chargeable would then be:-
        USD 232 on 5.746t   =   USD 1333.07
                USD 199 on 8.387m3 =   USD 1 669.01

NB: The matter of minimum charges for sea freight will be discussed later.

9.3.5 Groupage Multimodal Costs
These include the following:-
☐   collection from client's premises to container depot
☐   possible container depot storage charges
☐   container depot packing and documentation costs
☐   apportionment at groupage operator's tariff rates of the cost of movement of the containerised cargo from container depot to loading port
☐   groupage operator's apportionment of loading port costs
☐   groupage operator's tariff ocean freight charge (including surcharges)
☐   degrouping agent's apportionment of discharge port costs
☐   degroupage operator's charges on containerised cargo from discharge port to licensed container depot
☐   container depot unpack, storage and documentation charges
☐   cartage charges from container depot to importer's premises (including unloading thereat)

☐   groupage operator's commission, documentation and release fees.

The forwarder must appreciate, that circumstances may arise - and frequently do - when further costs become involved for which allowance must be made in any estimate or quotation. These further costs are not strictly transportation costs but they arise during the course of the total transportation. **They are items such as container demurrage, cargo rents, changes in currency exchange rates, delays and consequential costs arising from necessary cargo inspections, e.g. insurance inspection, governmental agency inspections, etc.**

Any estimate or quotation should be qualified to indicate that it is subject to adjustment for all of these reasons and in addition is subject to adjustment in the event of changes in the tariffs of the carriers, harbour authorities, etc., through whose hands the goods must necessarily pass.

Where the forwarder offers a groupage service and therefore endeavours never to use the shipping company's LCL service, then the rate comparisons are described in the preceding paragraphs must be made by reference to the forwarder's groupage rates instead to the break-bulk/LCL rates.

In broad terms it is correct to say that the groupage operator's rates will be higher than those offered by the shipping lien for its LCL service for a series of reasons, amongst which is the far more personalised service provided by the groupage operator. Put in a nutshell, the groupage operator provides a "premium service" having a greater value to the cargo owner than the routine LCL services offered by shipping lines.

Moreover, the shipping lines offering LCL services do not need to concern themselves with maximising container utilisation whereas it is vital to the groupage operator that he does so. In fact, the groupage operator is always taking commercial risks which involve financial considerations to him.

For these reasons he is justified in offering a rate which will be higher than the LCL rate, and experience over many years has shown clearly that international traders usually prefer to utilise a groupage operator rather than to employ a shipping line LCL service, preferring to leave his work to forwarders and their groupage services.

The forwarder offering a groupage service can quite simply do the calculations necessary to determine the break-even point discussed above but a further consideration always intrudes upon the decision whether the groupage service or the FCL service should be employed. This consideration is the "self-interest" of the forwarder. As a groupage operator he is constantly on the lookout for as much cargo as he can possibly obtain to maximise the volumes in his groupage containers in order to ensure that every groupage container makes for him a reasonable profit. A situation may arise in which, despite the fact that shipment FCL may be more economical for the client, it would nevertheless be to the advantage of the forwarder to incorporate the cargo in a groupage container giving him appreciable additional profits and perhaps the possibility of being in the position to ship that container on an earlier shipping opportunity to the benefit of all his clients with cargo in that container.

In such a situation the forwarder has a very important commercial decision to make in which the perceived interests of the trade and himself are in conflict.

9.4 LUMP SUM PRICES

Instances arise every now and then in a forwarder's life when he is asked to undertake a transaction in respect of which pricing by means of tariffs is impractical or inappropriate. These instances usually involve the movement of large volumes of mixed but disparate cargo from place to place. The transaction may involve the uprooting of an entire factory or an entire section of a factory from its site in one country and its transportation to a new site in another country inclusive of all the dismantling, protection and packing, of the goods at the place of origin, the utilisation of mobile cranes, heavy lift vehicles, containers, flat racks, and possibly shipment of certain parts of the cargo in a break-bulk fashion.

Where a forwarder is involved in this sort of work it may be quite impossible to price the job by means of reference to the forwarder's normal tariffs. The only practical alternative is by offering to undertake the work on the basis of a lump sum price.

The forwarder must ensure that the client defines as explicitly as possibly precisely what he requires the forwarder to do - both in the country of origin of the goods and also in Zimbabwe. There should be no risk that misunderstandings exist on this score.

Since the movement from site to site is involved it is clear that the forwarder's associate or agent in the country of origin will have to become deeply involved, and if the job is a major project it will pay the Zimbabwean forwarder to travel overseas to the site personally or to send his senior representative to inspect the entire operation personally and to agree on the spot with the overseas agent exactly how the operation overseas should proceed. This might sound an expensive exercise but it is only by personal contact of this nature that expensive misunderstandings, errors, and arguments can be avoided.

At the same time a thorough inspection of the destination site in Zimbabwe must also be undertaken with particular reference to access facilities, hard standing areas for cranes which will be required to move heavy lifts, if an existing building is to be utilised for housing the goods, whether the access doors are adequate or whether possibly a portion of the wall must be broken open, etc.

Where out-of-gauge items must be moved by road it is essential that the entire route be surveyed in association with provincial and other road authorities to ensure that culverts and bridges are of adequate strength, power lines and telecommunication lines are not placed at risk, that gradients and sharp bends are carefully assessed if any very heavy lifts or long lengths are involved, etc.

Consideration must also be given to the time of year when the movement will take place having in mind that at certain times of peak road traffic slow moving vehicles may be prohibited on main roads, and certainly abnormal loads requiring police escorts may only be permitted to move short distances at a time. Driving hours and the scheduling of drivers and drivers' mates must be considered.

These are but a very few of the complexities which can arise and it will be obvious that a total assessment of all costs must be made with suitable margins incorporated to cover contingencies.

It will be very clear to the forwarder that where this type of work is involved tariffs are useless. Major assessments of the costs involved must be made and the forwarder will be well advised to investigate the relative abilities of alternative sub-contractors who may be available to do portions of the work and are invited to quote him. This will equally apply to the relative merits of shipping by a Conference service as compared to the services offered by an independent shipping line.

In such an instance the forwarder must consider the advisability of applying to customs of the privilege of treating the entire transaction as a staged consignment rather than a series of separate importations. It may well be that the complete movement may involve a whole series of shipments and it is possible that while the bulk of the goods may move by sea others may require to be moved by air so that the full requirements of an application for a staged consignment ruling must be submitted for approval.

Furthermore, the question of ad valorem wharfage must not be forgotten. The rules for the determining of the maximum value of consignments for the purpose of ad valorem wharfage must be considered. The assumption is that these type of consignments, for the foreseeable future, will only move via South African ports.

It is vitally important in connection with this type of transaction that the forwarder elicits from his client a total co-operation with the fullest possible detail. Only if he is confident that he has received such co-operation will the forwarder be justified in submitting his tender or quotation for undertaking the transaction involved. Even then, he must qualify his tender or quotation with clauses which entitle him to vary his quoted lump sum price in accordance with fluctuations in shipping company and airline tariffs, in customs tariffs, and in consequence of changes in labour rates authorised by industrial councils and other statutory or quasi-statutory bodies.

Over and above this he must reserve to himself the right to vary the prices in accordance with fluctuations in the rates of exchange between the Zimbabwe dollar and those currencies in which the various portions of the costs will be incurred, e.g. overseas road transportation, overseas port charges, ocean freight rates, etc.

Finally, no tender or quotation should ever be submitted without a limiting date being specified within it for the acceptance of it by the organisation to which it is submitted.

A suitable clause in the forwarder's trading conditions is described in terms of which the offer of a fixed price for the accomplishment of any task shall not itself determine whether the task is to be arranged by the forwarder acting as agent or as principal. Particularly when the forwarder is dealing with a major task such as has been postulated above the forwarder has much greater protection from liability if he is employed as an agent than if the client insists that he acts as a principal.

Accordingly, when the forwarder is tendering on the basis of a lump sum price he should incorporate in the stipulations governing his tender that in all matters attendant upon the task he is acting as an agent.

9.5 QUOTATIONS AND TENDERS FOR PROJECT WORK
Quotations must be handled with care and a due sense of caution. If a quotation is issued without full knowledge of the transaction involved, or with insufficient skill on the part of the forwarder they can prove to be a source of severe embarrassment and of financial loss.

Since the forwarder is frequently called upon to provide quotations it is essential that he employs a skilled and experienced person for their compilation clearly defining the parameters of the job.

Frequently traders asking for quotations tend to couch their enquiries in vague terms without supplying details which are absolutely vital to the calculation of the costs involved.

"What will be the costs of getting a consignment of 5000 electric hair clippers from Munich to Bulawayo?"

No mention of the supplier's terms of delivery - ex works, FOB German or other port, whether required by sea or by air, no mention of value, no mention of any insurance requirements, - in fact, no details essential to the compilation of any quotation.

"I am a Harare manufacturer of ladies crocodile skin handbags and I have found a distributor in Paris who is interested and who will act as my agent for sales throughout Western Europe. He wants me to give him a price delivered to his warehouse in Paris. Can you help me, please?"

An enquiry such as this probably comes from a person who has never been in international trade previously and will need a great deal of schooling. He has not mentioned quantities, methods of packing, whether by sea or by air, who is to insure, etc.

It is quite obvious from the two quoted examples that a lot of additional information must be obtained.

Moreover, it may be quite essential to ascertain whether the traffic will be regular.

Should the forwarder in fact be responsible for marine insurance on the consignments expected to move, it will also be advisable to ascertain the formula by means of which the value of insurance purposes must be calculated.

9.5.1 Costs and Contingency Risks which must be provided for in any quotation

A list of all normal costs likely to be incurred in respect of imported goods from ex works to delivered importer's domicile follows. The list is divided by reference to the various possible terms of delivery (INCOTERMS).

Ex works (EXW) - all costs as enumerated below

Free Carrier (FCA) - loading to vehicle/wagon delivery to port/airport/container depot

Free Alongside Ship (FAS) - as for free carrier plus export licenses, permits, etc.
Free on Board (FOB) - dock charges and loading costs. Export customs clearance/bill of lading

Cost and Freight (CFR) - ocean freight plus surcharges to be added to or deducted from the freight

Cost Insurance and Freight (CIF) - as for CFR plus marine insurance

Carriage paid to (CPT) - dock charges, wharfage, inland transport charges or airfreight charges to destination. (This term applies to multimodal transportation in containers and to airfreight charges to destination airport.

Carriage and Insurance paid to (CIP) - marine insurance

In addition to normal costs as described in the previous paragraph care must be taken also to include all those additional costs which may be appropriate in certain instances. These may include any or all of the following:-

☐ dismantling costs at the location of origin
☐ costs for protection and packing of the goods suitable to the method of transportation
☐ preparation of detailed packing lists in respect of each shipment involved
☐ hire of cranage for loading goods to transport equipment at point of origin
☐ additional costs for hire of abnormal load vehicles
☐ cost of permits, etc for the conveyance of abnormal loads in the country of origin.
☐ hire of heavy lift or floating cranes at port of loading
☐ hire of similar cranes at port of discharge

- provision of abnormal load vehicles at the quayside at the port of discharge
- cost of permits for the transport of abnormal loads inland within Zimbabwe
- cost of inspection of routes and adjustments to obstacles along those routes
- hire of suitable cranes for discharge of vehicles at final destination etc, etc.

It is obvious that these additional costs will in the majority of instances not be involved but it is important that all who are engaged in compiling quotations consider thoroughly every aspect of work which will be needed and create their costing accordingly.

After consideration of all the costs and expenses which will be involved in the operation in question in the issue arises with regard to contingency margins essential to provide against unforeseen problems and profit margins.

9.5.2 Contingency Margins

It must be emphasised that despite every care brought to bear upon the compilation of quotations there are likely always to be unforeseen problems such as delays in customs clearance, delays in the availability of abnormal load vehicles, etc, which will involve additional costs and it must be within the competence of the compiler of a quotation to assess the risk in this regard and to provide for it in his total quotation.

It must be borne in mind that if a quotation is accepted or a tender for a major project is awarded, there will be substantial call upon the overhead expenses of the forwarding organisation involved, substantial travelling expenses, substantial involvement of the time and expense of senior staff, and the usual involvement of middle and lower management together with clerical staff in the detail for the achievement of the work and all of these must be accounted for within the quotation.

Once all these additional expenses are incorporated in the figure it still remains to say that a further addition must be made to provide for a reasonable percentage of net profitability for the company concerned. The quantum to be added in this regard is a matter of determination by senior management and should be discussed with them.

It will be obvious from a careful study of this Chapter that the compilation of quotations and tenders is a job requiring skill, expertise and research. It may also involve travelling and similar activities which may well involve expenses rather greater than at first may appear.

In fact, although an offer to quote or tender for major transportation may well be seen as glamorous and very interesting, it is better not to tender unless the company concerned has confidence that they have the inbred and in-house ability of undertake the work smoothly, efficiently, and to make adequate profit from it. This involves a consideration not only of the ability of the Zimbabwean forwarder but also the abilities of his overseas associates or agents. In this connection it must be pointed out that the most efficient

Zimbabwean organisation may find itself devastated by inefficiency or incompetence on the part of its overseas associates.

9.5.3 Surcharges on Freight Rates

Under normal circumstances shipping companies servicing the international trades of Zimbabwe endeavour as a matter of principle to limit increases in freight charges to once a year. The adoption of this principle has great benefits for both the importing and exporting community within Zimbabwe since it has assisted appreciably to stabilise costs and to enable estimates to be projected forward with a reasonable measure of confidence.

However, certain of the essential operating costs in the liner trades tend to be volatile, sometimes resulting in unacceptably high increases in operating costs which are impossible of prediction in advance. The most common of these is the fluctuations which take place in the cost of bunker fuel oils. On occasions, in addition, port congestion may involve unexpected delays in ship movements which increase operating costs without the possibility of any increase in operating revenues.

Fluctuations in international currency exchange rate and the development of warlike situations in some part of the world also have the same effect.

For these and certain other reasons shipping companies, while seeking to maintain their basic freight tariffs consistent for yearly periods, are compelled from time to time to impose surcharges on the basic freight rates - and such surcharges will, of necessity, fluctuate according to the circumstances which are involved. These surcharges, the reasons for them, and the methods of application of them must be considered.

Bunker Adjustment Factor (BAF)

"Bunkers" is the nautical term for the fuel oil which provides the energy necessary to ship movement.

Where the price for the purchase of fuel oils necessary to the bunkering of ships in a certain trade moves beyond the parameters already provided in the budgets of the shipping lines servicing that trade, a surcharge (BAF) will be imposed. This imposition will take effect in respect of all cargo shipped from a stated date but it is calculated on the prices already prevailing and the charges which the shipping line in question is already having to pay.

It may be expressed either as a percentage of the ocean freight rates or as a specific charge raised in the freight currency per freight ton for break-bulk or LCL cargo, or per container box or FAK rates.

Bunker adjustment factors are reviewed by the shipping lines at monthly intervals. They may remain static for a period or they may move upward or downward.

Currency Adjustment Factor (CAF)

In the great majority of international shipping trades the tariff currency which determines the revenue which is earned by shipping lines is the United States Dollar. By contrast, the expenses incurred by shipping lines e.g. port dues, harbour berthing charges, use of tugs, purchase of chandling supplies and drinking water, pilot charges, etc. - are incurred in the various currencies of the many different countries at which their ships call.

If the value of the tariff currency (USD) falls against a basket of the currencies in which the expenses are incurred this has the effect of increasing the operating expenses of the line involved. If the level of this increase becomes unacceptably high then the line will impose a surcharge (CAF) to compensate for the increase in the operating expenses.

If, of course, the value of the tariff currency rises against the currencies in which the expenses are incurred, then the surcharge can be decreased. In fact, it may be decreased to a negative factor where this is justified, effectively reducing the amount payable by the cargo owner.

Currency adjustment factors are normally quoted as a percentage upon the tariffied freight rate and they are reviewed monthly and adjusted where appropriate.

Congestion Surcharge
Where a regular port of call for any reason becomes chronically congested the effect is that vessels of a shipping line will be forced to anchor off the port awaiting their turn on a berth in that port. While any vessel is idle no revenue is being earned but expenses continue to be incurred very substantially on a daily basis. To compensate for the complete loss of revenue the shipping line will impose a congestion surcharge - normally a percentage uplift on the freight charges.

In practice, shipping lines accept for their own expense minor congestion, and will hesitate to impose a surcharge until it becomes clear that the congestion is going to continue for an appreciable period of time. Accordingly, by the time they consider themselves justified in imposing a congestion surcharge they have already suffered appreciable losses, all of which must ultimately be recouped.

For this reason it is important to understand that a congestion surcharge is not normally imposed at the commencement of the period of congestion but it may well continue for a period after the congestion has disappeared so that the recouping of losses is completed.

War Surcharges
Where a state of war or a warlike hostility develops in any areas of the world shipping lines trading to and from such an area are immediately faced with an increase in insurance premium which they must pay against the risk of damage and loss to the ship and its equipment and the life and limb of the ship's crew.

Depending upon the extent and severity of the war situation the increase in the insurance premiums required may be substantial and it is customary under such circumstances for the shipping lines in question to apportion the increase as equitably as possible over all the parties involved - the shipping line itself, the membership of the crew, and the cargo interests involved in each voyage.

Abnormal Cargo Surcharges

The major business of any forwarder involves the movement of goods on so-called "liner terms". These terms are embodied in the shipping line's tariff and the normal costs for loading and unloading of cargo and its manipulation where necessary within the ship's hold are included therein. However, where cargo exceeds the shipping line's definition of "normal" mass or dimensions so that special equipment must be employed for loading and discharge, etc, then the line will impose an abnormal cargo surcharge.

Where break-bulk cargo is concerned this surcharge may be referred to as either a long length surcharge or a heavy lift surcharge (or a combination of both). For containerised cargo it is commonly known as either an "out of gauge, over height, over width" or "over mass" surcharge.

These surcharges are normally raised in accordance with a sliding scale dependent upon the extent of the abnormality involved.

Application of Surcharges upon Seafreight

Because both currency exchange rates and costs of bunker fuel oils are subject to constant fluctuations throughout the world it must be accepted that CAF and BAF will be involved in virtually every calculation of seafreight charges.

In the major shipping trades to and from Zimbabwe e.g. ZSS, MSC, etc, these two forms of surcharge are separately applied to the basic freight rate. That is to say, they are not applied cumulatively, one upon the other.

This, however, is not a universal rule with the result that any enquiry from a shipping line with regard to a seafreight rate must not only include an enquiry with regard to the surcharges applicable but should also establish at the same time whether they are applied separately or cumulatively.

The other surcharges which have been described earlier are all applied separately. The application of any particular surcharge is a matter of simple arithmetic.

9.6   AIRFREIGHT COSTING

A very important difference between ocean freight rates and airfreight rates is that the latter are always quoted in the currency of the country in which the airfreight movement commences. There is no common worldwide tariff currency.

Airfreight rate structures are in general a great deal less complex than those applying to seafreight. With a few exceptions the unit used to calculate airfreight charges is the "chargeable weight".

Perhaps in Zimbabwe we ought to call it the "chargeable mass" but this is not the general term in use worldwide! On most routes this is defined as the greater of the volume of the consignment in cubic centimetres divided by a constant (usually 6000) or its actual gross weight in kilogrammes.

Thus, in the case of a consignment with a mass of 200kg and dimensions 590cm x 60cm x 20cm the volume of the cargo must first be determined and thereafter immediately divided by 6000. The quotient thus obtained must then be compared with the actual gross weight in kilogrammes. The higher of the two figures will be the "chargeable weight".

Calculation:

$$\frac{590 \times 60 \times 20}{6000} = 118$$

Compare 118 with the actual gross weight 200kgs
The chargeable weight is the actual gross weight of 200kg.

Where a number of dissimilar packages are involved in the consignment, the volume of each one must be calculated, the sum of these volumes must then be divided by 6000 and the comparison made as stated above.

Certain non-IATA airlines may use a different constant for the purpose of the division necessary in the above calculation. That constant may be perhaps 5000 instead of 6000. The effect of the use of a different constant - particularly a constant of a lower value - will be to increase the likelihood that the cargo in question will require to be freighted by its volume rather than its weight.

9.6.1 Cost Analysis: Air versus Sea
In international trade the question is constantly asked as to whether for a particular consignment, it will be economically advantageous to consign the goods by air or by sea and only too frequently decisions are made largely on the basis of a straight comparison of the alternative rates.

It can be stated categorically that decisions so made will invariably be faulty because they fail to take account of the numerous other factors which affect the true total costs of the goods when eventually taken into a production process or sold onwards. These additional factors are the following:-

- [ ]   Additional inland costs prior to shipment by sea and subsequent to discharge from the sea-going vessel
- [ ]   The time cost of the total transit
- [ ]   The foreign exchange risk exposure
- [ ]   Stock holding costs incurred by the buyer
- [ ]   Freight purchasing leverage
- [ ]   Stock obsolescence risks

The clearest way of describing the effects of these additional factors is to take a practical example.

Assume: A Harare importer requires 10 components per week for his uninterrupted manufacturing process. The component has the following characteristics:

Value each	-	$50 000
Dimensions each	-	100 x 20 x 40cms
Mass each	-	100kg
Time cost of money	-	20% per annum

Freight rates are:-
Airfreight	-	$12 per kg chargeable weight
Seafreight	-	Port to port $250 per freight ton
Durban-Harare	-	$30 per freight ton

Wharfage	-	1.78% of value for duty purposes (max value $22 000 per freight ton)

Airfreight lead time - 2 weeks

Seafreight lead time - 8 weeks

Assessment of total cost by Seafreight
Assume today that the importer had 40 units 4 weeks ago.
To maintain his production programme he must order a further 40 units today.

Total freight charges for each shipment of 40 units is:-

	3.2m3 @	250		=
$800				
Inland transportation	3.2m3 @	$130	=	$416
Wharfage	$22000 x 3.2 @ 1.78%		=	$1253
TOTAL			=	$2469

Total per unit (40 units) = $61.73 per unit (in round figures)

The units ordered 4 weeks ago will only arrive in 4 weeks time. The time cost of the money which consequently is "dead" for 8 weeks will therefore be:

$$40 \text{ units} \quad @ \quad \$50\,000 @ \$20\% \times \frac{8}{52} \quad = \quad \$61\,538$$

Consider importer's exposure to foreign exchange risks

Units ordered 4 weeks ago, 40 units @ $50 000	-	$2 000 000
New order placed this day, 40 units @ $50 000	-	$2 000 000
		$4 000 000

This exposure to the fluctuations is foreign exchange rates subsists for 8+4 = 12 weeks duration.

Consider the cost of the stock already held by the importer which has 40 units being utilised at a rate of 10 units per week. If the cost of money is 20% per annum then his stockholding is costing the following:-

Week 1:   40 units @ $50 000 x 20% x $\dfrac{1}{52}$ $7 692

Week 2:   30 units @ $50 000 x 20% x $\dfrac{1}{52}$ $5 769

Week 3:   20 units @ $50 000 x 20% x $\dfrac{1}{52}$ $3 846

Week 4:   10 units @ $50 000 x 20% x $\dfrac{1}{52}$ $1 923

Total   **$19 230**

The average weekly cost of the stock in hand therefore amounts to $4 808

Assessment of total costs by Airfreight
Assume the importer orders on a weekly basis, 10 units each week. Then he will have this day 10 units in stock, 10 units already ordered a week ago and he must order a further 10 units today.

The cost of airfreight on this day's order will be:-
1000kgs @ $12   = $12 000

The goods ordered this day will be in transit for 2 weeks and the time cost of money will be:-

10 units @ $50 000 @ 20% x $\dfrac{2}{52}$ = $3 846

Consider the importer's exposure to foreign exchange risks:-

Older order   10 units @ $50 000 $ 500 000
New order   10 units @ $50 000 $ 500 000
TOTAL   **$1 000 000**

This exposure will be for 1 + 2 = 3 weeks duration.

Consider the cost of stockholding (in weekly terms for simplicity's sake)

10 units @ $50 000   @ 20% x $\frac{1}{52}$ $ 1 923

To summarise and compare:-

	Sea	Air
Freight per unit	$43	$1 200
Time cost in transit	$61 538	$3 846
Forex risk Amount	$4 000 000	$1 000 000
Duration	12 weeks	3 weeks
Stockholding costs per week	$4 808	$1 923

It may be argued that this illustration - which indicates clearly the advantages of airfreight over seafreight - is somewhat extreme in that is postulates the movement of goods of a high value with low volume and weight. Nevertheless, it illustrates very clearly that despite the radical contrast between the seafreight and airfreight per unit, when true total costing is applied to the exercise and all factors are taken into account (not merely the freight costs) then airfreight can produce very substantial advantage indeed. The advantages of "Just-In-Time" (JIT) inventory coupled with the speed of airfreight must be very carefully assessed by every importer requiring regular supplies from overseas. In assessing the relative merits of air versus sea the forwarder can be of substantial assistance if he himself understands the nature of the assessments which must be made.

In addition to all the above considerations the importer in question should also realise that, if all his supplies moving along a particular trade route were to be switched from sea to air then he may find himself in a strong position to negotiate a more favourable airfreight rate with one or other of the forwarders servicing that route.

Also the appreciably smaller stockholding which the use of airfreight as a transport mode permits to him will also reduce the risk of stock obsolescence in the event that he has to initiate changes of design or function to his end product.

9.7   BUSINESS CAPITALISATION AND ASSET RATIOS

Money is a commodity just as is any other product, and that money which is "locked up" costs money for the duration of the period during which it is out of use. This is what is meant by the "time cost of money."

All the funds made available from various sources to the company in question can be broadly regarded as 'working capital' available to the directors to utilise as they think fit. However, it would be most unwise if they decided to utilise the entire funds in the erection of an office block or factory since they would have no further funds available to finance the day-to-day activities of the company.

Only a limited proportion of those funds dare be used in the purchase or creation of offices, of plant and equipment, of office equipment, or of vehicles and other transport equipment. The smaller the funds so used, the better; a larger proportion will be left for utilisation in day-to-day trading.

When goods are in transit the money that the goods represent is "dead" in the sense that it cannot be put to any other use in the course of trading. Thus, the different freight rates offered by different shipping lines must be evaluated against the different costs of the money involved resulting from the different sailing frequencies and transit times of the shipping lines being considered.

Example 1

A Consignment is valued at	$600 000
Shipping line A offer a freight rate of	$ 4 200
Shipping line B offer a freight rate of	$ 3 000
Difference in favour of shipping line B	**$ 1 200**
Sipping line A has sailing frequency of	9 days
Shipping line A has transit time of	21 days
Total effective transit time shipping line A	**30 days**
Sipping line B has sailing frequency of	12 days
Shipping line BV has transit time of	35 days
Total effective transit time shipping line B	**47 days**

Difference in effective transit time 47 - 30 = 17 days.

Assume that the cost of money is 14.5% per annum
Then the time cost of dead money if shipping line B is used is:-
$600 000 @ 14.5% per annum for 17 days

$$\frac{\$600\,000 \times 14.5 \times 17}{100 \times 365} = \mathbf{4\,052}$$

It is clear that if the cargo owner utilises the lower freight rate offered by shipping line B then the shipping will cost him $2 852 more ($4 052 less $1200) than if he had used shipping line A because of the time cost of dead money. In other words, in this example, the use of the cheaper freight rate will, in fact, prove to be more expensive due to the time cost of the money involved.

Moreover, this is not the end of the equation. The goods will be in transit at the cheaper freight rate for 47 days instead of 30 days which may also involve enhanced cash flow problems, dissatisfied customers - if the goods are for onward selling, etc.

Example 2

A consignment is valued at	$120 000
Shipping line A offers a freight rate of	$ 4 200
Shipping line B offers a freight rate of	$ 2 700
Difference in favour of shipping line B	**$ 1 500**

Shipping line A has a sailing frequency of	7 days	
Shipping line A has a transit time of	21 days	
Total effective transit time		**28 days**

Shipping line B has a sailing frequency of	10 days	
Shipping line B has a transit time of	28 days	
Total effective transit time		**38 days**

Difference in effective transit time   **10 days**

Assume the cost of money is 14.5% per annum.
Then the time cost of dead money if shipping line B is used is:-

$120 000 @ 14.5% per annum for 10 days

$$\frac{\$120\ 000 \times 14.5\% \times 10}{100 \times 365} \qquad = \qquad \mathbf{\$477}$$

In this example shipping line B could with advantage be used as the net saving by comparing the freight differential with the time cost of the dead money is :-

$1 500 - $477   =   **$1 023.**

If you substitute the value of the consignment in Example 2 by the value of the consignment in Example 1 - $600 000 of $120 000 - it will become very clear that, in general, the higher value of a consignment the faster its total transit time should be in order to minimise the time cost of the money which is "dead" during transit.

It has to be remarked here and now that this is a most important factor when considering the relative merits of seafreight versus airfreight.

9.7.1 Capitalisation
A very clear distinction must be drawn between "working capital" and the "capitalisation" of the company. The capitalisation is limited to the paid up ordinary shares, the paid up preferential shares, and any permanent loans provided to the company by the directors. In this context "permanent" means loans which the lender may not recover without the permission of the full board of directors of the company. Such loans will obviously bear a rate of interest payable to the lender but for all practical purposes the money lent is "locked in" to the company unless with the permission of the full board of directors the loan is released or a substitutionary loan from another party is arranged.

Capitalisation does not include overdraft and loan facilities granted by banks or other financial institutions.

It is acceptable that a carefully assessed proportion of the "capitalisation" of a company is utilised for the purchase or creation of fixed assets such as land, buildings, plant and equipment, office furnishings, etc., provided that a sufficient proportion of the capitalisation of the company is retained as "liquidity" or "cash in hand" with which to undertake its daily trading activities. The apportionment of the capitalisation of the company to be utilised on the acquisition of fixed assets and the amount to be retained for trading purposes is a matter for determination by the directors of the company and will vary according to the known or estimated trading requirement.

Capitalisation of a Forwarding Organisation

Forwarding, by its nature, is labour and liquidity intensive rather than fixed asset intensive. Assets such as motor vehicles, office equipment and machinery, with suitable office accommodation will obviously be essential. This, however, must be kept to the minimum consistent with efficient operation. By contrast, a forwarding business requires very substantial liquidity for the purpose of the payment of the many varieties of disbursement which a forwarder must outlay on behalf of his clientele. With comparatively few exceptions, it is wise if the forwarder endeavours to ensure that his ratio between liquidity and the cost of fixed assets is no less than 10:1. Even this ratio is unlikely in practice to be sufficient, with the result that the forwarder will have to go for the balance of the working capital which he requires to a bank or other financial institution for overdraft facilities or short term loans. It must be kept in mind at all times that bank overdraft facilities and loans are at the sole discretion of the bank. They may be called in or reduced without notice and at the entire discretion of the bank management.

Obviously, any bank granting such facilities will require guarantees from the company directors, by bonds over property, by cession of the company's debtor ledger, or from some other source. It is common bank policy to obtain if they can sell these different forms of security. The bank seek security to the maximum degree irrespective of the level of facility granted. It is important to a forwarding organisation to resist any attempt by its regular banker to take over all the possible sources of security which may be available. The bank does not really need very much greater security than the extent of the facility they have granted. If the forwarder can resist successfully the bank's attempts to take over all the security which the company can offer then the forwarder retains some proportion of those securities with which it can, at need, negotiate alternative facilities with a competing bank. If a forwarding organisation achieves success in thus obtaining facilities from more than one bank it reduces appreciably the risk of business failure should either one of the two banks involved decide to call in its facilities.

In addition, when "push comes to shove" the holding of the separate facilities matches the one bank with the other in a competitive position reducing in some degree the inclination of either bank to call in its facilities or unjustifiably increase its interest rate.

Interest on Overdraft Facilities

The level of interest on overdraft amounts is conditioned by the "bank rate" of the Zimbabwe Reserve Bank. The level of interest is therefore not easily within the control of the commercial bank with whom the forwarder deals.

However, if the facility granted is overdraft and not a loan, then the amount of interest due to the bank will be conditioned by the daily amount of the overdraft utilised.

This, in turn, leads to the consideration of the forwarder's efficiency in client selection and credit control. If the forwarder selects carefully the clients with which he chooses to do business and then exercises stringent credit control over the amounts outstanding from time to time he can ensure that his cash flow into his bank account is maintained at a satisfactory level which minimises the extent to which he has to rely on his overdraft facility and pay interest upon it.

9.7.2   Asset Ratios

The assets of a business organisation will include the following

- [ ] land and buildings where owned wholly or partly by the organisation
- [ ] factory, plant and equipment
- [ ] office equipment and machinery
- [ ] transport equipment
- [ ] goods handling equipment
- [ ] debtors accounts
- [ ] cash in hand and at bank (other than bank loans, overdraft, etc)

9.7.3   Liabilities

A business organisation's liabilities will include the following:-
paid up share capital - i.e.

- [ ] shareholder's funds invested in the organisation
- [ ] loans granted to the organisation
- [ ] lease agreements entered into
- [ ] bonds given
- [ ] all reserve accounts, i.e. undistributed profits
- [ ] creditors accounts unpaid
- [ ] overdrafts outstanding to bank(s)

9.7.3   Solvency

A company is solvent when its total assets exceed its total liabilities. It is an offense under the Companies Act for a business organisation to continue trading when its liabilities exceed its assets since it is then insolvent. When this occurs and the business is put into liquidation the directors may be held personally liable for the liabilities which are not covered by the assets.

A key ratio is therefore that of assets to liabilities but there are a number of others by which the viability and health of a business may be judged and these include the following:-

☐ debtors to creditors
☐ paid up share capital to fixed assets
☐ reserve accounts to share capital

9.8 CASHFLOW MANAGEMENT

9.8.1 Invoicing

Invoices will always be divided into two parts, the first covering disbursements made by the forwarding agent on behalf of his principal and the second listing the fees which he raises as his remuneration for the services which he renders. He will also include a fee for allowing his own ledger accounts to be used through which dock charges, railage, ocean freight or airfreight, are collected and paid by him so that he can pass those charges on to his client in a consolidated account. In addition to all this he will charge for such telephone, telefax, and other communication costs which he may incur and some form of "sundries" charge.

The agency fee which he will charge over and above the fees for services will be conditioned by a variety of formulae from amongst which he will charge the highest alternative.

Finally, since it is normal for the forwarding agent to allow credit for an agreed period to his client he must charge a finance fee to cover the cost of the money in respect of which he is giving the credit. This fee may be fairly substantial since it will not only be equal to the interest charge raised by the forwarder's bank for the bank overdraft facilities which the forwarder used but will be enhanced by at least 2% to compensate for the financial risk which the forwarder inevitably incurs as a result of granting his credit terms, together, with a further 1% as a modest profit margin on the financial transaction involved.

Example: The following is an example of a simple invoice issued by a forwarding agent in connection with an import consignment where no abnormalities or unusual features exist and where no examination by Customs nor freight collection was involved.

Disbursement Account:

Duty, etc		$10 000
Port Charges	250	
Wharfage		570
Insurance		350
Railage		1 420
Delivery		220	**$12 990**

Fees:

Documentation		175
Arranging insurance	7	
Finance fees	129	
Agency		650
Communication fees	25	
Sundries	12	1 383
Total		**$14**
373		

Fees as percentage of disbursements	10,65%
Fees as percentage of gross invoice	9,62%

NB: The actual level at which the various fees are raised is a matter to be determined by the forwarder after careful consideration of the fixed costs arising in this business, and his competitive position in the forwarding community. The fees listed above are not to be taken as correct or appropriate to any individual forwarder.

Taken in isolation the example has no particular impact but if it is taken to be one account out of 50 or 100 precisely similar accounts issued during a monthly accounting period then the impact on the funds of a clearing agent can be assessed and considered.

Assume: the clearing agent handles 50 precisely similar importations during a month then the funds which must be available to him in order to cope with the disbursements he must make, will be:

   50 x 12 990 = $649 500 ($650 000)

Assume: that in the course of the month the clearing agent deals with 100 similar importations then the funds he must command to cope with the disbursements will be:

   100 x 12990 = $1 299 999 ($1.3)

If the clearing agent allows normal credit terms - i.e. payment 30 days from monthly statement then to fund his first two months of trading he will require:-

For 50 shipments	$650 000 x 2 - $1.3m
For 100 shipments	41.3m x 2 = $2.6m

Thereafter, he will be receiving consistent cash flow from his debtor and his average funding requirement will drop to $975 000 or $1.95m respectively.

This emphasises how capital intensive the business of a forwarding agent can be when he is doing no more than acting as a clearing agent.

These hypothetical calculations take no account of the possibility that the client for whom the forwarding agent is acting delays his payments even by as much as one or two days in respect of every shipment - a situation which occurs commonly all the time. If the client delays his payments by an average of five days then the agent will find that his cash flow is so disrupted that he will be unable to continue servicing the client's account. This emphasises the vital importance to the agent of strict credit control to ensure that his client always pays on or before the due date.

It has already been noted that the gross revenue received by the agent from the fees is a comparatively small percentage of the gross invoice.

Assume : 50 shipments per month. Then the revenue received in one month from the agent's fees will be $69 150.

Assume: 100 shipments per month. Then the revenue received by the agent from fees will be $138 300.

This sounds a substantial amount but out of this revenue all the monthly expenses of the agent must be paid - salaries, rents, rates, motor vehicle and scooter expenses, depreciation of furniture and office equipment, director's fees, etc. After these have been provided for the net revenue may well be no more than 40% of those fees - and this is then subject to company taxation. The net profit after tax, assuming everything works strictly according to plan, is, in fact, quite small.

In the example quoted the duty, etc is a very substantial item. If the goods were duty free the situation would be substantially different for the reason that the disbursement account would be a great deal smaller and while the fees might also reduce to a modest extent the funding required by the agent would obviously be very much less and in proportion, the fees would be a much higher percentage.

This provides very clear evidence that it is important that a clearing agent avoids at all costs having "his eggs in one basket". He must diversify his clientele so as to endeavour to have a satisfactory "mix" within the various imports which he handles. A due proportion should, if possible, be free of duty, others should be at low rates of duty, and a limited number may then be permitted to be at higher rates of duty.

9.8.2 Credit Control

No client, however good he may be, should be allowed to slip into the habit of delaying payments. Even a small delay spread over a number of clients can seriously upset the agent's cash flow and cause substantial difficulties. In respect of many clients it may be possible with diplomacy and tact, to develop a relationship in terms of which, a few days before a payment is due, an offer is made to send a messenger to collect the cheque. Reasonable clients do not object to this. Where the agent's credit controller finds that this procedure is objected to it is policy for the matter to be reported to management so that at a suitable higher level management can intervene to achieve the desired objective.

Importance of continually monitoring clients' credit worthiness
It is unfortunately true that a client who last year was a solid and reliable organisation may within a few months find itself in financial difficulties and commence defaulting. When this takes place the agent concerned must take all possible measures for self-protection, including retention of goods under lien, taking out summary judgment for debt, and dispensing with the client in question. If this type of action is not taken forthwith the risk is substantial that when the defaulting organisation goes down it may take the agent with it.

The action suggested in the preceding paragraph may appear to be very drastic - and it is so. However, there remains the possibility that the client in question is merely facing temporary difficulties which, because of the inherent strength of its management and its capital reserves, may be overcome without too much difficulty. It is, therefore, very important indeed that the top management of the agent involved is brought into conference with the credit controller to determine the actual extent of the action required to regularise the situation. At that stage managerial wisdom and diplomacy must come into play and a carefully considered assessment made whether the client could be assisted in recovering his stability. Occasions have arisen where appropriate forbearance and help afforded by an agent have restored the ability of the client to maintain his trading viability, with the psychological result that the client has become a most loyal supporter of his agent for many further years.

9.8.3 Stock-in-Trade
In a manufacturing or wholesaling/retailing business stock-in-trade is also an asset but in the case of the forwarder who deals in services there is no corresponding equivalent. Perhaps the nearest that a forwarder can get to a form of stock-in-trade is a loyal, prompt-paying clientele. Possibly this might be termed the "goodwill" of the forwarder's business and although this has a very definite value the quantifying of that value is difficult. It is, however, a very important feature and this emphasises the vital importance of the right type of personality in the forwarding profession. Honesty, integrity, candour and responsiveness on the part of the forwarder and his entire staff and - even when, perhaps especially when, mistakes have been made - are the chief ingredients which attract loyalty on the part of clients. Sometimes this might cost money but most of the time it will not cost clients. In other words, it will conserve the forwarder's stock-in-trade.

9.9 INTERNATIONAL SETTLEMENTS
The forwarder is not directly involved in decisions with regard to the method of payment adopted by his client for his international transactions, nor with the means by which international transactions are funded.

Nevertheless, it is very important that the forwarder understands the mechanisms by which his clients pay for the goods they receive and also has a sound understanding of the means which his client adopts in order to fund his trading activities. The reason behind this is that the forwarder must ensure that the handling of the goods in transit and the documentation covering the movement of the goods in all its aspects conforms with the requirements of the manner by which funding is achieved.

9.9.1 Open Account

This is an agreement between the seller and the buyer in terms of which goods are supplied by the seller on the understanding that payment will be effected by the buyer at an agreed future date. The seller will forward all the documents relevant to the transaction, including the document of title to the goods, to the buyer directly. By doing so the seller is unconditionally releasing the goods to the buyer and is trusting to the buyer's integrity to pay him on due date.

Parties who trade on these terms are either sister companies within an international group, or one may be the subsidiary or the parent of the other, or their trading relationship has subsisted over so many years that they have complete trust in each other and need no form of security or assurance that all dealings will be completely honest. Payment of amounts due is not in any way controlled by any bank or other financial institution, other than, in the case of Zimbabwe, as authorised foreign exchange dealers through whom payment must be arranged.

9.9.2 Bank Collections
Documentary Collections

Where this term is employed the seller will put together the entire file of shipping documentation - invoices, packing lists, etc, - with the documents of title in complete set and will hand them to his bank with a standard letter or instruction requesting the bank to forward the documents to their correspondent bank in the buyer's country and to request the buyer to arrange unconditional payment for the goods in exchange for the release to him of the shipping documents. This arrangement is sometimes referred to as payment by "sight draft". Alternatively the shipping documents described above maybe accompanied by a draft payable at a fixed or determinable date in the future, in which case the collection is referred to as a usance collection. The drafts used are called usance drafts.

9.9.3 Clean Collections

Under some circumstances, especially where the buyer is a so called "blue chip" company, the seller may required that, once accepted, usance drafts are returned to him. These can then be used by the seller as collateral unit due.

Before due date the drafts (now referred to as "clean" collections, because they are not accompanied by other documents) are returned to the buyer's bank or his account to be debited and the proceeds remitted to the seller.

9.9.4 Bankers Acceptances

Where usance letters of credit are used, since it is the applicant's bank which is undertaking payment, it is that bank which must accept draft accompanying documents underlying goods shipped under a usance letter of credit.

Once accepted, such a draft is called a "bankers acceptance" and these drafts are very good collateral because of the fact that, at the end of the day, it is banks who are liable for payment of them.

It is therefore not unusual for the beneficiary to call for the banker's acceptance relating to a particular transaction to be returned to him. This he can exchange for cash with his bank for the amount of the draft less the interest payable on that amount for the period until the draft is due. This process is called "discounting".

9.9.5 Documentary Letters of Credit
A letter of credit is a contract entered into by a bank with the beneficiary named in the credit terms of which the bank undertakes to pay a stated amount to the beneficiary subject to exact fulfilment of the credit's specific conditions by that beneficiary.

Irrevocable Documentary Letters of Credit
Although letters of credit can be revocable or irrevocable it must be quite evident to the student that a revocable letter of credit is of no practical value in the context of international trade. A supplier of goods depending for payment upon a revocable letter of credit could discover after the goods have been shipped and are therefore beyond recall, that the buyer has revoked the credit with the result that the supplier has no means left to him to obtain payment except by going to enormous expense of litigation in the buyer's country. For this reason all documentary letters of credit issued in respect of international trading transactions must invariably be "irrevocable".

Confirmed Irrevocable Documentary Letters of Credit
A letter of credit issued in country A for the benefit of a beneficiary in country B constitutes a contract entered into directly between banker A and beneficiary B. The correspondent banker (B) in the seller's country acts merely as an "advising bank" without contractual obligation.

In respect of many transactions this is satisfactory but there are occasions when it may be important to the seller (beneficiary) that the correspondent bank in his own country (banker B) joins himself into the contract in terms of which the supplier anticipates being paid. The letter of credit is then said to be "confirmed". Alternatively, the seller may require that a third bank, usually outside the seller's country, confirms the letter of credit. Such a bank is then called the confirming bank.

9.9.6 Payments in Advance
From time to time the RBZ sets limits on payments in advance permissible. Under special circumstances special permission may be obtained for the pre-payment of higher amounts from the Reserve Bank.

For instance, where progressive payments have to be made for major machinery and plant as the manufacturer of the plant overseas proceeds. Also payments in advance are permitted where "tooling up" costs are called for where goods or components are being custom made for the particular buyer.

9.9.7 Off-Shore Finance Facilities
Companies of sound financial standing can secure off-shore facilities either directly from certain overseas banks or through their local representatives within Zimbabwe with exchange control approval.

9.9.8 Confirming Houses
Confirming houses are commercial enterprises set up for the purpose of supplying international finance (at a fee) to companies who are in a growth curve and possibly have not the ability from their own resources to fund their developments.

9.9.9 Bill of Exchange
A bill of exchange is frequently called a "sight draft" if payable at sight or a "draft". They should not be confused with a "bank draft" which is a bill of exchange or a cheque payable by a bank.

A bill of exchange is a written demand signed by the seller of the goods (the drawer) addressed to the buyer (the drawee) instructing the latter to pay a stated sum of money on a defined or determinable future date to the drawer or to his nominee in exchange for the goods (normally worded "for value received").

A "sight draft" is a bill of exchange in which the drawer demands payment of the amount stated at the moment that the draft is presented to the drawee.

A "period (or usance) draft" is a bill of exchange demanding the payment of the stated sum at a clearly defined or determinable future date. By endorsing the bill of exchange either across the front of it or upon the reverse of it, the drawee accepts unconditionally his liability to pay the stated sum on the determined date. An "accepted" bill of exchange is an extremely useful document because it is an unconditional acknowledgement of indebtedness. On presentation at the appropriate court of law the drawer can obtain immediate judgment in his favour without having to prove the detail of the underlying sale of goods in respect of which the bill of exchange was accepted.

9.10 ANALYSIS OR METHODS OF PAYMENT

9.10.1 Open Account Terms
Open account terms are particularly suitable for trading between associate companies and where there is a sound philosophy of trust between the buyer and the seller.

In addition, and broadly speaking, the majority of international transactions which involve the movement of the goods by airfreight must of necessity also be on open account terms. This is for the obvious reason that the speed of movement of airfreight together with the fact that an air waybill is not a document of title makes it difficult for an overseas supplier to insist that a bank must come between buyer and seller in order to control the remitting of funds to the latter.

Moreover, in the case of large trading corporations within Zimbabwe many have buying offices established in the major financial centres such as London, New York, Tokyo, Frankfurt, etc, through which orders are placed on behalf of the Zimbabwean Organisation which can complete transactions by arranging payment of suppliers in their local currency on receipt of the shipping documents or in accordance with the agreed credit terms.

Advantages to the Buyer
The buyer's bank facilities (overdraft or loans) are not tied up by the necessity, for instance, to open a letter of credit in favour of the seller at appreciable time before the shipping deadline. Neither are there any bank charges to pay.

The funds needed for payment of the seller need not be disbursed on presentation of a sight draft shortly after shipment has been effected.

The goods in question can be cleared, delivered and checked before payment.

Provided that the seller forwards the shipping documents promptly they will be received earlier with less consequential risk of demurrage on the shipment after arrival within Zimbabwe.

Under open account the buyer may demand more advantageous delivery terms - e.g. FOB or CFR as opposed to EXW - which defer the date from which his agreed credit period starts to run until after the shipment has actually been loaded onto the carrying vessel.

Disadvantages to the Buyer
The buyer has diminished control over the date of shipment or the completeness and accuracy of the documentation with consequential risk of customs clearance delays.

Advantages to the Seller
Offering open account terms has only a single advantage to the seller. Other considerations being reasonably equal, the offer of open account terms by the seller may give him a trading advantage over competitors offering the same products on more onerous terms - e.g. letter of credit.

Disadvantages to the Seller
The seller has to satisfy himself that the buyer is financially sound and trustworthy, and that he is not likely to withhold payment when the due payment date arrives.

The seller must himself assess the political and economic stability of the country in which the buyer is located since he is accepting the risk that the government of that country impose regulations which could delay or prevent payment of the funds due to him.

The seller will not receive an "accepted" bill of exchange through his banker which he might need to support a request by him to the banker for additional financial facilities to enhance his own cash flow.

It has been stressed that the prompt transmission of all the shipping documents from seller to buyer is of the utmost importance. Where the seller is obliged to use banking channels if he wishes to obtain payment:-

particularly where a documentary letter of credit is involved - he will act with a due sense of urgency in transmitting the documentation through such channels.

Since no such channels are necessary under open account terms, there is a natural and human tendency on the part of the seller's employees to put aside until a "convenient" moment the dispatch of the shipping documents. There is no incentive upon the seller to shift that documentation for the benefit of the buyer. Indeed, the seller's employees may be completely unaware that a delay to the documentation will create needless costs and expenses to the buyer in Zimbabwe - demurrage, overstay charges, etc.

NB: A mechanism does exist by which a seller can obtain the assistance of a bank to ensure that he receives due payment despite the dispatch of the goods by airfreight.

This mechanism involves showing the appropriate bank (by name and address) as the consignee on the air waybill and showing the actual importer's name and address in the "handling information" box together with an instruction "goods not to be released except under written authority of the consignee named above."

Obviously, a prior arrangement must be made with the named bank, and confirmed also by an instruction in the "consignor's letter" accompanying the goods in care of the pilot of the aircraft, in terms of which the bank is given clear-cut instructions only to release the goods to the named importer subject to his authority to debit the invoiced amount to his account and to remit the foreign exchange to the consignor in the country of origin.

This is a cumbersome procedure although quite commonly utilised.

A clearing agent receiving instructions to clear a consignment should always examine the air waybill carefully in order to ensure that where a restraint upon delivery is indicated in the air waybill the goods are not physically collected from the airline bond store until the authority in writing of the named bank has been received. If collection of the goods from the bond store and delivery of them to the importer is allowed to occur without the bank's written authority it could well involve the clearing agent in liability for the cost of the goods in the event that the importer defaulted.

9.10.2 Bank Collections

Advantages to the Buyer
As in the case of open account the buyer's bank facilities are not tied up.

If the buyer has, since placing his order, discovered that his market for the goods has shrunk or disappeared, he may simply refuse to take up the documentation. In other words, he is reneging on his contract to purchase them.

Even if he still wishes to obtain the goods he may, if he feels justified in so doing, attempt to renegotiate the seller's price for those goods on the basis that if he does not accept them the seller has the problem of finding an alternative buyer with all the additional attendant expenses which will be involved.

Disadvantages to the Buyer
As in the case of open account the buyer has diminished control over the date of shipment or the completeness and accuracy of the documents with possible delays in customs clearance.

Advantages to the Seller
Provided that the seller has sufficient knowledge of the buyer's business to be satisfied that the buyer will not reject the shipment, the seller is not constrained by the stringent terms of a letter of credit.

Disadvantages to the Seller
The seller has to satisfy himself as to the financial standing and trustworthiness of the buyer and that the latter is not likely to withhold payment or reject the goods.

The seller has the same risks with regard to the political and economic stability of the buyer's country as would be the case under open account terms.

Again, the seller will not receive an accepted bill of exchange through his banker which he may need to establish additional financial facilities to increase his own cash flow.

Clean Collections
The advantages and disadvantages of this method are exactly the same as they are for documentary collections.

Under all forms of bank conditions it is essential that the full set of negotiable documents moves through banking channels. Delays in the processing of documents can therefore be caused by buyers failing to issue comprehensive instructions to their suppliers in their initial order - including in particular the name and address of their own bankers.

Sellers who are submitting documentation to their banks for collection must themselves also ensure that they give comprehensive instructions including:-
- details of the name and address of the buyer's bank
- proper name of the buyer and his address
- whether the documents are to be released against immediate payment or on acceptance of the bill of exchange
- which party is to assume responsibility for the various bank charges and interest payable in the event of the buyer making a late payment.

The seller must clearly understand that his bank is under no obligation (although it may well do so) to check the accuracy, the completeness, or the relevance of any documents forwarded under a collection.

In turn, the buyer may experience problems arising from inadequacy of the documentation which may not have been apparent until after payment or acceptance of the bill of exchange.

Buyers must remember that the consequences of failing to meet an accepted bill of exchange on the date when the payment is due can be serious. The bank in question will immediately advise the seller of the default with negative consequences for future trading. The buyer's own bank will reconsider adversely the credit facilities they have extended to him and they will record the default - which may influence subsequent credit reports upon him which the bank may be asked to supply to other parties in other countries.

9.11 IRREVOCABLE DOCUMENTARY LETTERS OF CREDIT

A letter of credit is a conditional undertaking by a bank to pay a stated sum of money in a stated currency to a named beneficiary subject to the presentation to the bank of the documentation described therein drawn in a stipulated fashion evidencing shipment of the goods as described in the credit, within the time frame laid down therein.

Provided all the conditions stipulated in the credit are complied with, then the bank issuing the credit must pay.

If any single condition stipulated in the credit is not exactly fulfilled then the obligation upon the bank to pay falls away.

In the course of international trade very large sums of money may be involved in documentary letters of credit and for this reason all banks worldwide are thorough in their checking and verification of all details required in respect of documents presented under letters of credit to ensure absolutely that no funds are released to a beneficiary unless every stipulation is fulfilled.

It is within the discretion of the buyer requesting his bank to open a letter of credit, to determine for himself precisely what documents must be stipulated therein and in what form and manner they must be completed. In this context the buyer's bank will offer assistance to the buyer in compiling his application for the credit to ensure that the stipulations therein tie down the seller of the underlying goods in such a fashion as to provide the buyer with realistic evidence that the good supplied are in accordance with the underlying transaction in question.

9.11.1 Application for an Irrevocable Documentary Letter of Credit

It is normally the buyer of the goods who applies to his bank for the issue by that bank of the appropriate credit. The buyer thereupon becomes the Applicant.

In his application for the issue of the letter of credit the Applicant will nominate the overseas party who is to benefit by the receiving of the funds mentioned in the credit. This will normally be the seller/supplier of the underlying goods and he is termed the beneficiary.

Although the detail of the letter of credit application form is not discussed in this module, the forwarder is expected to have a complete understanding of the provisions in it and how they affect his clients hence completion of a Letter of Credit application may form part of the Final Examination.

9.11.2 Issuing Bank
The "issuing bank" is the bank in the applicant's country which will be responsible for "issuing" the credit through a bank in the beneficiary's country to the beneficiary.

The issue by the bank of an irrevocable credit constitutes a definite undertaking by that bank to pay the stated sum to the beneficiary in accordance with the provisions of the credit, provided that the stipulated documents are presented to it and that the terms and conditions of the credit are complied with.

By the issue of the credit the issuing bank is entering into its own specific contract with the beneficiary to pay over the stated sum provided that the beneficiary also fulfils the terms of the letter of credit, and this contract between the bank and the beneficiary is entirely separate from the contract to purchase the goods in question between the buyer and the seller.

Obviously, to protect itself, the issuing bank will ensure that the applicant for the credit has adequate funds or a sufficient facility with the bank from which those funds can be recouped by the bank. The issuing bank will block off the appropriate amount from the applicant's funds or facility as a safeguard to itself.

After the applicant's bank is satisfied in these respects it will issue the credit by means of a transmission (usually by telex or similar telecommunication means) to its correspondent bank in the beneficiary's country with the request that the issue of the credit is advised to the beneficiary. This bank in the beneficiary's country is known as "the advising bank."

9.11.3 Advising Bank
On receipt of the details from the issuing bank the advising bank accepts responsibility to "advise" the beneficiary of the issue of the credit. This advice to the beneficiary will name the bank of issue and will enumerate all the terms and conditions with which the beneficiary must comply in order to satisfy the issuing bank and to justify it in releasing the stated sum.

If the advising bank has not been requested to add its confirmation to the advice then that bank will explicitly state that in advising the beneficiary of the credit it is doing so "without commitment".

The effect of this is to relieve the advising bank of any responsibility for releasing funds to the beneficiary until the stipulated documents have not only been received by it but have been sent back to the issuing bank for scrutiny and checking and the issuing bank has itself released the appropriate funds to the advising bank. Only at that stage in the proceedings will the advising bank arrange for the payment to the beneficiary. This necessarily means that a period of time elapse - possibly as much as two or three weeks - between the date on which the beneficiary submits his documentation to the advising bank and the date when the advising bank releases to him the sum stated in the credit. During this interval the money involved is "floating" somewhere in the banking system. It is available to neither the applicant (buyer) nor the beneficiary (seller). One or other of the two banks involved has the benefit of it. It is, of course, the responsibility of the banks to limit as far as possible the duration of the interval but the student will appreciate that there must always be a temptation for the banks to stretch the interval by a day or two to their own advantage.

The way of overcoming this is to have the letter of credit payable in the beneficiary's country, in which case the beneficiary is paid a day or two after presentation of the documents: the advising bank will then be debited with the letter of credit proceeds once the documents are presented.

9.11.4 Confirmed Credits
If the seller of goods foresees that there may be a delay in the transfer of funds by the issuing bank for whatever reason he may require the applicant (buyer) to request the issuing bank to authorise the advising bank to confirm the credit. It must, however, be understood that the confirming of a credit by the advising bank is always within that bank's discretion.

In this situation the beneficiary has double assurance of payment provided his compliance with the credit is precise - the credit itself from the issuing bank together with the confirmation thereof by the confirming bank. If, however, the advising bank is for any reason not prepared to add its confirmation for the benefit of the beneficiary it must without delay inform the issuing bank but at the same time it must advise the beneficiary without the addition of its confirmation.

9.11.5 Irrevocability
The forwarder must remember that we are all at times discussing irrevocable documentary letter of credit. The irrevocability of the credits in question applies to the applicant, the issuing bank, the advising bank, the confirming bank and the beneficiary. All these parties are equally bound. However, the irrevocability of the credits in question clearly has it greatest value to the beneficiary.

Occasions do arise, however, when clearly the amendment of an irrevocable credit becomes necessary. When such a situation arises the prior and precise agreement of all the parties must be obtained before the amendment will be allowed.

9.11.6 Irrevocable Documentary Letters of Credit and Responsibilities of the Banks

"The banks issuing, advising and/or confirming a credit are responsible for examining all documents submitted to them with reasonable care to ascertain that they appear on their face to be in accordance with the terms and conditions of the credit."

It will be clear from these two statements - that banks acting in terms of credits deal with documents alone. They do not have, nor can they be expected to have, any means of verification concerning the underlying goods moving in terms of the contract of sale between the seller and the buyer.

"Banks assume no liability or responsibility for the format, sufficiency, accuracy, genuineness, falsification or legal effect of any documents, or for the general and/or particular conditions stipulated in the documents or superimposed thereon; nor do they assume any liability or responsibility for the description, quantity, weight, quality, condition, packing, delivery, value or existence of the goods represented by any documents, or for the good faith or acts and/or omissions, solvency, performance or standing of the consignor, the carriers, or the insurers of the goods, or any other person whomsoever."

Again, this emphasises categorically that in dealing with payments made under letters of credit, banks deal solely with documentation and the facts and statements made on the face of that documentation.

Banks assume no liability or responsibility for the consequences arising out of delay and/or loss in transit of any messages, letters or documents, or for delay, mutilation or other errors arising in the transmission of any telecommunication. Banks assume no liability or responsibility for errors in translation or interpretation of technical terms, and reserve the right to transmit credit terms without translating them.

Banks assume no liability or responsibility for consequences arising out of the interruption of their business by Acts of God, riots, civil commotions, insurrections, wars or any other causes beyond their control, or by any strikes or lock-outs. Unless specifically authorised, banks will not, upon resumption of their business, effect any payment under credits which expired during such interruption of their business.

Banks assume no liability or responsibility should the instructions they transmit not be carried out, even if they have themselves taken the initiative in the choice of such other bank(s).

The application for the credit shall be bound by and liable to indemnify the banks against all obligations and responsibilities imposed by foreign laws and usages.

The above conditions are those stipulated by the International Chamber of Commerce (ICC).

9.11.7 Irrevocable Documentary Letters of Credit Documentation - General Comments

It was made abundantly clear that banks deal with documents when they are acting in terms of documentary letters of credit. Just as the buyer will expect the goods supplied to him by the seller to be precisely correct as ordered, so also, the banks responsible for the issue of letters of credit will expect the documents supplied to them to be precisely as stipulated in those credits. No deviation from the stipulations of the credits will be accepted unless the credits themselves allow for stated tolerances.

For this reason the applicant for the issue of a credit and the issuing bank itself must state precisely the document(s) against which payment is to be allowed.

Vague terms such as "first class", "well known", "qualified", "independent" and the like should never be used to describe the issues of any documents to be presented under a credit. If such terms are incorporated in the credit then banks will accept the relative documents as presented, provided that they appear on their face to be in accordance with the other terms and conditions of the credit.

Unless the credit stipulates otherwise, banks will accept as originals, documents produced or appearing to have been produced:-
☐ by reprographic systems
☐ by, or as the result of, automated or computerised systems as carbon copies if marked as original and where necessary they appear to have been authenticated - as for instance by the insertion of the signature of the issuer.

Where a credit calls for documents other than the transport documents, the insurance documents and the commercial invoices, the credit should stipulate clearly by whom such documents are to be issued and also what their wording or data content should be. If the credit does not so stipulate, banks will accept such documents as presented, provided that their data content makes it possible to relate the goods referred to therein to those referred to in the commercial invoices.

Furthermore, unless the credit stipulates otherwise, banks will accept a document bearing a date of issue prior to the date of issue of the credit.

It must be clearly understood that banks invoiced with documentary letters of credit interpret their responsibilities so stringently that, if an error of wording of spelling appears in an application for a credit and that same error is carried forward into the credit by the issuing bank, then that error must be perpetuated through all relevant documentation despite the fact that it may be quite evident that the error was typographical or the result of ignorance.

9.12 IMPORT COSTING STRUCTURES
Most importers use landed cost valuation. Cook T. A. (2001) identify the following costs as being most common.
☐ currency conversion
☐ personnel travel and entertainment

- market research
- legal expenses
- consolidation and freight forwarding
- product modifications
- customs clearance, duties and taxes
- translation expenses
- international postage and communications
- international commissions
- packing, marking, labeling revisions
- international cargo insurance
- foreign inland freight and warehousing

9.12.1 Costing Terminology

- cost unit is a unit of quantity in which costs may be expressed e.g. kilometres, tonnes, packages,
- cost centre is a piece of equipment or location or person against which costs are charged
- direct costs are costs directly attributable to a cost centre
- indirect costs are costs like overheads, administration or establishment costs which are peripheral to the issue.
- fixed/standing costs are costs which are indifferent to activity level like operator's license or insurance
- variable costs/running costs are costs which vary with usage like fuel, engine oil, etc.

9.12.2 Vehicle Standing Costs

- depreciation (straight line or reducing balance)
- licenses (route authority, municipal discs)
- insurance
- interest on capital
- driver's basic wage

19.12.3 Vehicle running costs

- Cost of fuel (can be controlled : fuel leaks, worn engines, bad driving)
- engine oil and lubricants
- tyres
- repairs and maintenance (labour, spare parts, workshop)

19.12.4 Overhead Costs

- fleet overheads - 'back up' or reserve equipment and labour (spare tractors, spare drivers, and spare trailers)
- business overheads - transport department and company administration overheads

9.12.5 Transport Vessel Operating Costs

(a) Capital related - loan repayment, interest payment on mortgage

(b)   Direct operating - machinery insurance, cargo insurance, crew costs, lubrication costs, repairs and maintenance, stoves, administration, protection and indemnity insurance

(c)   Trip related - fuel costs, canal dues, port dues, cargo handling costs, crew provisions, pilotage and towage.

REFERENCES

Bailey C. A. (2007) **"A Guide to Qualitative Field Research."** Pine Forge Press. California.

Bedi K. (2004) **"Production and Operations Management"**. Oxford University Press. New Delhi.

Bhattacharyya D. K. (2003) **"Research Methodology."** Excel Books. New Delhi.

Cook T. A. (2001) **"The Ultimate Guide to Export Management."** AMACOM. New York.

Daniels, Raudebaugh, Sullivan (2004) **"Globalisation and Business."** Prentice Hall International. New Delhi

Frazelle E.H. (2004) **"Supply Chain Strategy."** Tata McGraw-Hill Publishing Co. Ltd. New Delhi.

Gubbins E. J. (2003) **"Managing Transport Operations."** Kogan Page. London.

House D. J. (2005) **"Cargo Work"** Elsevier. Amsterdam

Kapoor S. K. and Kansal P. (2003) **"Marketing Logistics: A Supply Chain Approach."** Pearson Education. New Delhi.

Kirby M., Kidd W et al (1997) **"Sociology in Perspective"** Heinnemann Educational Publishers. Oxford.

Raina H. K. (1990) **"Guide to Import Management"**. PRODEC. Helsinki

Rowland O.P. (1986) **"Imports and Exports: An Introductory Handbook."** Evans Brothers. Ltd. Nairobi

Silverman D. (2006) **"Interpreting Qualitative Data."** Sage Publications. London.

Sople V. V. (2004) **"Logistics Management: The Supply Chain Imperative."** Pearson Education. Singapore.

Thomas A. B. (2004**) "Research Skills for Management Studies."** Routledge, London

CHAPTER 10

BUSINESS ETHICS

10.1 INTRODUCTION TO BUSINESS ETHICS
Managers of organisations have obligations to various stakeholders whose values and expectations are sometimes in conflict with each other. Stakeholders are groups or individuals who have a stake in the organisation's performance (Johnson and Scholes (1996)). Internal stakeholders include group managers, shareholders and employees. External stakeholders include customers, suppliers, competitors, government and communities. The management strategies adopted to respond to these stakeholder expectations must be legitimate and sustainable.

10.2 CORPORATE SOCIAL RESPONSIBILITY
Even a freight forwarder can exercise corporate social responsibility towards its stakeholders. This can cover the following:-

(a)   **Employees -** provision of medical care, provision of mortgages, assist dependants, social and sporting clubs, observing safety standards, etc.

(b)   **Communities -** energy conservation, pollution reduction, local event sponsorship, monitoring jobs, minority employment.

(c)   **Customers -** safe and well priced products, etc.

(d)   **Competitors -** deciding not to enter some markets, ethical advertising

(e)   **Suppliers -** fair terms of trade, blacklisting some unethical supplier

(f)   **Government -** observing national and international laws, paying correct taxes, etc.

Individual managers can whistle blow against their employers or leave employers who are unethical. Managers who are members of professional institutes or associations are bound by the respective codes of conduct.

Whilst a forwarder is bound by the SFAAZ ethical code of conduct to be discussed later, professionals who are members of the Chartered Institute of Purchasing and Supply abide by the following code of conduct.
☐   maintain the highest standard of integrity in all business relationships.
☐   reject any business practice which might reasonably be deemed improper.
☐   never use authority or position for personal gain
☐   enhance proficiency and stature of the profession by acquiring and applying knowledge in the most appropriate way.

☐   foster highest standards of professional competence amongst those   for
whom one is responsible.

☐   optimise the use of resources which one can influence for benefit of
one's organisation.

☐   comply with both the letter and the intent of:-
-     the law of countries in which one practises
-     agreed contractual obligations
-     CIPs guidance on professional practice

☐   declare personal interest that might affect or be seen by others to   affect
one's impartiality or decision making.

☐   ensure that the information one gives in the course of one's work is
accurate.

☐   respect the confidentiality of information one receives and never use
it for personal gain.

☐   strive for genuine, fair and transparent competition

☐   not accept inducements or gifts other than items of small value like
diaries or calendars.

☐   always declare offer or acceptance of hospitality and never allow it to
influence a business decision

☐   remain impartial in all business dealing and not be influenced by
those with vested interests.

In Zimbabwe professionals who have previous criminal convictions cannot be admitted as company directors. A Police clearance is required for people who want to operate customs as directors or key operational staff. That makes integrity a very important asset.

10.3 COMMERCIAL AND CUSTOMS FRAUD

An ethical forwarder should be familiar with the manner and modus operandi of commercial fraudsters in international trade. This will enable the forwarder to escape from being used.

(a)   **Valuation fraud** which is fraud related to the value declared to customs for goods imported or exported. Undervaluation indicates lower value than actual - whilst overvaluation indicates higher value than actual. Fraudsters use false invoices, false transport or insurance costs, exchange rate manipulation or unusual payment method.

(b)   **Misdescription fraud** which is false declaration with regards to physical description or properties of the goods. It may take place with regard to tariff classification, origin, value, quantity or quality and quota limits.

(c)   **Origin/Preference fraud** which violates or abuses rules of origin and customs documentary requirements as dictated by bilateral or multilateral agreements in force. Fraud may involve false statement of country of origin, misdescription on customs documents, incorrect tariff codes, mixing goods from one country with goods from another country, transshipping goods through a third country and physically changing the presentation of the goods. (re-boxing, re-packaging, re-labeling).

(d)   Inward/Outward processing relief fraud which clears goods duty   free under specified conditions using false shipping documentation.

(e)   Temporary admission fraud evades duties and taxes on goods imported under a temporary admission regime. Such goods must be imported for a specific purpose then be exported within a certain time without having undergone any change. The fraud can be encountered at pre-entry, import, temporary stay or re-export phases.

(f)   Import/Export licensing fraud. It takes the form of fake license, altered genuine license, false statements made to obtain a license or failure to present a license.

(g)   End-use fraud which is diversion of imported goods from a specific end use in order to gain from a zero or lower rate of duty i.e. failure to use goods for the purpose originally declared. End use certificate may be requested by customs to support the declared end use since there is usually no duty or lower rate of duty on goods imported for a specific end use. End use provisions may cover agricultural, diplomatic, governmental, medical/scientific imports as well as specific economic promotion regimes.

(h)   Counterfeit/Pirated good fraud
Pirated goods are goods which are copies made without the consent of the right holder and which are made from an article where the marking of that copy would have constituted an infringement of a copyright under the law of the country of importation.

Counterfeit goods are:-
(i)   goods including packaging, bearing without authorisation a trademark which is identical to a registered trademark infringing the rights of the owner of the trademark in question or
(ii)   trademark designed without authorisation to be applied to goods or
(iii)   goods bearing marks identical to or indistinguishable from protected trade marks, used on goods differing from those for which a trademark   is registered.

(i)   Transit Fraud
Transit allows suspension of customs and other duties on goods destined for a third country while under transport across the territory of a defined customs area. The suspension remains in place until the goods either exit the territory concerned or are transferred to another customs regime or the duties and taxes are paid. Fraudsters make use of misdeclaration and fraudulent guarantees, tampering and substitution of documents, tampering with customs stamps and tampering with seals and locks.

**10.4   THE SHIPPING AND FORWARDING AGENTS' ASSOCIATION
            OF ZIMBABWE: ITS STRUCTURE, PURPOSE AND FUNCTIONS**

The Shipping and Forwarding Agents' Association of Zimbabwe is a voluntary
association of a national character.

The membership of SFAAZ consists of business organisations, whether companies, close
corporations or partnerships, which are engaged in forwarding and clearing of imports
and exports on behalf of the importing and exporting community generally.

10.4.1 The SFAAZ Ethical Code of Conduct

Since all international trade involves the passage of goods through Customs barriers and
submission to the statutory controls of Customs and of many other government
departments it remains true to say that the clearing function is a responsibility which all
forwarders must undertake. For this reason membership of SFAAZ uniformly requires
that business organisations seeking membership must:-
offer their services either as forwarders or as clearing agents or both to the trading
community as a whole, and must subscribe to, and be seen to subscribe to, the Code of
Ethical Conduct laid down by SFAAZ.

Recognising that the most important ethical consideration is the supreme good as the
ultimate end of human conduct, and because there are social customs and traditions
which carry much weight although not embodied in laws and regulations of the
legislative body, it is imperative to prescribe moral commitment to this code of Ethical
Conduct. Therefore:-

1.   Every member of the Association shall give its service to its clients with fidelity
        and shall conduct its business in a spirit of fairness to its clients and its fellow
        members, and by action shall seek to enhance the reputation of the profession by
        always discharging its responsibilities with integrity.

2.   Every member shall hold strictly confidential all information relating to the
        legitimate business affairs of its clients and shall not divulge any such information
        to a third party save with express consent of its clients or upon the legitimate
        demands of the authorities.

3.   No member shall knowingly associate itself with any enterprise or business
        transaction of a questionable nature which could bring it into contention with this
        Code of conflict with the lawful requirements of the authorities or reflect against
        the professional standing of the association.

4.   Every member shall accept the competitive private enterprise system as being the
        best means of ensuring the good of the community and of maintaining a high
        standard of service at fair prices.

5.   Every member shall market its services on their own merits and refrain from
        denigrating the service or questioning the legitimate fees of a fellow member.

6.   Every member shall bring its commitment to this Code of Conduct to the notice of its clients by displaying it prominently in a public area of each of its trading offices. It further undertakes to bring the Code to the notice of its staff, both now and in future, to ensure that the commitment to it is maintained.

The company being a member of the Shipping and Forwarding Agents' Association of Zimbabwe is committed to the Code of Ethical Conduct when discharging its professional responsibilities, SUBSCRIBED HERETO by the Chief Executive.

Any business organisation which fulfils these criteria is entitled to join SFAAZ. In addition, by joining SFAAZ that business organisation automatically becomes represented in the membership of SFAAZ and has power to influence the affairs of SFAAZ. For example, the appointed spokesman for the business organisation concerned may attend all general meetings of SFAAZ in question, may be elected to the Executive Committee of the Association or to any specialist sub-committees, and may be elected Chairman of the Association.

10.4.2 Associate Membership
The constitution of SFAAZ permits other associations having like objectives to become associate members of SFAAZ at the discretion of the SFAAZ Executive Committee.

However, Associate Members do not have the right to vote on matters arising at meetings.

10.3.3 Chairmanship
The constitutional head of SFAAZ is the Chairman who is elected anew each year at the Annual General Meeting.

The Chairman of SFAAZ is assisted in his responsibilities by a Vice Chairman and three others - this comprising the Executive Committee.

The Chairman is responsible to chair all formal meetings of SFAAZ.

10.4.4 The SFAAZ Executive
The Executive Office of SFAAZ is under the control of a Chief Executive who is an employee appointed and remunerated by decision of the SFAAZ Executive Committee. The Chief Executive is responsible at all times to ensure that the SFAAZ constitution is not violated, that decisions at general and special meetings of SFAAZ and also at meetings of the Executive Committee are carried out, to maintain the financial accounts, to assist the Chairman in all delegations of the Association meeting other bodies, including government departments, to prepare representations and submit them under the control of the Executive Committee wherever this is required, to receive information from all possible sources which is likely to affect the interests of the membership and to disseminate that information promptly and effectively.

In emergencies, and if requested to do so, the Chief Executive is responsible to take the chair at any SFAAZ meeting.

10.4.5 SFAAZ Meetings
The SFAAZ constitution requires that an annual general meeting shall be held each year. In addition, the Executive Committee of SFAAZ is required to meet at least twice during the course of each financial year. Regional Associations, or committees, having large autonomy to decide the frequency and the nature of the meetings they hold provided that they must call an annual general meeting at least once each year and must elect at that meeting a chairman.

Division of Functions between Regional Associations and SFAAZ
At regional level matters of concern within the area of responsibility of the Regional Association may be freely discussed, decisions taken, and action pursued. In this context Regional Associations may be as innovative and as active as they deem fit provided that they do not infringe the SFAAZ Constitution and that the actions they take are not inimical to other Regional Associations within SFAAZ.

SFAAZ, on the other hand, as the national organisation, is the point of reference for Regional Associations when circumstances, problems or difficulties arise in any context which also affect other Associations. It then becomes the responsibility of SFAAZ to coordinate views on matters in question, to suggest appropriate action and to obtain confirmation thereof from the Regional Associations. Thereafter, SFAAZ is responsible to pursue matters, keeping Regional Associations fully informed of progress made or otherwise.

10.4.6 The Power and Influence of SFAAZ
Because of the wealth of knowledge and expertise to be found within the grass roots membership of SFAAZ and the appreciable wisdom of its Officers, SFAAZ has an influence and exercises a power appreciably greater than would be anticipated from its numerically small membership. It is the medium through which policy changes proposed by customs, by the Ministry of Transport, by Exchange Control and many other government departments are discussed.

Regular meetings are held with the local officials of Customs throughout the country by Regional Associations. The Airfreight Committee has regular meetings also with Air Zimbabwe, and with other bodies relevant to the airfreight industry. Contacts are maintained with shipping conferences and with the operators of container depots. Regular meetings are also held with representatives of NRZ and the Transport Operators' Association.

10.4.7 Representation on other bodies
Both SFAAZ and the Regional Associations also have intimate links with Chambers of Commerce and Industry throughout the country. SFAAZ is represented on the CZI Transport and Communications Committee. SFAAZ is also represented on various regional committees involved in transport and associated infrastructure development, as

well as being a founder member and the Secretariat of the Federation of Clearing and Forwarding Agents of Southern Africa.

10.4.8 Basic Functions
The basic and primary function of SFAAZ is at all times to guard, care for and enhance the interests of its members.

It is also true to say that SFAAZ acts as the watchdog on behalf of the international trading community in all matters relating to the international movement of goods by whatever mode of transport. It can do this effectively because within its membership it has such intimate and extensive comprehension of the many facets of transportation.

10.5 THE INTERNATIONAL FEDERATION OF FREIGHT FORWARDERS ASSOCIATIONS (FIATA)

FIATA, with its headquarters in Zurich, Switzerland, is the international equivalent of SFAAZ. SFAAZ is one of its constituent members.

FIATA has as its dominant function the safeguarding of the interests of forwarders in a worldwide context just as SFAAZ has its function in a national context. FIATA is therefore a body recognised by the International Air Transport Association (IATA), by the United Nations Conference on Trade and Development (UNCTAD), by the European Union (EU), by the International Chamber of Commerce (ICC), by the World Bank and the International Monetary Fund. FIATA has a seat in many international policy-making conferences and has representation on many other United Nations committees and sub-committees. Forwarders in Zimbabwe have benefited greatly over the years by the work of FIATA.

10.6 THE ROLE OF TRADE UNIONS IN INTERNATIONAL TRANSPORT

There are many in the forwarding industry who regard the Trade Union movement as nothing more than an obstruction to progress and an unnecessary evil in the life of an intermodal operator.

Introduction
Fishermen from the Faroe islands, port workers from Pakistan, airline pilots in the United States, truck drivers in Ghana, or railway men from Argentina may have widely differing jobs and backgrounds, but they are all united through one powerful worldwide organisation - the International Transport Workers' Federation (ITF).

Transport workers - at sea, on land, on waterways or in the air - have always understood the need for solidarity in order to protect their jobs, wages, living and working conditions. Transport workers have also always shown solid support for strong and independent trade unions.

Trade Unions believe that to be truly effective, solidarity cannot be restricted to members of a single trade union. Nationally, unions have long recognised the need to provide support for each other's efforts.

Transport workers' trade unions have also long understood the value of international solidarity. While in some industries, international interdependence and the growth of multinational companies are relatively recent factors, much of the transport industry is, and has always been, international.

Some of the first direct acts of transport workers' international solidarity were between European dockers and seafarers. In July 1896 a group of trade unionists from Great Britain, Belgium, Sweden, United States, Germany, Holland and France formed the International Federation of Ship, Dock and Riverside Workers, an organisation which, two years later, changed its name to the International Transport Worker's Federation.

Since those days, the ITF has grown in strength and influence. Today it unites more than 400 trade unions in around 100 countries, representing over 5 million transport workers worldwide.

10.6.1 The Aims of the ITF
The aims of the ITF are set out in its constitution. They are:
☐   to promote respect for trade union and human rights workers
☐   to work for peace based on social justice and economic progress
☐   to help its affiliated unions defend the interests of their members
☐   to provide research and information services to its affiliates
☐   to provide general assistance to transport workers in difficulty

10.6.2 Trade Union Rights
Of all the ITF's aims, the most fundamental is respect for human and trade union rights. In addition to the basic rights laid down in the United Nations Universal Declaration on Human Rights, the ITF is deeply committed to securing respect, all over the world, for rights of freedom of association laid down in Conventions 7 and 98 of the International Labour Organisation (ILO).

The most important of those rights are:-
☐   the right of workers to establish and join unions of their own choice
☐   the right of unions to conduct their affairs free from government interference
☐   the right of unions to form federations and affiliate to international organisations.
☐   the right to protections from acts of anti-union discrimination
☐   the right to protection from interference by employers in the functioning of unions

Although all states which belong to the ILO are theoretically bound to ensure that these rights are exercised, evidence suggests that they are regularly violated. The ITF opposes all attempts by governments to restrict trade union rights for whatever reason. The transport industries are often singled out for special restrictions because of their nature as public services or "essential industries". The ITF is always ready to intervene to assist unions suffering from such attacks on their basic rights.

The special nature of the maritime industry, which is not under the authority of any single national government, makes violation of trade union rights by employers commonplace. The ITF's campaign against flags of convenience is a concrete example of its commitment to fight for workers' rights.

10.6.3 Membership
Membership of the ITF is open to any organisation with members in the transport industry upholding democratic principles, and able to operate independently of outside control.

Affiliated organisations pay annual fees related to their total membership. ITF affiliates are expected to uphold the ITF's Constitution and to cooperate in carrying out the decisions of its governing bodies. They remain, however, completely autonomous.

10.6.4 The International Trade Union Movement
Internationally, the ITF is part of a wider family of trade union organisations. This family includes 15 other International Trade Secretariats (ITS's) which, like the ITF in transport, look after the international interests of unions in different industries. It also includes the Brussels-based International Confederation of Free Trade Unions (ICFTU), which groups together national trade union centres. While co-operating closely with all these bodies, the ITF is, and has always been a completely independent and self governing organisation.

10.6.5 Who Runs the ITF?
The ITF is controlled by its affiliated unions. The main policy making body is the Congress which meets every four years and to which every affiliate is entitled to send voting delegates.

The Congress elects the chief officers of the ITF - the President and four Vice-Presidents (one each from Europe, North America, Latin America and the Caribbean, Africa and Asia/Pacific). It also elects the General Council and the Executive Board which is responsible for the direction of the ITF'S affairs between Congresses. The Executive Board normally meets twice a year. The Management Committee is a sub-committee of the Executive Board which special responsibilities in administrative matters. The Executive Board may refer other businesses to this committee.

Also elected by the Congress is the ITF'S full time chief executive officer, the General Secretary who is responsible for carrying out Executive Board and Congress decisions and policies and for the functioning of the ITF's Secretariat comprising the London headquarters as well as its regional offices.

10.6.6 Sectional Activities

At the heart of the ITF's industrial activities are its eight industrial sections, i.e.:
- railways
- road transport
- inland navigation
- ports and docks
- shipping
- fisheries
- civil aviation
- tourism services

Each section is serviced by a full time official in the ITF Secretariat. Sections elect their own committees and officers and hold regular meetings between congresses. They must also set up working groups or sub-committees to deal with special problems as necessary.

Sometimes sections meet together to tackle problems affecting more than one group of workers - road and rail workers cooperate in the ITF's Urban Transport Committee, for example, and there is regular close cooperation between the civil aviation and tourism services sections. Dockers' and seafarers' affiliates meet together regularly at joint conferences and in the ITF's Fair Practices Committee - the body charged with supervising its campaign against Flags of Convenience.

10.6.7 Flags of Convenience

The ITF is unique amongst international trade union organisations in having a direct influence on wages and conditions of one particular group of workers - seafarers working on ships flying flags of convenience (Focs).

For nearly fifty years the ITF and its affiliated seafarers' and dockers unions have been waging a vigorous campaign against ship-owners who abandon the flag of their own country in search of the cheapest possible crews and the lowest possible training and safety standards for their ships. The ability of ship-owners to change the registration of their ship and the nationality of the seafarers whenever they wish makes it impossible for this exploitation to be ended by the efforts of any one national trade union.

The ITF's campaign, which is conducted jointly by its seafarers' and dockers' affiliates has two main objectives:

To establish by international governmental agreement a genuine link between the flag a ship flies and the nationality or domicile of its owners, managers and seafarers, and to eliminate the flag of convenience system entirely.

To ensure that seafarers who serve on flag of convenience ships, whatever their nationality, are protected from exploitation by ship-owners.

The "political" side of the campaign (lobbying governments and international organisations) is dealt with through the ITF Seafarers' Section, while its "practical" side is handled through the Special Seafarers' Department (SSD) within the ITF Secretariat - both sides are under the same overall management.

The Special Seafarers' Department works under the direction of the Fair Practices Committee (FPC) - a body made up of ITF seafarers' and dockers' unions. The FPC coordinates affiliates' efforts to procure worldwide observance of minimum acceptable standards for wages and conditions of work laid down by the ITF.

10.6.8 The Campaign in Action
One practical symbol of the ITF's Flag of Convenience is the "Blue Certificate".

This document is issued by the ITF Secretariat in London to ship-owners who have signed an ITF acceptance agreement, either with the ITF's seafarers affiliates in the country of real ownership, with another ITF affiliate, or directly with the ITF SSD. The Certificate tells seafarers' and dockers' unions that a ship's crew is covered by an agreement which meets the ITF standards. Around 2000 Foc ships currently sailing are covered by such agreements.

Representatives of ITF affiliates (many of them full time Foc inspectors) regularly visit ships in port to check whether they are covered by a valid ITF-acceptance agreement and whether the ship-owner is cheating the crew by not keeping to an agreement which has been signed. Sometimes these visits are routine. Sometimes they are in response to a complaint to the ITF by members of the crew, port chaplains or other local organisations.

Affiliated unions who discover that the wages and conditions on board an Foc vessel do not conform to ITF policy may take legal or industrial action in support of claims by crew members. In the period 1974 - 1991, such action resulted in over US$140 million being secured in crew's back pay.

Regular information about the Foc campaign is given to the ITF Seafarers' Bulletin - a publication which appears in eleven languages and is widely distributed to seafarers and affiliates active in the campaign.

Seafarers' Welfare
Through the Seafarers' International Assistance, Welfare and Protection Fund funded by contributions from ship-owners who have signed ITF agreements, and through the ITF Seafarers' Trust, the ITF provides direct assistance to seafarers in difficulties. This ranges from practical support during industrial disputes, help with medical treatment where the ship-owner "disappears", to grants to seamen's missions for welfare and recreational purposes. Since 1986, the ITF Seafarers' Trust has supported the purchase or renovation of Seafarers' Welfare Centres in Rotterdam, Sydney, Antwerp, Tokyo and Genoa.

ITF Action
Although the range of ITF activities is very wide, they can be best summed up under three key headings - practical solidarity, representation and information.

Practical Solidarity

It is not only through the Flag of Convenience campaign that the ITF provides direct solidarity to trade unionists. When transport unions get involved in disputes with employers or governments, one of their first reactions is to approach the ITF for help.

This help takes many different forms. Sometimes just a telex or fax of support sent to a government or employer may help to tip the balance. Sometimes the ITF helps to get publicity of the union's case in the industrial press, and to bring it to the attention of international organisations which may be able to help.

Representation

Today, more and more decisions affecting workers in general and transport workers in particular are taken, not by national governments, but by international organisations or conferences.

Some of the more important of the organisations with the ITF deals, in cooperation with the ICFTU, are:

☐ The International Labour Organisation (ILO) - the tripartite (employers/workers/governments) United Nations agency dealing with labour issues. The ILO, based in Geneva, sets international labour standards in areas such as trade union rights, minimum working conditions and occupational safety and health. Since its foundation in 1919, the ILO has always devoted special attention to setting maritime standards, an activity in which the ITF has been centrally involved. More recently it has also adopted important Conventions on Hours of Work in Road Transport and Social Protection of Dockworkers.

☐ The International Maritime Organisation (IMO) - the London based UN agency dealing with maritime affairs, in particular, maritime safety and marine pollution.

☐ The International Civil Aviation Organisation (ICAO) - another UN body based in Montreal at which the ITF maintains a permanent representative dealing with questions such as aviation safety, personnel licensing and the carriage of dangerous goods.

☐ The European Union (EU) - Brussels, which lays down common rules for transport and social policy in the member states of the European Union.

☐ The Paris based Organisation for Economic Co-operation and Development (OECD) and the Trade Union Advisory Committee to the OECD (TUAC).

☐ The Central Rhine Commission (ZKR) in Strasbourg, which deals with inland waterways in continental Europe.

☐   The Joint Aviation Authorities (JAA), which lay down common aviation safety standards across Europe.

The ITF provides the machinery through which Transport workers' unions can speak with a single voice to international organisations, lobbying for respect for trade union rights, better social protection for the worlds' transport workers, and a more rational approach to transport policy.

Information
The third area where the ITF can be of help to its affiliates is in the provision of information on development affecting transport workers worldwide.

Some of this information work is carried out as a normal part of the ITF's sectional activities. The ITF also maintains a Research and Publications Department responsible for responding to requests for information, identifying areas of concern to affiliates, and producing reports, studies, information bulletins and special publications for direct use by negotiators, on education courses, or in union publications.

In addition to ITF News, published monthly in the five official languages, publications include regular sectional bulletins, surveys of salaries and working conditions, and in-depth studies. These deal with many issues such as:

Health and Safety - Airline security, the problems of stress and fatigue for long distance truck drivers, and the dangers involved in transporting dangerous goods are just a few examples of the health and safety problems with which the ITF is involved.

Multinational Companies - The ITF monitors the activities of key multinationalists, put unions organising the same company in different countries in touch, and works for binding international regulations governing their behaviour.

Technological change - the ITF keeps unions informed of new technological developments, provides a forum for exchanging experiences on dealing with them, and gives advice where necessary on how to cope with the problems which arise.

Deregulation and Privatisation - The ITF provides information and coordinates the response of unions of government measures which could threaten the conditions of transport workers or call in to question the concept of transport as a public service, a principle for which the ITF has long stood.

10.6.9 Transport Policy
Transport policy is obviously of major importance to the ITF and its affiliates in every part of the world. The ITF believes in a rational, cooperative and publicly planned transport system - both nationally and internationally coordinated to provide an efficient and integrated service of both goods and passenger transport.

343

The ITF believes that workers and transport users are best served by a system in which each mode of transport fulfils the task to which it is best suited and where competition between different forms of transport is based on genuinely equal conditions.

The principles of free competition cannot apply unmodified to an industry without which many individuals and entire communities could not survive. The decision to provide transport services must be taken on the basis of need, not just on whether they are profitable financially. Broader social costs and benefits must be taken into account in transport planning.

The current international trend to deregulate and liberalise transport is, in the ITF's view, a backward step from the public service concept. Changes can, and must of course, take place in the structure of transport services, but they should be carried out with the agreement of the representatives of the workforce and with the objective of providing a better transport service accessible to all.

10.7 OPERATING AGREEMENTS WITH OVERSEAS PARENT COMPANIES, ASSOCIATES AND AGENCIES

A modern forwarder must have in place a network of facilities as worldwide as possible through which he can achieve his objectives. Those facilities must be capable of servicing imports into Zimbabwe and exports there from.

Certain forwarders within Zimbabwe are themselves subsidiaries of major overseas forwarding companies; some of the larger Zimbabwean forwarders have branches of their own in certain countries overseas; others have developed operating agreements with large multinational overseas forwarders who by means of their worldwide representation can service the requirements of the Zimbabwean forwarder in question; the remainder arrange their operating agreements by means of appointments of one or more overseas forwarders in each country.

10.7.1   Agreements with Overseas Parent Companies
A number of well known Zimbabwean forwarders are subsidiaries of overseas parents. In almost every instance the Chief Executive of the Zimbabwean organisation is appointed directly by the overseas parent and is usually of the nationality of the parent company. In this country this applies particularly to European forwarding companies, German, Italian, and to a lesser extent, French.

The Zimbabwean organisations in question are characterised by the following:-

☐ Their international forwarding operations are conducted through other
subsidiaries of the parent company wherever such exist. Only where
no such subsidiary exists is the Zimbabwean organisation permitted
to appoint its own agent.

☐   Policies and procedures which must be adopted by the Zimbabwean organisation are determined by the parent company - as are all major investment decisions.

☐   Guidelines are normally laid down within which Zimbabwean top management may exercise their own discretion.

☐   A programme for the interchanging of middle and junior management personnel between the Zimbabwean organisation and their parent company/other major associate subsidiaries is usually a standard practice. Such a practice leads to an intimacy of operation and to valuable cross-fertilisation of ideas and of innovative concepts.

☐   The motivation of the parent company in setting up a Zimbabwean organisation is clearly to be able to repatriate profits which necessarily implies that investment within Zimbabwe is kept to a minimum compatible with efficiency in the Zimbabwean organisation.

☐   Consequent upon the international scope of the operations controlled by the parent company, cushioning is available to the Zimbabwean organisation to cover its risk of exposure to bad debts and similar problems, - a down turning the profitability in Zimbabwe is generally offset by an upturn in profitability in other areas.

☐   International carriers, e.g. shipping lines and airlines, are more amenable to providing favourable rates to the Zimbabwean organisation on account of the influence which the parent company and its other associates can bring to bear.

☐   The rigours of business discipline exercised by the parent company will have substantially greater influence on the Zimbabwe organisation than is possible under any other relationship.

10.7.2 Agreements with Overseas Subsidiaries
Because the Zimbabwean forwarding industry is comparatively small when compared with similar industries in European countries, and because Zimbabwe's international trade also is small compared with the trade of other developed countries, there are relatively few Zimbabwean forwarding organisations who can maintain overseas subsidiaries. Nevertheless, where this is possible then the overseas subsidiaries have characteristics which are comparable to those of a Zimbabwean forwarder who is itself a subsidiary of an overseas parent.

10.7.3 Agreements with Overseas Agencies
The majority of Zimbabwean forwarders appoint overseas agencies to undertake their overseas operations and to foster and develop their overseas interests.

Certain of these have been able to create operating agreements with overseas agencies having broad and worldwide branches with all of which business is conducted. Others, however, appoint separate and individual agencies in each country with whom they undertake business - the appointments developing as business itself develops.

In certain instances the agreements provide for the interchange of director appointments between the boards of the organisations in question as a means to ensure that the interests of each party are adequately protected in the deliberations of the other.

The interchange of directorships may be reinforced by an interchange of shareholdings to a degree which, while not amounting to common ownership, will be sufficient to develop an integration of company policies of mutual benefit.

Organisations operating within this type of relationship will usually agree that wherever each has branches, those branches will be utilised by the other party exclusively. No business will be conducted with "outsiders".

Nevertheless, in practical details differing profit sharing arrangements may be permitted between their respective branches depending on the nature of the traffic involved provided it comes within the broad supervision of the common directorships of each party.

By contrast, where a Zimbabwean organisation develops separate relationships with different organisations in different countries other criteria will influence the nature of those relationships.

For instance, where the overseas agency is a specialist in one mode of transport, the Zimbabwean organisation may enter into agreements with more than one agency - one servicing seafreight while the other services airfreight. Alternatively, one overseas agent may have an excellent distribution facility backed up by warehousing accommodation which may be suitable for one category of traffic only.

Not surprisingly, the Zimbabwean organisation will seek out partners which are comparable to itself in terms of shareholding, size and method of operation.

Since such arrangements are by their nature fluid and might be subject to market fluctuations, it is fairly simple for the Zimbabwean organisation to drop one overseas agency and appoint another. Unfortunately, this freedom to change can result in regrettable effects. A change may be made an excuse on the part of one party to attempt to avoid or seriously delay settlement of accounts due to the other party. There is rarely a cause of greater bitterness between forwarders in different countries than problems of this nature and it is particularly regrettable when they are permitted to impinge upon client relationships at either end.

10.7.4 Content and Scope of an Operation Agreement

The objective to be achieved by the appointment of overseas agents is the provision of a door-to-door forwarding service at a profit which is acceptable both to the Zimbabwean and to the overseas forwarder. The operating agreement between them must therefore stipulate in some detail the functions which each party must perform and the procedures necessary to that performance so as to ensure in the first place client satisfaction and in the second place - but equally important - mutual satisfaction the one with the other. The latter must include agreement with regard to profit sharing and the frequency and method by which balances owed from one to the other should be remitted.

10.7.5 Exclusivity
An exclusive operating agreement is somewhat similar to a contract of marriage. Each party to the agreement undertakes to ensure that he will undertake no business with the country where the other is located except through the other party.

Thus, if Jimmy in Zimbabwe has an exclusive operating agreement with Johnny in the UK then sales leads, routing orders, export traffic, etc., acquired by Jimmy may only be handled in the UK by Johnny. Johnny is under the same obligations with regard to traffic which he acquires. Neither of them may deliberately deal with anyone else.

Provided the two parties concerned in such an agreement are well matched and have comparable skills in forwarding, exclusive agreements can be very beneficial. This is particularly true where such agreements are entered into separately with individual agents in each country to or from which traffic moves.

Where, however, an exclusive agreement is entered into with a multinational forwarder overseas and that agreement provides for exclusivity in relation to all the worldwide offices of the overseas organisation, there is always risk that while benefits accrue in relation to certain traffic where the overseas offices are efficient, it may not be so effective if it involves business with overseas offices which are less than efficient.

In any overseas country in which the overseas multinational organisation has no offices of its own the agreement may stipulate one of the two following alternatives:-

☐ that the Zimbabwean organisation may appoint any independent agent of his choice, or

☐ the Zimbabwean organisation may be required to use an appointee of the overseas organisation.

Where this is involved it will be a matter for negotiation and the Zimbabwean organisation must watch very clearly its own interests.

A word of caution must be stated in relation to exclusive agreements. Experience may prove that while the Zimbabwean organisation has a highly trained and effective sales force capable of developing steadily increasing business, the overseas party may prove to perform poorly in its selling activities with the result that the traffic which is developed

347

may be largely "one way" with the result that the profit sharing stipulations in the agreement will operate for the benefit of one party while the other gains little. The risk that this may prove to be the case should have been investigated thoroughly before the agreement was signed.

This word of caution points to another. Because the agreement is exclusive the party finding itself disadvantaged may find that it is inhibited by the agreement's exclusivity from taking any remedial action.

Finally, there must be within any exclusive agreement a clearly defined process in terms of which the agreement can be terminated. This process must stipulate the following:-

☐ An agreed form of notice of termination communicated in an agreed manner - possibly air mail or telefax.

☐ An agreed period of notice during which all commitments to traffic moving or to move must be honoured. The period might be 3 months from date of notice.

☐ An agreed formula for the reconciliation of all accounts rendered between the parties concerned allowing an additional briefer period - say 2 months - after termination of the agreement within which all outstanding accounts must be settled.

☐ An agreement incorporating these points will not necessarily eliminate all difficulties and disputes but it will materially assist. As regards the settlement of disputes by means of arbitration, comments are made later.

10.7.6 Confidentiality

All operating agreements - but particularly exclusive agreements - must stipulate that the parties to the agreement will not divulge any details of their mutual business to third parties.

Confidentiality assumes particular importance where trade between an overseas country and Zimbabwe is discouraged for political reasons or where trade in certain classes of goods, e.g. computer software, arms and ammunition, etc., - is subject to governmental prohibition or governmental restraint.

Moreover, confidentiality must include:-
☐ names of clients and the entire client base
☐ rate structures
☐ cargo flows in both directions
☐ profit sharing stipulations

In the context of confidentiality, there are, of course, certain circumstances in which both parties to an operational agreement may find difficulty in fulfilment. Operational staff within the offices of forwarders have a tendency to move from one employer to another and it is very natural that in order to please a new employer, such staff may well seek to take with them knowledge of the old employer's business. This is a form of industrial espionage which cannot entirely be eliminated. It must, however, be limited as completely as possible. Where senior or management staff move from one organisation to another or move from one organisation in order to establish their own businesses, it is sometimes possible to obtain their signatures to "restraint of trade" contracts which are enforceable at law provided that a financial consideration is paid by the old employer to the individuals concerned as a fee in exchange for the restraint.

The form of restraint must also be reasonable. One could not, for instance, prohibit a previous employee from participating in the freight industry for 10 years if he leaves your company. One year may be considered reasonable under some circumstances.

10.7.7 Marketing Activities and Reporting Procedures

In many countries worldwide trade practices have developed in terms of which control over the routing of international trade is determined.

Before the advent of containerisation and the development of intermodal transportation, the rule in the countries of Western Europe was that the forwarder's commission for his services was payable by the party - exporter or importer - who paid the ocean or air freight. This freight charge was obviously the major outlay involved in any international movement and the party paying this major outlay was regarded as having the right to appoint the forwarder through whose services the goods would move. In other words, "who pays the piper, call the tune".

In the case of exports from Zimbabwe, however, the position differed in that even though the overseas consignee paid the freight, it was the exporter who always paid the fees raised by the forwarder.

With the advent of containerisation and the development of new transportation technologies and new practices, the position is not now so clearly defined with the result that it is not easy to define with precision whether it is the exporter of goods or the importer of those same goods who must be targeted in an effort to acquire the handling of traffic.

Traffic acquisition is now frequently the result of a joint effort mutually undertaken by both the Zimbabwean forwarder and his appointed agent overseas. Accordingly, consistent and reliable communication of information must be an objective. In this connection it must be emphasised that international communication is no longer a slow and time consuming business. Telefax and e-mail communication is now the norm and anything which takes longer is likely to be ineffective.

Coupled with speed of communication, speed of action must go hand in hand. Hesitancy in taking decisive action can be disastrous since it must never be forgotten that there are many other forwarders "out there" who are hungry for the very same traffic.

If a Zimbabwean forwarder is fortunate enough to have an active and energetic overseas agent with an efficient sales force which is constantly feeding leads and enquiries to the Zimbabwean forwarder, it may become essential that a salesman in Zimbabwe is dedicated to servicing the interests of that overseas agent. This may not always be possible, of course, but where it is not possible it may still be wise to arrange for one competent salesman or more to devote a given percentage of their time and energy to the leads generated by the overseas agent in question.

Sales Leads
Sales leads may take a variety of forms.

☐ They may refer to traffic existing but passing through other hands - both imports into Zimbabwe and exports from Zimbabwe.

☐ They may concern new traffic which will arise but which is only in the developmental stage.

☐ They may involve "routing requests" indicating that it is the wish   either of the exporter or the importer involved that the traffic moves   through a particular forwarder. The request may be based upon better   freight rates, better service, reduction of damage and loss, or for a   variety of other reasons.

☐ For any sales lead to be efficient and capable of being responded to it must contain certain essential elements of information.

☐ The names, addresses, telephones and fax numbers of the trading Partners and their email addresses

☐ The nature of the traffic moving

☐ Whether break-bulk, LCL, groupage, or FCL.

☐ Whether airfreight under direct IATA air waybills, whether via a non IATA airline, or in a general cargo consolidation or a commodity cargo consolidation.

☐ The volume of cargo moving in a named period of time

☐ The manner in which the transport documents are drawn

☐ The method of payment agreed between the seller and the buyer

☐ The terms of delivery - i.e. the INCOTERM

☐ If appropriate, the level of freight charges currently imposed by the competition.

☐ etc, etc

Obviously, it is not always possible to acquire all this information but it must be emphasised that the more information which can be supplied, the more effectively will the sales representative appointed to deal with the lead be able to make progress and hopefully acquire the traffic.

10.7.8 Interchange of Senior Personnel
It has already been emphasised that it is a tremendous advantage if senior management from the Zimbabwean organisation can pay regular visits overseas to consolidate the relationship with the appointed overseas agent and also to visit those trading

organisations overseas on whose behalf traffic is moved. This evidence of personal interest serves to cement relationships - and can possibly pre-empt difficulties and snags before they become irritants and frustrations which could well ultimately lead to loss of traffic.

10.7.9 Rate Structures

The severely competitive environment within which forwarders throughout the world operate necessarily requires that the rates which they devise and apply to traffic which they handle are based upon realistic considerations. They must provide a satisfactory level of profit between the partners in any operating agreement, while at the same time they must be commercially satisfactory to the client or clients for whose benefit the traffic moves.

The forwarders in question must provide a service which meets the requirements of the clients both in relation to speed of movement of the goods and the cost thereof.

Obviously, when considering speed of movement the issues are completely different between seafreight transportation, airfreight transportation, and movement by road or rail, but the principle underlying the concept is maximising speed while, if possible, minimising cost.

Nevertheless, it is completely useless offering over-optimistic transit times, or alternatively, rates so modest that they do not produce the requisite profit margins.

Compilation of Through Rates involving Ocean Transportation

Fortunately, seafreight rates have, over recent years, become increasingly negotiable. This applies to rates offered by Conferences as well as independent operators. The ability of a forwarder to negotiate rates downward will depend first upon the total volume which that forwarder already offers to the shipping line in question and secondly, to the volume of traffic which emanates from the particular shipper. However, as regards the second point just mentioned, the forwarder must recognise that he can only utilise the leverage afforded by the volume of traffic from the shipper in question provided that same traffic is not already moving through the same shipping company. If it is so doing, then that shipping company is acquiring no additional traffic although the traffic may be additional to the business of the particular forwarder.

The same considerations apply in the context of airfreight.

Who should negotiate - the Zimbabwean Forwarder or his Overseas Agent?

The answer to this question depends to an appreciable degree on the level of business which the two parties respectively hand to the international carrier. It is possible that one of them may have comparatively little business with that carrier while the other may have substantial business. The negotiation of the rate should always be left in the care of the party providing the carrier with the most substantial business.

10.7.10 Negotiation of Rates in respect of Landside Legs of International Transportation

The general rule is that the compilation of rates for the landside leg overseas is left to the overseas agent while the compilation of landside rates within Zimbabwe is the responsibility of the Zimbabwean forwarder. It is helpful if this rule is stated clearly in any operating agreement.

10.7.11 Profit Sharing Between the Parties to an Operating Agreement

The manner in which profitability is divided between the Zimbabwean forwarder and his overseas agent is a matter entirely for negotiation and a specific clause in the operating agreement should clearly enunciate the formula by which the profit is shared.

10.6.12 Jurisdiction

Where an operating agreement exists between a parent or holding company and its subsidiaries, or between two of those subsidiaries in different countries, a clause concerning jurisdiction is hardly appropriate since it will usually be the parent or holding company who dictates decisions when disputes arise.

Where operating agreements are entered into between independent parties such as a Zimbabwean forwarder and his agent in the UK or France, it is clear that the agreement is concluded "at arm's length", and has the nature of a contract.

As in all other contracts, such as operating agreement should have within it a clause indicating whose national law and courts of jurisdiction are to be used in the event of an intractable dispute arising - those of the Zimbabwean forwarder or those of the overseas agent.

This can be a thorny issue in the creation of an operating agreement since each of the parties would obviously prefer that the law and courts of his own country should have jurisdiction - he is familiar with the law and is familiar with the procedures in courts. For this reason some hard bargaining may be necessary before a compromise is reached and it may well be that the preferences of the party who will bring the greatest benefit to the agreement will prevail.

If, in the event, it is the law of the overseas country which takes jurisdiction then the Zimbabwean forwarder must endeavour to familiarise himself with all relevant legislation, with the basics of the common law of the country, and with court procedures. It may even be wise that he employs legal counsel to investigate these matters on his behalf. Initially this may be expensive but in the long term it may prove to be money well spent.

Having discussed jurisdiction thus far, it must be emphasised that it is in the interests of neither party that disputes ever find themselves actually submitted to a court of law. It is far better that provision is made in the operating agreement by which disputes which cannot be settled by simple commercial negotiations are settled by means of arbitration.

Hare J. (1999) prefers resolution of shipping disputes by arbitration rather than litigation because of the following reasons:-

it is a specialised field which many judicial officers are not familiar with
trial and judgment delay due to costly and cumbersome court practices.
arbitration procedures are generally conduced in private suiting the desire of international enterprises
arbitration award is facilitated by the UN Convention on the recognition and enforcement of Foreign Arbitral Awards 1958 as opposed to more difficult enforcement of a judgment.

10.7.3 Resolution of Disputes by Arbitration

Arbitration may be by the submission of disputes to a single, mutually agreed, arbitrator, or by submission to a panel of two arbitrators - possibly three - one each appointed by the respective parties and if three are involved, the third one being a chairman appointed with mutual agreement between the parties.

Where resolution of disputes by arbitration is accepted by the parties the operating agreed, arbitrator, or by submission to a panel of arbitrators - possibly three - one each appointed by the respective parties and if three are involved, the third one being a chairman appointed with mutual agreement between the parties.

Where resolution of disputes by arbitration is accepted by the parties the operating agreement should be unequivocal and absolute in this respect. Each part must agree that the decision of the appointed arbitrator(s) is final without subject to any review. This commitment is quite essential since it is almost impossible to get any court of law to intervene in a dispute in which the disputants have agreed to go to arbitration.

Risks Clement in Arbitration

One of the difficulties with arbitration is that a lawyer or attorney appointed as an arbitrator may be very conversant with the law concerning the subject matter of the dispute but may be ignorant of business practices involved in the dispute. Alternatively, an independent experienced businessman thoroughly knowledgeable in the business practices and for this reason appointed as arbitrator, may be ignorant of legal implications.

Again, an arbitrator lacking legal training may have difficulty in assessing how much weight or importance he should allow to the various contending arguments placed before him.

Moreover, an arbitrator is not bound by the law of precedent - as are courts of law in most civilized countries - with the result that his decisions may be capricious and inconsistent. To minimise the risk of this an arbitration panel is usually to be preferred rather than a single arbitrator.

Conclusion

Despite the problems with arbitration it is always true to say that the resolution of disputes by means of arbitration is far less expensive and far more speedy than resolution by litigation.

For this reason it is very advantageous if a satisfactory arbitrator can be found and appointed in the agreement between the parties. He needs to be an individual with both legal knowledge and knowledge of business practices in the forwarding and shipping professions. Such an individual is not readily found with the result that only too often the procedure for the resolution of disputes is not covered in the agreement at all. Where this is the case any severe and irreconcilable dispute inevitably means taking the matter to a court of law - which is the worst possible thing to do. On occasion, it may even be preferable for the parties concerned to break their agreement by mutual consent and the disadvantaged party to cut his losses and write them off to experience.

Operations
Responsibilities for Cargo Handling
Depending upon the amount of traffic being handled and the area or areas of origin, the parties to the agreement will wish to establish whether the overseas forwarder has liberty to consolidate his own cargo into groupage FCLs (seafreight) or airline unit load devices (ULDS) - (airfreight) or whether as an alternative the cargo available should be co-loaded with a third party groupage operator or airfreight consolidator. In the event that the latter is to be the mode of operation then the agreement should stipulate who the third party should be with respect to each of the alternative modes of transport, or which of the parties - overseas forwarder or Zimbabwean forwarder - has the right to appoint the third party.

Where the decision is left to the overseas forwarder it may frequently happen that upon one occasion the overseas forwarder himself has the majority of the cargo required for a groupage container (or consolidation by airfreight) while the third party has comparatively little. In such an event the responsibility for grouping or consolidating could lie with the overseas forwarder to the agreement. On another occasion, however, the comparative volumes of cargo might be reversed and in such an instance the co-loading facility would also be reversed.

Where this type of flexible arrangement is permitted - and it is frequently very important that it is so permitted since by this means cargo movement can take place with the minimum of delay - it is important that agreements are arranged between not only the overseas forwarder and his Zimbabwean counterpart but also with the third parties to the co-loading agreement so as to ensure that the third parties concerned in the operations are not allowed to utilise for their own special benefit the knowledge which they gain about each other's clientele. Should such knowledge be utilised for the purpose of "poaching" then immediately the agreement must be rendered null and void.

Operations within Zimbabwe

Customs controls on goods imported into Zimbabwe are such that the physical carrier of the goods remains responsible for the custody of them until such time a valid bill of entry has been passed and the goods released.

The only exception to this rule is that the carrier of goods by sea may pass them into the custody of a customs licensed depot when the responsibility for their safe custody passes to the depot operator.

As regards groupage containerised traffic therefore it is the depot operator who unloads the cargo from the container and stores it upon the depot floor until such time as a release is permitted.

In the case of airfreight it is the airline who must retain custody. In Zimbabwe the custody is effectively with either Air Zimbabwe or AGS.

Operating agreements between Zimbabwean forwarders and their overseas counterparts do not normally stipulate the detail concerning these local matters since the options are in any event limited and decisions as to these details can safely be left in the hands of the Zimbabwean forwarder.

Responsibility for Document Flows
The timeous and efficient movement of documents is the secret of every successful groupage operation. Unfortunately, it is all too frequently the cause of disputes between overseas forwarders and their Zimbabwean counterparts.

10.7.17 Airfreight Documentation
Because of the rapidity with which goods are transported by airfreight from one country to another it is uniform and universal practice that all documentation relevant to a particular consignment accompanies that consignment on the flight. In consequence there are normally few problems with documentation flow for airfreight traffic. Nevertheless, the operating agreement should stipulate:-

☐   the master waybill - to whom this should be addressed, and what freighting details require to be reflected upon it

☐   cargo manifest - precisely what details of each consignment in a consolidation must be reflected thereon.

☐   house air waybills - addressee details, routing details, - and of great importance - precisely how "prepaid" and "collect" charges must be reflected so that there shall be no ambiguity or reason for misunderstanding. In addition, and separately reflected, must be any COD amounts which the consignee de-consolidator must collect on behalf of the supplier of the goods.

355

☐ pre-shipment advises - these are vitally important since they supply advance information not only to the de-consolidator but also to the importer who is doubtless anxiously awaiting the arrival of his supplies. It is vital that the operating agreement stipulates precisely what details of each consignment must be reflected in these advises and also the precise method by which these advises must be transmitted - e.g., telex, fax, EDI, or other.

10.7.18 Seafreight Documentation

The position with regard to the transmission of seafreight documentation is vastly different to that for airfreight, with the result that quite a variety of problems can arise.

Documentation covering seafreight shipments must be transmitted by the overseas seller to the Zimbabwean importer in accordance with the terms of purchase stipulated in the indent for the goods.

The terms of purchase may be any of the following:-

☐ open account
☐ cash against documents
☐ documentary acceptance
☐ letter of credit

Each of these alternatives will be discussed briefly below.

Open Account

Where the two parties to the contract of sale are dealing on an open account basis there is no reason to restrict the method by which the documentation is transmitted. Accordingly, any of the following routes may be utilised:

☐ The seller may demand the full set of shipping documents and himself forward them direct to the customer in Zimbabwe.

☐ The seller may instruct the overseas forwarder to send the full set of shipping documents to the Zimbabwean customer.

☐ The seller may instruct the overseas forwarder to send the full set of shipping documents direct to the Zimbabwean forwarder's clearing agent at the port of destination.

☐ As a final alternative the documentation may be split into two complete parts, one of which is sent to the Zimbabwean clearing agent while the other is sent to the Zimbabwean customer.

Of these four alternatives the last is the most effective since firstly it helps to eliminate the risk that the documentation goes adrift in transmission (if one set goes adrift the other set will almost certainly arrive safely), and secondly, it has the effect of informing both the Zimbabwean parties concerned that the goods have been safely shipped and when they are likely to arrive. Nevertheless, a difficulty may still arise if the transport document evidencing the shipment of the goods is a bill of lading which is drawn only to the order of the customer: if it is so drawn it will require the customer's endorsement before the clearing agent can obtain release of the goods even though he may have in his possession one of the original bills of lading.

A peculiar situation can, however, arise when purchases are made on an open account basis. Because of the trust which exists mutually between the seller and the buyer there is no financial incentive upon the seller to dispatch the documents speedily; he is confident that he is going to get paid on the agreed due date and only too frequently it does not occur to him that even though his payment is secure unless the documents are promptly dispatched, the buyer in Zimbabwe will be unable to clear the goods and obtain release. As a, the seller may put the documentation aside while he deals with other documentation required in terms of letters of credit where there is a very strictly defined time limit within which the documents must be put into the appropriate banking channel - and we all realise that once the correct action has been deferred "until tomorrow" it tends to get deferred again and again.

Documentary Collections

The documentary collection system requires the seller to give to his bank a letter of instruction to forward the shipping documentation to the bank's correspondent in Zimbabwe and to release those shipping documents only against settlement of the seller's account or agreement to do so if there is a period of credit involved.

Although this method is occasionally adopted it lacks security and any certainty of payment unless the goods are being sold on extended terms, there is no payment instrument such as a bill of exchange included with the documents.

Documentary collections which are payable "at sight" of the documents are commonly referred to as "sight drafts" by traders, although this is a misnomer. The true definition of a sight draft is shown below.

Sight Draft

A similar arrangement to the documentary collection involves the preparation by the seller of a bill of exchange drawn upon the buyer who will be required to "accept" that bill of exchange before he obtains release of the documentation.

A bill of exchange - commonly called a draft - is a written demand signed by the seller of the goods (the drawer) addressed to the buyer (the drawee) instructing the latter to pay a stated sum of money on a defined date to the drawer or to the drawer's nominee in exchange for the goods. The defined date may be "at sight" (a sight draft) or at a future date (a term or period draft).

Letter of Credit

A letter of credit is a contract entered into by a bank with a beneficiary in terms of which the bank undertakes to pay a stated amount to the beneficiary subject to exact fulfilment by him of the specific conditions stipulated in the letter of credit.

In international trade a letter of credit has very great value provided that it is irrevocable on the part of the opening bank and on the part of the buyer who has requested the bank to open it.

It is normal practice that a letter of credit stipulates precisely what documentation must be submitted by the beneficiary in order to justify the bank in paying the stated amount to him. Furthermore, the buyer who requests the opening of a letter of credit is entitled to stipulate deadlines for the physical shipment of the goods on board a carrying ship, whether or not transshipment at an intermediate port is permissible, within what defined period the documentation called for by the credit must be submitted to the bank, and whether the full set is to be demanded or alternatively, the full set should be split into two portions only, one of which passes through the bank while the other is dispatched direct to the importer in Zimbabwe. Where the latter alternative is utilised it is very important that an additional stipulation is inserted into the letter of credit to the effect that the beneficiary shall issue a certificate that the second set of documents have been dispatched by airmail/courier direct to the Zimbabwean importer within a stated number of days from the sailing date of the carrying vessel.

10.7.19 Document Distribution

In the context of airfreight, documentation moves through a clearly defined route - that is to say, it accompanies the goods on the flight under cover of the air waybill. Little more need to be said, therefore, with regard to the distribution of airfreight documentation.

In the context of seafreight, however, it will be clear from the remarks in the preceding paragraphs that the situation is very different. Where any form of bill of lading is involved it is essential that the original bill of lading, being a document of title to the goods, must move so that ultimately it arrives in the possession of the Zimbabwean buyer. It is only when he has that document in his possession that he is enabled to obtain release of the goods.

However, it is always essential that copies of all shipping documents are promptly transmitted from the overseas forwarder to his Zimbabwean counterpart even though the original of the document of title is, of necessity, passing through another channel. The operating agreement must be very clear on this point.

10.7.20 Trading Conditions and Operating Agreements

To every operating agreement there are two parties - the overseas forwarder and the Zimbabwean forwarder - each of which has its own trading terms and conditions which may differ in a number of material aspects.

It is essential that each party obtains, studies, and makes itself familiar with the trading terms and conditions of the other, identifying those aspects which are compatible and those which differ. It is those differences which are important and to which attention must be directed. They should be addressed within the operating agreement in such a fashion that where there is a risk of claims arising during any part of the transit of goods there can be no doubt as to which of the two parties is to accept liability and how the financial consequences of that liability are to be apportioned between them.

The problem is an obvious one; where traffic is, for instance, acquired by the Zimbabwean forwarder on a door-to-door basis it will be the Zimbabwean forwarder who has introduced his own trading conditions which have been found to be acceptable by the new client. Nevertheless, incidents resulting in claims may arise while the traffic is under the control of the overseas forwarder whose trading conditions differ and whose liability is therefore different. If there is no prior and efficient agreement between the two forwarders in terms of which the problem can be resolved, it is likely that the client will suffer and remove all future business to the detriment of both parties. The client may even determine to take the issue in question to litigation and where the client is in Zimbabwe and the litigation is successful the result may well be that the Zimbabwean forwarder has to bear alone the financial consequences.

REFERENCES
Bailey C. A. (2007) **"A Guide to Qualitative Field Research."** Pine Forge Press. California.

Bedi K. (2004) **"Production and Operations Management"**. Oxford University Press. New Delhi.

Bhattacharyya D. K. (2003) **"Research Methodology."** Excel Books. New Delhi.

Cook T. A. (2001) **"The Ultimate Guide to Export Management."** AMACOM. New York.

Daniels, Raudebaugh, Sullivan (2004) **"Globalisation and Business."** Prentice Hall International. New Delhi

Frazelle E.H. (2004) **"Supply Chain Strategy."** Tata McGraw-Hill Publishing Co. Ltd. New Delhi.

Gubbins E. J. (2003) **"Managing Transport Operations."** Kogan Page. London.

House D. J. (2005) **"Cargo Work"** Elsevier. Amsterdam

Kapoor S. K. and Kansal P. (2003) **"Marketing Logistics: A Supply Chain Approach."** Pearson Education. New Delhi.

Kirby M., Kidd W et al (1997) **"Sociology in Perspective"** Heinnemann Educational Publishers. Oxford.

Raina H. K. (1990) **"Guide to Import Management".** PRODEC. Helsinki

Rowland O.P. (1986) **"Imports and Exports: An Introductory Handbook."** Evans Brothers. Ltd. Nairobi

Silverman D. (2006) **"Interpreting Qualitative Data."** Sage Publications. London.

Sople V. V. (2004) **"Logistics Management: The Supply Chain Imperative."** Pearson Education. Singapore.

Thomas A. B. (2004**) "Research Skills for Management Studies."** Routledge, London

CHAPTER 11

WAREHOUSING AND STORES MANAGEMENT

11.1 INVENTORY MANAGEMENT
Inventory consists of raw materials, components, production consumables, tools, stationery, packing materials, semi-finished goods and finished products.

Inventory can be classified into the following categories:-
☐　　Cycle stock - portion of inventory which gets depleted through normal sales or usage in the production process. It is replenished through routine ordering process.

☐　　Safety/buffer stock - protects enterprises against uncertainties in demand or length of lead-time. Enterprises should hold safety stock in addition to cycle stock to cater for unforeseen situations like late deliveries or rapid change in demand.

☐　　In-transit inventories are inventories in the process of being transported to a buyer.

☐　　Speculative stock-stock which protects an enterprise against price increases and constrained availability.

☐　　Seasonal stock - stock kept to accommodate seasonal harvesting of products for sale throughout the year. It can also be stock accumulated for sale during next season.

☐　　Dead stock - stock that has no value for an enterprise. It can be products that do not sell or raw materials, semi-finished products and components not needed in the production process anymore.

　　　　Enterprises with dead stock may adopt any of the following:-
(i)　　sell to retailers who may need them at reduced prices
(ii)　　sell them to scrap metal dealers for recycling
(iii)　　products nearing expiry date can be sold at reduced price or handed out to regular customers as gifts.

NB:　　Keeping dead stock inflates balance sheet figures inflating net profits and hence tax payable.

Inventory is held for the following reasons:-
☐　　economies of scale e.g. price discounts
☐　　minimising uncertainties in the demand and order cycle
☐　　balancing supply and demand to contain seasonality
☐　　ensure stable employment
☐　　buffering

11.2　STORES MANAGEMENT

Efficient management of stores require different storage methods and facilities for different products considering physical, chemical and metallurgical properties of goods, shelf life, susceptibility to moisture, dust, heat contact with other materials, etc. Bulky products may be difficult to handle manually. A warehouse may be a building or a stock yard, a covered place or an open place. Warehouse buildings should enable mechanical equipment to be maneuvered with ease. The building should allow for through flow of materials that is receipts and issues should not be handled through the same door or side of the building. Special rooms should be provided with air conditioners and refrigerators for items like vaccines and antibiotics. Items not suitable for indoor storage may go to open stock yards e.g. structural steel sections, pipes, bricks, sand, concrete products.

Outdoor space for storage should be paved in concrete which is more durable than tarred surfaces. Stacking goods in direct contact with the ground should be avoided and in some cases tarpaulin protection should be provided. The warehouse should be fitted with fixtures, fittings and equipment such as:-
☐   pallets and skids
☐   open and closed shelving
☐   cabinets
☐   bins, stacking boxes, special storage racks, outdoor platforms and   racks, trolleys, mechanical trucks, pallet stackers, forklifts, etc.

11.3 RECEIVING AND INSPECTION OF GOODS
Receiving means checking identity of goods, counting, weighing and any visible loss or damage. Inspection involves checking for quality to ensure that goods conform to specifications and standards agreed to as per contract or as normally associated with product by trade and industry.

11.3.1 Receiving
☐   check delivery note or packing list details against requisition and purchase documents
☐   verify discrepancies with the supplier and/or transporter
☐   check for loss or damage if any and report to transporter, insurance company, supplier or any other stakeholders. For short shipped goods buyer claims from supplier.
☐   Services of recognised inspection company may be employed to survey   the extend of the loss or discrepancy.

11.3.2 Inspection
Commodities or products purchased with reference to trade grades or market are generally checked on a sample basis. Occasional inspection and sample testing is used for goods bought on basis of brands or trademarks. Plant and machinery, capital goods or equipment require thorough inspection. Some contracts include installation and commissioning of plant and machinery necessitating final testing before acceptance. Parties should agree on place of inspection during contract stage considering that it is costly. Alternatives are pre-shipment inspection or post-shipment inspection. Inspection before shipment is suitable:-

362

- where purchases are procured from a distant source
- where transportation costs are significant in total cost
- where return of rejected merchandise would be impracticable
- where inspection at the point of destination would be unsatisfactory

Large procurement agencies may have a contingent of qualified staff to carry out inspection responsibilities. In some cases outside laboratories or testing facilities may be used.

11.4 MATERIAL STORAGE AND STOCK RECORDS
Stock records indicate the amount of items in stock without the necessity of making a physical count. They provide a link between physical supplies and stores accounting and also the means of determining replenishment times and quantities.

Stock records also indicate stock location and provide information for stock taking. They assist during cataloguing and pricing of stock.

NB: A stock record system is determined by the type of product handled, number of items stocked and the inventory transactions in a period of time.

A manual stock control and record system uses cards to record stock movements for each item of stock.

A bin card is attached to the bin or shelf with the item and gives item description, catalogue number and unit of account. Whenever stock movement occurs opening stock, quantities received or issued and balance of physical stock is recorded.

Stock record card supplements bin card by giving broader information coverage. It includes information on unit prices, value of each transaction and value of balance of stock.

Stock review card is prepared for an item of stock when its status is under review for procurement action. It records latest balance of stock and pipeline of orders and past consumption.

11.5 BONDED WAREHOUSES
Bonded warehouses are licensed by customs for storage of goods upon which duty and tax has not been paid except dumping duty. Customs inspects warehouses randomly for compliance. Duty-free goods or broken packages cannot be warehoused. Dangerous goods can only be warehoused separately from other goods. Maximum storage period range from one year to two years depending on source of funds.

Inspecting customs officers check to ascertain that:-
- general condition of warehouse is satisfactory

- security is adequate
- stacking and ticketing are satisfactory
- there are no broken or damaged goods
- there are no goods warehoused for longer than prescribed period
- current license is prominently displayed
- no alterations have been made to the structure

NB: Customs authority is required to sort, separate, pack and repack goods in a bonded warehouse.

11.6 STATE WAREHOUSES
There are warehouses operated by customs for the storage of:-
- seized or forfeited goods
- uncleared goods
- goods abandoned by the importer without clearance
- goods held pending production of permits and licenses

NB: Customs charges state warehouse rent for goods placed in the state warehouse.

11.7 MATERIAL HANDLING SYSTEMS

Warehouse material handling stages
- Off-loading incoming materials from transport vessels
- moving off-loaded material to storage places assigned
- lifting material from storage place during order picking
- moving material for inspection and packing
- loading packages/boxes/cartons onto transport vehicles

Material handling system choice depends on:-
- volumes to be handled
- speed in handling
- productivity
- product characteristics (weight, size, shape)
- nature of the product (hazardous, perishable, crushable)

A manual system is ideal for countries with abundant cheap labour
A mechanical system involve its use of equipment like wheeled trolley, forklift, pallet truck, truck-trailer, device, conveyors, cranes and carousels.

A forklift truck has the following advantages:-
- Movement of larger loads over a longer distance
- Picking and dropping of loads as it travels
- Moving the load vertically into vertical storage systems
- Vertical and horizontal movement of load positioning for loading or off-loading

☐   Excellent maneuverability of load in all directions

Conveyors can be in types like wheel conveyor, roller conveyor, belt conveyor and chain conveyor. A semi-automatic system involve the use of sorting devices, robotics and automatic guided vehicle systems. In automatic systems human factor is restricted to programming and control.

11.8 WAREHOUSE ESTABLISHMENT
According to Bedi K. (2004) a warehouse establishment project consists of:-
☐   warehouse construction
☐   creation of establishment to run the warehouse
☐   creating computer systems to operate the warehouse
☐   employee deployment and training
☐   coordination with buying function and budgeting
☐   warehouse commissioning

BONDED WAREHOUSE

A **Bonded warehouse** is a warehouse in which goods on which the duties are unpaid are stored under bond and in the joint custody of the importer, or his agent, and the customs officers. It may be managed by the state or by private enterprise. In the latter case a customs bond must be posted with the government. This system exists in all developed countries of the world.

History

Previous to the establishment of bonded warehouses in England the payment of duties on imported goods had to be made at the time of importation, or a bond with security for future payment given to the revenue authorities. The inconveniences of this system were many:

- it was not always possible for the importer to find sureties, and he had often to make an immediate sale of the goods, in order to raise the duty, frequently selling when the market was depressed and prices low;
- the duty, having to be paid in a lump sum, raised the price of the goods by the amount of the interest on the capital required to pay the duty;
- competition was stifled from the fact that large capital was required for the importation of the more heavily taxed articles;

To obviate these difficulties and to put a check upon frauds on the revenue, Sir Robert Walpole proposed in his "excise scheme" of 1733, the system of warehousing for tobacco and wine. The proposal was unpopular, and it was not till 1803 that the system was actually adopted. By an act of that year imported goods were to be placed in warehouses approved by the customs authorities, and importers were to give bonds for payment of duties when the goods were removed.

The Customs Consolidation Act 1853 dispensed with the giving of bonds, and laid down various provisions for securing the payment of customs duties on goods warehoused. These provisions are contained in the Customs Consolidation Act 1876, and the amending statutes, the Customs and Inland Revenue Act 1880, and the Revenue Act 1883. The warehouses are known as "king's warehouses," and by s. 284 of the act of 1876 are defined as "any place provided by the crown or approved by the commissioners of customs, for the deposit of goods for security thereof, and the duties due thereon."

By s. 12 of the same act the treasury may appoint warehousing ports or places, and the commissioners of customs may from time to time approve and appoint warehouses in such ports or places where goods may be warehoused or kept, and fix the amount of rent payable in respect of the goods. The proprietor or occupier of every warehouse so approved (except existing warehouses of special security in respect of which security by bond has hitherto been dispensed with), or someone on his behalf, must, before any goods be warehoused therein, give security by bond, or such other security as the commissioners may approve of, for the payment of the full duties chargeable on any goods warehoused therein, or for the due exportation thereof (s. 13).

All goods deposited in a warehouse, without payment of duty on the first importation, upon being entered for home consumption, are chargeable with existing duties on like goods under any customs acts in force at the time of passing such entry (s. 19). The act also prescribes various rules for the unshipping, landing, examination, warehousing and custody of goods, and the penalties on breach. The system of warehousing has proved of great advantage both to importers and purchasers, as the payment of duty is deferred until the goods are required, while the title-deeds, or warrants, are transferable by endorsement.

While the goods are in the warehouse ("in bond") the owner may subject them to various processes necessary to fit them for the market, such as the repacking and mixing of tea, the racking, vatting, mixing and bottling of wines and spirits, the roasting of coffee, the manufacture of certain kinds of tobacco, &c., and certain specific allowances are made in respect of waste arising from such processes or from leakage, evaporation and the like.

Modern

Bonded warehouses provide specialized storage services such as deep freeze or bulk liquid storage, commodity processing, and coordination with transportation, and are an integral part of the global supply chain.

What is a Customs Bonded Warehouse – the USA System?

A Customs bonded warehouse is a building or other secured area in which dutiable goods may be stored, manipulated, or undergo manufacturing operations without payment or duty. Authority for establishing bonded storage warehouses is set forth in Title 19, United States Code (U.S.C.), section 1555. Bonded manufacturing and smelting and refining warehouses are established under Title 19, U.S.C., sections 1311 and 1312.

Upon entry of goods into the warehouse, the importer and warehouse proprietor incur liability under a bond. This liability is generally cancelled when the goods are:
- Exported; or deemed exported
- Withdrawn for supplies to a vessel or aircraft international traffic;
- Destroyed under Customs supervisions; or
- Withdrawn for consumption within the United States after payment of duty.

Types of Customs Bonded Warehouses

Eleven different types or classes of Customs bonded warehouses are authorized under section 19.1, Customs Regulations (19 C.F.R. 19.1, Amendments Pending):
1. Premises owned or leased by the government and used for the storage of merchandise that is undergoing Customs examination, is under seizure, or is pending final release for Customs custody. Unclaimed merchandise stored in such premises shall be held under "general order." When such premises are not sufficient or available for the storage of seized or unclaimed goods, such goods may be stored in a warehouse of Class 3, 4, or 5.
2. Importers' private bonded warehouses used exclusively for the storage of merchandise belonging or consigned to the proprietor thereof. A Class 4 or 5 warehouse may be bonded exclusively for the storage of goods imported by the proprietor thereof, in which case it should be known as a private bonded warehouse.
3. Public bonded warehouse used exclusively for the storage of imported merchandise.
4. Bonded yards or sheds for the storage of heavy and bulky imported merchandise; stables, feeding pens, corrals, other similar buildings or limited enclosures for the storage of imported animals; and tanks for storage of imported liquid merchandise in bulk.
5. Bonded bins or parts of buildings or elevators to be used for the storage of grain.
6. Warehouses for the manufacture in bond, solely for exportation, of articles made in whole or in part of imported materials or of materials subject to internal revenue tax; and for the manufacture for domestic consumption or exportation of cigars made in whole of tobacco imported from one country.
7. Warehouses bonded for smelting and refining imported metal-bearing materials for exportation or domestic consumption.
8. Bonded warehouses established for the cleaning, sorting, repacking, or otherwise changing the condition of, but not the manufacturing of, imported merchandise, under Customs supervision, and at the expense of the proprietor.
9. Bonded warehouses, known as "duty-free stores," used for selling conditionally duty-free merchandise for use outside the Customs territory. Merchandise in this class must be owned or sold by the proprietor and delivered from the warehouse to an airport or other exit point for exportation by, or on behalf of, individuals departing from the Customs territory or foreign destinations. These stores may also sell other than duty-free merchandise.
10. Bonded warehouses for international travel merchandise, goods sold conditionally duty-free aboard aircraft and not at a duty-free store. This is based on amendments to 19 U.S.C., section 1555(c), approved 11/00. Regulations governing this type of warehouse are being written.
11. Bonded warehouses established for the storage of General Order (G.O.) merchandise. G.O. is any merchandise not claimed or entered for 15 days after arrival in the U.S. (or final U.S. destination for in-bond shipments). The amended regulations

establishing this class of warehouse are awaiting final approval and publication in the Federal Register.

Advantages of Using a Bonded Warehouse

No duty is collected until merchandise is withdrawn for consumption. An importer, therefore, has control over use of his money until the duty is paid upon withdrawal of merchandise for the bonded warehouse. If no domestic buyer is found for the imported articles, the importer can sell merchandise for exportation, thereby eliminating his obligation to pay duty.

Many items subject to quota or other restrictions may be stored in a bonded warehouse. Check with the nearest Customs office before assuming that such merchandise may be placed in a bonded warehouse. Duties owed on articles that have been manipulated are determined at the time of withdrawal from the Customs bonded warehouse.

Merchandise: Entry, Storage, Treatment

All merchandise subject to duty may be entered for warehousing except perishables and explosive substances other than firecrackers and merchandise other than duty-free merchandise may be stored in the retail sales facility of a class 9 warehouse and sold to persons departing the U.S.

Full accountability for all merchandise entered into a Customs bonded warehouse must be maintained; that merchandise will be inventoried and the proprietor's records will be audited on a regular basis. Bonded merchandise may not be commingled with domestic merchandise and must be kept separate from unbonded merchandise.

Merchandise in a Customs bonded warehouse may, with certain exceptions, be transferred from one bonded warehouse to another in accordance with the provisions of Customs Regulations. Merchandise placed in a Customs bonded warehouse, other than Class 6 or 7, may be stored, cleaned, sorted, repacked, or otherwise changed in condition, but not manufactured (Title 19, U.S.C., section 1562).

Articles manufactured in a Class 6 warehouse other than cigars made from imported tobacco must be exported in accordance with Customs Regulations. Waste or a by-product from a Class 6 warehouse may be withdrawn for consumption upon payment or applicable duties. Imported merchandise may be stored in a Customs bonded warehouse for a period of 5 years (Title 19, U.S.C., section 1557 (a)).

How to Establish a Customs Bonded Warehouse
Application

An owner or lessee seeking to establish a bonded warehouse must make written application to his or her local Customs port director describing the premises, giving the location, and stating the class of warehouse to be established.

Except in the case of a Class 2 or Class 7 warehouse, the application must state whether the warehouse is to be operated only for the storage or treatment of merchandise belonging to the applicant, or whether it is to be operated as a public bonded warehouse.

If the warehouse is to be operated as a private bonded warehouse, the application must also state the general character of the merchandise to be stored therein, with an estimate of the maximum duties and taxes that will be due on the merchandise at any one time.

Other Requirements

368

The application must be accompanied by the following:
- A certificate signed by the president or a secretary of a board of fire underwriters that the building is a suitable warehouse and acceptable for fire-insurance purposes. At ports where there is no board of fire underwriters, certificates should be obtained and signed by officers of agents of two or more insurance companies.
- A blueprint showing measurements of the building or space to be bonded.

If the warehouse to be bonded is a tank, the blueprint should identify all outlets, inlets, and pipelines and be certified as correct by the proprietor of the tank. A gauge table showing the capacity of the tank in U.S. gallons per inch or fraction of an inch of height, should be included and certified by the proprietor as correct.

When a part or parts of the building are to be used as a warehouse, a detailed description of the materials and construction of all partitions shall be included.

The Customs port director may ask for a list of names and addresses and a set of fingerprints for all company officers, principals, and employees of the applicant.

Duty-free shops (Class 9) have specific requirements governing their establishment. These requirements include location, exit points, record-keeping systems, and the approval of local governments.

Bonds Required

Bonds for each class of warehouse shall be executed on Customs Bond, Form 301.

Where are Customs Offices Located?

The U.S. Customs Service has more than 300 ports of entry in the United States, Puerto Rico, and the U.S. Virgin Islands. Please consult your local telephone directory under Federal government listings. You will find your local port director under "U.S. Treasury Department, Customs Service."

The material contained in this brochure is for information purposes only. The warehouse proprietor and/or importer must comply with all the legal and technical requirements set forth in the law and in the regulations. The U.S. Customs Service is unable to recommend existing Customs bonded warehouses for the use of individual importers. Any additional questions regarding Customs bonded warehouses should be directed to the Customs office nearest you.

Practice areas > Bonded Warehouse Applications

With over 300 ports of entry in the United States, including the Virgin Islands and Puerto Rico, many businesses find establishing their own bonded warehouse(s) to be advantageous.

To do so, a lengthy application must be completed and filed with the local port's U.S. Customs' director. Information must be provided that gives detailed information about

369

the physical features of the warehouse site (including a blueprint), as well as giving its location, a certificate of fire insurability by an independent underwriter, and the intended warehouse classification.

The U.S. government recognizes **eleven types of bonded warehouses**, each defined within its own class. (These are listed below, as they are described under federal law.)

Bonded Warehouse Application Requirements Vary According to Classification

All applications for warehouses except Class 2 or Class 7 facilities must reveal if they will be operated as public bonded warehouses or used solely by the applicant. Private use will require that the applicant report to the federal officials not only what type of merchandise will be stored in its private warehouse, but the maximum duties and taxes that will be due on the goods at any set time.

Customs officials can also require identification of the applicant's personnel, including not only their names and personal addresses, but their fingerprints, as well. The list can require officers and principals of the company along with all of its employees. This is true, regardless of the warehouse's intended classification.

Duty free shops have special requirements. Designated as a Class 9 Bonded Warehouse under federal law, duty free shop applicants must provide Customs officials with information regarding the location, exit-points, record keeping systems, and confirmation of local government approvals of the facility.

List of Bonded Warehouse Classifications

According to 19 C.F.R. 19.1, bonded warehouses are classified as:

(1) **Class 1.** Premises that may be owned or leased by the Government, when the exigencies of the service as determined by the port director so require, and used for the storage of merchandise undergoing examination by Customs, under seizure, or pending final release from Customs custody. Merchandise will be stored in such premises only at Customs direction and will be held under general order.

(2) **Class 2.** Importers' private bonded warehouses used exclusively for the storage of merchandise belonging or consigned to the proprietor thereof. A warehouse of class 4 or 5 may be bonded exclusively for the storage of goods imported by the proprietor thereof, in which case it shall be known as a private bonded warehouse.

(3) **Class 3.** Public bonded warehouses used exclusively for the storage of imported merchandise.

(4) **Class 4**. Bonded yards or sheds for the storage of heavy and bulky imported merchandise; stables, feeding pens, corrals, or other similar buildings or limited enclosures for the storage of imported animals; and tanks for the storage of imported

liquid merchandise in bulk. If the port director deems it necessary, the yards shall be enclosed by substantial fences with entrances and exit gates capable of being secured by the proprietor's locks. The inlets and outlets to tanks shall be secured by means of seals or the proprietor's locks.

(5) **Class 5**. Bonded bins or parts of buildings or of elevators to be used for the storage of grain. The bonded portions shall be effectively separated from the rest of the building.

(6) **Class 6**. Warehouses for the manufacture in bond, solely for exportation, of articles made in whole or in part of imported materials or of materials subject to internal-revenue tax; and for the manufacture for home consumption or exportation of cigars in whole of tobacco imported from one country.

(7) **Class 7**. Warehouses bonded for smelting and refining imported metal-bearing materials for exportation or domestic consumption.

(8) **Class 8**. Bonded warehouses established for the purpose of cleaning, sorting, repacking, or otherwise changing in condition, but not manufacturing, imported merchandise, under Customs supervision and at the expense of the proprietor.

(9) **Class 9**. Bonded warehouse, known as duty-free stores, used for selling, for use outside the Customs territory, conditionally duty-free merchandise owned or sold by the proprietor and delivered from the Class 9 warehouse to an airport or other exit point for exportation by, or on behalf of, individuals departing from the Customs territory for destinations other than foreign trade zones. Pursuant to 19 U.S.C. 1555(b)(8)(C), Customs territory, for purposes of duty-free stores, means the Customs territory of the U.S. as defined in 101.1(e) of this chapter, and foreign trade zones (see part 146 of this chapter). All distribution warehouses used exclusively to provide individual duty-free sales locations and storage cribs with conditionally duty-free merchandise are also Class 9 warehouses.

(10) [Reserved]

(11) **Class 11**. Bonded warehouses, known as general order warehouses, established for the storage and disposition exclusively of general order merchandise as described in 127.1 of this chapter.

FHI Assists Clients in Applying for Bonded Warehouses

Customs Bonded Warehouse Program – the Canadian System

Canada Border Services Agency (CBSA) **Act:** Customs Tariff, S.C. 1997.e.36 as amended by 1998, c. 19, 1999, c.17

Regulation: Customs Bonded Warehouses Regulations, SOR/96-46, as amended by SOR/99-106

To Whom Does This Apply?

Anyone wishing to operate a customs bonded warehouse.

Summary

- have a duly completed bonded application, Form E401;
- have a site plan;
- agree to a site visit from a CBSA official;
- pay an annual license fee; and
- post a security deposit.

Licensees have to keep inventory-related records of receipt, removal, transfer and alteration of goods. They also have to provide specified facilities, equipment and personnel. Licensees also have to meet appropriate operational standards.

Most goods waiting to be exported or for CBSA release can be stored in these warehouses for up to four years, although certain goods can be stored for up to 15 years. The warehouses defer total duties and taxes payable until the goods are either consumed domestically, exported, or the time limits noted above have expired.

What Are the Benefits to Importers?

Importers who use these warehouses enjoy one or more of the following advantages:

- on-site storage;
- just-in-time delivery;
- less cash tied up in duties and taxes.

All shipments of goods moving into or out of these warehouses must be documented on a B3, *Canada Customs Coding* form. If good are removed or for consumption in Canada, then they must be accounted for on the B3 with full duty and tax payment.

Requirements and Restrictions

Customs bonded warehouse operators have to let the CBSA see their warehoused goods and have to make their records available. They must keep records on goods for six years after the goods are removed from the warehouse.

Certain restrictions apply to the storage of imported alcohol and tobacco.

CBSA customs bonded warehouses are licensed under Section 91 of the *Customs Tariff*. The Act governs the issuing of licenses for the operation of any place as a bonded warehouse. Such warehouses store goods that have not been released or are destined for exportation. The **Customs Bonded Warehouses Regulations** specify the requirements for the licensing and operation of bonded warehouses.

For more information, please contact the Canada Border Services Agency of visit the Web site.

DISCLAIMER
Information contained in this section is of a general nature only and is not intended to constitute advice for any specific fact situation. For particular questions, the users are invited to contact their lawyer. For additional information, see contact(s) listed below.

Alberta, British Columbia, Manitoba, New Brunswick, Newfoundland and Labrador, Northwest Territories, Nova Scotia, Nunavut, Ontario, Prince Edward Island, Quebec, Saskatchewan, Yukon Contact(s):
See National Contact.

National Contact(s):
Border Information Service - BIS
Canada Border Services Agency
Telephone: 204-983-3500 or 506-636-5064 (for calls outside Canada)
Toll-free (information): 1-800-461-9999 (for calls within Canada)
Web site: http://www.cbsa.gc.ca/menu-eng.html

Packaging Guidelines

Here are some general packaging guidelines that will help you prepare your package for shipping. Please visit related links to other guideline areas for more detailed information.

Guidelines for Good Packaging

You can help to ensure that your package arrives safely and on time with these packaging guidelines and procedures developed from UPS research.

- Use a rigid box with flaps intact
- Remove any labels, hazardous materials indicators, and other previous shipment markings on the box that are no longer applicable
- Wrap all items separately
- Use adequate cushioning material
- Use strong tape designed for shipping

- Do not use string or paper over-wrap
- Use a single address label that has clear, complete delivery and return information
- Place a duplicate address label inside the package

REFERENCES

Bailey C. A. (2007) **"A Guide to Qualitative Field Research."** Pine Forge Press. California.

Bedi K. (2004) **"Production and Operations Management"**. Oxford University Press. New Delhi.

Bhattacharyya D. K. (2003) **"Research Methodology."** Excel Books. New Delhi.

Cook T. A. (2001) **"The Ultimate Guide to Export Management."** AMACOM. New York.

Daniels, Raudebaugh, Sullivan (2004) **"Globalisation and Business."** Prentice Hall International. New Delhi

Frazelle E.H. (2004) **"Supply Chain Strategy."** Tata McGraw-Hill Publishing Co. Ltd. New Delhi.

Gubbins E. J. (2003) **"Managing Transport Operations."** Kogan Page. London.

House D. J. (2005) **"Cargo Work"** Elsevier. Amsterdam

Kapoor S. K. and Kansal P. (2003) **"Marketing Logistics: A Supply Chain Approach."** Pearson Education. New Delhi.

Kirby M., Kidd W et al (1997) **"Sociology in Perspective"** Heinnemann Educational Publishers. Oxford.

Raina H. K. (1990) **"Guide to Import Management"**. PRODEC. Helsinki

Rowland O.P. (1986) **"Imports and Exports: An Introductory Handbook."** Evans Brothers. Ltd. Nairobi

Silverman D. (2006) **"Interpreting Qualitative Data."** Sage Publications. London.

Sople V. V. (2004) **"Logistics Management: The Supply Chain Imperative."** Pearson Education. Singapore.

Thomas A. B. (2004) **"Research Skills for Management Studies."** Routledge, London

CHAPTER 12

CARGO PROTECTION AND MARINE INSURANCE

12.1 PROTECTION AND PACKING OF GOODS IN INTERNATIONAL TRADE

A study conducted into the movement to which a consignment was subjected during shipment from quayside Hamburg to delivered on pier in New York by seafreight, controlled and compiled by a computer, indicated that the shipment experienced more than 80 000 separate movements - forward, backward, up, down, to the left, to the right, and in circular fashion corkscrew motion.

The voyage from Hamburg to New York took five and a half days. Not all of those movements were severe but they were all repetitious and all created strains and tensions within the contents against which the protection and packing of the goods had to contend. The voyage was not abnormal in terms of weather and/or sea conditions.

This fairly sophisticated exercise took no account of the additional stresses imposed upon the goods during the landslide movement of the cargo from the point of origin within Germany and to the point of destination in the USA. Moreover, the exercise ignored the additional problems created by changes in temperature, in atmospheric pressure and in humidity, all of which have a deleterious effect on cargo if precautions are not taken against them.

It is an elementary exercise in arithmetic to discover to what extent stresses and strains apply to cargo shipped from the same loading port to Harare - voyage more than three times as long.

What has been said above takes no account of the specialised nature of many cargoes which require special types of protection and packing, or alternatively, have peculiarities which create hazards and dangers which must be brought into account when deciding methods of packing, quantities to be allowed within each pack, or which require special rules and regulations relevant to the mode of transport by which the commodities will be moved. All these must be considered within the broad subject to protection and packing.

Protection and packing of cargo is never completed until suitable identification and other marking is applied to the package and every package is uniquely identified by a number - to which must be added special markings to indicate how the packages must be handled, centers of gravity, etc.

Protection is the means employed to preserve the goods from damage within the case, crate, drum, etc, in which they are shipped.

Packing
Packing is the means employed to surround the goods in a suitable envelope which may consist of a case, carton, crate, drum, etc.

It follows from this that protection of cargo is designed to prevent movement of the goods outer packing, to preserve the goods from corrosion, rust, dampness, etc., within that same outer envelope, to prevent the goods within the pack damaging themselves by movement against one another, etc.

By contrast, packing is intended to protect the goods from dropping, crushing, contamination by the contents of other packages, the ingress of moisture or water, etc.

'Packaging' is intended to be a sales asset and money spent upon it is money well spent if it improves sales. In fact, sometimes the packaging may be as expensive as the product.

'Packing', on the other hand, is a necessary nuisance - essential to ensure that goods travel safely but likely to be discarded once it has achieved its purpose. Too little packing can be a disaster but too much packing can be a waste of money - not only because the packing may be expensive in itself, but also because it may increase the weight or volume of the consignment with resultant increases in freight charges.

12.2 PRINCIPLE CAUSES OF LOSS OR DAMAGE

12.2.1 Loses arising from Handling and Stowage
Inefficient handling of cargo does not occur only during the loading/discharge of goods to and from ships. It can occur during any loading/discharge operation from any form of vehicle and also on the quayside or in transit sheds or warehouses. It usually arises from inefficient labour, inadequate mechanical equipment, carelessness in the handling of such mechanical equipment, as well as mechanical breakdown or failure of such equipment. The immediate cause is therefore outside the control of the cargo owner but in deciding the level of protection and packing required for the product in question the cargo owner must take account of the efficiency or otherwise of the many various handling points through which the cargo must pass from source to destination. In countries in the more sophisticated parts of the world the risks are obviously likely to be less than in the less developed countries such as those of Central Africa and parts of South America.

12.2.2 Loses Arising from Stowage
Break-bulk cargo being loaded by traditional methods into a ship normally requires approximately 37 different handlings before it is secured finally in the ship's hold. A similar series of handlings must occur in order to extract it at the destination port.

The advent of containers has been assumed to be the answer to the risks involved in the matter of stowage but while this may be largely true with regard to the activities within the hold of a ship, stowage of goods in a container whether at the supplier's premises or at a container depot also involves risks of which account must be taken at both ends of the journey.

12.2.3 Losses Arising from Theft/Pilferage
While this cause of loss will never be totally eliminated it can be substantially minimised with intelligent forethought and the use of an appropriate method of packing.

376

Identification also has a bearing on the matter since external marks applied to the packing can attract thieves and pilferers - for which reason such marks should be anonymous.

It is worth noting that thieves try by every possible means to avoid leaving traces of their activities. For this reason, goods in stout cartons are far less easy to broach by thieves without leaving traces provided that the tops and bottoms of the cartons are securely gummed down with a heavy duty gum. Wooden cases, on the other hand, can, by a skilful thief, be opened and reclosed without leaving scarcely a mark to indicate what has happened.

12.2.4 Losses arising from Water Damage
The water may be fresh water, sea water, or condensation developing within the packing. The resulting damage may be rust, corrosion, mould, contamination, etc. All these risks are largely avoidable unless they arise consequent upon a major catastrophe.

Although it is generally correct that airfreight traffic is less subject to the types of loss and damage referred to hitherto, it must always be remembered that prior to loading to aircraft goods still have to be handled, stowed, protected from moisture, and also from theft and pilferage just as is the case with seafreight traffic.

Furthermore, while direct dispatch in a single aircraft from the airport of departure to the airport of intended destination involves no further handling en route, if transshipment from one airline to another is involved there will be intermediate handling to be taken into account.

Airfreight also has its own peculiar problems. The great proportion of airfreight moves in the belly holds of passenger aircraft which are not necessarily themselves pressurised. In consequence of this commodities which are placed in sealed tins, cans, or bottles - whether of plastic or glass - may be subject to bursting with resultant leakage and contamination of other cargo. Liquids which thus escape from their containers can have very serious consequences on the air frame, hydraulics and electrical equipment within aircraft. Where this occurs the consequences of inappropriate packing may be incredibly more devastating than expected.

12.3   INTERNAL PROTECTION OF CARGO
The method of protection of the cargo will be dependent upon this nature and there are many tried and tested methods which may be adopted. These will be considered each in turn.

Greasing, Painting, Spraying, with a Protective Film to prevent rusting, oxidation, corrosion, or the effects of internal condensation.
Condensation is a very common cause of damage. If the process of packing the goods in question takes place in a damp or humid atmosphere then the ambient air within the packing may well be saturated with moisture which later may condense upon metal parts which have not been coated with a protective film. The same moisture may also be absorbed by shredded newspaper or wood wool used as cushioning between articles in

the package with the result that the cushioning beds down and ceases to be resilient and capable of doing its job.

It is also a fact that even dry timber utilised for the making and packing cases, etc., still retains moisture within itself to at least 105 of its absolute dry weight. This moisture can evaporate from the timer inside the case and subsequently condense with detrimental effects on the
goods.

In addition to petroleum greases and oils, there are many proprietary brands of anti-rust anti-corrosion compounds available which can be readily applied by spray or brush.

Sealing in Plastic Containers or Shrink Wrapping to minimise the risk of pilferage, and also the risk of rusting, oxidation, corrosion, other water damage, and also evaporation and contamination.

However, where goods are sealed in this fashion the problem of ambient moisture in the air sealed in with the goods must always be remembered.

A desiccant should invariably in appropriate instances be placed within the seal. Silica gelin small quantities in muslin bags can be thrown in prior to sealing. It is cheap, it can absorb and retain within itself up to 20 times its own weight of moisture, and on completion of the journey it can be reused after it has been dried out afresh by gentle heat.

Where repetitive sets of articles are being shipped, pre-formed moulded polystyrene shapes are very useful to hold each individual item secure from damage. Alternatively, wood wool, foam rubber, polystyrene chips, and the like can also prevent movement within a packing case so as to avoid damage such as breaking, chipping, or bending. Resin bonded horsehair achieves the same objective but it relatively more expensive.

Shock absorbers may consist of springs arranged so as to hold a delicate object (e.g. an X-ray tube) clear of the sides of a case or crate. Heavy duty rubber banding can also be used.

Robust cargo such as road graders, earth moving equipment, etc., is frequently shipped without casing. Nevertheless, it must always be remembered that such cargo usually has "bright parts" such as hydraulic pistons, axle bearings, etc, all of which require special attention to avoid rusting, corrosion, etc. In addition, the electrical controls and electric motors which may be part of the equipment will require special attention.

On the other hand, blooms, billets, etc., of iron, steel or copper normally need no protection at all.

Although containers provide comparatively substantial protection externally, they can themselves create problems which have to be considered. Shipping containers are normally structures of steel with doors which are provided with sealing rubbers so as to ensure that in transit the container remains waterproof. This, however, means that a large volume of ambient air becomes sealed in together with all water vapour which forms part of that air. Condensation upon the roof and sides of a container can therefore be appreciable.

Containers in the trades between the northern and southern hemispheres obviously pass through tropical and equatorial climates where they are subject to appreciable heat which can drive water vapour out of wooden packages enclosed within them with, again, risk or condensation and resultant cargo damage. For these reasons containerised cargo which is susceptible to damage by moisture must be thoroughly protected by desiccants at all times.

Finally, even the heaviest piece of machinery shipped in a container will move and slide upon the container or floor when subject to the strains arising from heavy seas. The lashing and securing of the equipment within the container is essential. All general purpose containers are provided with lashing points in the angles between the container walls and the container floor which are capable of standing very substantial strains. The lashing may be by heavy duty nylon webbing, by wire rope, or by chains and grapples. It must be remembered, however, that the lashings themselves can cause damage to the cargo unless they are intelligently applied so as to eliminate this eventuality.

No commodity or product moving in the course of international trade should ever be packed in hay, straw, chaff, or similar material. These materials are carriers of insects, bugs, bacteria, etc., with the result that their use in international trade could spread disease, infestation, etc., from country to country. If the authorities in any port of airport in the world discover goods packed or protected by these materials they will instantly refuse to permit the shipments into the country.

In addition, such materials can, under certain circumstances, spontaneously develop heat within themselves which can lead to spontaneous combustion.

12.4 EXTERNAL PACKING
Packing can take a variety of forms:
- wooden cases/crates
- metal boxes/drums/cans
- fibre drums with clip-on lids
- plastic drums
- corrugated cardboard cartons
- bags of paper, synthetic or vegetable fibres
- bales
- trusses

All of these may be secured to one another or secured upon pallets, by means of steel or nylon strapping or by means of shrink wrapping of heavy duty plastic sheeting. Where such combination packs are created they provide further protection against damage resulting from movement and losses resulting from theft/pilferage.

Where goods are secured to pallets or upon bolsters - which are essentially steel pallets - which are constructed to internationally recognised dimensions, then they are said to have been unitised. Unitisation affords the additional protection of the cargo mentioned above and also unitised loads are much easier to handle by mechanical means such as forklifts, than are individual packages.

The intention of packing is to provide protection against the risks arising from impact, crushing, dropping, lateral pressure, contamination, evaporation, theft and pilferage. It is also intended to contain spillage of liquids, and sifting of powders and granules.

In the case of goods moving by **seafreight**, it is the seafreight leg which is the roughest.

In the case of goods moving by **airfreight**, a lighter form of packing may be utilised but the exporter must realise that overland transport by some form of road or rail vehicle is inevitably going to be involved either within this country or overseas unless the destination address is very close to the destination airport.

In the case of transportation by **rail** problems concerning shunting and vibration must be considered together with handling at rail depots.

In the case of goods moving by **road,** the nature of the roads - e.g. in Southern African countries - and of the handling at road depots, must be considered.

Unitisation
Where goods are unitised their individual packing requirements may not need to be quite substantial as would be necessary if the goods were conveyed in single separate parcels.

Containerisation
Where goods are to be containerised a distinction must be drawn between LCL groupage consignments and FCL consignments. The strength of the packing required for LCL groupage consignments must be equal to that which would be provided for break-bulk consignments.

In the case of FCL consignments - which are normally packed at the exporter's premises - the packing strength can be reduced substantially provided that efficient securing provisions are made within the container. This provision must be against any lateral or end-to-end movement and must also provide against the crushing of lower layers of packages as a result of excessive weight above them. Where the packages in an FCL consignment are homogeneous endeavour should be to ensure that they interlock so that the natural friction between every package assists in holding the whole consignment together with minimum movement in any direction.

Spaces within containers which are insufficient to hold additional air imprisoned within the packing at the time that the goods were packed, or from the time a packing case was made, or from the ambient air within a container in which the goods travel. The effects of humidity are substantially enhanced in the case of exports from Zimbabwe to northern hemisphere destinations as a result of the journey through the tropics and across the equator. Silica gel is the most economic and efficient method of sopping up humidity.

Ease of Handling and Stowage
Where labour is scarce and/or expensive then packing should be designed so that cargo can be handled with relative ease by mechanical means such as forklifts.

The exporter must, however, take account of the methods of cargo handling which will be employed at the destination port or airport.

Palletised and unitised cargo should be capable of forklift handling. As regards airfreight, unit load devices (ULDS) are in constant use in respect of all four engined aircraft in service in Zimbabwe where "scissor-lifts" are available at all major airports. However, in less developed countries, appropriate equipment is not always available. Where transshipment to smaller aircraft - e.g. DC3s - will be required, then it may be inevitable that the unitised/palletised loads or the UDLs, will have to be broken down at the transshipping point in order to cope with cargo handling into and out of the smaller aircraft. Packing must take account of these contingencies whenever they are likely to arise.

As regards shipments moved by seafreight, the exporter should be aware that at certain destinations in the less developed countries of the world, full quayside water depth and crane facilities may not be available with the result that cargo must be discharged from ocean vessels into lighters for conveyance to shallow draft quays for ultimate discharge to land. It is obvious that where this occurs substantial additional hazards arise.

12.5 INSURANCE CONSIDERATIONS
Every policy or cover of marine insurance issued in Zimbabwe contains the following clause:

"In no case shall this insurance cover ... loss, damage or expense caused by insufficiency or unsuitability of packing or preparation of the subject-matter insured (for the purpose of this clause "packing" shall be deemed to include stowage in a container or lift van but only when such stowage is carried out prior to attachment of this insurance or by the assured or their servants)."

The effect of this exclusion in the marine insurance cover is that if the loss or damage arises as a result of insufficiency or inadequacy of the packing of the goods, then the insurers may avoid their responsibility to pay a claim.

It is quite impossible to define what type of packing is "sufficient or adequate" or what type of packing is to be regarded as "insufficient or inadequate". Obviously, the sufficiency or adequacy of the packing will vary according to the mode of transport employed, the frequency of handling to which the goods are subjected, the circumstances to which the good are normally subjected during transit, and the destination to which the goods are consigned.

Where a claim is lodged with the underwriters and the underwriters contend that the packing was insufficient or inadequate, they will not pay. If the claimant continues to insist that his claim is justified, then it becomes his responsibility to sue the underwriters and to produce adequate evidence that the packing of the goods was, in fact sufficient and adequate. It is not necessary for the underwriters to prove insufficiency or inadequacy. The onus is on the claimant and it is extremely difficult for the claimant to prove his point.

The exporter from Zimbabwe must satisfy himself that the packing which he has provided is of a strength and character which a reasonable man would employ to ensure the safety of the goods against the normal risks and hazards to which the goods will be subjected throughout their journey. To achieve this, and if the goods are in any way unusual, delicate or sophisticated, it is always open to an exporter to consult with his underwriters as regards the nature of the packing which he proposes to employ so as to obtain their concurrence to it in advance.

Size and Mass
Clearly the strength and robustness of packing must increase in relation to both the size and the mass of the goods in question. In particular, the packing must take account of the center of gravity of the goods so as to ensure that there is no weakness at this point.

There is a natural tendency on the part of Zimbabwean importers to assume that the supplier of the goods they have ordered will know best how to pack them and that there will be no need for any instructions to be given to him. This is not necessarily the case.

While the terms of delivery (INCOTERMS) all state that it is the responsibility of the seller of goods to pack those goods suitable to protect them from the normal risks and hazards which they will face during the course of their journey provided that the seller knows the mode of transport and the nature of the journey, there is little satisfaction for an importer to blame his supplier because his goods have arrived crushed, dented, smashed and generally obliterated when, by the application of a little forethought he could have given instructions how he wished the goods to be packed and protected so that he would receive them safe and sound.

There will be even less satisfaction for that importer when he discovers that the insurance which he took out for the goods will not pay him for the reason that they were "insufficiently or inadequately' packed.

It is important for every importer - especially when he is entering into business with a new supplier overseas - to make diligent enquiry with regard to the method which the supplier will adopt for the packing of the goods. If he is not satisfied then he must stipulate the method of packing and the quality of the packing materials to be used so as to safeguard himself from the frustration of receiving damaged goods or finding that some part of his supplies has been pilfered or lost.

Marking, Numbering and Labeling

Marking and numbering is essential for all packages whether forwarded by sea, by air, by rail or by road. Marking and numbering is essential for all packages shipped as LCL groupage cargo in shipping containers, rail containers, volume vans by road, or ULDs by airfreight.

Numbering is essential for all packages in a consignment shipped as FCL cargo by sea, full ULD cargo by air, full container by rail, or full volume van by road.

Marking/labeling with cautionary marks is essential in respect of packages which require special slinging, special stowage, retention one way up, special handling, etc., by all modes of transport.

Labeling with dangerous/hazardous cargo labels is mandatory in respect of all cargoes regarded as dangerous under the International Maritime Dangerous Goods Regulations in respect of articles carried by sea. Within Zimbabwe and the neighbouring territories stringent regulations for the carriage of dangerous/hazardous good by rail and road have been laid down. In addition, dangerous/hazardous goods require special documentation.

Marking

For break-bulk traffic by sea three separate marks must be considered
- an identification mark
- a destination mark
- a route mark where necessary

The identification mark should be a mark sufficient to identify the consignee. However, attractive good - portable radios, cigarettes, clothing, footwear, etc. should not be identified by means of the name of the consignee and also should not incorporate in the identification any indication of the nature of the goods.

Company initials consistently used could be sufficient; a pseudonym would be acceptable; even the initials of the shipping company could serve.

Any of these would be adequate bearing in mind that the mark shown on the goods would be repeated on the transport document, in the invoices, and upon the packing specifications.

The reason for ensuring a measure of anonymity is to avoid advertising the nature of the contents to thieves and pilferers. If such precautions are not taken and as a result claims keep recurring, the risk is that the insurance underwriters will complain and will lift premium rates as a mechanism for compensation for their losses.

The destination mark is essential so as to inform handlers where the goods must go. It should be clear and complete - not merely abbreviations such as HRE or BYO - respectively Harare or Bulawayo.

Similarly, the route mark must be clear and specific. The route mark normally indicates the port of destination where goods moving by ship will first be discharged.

Examples of route marks are:
Via Durban
Via Beira

Such route marks are very important at the overseas loading port since they assist the stevedores responsible for loading the ship to determine the correct stowage for the goods within the ship's holds.

Marking in respect of containerised cargo
A consignment which constitutes a full container load intended for a single consignee will normally move within the container all the way to the consignee's premises. When this is the intention, it may not be considered necessary to put a separate identification mark upon every package unless there is a requirement that the consignment will have to be transferred from container to container at a transshipping port. This is however unusual with the result that the general rule is that identification marks upon the packages are unnecessary.

In fact the container number becomes the identification mark. Moreover, there is no need for any destination mark nor for any route mark since the documentation for the container movement will stipulate fully these elements of information.

Despite this however it still remains important that every package in an FCL consignment is numbered and that a packaging specification is supplied.

In the case of LCL/groupage traffic full marking in every respect needs to be applied to every package together with numbering.

Marking of airfreight consignments
In the case of goods moving by airfreight it is desirable, although not essential, that identification, destination, and route marks are applied together with numbering. However, it is vital that a further mark is also applied. This is the air waybill number. Airlines normally supply a number of pre-gummed labels already printed with the air waybill number along with each set of air waybills. If the quantity of pre-gummed labels is insufficient then the air waybill number should be stenciled upon the packages.

Furthermore, every airport in the world is identified by a 3-alpha code such as LHR (London Heathrow), JHB (Johannesburg International), HRE (Harare), BUQ (Bulawayo). The mark for a destination airport need only consist of the appropriate 3-alpha code.

Numbering

There are a number of reasons why every package in a multi-package consignment should bear a unique number and that a packing specification should be provided in which the contents of every numbered package is described.

- ☐ The details shown on the packing specification will indicate whether the complete shipment of goods covered by the invoice have been supplied.
- ☐ How many packages make up the complete shipment
- ☐ So that customs can determine which packages out of the total shipment they require to detain for examination of contents.
- ☐ To determine, for the purpose of creating a claim for goods lost, the quantity of goods missing from the total consignment.

The identification of packages by number on a packing specification can also be valuable so that the importer can determine which packages he requires immediately and which other packages he may place in his warehouse for utilisation at a later date.

Labeling / Marking with Cautionary Marks

The purpose of cautionary marks is to communicate to parties who need to know, the handling requirements appropriate to the goods in the packages in question. These cautionary marks are pictorial so that they are comprehensible irrespective of differences in language or culture.

It will be obvious that where cautionary marks need to be applied to any package they should be applied on all four side of it.

Labeling with Dangerous / Hazardous Cargo Labels

All goods which are for any reason hazardous must be distinguished by the application of special very colourful labels all of which are basically pictorial although certain of them may of necessity have to bear additional information in words. In addition to being colourful and therefore highly visible, these labels are printed in such a fashion that they have to placed upon packages in a diamond shape rather than merely square.

The range of goods which are classified as hazardous is very extensive. In fact there are many products in common use in homes and offices which constitute hazards when being transported internationally.

The broad classifications are as follows:-

Class I	Explosives
Class II	Gases - compressed, liquefied or dissolved under pressure
Class III	Flammable liquids
Class IV	Flammable solids, substances subject to spontaneous combustion, and solids which emit flammable gases when wet
Class V	Oxidising substances and organic peroxides
Class VI	Poisonous substances, infectious substances, etc

Class VII	Radioactive substances
Class VIII	Corrosives
Class IX	Miscellaneous dangerous substances

Within each of the classes enumerated above there are in each instance three "Packaging Groups". Packing Group 1 stipulates the packing requirements for the most dangerous of the goods within that classification while Packing Group III stipulates the packing requirements for those which are least dangerous within that classification.

The classification and labeling of dangerous goods have been universally adopted by all the major trading nations of the world. Within the packaging groups for each classification the type of label and where the label must be located on each package is stipulated.

It is probably unnecessary to emphasize that a higher degree of knowledge and of expertise is required on the part of any international trader to ensure compliance with the packing and labeling of hazardous cargoes.

The International Maritime Dangerous Goods Code is the authoritative Publication in respect of requirements for goods being transported by sea, the IATA Dangerous Goods Regulations are the authoritative guide in respect of hazardous cargo being transported by air.

12.6   MARINE INSURANCE
Marine Insurance is an essential ingredient in international trade. International trade is normally achieved by means of four contracts which can be stated as follows:-

☐   The contract of sale
☐   The contract of carriage
☐   The contract of insurance
☐   The contract of finance

Each of these contracts are independent from the others but they cannot be disassociated because they complement each other and form the basis necessary to protect the interests of both the seller and the buyer of the goods which are the subject of the international trade transaction.

If any one of these separate contracts is ignored or is not efficiently concluded bearing in mind the nature of the goods, the nature of the journey, and the nature of the means of transport to be employed, then the balance of the entire commercial transaction is disturbed and the result can be disaster.

The term "marine insurance" is used to indicate the insurance to be taken out for any form of international transportation even though the marine distance involved is only a small part of the whole journey, and also even if there is, in fact, no marine movement actually involved, as for instance when goods are forwarded by airfreight.

A marine insurance policy of cover can attach to goods from the moment they are loaded into a form of conveyance at the premises of the supplier until they arrive at the premises of the buyer or at the premises nominated by him as the place of delivery. Such a form of marine insurance is commonly called a "warehouse to warehouse" cover.

12.6.1 Motivation for Marine Insurance
The importer purchasing goods from a supplier in another country relies on the receipt of those goods for the purpose of his business. He cannot himself afford to bear the risks which can arise from the many hazards involved in the international movement of the goods in question.

Loss of any part of the goods will mean of loss of money paid for them, loss of profit upon them, loss of goodwill which has painstakingly been built up with customers, while damage to the goods in question will result in delay of trading returns, delay in utilisation, delay in fulfilment of contractual obligations which may possibly result in penalties, expensive repairs, and/or replacement of the goods damaged.

Any one or more of these factors can put a small business "out of business". Even a large business can find itself substantially embarrassed.

For these many and vital reasons the prudent international trader will make quite certain that he has a suitable insurance cover for the correct insurance value which will persist for the essential duration of the transit.

12.7 THE NATURE OF INSURANCE CONTRACTS
12.7.1 The Principle of Indemnity
A contract of insurance is a contract of indemnity, i.e. the insurers undertake to indemnify the assured against financial loss or expense resulting from any of the risks and hazards which are defined in the policy document. Another way of putting this is to say that, in the event of loss or damage resulting from the action of a risk insured against, the insurer undertakes to place the insured in the same position as would have been had such loss or damage not incurred.

The insurers will, by the wording of the policy document, define their liabilities in such a manner that they do not become responsible for loss or damage resulting from any neglect by the assured to take prudent and reasonable care of the goods by means of packing, marking, securing, dunnaging, and other forms of protection. They will also limit their liability by excluding losses which arise inevitably from the nature of the goods, such as evaporation or natural deterioration. Normally, they will also disclaim responsibility for deliberate or malicious or willful mishandling or damage on the part of the assured or his employees.

12.7.2 Utmost Good Faith (Uberrimae Fides)
Every contract of marine insurance is a contract entered into by the insurers on the assumption of the assured's utmost good faith.

387

Insurers do not see the packing by which the goods are protected; they do not see the transport equipment in which the goods will move. They have no direct knowledge of the means by which the goods will be conveyed to their ultimate destination.

In fact, they rely on an accurate, complete, and truthful declaration of all these facts by the party who is seeking the insurance cover. The good faith and honesty of the party seeking insurance is therefore of essence in every contract of insurance.

It is therefore the duty of every party seeking insurance cover to disclose every relevant fact which affects the risks which the insurers are being asked to accept. If the insurers can point to any lack of disclosure of relevant facts they become entitled to avoid liability. Courts of law in many countries of the world have upheld this view.

It is also important to know that this obligation of disclosure extends to information which the insured knows but also to that which he is deemed to know by the nature of the business in which he operates.

Essential information which must be disclosed when seeking insurance cover will include the following:

☐ The precise nature of the goods, including any inherent property of the goods which might affect the risk, e.g. flammability, corrosiveness, fragility, etc.

☐ The nature of the protection and of the packing provided for the goods while in transit.

☐ The identification marks and numbers applied to the packages

☐ The nature of the route over which the goods will move, including especially the mode or modes of transport which will be utilised.

☐ Whether or not the goods will be containerised and, if so, whether as FCL or LCL / groupage.

☐ Whether the goods are new or second-hand

☐ Any other particulars which, in the view of a reasonable and prudent businessman, would be likely to affect or to increase the risk which the insurers are being asked to accept.

The courts have held that non-disclosure of the previous claims history of the organisation asking for the insurance cover is not a breach of this principle - it is up to the prudent insurer to require this information, if, however, it has been sought and false information is given, this is fraud.

Good faith also requires that the assured, either himself or through his servants or agents, will take all reasonable steps to reduce any loss or damage for which the insurers may become liable.

Responsibilities in this regard will include the following:-

☐ Removing the goods from the cause of damage -e.g. from the site of a fire or from a pool of oil which is soaking into the packing

☐ Conserving and protecting the undamaged portion of the goods

☐ Repairing torn or broken packages to prevent further loss

☐ Claiming promptly upon all parties who may be liable for the damage

☐ Notifying the insurance organisation or its broker or agency promptly, and facilitating any survey or inspection which may be deemed to be necessary.

In practice, it is frequently the forwarder who has first hint of possible loss and/or damage to his client's consignments and it is therefore important that the forwarder understands what his responsibilities are as the representative of the client in question. He must act with competence to safeguard his client's interests by taking appropriate measures to mitigate the loss or damage.

A forwarder who understands the requirements of a policy of marine insurance and is aware of the importance of taking effective action immediately an apparent loss or damage is defected, will be able to act in the best interests of his client and will cement the relationship which is desirable between forwarder and client.

12.7.3 Insurable Interest
This concept simply means that, in order to insure goods, the party insuring them must stand to lose financially from the loss of, or damage to the goods.

Thus, for example, an INCOTERMS FOB seller has an insurable interest in the goods he sells until they have effectively passed the ship's rail at port of shipment: at that point his insurable interest passes to the buyer.

12.7.4 Subrogation
Although a big word, the concept is straight forward. Where the insured has had a claim for loss or damage settled to his satisfaction, he must pass on his rights to claim for that loss or damage from any party who may have been responsible to his insurer.

In the case of a break-bulk consignment damaged at port of discharge and final destination, the insured may have a right of recovery against the trucker or rail authority which delivered the goods. This right must be handed over, or subrogated, to the insurer once the insurance claim has been settled.

The above are the broad issues with which the forwarder must be thoroughly conversant and in terms of which he must be prepared at all times to take prompt action.

12.8 FORMAT OF THE MARINE INSURANCE POLICY

While it is true that in certain (relatively few) overseas countries there are "local" forms of marine insurance policy based on so-called "local" conditions - and possibly local prejudices, it is fair to state that the form of marine insurance policy devised by the Institute of London Underwriters at Lloyds in the early 80s has received very broad acceptance throughout the international trading world. Even where there are "local" forms of policy in use the clauses devised by the Institute of London Underwriters at Lloyds have had substantial influence in the design of such "local" policies.

12.8.1 The Three Major Sets of Clauses

Institute of Clauses A
These clauses provide for insurance cover to the broadest extent acceptable to underwriters. They are roughly equivalent to what was in earlier days called "all risks" cover.

However, it must be clearly understood from the very outset that the colloquial reference to these clauses as being "all risks" is not in any way accurate. It would be more precise to refer to "all insurable risks" cover since there are a number of risks to which goods in international trade may be subject which underwriters will decline to accept save upon payment of an additional premium. There are yet further risks which underwriters specifically exclude under all circumstances.

Institute Cargo Clauses B
The B clauses provide a more limited extend of cover. Where the assured is content to accept such a cover the premium rate charged by the underwrite will be reduced proportionately to the risks which have thereby been excluded from the underwriter's liability.

Institute Cargo Clauses C
The C clauses are the clauses offering the minimum insurance cover. The exclusions from the C clauses are substantial with the result that these clauses approximate roughly to those which were formerly known as "total loss only".

Institute Cargo Clauses (Air) Excluding Sendings by Post
There are differences in the risks involved between sending goods by sea or overland and sending goods by air.

Where the main transport mode is air and all sea transportation is excluded, the "air" clauses are the most appropriate.

The special clauses to which reference is made here are those where the risks or loss of, or damage to, the cargo are not accidental or fortuitous. In each case the risks arise from the deliberate activities of third parties over whom the assured cannot be expected to be capable of exercising any control e.g. strikes, war.

12.8.2 Other Marine Policies
All types of policy referred to above relate to the general cargo, and these are the types of cover which forwarders are normally concerned.

However, in relation to special categories of cargo such as hides and skins, cargo subject to spontaneous combustion, etc, special clauses have been devised by the Institute of London Underwriters.

12.9 MARINE INSURANCE - DURATION OF COVER
It is quite clear that the underwriters of any marine insurance policy must limit the duration - whether of time or of geographical distance, during which they remain at risk. If they were not to do so it would be analogous to giving the assured a "blank cheque".

It must be understood that there has to be a clearly defined moment both in time and in place when the risk in the goods attaches to the underwriters and also a similar defined moment in both time and place when the underwriters become relieved of that risk.

The "transit clauses" within the policy create these definitions. Meantime, it is sufficient for the forwarder to understand the following:

1.   The risk attaches to the underwriter from the time the goods leave the warehouse or place of storage at the place named for the commencement of the transit.

The risk terminates either:-

☐   on delivery of the goods to the consignee or on any other final warehouse or place of storage at the destination named in the policy, or

☐   on delivery to any other warehouse or place of storage, even if prior   to arrival at the destination named in policy, which the assured elects to use either.

        -       for storage other than in the ordinary course of transit, or
        -       for allocation or distribution, or

☐   on the expiry of 60 days after completion of discharge over side of the goods insured from the overseas vessel at the final port of discharge,

☐   whichever of these shall first occur.

However, if, after discharge over side from the overseas vessel at the final port of destination but prior to the normal termination of the insurance as described above, the assured elects to forward the goods to a destination other than that to which they were insured, then the insurance shall not extend beyond the commencement of the transit to that other destination.

If owing to circumstances beyond the control of the assured either the contract of carriage is terminated at a port or place other than the destination named in the policy or the transit is otherwise terminated before delivery of the goods as described above, then the insurance shall also terminate unless prompt notice is given to the underwriters and a continuation of cover is requested. Then the insurance shall remain in force subject strictly to the payment of an additional premium if required by the underwriters, unless the goods are sold and delivered at such port or place, or, unless otherwise specially agreed, until the expiry of 60 days after arrival of the goods insured at such port or place whichever shall first occur, **or**

if the goods are forwarded within the said period of 60 days (or any agreed extension thereof) to the destination named in the policy or to any other destination, until terminated in accordance with the clauses governing termination described above.

Where, however, delay beyond the control of the assured, deviation, forced discharge, reshipment or transshipment, is involved then the insurance will remain in force if the circumstances described arise from the exercise of a liberty granted to ship owners or charterers under the contract of affreightment.

The policy provides that where, after attachment of the risk to the underwriters, the destination is changed by the assured, the risk will be held covered at a premium and on conditions to be arranged, subject to prompt notice being given to the underwriters.

"Insurable interest" vests in the party to an international transaction who will suffer a financial loss or incur an expense arising from loss of, or damage to, cargo resulting from a peril covered by the insurance policy in question.

We must relate the discussion to INCOTERMS. It will be recalled that INCOTERMS codify the definitions of various terms of delivery and in particular clarify the points under those terms where the risk of loss of, or damage to, the goods passes from the seller to the buyer.

It necessarily follows that where during the course of the transit a peril arises which results in loss or damage then it is the party bearing the risk in accordance with the definition in INCOTERMS which is holding the insurable interest in the goods.

The wording of the clause in the London Institute of Underwriters policies reads are follows:

> *"In order to recover under this insurance the assured must have an insurable interest in the subject matter insured at the time of the loss."*

The key words in this clause are "at the time of the loss".

A careful study and comprehension of INCOTERMS will enable the forwarder to determine with confidence which party - seller or buyer - holds the insurable interest in goods which are in transit.

We have discussed insurable interest as if it is only the buyer or the seller who can hold such an interest in the goods. This is not necessarily the end of the story. A bank who has paid for the goods in terms of a documentary letter of credit but who cannot obtain recovery of the amounts outlaid would thereby acquire an insurable interest.

A confirming house which had made an irrevocable commitment to pay for goods may acquire an insurable interest in them.

In the very unlikely event that a forwarder had agreed in his own right to purchase goods from a foreign supplier on behalf of a client in Zimbabwe but who then found that the client was unable to reimburse the amount involved, would also acquire thereby an insurable interest in the goods.

12.10 INSURABLE VALUE
Marine insurance can be taken out either by the seller or the buyer. It is obvious that the term of delivery (INCOTERM) employed in the contract between the two parties will dictate which of the two parties is responsible to provide the insurance cover.

It is true to say that under most circumstances the insurance cover taken out is for the benefit of the buyer who will be the party from whom a claim upon the underwriters will arise.

The insured value must be that value which provides a sufficient indemnity so that the buyer (importer) will be put in the same position financially after settlement of the claim, as if the loss or damage had not occurred.

The insured value must therefore be inclusive of all costs, charges and expenses which the importer will pay right up to the moment when the goods are finally delivered at the destination warehouse. In addition, the value so calculated may be increased by a percentage agreed between the holder of the insurance policy and the insurers which will cover the reasonable anticipated profit on the goods.

In the case of goods to be sold by retail this can be readily assessed. In the case, however, of goods which are intended as components for incorporation within other goods, a balance of reasonableness must prevail. No underwriter will permit the assured to uplift the calculated value to so great an extent as to provide an incentive to him to "arrange" the loss of the goods for the purpose of making a claim for the insured value.

12.10.1 The Ingredients of the Insurable Value

i)   The seller's invoice - this forms the first element in the value and the forwarder will understand that the invoiced price will be expressed in accordance with the delivery terms (INCOTERMS) under which the seller supplies the goods.

ii)   Transportation costs, dock and harbour charges, delivery costs, costs   of clearance through customs, etc. In fact, every cost which is not already included in the seller's invoiced price must be added.

ii)   As regards imports in transit through Zimbabwe or Mozambique, the ad valorem wharfage change must be added.

iii)   Duty, excise duty, surcharge, etc, as appropriate must be included.

iv)   Finally, the agreed percentage uplift must be added on.

v)   VAT payable upon entry of the goods for home consumption.

Having by these calculations arrived at a satisfactory insurable value for a consignment, the question arises whether, in the event of the goods being totally lost or irreparably damaged, the assured is entitled under all circumstances to claim for that value.

The answer is no. It depends upon the point in the transportation chain where the total loss or irreparable damage occurred.

If the loss of damage occurred prior to the moment when certain of the costs became due, then the claim can only be for the costs actually incurred plus the agreed uplift. An assured is not entitled to claim costs which he has never incurred - as for instance duty, etc, if the goods were totally lost prior to importation.

It frequently happens that the duty has, in fact, been paid along with dock charges, etc, prior to the actual arrival of the ship in the destination port. If the loss occurred prior to such arrival but after such payments were made, the assured would be under an obligation to lodge claims for refunds from the parties concerned but in the event that such refunds were not allowed for any reason then the assured would be entitled to claim for those costs under the insurance policy.

12.10.2 The problem of value added to goods during the course of transit
The added value in question is normally the customs duties, etc. On certain categories of goods the duty is high, but it only becomes a charge upon the importer when the goods are landed in Zimbabwe. In terms of the calculation described above by which an appropriate insurable value must be arrived at it will be true to say that the underwriters will require a premium at a level which will justify them in accepting the risk in the goods to the extent of that entire value despite the fact that the value added by the payment of the duty, etc, will only arise at the time of entry with the customs authorities and it may not be reasonable for an importer to be required to cover a duty-inclusive value from the point of origin far overseas through to destination.

Marine underwriters acknowledge the reasonableness of this contention where the traffic involved is substantial, is moving continually and the duty involvement is high. In these circumstances underwriters are prepared, upon request, to negotiate special arrangements in terms of which the marine insurance cover (warehouse-to-warehouse) excludes the value added by the duty, etc, so that the marine insurance premium payable in respect of the marine insurance cover is a lower figure. Underwriters will then charge a separate premium based on the value added by the duty, etc, from the moment when the duty, etc, becomes payable so that the higher value for the goods is brought to account only during the residual transit from the port of customs entry to the final destination.

It will normally be found that the premium rate which will be applied to the added value in such instances will normally be in the region of 40 - 50% of the premium rate applicable to the full marine insurance.

12.10.3 Insurable Value for Goods Bought on Terms CIF or CIP

It was pointed out that almost invariably the insurance cover taken out is for the benefit of the buyer who will be the party from whom a claim upon the underwriters will arise. Under those INCOTERMS where it is the responsibility of the buyer to create the insurance cover the intelligent buyer will make quite sure that the value for which he seeks insurance includes - in financial terms all the risks of loss or damage which will fall upon him.

Where the delivery terms for the transaction in question are CIF or CIP, however, it will be the seller who is responsible to take out an appropriate insurance cover and make it available promptly to the buyer in such a form that the buyer is able to claim directly upon the underwriter's local agent in the buyer's country.

Under both terms - CIF and CIP - responsibility of the seller is to provide insurance in accordance with the minimum cover of the Institute Cargo Clauses on a warehouse-to-warehouse basis, and for a value of 110% of the contract price unless by agreement in the international contract he is required to cover broader risks and a higher insured value.

INCOTERMS impose no obligation upon the seller to provide cover in respect of risks of war as per the Institute War Clauses (Cargo), or strikes, riots and civil commissions as per the Institute Strikes Clauses (Cargo), unless the buyer has required him to do so.

While it may be true that in the majority of instances the seller will realise without being specifically instructed, that he must take out insurance against the broadest possible risks (the A Clauses), and he may also automatically take out insurance against war, strikes, riots and civil commotions, instances occur regularly where the seller will only take out the minimum cover for the minimum obligatory value, either through ignorance or because the buyer, when ordering the goods, has failed to stipulate his insurance instructions. The effect of this is, of course, that the buyer may find himself severely under-listed, and the fault will be entirely his own.

395

The international contract may omit to define the value for insurance purposes needed by the buyer with the result that the insured value is merely 110% of the contract price. When this occurs it is entirely the fault of the buyer.

12.10.4 Duration of Insurance arranged by the Seller under CIF and CIP

This Module deals with duration of cover in terms of the clauses in the marine policy but does not refer to a problem which only too frequently occurs where the seller is responsible for arranging the insurance on the buyer's behalf.

In respect of both terms CIF and CIP the forwarder will already know from his studies of INCOTERMS that these two terms require to be qualified by the naming of either the destination port (CIF) or the place (CIP).

Where the delivery term is CIF the definition of the term makes it quite clear that it is for use in the context of maritime transit only, with the result that "delivery" of the goods takes place at the destination port. On many occasions, however, and particularly in Zimbabwe, the destination port is not the final destination for the transit of the goods. For example, a substantial proportion of imports arriving in the port of Durban are for destination on the Reef.

It therefore becomes vitally important to make certain that the insurance covers the full duration of the transit, that the buyer stipulates that the insurance cover must persist to the warehouse at the final delivery location.

Under the term CIP, the point of delivery must be added as a qualification to the term and in, perhaps, the majority of instances that point will, in fact, be the final delivery location. Nevertheless, there may be instances when that point is a rail depot, container depot or the container terminal at Dabuka whence the goods will still remain to be transported to the warehouse at the final destination location.

In both instances it is important to ensure that the insurance cover taken out by the seller is so worded as to make certain that the duration stated in the policy correctly covers the full transit to which the goods are to be subjected.

In fact, so far as concerns imports into Zimbabwe it is normally sufficient for the ultimate destination to be stated as "interior of Zimbabwe". This form of wording is sufficient to cover all contingencies.

A small word of caution must still be given. In the case of exports from Zimbabwe on these terms into the less developed countries elsewhere in the world where the transport infrastructure may be inferior the extending of the duration to the warehouse of final destination might involve some increase in the premium rate.

There are a number of other clauses which form an integral part of all policies of insurance worded in accordance with the London Institute of underwriters.

12.11 INSURE LOCALLY OR BUY CIF/CIP

12.11.1 Advantages of Insuring Imports Locally

☐   The full marine insurance cover on a warehouse-to-warehouse basis can be arranged with the same company which is already undertaking the insurance of the importer's warehouse stocks and commodities in trade.

This can assist in the settlement of claims provided the policy includes cover as per the concealed damage extension clause when loss or damage is discovered subsequent to the taking of an import consignment into stock when the damage was "concealed" and therefore not discovered until a package or packages were finally opened and unpacked. In such instance no question can occur with regard to the underwriter upon whom the claim must be made.

☐   The importer may, with the assistance of his broker or from the insurance company itself, select tailor-made terms and conditions to suit his particular requirements.

☐   The importer will be in a position to negotiate a claim settlement with the people who arranged the insurance locally instead of having to deal with the agents for foreign underwriters with whom he has no direct business relationship.

☐   Zimbabwean marine insurers utilise the insurance clauses of the Institute of London Underwriters which are without question the most lucid and the most fair insurance conditions to be found anywhere in the world.

By insuring locally the importer can make certain that the complete transit is covered and also that an adequate insured value is declared.

Marine insurance arranged with a local underwriter is paid for in local currency which is one means by which the Zimbabwean economy can be supported and the balance of payments of the country assisted.
In the context of exports to less developed countries it may be possible to obtain better insurance terms from the local underwriting market in Zimbabwe than the overseas buyer could obtain in his own market.

Offering terms which are inclusive of marine insurance have the advantage to the overseas buyer of relieving him of the onus of arranging insurance at this end of the transit chain.

Insurance arranged within Zimbabwe will be in accordance with the clauses of the Institute of London Underwriters - with their substantial recognition worldwide.

If the insurance premium payable is substantial and the credit terms extended to the overseas buyer are fairly long (e.g. 90 or 120 days) then it will be an advantage to the overseas buyer that the insurance premium is included within the credit terms.

By arranging the insurance locally the exporter is assisting Zimbabwe to earn additional foreign currency for the benefit of the balance of payments.

Selling on CIF/CIP terms necessarily demands that the Zimbabwean exporter makes quite certain that he is providing insurance cover against the required risks, for the appropriate duration, and for the correct value, as required by the overseas buyer.

Where extended credit terms are offered to the overseas buyer the Zimbabwean exporter will be subject to bank interest charges on the total amount outstanding for the transaction in question until the payment is received. That total amount will be inclusive of the marine insurance premium.

Where the Zimbabwean exporter insures his credit risk with the Export Credit Guarantee Company the amount of the insured value under credit insurance policy will be increased together with the premium payable.

12.11.2 Disadvantages of Overseas Seller Arranging Insurance Cover

This inevitably leads to a "split" in the insurance cover between that cover provided for purposes of transportation and that cover which is provided for stocks in warehouse or in course of trade. Where hidden damage is discovered after the termination of the marine insurance the challenge will be made to determine whether that damage occurred during the validity of the marine insurance or subsequent thereto.

In the event of a claim arising the importer will find himself dealing with the local claims settling agent of an overseas (foreign) underwriter with whom he normally has no business dealings, with the result that his negotiating ability is limited. He will have no "goodwill" which may enable him to influence a satisfactory settlement when the circumstances may admittedly be obscure.

There is a possibility that the insurance arranged for him by the seller may be on terms which are more restrictive than those of the London Institute of Underwriters and therefore against his financial interest.

He may find that, despite instructions given in correct detail to the seller, those instructions are not completely fulfilled which may leave him short of the cover which he requires.

General Comments
In the context of both imports and exports the following comments apply with equal force.

If the seller - whether in Zimbabwe or overseas - is a large multinational organisation with substantial traffic moving worldwide he may be able to obtain from his own insurers rates which are appreciably better than the rates which are available to the small organisation desirous of insuring only periodic shipments. The reason for this is obvious - the underwriter's risk is spread broadly over many shipments moving over a variety of routes to many different destinations with two important results:-

☐   the underwriter's revenue is substantial and

☐   in an actuarial sense, the incidence of claims in proportion to total traffic value will reduce.

Where this is true benefits of lower premium rates are therefore available to the trader buying from or selling to such an organisation. On the other hand, the multinational organisation could have a poor worldwide loss ratio - with the reverse effect upon his premium rates - making it preferable for his Zimbabwean buyer to negotiate separate insurance locally which would not be influenced by the supplier's poor record.

The multinational organisation may be content to carry excesses under their policies which would be unacceptable to the Zimbabwean buyer.

12.12 OPEN MARINE POLICIES
An open marine policy is not, in fact, an insurance policy. It is a contract entered into by mutual agreement between the insurance underwriters and the assured which is subject to stipulations which must be complied with by both parties. Individual insurance policies or certificates are then issued with regard to each transaction declared under the open policy.

Open marine policies are particularly useful to international traders - whether importers or exporters - for use when they are responsible for the arranging of the appropriate insurance for goods in the process of transportation.

12.12.1 Open Marine Policy - A Legally Binding Contract
An open marine policy is a legally binding contract in which the following stipulations are obligatory on the parties:-

☐   the assured undertakes to declare under the open policy all shipments in respect of which no insurance has been arranged by the supplier, and

☐   the insurance underwriters agree to hold covered all shipments
      declared to them by the assured even though the declarations in   question have been made after the goods have been shipped.

Provided that the underwriters are satisfied with the good faith of the assured, they are normally prepared not only to accept declarations made to them after shipment of the goods, but also declarations made to them even after the goods have arrived. The intention of the underwriters is to hold covered those shipments which by clerical error are not timeously declared. It will be obvious that by extending this facility the underwriters are placing themselves in a vulnerable situation with the result that they will not maintain an open policy while they are satisfied with the good faith of the assured.

12.12.2 Important Features of an Open Marine Policy

An open marine policy always places a limit upon the insured value which is declarable in respect of any one vessel, mode of conveyance, or at any one location.

These are referred to as bottom and location limits respectively. It is therefore important that the assured sets these limits at the maximum amount which he may require. These limits do not affect the premium payable which will be based on the value of the shipments actually declared.

The open policy must state the basis of the calculation of the insured value. This can vary from commodity to commodity, from voyage to voyage, and from client to client. Whatever the basis selected, the final formula for the calculation of the insured value should equate to at least the delivered cost at the final destination. And, as is the case with marine insurance policies, it is permissible to insure for a reasonable anticipated profit.

The open policy will normally describe the nature of the cargo which will be insured there under. This can be "general", although the underwriters would normally wish to know the nature of the goods which are normally traded.

Underwriters normally require that the countries of source/destination for the cargoes involved are stated.

The conditions of cover should also be indicated. Where an open policy is negotiated, all possible conditions of cover should be discussed.

In the instance of many open policies it is possible for the premium rates which will be applied to be enumerated, but, where this is impractical, the open policy will normally state "at rates to be determined".

General Comments

It is obvious that an open marine policy is a very useful asset to any forwarder. It may not be possible for a forwarder to stipulate within his open policy either the nature of the goods which he will have to declare, nor the source and destination thereof. It is evident that in relation to certain goods, he may require somewhat less cover. It is quite normal for an underwriter to organise an open policy in the name of the forwarder but for the benefit of the forwarder's clients. Provided that such an open policy is approximately worded, it is possible for a forwarder to arrange insurance for every type of goods which he is called upon to handle.

Payment of Premiums Due

It is a basic principle of marine insurance (as of all other insurances) that claims will be considered only provided the premium due in respect of the cover provided has been paid. This principle is maintained in relation to declarations made in terms of open policies. It is important therefore that a forwarder acting for insurance purposes under his own open policy makes certain that all premiums payable by him are duly settled on a monthly basis without delay or any attempt to offset.

12.13 THE C CLAUSES - RISKS COVERED AND EXCLUSIONS

Risks Covered under Institute Cargo Clauses C

These are quoted in full as follows:-
This insurance covers, except as provided in Clauses 4,5,6 and 7 below,
Loss of or damage to the subject-matter insured reasonably attributable to:
- *Fire or explosion*
- *Vessel or craft being stranded, grounded, sunk or capsized*
- *Overturning or derailment and land conveyance*
- *Collision or contact of vessel, craft or conveyance with an external object other than water*
- *Discharge of cargo at a port of distress*
- *Loss of or damage to the subject-matter insured caused by general average sacrifice and or jettison*

This insurance covers General Average and salvage charges, adjusted or determined according to the contract of affreightment and/or the governing law and practice, incurred to avoid or in connection with the avoidance of loss from any cause except those excluded in Clauses 4,5,6 and 7 or elsewhere in this insurance.

This insurance is extended to indemnify the assured against such proportion of liability under the contract of affreightment "both to blame collision" clause as is in respect of a loss recoverable hereunder. In the event of any claim by ship owners under the said clause the assured agree to notify the underwriters who shall have the right at their own cost and expense, to defend the assured against such claim.

Comments on the risks covered
Contact of the vessel, craft or conveyance with water, whether salt or fresh or river water, will not justify any claim since it is in the nature of the conveyances involved that they shall, at all times, be in contact with water.

However, contact with ice, contact with floating flotsam, with floating jetsam, with floating wreckage, etc, which results in loss or damage will be claimable.

The definition of a port of distress is highly sophisticated but put in rather simplistic terms it is that port into which the vessel or craft is compelled to put for any of the following reasons:-

- for protection from severe weather
- for such repairs to ship's machinery, navigational aids, and similar, which are essential to the completion of the voyage.
- for the landing of members of the ship's complement requiring urgent medical or surgical treatment
- etc, etc.

However, while these may be the reasons for a ship to call at a port of distress, none of these justify a claim on the underwriters to the cargo unless the cargo itself or some part of it, has to be discharged at that port. Where this occurs, there are obviously expenses arising and additional risks of loss or damage to the cargo in question. It is these expenses and these risks of loss or damage which are acceptable risks under the C Clauses.

'Jettisoning' is the voluntary and deliberate throwing overboard of cargo for the purpose of lightening the ship in time of danger. Thus a ship which is stranded on a reef, sandbank or rock, may be floated off if a proportion of the cargo is jettisoned. Where jettison takes place, then the C Clauses provide an insurance for the cargo owner against this occurrence.

12.13.2 Exclusions Under the C Clauses
The exclusions from the cover provided by the C Clauses are defined as follows:-

In no case shall this insurance cover.
- Loss or damage or expense attributable to willful misconduct of the assured.

- Ordinary leakage, ordinary loss in weight or volume, or ordinary wear and tear of the subject-matter insured.

- Loss, damage or expense caused by insufficiency or unsuitability of packing or preparation of the subject-matter insured (for the purpose of this clause 4.3 "Packing" shall be deemed to include stowage in a container or lift van but only when such stowage is carried out prior to attachment of this insurance or by the assured or their servants.

- Loss, damage or expense caused by inherent vice or nature of the subject matter insured.

- Loss damage or expense approximately caused by delay even though the delay be caused by a risk insured against (except expenses payable under general average).

- Loss, damage or expense arising from insolvency or financial default of the owners, manager, charterers or operators of the vessel.

- Deliberate damage to or deliberate destruction of the subject-matter insured or any part thereof by the wrongful act of any person or persons.

402

☐ Loss, damage or expense arising from the use of any weapon of war employing atomic or nuclear fission and/or fusion or other like reaction or radioactive force or matter.

☐ In no case shall insurance cover loss damage or expense arising from unseaworthiness of vessel or craft, unfitness of vessel, craft, conveyance, container or lift van for the safe carriage of the subject-matter insured where the assured or their servants are privy to such unseaworthiness or unfitness at the time the subject-matter insured is loaded therein.

The underwriters waive any breach of the implied warranties of seaworthiness of the ship and fitness of the ship to carry the subject-matter insured to destination unless the assured or their servants are privy to such unseaworthiness or unfitness.

☐ In no case shall this insurance cover loss, damage or expense caused by:- War, civil war, revolution, rebellion, insurrection, or civil strife arising there from, or any hostile act by or against a belligerent power.

☐ Capture, seizure, arrest, restraint or detainment (piracy excepted) and the consequences thereof or any attempt thereat.

☐ Derelict mines, torpedoes, bombs and other derelict weapons of war.

In no case shall this insurance cover loss, damage or expense:-

☐ Caused by strikes, locked-out workmen or persons taking part in labour disturbance, riots or civil commotions.

☐ Resulting from strikes, lock-outs, labour disturbances, riots or civil commotions.

☐ Caused by any terrorist or any other person acting from a political motive.

Comments on the Exclusions
There is a clause which excludes all losses or damages caused to the assured which arise directly (proximately) from delay in the completion of the transit. That delay might result in loss of market, deterioration of perishable goods, the incurring of a penalty for failure to fulfill a deadline, etc, even when that delay is consequent upon a risk insured against.

If the assured allows his goods to be shipped on a vessel owned or operated by an organisation which is financially unsound, and that organisation goes insolvent or defaults upon its financial obligations, then losses incurred by such cargo owners are not covered. This emphasises the importance of shipping through shipping lines which are financially sound, are well managed, and which have no track record of delinquency.

Another clause refers to "the use of any weapon of war employing atomic or nuclear fission/fusion, etc." Use, in this context, appears to presuppose international hostilities in which atomic weapons are being utilised. The development of such hostilities are likely to have so severe effects worldwide that the clause would appear to be largely academic. Nevertheless, if a claim arose in which the loss or damage or expense arose from the use of such weapons that claim would be excluded.

For practical purposes, it is hardly possible for the shipper of cargo to obtain for his own satisfaction first-hand knowledge that a ship or other craft is, in fact, seaworthy. There are organisations who codify the seaworthiness of ships utilised in international trade. For instance, Lloyds Register of Shipping classifies a vessel of top quality as "A1". The corresponding Register in the United States, Germany, Japan, etc, will have a corresponding code for a vessel of a corresponding quality.

Furthermore, every ship engaged in ocean transportation must undergo an annual inspection which is stringent in its detail. If there is any element of the ship which is in a deteriorated or deteriorating state, that ship rating will be reduced.

It is by these means that international traders can, if they feel it desirable, ascertain the relative seaworthiness or otherwise of the ship(s) on which they intend to load their goods. Nevertheless, underwriters recognise that "seaworthiness" is a highly technical study and it would not be reasonable that claims be rejected on the basis of unseaworthiness unless the assured or its servants were privy to that fact.

Exclusion of War Risks
The three sub-clauses above deal with the whole question of war risks. There clauses are self-explanatory but it must be emphasised that the definition of "war" is very broad. It covers virtually all forms of hostility and hostile action deliberately undertaken by any party; it is not confined to parties who have made a formal declaration of war between each other.

Furthermore, risks arising from derelict weapons of war are also excluded. In consequence, the mere cessation of hostilities does not obviate war risks. Marine casualties have occurred very many years after the termination of World War 2 and may still occur. The normal marine insurance cover excludes all such risks but the London Institute of Underwriters have devised a set of clauses - the Institute War Clause (Cargo) - by means of which they can be reincorporated subject to the payment of an additional premium.

Risks Arising from Strikes, Riots and Civil Commotions
This clause excludes from marine insurance cover the risks of loss, damage or expense caused by individuals taking part in labour disturbances, riots and civil commissions and also loss, damage or expense resulting from strikes, lock-outs, labour disturbances, riots or civil commissions.

A subtle distinction will be noted between these two aspects of the exclusions. In the first instance the exclusion is from loss, etc, caused by individuals taking part in such activities, and in the second instance, loss, etc, resulting from the existence of such activities.

In other words, if the assured permits his goods to be shipped over a route affected either by participants in those activities or by the existence, per se, of such activities the responsibility is his own. The underwriters will not accept the consequential risks.

In addition, the normal marine policy excludes loss, etc, caused by any terrorist or any person acting from a political motive. Unfortunately, this particular clause is subject to a very broad interpretation.

12.14 THE B CLAUSES - RISKS COVERED AND EXCLUSIONS

The differences between the C and the B Clauses are entirely the inclusion of one further set of risks.

12.14.1 Risks covered under Institute Cargo Clauses B

These are quoted in full as follows:-

This insurance covers, except as provided in Clauses below:-
Loss of or damage to the subject-matter insured reasonably attributable to.
☐ *Fire or explosion*
☐ *Vessel or craft being stranded, grounded, sunk or capsized.*
☐ *Overturning or derailment of land conveyance*
☐ *Collision or contact of vessel, craft or conveyance with an external object other than water.*
☐ *Discharge of cargo at port of distress.*

Earthquake, volcanic eruption or lightning

☐ General average sacrifice
☐ Jettison or washing overboard
☐ Entry of sea, lake or river water into vessel, craft, hold, conveyance, container, lift van or place of storage.
☐ ...The same paragraph regarding General Average as in the C Clauses
☐ ...The same paragraph with regard to the "both to blame collision" clause as in the C Clauses.

12.14.2 Exclusions under the B Clauses

The exclusions from the cover provided by the B Clauses are precisely the same as those excluded under the C Clauses.

In practice, therefore, the forwarder will understand that if the goods which are the subject of the transaction in question do not justify the additional premium expense required by the use of the A Clauses then the probability is that in most instances the reduced cover provided by the C Clauses will be adequate.

The B Clauses continue to exclude war risks and the risks arising from strikes, riots and civil commissions and also a sub-clause (above) is frequently deleted because of the difficulty in establishing the nature of the water causing the damage (e.g. rain water is not mentioned but may be the cause of the damage).

12.15 THE A CLAUSES - RISKS COVERED AND EXCLUSIONS
The A Clauses extend very substantially the risks covered by the underwriter. In the liner and general cargo trades the great majority of insurance covers are based upon the A Clauses.

12.15.1 Risks covered under Institute Cargo Clauses A
The operative clause dealing with risks covered under the A Clauses is a simple one and is worded as follows:-

☐   This insurance covers all risks of loss of or damage to the subject-matter insured except as provided in Clauses 4, 5, 6 & 7.
☐   ... The General Average clause as in the C Clauses
☐   ... The "both to blame collision" clause as in the C Clauses.

In the A Clauses, therefore, all risks of loss of or damage to the cargo are covered by the insurance except for those which are specifically listed as the exclusions.

12.15.2 Exclusions under the A Clauses
The exclusions from the cover provided by the A Clauses are defined as follows:-

In no case shall this insurance cover:-
☐   *Loss, damage or expense attributable to willful misconduct of the   assured.*
☐   *Ordinary leakage, ordinary loss in weight or volume or ordinary wear   and tear of the subject matter insured.*
☐   *Loss, damage or expense caused by insufficient or unsuitability of packing or preparation of the subject matter insured (for the purpose of this Clause 4.3 'packing' shall be deemed to include stowage in a container or lift van but only when such stowage is carried out prior   to attachment of this insurance or by the assured or their servants.*
☐   *Loss, damage or expense caused by inherent vice or nature of the subject matter insured.*
☐   *Loss, damage or expense proximately caused by delay even though the delay be caused by a risk insured against (except expenses payable under Clause 2 above.*
☐   *Loss, damage or expense arising from insolvency or financial default of the owners, managers, charterers or operators of the vessel.*
☐   *Loss, damage or expense arising from the use of any weapon of war employing atomic or nuclear fission and/or fusion or other like reaction or radioactive force or matter.*

□ *In no case shall this insurance cover loss, damage or expense arising from unseaworthiness of vessel or craft, unfitness of vessel, craft, conveyance, container or lift van for the safe carriage of the subject matter insured, where the assured or their servants are privy to such unseaworthiness or unfitness, at the time the subject matter insured is loaded therein.*

□ *The underwriters waive any breach of the implied warranties of seaworthiness of the ship and fitness of the ship to carry the subject matter insured to destination, unless the assured or their servants are privy to such unseaworthiness or unfitness.*

In no case shall this insurance cover loss, damage or expense caused by:-

□ *War, civil war, revolution, rebellion, insurrection, or civil strife arising there from, or any hostile act by or against a belligerent power.*
□ *Capture, seizure, arrest restraint or detainment (piracy excepted), and the consequences thereof or any attempt thereat.*
□ *Derelict mines, torpedoes, bombs or other derelict weapons of war.*

In no case shall this insurance cover loss, damage or expense:-
□ *Caused by strikers, locked-out workmen, or persons taking part in labour disturbance, riots or civil commotion.*
□ *Resulting from strikes, lock-outs labour disturbances, riots or civil commissions*
□ *Caused by any terrorist or any person acting from a political motive.*

The exception is the omission from the A Clauses Exclusions of the following clause which is in the B and C Clauses Exclusions:-

"deliberate damage to or deliberate destruction of the subject-matter insured or any part thereof by the wrongful act of any person or persons"

NB: The exclusion of this "malicious damage" clause from the B and C Clauses can upon request be reinstated in those Clauses upon payment of an additional premium.

12.15.3 Institute Cargo Clauses (AIR) - Risks Covered and Exclusions
It will be quite evident to the student that certain risks which are inherent in the transportation of goods by sea are irrelevant when the same goods are transported by airfreight.

There can be no such thing as a General Average sacrifice where goods are transported by airfreight. It is manifestly quite impossible to "jettison" some of the cargo from an aircraft, and it is also equally evident that there is no such thing as a minor collision between two aircraft where a "both to blame clause" could apply. Mid-air collisions are always catastrophes.

Accordingly, the risks of a General Average sacrifice or a "both to blame collision" are simply not relevant.

The Air Clauses cover all risks of, or damage to the goods except those covered by the exclusions which are for practical purposes identical, mutatis mutandis, with those to be found in the A Clauses.

12.16 INSURANCE STRIKES CLAUSES (CARGO) - RISKS AND EXCLUSIONS

NB: The Strikes Clauses, whilst optional, should always be added to the standard marine insurance policy and may be incorporated by request of the assured and with the agreement of the underwriters.

The effect of their incorporation in a marine insurance policy is to incorporate into the policy certain of the risks which are normally excluded by the wording of Clauses 7.1, 7.2 and 7.3 in the A, B and C Clauses.

12.16.1 Risks Covered in the Institute Strikes Clauses (Cargo)
The risks covered are defined as follows:-
This insurance covers except as provided in Clauses 3 and 4 below loss of or damage to the subject-matter insured caused by:-

☐   *Strikers, locked-out workmen or persons taking part in labour disturbances, riots or civil commotions*
☐   *Any terrorists or any person acting from a political motive*
      This insurance covers General Average and salvage charges adjusted or determined according to the contract of affreightment and/or the governing law and practice, incurred to avoid or in connection with the avoidance of loss from a risk covered under these Clauses.

Comments on the Risks Covered
It is essential to notice that the Institute Strikes Clauses restores to a marine insurance policy two out of the three exclusions in the normal policy.

It restores to the policy cover for losses caused by strikers, locked-out workmen, or persons taking part in labour disturbances, riots or civil commissions and it also restores losses caused by any terrorist or person acting from a political motive. It does not restore to the policy losses 'resulting from strikes, lock-outs, labour disturbances, riots and civil commotions'.

In other words, deliberate willful and wanton actions by persons involved in strikes, lock-outs, etc, are covered but losses or damage caused by the mere existence, per se, of strikes, lock-outs, etc, remain excluded. To illustrate, a consignment of goods awaiting shipment at a port where a strike is declared before the goods have been successfully shipped, with the result that those goods are delayed and possibly deteriorate in consequence, are not covered. Put another way, it is the responsibility of the assured to anticipate as intelligently as possible whether the route which he has chosen for the movement of his goods is likely to be affected by one of the contingencies named and if in his opinion that is a likelihood then he must on his own responsibility vary the route so as to avoid the location where the risks could occur.

As regards the Clause above referring to terrorist or other person acting from a political motive, there are problems because there is no clearly defined definition for "terrorist" nor for "a person acting from a political motive".

The forwarder must also note the difference in the wording of the clause dealing with General Average sacrifice. It must be recognised that the clause dealing with General Average sacrifice in the normal marine policy remains intact with the effect that the clause dealing with General Average sacrifice in the Strikes Clauses (Cargo) is, in effect, additional and is intended to make it clear that a General Average sacrifice arising as a result of the additional risks covered will itself be covered.

12.16.2 Exclusions from Institute Strikes Clauses (Cargo)
The exclusions within these clauses are identical to those which are common to the A, B and C Clauses but they have the following additions:-

☐ Loss, damage or expense arising from the absence, shortage or withholding of labour of any description whatsoever resulting from any strike, lock-out, labour disturbance, riot or civil commodity.

☐ Any claim based upon loss of, or frustration of the voyage or adventure.

12.17 INSTITUTE WAR CLAUSES (CARGO) - RISKS COVERED AND EXCLUSIONS

NB: The War Clauses are optional and may be incorporated in a marine insurance policy by request of the assured and with the agreement of the underwriters.

The effect of their incorporation in a marine insurance policy is to incorporate into the policy the risks which are normally excluded by the wording of Clauses 6.1, 6.2 and 6.3 in the A, B and C Clauses.

12.17.1   Risks Covered in the Institute War Clauses (Cargo)
The risks covered are defined as follows:-

☐ This insurance covers, except as provided in Clauses 3 and 4 below, loss of or damage to the subject-matter insured caused by:-

☐ War, civil war, revolution, rebellion, insurrection, or civil strife arising there from, or any hostile act by or against a belligerent power

☐ Capture, seizure, arrest, restraint, or detainment arising from risks covered under 1.1 above, and the consequences thereof or any attempted threat.

☐ Derelict mines, torpedoes, bombs or other derelict weapons of war.

This insurance covers General Average and salvage charges, adjusted or determined according to the contract of affreightment and/or the governing law and practice, incurred to avoid or in connection with the avoidance of loss from a risk covered under these Clauses.

Comments on the Risks Covered
It will be noted by the forwarder that while the exclusions from the normal marine policy are reinstated there is a slight difference in the wording of one Clause above.

First of all, there is no reference to piracy. There is no need for such a reference since loss of, or damage to, goods arising from piracy is covered in any event in the A Clauses - although not in the B or C Clauses.

Secondly, a Clause quoted above makes it clear that the circumstances mentioned within it must arise from the risks referred to.

12.17.2 Exclusions from Institute War Clauses (Cargo)

The exclusions within these clauses are identical to those which are common to the A, B and C Clauses with the following single addition.

In no case shall this insurance cover any claim based upon loss of or frustration of the voyage or adventure.

12.18 INSTITUTE RADIO ACTIVE CONTAMINATION EXCLUSION CLAUSE

The Radioactive Contamination Exclusion Clause is worded as follows:-

"This Clause shall be paramount and shall override anything contained in this insurance inconsistent therewith.

☐ *In no case shall this insurance cover loss damage liability or expense directly or indirectly caused by or contributed to by or arising from -*
☐ *Ionising radiators from or contamination by radioactivity from any nuclear fuel or from any nuclear waste or from the combination of nuclear fuel.*

- *The radioactive, toxic, explosive or other hazardous or contaminating properties of any nuclear installation, reactor or other nuclear assembly or nuclear component thereof.*
- *Any weapon of war employing atomic or nuclear fission and/or fusion or other like reaction or radioactive force or matter.*

This Clause is uniformly inserted in every policy of marine insurance issued within the Republic of Zimbabwe and is also now included in many policies of marine insurance issued elsewhere in the world.

The commanding wording - "This Clause shall be paramount and shall override..." is important. The implication of these words is quite clear - that no loss or damage or liability or expense caused directly or indirectly from the risks enumerated is covered by any marine policy.

While, up to the present time, the breadth of application of the clause has not been tested in courts of law, it would appear that contamination of cargo by radioactive fall-out which in turn may cause loss of life or health at a later date with resultant expense is totally excluded from a marine policy.

It would further appear that marine underwriters will not be prepared to reinstate this exclusion even on payment of a substantial additional premium.

12.19 GENERAL AVERAGE

A General Average loss is loss, damage and expense arising as the direct result of:-

- a voluntary action taken by the ship owner or the ship's master,
- in a time of genuine peril of such a nature that the entire voyage is put in jeopardy,
- voluntarily incurred for the purpose of preserving to the greatest   extent possible the interests of all parties involved in the voyage,
- with the result that the voyage is saved.

It may be essential that a portion of the ship's cargo is thrown overboard in order to lighten a ship which is stranded on a reef or sandbank, or water may have to be pumped into the ship's hold to quench a fire which may cause water damage to cargo which in itself was not damaged by the fire. An engine breakdown may result in the ship's master having to radio for assistance - possible for towage into a port of refuge where the necessary repairs can be carried out - and the costs so incurred will be a General Average expense.

Note the criteria which must be fulfilled in order to justify a declaration by the ship owner of a General Average.

- A direct result of a peril

- ☐ The peril must be genuine
- ☐ The actions or the expenses incurred must be voluntary for the purpose of mitigating or avoiding the results of the peril.
- ☐ The voyage must be saved

It will be obvious from the definition that as a result of the voluntary actions taken by the ship's owner or the ship's master certain parties involved in the voyage will have suffered losses. Possibly their cargo has been thrown overboard; possibly their cargo has been voluntarily damaged; possibly the ship is being taken to a port of refuge with the consequence that major expenses have fallen upon the ship owner.

All these circumstances mean that certain parties have been put to loss, damage or expense for the greater good of all other parties involved in the voyage. The concept of General Average is that under such circumstances each party whose interest in the voyage was preserved as a consequence of the sacrifice of others, must contribute a ratable proportion for the benefit of those who have suffered the losses in order that the total burden of loss shall fall equally upon all involved.

When the term "Average" is used in the context of Marine Insurance, it must be clearly understood that the meaning of the word has nothing to do with the common meaning, that is, the average between two numbers, in this context is meaning is taken from the Ancient French word "avarie", meaning damage, especially to a ship of her cargo.

NB: **General Average is not in itself an insurance subject but it is convenient to discuss it in the context of marine insurance since loss, damage and expense resulting from a General Average event are risks which are covered in all marine insurance policies based on the clauses of the London Institute of Underwriters.**

12.19.1 The Assessment of the Contributions Due
The assessment of the contributions due from the parties whose interests were preserved is highly complex and there is no need to go into those complexities now. Suffice it to say that the assessments may take several years to finalise. It would be manifestly very unwise to allow the cargo, etc. ensure payment of the contributions when the assessment is completed. Accordingly, once a General Average has been declared the shipping company will not release any cargo under any circumstances until one of two alternatives have been provided:-

- ☐ A deposit in cash has been lodged with the shipping company of a size sufficient to cover the likely contributions due, or

- ☐ A General Average guarantee has been given to the shipping company by an insurance organisation of good standing acceptance to the company.

When a General Average is declared, it is vital for the importer to make speedy contact with his underwriters in order to arrange that they sign the appropriate General Average guarantee so as to enable the importer to obtain release of his goods. Once the guarantee has been given by the underwriter and accepted by the shipping company the importer has no further concern with the matter. Shipping companies accept a General Average guarantee given by any Zimbabwean based underwriting organisation.

It is worth noting that somewhere in the world incidents occur virtually every day which involve the declaration of a General Average by the shipping company concerned. if the incident is a serious one, the contribution which will be demanded from the cargo owner may well be an appreciable proportion of the value of the cargo.

The mere fact that over a period such as ten years a Zimbabwean international trader has never had occasion to claim upon his insurance should never delude that trader into assuming that he is paying out insurance premiums needlessly. He still, for another twenty years, may not have an occasion to claim for loss or damage to the cargo but within seven days of his decision to abandon the insuring of his goods a ship carrying his cargo may be involved in a General Average incident which will cost him dearly through lack of that insurance.

In other words, the risk of being called on to contribute to general average and/or salvage charges is not avoided by non-insurance of the cargo.

12.20 INSURANCE CLAIMS PROCEDURE
☐ notify insurance company or its agent of the damage.
☐ make a written claim against the carrier, port authorities or third   parties
☐ apply a survey by the carrier's representative, port authority and file claim on them
☐ within **three** days from delivery give notice to carrier's representative where damage was not apparent at the time of taking delivery
☐ in case of non-delivery, obtain a copy of non-delivery certificate from   the carrier's representative
☐ where appropriate obtain a copy of a master's protest certifying unusual transit conditions

12.20.1   Claim Filing
File as soon as possible attaching:-
☐ insurance certificate
☐ damage/loss survey report
☐ master's protest (where appropriate)
☐ certificate of non-delivery or short delivery
☐ certificate of loss overboard
☐ copy claim against carrier and reply if any
☐ port or customs landing certificate or bill of entry
☐ invoice, original bill of lading, packing list
☐ a loss or damage statement giving details of loss/damage to facilitate loss assessment and claim adjustment.

REFERENCES

Bailey C. A. (2007) **"A Guide to Qualitative Field Research."** Pine Forge Press. California.

Bedi K. (2004) **"Production and Operations Management"**. Oxford University Press. New Delhi.

Bhattacharyya D. K. (2003) **"Research Methodology."** Excel Books. New Delhi.

Cook T. A. (2001) **"The Ultimate Guide to Export Management."** AMACOM. New York.

Daniels, Raudebaugh, Sullivan (2004) **"Globalisation and Business."** Prentice Hall International. New Delhi

Frazelle E.H. (2004) **"Supply Chain Strategy."** Tata McGraw-Hill Publishing Co. Ltd. New Delhi.

Gubbins E. J. (2003) **"Managing Transport Operations."** Kogan Page. London.

House D. J. (2005) **"Cargo Work"** Elsevier. Amsterdam

Kapoor S. K. and Kansal P. (2003) **"Marketing Logistics: A Supply Chain Approach."** Pearson Education. New Delhi.

Kirby M., Kidd W et al (1997) **"Sociology in Perspective"** Heinnemann Educational Publishers. Oxford.

Raina H. K. (1990) **"Guide to Import Management".** PRODEC. Helsinki

Rowland O.P. (1986) **"Imports and Exports: An Introductory Handbook."** Evans Brothers. Ltd. Nairobi

Silverman D. (2006) **"Interpreting Qualitative Data."** Sage Publications. London.

Sople V. V. (2004) **"Logistics Management: The Supply Chain Imperative."** Pearson Education. Singapore.

CHAPTER 13

HUMAN RESOURCE MANAGEMENT

If human resources are not managed correctly and professionally the shipping,
forwarding and customs clearing function would be a complete failure. You need the best
brains for success. **Human resource management** (HRM) is the strategic and coherent
approach to the management of an organization's most valued assets - the people working
there who individually and collectively contribute to the achievement of the objectives of
the business. The terms "human resource management" and "human resources" (HR)
have largely replaced the term "personnel management" as a description of the processes
involved in managing people in organizations. In simple sense, HRM means employing
people, developing their resources, utilizing, maintaining and compensating their services
in tune with the job and organizational requirement.

Features

Its features include:

- Organizational management
- Personnel administration
- Manpower management
- Industrial management

But these traditional expressions are becoming less common for the theoretical discipline.
Sometimes even employee and industrial relations are confusingly listed as synonyms,
although these normally refer to the relationship between management and workers and
the behavior of workers in companies.

The theoretical discipline is based primarily on the assumption that employees are
individuals with varying goals and needs, and as such should not be thought of as basic
business resources, such as trucks and filing cabinets. The field takes a positive view of
workers, assuming that virtually all wish to contribute to the enterprise productively, and
that the main obstacles to their endeavors are lack of knowledge, insufficient training,
and failures of process.

HRM is seen by practitioners in the field as a more innovative view of workplace
management than the traditional approach. Its techniques force the managers of an
enterprise to express their goals with specificity so that they can be understood and
undertaken by the workforce, and to provide the resources needed for them to
successfully accomplish their assignments. As such, HRM techniques, when properly
practiced, are expressive of the goals and operating practices of the enterprise overall.
HRM is also seen by many to have a key role in risk reduction within organizations.[5]

Synonyms such as *personnel management* are often used in a more restricted sense to
describe activities that are necessary in the recruiting of a workforce, providing its

members with payroll and benefits, and administrating their work-life needs. So if we move to actual definitions, Torrington and Hall (1987) define personnel management as being:

"a series of activities which: first enable working people and their employing organisations to agree about the objectives and nature of their working relationship and, secondly, ensures that the agreement is fulfilled" (p. 49).

While Miller (1987) suggests that HRM relates to:

".......those decisions and actions which concern the management of employees at all levels in the business and which are related to the implementation of strategies directed towards creating and sustaining competitive advantage" (p. 352).

Academic theory

The goal of human resource management is to help an organization to meet strategic goals by attracting, and maintaining employees and also to manage them effectively. The key word here perhaps is "fit", i.e. a HRM approach seeks to ensure a fit between the management of an organization's employees, and the overall strategic direction of the company (Miller, 1989).

The basic premise of the academic theory of HRM is that humans are not machines, therefore we need to have an interdisciplinary examination of people in the workplace. Fields such as psychology, industrial engineering, industrial, Legal/Paralegal Studies and organizational psychology, industrial relations, sociology, and critical theories: postmodernism, post-structuralism play a major role. Many colleges and universities offer bachelor and master degrees in Human Resources Management.

One widely used scheme to describe the role of HRM, developed by Dave Ulrich, defines 4 fields for the HRM function:

- Strategic business partner
- Change management
- Employee champion
- Administration

However, many HR functions these days struggle to get beyond the roles of administration and employee champion, and are seen rather as reactive than strategically proactive partners for the top management. In addition, HR organizations also have the difficulty in proving how their activities and processes add value to the company. Only in the recent years HR scholars and HR professionals are focusing to develop models that can measure if HR adds value.

Business practice

Human resources management comprises several processes. Together they are supposed to achieve the above mentioned goal. These processes can be performed in an HR department, but some tasks can also be outsourced or performed by line-managers or other departments. When effectively integrated they provide significant economic benefit to the company.[8]

- Workforce planning
- Recruitment (sometimes separated into attraction and selection)
- Induction and Orientation
- Skills management
- Training and development
- Personnel administration
- Compensation in wage or salary
- Time management
- Travel management (sometimes assigned to accounting rather than HRM)
- Payroll (sometimes assigned to accounting rather than HRM)
- Employee benefits administration
- Personnel cost planning
- Performance appraisal

Careers and education

The sort of careers available in HRM are varied. There are generalist HRM jobs such as human resource assistant. There are careers involved with employment, recruitment and placement and these are usually conducted by interviewers, EEO (Equal Employment Opportunity) specialists or college recruiters. Training and development specialism is often conducted by trainers and orientation specialists. Compensation and benefits tasks are handled by compensation analysts, salary administrators, and benefits administrators.

Several universities offer programs of study pertaining to HRM and broader fields. Cornell University created the world's first school for college-level study in HRM (ILR School).[9] University of Illinois at Urbana-Champaign also now has a school dedicated to the study of HRM, while several business schools also house a center or department dedicated to such studies; e.g., Michigan State University, Ohio State University, and Purdue University.

Professional organizations

Professional organizations in HRM include the Society for Human Resource Management, the Australian Human Resources Institute (AHRI), the Chartered Institute of Personnel and Development (CIPD), the International Public Management Association for HR (IPMA-HR), Management Association of Nepal (MAN) and the International Personnel Management Association of Canada (IPMA-Canada), Human Capital Institute (HCI)

Functions

The Human Resources Management (HRM) function includes a variety of activities, and key among them is deciding what staffing needs you have and whether to use independent contractors or hire employees to fill these needs, recruiting and training the best employees, ensuring they are high performers, dealing with performance issues, and ensuring your personnel and management practices conform to various regulations. Activities also include managing your approach to employee benefits and compensation, employee records and personnel policies. Usually small businesses (for-profit or nonprofit) have to carry out these activities themselves because they can't yet afford part- or full-time help. However, they should always ensure that employees have -- and are aware of -- personnel policies which conform to current regulations. These policies are often in the form of employee manuals, which all employees have.

Note that some people distinguish a difference between HRM (a major management activity) and HRD (Human Resource Development, a profession). Those people might include HRM in HRD, explaining that HRD includes the broader range of activities to develop personnel inside of organizations, including, e.g., career development, training, organization development, etc. There is a long-standing argument about where HR-related functions should be organized into large organizations, e.g., "should HR be in the Organization Development department or the other way around?" The HRM function and HRD profession have undergone tremendous change over the past 20-30 years. Many years ago, large organizations looked to the "Personnel Department," mostly to manage the paperwork around hiring and paying people. More recently, organizations consider the "HR Department" as playing a major role in staffing, training and helping to manage people so that people and the organization are performing at maximum capability in a highly fulfilling manner.

Recruitment

Recruitment refers to the process of screening, and selecting qualified people for a job at an organization or firm, or for a vacancy in a volunteer-based some components of the recruitment process, mid- and large-size organizations and companies often retain professional recruiters or outsource some of the process to recruitment agencies. External recruitment is the process of attracting and selecting employees from outside the organization.

The recruitment industry has four main types of agencies: employment agencies, recruitment websites and job search engines, "headhunters" for executive and professional recruitment, and in-house recruitment. The stages in recruitment include sourcing candidates by advertising or other methods, and screening and selecting potential candidates using tests or interviews.

Agency types

The recruitment industry has four main types of agencies. Their recruiters aim to channel candidates into the hiring organizations application process. As a general rule, the agencies are paid by the companies, not the candidates.

Traditional Agency

Also known as a employment agencies, recruitment agencies have historically had a physical location. A candidate visits a local branch for a short interview and an assessment before being taken onto the agency's books. Recruitment consultants then work to match their pool of candidates to their clients' open positions. Suitable candidates are short-listed and put forward for an interview with potential employers on a temporary ("temp") or permanent ("perm") basis.

Compensation to agencies take several forms, the most popular:

- A contingency fee paid by the company when a recommended candidate accepts a job with the client company (typically 20%-30% based and calculated of the candidates first-year base salary – though fees as low as 12.5% can be found online[1]), which usually has some form of guarantee (30–90 days standard), should the candidate fail to perform and is terminated within a set period of time (refundable fully or prorated)
- An advance payment that serves as a retainer, also paid by the company, non-refundable paid in full depending on outcome and success (e.g. 30% up front, 30% in 90 days and the remainder once a search is completed). This form of compensation is generally reserved for high level executive search/headhunters
- Hourly Compensation for temporary workers and projects. A pre-negotiated hourly fee, in which the agency is paid and pays the applicant as a consultant for services as a third party. Many contracts allow a consultant to transition to a full-time status upon completion of a certain number of hours with or without a conversion fee.

Headhunters

A "headhunter" is industry term for a third-party recruiter who seeks out candidates, often when normal recruitment efforts have failed. Headhunters are generally considered more aggressive than in-house recruiters or may have preexisting industry experience and contacts. They may use advanced sales techniques, such as initially posing as clients to gather employee contacts, as well as visiting candidate offices. They may also purchase expensive lists of names and job titles, but more often will generate their own lists. They may prepare a candidate for the interview, help negotiate the salary, and conduct closure to the search. They are frequently members in good standing of industry trade groups and associations. Headhunters will often attend trade shows and other meetings nationally or even internationally that may be attended by potential candidates and hiring managers.

Headhunters are typically small operations that make high margins on candidate placements (sometimes more than 30% of the candidate's annual compensation). Due to their higher costs, headhunters are usually employed to fill senior management and executive level roles. Headhunters are also used to recruit very specialized individuals; for example, in some fields, such as emerging scientific research areas, there may only be a handful of top-level professionals who are active in the field. In this case, since there are so few qualified candidates, it makes more sense to directly recruit them one-by-one, rather than advertise internationally for candidates. While in-house recruiters tend to attract candidates for specific jobs, headhunters will both attract candidates and actively seek them out as well. To do so, they may network, cultivate relationships with various companies, maintain large databases, purchase company directories or candidate lists, and cold call prospective recruits

In-House Recruitment

Larger employers tend to undertake their own in-house recruitment, using their human resources department, front-line hiring managers and recruitment personnel who handle targeted functions and populations. In addition to coordinating with the agencies mentioned above, in-house recruiters may advertise job vacancies on their own websites, coordinate internal employee referrals, work with external associations, trade groups and/or focus on campus graduate recruitment. While job postings are common, networking is by far the most significant approach when reaching out to fill positions. Alternatively a large employer may choose to outsource all or some of their recruitment process(recruitment process outsourcing).

Passive Candidate Research Firms / Sourcing Firms

These firms provide competitive passive candidate intelligence to support company's recruiting efforts. Normally they will generate varying degrees of candidate information from those people currently engaged in the position a company is looking to fill. These firms usually charge a per hour fee or by candidate lead. Many times this uncovers names that cannot be found with other methods and will allow internal recruiters the ability to focus their efforts solely on recruiting.

Process

Job Analysis

The proper start to a recruitment effort is to perform a job analysis, to document the actual or intended requirement of the job to be performed. This information is captured in a job description and provides the recruitment effort with the boundaries and objectives of the search. [2] Oftentimes a company will have job descriptions that represent a historical collection of tasks performed in the past. These job descriptions need to be reviewed or updated prior to a recruitment effort to reflect present day requirements. Starting a recruitment with an accurate job analysis and job description insures the recruitment effort starts off on a proper track for success.

Sourcing

Sourcing involves 1) advertising, a common part of the recruiting process, often encompassing multiple media, such as the Internet, general newspapers, job ad newspapers, professional publications, window advertisements, job centers, and campus

420

graduate recruitment programs; and 2) recruiting research, which is the proactive identification of relevant talent who may not respond to job postings and other recruitment advertising methods done in #1. This initial research for so-called passive prospects, also called name-generation, results in a list of prospects who can then be contacted to solicit interest, obtain a resume/CV, and be screened (see below).jh

Screening and selection

Suitability for a job is typically assessed by looking for skills, e.g. communication, typing, and computer skills. Qualifications may be shown through résumés, job applications, interviews, educational or professional experience, the testimony of references, or in-house testing, such as for software knowledge, typing skills, numeracy, and literacy, through psychological tests or employment testing. In some countries, employers are legally mandated to provide equal opportunity in hiring. Business management software is used by many recruitment agencies to automate the testing process. Many recruiters and agencies are using an Applicant tracking system to perform many of the filtering tasks, along with software tools for psychometric testing

On boarding

"On boarding" is a term which describes the introduction or "induction" process. A well-planned introduction helps new employees become fully operational quickly and is often integrated with a new company and environment. On boarding is included in the recruitment process for retention purposes. Many companies have on boarding campaigns in hopes to retain top talent that is new to the company, campaigns may last anywhere from 1 week to 6 months.

Internet Recruitment / Websites

Such sites have two main features: job boards and a résumé/curriculum vitae (CV) database. Job boards allow member companies to post job vacancies. Alternatively, candidates can upload a résumé to be included in searches by member companies. Fees are charged for job postings and access to search resumes. Since the late 1990s, the recruitment website has evolved to encompass end-to-end recruitment. Websites capture candidate details and then pool them in client accessed candidate management interfaces (also online). Key players in this sector provide e-recruitment software and services to organizations of all sizes and within numerous industry sectors, who want to e-enable entirely or partly their recruitment process in order to improve business performance.

The online software provided by those who specialize in online recruitment helps organizations attract, test, recruit, employ and retain quality staff with a minimal amount of administration. Online recruitment websites can be very helpful to find candidates that are very actively looking for work and post their resumes online, but they will not attract the "passive" candidates who might respond favorably to an opportunity that is presented to them through other means. Also, some candidates who are actively looking to change jobs are hesitant to put their resumes on the job boards, for fear that their current companies, co-workers, customers or others might see their resumes.

Job search engines

The emergence of meta-search engines, allow job-seekers to search across multiple websites. Some of these new search engines index and list the advertisements of traditional job boards. These sites tend to aim for providing a "one-stop shop" for job-seekers. However, there are many other job search engines which index pages solely from employers' websites, choosing to bypass traditional job boards entirely. These vertical search engines allow job-seekers to find new positions that may not be advertised on traditional job boards, and online recruitment websites.

Skills management

Skills Management is the practice of understanding, developing and deploying people and their skills. Well-implemented skills management should identify the skills that job roles require, the skills of individual employees, and any gap between the two.

Overview

The skills involved can be defined by the organization concerned, or by third party institutions. They are usually defined in terms of a skills framework, also known as a competency framework or skills matrix. This consists of a list of skills, and a grading system, with a definition of what it means to be at particular level for a given skill. (For an example of a mature skills framework, see the Skills Framework for the Information Age, [1], a technical IT skills framework owned by a British not-for-profit organization.)

To be most useful, skills management needs to be conducted as an ongoing process, with individuals assessing and updating their recorded skill sets regularly. These updates should occur at least as frequently as employees' regular line manager reviews, and certainly when their skill sets have changed.

Skills management _systems_ record the results of this process in a database, and allow analysis of the data.

In order to perform the functions of management and to assume multiple roles, managers must be skilled. Robert Katz identified three managerial skills that are essential to successful management: technical, human, and conceptual*. Technical skill involves process or technique knowledge and proficiency. Managers use the processes, techniques and tools of a specific area. Human skill involves the ability to interact effectively with people. Managers interact and cooperate with employees. Conceptual skill involves the formulation of ideas. Managers understand abstract relationships, develop ideas, and solve problems creatively. Thus, technical skill deals with things, human skill concerns people, and conceptual skill has to do with ideas. A manager's level in the organization determines the relative importance of possessing technical, human, and conceptual skills. Top level managers need conceptual skills in order to view the organization as a whole. Conceptual skills are used in planning and dealing with ideas and abstractions. Supervisors need technical skills to manage their area of specialty. All levels of management need human skills in order to interact and communicate with other people successfully.

As the pace of change accelerates and diverse technologies converge, new global industries are being created (for example, telecommunications). Technological change alters the fundamental structure of firms and calls for new organizational approaches and management skills.

Employees who benefit

Skills management provides a structured approach to developing individual and collective skills, and gives a common vocabulary for discussing skills. As well as this general benefit, three groups of employees receive specific benefits from skills management.

Individual Employees

As a result of skills management, employees should be aware of the skills their job requires, and any skills gaps that they have. Depending on their employer, it may also result in a personal development plan (PDP) of training to bridge some or all of those skills gaps over a given period.

line manager

Skills management enables managers to know the skill strengths and weaknesses of employees reporting to them. It can also enable them to search for employees with particular skill sets (e.g. to fill a role on a particular job).

Organization Executives

A rolled-up view of skills and skills gaps across an organization can enable its executives to see areas of skill strength and weakness. This enables them to plan for the future against the current and future abilities of staff, as well as to prioritise areas for skills development.

Professional development

Professional development refers to skills and knowledge attained for both personal development and career advancement. Professional development encompasses all types of facilitated learning opportunities, ranging from college degrees to formal coursework, conferences and informal learning opportunities situated in practice. It has been described as intensive and collaborative, ideally incorporating an evaluative stage. There are a variety of approaches to professional development, including consultation, coaching, communities of practice, lesson study, mentoring, reflective supervision and technical assistance.

Who Participates and Why

A wide variety of people, such as teachers, military officers and non-commissioned officers, health care professionals, lawyers, accountants and engineers engage in professional development. Individuals may participate in professional development because of an interest in lifelong learning, a sense of moral obligation, to maintain and improve professional competence, enhance career progression, keep abreast of new technology and practice, or to comply with professional regulatory organizations. [3] [4] [5] Many American states have professional development requirements for school teachers. For example, Arkansas teachers must complete 60 hours of documented professional development activities annually. [6] Professional development credits are named differently from state to state. For example, teachers: in Indiana are required to earn 90 Continuing Renewal Units (CRUs) per year [7]; in Massachusetts, need 150 Professional Development Points (PDPs) [8]; and in Georgia, must earn 10 Professional Learning Units (PLUs) [9]. American and Canadian nurses, as well as those in the United Kingdom, are required to participate in formal and informal professional development (earning Continuing education units, or CEUs) in order to maintain professional registration Other groups such as engineering and geoscience regulatory bodies also have mandatory professional development requirements.

Approaches to Professional Development

In a broad sense, professional development may include *formal* types of vocational education, typically post-secondary or poly-technical training leading to qualification or credential required to obtain or retain employment. Professional development may also come in the form of pre-service or in-service professional development programs. These programs may be formal, or informal, group or individualized. Individuals may pursue professional development independently, or programs may be offered by human resource departments. Professional development on the job may develop or enhance process skills, sometimes referred to as leadership skills, as well as task skills. Some examples for process skills are 'effectiveness skills', 'team functioning skills', and 'systems thinking skills'.

Professional development opportunities can range from a single workshop to a semester-long academic course, to services offered by a medley of different professional development providers and varying widely with respect to the philosophy, content, and format of the learning experiences. Some examples of approaches to professional development include: [13]

- **Case Study Method** - The case method is a teaching approach that consists in presenting the students with a case, putting them in the role of a decision maker facing a problem (Hammond 1976)

- **Consultation** - to assist an individual or group of individuals to clarify and address immediate concerns by following a systematic problem-solving process.
- **Coaching** - to enhance a person's competencies in a specific skill area by providing a process of observation, reflection, and action.
- **Communities of Practice** - to improve professional practice by engaging in shared inquiry and learning with people who have a common goal
- **Lesson Study** - to solve practical dilemmas related to intervention or instruction through participation with other professionals in systematically examining practice
- **Mentoring** - to promote an individual's awareness and refinement of his or her own professional development by providing and recommending structured opportunities for reflection and observation
- **Reflective Supervision** - to support, develop, and ultimately evaluate the performance of employees through a process of inquiry that encourages their understanding and articulation of the rationale for their own practices
- **Technical Assistance** - to assist individuals and their organization to improve by offering resources and information, supporting networking and change efforts

Professional development is a broad term, encompassing a range of people, interests and approaches. Those who engage in professional development share a common purpose of enhancing their ability to do their work. At the heart of professional development is the individual's interest in lifelong learning and increasing their own skills and knowledge. The 21st century has seen a significant growth in online professional development. Content providers incorporate collaborative platforms such as discussion boards and wikis, thereby encouraging and facilitating interaction, and optimizing training effectiveness.

Remuneration

Remuneration is pay or salary, typically a monetary payment for services rendered, as in an employment. Usage of the word is considered formal.

Types

Remuneration can include:

- Commission
- Compensation methods (in online advertising and internet marketing)
- Compensation
  - Executive compensation
  - Deferred compensation
- Employee stock option

- Fringe benefit
- Salary
  - Performance Linked Incentives
- Wage

EMPLOYEE BENEFIT

Employee benefits and (especially in British English) **benefits in kind** (also called **fringe benefits, perquisites, perqs** or **perks**) are various non-wage compensations provided to employees in addition to their normal wages or salaries. Where an employee exchanges (cash) wages for some other form of benefit, this is generally referred to as a 'salary sacrifice' arrangement. In most countries, most kinds of employee benefits are taxable to at least some degree.

Some of these benefits are: housing (employer-provided or employer-paid), group insurance (health, dental, life etc.), disability income protection, retirement benefits, daycare, tuition reimbursement, sick leave, vacation (paid and non-paid), social security, profit sharing, funding of education, and other specialized benefits.

The purpose of the benefits is to increase the economic security of employees.

The term **perqs** or **perks** is often used colloquially to refer to those benefits of a more discretionary nature. Often, perks are given to employees who are doing notably well and/or have seniority. Common perks are take-home vehicles, hotel stays, free refreshments, leisure activities on work time (golf, etc.), stationery, allowances for lunch, and—when multiple choices exist—first choice of such things as job assignments and vacation scheduling. They may also be given first chance at job promotions when vacancies exist.

United States

Employee benefits in the United States might include relocation assistance; medical, prescription, vision and dental plans; health and dependent care flexible spending accounts; retirement benefit plans (pension, 401(k), 403(b)); group-term life and long term care insurance plans; legal assistance plans; adoption assistance; child care benefits; transportation benefits; and possibly other miscellaneous employee discounts (*e.g.*, movies and theme park tickets, wellness programs, discounted shopping, hotels and resorts, and so on).

Some fringe benefits (for example, accident and health plans, and group-term life insurance coverage up to US$50,000) may be excluded from the employee's gross income and, therefore, are not subject to federal income tax in the United States. Some function as tax shelters (for example, flexible spending accounts, 401(k)'s, 403(b)'s). Fringe benefits are also thought of as the costs of keeping employees other than salary. These benefit rates are typically calculated using fixed percentages that vary depending on the employee's classification and often change from year to year.

426

Normally, employer provided benefits are tax-deductible to the employer and non-taxable to the employee. The exception to the general rule includes certain executive benefits (e.g. golden handshake and golden parachute plans).

American corporations may also offer cafeteria plans to their employees. These plans would offer a menu and level of benefits for employees to choose from. In most instances, these plans are funded by both the employees and by the employer(s). The portion paid by the employees are deducted from their gross pay before federal and state taxes are applied. Some benefits would still be subject to the FICA tax, such as 401(k)[and 403(b) contributions; however, health premiums, some life premiums, and contributions to flexible spending accounts are exempt from FICA.

If certain conditions are met, employer provided meals and lodging may be excluded from an employee's gross income. If meals are furnished (1) by the employer; (2) for the employer's convenience; and (3) provided on the business premises of the employer they may be excluded from the employee's gross income per Section 119(a). In addition, lodging furnished by the employer for its convenience on the business premise of the employer (which the employee is required to accept as a condition of employment) is also excluded from gross income. Importantly, section 119(a) only applies to meals or lodging furnished "in kind." Therefore, cash allowances for meals or lodging received by an employee are included in gross income .
The term "fringe benefits" was coined by the War Labor Board during World War II to describe the various indirect benefits which industry had devised to attract and retain labor when direct wage increases were prohibited.

United Kingdom

In the UK, Employee Benefits are categorised by three terms: Flexible Benefits (Flex) and Flexible Benefits Packages, Voluntary Benefits and Core Benefits.

Flexible Benefits, usually called a "Flex Scheme", is where employees are allowed to choose how a proportion of their remuneration is paid. Currently around a quarter of UK employers operate such a scheme.[3] . This is normally delivered by allowing employees to sacrifice part of their pre-tax pay in exchange for a car, additional holiday, a shorter working week or other similar benefits, or give up benefits for additional cash remuneration. A number of external consultancies exist that enable organizations to manage Flex packages and they centre around the provision of an Intranet or Extranet website where employees can view their current flexible benefit status and make changes to their package. Adoption of flexible benefits has grown considerably over the five years to 2008, with The Chartered Institute of Personnel and Development additionally anticipating a further 12% rise in adoption within 2008/9. This has coincided with increased employee access to the internet and studies suggesting that employee engagement can be boosted by their successful adoption..

Voluntary Benefits is the name given to a collection of benefits that employees choose to opt-in for and pay for personally. These tend to be schemes such as the government-backed (and therefore tax-efficient) Bike2Work and Childcare Vouchers (Accor Services, Busybees, Sodexho, Fideliti, KiddiVouchers, Imagine, Early Years Vouchers Ltd) and also specially arranged discount schemes for employees such as group ISAs. Employee Discount schemes are often setup by employers as a perk of working at the organization. They can be run in-house or arranged by an external employee benefits consultant.

Core Benefits is the term given to benefits which all staff enjoy, such as holiday, sick pay and sometimes flexible hours.

In recent years many UK companies have used the tax and national insurance savings gained through the implementation of salary sacrifice benefits to fund the implementation of flexible benefits. In a salary sacrifice arrangement an employee gives up the right to part of the cash remuneration due under their contract of employment. Usually the sacrifice is made in return for the employer's agreement to provide them with some form of non-cash benefit. The most popular types of salary sacrifice benefits include childcare vouchers and pensions.

In the UK, the employee benefit market is split between larger employee benefit consultancies (Aon Consulting, Mercers, Watson Wyatt, Towers Perrin, Hewitt), the mid-market (Vebnet Limited, Buck Consultants, SBJ, Thomsons Online Benefits, Gissings, Foster Denovo) and smaller bespoke advice and consultancy organisations. Technology provision is led by companies such as Vebnet Limited with their FIX&FLEX product and Thomsons Online Benefits with their Perquisite product.

Fringe Benefits Tax

In a number of countries (e.g., Australia, New Zealand, Pakistan and India) the 'fringe benefits' are subject to the Fringe Benefits Tax (FBT), which applies to most, although not all, fringe benefits.

Advantages of employee benefits

There are a number of advantages to employee benefits for both employer and employee.[6]

Employer advantages

- Helps attract and retain better qualified employees.
- Provides high risk coverage at low costs easing the company's financial burden.
- Improves efficiency and productivity as employees are assured of security for themselves and their families.
- Premiums are tax deductible as corporation expense, which means savings with quality coverage.

Employee advantages

- Peace of mind leading to better productivity as employees are assured of provision for themselves and families in any mishap.
- Employees with personal life insurance enjoy additional protection
- Confidence in company's EB schemes boost staff morale and pride in company
- Employees enjoy cheaper rates negotiated through their employer than they could obtain as an individual

Employee disadvantages

In the UK these benefits are often taxed at the individuals normal tax rate, which can prove expensive if there is no financial advantage to the individual from the benefits.

EXECUTIVE COMPENSATION

Executive compensation is how top executives of business corporations are paid. This includes a basic salary, bonuses, shares, options and other company benefits. Over the past three decades, executive compensation has risen dramatically beyond the rising levels of an average worker's wage. Executive compensation is an important part of corporate governance, and is often determined by a company's board of directors.

Types of compensation

There are six basic tools to compensation or remuneration.

- a base salary
- short-term incentives, or bonuses
- long-term incentive plans (LTIP)
- employee benefits
- perquisites, or perks
- compensation protection (Golden parachute)

In a typical modern US corporation, the CEO and other top executives are paid salary plus short-term incentives or bonuses. This combination is referred to as Total Cash Compensation (TCC). Short-term incentives usually are formula-driven and have some performance criteria attached depending on the role of the executive. For example, the Sales Director's performance related bonus may be based on incremental revenue growth turnover; a CEO's could be based on incremental profitability and revenue growth. Bonuses are after-the-fact (not formula driven) and often discretionary. Executives may also be compensated with a mixture of cash and shares of the company which are almost always subject to vesting restrictions (a long-term incentive). To be considered a long-term incentive the measurement period must be in excess of one year (3–5 years is common). The vesting term refers to the period of time before the recipient has the right to transfer shares and realize value. Vesting can be based on time, performance or both. For example a CEO might get 1 million in cash, and 1 million in company shares (and share buy options used). Other components of an executive compensation package may

429

include such perks as generous retirement plans, health insurance, a chauffeured limousine, an executive jet[2], interest free loans for the purchase of housing, etc.

Stock options

Supporters of stock options say they align the interests of CEOs to those of shareholders, since options are valuable only if the stock price remains above the option's strike price. Stock options are now counted as a corporate expense (non-cash), which impacts a company's income statement and makes the distribution of options more transparent to shareholders. Critics of stock options charge that they are granted excessively and that they invite management abuses such as the options backdating of such grants. Stock options also pose a conflict of interest in which a CEO can artificially raise the stock price to cash in stock options at the expense of the company's long-term health, although this is a problem for any type of incentive compensation that goes unmonitored by directors. Indeed, "reload" stock options allow executives to exercise options and then replace them in part (and sometimes in whole), essentially selling the company stock short (i.e., profiting from the stock's decline). For various reasons, including the accounting charge, concerns about dilution and negative publicity related to stock options, companies have reduced the size of grants to executives.

Stock options also incentivize executives to engage in risk-seeking behavior. This is because the value of a call option increases with increased volatility. (cf. options pricing). Stock options therefore - even when used legitimately - can incentivize excessive risk seeking behavior that can lead to catastrophic corporate failure.

Restricted stock

Executives are also compensated with restricted stock, which is stock given to an executive that cannot be sold until certain conditions are met and has the same value as the market price of the stock at the time of grant. As the size of stock option grants have been reduced, the number of companies granting restricted stock either with stock options or instead of, has increased. Restricted stock has its detractors, too, as it has value even when the stock price falls. As an alternative to straight time vested restricted stock, companies have been adding performance type features to their grants. These grants, which could be called performance shares, do not vest or are not granted until these conditions are met. These performance conditions could be earnings per share or internal financial targets.

Tax issues

Cash compensation is taxable to an individual at a high individual rate. If part of that income can be converted to long-term capital gain, for example by granting stock options instead of cash to an executive, a more advantageous tax treatment may be obtained by the executive.

Levels of compensation

430

The levels of compensation in all countries has been rising dramatically over the past decades. Not only is it rising in absolute terms, but also in relative terms.

Fortune 500 compensation

During 2003, about half of Fortune 500 CEO compensation was in cash pay and bonuses, and the other half invested restricted stock, and gains from exercised stock options according to Forbes magazine.[2] Forbes magazine counted the 500 CEOs compensation to $3.3 billion during 2003 (which makes $6.6 million a piece). Notice that this figure includes gains from stock call options used; the options may have been rewarded many years before the option to buy is used.

Forbes categories of compensation

The categories that Forbes use are (1) salary (cash), (2) bonus (cash), (3) other (market value of restricted stock received), and (4) stock gains from option exercise (the gains being the difference between the price paid for the stock when the option was exercised and that days market price of the stock). If you see someone "making" $100 million or $200 million during the year, chances are 90% of that is coming from options (earned during many years) being exercised.

Typical compensation

The typical salary in the top of the list is $1 million - $3 million. The typical top cash bonus is $10 million - $15 million. The highest stock bonus is $20 million. The highest option exercise have been in the range of $100 million - $200 million.

Compensation Protection

Senior executives may enjoy considerable income protection unavailable to many other employees. Often executives may receive a Golden Parachute that rewards them substantially if the company gets taken over or they lose their jobs for other reasons. This can create perverse incentives.

One example is that overly attractive Golden Parachutes may incentivize executives to facilitate the sale of their company at a price that is not in their shareholders' best interests.

It is fairly easy for a top executive to **reduce** the price of his/her company's stock - due to information asymmetry. The executive can accelerate accounting of expected expenses, delay accounting of expected revenue, engage in off balance sheet transactions to make the company's profitability appear temporarily poorer, or simply promote and report severely conservative (eg. pessimistic) estimates of future earnings. Such seemingly adverse earnings news will be likely to (at least temporarily) reduce share price. (This is again due to information asymmetries since it is more common for top executives to do everything they can to window dress their company's earnings forecasts).

431

A reduced share price makes a company an easier takeover target. When the company gets bought out (or taken private) - at a dramatically lower price - the takeover artist gains a windfall from the former top executive's actions to surreptitiously reduce share price. This can represent 10s of billions of dollars (questionably) transferred from previous shareholders to the takeover artist. The former top executive is then rewarded with a golden handshake for presiding over the firesale that can sometimes be in the 100s of millions of dollars for one or two years of work. (This is nevertheless an excellent bargain for the takeover artist, who will tend to benefit from developing a reputation of being very generous to parting top executives).

Similar issues occur when a publicly held asset or non-profit organization undergoes privatization. Top executives often reap tremendous monetary benefits when a government owned, mutual or non-profit entity is sold to private hands. Just as in the example above, they can facilitate this process by making the entity appear to be in financial crisis - this reduces the sale price (to the profit of the purchaser), and makes non-profits and governments more likely to sell. Ironically, it can also contribute to a public perception that private entities are more efficiently run reinforcing the political will to sell of public assets.

Again, due to asymmetric information, policy makers and the general public see a government owned firm that was a financial 'disaster' - miraculously turned around by the private sector (and typically resold) within a few years.

Regulation

There are a number of strategies that could be employed as a response to the growth of executive compensation.

- In the United States, shareholders must approve all equity compensation plans. Shareholders can simply vote against the issuance of any equity plans. This would eliminate huge windfalls that can be due to a rising stock market or years of retained earnings.

- Independent non-executive director setting of compensation is widely practised. Remuneration is the archetype of self dealing. An independent remuneration committee is an attempt to have pay packages set at arms' length from the directors who are getting paid.

- Disclosure of salaries is the first step, so that company stakeholders can know and decide whether or not they think remuneration is fair. In the UK, the Directors' Remuneration Report Regulations 2002[7] introduced a requirement into the old Companies Act 1985, the requirement to release all details of pay in the annual accounts. This is now codified in the Companies Act 2006. Similar requirements exist in most countries, including the U.S., Germany, and Canada.

- A say on pay - a non-binding vote of the general meeting to approve director pay packages, is practised in a growing number of countries. Some commentators have advocated a mandatory binding vote for large amounts (e.g. over $5 million). The aim is that the vote will be a highly influential signal to a board to not raise salaries beyond reasonable levels. The general meeting means shareholders in most countries. In most European countries though, with two-tier board structures, a supervisory board will represent employees and shareholders alike. It is this supervisory board which votes on executive compensation.

- Progressive taxation is a more general strategy that affects executive compensation, as well as other highly paid people. There has been a recent trend to cutting the highest bracket tax payers, a notable example being the tax cuts in the U.S. For example, the Baltic States have a flat tax system for incomes. Executive compensation could be checked by taxing more heavily the highest earners, for instance by taking a greater percentage of income over $200,000.

- Maximum wage is an idea which has not been implemented anywhere.[citation needed] The argument is to place a cap on the amount that any person may legally make, in the same way as there is a floor of a minimum wage so that people can not earn too little.

- Indexing Operating Performance is a way to make bonus targets business cycle independent. Indexed bonus targets move with the business cycle and are therefore fairer and valid for a longer period of time.

Criticism

Many newspaper stories show people expressing concern that CEOs are paid too much for the services they provide. In *Searching for a Corporate Savior: The Irrational Quest for Charismatic CEOs*, Harvard Business School professor Rakesh Khurana documents the problem of excessive CEO compensation, showing that the return on investment from these pay packages is very poor compared to other outlays of corporate resources.

Defenders of high executive pay say that the global war for talent and the rise of private equity firms can explain much of the increase in executive pay. For example, while in conservative Japan a senior executive has few alternatives to his current employer, in the United States it is acceptable and even admirable for a senior executive to jump to a competitor, to a private equity firm, or to a private equity portfolio company. Portfolio company executives take a pay cut but are routinely granted stock options for ownership of ten percent of the portfolio company, contingent on a successful tenure. Rather than signaling a conspiracy, defenders argue, the increase in executive pay is a mere byproduct of supply and demand for executive talent. However, U.S. executives make substantially more than their European and Asian counterparts.[9]

Shareholders, often members of the Council of Institutional Investors or the Interfaith Center on Corporate Responsibility have often filed shareholder resolutions in protest. 21

such resolutions were filed in 2003. About a dozen were voted on in 2007, with two coming very close to passing (at Verizon, a recount is currently in progress). The U.S. Congress is currently debating mandating shareholder approval of executive pay packages at publicly traded U.S. companies.

The U.S. stood first in the world in 2005 with a ratio of 39:1 CEO's compensation to pay of manufacturing production workers. Britain second with 31.8:1; Italy third with 25.9:1, New Zealand fourth with 24.9:1.

United States

The U.S. Securities and Exchange Commission has asked publicly traded companies to disclose more information explaining how their executives' compensation amounts are determined. The SEC has also posted compensation amounts on its website to make it easier for investors to compare compensation amounts paid by different companies. It is interesting to juxtapose SEC regulations related to executive compensation with Congressional efforts to address such compensation. In 2005, the issue of executive compensation at American companies has been harshly criticized by columnist and Pulitzer Prize winner Gretchen Morgenson in her *Market Watch* column for the Sunday "Money & Business" section of the New York Times newspaper.

A February 2009 report, published by the Institute for Policy Studies notes the impact excessive executive compensation has on taxpayers:

U.S. taxpayers subsidize excessive executive compensation — by more than $20 billion per year — via a variety of tax and accounting loopholes. For example, there are no meaningful limits on how much companies can deduct from their taxes for the expense of executive compensation. The more they pay their CEO, the more they can deduct. A proposed reform to cap tax deductibility at no more than 25 times the pay of the lowest-paid worker could generate more than $5 billion in extra federal revenues per year. Although a proposal such as this one would tighten controls on pay to executives, this study does take into consideration (or at least does not address) the tax obligations of the individual (CEO) that receives this compensation. Every dollar that is deducted from the firm's income is subject to the personal tax of the individual receiving such pay.

Unions have been very vocal in their opposition to high executive compensation. The AFL-CIO sponsors a website called Executive Paywatch which allows users to compare their salaries to the CEOs of the companies where they work.

In 2007, CEOs in the S&P 500, averaged $10.5 million annually, 344 times the pay of typical American workers. This was a drop in ratio from 2000, when they averaged 525 times the average pay.

To work around the restrictions and the political outrage concerning executive pay practices, banks in particular turned to using life insurance policies to fund bonuses, deferred pay and pensions owed to its executives. Under this scenario, a bank insures thousands of its employees under the life insurance policy, naming itself as the beneficiary of the policy. Bank undertake this practice often without the knowledge or consent of the employee and sometimes with the employee misunderstanding the scope of the coverage or the ability to maintain employee coverage after leaving the company. In recent times, a number of families became outraged by the practice and complained that banks should not profit from the death of the deceased employees. In one case, a family of a former employee filed a lawsuit against the bank after the family questioned the practices of the bank in its coverage of the employee. The insurance company accidentally sent the widow of the deceased employee a check for a $1.6 million that was payable to the bank after the former employee died in 2008. In that case, bank allegedly told the employee in 2001 that the employee was eligible for a $150,000 supplemental life insurance benefit if the employee signed a consent form to allow the bank to add the employee to the bank's life insurance policy. The bank fired the employee four months after the employee consented to the arrangement. After that employee's death, the family collect no benefits from the employee life insurance policies provided by the bank, since the bank had canceled the employee's benefit after the firing. The family claimed that the former employee was "cognitively disabled" because of brain surgery and medical treatments at the time of signing the consent form to understand fully the scope of insurance coverage under the bank's master insurance benefit plan.

The practice of financing executive compensation using corporate-owned life insurance policies remain controversial. On the one hand, observers in the insurance industry note that "businesses enjoy tax-deferred growth of the inside buildup of the [life insurance] policy's cash value, tax-free withdrawals and loans, and income tax-free death benefits to [corporate] beneficiaries." On the other hand, critics frowned upon the use of "janitor's insurance" to collect tax-free death benefits from insurance policies covering retirees and current and former non-key employees that companies rely on as informal pension funds for company executives. To thwart the abuse and reduce the attractiveness of corporate-owned life insurance policies, changes in tax treatment of corporate-owned insurance life insurance policies are under consideration for non-key personnel. These changes would repeal "the exception from the pro rata interest expense disallowance rule for [life insurance] contracts covering employees, officers or directors, other than 20% owners of a business that is the owner or beneficiary of the contracts."

Australia

In Australia, shareholders can vote against the pay rises of board members, but the vote is non-binding.[22] Instead the shareholders can sack some or all of the board members.

Trends in Executive Compensation

According to the independent research firm Equilar, median S&P 500 CEO compensation fell significantly for the first time since 2002. From 2007 to 2008, median total compensation declined by 7.5 percent.

A sharp decline in bonus payouts contributed most to declines in total pay, with median annual bonus payouts for S&P 500 CEOs dropping to $1.2 million in 2008, down 24.5 percent from the 2007 median of $1.6 million. Additionally, 20.6 percent of CEOs received no bonus payout at all for 2008.

On the other hand, Equity compensation changed little from 2007 to 2008, despite the market turmoil. The median value of option awards and stock awards rose by 3.5 percent and 1.4 percent, respectively. Options maintained its place as the most prevalent equity award vehicle, with 72.2 percent of CEOs receiving option awards. In 2008, nearly two-thirds of total CEO compensation was delivered in the form of stock or options.

Though overall pay composition changed little, more companies have slowly moved toward increasing their use of performance shares for CEOs. In 2008, fewer companies awarded a single equity vehicle as companies expanded their equity mix to include performance shares.

PERFORMANCE APPRAISAL

A **performance appraisal**, **employee appraisal**, or **performance review** is a method by which the job performance of an employee is evaluated (generally in terms of quality, quantity, cost, and time). Performance appraisal is a part of career development.

Performance appraisals are regular reviews of employee performance within organizations.

Generally, the aims of a performance appraisal are to:

- Give feedback on performance to employees.
- Identify employee training needs.
- Document criteria used to allocate organizational rewards.
- Form a basis for personnel decisions: salary increases, promotions, disciplinary actions, etc.
- Provide the opportunity for organizational diagnosis and development.
- Facilitate communication between employee and administration
- Validate selection techniques and human resource policies to meet federal Equal Employment Opportunity requirements.

A common approach to assessing performance is to use a numerical or scalar rating system whereby managers are asked to score an individual against a number of objectives/attributes. In some companies, employees receive assessments from their manager, peers, subordinates and customers while also performing a self assessment. This is known as 360° appraisal. forms good communication patterns

The most popular methods that are being used as performance appraisal process are:

- Management by objectives
- 360 degree appraisal
- Behavioral Observation Scale
- Behaviorally Anchored Rating Scale

Trait based systems, which rely on factors such as integrity and conscientiousness, are also commonly used by businesses. The scientific literature on the subject provides evidence that assessing employees on factors such as these should be avoided. The reasons for this are two-fold:

1) Because trait based systems are by definition based on personality traits, they make it difficult for a manager to provide feedback that can cause positive change in employee performance. This is caused by the fact that personality dimensions are for the most part static, and while an employee can change a specific behavior they cannot change their personality. For example, a person who lacks integrity may stop lying to a manager because they have been caught, but they still have low integrity and are likely to lie again when the threat of being caught is gone.

2) Trait based systems, because they are vague, are more easily influenced by office politics, causing them to be less reliable as a source of information on an employee's true performance. The vagueness of these instruments allows managers to fill them out based on who they want to/feel should get a raise, rather than basing scores on specific behaviors employees should/should not be engaging in. These systems are also more likely to leave a company open to discrimination claims because a manager can make biased decisions without having to back them up with specific behavioral information.

In the PTF Report it was claimed that "although annual Reports by ministries and departments are obligatory, they are hardly ever prepared and submitted to government, and where they, they are scanty and hardly confirms with any standards, either in terms of contents or format. The recommendation was that there should be target setting by ministries where concrete and measurable achievement can be inferred (PTF Report Section 10 Sub10.1).

EFFECTIVE SUCCESSION PLANNING

Failing to plan

There is an old adage, "Failing to plan is planning to fail". Like any other organisation that wants to thrive and compete, a training organisation must have plans in place so that the right people are in the right place at the right time to achieve successful organisational outcomes. The purpose of this short review is to provide an explanation of succession planning, to discuss its relationship to building capabilities that ensure the continued ability of an organisation to compete and to grow, and to provide some practical tips.

Being proactive or reactive

There are significant demographic changes facing Australian training organisations. Numerous reports, for example, have detailed the ageing of the Vocational Education and Training (VET) workforce in Australia, the increased use of part-time and casual staff, and the challenges of attracting and retaining younger generations to replace retiring staff:-

The new reality is that a deep bench of talent is the most important asset if organisations want to operate successfully into the future. Those training organisations that will move from being good to great over the next decade will be those that have put in place effective succession planning. Those that choose not to plan will most likely continue to adopt very reactive approaches that rely overwhelmingly on outside hiring. They are most at risk of failing to replace talented staff in a period of increasingly large skills shortages.

As numerous reports show, the more innovative of our VET organisations are already very much:-

- **Engaged in planning** around the types of people and the capabilities that will be required to meet the needs of the increasingly diverse training market
- **Challenging traditional views** about who can be the leaders
- Identifying and **resolving blockages** that are preventing staff from more diverse backgrounds from aspiring to higher positions of responsibility
- Incorporating into their approach to **talent management**, the more specific challenge of effective succession planning around key roles and responsibilities
- Employing a wide range of **developmental opportunities** to support their talent through on-the-job experiences, challenging assignments, 360 degree assessments, and opportunities to be involved in new forms of partnering with industry.

Succession planning

The practice of succession planning has been around for hundreds of years. Its roots exist in the dilemmas of managing transitions of power in royal families and in business dynasties. In organisations succession planning is about building pools of candidates who possess critical capabilities that are required to meet the short and longer term objectives of the organisation. Effective succession planning is a form of future proofing. It assists the enterprise to adopt and sustain specific strategic positions into the future that will allow the achievement of its vision, goals and specific objectives. Succession planning involves a projection of future needs in terms of the capabilities that staff will need to have to fill key positions that support the business.

In the past, most of this planning centred upon key management and leadership roles. Today succession planning is focused not only upon filling the most senior positions, but also upon developing leaders, managers and team leaders at all levels. This new positioning of succession planning reflects the move away from leadership development being a discrete activity to leadership development being more about building a culture of leaders throughout the organisation.

Evidence about the impact of succession planning

The majority of reviews about the impact of effective succession planning are anecdotal reports or the experiences of very large corporations. There is not a lot of evidence-based research. However, in a recent review into the practice and art of succession planning, Andrew Garman and Jeremy Glawe brought together over 150 research papers to address a number of key questions[3]. On the question should succession planning be done, they found that the most compelling evidence was at the executive level when the CEO "gets hit by the proverbial bus". In these cases, organisations fared much better if they could immediately name an internal successor.

This same review also revealed that organisations with a reputation for excellence in their management of talent and succession planning gave higher returns to their shareholders than their industries' average.

That is, major stakeholders today (i.e. governments, customers, industry partners) expect businesses and organisations to have a plan in place that covers the replacement of its senior leaders.

Some practical tips in planning for succession

A priority of the senior leaders. Senior leaders must be actively committed to and involved in the process of succession management. They need to convey that succession management is a key organisational priority and one that requires collaboration across the organisation. With this high level of commitment in place, lower level managers can challenge built-in rigidities and biases that might turn talent away. In addition, senior leaders need to accept responsibility for creating a succession culture or a culture of leadership. In these environments, the thinking and planning around succession planning and talent management is not just the purview of the CEO. The task of succession planning becomes a partnership between the senior executive group, senior and middle managers and supervisors in identifying, nurturing and retaining this talent.

Fundamental to effective succession planning is a healthy and robust performance management system that manages the expectations of all employees who aspire to higher positions. It needs to be used well to judge, identify and to build the capabilities of top performers.

Succession planning as a strategic activity. It is important to link succession planning to the organisation's long-term strategic plans. Strategic planning identifies the capabilities required by the organisation and its staff to achieve its objectives. Strategic plans should inform future needs around staffing, and in turn identify required capabilities, career progression, promotion processes, and the strategies being used on and off-the-job to grow talent.

Capability pathways. The VET sector has been developing Management and Leadership Capability Frameworks that define the capabilities required for now and into the future. A number of VET publications provide examples of such capability frameworks that can support the activities around succession planning. These frameworks do provide "capability pathways" that can help staff to know what knowledge, skills and experiences are needed if they are to move into more senior and challenging roles in VET. These capability frameworks, as well as the feedback provided through performance reviews, provide important opportunities for honest conversations with staff about their future within the organisation and the training sector.

Succession planning requires a major re-think about who could be future leaders at all levels of the training organisation.

Review opinions about who can lead. Effective succession planning really requires VET organisations to throw away the book about the type of people that they see as potential leaders. More training organisations need to review, challenge and update their definitions of leadership and to develop succession and workforce plans that attract, recruit, select, train and advance those individuals with the skills most aligned with current realities. This re-thinking especially needs to recognise the utility of greater diversity in the VET leadership pipeline.

Effective succession planning can provide better pathways for more people to lead at younger ages than they do at present, for more women to be in key leadership positions, and for more individuals with non-VET experiences to join the sector in key positions of responsibility. Assumptions need to be challenged around the commonly-held view that outsiders to VET cannot perform as well as insiders due to what are seen as almost insurmountable challenges in learning about the complexities of VET.

Be able to make a case for the need to succession plan. If you are managing staff that you think have the talent to lead in the future, and want to get access to a budget to develop them, mount a business case to more senior managers. For example, to gain entry into new training markets, VET organisations need to promote into leadership roles those employees who are more similar to existing or targeted clients. Also influential is what might be called the integration, learning and innovation case. That is, a training organisation that has more diversity in its leadership group (e.g. around the gender, generational, cultural and industry backgrounds of its leaders) should demonstrate more creativity and innovation around its purpose, strategic direction, core business, and potential opportunities for growth.

Seek transparency. There is evidence from best practice, as well as from research, that the succession process needs to be as transparent as possible[5]. In particular, this requires good communications, clear policy and numerous opportunities for the succession planning process to be reviewed to assist its continued development. If an organisation is not open to regular review, for example, succession planning can come to be seen as a highly political process. One symptom is when the views of individual managers around the capabilities of their staff are frequently at odds with advice from other sources. This is where the organisation needs to clearly define and communicate the standards of performance. In addition, through job rotations, special assignments and leadership and management development programs talented staff can be judged by a wider group of senior staff, as well as by their peers, around their potential to lead.

There are related concerns around the use of terms such as high potentials, leaders of the future, acceleration pools, and the Top 100. Most recommendations around getting the right selection process in place cite the need to develop formal criteria, to use multiple methods for selection, and to provide managers with the training and skills to identify those who might become part of the talent management and succession planning programs.

Watch out for too much process. Another risk that needs to be managed is that the succession planning processes can become an administrative nightmare. Succession planning in larger organisations can take on many dinosaur-like qualities, moving too slowly to identify, support and to build the pool of successors. Effective succession planning has to move along at pace to ensure that the right people are in the right place at the right time.

Conclusion

In summary, succession planning has broadened its focus. It is more than just about replacing the CEO. As a strategic endeavour, succession planning is an integral part of talent management in today's organisations. For the reader interested in more in-depth treatments, the following texts explore succession planning processes, systems, and specific cases. These include:

- Byham, W.C., Smith, A.B., & Paese, M.J. (2002). *Grow your own leaders: How to identify, develop and retain leadership talent.* New York: Prentice-Hall.
- Charan, R. (2008) *Leaders at all levels: Deepening your talent pool to solve the succession crisis.* San Francisco: Jossey-Bass.
- McCall, M.W. (1998). *High flyers: Developing the next generation of leaders.* Boston: Harvard Business School Press.

To gain a more Australian public sector examination of the merits of succession planning, as well as case studies of good practice, look at:

- http://www.apsc.gov.au/# which is the site of Australian Public Service Commission. The site provides access to special publications relevant to succession planning, public sector cases, and access to various capability frameworks around its Integrated Leadership System.
- http://www.apsc.gov.au/publications03/managingsuccession.pdf . This paper titled '*Managing succession*" reports on research undertaken by the Australian

Public Service Commission, and provides many insights into best practice in succession planning.

- http://www.apsc.gov.au/publications08/leadingproductivepeople.pdf, has the publication titled "*Leading productive people: A manager's seven steps to success.*" This report has been developed to help new managers build their people management skills. It identifies the essential steps and best approaches that managers can take to build the productivity and effectiveness of their people.

- http://www.apsc.gov.au/publications01/indigenousrecruitment.pdf provides the booklet titled "*Recruitment of Indigenous Australians in the Australian public service*". It covers the legal framework that applies to the recruitment and development of Indigenous Australians, as well as providing ideas regarding strategies that organisations might adopt and develop.

Reference

[1] Dickie, M., Eccles, C., FitzGerald, I., McDonald, R., Cully, M., Blythe, A., Stanwick, J. & Brooks, L. (2004) *Enhancing the capability of VET professionals project: Final report.* Brisbane: NCVER.

[2] Callan, V.J. (2004) *Building innovative VET organisations.* Adelaide: NCVER; Mitchell, J., Clayton, B., Hedberg, J. & Paine, N. (2003) *Emerging futures: Innovation in teaching and learning in VET. A report on current practice.* Melbourne: ANTA.

[3] Garman, A. & Glawe, J. (2004) Succession planning. *Consulting Psychology Journal: Practice and Research,* 56, 2, pp. 119-128.

[4] Callan, V.J., Mitchell, J., Clayton, B. & Smith, L. (2007) *Approaches for sustaining and building management and leadership capability in VET providers.* Adelaide: NCVER.

[5] Conger, J.A. & Fulmer, R.M. (2003) Developing your leadership pipeline. *Harvard Business Review,* 81, pp. 76-85.

STAFF SUCCESSION PLANNING
Steps
Employees express interest in becoming potential candidates for succession planning positions in the academic or non-academic stream or both (see schedule A). Supervisors should ask employees, who show potential to advance within management, if they are interested. This applies to all employees.
The employee and supervisor determine the level of readiness of the employee given assessment of their outputs, leadership competencies, job specific education, experience, and skills and their ongoing commitment to management development. The Executive may assist with this decision at the start of the program and as needed thereafter. If the employee is still interested but does not demonstrate ability to be ready within two years,

the employee with the assistance of the supervisor should complete and implement a staff-learning plan targeted to increase their ability in the development areas needed for succession readiness.

Employees who currently demonstrate ability or have potential to be ready within the next two years make a commitment to the succession planning process and the supervisor submits their name and the stream of interest to their Executive Officer.

Executive Group endorses succession-planning candidates. Most candidates will be identified to be in the academic or non-academic succession planning pool or in both rather than attached to a specific position. Succession Planning candidates participate in a multisource feedback process based on the leadership competencies for development purposes. Employees who are not yet ready to be a succession planning candidate as determined in step 2 or 4 and for whom the leadership competencies is the greatest development need may also participate in the multisource feedback process to acquire better information for the basis of their staff learning plans. Based on the multisource feedback and any job specific gaps, succession-planning candidates formulate and implement a staff-learning plan with their supervisor and executive officer. Succession planning candidates with their supervisors and the executive group review their development progress annually around performance assessment time. New succession planning candidates can be added to the program each year; likewise current candidates who do not maintain good performance and/or do not live up to their commitments under the program (see below) can be dropped from the program. In all cases the employee is to be told of their status regarding the potential for succession.

Employee Role

Willingness to participate in a multisource feedback process and use the results to develop.

Willingness to take on additional development/broadening activities, often in addition to one's own workload.

Willingness to work with and share progress with their supervisor and Executive Officer. Understand that the succession planning process is designed to assist with readiness preparation but there are no guarantees of progression.

Supervisor Role

Encourage employees who show leadership/management potential to become potential succession planning candidates.

Support the employee, remove obstacles to management development, and create or allow for the creation of management development opportunities.

Give honest balanced feedback to the employee.

Report potential candidates and their progress to the Executive Officer

Executive Group's Role

Review the progress of all succession planning candidates annually.

Work together to remove obstacles and create or allow for the creation of management development opportunities.

Provide honest balanced feedback to the employee and their supervisor on development gaps and progress expectations.

Effective succession planning is about ensuring leadership continuity and building talent by implementing strategies to identify and develop high-potential staff within the organisation. Succession planning demonstrates a genuine commitment to the development of the existing workforce and to ensuring that staff have the skills, experience and knowledge to meet changing work requirements.

The benefits of succession planning include the creation of a diverse talent pool within the Department, retention of valued staff, a saving in the cost and time of external personnel searches, an improvement in staff morale and reduced effects of restructuring.

The philosophy of succession planning aims to foster communication between Branches, Regions and Divisions, to exchange expertise and innovative techniques and to provide a vehicle for the development of the skills of staff.

A good succession planning process should begin with an informed evaluation of the knowledge and skills required for success in a particular job - the target profile. The next step is to undertake accurate assessments and evaluations of staff members' knowledge and skills which would be matched against the target profile. The final step is the creation of development plans to close any gaps between target profiles and current staff profiles.

As part of their professional development plan all staff members should be encouraged to consider personal development goals as well as organisational knowledge and skill needs which may enhance their career aspirations.

Succession plans can be achieved through a variety of innovative workforce management strategies such as:

- staff interchange

- formal or informal mentoring arrangements

- coaching of staff

- identification of suitable professional development activities for high performing and aspirant staff

- the formulation of forward-thinking internal promotion policies

- supporting staff member/s to take increased responsibility in the context of work unit tasks

- the allocation of project or higher class duties assignments.

A range of targeted professional development programs are available for staff at all classification levels, which address individual and organisational development needs. High level development opportunities are available for staff who have potential as future leaders, including leadership programs for women.

OCCUPATIONAL SAFETY AND HEALTH

Occupational safety and health is a cross-disciplinary area concerned with protecting the safety, health and welfare of people engaged in work or employment. The goal of all occupational safety and health programs is to foster a safe work environment. As a secondary effect, it may also protect co-workers, family members, employers, customers, suppliers, nearby communities, and other members of the public who are impacted by the workplace environment. It may involve interactions among many subject areas, including occupational medicine, occupational (or industrial) hygiene, public health, safety engineering, chemistry, health physics, ergonomics, toxicology, epidemiology, environmental health, industrial relations, public policy, sociology, and occupational health psychology.

Definition

Since 1950, the International Labour Organization (ILO) and the World Health Organization (WHO) have shared a common definition of occupational health. It was adopted by the Joint ILO/WHO Committee on Occupational Health at its first session in 1950 and revised at its twelfth session in 1995. The definition reads: "Occupational health should aim at: the promotion and maintenance of the highest degree of physical, mental and social well-being of workers in all occupations; the prevention amongst workers of departures from health caused by their working conditions; the protection of workers in their employment from risks resulting from factors adverse to health; the placing and maintenance of the worker in an occupational environment adapted to his physiological and psychological capabilities; and, to summarize, the adaptation of work to man and of each man to his job."

Reasons for safety and health

The reasons for establishing good occupational safety and health standards are frequently identified as:

- Moral - An employee should not have to risk injury or death at work, nor should others associated with the work environment.
- Economic - many governments realize that poor occupational safety and health performance results in cost to the State (e.g. through social security payments to the incapacitated, costs for medical treatment, and the loss of the "employability" of the worker). Employing organizations also sustain costs in the event of an incident at work (such as legal fees, fines, compensatory damages, investigation time, lost production, lost goodwill from the workforce, from customers and from the wider community).
- Legal - Occupational safety and health requirements may be reinforced in civil law and/or criminal law; it is accepted that without the extra "encouragement" of potential regulatory action or litigation, many organisations would not act upon their implied moral obligations.

445

National implementing legislation

Different states take different approaches to legislation, regulation, and enforcement.

In the European Union, member states have enforcing authorities to ensure that the basic legal requirements relating to occupational safety and health are met. In many EU countries, there is strong cooperation between employer and worker organisations (e.g. Unions) to ensure good OSH performance as it is recognized this has benefits for both the worker (through maintenance of health) and the enterprise (through improved productivity and quality). In 1996 the European Agency for Safety and Health at Work was founded.

Member states of the European Union have all transposed into their national legislation a series of directives that establish minimum standards on occupational safety and health. These directives (of which there are about 20 on a variety of topics) follow a similar structure requiring the employer to assess the workplace risks and put in place preventive measures based on a hierarchy of control. This hierarchy starts with elimination of the hazard and ends with personal protective equipment.

In the UK, health and safety legislation is drawn up and enforced by the Health and Safety Executive and local authorities (the local council) under the Health and Safety at Work etc. Act 1974. Increasingly in the UK the regulatory trend is away from prescriptive rules, and towards risk assessment. Recent major changes to the laws governing asbestos and fire safety management embrace the concept of risk assessment.

In the United States, the Occupational Safety and Health Act of 1970 created both the National Institute for Occupational Safety and Health (NIOSH) and the Occupational Safety and Health Administration (OSHA).[2] OSHA, in the U.S. Department of Labor, is responsible for developing and enforcing workplace safety and health regulations. NIOSH, in the U.S. Department of Health and Human Services, is focused on research, information, education, and training in occupational safety and health.[3]

OSHA have been regulating occupational safety and health since 1971. Occupational safety and health regulation of a limited number of specifically defined industries was in place for several decades before that, and broad regulations by some individual states was in place for many years prior to the establishment of OSHA.

In Canada, workers are covered by provincial or federal labour codes depending on the sector in which they work. Workers covered by federal legislation (including those in mining, transportation, and federal employment) are covered by the Canada Labour Code; all other workers are covered by the health and safety legislation of the province they work in. The Canadian Centre for Occupational Health and Safety (CCOHS), an agency of the Government of Canada, was created in 1978 by an Act of Parliament. The act was based on the belief that all Canadians had "...a fundamental right to a healthy and safe working environment." CCOHS is mandated to promote safe and healthy workplaces to help prevent work-related injuries and illnesses.

In Malaysia, the Department of Occupational Safety and Health (DOSH) under the Ministry of Human Resource is responsible to ensure that the safety, health and welfare of workers in both the public and private sector is upheld. DOSH is responsible to enforce the Factory and Machinery Act 1969 and the Occupational Safety and Health Act 1994.

Hazards, risks, outcomes

The terminology used in OSH varies between states, but generally speaking:

- A hazard is something that can cause harm if not controlled.
- The outcome is the harm that results from an uncontrolled hazard.
- A risk is a combination of the probability that a particular outcome will occur and the severity of the harm involved.

"Hazard", "risk", and "outcome" are used in other fields to describe e.g. environmental damage, or damage to equipment. However, in the context of OSH, "harm" generally describes the direct or indirect degradation, temporary or permanent, of the physical, mental, or social well-being of workers. For example, repetitively carrying out manual handling of heavy objects is a hazard. The outcome could be a musculoskeletal disorder (MSD) or an acute back or joint injury. The risk can be expressed numerically (e.g. a 0.5 or 50/50 chance of the outcome occurring during a year), in relative terms (e.g. "high/medium/low"), or with a multi-dimensional classification scheme (e.g. situation-specific risks).

Risk assessment

Further information: Risk assessment#Risk assessment in public health

Modern occupational safety and health legislation usually demands that a risk assessment be carried out prior to making an intervention. It should be kept in mind that risk management requires risk to be managed to a level which is as low as is reasonably practical.

This assessment should:

- Identify the hazards
- Identify all affected by the hazard and how
- Evaluate the risk
- Identify and prioritise appropriate control measures

The calculation of risk is based on the likelihood or probability of the harm being realised and the severity of the consequences. This can be expressed mathematically as a

447

quantitative assessment (by assigning low, medium and high likelihood and severity with integers and multiplying them to obtain a risk factor, or qualitatively as a description of the circumstances by which the harm could arise.

The assessment should be recorded and reviewed periodically and whenever there is a significant change to work practices. The assessment should include practical recommendations to control the risk. Once recommended controls are implemented, the risk should be re-calculated to determine of it has been lowered to an acceptable level. Generally speaking, newly introduced controls should lower risk by one level, i.e., from high to medium or from medium to low

Common workplace hazard groups

- **Mechanical hazards** include:

  By type of agent:

  -
    - Impact force
      - Collisions
      - Falls from height
    - Struck by objects
    - Confined space
    - Slips and trips
    - Falling on a pointed object
    - Compressed air/high pressure fluids (such as cutting fluid)
    - Entanglement
    - Equipment-related injury

  By type of damage:

  -
    - Crushing
    - Cutting
    - Friction and abrasion
    - Shearing
    - Stabbing and puncture

- Other **physical hazards**:
  - Noise
  - Vibration
  - Lighting
  - Barotrauma

Harry McShane, age 16, 1908. Pulled into machinery in a factory in Cincinnati. His arm was ripped off at the shoulder and his leg broken. No compensation paid. Photograph by Lewis Hine.

- **Chemical hazards** include:
  - Acids
  - Bases
  - Heavy metals
    - Lead
  - Solvents
    - Petroleum
  - Particulates
    - Asbestos and other fine dust/fibrous materials
    - Silica
  - Fumes (noxious gases/vapors)
  - Highly-reactive chemicals
  - Fire, conflagration and explosion hazards:
    - Explosion
    - Deflagration
    - Detonation
    - Conflagration

- **Psychosocial issues** include:
  - Work-related stress, whose causal factors include excessive working time and overwork
  - Violence from outside the

(hypobaric/hyperbaric pressure)
- o Ionizing radiation
- o Electricity
- o Asphyxiation
- o Cold stress (hypothermia)
- o Heat stress (hyperthermia)
  - Dehydration (due to sweating)

- **Biological hazards** include:
  - o Bacteria
  - o Virus
  - o Fungi
    - Mold
  - o Blood-borne pathogens
  - o Tuberculosis

organisation
- o Bullying, which may include emotional, verbal, and sexual harassment
- o Mobbing
- o Burnout
- o Exposure to unhealthy elements during meetings with business associates, e.g. tobacco, uncontrolled alcohol

- **Musculoskeletal disorders**, avoided by the employment of good ergonomic design

Fire prevention (fire protection/fire safety) often comes within the remit of health and safety professionals as well.

Future developments

Occupational health and safety has come a long way from its beginnings in the heavy industry sector. It now has an impact on every worker, in every work place, and those charged with managing health and safety are having more and more tasks added to their portfolio. The most significant responsibility is Environmental Protection. The skills required to manage occupational health and safety are compatible with environmental protection, which is why these responsibilities are so often bolted onto the workplace health and safety professional.

TIME MANAGEMENT

Time management refers to a range of skills, tools, and techniques used to manage time when accomplishing specific tasks, projects and goals. This set encompasses a wide scope of activities, and these include planning, allocating, setting goals, delegation, analysis of time spent, monitoring, organizing, scheduling, and prioritizing. Initially time management referred to just business or work activities, but eventually the term broadened to include personal activities also. A time management system is a designed combination of processes, tools and techniques.

Some authors (such as Stephen R. Covey) offered a categorization scheme for the hundreds of time management approaches that they reviewed

- First generation: reminders based on clocks and watches, but with computer implementation possible; can be used to alert a person when a task is to be done.
- Second generation: planning and preparation based on calendar and appointment books; includes setting goals.
- Third generation: planning, prioritizing, controlling (using a personal organizer, other paper-based objects, or computer or PDA-based systems) activities on a daily basis. This approach implies spending some time in clarifying values and priorities.
- Fourth generation: being efficient and proactive using any of the above tools; places goals and roles as the controlling element of the system and favors importance over urgency.

Some of the recent general arguments related to "time" and "management" point out that the term "time management" is misleading and that the concept should actually imply that it is "the management of our own activities, to make sure that they are accomplished within the available or allocated time, which is an unmanageable continuous resource".

Time management literature paraphrased: "Get Organized" - paperwork and task triage "Protect Your Time" - insulate, isolate, delegate "set gravitational goals" - that attract actions automatically "Achieve through Goal management Goal Focus" - motivational emphasis

- "Work in Priority Order" - set goals and prioritize
- "Use Magical Tools to Get More Out of Your Time" - depends on when written
- "Master the Skills of Time Management"
- "Go with the Flow" - natural rhythms, Eastern philosophy
- "Recover from Bad Time Habits" - recovery from underlying psychological problems, e.g. procrastination

Time management and related concepts

Time management has been considered as subsets of different concepts such as:

- Project management. Time Management, can be considered as a project management subset, and is more commonly known as project planning and project scheduling. Time Management is also been identified as one of the core functions identified in project management.
- Attention management: Attention management relates to the management of cognitive resources, and in particular the time that humans allocate their mind (and organizations the minds of their employees) to conduct some activities.
- Personal knowledge management: see below (Personal time management).

Personal Time Management

Time management strategies are often associated with the recommendation to set goals. These goals are recorded and may be broken down into a project, an action plan, or a simple task list. For individual tasks or for goals, an importance rating may be established, deadlines may be set, and priorities assigned. This process results in a plan with a task list or a schedule or calendar of activities. Authors may recommend a daily, weekly, monthly or other planning periods, usually fixed, but sometimes variable. Different planning periods may be associated with different scope of planning or review. Authors may or may not emphasize reviews of performance against plan. Routine and recurring tasks may or may not be integrated into the time management plan and, if integrated, the integration can be accomplished in various ways.

How We Use Time

When we spend time, there is no improvement in efficiency, productivity, or effectiveness. The time is gone without a return. We save time when we perform tasks in less time or with less effort than previously. We use shortcuts and processes that streamline activities. We invest time when we take time now to save time later.

We spend time when we go to a movie; however, if we are a screenwriter, the time spent in the movie is an investment since it will help hone our writing skills. If we invest time to learn screenwriting software, we will save time in the future when we compose our scripts. However, this is still relative to the point that we are able to turn better writing skills and faster script development into profit - if we are able to sell it. In capitalism our investment, might very well be someone else's profit.

Delegation is a valuable investment of our time. When we delegate, we teach someone to perform tasks we usually perform. While the training process takes time now, the investment pays off later since we free our time to perform higher-payoff activities.

The goal is to look for ways a person can save and invest time.

Task list

A **task list** (also *to-do list*) is a list of tasks to be completed, such as chores or steps toward completing a project. It is an inventory tool which serves as an alternative or supplement to memory.

Task lists are used in self-management, grocery lists, business management, project management, and software development. It may involve more than one list.

When you accomplish one of the items on a task list, you *check* it off or *cross* it off. The traditional method is to write these on a piece of paper with a pen or pencil, usually on a note pad or clip-board. Numerous digital equivalents are now available, including PIM (Personal information management) applications and most PDAs. There are also several web-based task list applications, many of which are free.

Task list organization

Task lists are often tiered. The simplest tiered system includes a general to-do list (or task-holding file) to record all the tasks the person needs to accomplish, and a daily to-do list which is created each day by transferring tasks from the general to-do list.

Task lists are often prioritized:

- An early advocate of "ABC" prioritization was Alan Lakein (See Books below.). In his system "A" items were the most important ("A-1" the most important within that group), "B" next most important, "C" least important.

- A particular method of applying the *ABC method* assigns "A" to tasks to be done within a day, "B" a week, and "C" a month.

- To prioritize a daily task list, one either records the tasks in the order of highest priority, or assigns them a number after they are listed ("1" for highest priority, "2" for second highest priority, etc.) which indicates in which order to execute the tasks. The latter method is generally faster, allowing the tasks to be recorded more quickly.

Alternatives to Prioritizing:

A completely different approach which argues against prioritising altogether was put forward by British author Mark Forster in his book "Do It Tomorrow and Other Secrets of Time Management". This is based on the idea of operating "closed" to-do lists, instead of the traditional "open" to-do list. He argues that the traditional never-ending to-do lists virtually guarantees that some of your work will be left undone. This approach advocates getting all your work done, every day, and if you are unable to achieve it helps you diagnose where you are going wrong and what needs to change. Recently, Forster developed the "Autofocus Time Management System", which further systematizes working a to-do list as a series of closed subsists and emphasizes intuitive choices.

Software applications

Modern task list applications may have built-in task hierarchy (tasks are composed of subtasks which again may contain subtasks), may support multiple methods of filtering and ordering the list of tasks, and may allow one to associate arbitrarily long notes for each task.

In contrast to the concept of allowing the person to use multiple filtering methods, at least one new software product additionally contains a mode where the software will attempt to dynamically determine the best tasks for any given moment.

Many of the software products for time management support multiple users. It allows the person to give tasks to other users and use the software for communication.

Task list applications may be thought of as lightweight personal information manager or project management software.

Resistors

Fear of change: Change can be daunting and one may be afraid to change what's proven to work in the past.

- Uncertainty: Even with the change being inevitable, one may be hesitant as being not sure where to start. Uncertainty about when or how to begin making a change can be significant.

- Time pressure: To save time, one has to invest time, and this time investment may be a cause of concern. Fearing that changing may involve more work at the start—and thus, in the very short term, make things worse—is a common resistor.

Attention Deficit Disorder

Excessive and chronic inability to manage time effectively may be a result of Attention Deficit Disorder (ADD). Diagnostic criteria includes: A sense of underachievement, difficulty getting organized, trouble getting started, many projects going simultaneously and trouble with follow-through.[6]

- The Prefrontal Cortex: The Prefrontal Cortex is the most evolved part of the brain. It controls the functions of attention span, impulse control, organization, learning from experience and self-monitoring, among others. Daniel Amen, M.D. offers possible solutions in Change Your Brain Change Your Life.

Drivers

- Increased effectiveness: One may feel the need to make more time so as to be more effective in performing the job and carrying out responsibilities.

- Performance improvement: Time management is an issue that often arises during performance appraisals or review meetings.

- Personal development: One may view changing the approach to time management as a personal development issue and reap the benefit of handling time differently at work and at home.

- Increased responsibilities: A change in time-management approach may become necessary as a result of a promotion or additional responsibilities. Since there is more work to do, and still the same amount of time to do it in, the approach must change.

Caveats

Dwelling on the lists

- According to Sandberg, task lists "aren't the key to productivity [that] they're cracked up to be". He reports an estimated "30% of listers spend more time managing their lists than [they do] completing what's on them".

- This could be caused by procrastination by prolonging the planning activity. This is akin to analysis paralysis. As with any activity, there's a point of diminishing returns.

Rigid adherence

- Hendrickson asserts[9] that rigid adherence to task lists can create a "tyranny of the to-do list" that forces one to "waste time on unimportant activities".

- Again, the point of diminishing returns applies here too, but toward the size of the task. Some level of detail must be taken for granted for a task system to work. Rather than put "clean the kitchen", "clean the bedroom", and "clean the bathroom", it is more efficient to put "housekeeping" and save time spent writing and reduce the system's administrative load (each task entered into the system generates a cost in time and effort to manage it, aside from the execution of the task). The risk of consolidating tasks, however, is that "housekeeping" in this example may prove overwhelming or nebulously defined, which will either increase the risk of procrastination, or a mismanaged project.

- Listing routine tasks wastes time. If you are in the habit of brushing your teeth every day, then there is no reason to put it down on the task list. The same goes for getting out of bed, fixing meals, etc. If you need to track routine tasks, then a standard list or chart may be useful, to avoid the procedure of manually listing these items over and over.

- To remain flexible, a task system must allow adaptation, in the form of rescheduling in the face of unexpected problems and opportunities, to save time spent on irrelevant or less than optimal tasks.

- To avoid getting stuck in a wasteful pattern, the task system should also include regular (monthly, semi-annual, and annual) planning and system-evaluation sessions, to weed out inefficiencies and ensure the user is headed in the direction he or she truly desires.[citation needed][10]

- If some time is not regularly spent on achieving long-range goals, the individual may get stuck in a perpetual holding pattern on short-term plans, like staying at a particular job much longer than originally planned.

Set goals for oneself and work on achieving these goals. Some people study in different ways so you are to find out how you are able to study and put that into action. Some people are able to understand their work if they can see it. Some need to touch and feel whatever is being spoken about in the book. Some people need to see what they are studying in order to understand what is coming out of the book.

Techniques for setting priorities

ABC analysis

A technique that has been used in business management for a long time is the categorization of large data into groups. These groups are often marked A, B, and C— hence the name. Activities are ranked upon these general criteria:

- **A** – Tasks that are perceived as being urgent and important.
- **B** – Tasks that are important but not urgent.
- **C** – Tasks that are neither urgent nor important.

Each group is then rank-ordered in priority. To further refine priority, some individuals choose to then force-rank all "B" items as either "A" or "C". ABC analysis can incorporate more than three groups. ABC analysis is frequently combined with Pareto analysis.

Pareto analysis

This is the idea that 80% of tasks can be completed in 20% of the disposable time. The remaining 20% of tasks will take up 80% of the time. This principle is used to sort tasks into two parts. According to this form of Pareto analysis it is recommended that tasks that fall into the first category be assigned a higher priority.

The 80-20-rule can also be applied to increase productivity: it is assumed that 80% of the productivity can be achieved by doing 20% of the tasks. If productivity is the aim of time management, then these tasks should be prioritized higher.

Fit

Essentially, fit is the congruence of the requirements of a task (location, financial investment, time, etc.) with the available resources at the time. Often people are constrained by externally controlled schedules, locations, etc., and "fit" allows us to maximize our productivity given those constraints. For example, if one encounters a gap of 15 minutes in their schedule, it is typically more efficient to complete a task that would require 15 minutes, than to complete a task that can be done in 5 minutes, or to start a task that would take 4 weeks. This concept also applies to time of the day: free time at 7am is probably less usefully applied to the goal of learning the drums, and more productively a time to read a book. Lastly, fit can be applied to location: free time at home would be used differently from free time at work, in town, etc.

POSEC method

POSEC is an acronym for *Prioritize by Organizing, Streamlining, Economizing and Contributing*.

The method dictates a template which emphasises an average individual's immediate sense of emotional and monetary security. It suggests that by attending to one's personal responsibilities first, an individual is better positioned to shoulder collective responsibilities.

Inherent in the acronym is a hierarchy of self-realization which mirrors Abraham Maslow's "Hierarchy of needs".

1. PRIORITIZE-Your time and define your life by goals.
2. ORGANIZING-Things you have to accomplish regularly to be successful. (Family and Finances)
3. STREAMLINING-Things you may not like to do, but must do. (Work and Chores)
4. ECONOMIZING-Things you should do or may even like to do, but they're not pressingly urgent. (Pastimes and Socializing)
5. CONTRIBUTING-By paying attention to the few remaining things that make a difference. (Social Obligations)

The Eisenhower Method

All tasks are evaluated using the criteria important/unimportant and urgent/not urgent and put in according quadrants. Tasks in unimportant/not urgent are dropped, tasks in important/urgent are done immediately and personally, tasks in unimportant/urgent are delegated and tasks in important/not urgent get an end date and are done personally. This method is said to have been used by US President Dwight D. Eisenhower, and is outlined in a quote attributed to him: *"What is important is seldom urgent and what is urgent is seldom important."*

GAP ANALYSIS

In business and economics, **gap analysis** is a tool that helps a company to compare its actual performance with its potential performance. At its core are two questions: "Where are we?" and "Where do we want to be?". If a company or organization is not making the best use of its current resources or is forgoing investment in capital or technology, then it may be producing or performing at a level below its potential. This concept is similar to the base case of being below one's production possibilities frontier.

The goal of gap analysis is to identify the gap between the optimized allocation and integration of the inputs, and the current level of allocation. This helps provide the company with insight into areas which could be improved. The gap analysis process involves determining, documenting and approving the variance between business

456

requirements and current capabilities. Gap analysis naturally flows from benchmarking and other assessments. Once the general expectation of performance in the industry is understood, it is possible to compare that expectation with the company's current level of performance. This comparison becomes the gap analysis. Such analysis can be performed at the strategic or operational level of an organization.

Gap analysis is a formal study of what a business is doing currently and where it wants to go in the future. It can be conducted, in different perspectives, as follows:

1. Organization (e.g., human resources)
2. Business direction
3. Business processes
4. Information technology

Gap analysis provides a foundation for measuring investment of time, money and human resources required to achieve a particular outcome (e.g. to turn the salary payment process from paper-based to paperless with the use of a system). Note that 'GAP analysis' has also been used as a means for classification of how well a product or solution meets a targeted need or set of requirements. In this case, 'GAP' can be used as a ranking of 'Good', 'Average' or 'Poor'. This terminology does appear in the PRINCE2 project management publication from the OGC.

Gap analysis and new products

The need for new products or additions to existing lines may have emerged from portfolio analyses, in particular from the use of the Boston Consulting Group Growth-share matrix, or the need will have emerged from the regular process of following trends in the requirements of consumers. At some point a gap will have emerged between what the existing products offer the consumer and what the consumer demands. That gap has to be filled if the organization is to survive and grow.

To identify a gap in the market, the technique of gap analysis can be used. Thus an examination of what profits are forecasted for the organization as a whole compared with where the organization (in particular its shareholders) 'wants' those profits to be represents what is called the 'planning gap': this shows what is needed of new activities in general and of new products in particular.

The planning gap may be divided into three main elements:

Usage gap

This is the gap between the total potential for the market and the actual current usage by all the consumers in the market. Clearly two figures are needed for this calculation:

- market potential
- existing usage

457

Market potential

The most difficult estimate to make is that of the total potential available to the whole market, including all segments covered by all competitive brands. It is often achieved by determining the "maximum potential individual usage", and extrapolating this by the maximum number of potential consumers. This is inevitably a judgment rather than a scientific extrapolation, but some of the macro-forecasting techniques may assist in making this estimate more soundly based.

The *maximum number of consumers* available will usually be determined by market research, but it may sometimes be calculated from demographic data or government statistics. Ultimately there will, of course, be limitations on the number of consumers. For guidance one can look to the numbers using similar products. Alternatively, one can look to what has happened in other countries. It is often suggested that Europe follows patterns set in the USA, but after a time-lag of a decade or so. The increased affluence of all the major Western economies means that such a lag can now be much shorter.

The maximum potential individual usage, or at least the maximum attainable average usage (there will always be a spread of usage across a range of customers), will usually be determined from market research figures. It is important, however, to consider what lies behind such usage.

Existing usage

The existing usage by consumers makes up the total current market, from which market shares, for example, are calculated. It is usually derived from marketing research, most accurately from panel research such as that undertaken by the Nielsen Company but also from ad hoc work. Sometimes it may be available from figures collected by government departments or industry bodies; however, these are often based on categories which may make sense in bureaucratic terms but are less helpful in marketing terms.

The **'usage gap'** is thus:

usage gap = market potential – existing usage

This is an important calculation to make. Many, if not most marketers, accept the existing market size, suitably projected over the timescales of their forecasts, as the boundary for their expansion plans. Although this is often the most realistic assumption, it may sometimes impose an unnecessary limitation on their horizons. The original market for video-recorders was limited to the professional users who could afford the high prices involved. It was only after some time that the technology was extended to the mass market.

In the public sector, where the service providers usually enjoy a monopoly, the usage gap will probably be the most important factor in the development of the activities. But persuading more consumers to take up family benefits, for example, will probably be more important to the relevant government department than opening more local offices.

The usage gap is most important for the brand leaders. If any of these has a significant share of the whole market, say in excess of 30 per cent, it may become worthwhile for the firm to invest in expanding the total market. The same option is not generally open to the minor players, although they may still be able to target profitably specific offerings as market extensions.

All other gaps relate to the difference between the organization's existing sales (its market share) and the total sales of the market as a whole. This difference is the share held by competitors. These gaps will, therefore, relate to competitive activity.

Product Gap

The product gap, which could also be described as the segment or positioning gap, represents that part of the market from which the individual organization is excluded because of product or service characteristics. This may have come about because the market has been segmented and the organization does not have offerings in some segments, or it may be because the positioning of its offering effectively excludes it from certain groups of potential consumers, because there are competitive offerings much better placed in relation to these groups.

This segmentation may well be the result of deliberate policy. Segmentation and positioning are very powerful marketing techniques; but the trade-off, to be set against the improved focus, is that some parts of the market may effectively be put beyond reach. On the other hand, it may frequently be by default; the organization has not thought about its positioning, and has simply let its offerings drift to where they now are.

The product gap is probably the main element of the planning gap in which the organization can have a productive input; hence the emphasis on the importance of correct positioning.

Competitive gap

What is left represents the gap resulting from the competitive performance. This competitive gap is the share of business achieved among similar products, sold in the same market segment, and with similar distribution patterns - or at least, in any comparison, after such effects have been discounted. Needless to say, it is not a factor in the case of the monopoly provision of services by the public sector.

The competitive gap represents the effects of factors such as price and promotion, both the absolute level and the effectiveness of its messages. It is what marketing is popularly supposed to be about.

Market gap analysis

In the type of analysis described above, gaps in the product range are looked for. Another perspective (essentially taking the `product gap' to its logical conclusion) is to look for gaps in the 'market' (in a variation on `product positioning', and using the multidimensional `mapping'), which the company could profitably address, regardless of where the current products stand.

Many marketers would, question the worth of the theoretical gap analysis described earlier. Instead, they would immediately start proactively to pursue a search for a competitive advantage.

PARETO'S PRINCIPLE - THE 80-20 RULE

In 1906, Italian economist Vilfredo Pareto created a mathematical formula to describe the unequal distribution of wealth in his country, observing that twenty percent of the people owned eighty percent of the wealth. In the late 1940s, Dr. Joseph M. Juran inaccurately attributed the 80/20 Rule to Pareto, calling it Pareto's Principle. While it may be misnamed, Pareto's Principle or Pareto's Law as it is sometimes called, can be a very effective tool to help you manage effectively.

Where It Came From

After Pareto made his observation and created his formula, many others observed similar phenomena in their own areas of expertise. Quality Management pioneer, Dr. Joseph Juran, working in the US in the 1930s and 40s recognized a universal principle he called the "vital few and trivial many" and reduced it to writing. In an early work, a lack of precision on Juran's part made it appear that he was applying Pareto's observations about economics to a broader body of work. The name Pareto's Principle stuck, probably because it sounded better than Juran's Principle.

As a result, Dr. Juran's observation of the "vital few and trivial many", the principle that 20 percent of something always are responsible for 80 percent of the results, became known as Pareto's Principle or the 80/20 Rule.

What It Means

The 80/20 Rule means that in anything a few (20 percent) are vital and many(80 percent) are trivial. In Pareto's case it meant 20 percent of the people owned 80 percent of the wealth. In Juran's initial work he identified 20 percent of the defects causing 80 percent of the problems. Project Managers know that 20 percent of the work (the first 10 percent and the last 10 percent) consume 80 percent of your time and resources. You can apply the 80/20 Rule to almost anything, from the science of management to the physical world.

You know 20 percent of your stock takes up 80 percent of your warehouse space and that 80 percent of your stock comes from 20 percent of your suppliers. Also 80 percent of your sales will come from 20 percent of your sales staff. 20 percent of your staff will cause 80 percent of your problems, but another 20 percent of your staff will provide 80 percent of your production. It works both ways.

How It Can Help You

The value of the Pareto Principle for a manager is that it reminds you to focus on the 20 percent that matters. Of the things you do during your day, only 20 percent really matter. Those 20 percent produce 80 percent of your results. Identify and focus on those things. When the fire drills of the day begin to sap your time, remind yourself of the 20 percent you need to focus on. If something in the schedule has to slip, if something isn't going to get done, make sure it's not part of that 20 percent.

There is a management theory floating around at the moment that proposes to interpret Pareto's Principle in such a way as to produce what is called Superstar Management. The theory's supporters claim that since 20 percent of your people produce 80 percent of your results you should focus your limited time on managing only that 20 percent, the superstars. The theory is flawed, as we are discussing here because it overlooks the fact that 80 percent of your time should be spent doing what is really important. Helping the good become better is a better use of your time than helping the great become terrific. Apply the Pareto Principle to all you do, but use it wisely.

Manage This Issue

Pareto's Principle, the 80/20 Rule, should serve as a daily reminder to focus 80 percent of your time and energy on the 20 percent of you work that is really important. Don't just "work smart", work smart on the right things.

Understanding the Pareto Principle (The 80/20 Rule)

Originally, the Pareto Principle referred to the observation that 80% of Italy's wealth belonged to only 20% of the population.

More generally, the Pareto Principle is the observation (not law) that **most things in life are not distributed evenly**. It can mean all of the following things:

- 20% of the input creates 80% of the result
- 20% of the workers produce 80% of the result
- 20% of the customers create 80% of the revenue
- 20% of the bugs cause 80% of the crashes
- 20% of the features cause 80% of the usage
- And on and on...

But be careful when using this idea! First, there's a common misconception that the numbers 20 and 80 must add to 100 — they don't!

461

20% of the workers could create 10% of the result. Or 50%. Or 80%. Or 99%, or even 100%. Think about it — in a group of 100 workers, 20 could do all the work while the other 80 goof off. In that case, 20% of the workers did 100% of the work. Remember that the 80/20 rule is a rough guide about **typical distributions**.

Also recognize that the numbers don't have to be "20%" and "80%" exactly. The key point is that **most things in life (effort, reward, output) are not distributed evenly – some contribute more than others**.

Life Isn't Fair

What does it mean when we say "things aren't distributed evenly"? The key point is that each unit of work (or time) doesn't contribute the same amount.

In a perfect world, every employee would contribute the same amount, every bug would be equally important, every feature would be equally loved by users. Planning would be so easy.

But that isn't always the case:

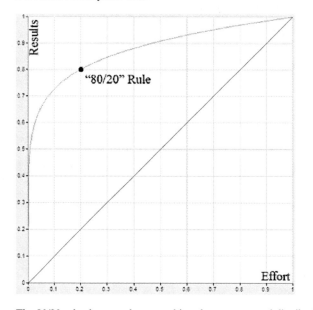

The 80/20 rule observes that most things have an unequal distribution. Out of 5 things, perhaps 1 will be "cool". That cool thing/idea/person will result in majority of the impact of the group (the green line). We'd like life to be like the red line, where every piece contributes equally, but that doesn't always happen.

Of course, this ratio can change. It could be 80/20, 90/10, or 90/20 (remember, the numbers don't have to add to 100!).

The key point is that most things are **not** 1/1, where each unit of "input" (effort, time, labor) contributes exactly the same amount of output.

So Why Is This Useful?

The Pareto Principle helps you realize that the majority of results come from a minority of inputs. Knowing this, if...

20% of workers contribute 80% of results: Focus on rewarding these employees.
20% of bugs contribute 80% of crashes: Focus on fixing these bugs first.
20% of customers contribute 80% of revenue: Focus on satisfying these customers.

The examples go on. The point is to realize that you can often focus your effort on the 20% that makes a difference, instead of the 80% that doesn't add much.

In economics terms, there is **diminishing marginal benefit**. This is related to the law of diminishing returns: each additional hour of effort, each extra worker is adding less "oomph" to the final result. By the end, you are spending lots of time on the minor details.

A Fun, Non-Math Example, Please

Everything is nice and rosy in the abstract. I want to give you a real example. Take a look at this awesome video of an artist drawing a car in Microsoft Paint. It's pretty phenomenal what can be accomplished with such a basic tool:

Now let's deconstruct this video. It's about 5 minutes long, so each minute is about 20% of the way to completion (of course the video is sped up, but we are only interested in relative times anyway). Take a look at how the car evolved over time:

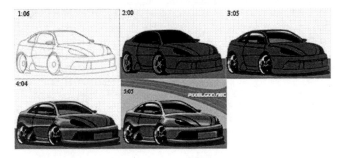

1:06 (Level 1) – Wireframe
2:00 (Level 2) – Basic coloring
3:05 (Level 3) – Beginning details: rims, windshield
4:04 (Level 4) – Advanced details: shading, reflections
5:05 (Level 5) – Finishing touches: headlights, background

Now, let's say the artist was creating potential designs for a client. Given 5 minutes of time, he could present:

- A single car at top quality (Level 5)
- A reasonably detailed car (Level 3) and a colorized wireframe (Level 2)
- 5 cars at a wireframe level (5 Level 1s)

"But #5 is way better than #1!!!" someone will inevitably shout.

The point isn't that #5 is better than #1 — it clearly is. The question is whether #5 is better than five #1s, or some other combination.

Let's say your customer doesn't know whether they want a car, a truck, or a boat, let alone the color. Spending the time to create a Level 5 drawing wouldn't make sense — show some concepts, get a general direction, and then work out the details.

The point is to put in the amount of effort needed to get the most bang for your buck — it's usually in the first 20% (or 10%, or 30% — the exact amount can vary). In the planning stage, it may be better to get 5 fast prototypes rather than 1 polished product.

In this example, after 1 minute (20% of the time) we have a great understanding of what the final outcome will be. Most of the "work" is done up front, in the sense of deciding the type of vehicle, body style, and perspective. The rest is "filling in details" like colors and shading.

This isn't to say the details are easy — they're not — but each detail does not add as much to the picture as the broad strokes in the beginning. The difference between #4 and #5 is not as great as #1 and #2, or better yet, a blank drawing and #1 (the time from 0:00 to 1:06). You really have to look to see the differences on the car between #4 and #5, while the contribution #1 makes is quite obvious.

Concluding Thoughts

This may not be the best strategy in every case. The point of the Pareto principle is to **recognize that most things in life are not distributed evenly**. Make decisions on allocating time, resources and effort based on this:

- Instead of 1 hour on a rough draft for an article you may write, spend 10 minutes on 6 outlines for a paper / blog article and pick the best topic.

- Instead of investing 3 hours on a website, spend 30 minutes and create 6 different template layouts.
- Rather than spending 3 hours to read 3 articles in detail (which may not be relevant to you), spend 5 minutes glancing through 12 articles (1 hour) and then spend an hour each on the two best ones (2 hours).

These techniques may or may not make sense – the point is to realize you have the option to focus on the important 20%.

Lastly, don't think the Pareto Principle means only do 80% of the work needed. It may be true that 80% of a bridge is built in the first 20% of the time, but you still need the rest of the bridge in order for it to work. It may be true that 80% of the Mona Lisa was painted in the first 20% of the time, but it wouldn't be the masterpiece it is without all the details. **The Pareto Principle is an observation, not a law of nature.**

When you are seeking top quality, you need all 100%. When you are trying to optimize your bang for the buck, focusing on the critical 20% is a time-saver. See what activities generate the most results and give them your appropriate attention.

Pareto principle

The **Pareto principle** (also known as the **80-20 rule**, the **law of the vital few,** and the **principle of factor sparsity**) states that, for many events, roughly 80% of the effects come from 20% of the causes. Business management thinker Joseph M. Juran suggested the principle and named it after Italian economist Vilfredo Pareto, who observed in 1906 that 80% of the land in Italy was owned by 20% of the population; he developed the principle by observing that 20% of the pea pods in his garden contained 80% of the peas.[4] It is a common rule of thumb in business; e.g., "80% of your sales come from 20% of your clients." Mathematically, where something is shared among a sufficiently large set of participants, there must be a number k between 50 and 100 such that k% is taken by $(100 - k)$% of the participants. k may vary from 50 (in the case of equal distribution, i.e. 100% of the population is assigned the same value) to nearly 100 (when a tiny number of participants account for almost all of the resource). There is nothing special about the number 80% mathematically, but many real systems have k somewhere around this region of intermediate imbalance in distribution.

The Pareto principle is only tangentially related to Pareto efficiency, which was also introduced by the same economist. Pareto developed both concepts in the context of the distribution of income and wealth among the population.

In economics

The original observation was in connection with income and wealth. Pareto noticed that 80% of Italy's wealth was owned by 20% of the population.[4] He then carried out surveys on a variety of other countries and found to his surprise that a similar distribution applied.

Because of the scale-invariant nature of the power law relationship, the relationship applies also to subsets of the income range. Even if we take the ten wealthiest individuals in the world, we see that the top three (Warren Buffett, Carlos Slim Helú, and Bill Gates) own as much as the next seven put together.[5]

A chart that gave the inequality a very visible and comprehensible form, the so-called 'champagne glass' effect,[6] was contained in the 1992 United Nations Development Program Report, which showed the distribution of global income to be very uneven, with the richest 20% of the world's population controlling 82.7% of the world's income.

Distribution of world GDP, 1989

Quintile of population	Income
Richest 20%	82.70%
Second 20%	11.75%
Third 20%	2.30%
Fourth 20%	1.85%
Poorest 20%	1.40%

The Pareto Principle has also been used to attribute the widening economic inequality in the USA to 'skill-biased technical change' – i.e. income growth accrues to those with the education and skills required to take advantage of new technology and globalisation. However, Nobel Prize winner in Economics Paul Krugman in the *New York Times* dismissed this "80-20 fallacy" as being cited "not because it's true, but because it's comforting." He asserts that the benefits of economic growth over the last 30 years have largely been concentrated in the top 1%, rather than the top 20%.

In software

In computer science and engineering control theory such as for electromechanical energy converters, the Pareto principle can be applied to optimization efforts. For example, this rule is currently being implemented into Mozilla Firefox, a popular internet browser.

Microsoft also noted that by fixing the top 20% of the most reported bugs, 80% of the errors and crashes would be eliminated.

In computer graphics the Pareto principle is used for ray-tracing: 80% of rays intersect 20% of geometry.

Other applications

In the systems science discipline, Epstein and Axtell created an agent-based simulation model called Sugarscape, from a decentralized modeling approach, based on individual behavior rules defined for each agent in the economy. Wealth distribution and Pareto's 80/20 Principle became emergent in their results, which suggests that the principle is a natural phenomenon.

466

The Pareto principle has many applications in quality control. It is the basis for the Pareto chart, one of the key tools used in total quality control and six sigma. The Pareto principle serves as a baseline for ABC-analysis and XYZ-analysis, widely used in logistics and procurement for the purpose of optimizing stock of goods, as well as costs of keeping and replenishing that stock. The Pareto principle was a prominent part of the 2007 bestseller *The 4-Hour Workweek* by Tim Ferriss. Ferriss recommended focusing one's attention on those 20% that contribute to 80% of the income. More notably, he also recommends firing those 20% of customers who take up the majority of one's time and cause the most trouble. In human developmental biology the principle is reflected in the gestation period where the embryonic period constitutes 20% of the whole, with the foetal development taking up the rest of the time. In health care in the United States, it has been found that 20% of patients use 80% of health care resources. Several criminology studies have found that 80% of crimes are committed by 20% of criminals

Mathematical notes

The idea has rule-of-thumb application in many places, but it is commonly misused. For example, it is a misuse to state that a solution to a problem "fits the 80-20 rule" just because it fits 80% of the cases; it must be implied that this solution requires only 20% of the resources needed to solve all cases. Additionally, it is a misuse of the 80-20 rule to interpret data with a small number of categories or observations. This is a special case of the wider phenomenon of Pareto distributions. If the parameters in the Pareto distribution are suitably chosen, then one would have not only 80% of effects coming from 20% of causes, but also 80% of that top 80% of effects coming from 20% of that top 20% of causes, and so on (80% of 80% is 64%; 20% of 20% is 4%, so this implies a "64-4" law; and a similarly implies a "51.2-0.8" law).

80-20 is only a shorthand for the general principle at work. In individual cases, the distribution could just as well be, say, 80-10 or 80-30. (There is no need for the two numbers to add up to 100%, as they are measures of different things, e.g., 'number of customers' vs 'amount spent'). The classic 80-20 distribution occurs when the gradient of the line is −1 when plotted on log-log axes of equal scaling. Pareto rules are not mutually exclusive. Indeed, the 0-0 and 100-100 rules always hold. Adding up to 100 leads to a nice symmetry. For example, if 80% of effects come from the top 20% of sources, then the remaining 20% of effects come from the lower 80% of sources. This is called the "joint ratio", and can be used to measure the degree of imbalance: a joint ratio of 96:4 is very imbalanced, 80:20 is significantly imbalanced (Gini index: 60%), 70:30 is moderately imbalanced (Gini index: 40%), and 55:45 is just slightly imbalanced. The Pareto Principle is an illustration of a "power law" relationship, which also occurs in phenomena such as brush-fires and earthquakes[19] Because it is self-similar over a wide range of magnitudes, it produces outcomes completely different from Gaussian distribution phenomena. This fact explains the frequent breakdowns of sophisticated financial instruments, which are modeled on the assumption that a Gaussian relationship is appropriate to, for example, stock movement sizes.

CHAPTER 14

IMMIGRATION

Immigration is the arrival of new individuals into a habitat or population. It is a biological concept and is important in population ecology, differentiated from emigration and migration. Dual citizenship is now being adopted by most nations the world over and African governments need to move with speed to adopt dual citizenship because of their large diaspora populations now. South Africa and many others in Africa have already embraced dual citizenship. There are lots of benefits for dual citizenship, the first one being investment, technology transfer, benchmarking and creation of solid relations with other nations. Resistance to dual citizenship in the 3rd world by some die hard village politicians with no international exposure beyond their villages will not help national economies in Africa. Politics and political policies have to embrace the realities of the new international demographic landscape, that is why Republicans lost the American election through misguided conservative policies which cost them a ticket to the White House and realised their mistake too late to correct. *One of the most dangerous mistakes that countries make (especially in the 3rd world and in Africa) is to accept valueless immigrants and refugees in unlimited numbers.* Sooner or later serious social and economic problems naturally develop as foreigners fight your people for jobs, land, space, business control, food, other scarce resources and political control of the country. The worst risk is political dispossession and you lose your country completely. There are many stories of countries that lost their sovereignty and countries to foreigners and foreign control completely. Politics is all about numbers. The number of Nigerians in Zimbabwe today is a serious cause of concern and this trend needs to be reversed as a matter of urgency for the goodness of political and economic security. These Nigerians are now too many and are a big political and economic risk for the country. You find whole streets and business centres in a business district in Harare, Zimbabwe (Gulf Complex and Cameroon Street) all controlled by Nigerians without a single Zimbabwean there. This is completely indefensible, unacceptable and dangerous. The same pattern exists in other countries, especially South Africa but is a time bomb. There is a difference when a country admits skilled labour which adds a lot of value to a country as well as investors who bring in much needed investment funds. Some countries have gone further with innovative policies and now give automatic citizenship to people who bring investment funds worth US$500 000 to US$2 000 000 of clean money and above, as long as people get full INTERPOL security clearance and background checks. The United States of America is known for offering citizenship to people who complete PhDs in the USA as a way to retain those critical skills. Actually retention of PhDs is one of the major reasons why the USA became the largest and most sophisticated economy in the world, when this was combined with other strategic natural resources and factors of production as well as freedom of expression as it resulted in the most breakthrough researches being done there. They allowed a lot of dissident academics from all over the world to settle in America and use their skills in America rather than fighting senseless hide and seek battles with dictators in their countries of origin. The first helicopter was built in the USA by Russian dissident academics who ran away from persecution and suppression of their ideas in Russia. Their invention was patented in the USA rather than Russia their country of origin and one can imagine how much Russia lost in not pioneering this discovery and invention of its own people.

In Britain the Labour Party lost the May 2010 elections partly because of irresponsible open door immigration policies which brought into Britain unsustainable large numbers of foreigners some of whom displaced the British in the labour market. This is not a secret and the new coalition Conservative Government of David Cameroon and Nick Clegg of the Liberal Democrats is beginning to seriously reverse this. Frivolous asylum applications were entertained to discredit African/Latin American and former East European countries as undemocratic, violent and repressive but this became very costly for the UK and proved unsustainable and this debate rages on. Some of these people were dangerous thieves, criminals and fugitives from justice in their countries of origin with very serious proven cases. And most of them were simple economic refugees who were prepared to tell the British the lies which they knew would earn them a ticket to stay in Britain – an asylum application on the pretext of persecution at home, simple. As a result of this costly mistake the crime rate in Britain short up terribly as confirmed in the media everyday and as confirmed during the recent election campaign by the politicians themselves. *It was naturally expected that when you admit wanted thieves, murderers, fraudsters and prostitutes into your country they bring their evil deeds too.*

EXCHANGE RATES

International business is strategically and heavily driven by exchange rates due to the unavoidable use of multiple currencies. In finance, the **exchange rates** (also known as the **foreign-exchange rate**, **forex rate** or **FX rate**) between two currencies specifies how much one currency is worth in terms of the other. It is the value of a foreign nation's currency in terms of the home nation's currency. For example an exchange rate of 91 Japanese yen (JPY, ¥) to the United States dollar (USD, $) means that JPY 91 is worth the same as USD 1. The foreign exchange market is one of the largest markets in the world. By some estimates, about 3.2 trillion USD worth of currency changes hands every day.

The **spot exchange rate** refers to the current exchange rate. The **forward exchange rate** refers to an exchange rate that is quoted and traded today but for delivery and payment on a specific future date.

Quotations

An exchange system quotation is given by stating the number of units of "quote currency" (price currency, payment currency) that can be exchanged for one unit of "base currency" (unit currency, transaction currency). For example, in a quotation that says the EURUSD exchange rate is 1.4320 (1.4320 USD per EUR, also known as EUR/USD; see foreign exchange market), the quote currency is USD and the base currency is EUR.

There is a market convention that determines which is the base currency and which is the term currency. In most parts of the world, the order is: EUR – GBP – AUD – NZD –

USD – others. Thus if you are doing a conversion from EUR into AUD, EUR is the base currency, AUD is the term currency and the exchange rate tells you how many Australian dollars you would pay or receive for 1 euro. Cyprus and Malta which were quoted as the base to the USD and others were recently removed from this list when they joined the euro. In some areas of Europe and in the non-professional market in the UK, EUR and GBP are reversed so that GBP is quoted as the base currency to the euro. In order to determine which is the base currency where both currencies are not listed (i.e. both are "other"), market convention is to use the base currency which gives an exchange rate greater than 1.000. This avoids rounding issues and exchange rates being quoted to more than 4 decimal places. There are some exceptions to this rule e.g. the Japanese often quote their currency as the base to other currencies.

Quotes using a country's home currency as the price currency (e.g., EUR 0.63 = USD 1.00 in the euro zone) are known as direct quotation or price quotation (from that country's perspective)[2] and are used by most countries.

Quotes using a country's home currency as the unit currency (e.g., EUR 1.00 = USD 1.58 in the euro zone) are known as indirect quotation or quantity quotation and are used in British newspapers and are also common in Australia, New Zealand and the euro zone.

- direct quotation: 1 foreign currency unit = x home currency units
- indirect quotation: 1 home currency unit = x foreign currency units

Note that, using direct quotation, if the home currency is strengthening (i.e., appreciating, or becoming more valuable) then the exchange rate number decreases. Conversely if the foreign currency is strengthening, the exchange rate number increases and the home currency is depreciating.

Market convention from the early 1980s to 2006 was that most currency pairs were quoted to 4 decimal places for spot transactions and up to 6 decimal places for forward outrights or swaps. (The fourth decimal place is usually referred to as a "pip"). An exception to this was exchange rates with a value of less than 1.000 which were usually quoted to 5 or 6 decimal places. Although there is no fixed rule, exchange rates with a value greater than around 20 were usually quoted to 3 decimal places and currencies with a value greater than 80 were quoted to 2 decimal places. Currencies over 5000 were usually quoted with no decimal places (e.g. the former Turkish Lira). e.g. (GBPOMR : 0.765432 - EURUSD : 1.5877 - GBPBEF : 58.234 - EURJPY : 165.29). In other words, quotes are given with 5 digits. Where rates are below 1, quotes frequently include 5 decimal places.

In 2005 Barclays Capital broke with convention by offering spot exchange rates with 5 or 6 decimal places on their electronic dealing platform[3]. The contraction of spreads (the difference between the bid and offer rates) arguably necessitated finer pricing and gave the banks the ability to try and win transaction on multibank trading platforms where all banks may otherwise have been quoting the same price. A number of other banks have now followed this.

471

Free or pegged

If a currency is free-floating, its exchange rate is allowed to vary against that of other currencies and is determined by the market forces of supply and demand. Exchange rates for such currencies are likely to change almost constantly as quoted on financial markets, mainly by banks, around the world. A movable or adjustable peg system is a system of fixed exchange rates, but with a provision for the devaluation of a currency. For example, between 1994 and 2005, the Chinese Yuan renminbi (RMB) was pegged to the United States dollar at RMB 8.2768 to $1. China was not the only country to do this; from the end of World War II until 1967, Western European countries all maintained fixed exchange rates with the US dollar based on the Bretton Woods system.

The RER is based on the GDP deflator measurement of the price level in the domestic and foreign countries (P,P'), which is arbitrarily set equal to 1 in a given base year. Therefore, the level of the RER is arbitrarily set, depending on which year is chosen as the base year for the GDP deflator of two countries. The changes of the RER are instead informative on the evolution over time of the relative price of a unit of GDP in the foreign country in terms of GDP units of the domestic country. If all goods were freely tradable, and foreign and domestic residents purchased identical baskets of goods, purchasing power parity (PPP) would hold for the GDP deflators of the two countries, and the RER would be constant and equal to one.

Bilateral vs. effective exchange rate

Bilateral exchange rate involves a currency pair, while effective exchange rate is weighted average of a basket of foreign currencies, and it can be viewed as an overall measure of the country's external competitiveness. A nominal effective exchange rate (NEER) is weighted with the inverse of the asymptotic trade weights. A real effective exchange rate (REER) adjust NEER by appropriate foreign price level and deflates by the home country price level. Compared to NEER, a GDP weighted effective exchange rate might be more appropriate considering the global investment phenomenon.

Uncovered interest rate parity

Uncovered interest rate parity (UIRP) states that an appreciation or depreciation of one currency against another currency might be neutralized by a change in the interest rate differential. If US interest rates increase while Japanese interest rates remain unchanged then the US dollar should depreciate against the Japanese yen by an amount that prevents arbitrage. The future exchange rate is reflected into the forward exchange rate stated today. In our example, the forward exchange rate of the dollar is said to be at a discount because it buys fewer Japanese yen in the forward rate than it does in the spot rate. The yen is said to be at a premium.

UIRP showed no proof of working after 1990s. Contrary to the theory, currencies with high interest rates characteristically appreciated rather than depreciated on the reward of the containment of inflation and a higher-yielding currency.

This model holds that a foreign exchange rate must be at its equilibrium level - the rate which produces a stable current account balance. A nation with a trade deficit will experience reduction in its foreign exchange reserves which ultimately lowers (depreciates) the value of its currency. The cheaper currency renders the nation's goods (exports) more affordable in the global market place while making imports more expensive. After an intermediate period, imports are forced down and exports rise, thus stabilizing the trade balance and the currency towards equilibrium.

Like PPP, the balance of payments model focuses largely on tradable goods and services, ignoring the increasing role of global capital flows. In other words, money is not only chasing goods and services, but to a larger extent, financial assets such as stocks and bonds. Their flows go into the capital account item of the balance of payments, thus, balancing the deficit in the current account. The increase in capital flows has given rise to the asset market model.

Asset market model

The explosion in trading of financial assets (stocks and bonds) has reshaped the way analysts and traders look at currencies. Economic variables such as economic growth, inflation and productivity are no longer the only drivers of currency movements. The proportion of foreign exchange transactions stemming from cross border-trading of financial assets has dwarfed the extent of currency transactions generated from trading in goods and services.

The asset market approach views currencies as asset prices traded in an efficient financial market. Consequently, currencies are increasingly demonstrating a strong correlation with other markets, particularly equities.

Like the stock exchange, money can be made or lost on the foreign exchange market by investors and speculators buying and selling at the right times. Currencies can be traded at spot and foreign exchange options markets. The spot market represents current exchange rates, whereas options are derivatives of exchange rates

Fluctuations in exchange rates

Exchange rates display

A market based exchange rate will change whenever the values of either of the two component currencies change. A currency will tend to become more valuable whenever demand for it is greater than the available supply. It will become less valuable whenever demand is less than available supply (this does not mean people no longer want money, it just means they prefer holding their wealth in some other form, possibly another currency).

Increased demand for a currency is due to either an increased transaction demand for money, or an increased speculative demand for money. The transaction demand for money is highly correlated to the country's level of business activity, gross domestic product (GDP), and employment levels. The more people there are unemployed, the less the public as a whole will spend on goods and services. Central banks typically have little difficulty adjusting the available money supply to accommodate changes in the demand for money due to business transactions.

The speculative demand for money is much harder for a central bank to accommodate but they try to do this by adjusting interest rates. An investor may choose to buy a currency if the return (that is the interest rate) is high enough. The higher a country's interest rates, the greater the demand for that currency. It has been argued that currency speculation can undermine real economic growth, in particular since large currency speculators may deliberately create downward pressure on a currency in order to force that central bank to sell their currency to keep it stable (once this happens, the speculator can buy the currency back from the bank at a lower price, close out their position, and thereby take a profit).

LETTER OF CREDIT

After a contract is concluded between buyer and seller, buyer's bank supplies a letter of credit to seller. A standard, commercial **letter of credit** is a document issued mostly by a financial institution, used primarily in trade finance, which usually provides an irrevocable payment undertaking. The LC can also be the source of payment for a transaction, meaning that redeeming the letter of credit will pay an exporter. Letters of credit are used primarily in international trade transactions of significant value, for deals between a supplier in one country and a customer in another. They are also used in the land development process to ensure that approved public facilities (streets, sidewalks, stormwater ponds, etc.) will be built. The parties to a letter of credit are usually a **beneficiary** who is to receive the money, the **issuing bank** of whom the applicant is a client, and the **advising bank** of whom the beneficiary is a client. Almost all letters of credit are irrevocable, i.e., cannot be amended or cancelled without prior agreement of the beneficiary, the issuing bank and the confirming bank, if any. In executing a transaction, letters of credit incorporate functions common to giros and Traveler's cheques. Typically, the documents a beneficiary has to present in order to receive payment include a commercial invoice, bill of lading, and documents proving the shipment was insured against loss or damage in transit. However, the list and form of documents is open to imagination and negotiation and might contain requirements to present documents issued by a neutral third party evidencing the quality of the goods shipped, or their place of origin.

Terminology

The English name "letter of credit" derives from the French word "accreditation", a power to do something, which in turn is derivative of the Latin word "accreditivus", meaning trust. S.'The Application any defence relating to the underlying contract of sale. This is as long as the seller performs their duties to an extent that meets the requirements contained in the LC.

- Note that banks deal only with documents required in the letter of credit and not the underlying transaction.
- Many exporters have mistakenly assumed that the payment is guaranteed after receiving the LC. The issuing bank is obligated to pay under the letter of credit only when the stipulated documents are presented and the terms and conditions of the letter of credit have been met.

Availability

LC being an irrevocable undertaking of the issuing bank makes available the Proceeds, to the Beneficiary of the Credit provided, stipulated documents strictly complying with the provisions of the LC, UCP 600 and other international standard banking practices, are presented to the issuing bank, then:

- i.if the Credit provides for **sight payment** – by payment at sight against compliant presentation
- ii.if the Credit provides for **deferred payment** – by payment on the maturity date(s) determinable in accordance with the stipulations of the Credit; and of course undertaking to pay on due date and confirming maturity date at the time of compliant presentation
- iii.a.if the Credit provides for **acceptance by the Issuing Bank** – by acceptance of Draft(s) drawn by the Beneficiary on the Issuing Bank and payment at maturity of such tenor draft, or
- iii.b. if the Credit provides for **acceptance by another drawee bank** – by acceptance and payment at maturity Draft(s)drawn by the Beneficiary on the Issuing Bank in the event the drawee bank stipulated in the Credit does not accept Draft(s) drawn on it,

or by payment of Draft(s) accepted but not paid by such drawee bank at maturity;

- iv. if the Credit provides for **negotiation** by another bank – by payment without recourse to drawers and/or bona fide holders, Draft(s) drawn by the Beneficiary and/or document(s) presented under the Credit, (and so negotiated by the nominated bank)

- Negotiation means the giving of value for Draft(s) and/or document(s) by the bank authorized to negotiate, viz the nominated bank. Mere examination of the documents and forwarding the same to LC issuing bank for reimbursement, without giving of value / agreed to give, does not constitute a negotiation.

Some of the Documents Called for under a LC

- **Financial Documents**

    Bill of Exchange, Co-accepted Draft

- **Commercial Documents**

  Invoice, Packing list

- **Shipping Documents**

  Transport Document, Insurance Certificate, Commercial, Official or Legal Documents

- **Official Documents**

  License, Embassy legalization, Origin Certificate, Inspection Cert , Phyto-sanitary Certificate

- **Transport Documents**

  Bill of Lading (ocean or multi-modal or Charter party), Airway bill, Lorry/truck receipt, railway receipt, CMC Other than Mate Receipt, Forwarder Cargo Receipt, Deliver Challan...etc

- **Insurance documents**

  Insurance policy, or Certificate but not a cover note.

Legal principles governing documentary credits

One of the primary peculiarities of the documentary credit is that the payment obligation is abstract and independent from the underlying contract of sale or any other contract in the transaction. Thus the bank's obligation is defined by the terms of the credit alone, and the sale contract is irrelevant. The defences of the buyer arising out of the sale contract do not concern the bank and in no way affect its liability.[1] Article 4(a) UCP states this principle clearly. Article 5 the UCP further states that banks deal with documents only, they are not concerned with the goods (facts). Accordingly, if the documents tendered by the beneficiary, or his or her agent, appear to be in order, then in general the bank is obliged to pay without further qualifications.

The policies behind adopting the abstraction principle are purely commercial and reflect a party's expectations: firstly, if the responsibility for the validity of documents was thrown onto banks, they would be burdened with investigating the underlying facts of each transaction and would thus be less inclined to issue documentary credits as the transaction would involve great risk and inconvenience. Secondly, documents required under the credit could in certain circumstances be different from those required under the sale transaction; banks would then be placed in a dilemma in deciding which terms to follow if required to look behind the credit agreement. Thirdly, the fact that the basic function of the credit is to provide the seller with the certainty of receiving payment, as long as he performs his documentary duties, suggests that banks should honour their

476

obligation notwithstanding allegations of misfeasance by the buyer. [2] Finally, courts have emphasised that buyers always have a remedy for an action upon the contract of sale, and that it would be a calamity for the business world if, for every breach of contract between the seller and buyer, a bank were required to investigate said breach.

The "principle of strict compliance" also aims to make the bank's duty of effecting payment against documents easy, efficient and quick. Hence, if the documents tendered under the credit deviate from the language of the credit the bank is entitled to withhold payment even if the deviation is purely terminological.[3] The general legal maxim *de minimis non curat lex* has no place in the field of documentary credits.

The price of LCs

All the charges for issuance of Letter of Credit, negotiation of documents, reimbursements and other charges like courier are to the account of applicant or as per the terms and conditions of the Letter of credit. If the LC is silent on charges, then they are to the account of the Applicant. The description of charges and who would be bearing them would be indicated in the field 71B in the Letter of Credit.

Legal Basis for Letters of Credit

Although documentary credits are enforceable once communicated to the beneficiary, it is difficult to show any consideration given by the beneficiary to the banker prior to the tender of documents. In such transactions the undertaking by the beneficiary to deliver the goods to the applicant is not sufficient consideration for the bank's promise because the contract of sale is made before the issuance of the credit, thus consideration in these circumstances is past. In addition, the performance of an existing duty under a contract cannot be a valid consideration for a new promise made by the bank: the delivery of the goods is consideration for enforcing the underlying contract of sale and cannot be used, as it were, a second time to establish the enforceability of the bank-beneficiary relation.

Legal writers have analyzed every possible theory from every legal angle and failed to satisfactorily reconcile the bank's undertaking with any contractual analysis. The theories include: the implied promise, assignment theory, the novation theory, reliance theory, agency theories, estoppels and trust theories, anticipatory theory, and the guarantee theory. [4] Davis, Treitel, Goode, Finkelstein and Ellinger have all accepted the view that documentary credits should be analyzed outside the legal framework of contractual principles, which require the presence of consideration. Accordingly, whether the documentary credit is referred to as a promise, an undertaking, a chose in action, an engagement or a contract, it is acceptable in English jurisprudence to treat it as contractual in nature, despite the fact that it possesses distinctive features, which make it sui generis.

A few countries including the US (see Article 5 of the Uniform Commercial Code) have created statutes in relation to the operation of LCs. These statutes are designed to work with the rules of practice including the UCP and the ISP98. These rules are practice are incorporated into the LC transaction by agreement of the parties. The latest version of the UCP is the UCP600 effective July 1, 2007[5]. The previous revision was the UCP500 and became effective on 1 January 1994. Since the UCP are not laws, parties have to include them into their arrangements as normal contractual provisions.

International Trade Payment methods

- **Advance payment** (most secure for seller)

Where the buyer parts with money first and waits for the seller to forward the goods

- **Documentary Credit** (more secure for seller as well as buyer)

subject to ICC's UCP 600, where the bank gives an undertaking (on behalf of buyer and at the request of applicant) to pay the shipper (beneficiary) the value of the goods shipped if certain docs are submitted and if the stipulated terms and conditions are strictly complied. Here the buyer can be confident that the goods he is expecting only will be received since it will be evidenced in the form of certain docs called for meeting the specified terms and conditions while the supplier can be confident that if he meets the stipulations his payment for the shipment is guaranteed by bank, who is independent of the parties to the contract.

- **Documentary collection** (more secure for buyer and to a certain extent to seller)

subject to ICC's URC 525, sight and usance, for delivery of shipping documents against payment or acceptances of draft, where shipment happens first, then the title documents are sent to the [collecting bank] buyer's bank by seller's bank [remitting bank], for delivering documents against collection of payment/acceptance

- **Direct payment** (most secure for buyer)

Where the supplier ships the goods and waits for the buyer to remit the bill proceeds, on open account terms

Risk situations in LC transaction

General Risks

- If goods are being offered for sale at a price that is too good to be true, then it probably is too good to be true'

Fraud Risks

- The payment will be obtained for nonexistent or worthless merchandise against presentation by the Beneficiary of forged or falsified documents.
- Credit itself may be forged.

Sovereign and Regulatory Risks

- Performance of the Documentary Credit may be prevented by government action outside the control of the parties.

Legal Risks

- Possibility that performance of a Documentary Credit may be disturbed by legal action relating directly to the parties and their rights and obligations under the Documentary Credit

Force Majeure and Frustration of Contract

- Performance of a contract – including an obligation under a Documentary Credit relationship – is prevented by external factors such as natural disasters or armed conflicts

Risks to the Applicant

- Non-delivery of Goods
- Short Shipment
- Inferior Quality
- Early /Late Shipment
- Damaged in transit
- Foreign exchange
- Failure of Bank viz Issuing bank / Collecting Bank

Risks to the Issuing Bank

- Insolvency of the Applicant
- Fraud Risk, Sovereign and Regulatory Risk and Legal Risks

Risks to the Reimbursing Bank

- no obligation to reimburse the Claiming Bank unless it has issued a reimbursement undertaking.

Risks to the Beneficiary

- Failure to Comply with Credit Conditions
- Failure of, or Delays in Payment from, the Issuing Bank
- Credit Issued by Party other than Bank

Risks to the Advising Bank

- The Advising Bank's only obligation – if it accepts the Issuing Bank's instructions – is to check the apparent authenticity of the Credit and advising it to the Beneficiary

Risks to the Nominated Bank

- Nominated Bank has made a payment to the Beneficiary against documents that comply with the terms and conditions of the Credit and is unable to obtain reimbursement from the Issuing Bank

Risks to the Confirming Bank

- If Confirming Bank's main risk is that, once having paid the Beneficiary, it may not be able to obtain reimbursement from the Issuing Bank because of insolvency of the Issuing Bank or refusal of the Issuing Bank to reimburse because of a dispute as to whether or not payment should have been made under the Credit

Risks in International Trade

- A Credit risk risk from change in the credit of an opposing business.
- An Exchange risk is a risk from a change in the foreign exchange rate.
- A Force majeure risk is **1.** a risk in trade incapability caused by a change in a country's policy, and **2.** a risk caused by a natural disaster.
- Other risks are mainly risks caused by a difference in law, language or culture. In these cases, the cargo might be found late because of a dispute in import and export dealings.

POLITICAL AND ECONOMIC RISK

This aspect of international business can be ruinous and fatal if not managed and planned properly. Political and economic risk is always a factor in international management due to the unavoidable differences between the laws, customs and policies of foreign governments. As foreigners entering new markets, we often lack the local market knowledge and culture to understand these differences and must depend on outside sources for information and forecasts. In most Westernized nations, a vast library of economic statistics and political analysis is publicly available for review. These countries tend to have well-developed and predictable economies and relatively stable governments. Developing countries offer less transparency and access to accurate economic or industry statistics may not exist at all. By understanding the elements of political and economic risk, it is easier to define a model for risk management and decision-making and to collect appropriate data for analysis. This article will review the various components of economic and political risk and offer a method used for quantifying and comparing the "riskiness" of doing business in different countries.

Political Risk

Political risk is the risk that a government will unexpectedly change the roles of the game under which businesses in that country operate. Political risk is often characterized by the stability (or instability) of the government and the presence, or lack thereof, of an independent judiciary and legal system. The relationship with other countries is also very important in determining the level of political risk involved in entering a new market. Political differences between countries can create significant and unexpected business challenges, including international or home-country sanctions, consumer boycotts or even violent attacks against the country or firms that trade there.

Political and economic risk is always a factor in international commerce due to the unavoidable differences between the laws, customs and policies of foreign governments. As foreigners entering new markets, we often lack the local market knowledge and culture to understand these differences and must depend on outside sources for information and forecasts.

In most Westernized nations, a vast library of economic statistics and political analysis is publicly available for review. These countries tend to have well-developed and predictable economies and relatively stable governments. Developing countries offer less transparency and access to accurate economic or industry statistics may not exist at all.

By understanding the elements of political and economic risk, it is easier to define a model for risk management and decision-making and to collect appropriate data for analysis. This article will review the various components of economic and political risk and offer a method used for quantifying and comparing the "riskiness" of doing business in different countries.

Political Risk

Political risk is the risk that a government will unexpectedly change the roles of the game under which businesses in that country operate. Political risk is often characterized by the stability (or instability) of the government and the presence, or lack thereof, of an independent judiciary and legal system. The relationship with other countries is also very important in determining the level of political risk involved in entering a new market. Political differences between countries can create significant and unexpected business challenges, including international or home-country sanctions, consumer boycotts or even violent attacks against the country or firms that trade there.

Corruption and Other Issues

Corruption and nepotism can be a major challenge when doing business in some countries. The annual Corruption Perceptions Index provides a reliable annual index of corruption based on data from several sources. It ranks countries in terms of the degree to which corruption is perceived to exist among public officials and politicians. The CPI is sponsored by Transparency International and can be found at www.transparency.org.

"CORRUPTION IN large-scale public projects is a daunting obstacle to sustainable development and results in a major loss of public funds needed for education, health care, and poverty alleviation, both in developed and developing countries," said Transparency International (TI) Chairman Peter Eigen at the launch of the TI Corruption Perceptions Index (CPI) 2004 in London last month. A poll of polls, the CPI reflects the perceptions of business people and country analysts, both resident and nonresident, compiled from 18 surveys conducted by 12 independent institutions.

Of the 146 countries listed on the CPI, 60 countries scored less than three out of 10, indicating rampant corruption. According to the composite index, corruption is perceived to be most acute in Bangladesh, Haiti, Nigeria, Chad, Myanmar, Azerbaijan, and Paraguay, all of which received a score of less than 2. As well, oil-rich Angola, Iran, Iraq, Kazakhstan, Libya, Russia, Sudan, Venezuela, and Yemen have extremely low scores. According to Eigen, public contracting in the oil sector is plagued by revenues vanishing into the pockets of Western oil executives, middlemen, and local officials. TI, the leading non-governmental organization fighting corruption worldwide, urges Western governments to oblige their oil companies to publish what they pay in fees, royalties, and other payments to host governments and state oil companies. "Access to this vital information will minimize opportunities for hiding the payment of kickbacks to secure oil tenders, a practice that has blighted the oil industry in transition and post-war economies," Eigen said.

Also speaking at the CPI launch, TI Vice Chair Rosa Ines Ospina Robledo challenged national governments to introduce no-bribery clauses into all major projects and make non-compliance punishable with tough sanctions, including forfeiting the contract and blacklisting the offender from future bidding. She continued: "Tenders should include objective award criteria and public disclosure of the entire process. Exceptions to open competitive bidding must be kept to a minimum, and explained and recorded, because limited bidding and direct contracting are particularly prone to manipulation and corruption. Public contracting must be monitored by independent oversight agencies and civil society. With the spread of anti-bribery legislation, corporate governance, and anti-compliance codes, managers have no excuse for paying bribes."

The most common type of political risk consists of selective intervention. These risks are usually less dramatic changes in the rules of the game that may affect foreign-owned companies more than domestic ones. These include a wide variety of issues such as restrictions on cross-border transfer of resources, taxation concerns, investment restrictions, legal conventions and operating restrictions.

Restrictions on cross-border transfer of resources can affect everything from securing equipment and supplies, to the travel and assignments of management talent. Tariffs and export restrictions can be significant, requiring the development of a local supplier network. In many regions, trade agreements and international conventions can provide the incentive to develop regional supplier networks benefiting the different business units operating in the participating treaty countries. Non-trade cross-border restrictions include immigration laws, environmental safeguards and capital and currency exchange controls.

Restrictions on currency exchange can occur for short or long periods of time and may make it difficult, if not impossible, to transfer funds or to collect royalties and profits.

Understanding the effects of taxation between countries requires knowledge that can most accurately be provided by attorneys and accountants specializing in the field. For companies operating subsidiaries in foreign countries, the issue of unitary taxation must be considered. The unitary method of taxation is used by countries to close the "subsidiary loophole" by treating integrated subsidiaries of corporations as a single business entity for tax purposes. The unitary method apportions the profits of integrated offshore business operations to a specific country based on the share of the businesses sales, employment and property located in that country. Many countries also apply withholding taxes on foreign remittances and restrict transfer pricing to ensure they collect their fair share of tax revenue from foreign-owned corporations.

The effect of restrictions on investments and on business operations will depend on the structure of the organization. For companies that choose to invest directly, there may be sectoral restrictions that protect domestic suppliers or ownership requirements that specify joint venture or local ownership. A number of countries require new franchisors to secure government approval. For example, in China, foreign franchisors must be registered and are also required to own and operate two pilot locations for a minimum of one year before being allowed to offer franchises for sale.

Economic Risk

Economic risk is the likelihood that events, including economic mismanagement, will cause drastic changes in a country's business environment that would adversely affect profits and other goals of a particular business enterprise. Economic risk consists of both internal and external factors. Internal factors include monetary stability, the type of currency exchange system (fixed vs. floating), government spending policies and the country's resource base. External economic risks consist of uncontrollable events such as supply shocks, currency fluctuations, trade deficits, natural disasters, and the health of the overall global economy. How well a nation responds to the impact of external economic shocks will vary from country to country. Monetary stability can be measured by a variety of economic statistics. The relative size of government deficits, rate of money supply expansion and capital flight are all excellent indicators of economic risk. High government deficits and a rapidly growing money supply can lead to runaway inflation and currency devaluation. A certain amount of exchange rate volatility can be managed by hedging anticipated offshore revenues in the foreign exchange market. Capital flight is defined as the export of savings by a country's citizens due to fears caused by the expectation of currency devaluation. It is an excellent up-to-date indicator of consumer confidence. Capital flight is typically caused by inappropriate economic policies or high political risk and is measured using the country's balance-of-payments account.

Competitive factors aside, managing political and economic risk can be as simple as focusing business expansion on proven and familiar markets. Following the development path of other successful international franchisors is a logical and legitimate strategy.

However, a more empirical approach will allow for a valid comparison between target markets on an equivalent basis. One of the most well known sources for political risk data is The PRS Group which has implemented a methodology that uses the Coplin-O'Leary system for forecasting the risks related to regime stability, turmoil, financial transfer, direct investment, and export markets. It also provides country datasets of more than 75 individual economic variables and risk ratings covering more than 140 countries.

CHAPTER 15

NATIONAL BRANDING

National branding is at the heart of any successful nation. **Nation branding** is an "idea [that] has been generating more interest in recent years as countries including the United States, Germany, France, Portugal, Estonia and Poland have brought in experts to help them tinker with their identities." "'Branding' is the ways in which an organization communicates, differentiates and symbolizes itself to all of its audiences. **National branding** is doing the same thing, but to a whole country. This may be to encourage foreign direct investment, create internal pride, or be a support for exports or any enterprise that a nation may undertake."

- "Although it means more than image and perception, 'national branding may be briefly defined as the way a country or a nation--for instance, Palestine--is perceived by the audience.
- "It is very important to underline that the audience is split into two major categories: that nation's people and everyone else. It seems that most national branding programs are aimed at foreigners--improving one nation's image in the eye of the rest of the world--but it is equally important to create programs that aim at that nation's own people, because on a long-term basis, a nation is perceived also through its individuals."
- "Every nation has a brand. The nation's brand is defined by the people, by their temper, education, look, by their endeavors. This is why national branding is not easy. It is very hard to change a nation's values. It means education, it means economic status, standard of life. It takes generations to change how people are.
- "This is not the work of a branding agency, not even of a government. Instead, national branding programs aim at something different: making [the country's] values better known, minimize the effect of several accidents caused by individuals that affect the nation's brand, promote tourism, or attract investors."
- Source: LogoLounge.com.
- ⸻⸻⸻⸻⸻⸻⸻⸻
- "Branding experts" like Simon Anholt, who established Placebrands early in 2003 but now works as an independent policy advisor to several governments, help "countries develop and communicate strong brand identities [which] could help speed up development by attracting foreign investors and tourists. That, in turn, could increase political influence and help a country's corporations grow."[2]
- "Next year, Finland will start a campaign to enhance its image as a center of high-tech innovation, with the hope of helping its technology companies fare better in the United States. Branding is also seen as crucial to many Central European countries that have realized that their timelines for acceptance into the European Union, and their ability to compete against their neighbors for investment, depend in part on how they are perceived by more developed European countries like France and Germany.
- "Changing the image of a country is no easier than changing the image of a company or an individual. While branding may be able to help a country improve its communication with the world, it won't work if the country sends out lies or

485

hype, said Erich Joachimsthaler, chief executive of Vivaldi Partners, a four-year-old agency that specializes in branding. Mr. Joachimsthaler said that when working with Germany, he had run into a perception gap that is common in such work. His German clients wanted to portray themselves as a passionate, emotional, flexible people, an image that he said was 'a whole bunch of baloney.'

- "Charlotte Beers, the former chief executive of the advertising agency Ogilvy & Mather, served for a year and a half as President George Walker Bush's under secretary of state for public diplomacy and public affairs - and part of the job was the task of selling America to the Middle East.

- "Jennifer L. Aaker, an associate professor of marketing at Stanford University's Graduate School of Business, said that task was almost impossible. 'One of the reasons that effort failed was because of the underlying product - our policies were not perceived as pro-Middle East. We failed to understand the media, the culture, even the language in that region. It is difficult to garner favorable perceptions of the American brand in that context.'

- "While most countries have complicated identities, Croatia, one of Mr. Anholt's clients, is a particularly vexing case. To the extent that people in Western Europe think of the country at all, they associate it with Nazi complicity in World War II, Mr. Anholt said, or with the bloody conflicts in the 1990's between the Serbs and the Croats. Stjepo Martinovic, editor of Croatia's national heritage magazine, *Matica*, and a former adviser to the Croatian government on European integration, said that because Croatia is scheduled to join the European Union as early as 2007, it was particularly important that the country project a positive image.

- "'We are trying to present Croatia as a normal country, a market economy, a democratic society, a Mediterranean country,' Mr. Martinovic said. He argues that Croatia can be made attractive to the rest of the world by letting people know about its inexpensive work force, its livable cities and its schools that offer classes in English - as well as its ballet, theater and contemporary artists."

- Read remainder of article at When Nations Need a Little Marketing by Jim Rendon, *NYT*, November 23, 2003.

-
- "Since 9/11 : Brand Usa has received huge coverage, particularly because of the high visibility battle between gurus with 2 very different belief systems about branding: Charlotte Beers a doyen of the ad industry hired by George W. Bush to get the USA's message out and Naomi Klein of Nologo & Globalisation who furiously criticises global identities of all sorts. Whilst apparently disagreeing about almost everything, they both are reported to use the word brand almost synonymously with image & message-making. Actually this is only the visible tip of why global identities can have huge value for almost anyone who produces or is served by the economics of the system of leadership and the value exchanges they represent. It is time nations as the biggest general influencer on people's livelihoods learnt all about this.

- "Historically **nation branding** and invention of tradition has always happened by accident more than continuous economic planning. However, serious economic planning around nation branding is now at least 10 years old with the New Zealand government being one of the practice leaders in this field since early 1990s . And before that both Singapore and Japan over decades represented much more consistent brand leadership than most global companies exhibited. However, the most important recent understanding in nation brand architectures may be that in a networked world it's not just a big/rich country topic but a vital one to involve developing countries in. Start with the question who does a nation brand represent?: and you can map out hundreds of detailed possibilities most of which get ignored if you are trying to govern one brand for everyone. Start with the different question series: what are the 3 most desperate developing needs in this country? can we sub-brand an activist network around each one? can that national seal of honour of doing good work most desperately needed human areas of development then be awarded by the activist networks to global companies and other who really help them - if you will a poor nation's 'virtual oscars ceremony' to the big organisational powers among the World Economic Forum's members that provide the most consistent grassroots help in developing communities and you have a different dynamic of nation branding by the people for the people. There then may emerge direct links between competent branding of nations and United Nations global compacts, WEF corporate citizenships and the whole practice of Corporate Social Responsibility."

• ==
========================

Mapping a Country's Future

By Randall Frost

Imagine France without fashion, Germany without automotive excellence or Japan without consumer electronics. There's no arguing that the image we have of another country says a lot about how we view it as a tourist destination, a place to invest or a source of consumer goods. How does a country brand differ from a product or service brand? Who controls it? And how do you ensure "internal" alignment?

" The idea of a nation as a brand – as Kellogg's Corn Flakes is a brand – is a very big mistake. "

Many think a country, place or region constitutes a brand, and now a few countries are currently working on strategies to spruce up their brand images. In the case of exports, the thinking goes something like this: once a country has become known as an exporter of quality branded goods, the country's product brands and its place brand will work together to raise expectations overseas. Country branding should then become part of a self-perpetuating cycle: as the country promotes its consumer brands, those brands will promote the country.

487

Does it work? Sometimes, but the relationship between product and place brands is by no means simple. While there may be similarities between product and place brands, "the idea of a nation as a brand – as Kellogg's Corn Flakes is a brand – is a very big mistake," cautions Wally Olins, chairman of the branding consultancy Saffron in London and Madrid.

Magne Supphellen, a professor at the Norwegian School of Economics and Business Administration in Bergen, explains, "In *principle*, [product] and place branding is the same. It's all about identifying, developing and communicating the parts of the identity that are favorable to some specified target groups...." But the analysis of identity and of target group perceptions, coupled with brand building activities, he notes, are much more complex for places than for products. "It is far more difficult to obtain a fully integrated communication mix in place branding," he says.

Philip Kotler, a professor at the Kellogg Graduate School of Management at Northwestern University in Chicago, acknowledges the complexity by explaining that a new product comes into existence as a *tabula rasa*, to which a set of associations can later be mapped. Even after a product has been launched, companies are free to make modifications in response to consumer demand. Countries, however, may be more limited in altering their place brands. Obviously a country can't replace its beaches with mountains, or grow bananas if its climate favors snow. Although it may be possible for a nation to attract more foreign direct investment or shift its economic base, there will always be some constraints over which it has little or no control.

Professor David Gertner of the Lubin School of Business at Pace University in New York City explains, "Products can be discontinued, modified, withdrawn from the market, re-launched and re-positioned or replaced by improved products. Places do not have most of these choices. Their image problems may be founded in structural problems that take years to fix."

Professor Nicolas Papadopoulos of the Sprott School of Business at Carleton University in Ottawa, believes the most important challenges currently facing place branding are "lack of unity of purpose, difficulty in establishing actionable and measurable objectives, lack of authority over inputs and control over outputs, restricted flexibility, and relative lack of marketing know-how." Consider the following examples:

- Place marketing involves multiple stakeholders, often with competing interests. Trying to market a country to tourists as a mountain hideaway inhabited by rustic peasants may not serve the interests of those wishing to promote the country's budding industrial infrastructure to foreign investors.

- Measuring the effectiveness of place marketing is fraught with difficulties. The decision of a multinational firm to locate a plant in an offshore country may have little or nothing to do with promotional activities by members of the host country. Likewise, trying to measure success in meeting broad objectives, not to mention identifying the separate contributions to marketing outcome, can be a nightmare.

- Unlike product branding, place branding is seldom under the control of a central authority.

Government or industry associations are rarely in a position to dictate policy to stakeholders.

- Marketers have far less control over place brands than over product brands. Besides country marketing campaigns, people may learn about a country in school; from media sources (including newspapers, books, TV and movies); from purchases; and from trips abroad or from contact with citizens or former residents.

- A typical business will have more experience with marketing issues than most countries. Many government officials who become involved in country branding are drawn to product marketing approaches because their countries are in desperate need of exports, tourism or foreign direct investment. But few in government have the skill sets required to design major marketing campaigns.

When marketing expertise is lacking within government, however, it may be possible for countries to enlist the help of outside professionals. Costa Rica beat out Brazil, Chile and Mexico to become the site of Intel's first Latin American plant in 1996 by drawing on the resources of its own investment promotion agency and the Irish Development Agency. Likewise, Colombia is today the major exporter of coffee to the US, largely because the National Federation of Coffee Growers of Colombia built a successful marketing campaign for Café de Colombia.

Matthew Healey, former brand manager for T-Mobile in the Czech Republic, believes there are many paths to achieving a unique national identity. As examples, he observes that Spain has made tremendous strides in branding itself as a modern and developed country, while Denmark has successfully branded all of its government ministries and departments. Croatia for its part, he notes, has been working to reform its image in sports and tourism, and Poland has begun asserting itself in foreign policy.

According to Saffron's Olins, some nations develop a national brand in a kind of controlled or formalized way, but with others it happens almost spontaneously. "If you look at what is happening in India today, and the perceptions around India, none of these are controlled. India has emerged in the last five years in terms of perceptions in a quite different way from the way it was perceived ten or fifteen years ago. It was spirituality and poverty, and now it's software; it's highly educated people. And in some countries, Indian clothing — textiles and fabrics, are fashionable.... None of this is managed. It's all spontaneous."

In other cases, promoting a country has involved identifying spokespeople, product brands, and events that can favorably influence public opinion in other countries. But because countries usually produce many products — not just one, a variety of marketing strategies may be needed. Tourism and exports often employ mass marketing techniques, for example, but personal selling may be better adapted to investment marketing.

Besides being brands, countries can also be products, particularly when they serve as tourist destinations or factory sites. In many cases the country brand must serve as an umbrella, in much the same way that General Electric serves as an umbrella brand for all its subsidiaries.

Says Papadopoulos, "Once an umbrella brand concept that is unitary and clear is established, individual constituents can go their merry separate ways within it, without the risk of inconsistent messaging. Achieving this, of course, will take a lot of doing. There's a steep learning curve, and there's a great need to devise approaches for coordinating within and across diverse constituents."

According to Juergen Gnoth, a senior lecturer in the Department of Marketing at the University of Otago in New Zealand, there are still other challenges in the offing. "The determining issue in place branding will be, how effectively has the brand been designed and who is to be its messenger. What qualities do these messengers have, and does that constitute a constructive basis? Does the brand fit with its environment? What is the relationship of the brand to other place brands in the area, country, or continent? And how will the brand attributes be perpetuated through time and from generation to generation?"

One of the chief difficulties for many countries has been deciding who should run their national branding campaigns. Allan Steinmetz, CEO of Inward Strategic Consulting in Massachusetts, does not see classical top-down brand building strategies working for most governments, citing by way of example the failure of the Bush administration's Brand America campaign. "That [type of brand building] typically has to be done in a corporate environment by the CEO or senior leadership," he says. Steinmetz believes that relying on government leaders to devise a country's branding campaign is particularly risky if politicians have image problems of their own.

Adds Olins, "Inevitably [national branding campaigns] are inspired at least partially by governments. And governments like quick results. But governments [...] often don't stay in power for very long." Olins therefore thinks that governments should work closely with the private sector when developing branding strategies.

But public opinion clearly counts for something too. Thomas Cromwell, president of East West Communications in Washington, DC, observes that Liechtenstein's government had to abandon its attempts to brand that country as a convention destination after the population objected that the brand emphasized the country's weak points (tiny size) but none of its pluses (strong economy and lovely countryside).

In principle, it is a country's citizens who stand to gain the most from a successful nation branding campaign. Just as corporate branding campaigns can raise the morale, team spirit, and sense of purpose of a company's employees, national branding campaigns can provide a country with a common sense of purpose and national pride – not to mention a higher standard of living.

According to Papadopoulos, however, most governments currently do not bother to consult their citizens when putting together national branding campaigns. That may change, he says, because "widespread buy-in by the population is a critical precondition of the success of any branding program.... To deliver, everyone in the 'organization' must believe in the brand." Papadopoulos also foresees "a lot of soul-searching" as nations attempt to come to grips with their national images. Just as companies must solicit the trust of consumers by

490

behaving transparently and accountably, so will country brands have to work at maintaining credible reputations.

In spite of the challenges, Olins sees a bright future for country branding. "What has always been part of the national attempt to influence the world around it will continue, and will continue to use sophisticated elements of marketing techniques," he says. Presumably part of the reason for this is that competition between country brands need not be a zero-sum game. There will always be room in the global marketplace for many brands, including niche brands and brands that compete on cultural excellence. The presence of multiple country brands in the market place will almost certainly enhance overall interest in the offerings.

Nation branding is a field of theory and practice which aims to measure, build and manage the reputation of countries (closely related to place branding). Some approaches applied, such as an increasing importance on the symbolic value of products, have led countries to emphasize their distinctive characteristics. The branding and image of a nation-state "and the successful transference of this image to its exports - is just as important as what they actually produce and sell."[1]

Simon Anholt is credited as a pioneer in the field. He regularly conducts two global surveys known as the Anholt-GfK Roper Nation Brands Index and Anholt-GfK Roper City Brands Index. There is one professional/academic journal in the field, Place Branding and Public Diplomacy, published by Palgrave Macmillan and edited by Simon Anholt.

Simon Anholt also conducts the Nation Branding Masterclass, a series of one-day events designed to support the more effective stewardship of the national identity. Combining his own expertise with the expertise of regional public leaders and key national stakeholders, each event is designed to further the understanding of best practice in national branding techniques, helping countries to understand and develop their competitive identities within a rapidly changing global marketplace. Delegates will learn how nations are currently perceived and how reputations can be changed for the better. They will leave the Masterclass with a better understanding of how a comprehensive national strategy can benefit domestic industries and exports as well as improve inward investment and the general health of the economy.

Nation branding appears to be practised by many states, including the United States and United Kingdom (where it is officially referred to as Public Diplomacy), South Africa, Canada, New Zealand, and most Western European countries. There is increasing interest in the concept from poorer states on the grounds that an enhanced image might create more favorable conditions for foreign direct investment, tourism, trade and even political relations with other states.

Scholars such as Evan H. Potter at the University of Ottawa have conceptualized nation brands as a form of national soft power. All efforts by government (at any level) to support the nation brand - either directly or indirectly - becomes public diplomacy. Anti-globalisation proponents often claim that globalisation diminishes and threatens local diversity, but there is evidence that in order to compete against the backdrop of global cultural homogenity, nations strive to accentuate and promote the distinctiveness of local characteristics and competitive advantages.

The concept of measuring the global perception of a country in several spheres has been developed by Simon Anholt. A subsequent ranking of nations following his surveys was first released in 2005 known as the Anholt Nation Brands Index and was initially published four times a year. Since 2008 research activities from GfK Roper Public Affairs & Media and Simon Anholt are joined and resulted in an expanded version of the index which is since then known as the Anholt-GfK Roper Nation Brands Index (NBI). Published on an annual basis, 20,157 interviews have been conducted with approximately 1,000 interviews per country for the 2008 Index to determine how countries are perceived by others. People over the age of seventeen have been interviewed in twenty core countries such as the United States, Canada, the United Kingdom, Germany, France, Italy, Sweden, Russia, Poland, Turkey, Japan, China, India, South Korea, Australia, Argentina, Brazil, Mexico, Egypt, South Africa. The criteria underlying the NBI ranking are:

People: Measures the population's reputation for competence, education, openness and friendliness and other qualities, as well as perceived levels of potential hostility and discrimination.

Governance: Measures public opinion regarding the level of national government competency and fairness and describes individuals' beliefs about each country's government, as well as its perceived commitment to global issues such as democracy, justice, poverty and the environment.

Exports: Determines the public's image of products and services from each country and the extent to which consumers proactively seek or avoid products from each country-of-origin.

Tourism: Captures the level of interest in visiting a country and the draw of natural and man-made tourist attractions.

Culture & Heritage: Reveals global perceptions of each nation's heritage and appreciation for its contemporary culture, including film, music, art, sport and literature.

Investment & Immigration Determines the power to attract people to live, work or study in each country and reveals how people perceive a country's economic and social situation.

492

BRANDING STRATEGIES

Some people distinguish the psychological aspect of a brand from the experiential aspect. The experiential aspect consists of the sum of all points of contact with the brand and is known as the **brand experience**. The psychological aspect, sometimes referred to as the **brand image**, is a symbolic construct created within the minds of people and consists of all the information and expectations associated with a product or service.

People engaged in branding seek to develop or align the expectations behind the brand experience, creating the impression that a brand associated with a product or service has certain qualities or characteristics that make it special or unique. A brand is therefore one of the most valuable elements in an advertising theme, as it demonstrates what the brand owner is able to offer in the marketplace. The art of creating and maintaining a brand is called brand management. Orientation of the whole organization towards its brand is called integrated marketing.

Careful brand management, supported by a cleverly crafted advertising campaign, can be highly successful in convincing consumers to pay remarkably high prices for products which are inherently extremely cheap to make. This concept, known as creating value, essentially consists of manipulating the projected image of the product so that the consumer sees the product as being worth the amount that the advertiser wants him/her to see, rather than a more logical valuation that comprises an aggregate of the cost of raw materials, plus the cost of manufacture, plus the cost of distribution. Modern value-creation branding-and-advertising campaigns are highly successful at inducing consumers to pay, for example, 50 dollars for a T-shirt that cost a mere 50 cents to make, or 5 dollars for a box of breakfast cereal that contains a few cents' worth of wheat.

Brands should be seen as more than the difference between the actual cost of a product and its selling price - they represent the sum of all valuable qualities of a product to the consumer. There are many intangibles involved in business, intangibles left wholly from the income statement and balance sheet which determine how a business is perceived. The learned skill of a knowledge worker, the type of metal working, the type of stitch: all may be without an 'accounting cost' but for those who truly know the product, for it is these people the company should wish to find and keep, the difference is incomparable. Failing to recognize these assets that a business, any business, can create and maintain will set an enterprise at a serious disadvantage.

A brand which is widely known in the marketplace acquires **brand recognition**. When brand recognition builds up to a point where a brand enjoys a critical mass of positive sentiment in the marketplace, it is said to have achieved **brand franchise**. One goal in brand recognition is the identification of a brand without the name of the company present. For example, Disney has been successful at branding with their particular script font (originally created for Walt Disney's "signature" logo), which it used in the logo for go.com.

Consumers may look on branding as an important value added aspect of products or services, as it often serves to denote a certain attractive quality or characteristic (see also brand promise). From the perspective of brand owners, branded products or services also command higher prices. Where two products resemble each other, but one of the products has no associated branding (such as a generic, store-branded product), people may often select the more expensive branded product on the basis of the quality of the brand or the reputation of the brand owner.

Brand name

The brand name is quite often used interchangeably within "brand", although it is more correctly used to specifically denote written or spoken linguistic elements of any product. In this context a "brand name" constitutes a type of trademark, if the brand name exclusively identifies the brand owner as the commercial source of products or services. A brand owner may seek to protect proprietary rights in relation to a brand name through trademark registration. Advertising spokespersons have also become part of some brands, for example: Mr. Whipple of Charmin toilet tissue and Tony the Tiger of Kellogg's.

Brand names will fall into one of three spectrums of use - Descriptive, Associative or Freestanding.

Descriptive brand names assist in describing the distinguishable selling point(s) of the product to the customer (eg Snap, Crackle and Pop or Bitter Lemon).

Associative brand names provide the customer with an associated word for what the product promises to do or be (e.g. Walkman, Sensodyne or Natrel)

Finally, **Freestanding brand names** have no links or ties to either descriptions or associations of use. (eg Mars Bar or Pantene)

The act of associating a product or service with a brand has become part of pop culture. Most products have some kind of brand identity, from common table salt to designer jeans. A brandnomer is a brand name that has colloquially become a generic term for a product or service, such as Band-Aid or Kleenex, which are often used to describe any kind of adhesive bandage or any kind of facial tissue respectively.

Brand identity

A product identity, or brand image are typically the attributes one associates with a brand, **how the brand owner wants the consumer to perceive the brand** - and by extension the branded company, organization, product or service. The brand owner will seek to bridge the gap between the brand image and the brand identity.[2] Effective brand names build a connection between the brand personality as it is perceived by the target audience and the actual product/service. The brand name should be conceptually on target with the product/service (what the company stands for). Furthermore, the brand name should be on target with the brand demographic.[3] Typically, sustainable brand names are easy to

494

remember, transcend trends and have positive connotations. Brand identity is fundamental to consumer recognition and symbolizes the brand's differentiation from competitors.

Brand identity is what the owner wants to communicate to its potential consumers. However, over time, a products brand identity may acquire (evolve), gaining new attributes from consumer perspective but not necessarily from the marketing communications an owner percolates to targeted consumers. Therefore, brand associations become handy to check the consumer's perception of the brand.[4]

Brand identity needs to focus on authentic qualities - real characteristics of the value and brand promise being provided and sustained by organisational and/or production characteristics[5][6].

Brand parity

Brand parity is the perception of the customers that all brands are equivalent.[7]

Branding approaches

Company name

Often, especially in the industrial sector, it is just the company's name which is promoted (leading to one of the most powerful statements of "branding"; the saying, before the company's downgrading, "No one ever got fired for buying IBM").

In this case a very strong brand name (or company name) is made the vehicle for a range of products (for example, Mercedes-Benz or Black & Decker) or even a range of subsidiary brands (such as Cadbury Dairy Milk, Cadbury Flake or Cadbury Fingers in the United States).

Individual branding

Each brand has a separate name (such as Seven-Up, Kool-Aid or Nivea Sun (Beiersdorf)), which may even compete against other brands from the same company (for example, Persil, Omo, Surf and Lynx are all owned by Unilever).

Attitude branding and Iconic brands

Attitude branding is the choice to represent a larger feeling, which is not necessarily connected with the product or consumption of the product at all. Marketing labeled as attitude branding include that of Nike, Starbucks, The Body Shop, Safeway, and Apple Inc.. In the 2000 book *No Logo*, Naomi Klein describes attitude branding as a "fetish strategy".

"A great brand raises the bar -- it adds a greater sense of purpose to the experience, whether it's the challenge to do your best in sports and fitness, or the affirmation that the cup of coffee you're drinking really matters." - Howard Schultz (president, CEO, and chairman of Starbucks)

Iconic brands are defined as having aspects that contribute to consumer's self-expression and personal identity. Brands whose value to consumers comes primarily from having identity value comes are said to be "identity brands". Some of these brands have such a strong identity that they become more or less "cultural icons" which makes them iconic brands. Examples of iconic brands are: Apple Inc., Nike and Harley Davidson. Many iconic brands include almost ritual-like behaviour when buying and consuming the products.

There are four key elements to creating iconic brands (Holt 2004):

1. "Necessary conditions" - The performance of the product must at least be ok preferably with a reputation of having good quality.
2. "Myth-making" - A meaningful story-telling fabricated by cultural "insiders". These must be seen as legitimate and respected by consumers for stories to be accepted.
3. "Cultural contradictions" - Some kind of mismatch between prevailing ideology and emergent undercurrents in society. In other words a difference with the way consumers are and how they some times wish they were.
4. "The cultural brand management process" - Actively engaging in the myth-making process making sure the brand maintains its position as an icon.

"No-brand" branding

Recently a number of companies have successfully pursued "No-Brand" strategies, examples include the Japanese company Muji, which means "No label" in English (from 無印良品 – "Mujirushi Ryohin" – literally, "No brand quality goods"). Although there is a distinct Muji brand, Muji products are not branded. This no-brand strategy means that little is spent on advertisement or classical marketing and Muji's success is attributed to the word-of-mouth, a simple shopping experience and the anti-brand movement.[9][10][11] "No brand" branding is actually branding as the brand is made conspicous through its absence.

Derived brands

In this case the supplier of a key component, used by a number of suppliers of the end-product, may wish to guarantee its own position by promoting that component as a brand in its own right. The most frequently quoted example is Intel, which secures its position in the PC market with the slogan "Intel Inside".

Brand extension

The existing strong brand name can be used as a vehicle for new or modified products; for example, many fashion and designer companies extended brands into fragrances, shoes and accessories, home textile, home decor, luggage, (sun-) glasses, furniture, hotels, etc.

Mars extended its brand to ice cream, Caterpillar to shoes and watches, Michelin to a restaurant guide, Adidas and Puma to personal hygiene. Dunlop extended its brand from tires to other rubber products such as shoes, golf balls, tennis racquets and adhesives.

There is a difference between brand extension and line extension. When Coca-Cola launched "Diet Coke" and "Cherry Coke" they stayed within the originating product category: non-alcoholic carbonated beverages. Procter & Gamble (P&G) did likewise extending its strong lines (such as Fairy Soap) into neighboring products (Fairy Liquid and Fairy Automatic) within the same category, dish washing detergents.

Multi-brands

Alternatively, in a market that is fragmented amongst a number of brands a supplier can choose deliberately to launch totally new brands in apparent competition with its own existing strong brand (and often with identical product characteristics); simply to soak up some of the share of the market which will in any case go to minor brands. The rationale is that having 3 out of 12 brands in such a market will give a greater overall share than having 1 out of 10 (even if much of the share of these new brands is taken from the existing one). In its most extreme manifestation, a supplier pioneering a new market which it believes will be particularly attractive may choose immediately to launch a second brand in competition with its first, in order to pre-empt others entering the market.

Individual brand names naturally allow greater flexibility by permitting a variety of different products, of differing quality, to be sold without confusing the consumer's perception of what business the company is in or diluting higher quality products.

Once again, Procter & Gamble is a leading exponent of this philosophy, running as many as ten detergent brands in the US market. This also increases the total number of "facings" it receives on supermarket shelves. Sara Lee, on the other hand, uses it to keep the very different parts of the business separate — from Sara Lee cakes through Kiwi polishes to L'Eggs pantyhose. In the hotel business, Marriott uses the name Fairfield Inns for its budget chain (and Ramada uses Rodeway for its own cheaper hotels).

Cannibalization is a particular problem of a "multibrand" approach, in which the new brand takes business away from an established one which the organization also owns. This may be acceptable (indeed to be expected) if there is a net gain overall. Alternatively, it may be the price the organization is willing to pay for shifting its position in the market; the new product being one stage in this process.

Private labels

With the emergence of strong retailers, private label brands, also called own brands, or store brands, also emerged as a major factor in the marketplace. Where the retailer has a particularly strong identity (such as Marks & Spencer in the UK clothing sector) this "own brand" may be able to compete against even the strongest brand leaders, and may outperform those products that are not otherwise strongly branded.

History

The word "brand" is derived from the Old Norse *brandr*, meaning "to burn." It refers to the practice of producers burning their mark (or brand) onto their products.[12]

Although connected with the history of trademarks[13] and including earlier examples which could be deemed "protobrands" (such as the marketing puns of the "Vesuvinum" wine jars found at Pompeii),[14] brands in the field of mass-marketing originated in the 19th century with the advent of packaged goods. Industrialization moved the production of many household items, such as soap, from local communities to centralized factories. When shipping their items, the factories would literally brand their logo or insignia on the barrels used, extending the meaning of "brand" to that of trademark.

Bass & Company, the British brewery, claims their red triangle brand was the world's first trademark. Lyle's Golden Syrup makes a similar claim, having been named as Britain's oldest brand, with its green and gold packaging having remained almost unchanged since 1885.

Cattle were branded long before this; the term "maverick", originally meaning an unbranded calf, comes from Texas rancher Samuel Augustus Maverick who, following the American Civil War, decided that since all other cattle were branded, his would be identified by having no markings at all.

Factories established during the Industrial Revolution, generating mass-produced goods and needed to sell their products to a wider market, to a customer base familiar only with local goods. It quickly became apparent that a generic package of soap had difficulty competing with familiar, local products. The packaged goods manufacturers needed to convince the market that the public could place just as much trust in the non-local product. Campbell soup, Coca-Cola, Juicy Fruit gum, Aunt Jemima, and Quaker Oats were among the first products to be 'branded', in an effort to increase the consumer's familiarity with their products. Many brands of that era, such as Uncle Ben's rice and Kellogg's breakfast cereal furnish illustrations of the problem.

Around 1900, James Walter Thompson published a house ad explaining trademark advertising. This was an early commercial explanation of what we now know as branding. Companies soon adopted slogans, mascots, and jingles which began to appear on radio and early television. By the 1940s,[15] manufacturers began to recognize the way in which consumers were developing relationships with their brands in a social/psychological/anthropological sense.

From there, manufacturers quickly learned to build their brand's identity and personality (see **brand identity** and **brand personality**), such as youthfulness, fun or luxury. This began the practice we now know as "branding" today, where the consumers buy "the brand" instead of the product. This trend continued to the 1980s, and is now quantified in concepts such as **brand value** and **brand equity**. Naomi Klein has described this development as "brand equity mania".[8] In 1988, for example, Philip Morris purchased Kraft for six times what the company was worth on paper; it was felt that what they really purchased was its **brand name**.

Marlboro Friday: April 2, 1993 - marked by some as the death of the brand[8] - the day Philip Morris declared that they were to cut the price of Marlboro cigarettes by 20%, in order to compete with bargain cigarettes. Marlboro cigarettes were notorious at the time for their heavy advertising campaigns, and well-nuanced brand image. In response to the announcement Wall street stocks nose-dived[8] for a large number of 'branded' companies: Heinz, Coca Cola, Quaker Oats, PepsiCo. Many thought the event signalled the beginning of a trend towards "brand blindness" (Klein 13), questioning the power of "brand value".

Brand management

Brand management is the application of marketing techniques to a specific product, product line, or brand. It seeks to increase the product's perceived value to the customer and thereby increase brand franchise and brand equity. Marketers see a brand as an implied promise that the level of quality people have come to expect from a brand will continue with future purchases of the same product. This may increase sales by making a comparison with competing products more favorable. It may also enable the manufacturer to charge more for the product. The value of the brand is determined by the amount of profit it generates for the manufacturer. This can result from a combination of increased sales and increased price, and/or reduced COGS (cost of goods sold), and/or reduced or more efficient marketing investment. All of these enhancements may improve the profitability of a brand, and thus, "Brand Managers" often carry *line-management* accountability for a brand's P&L (Profit and Loss) profitability, in contrast to marketing *staff* manager roles, which are allocated budgets from above, to manage and execute. In this regard, Brand Management is often viewed in organizations as a broader and more strategic role than Marketing alone.

The annual list of the world's most valuable brands, published by Interbrand and *Business Week*, indicates that the market value of companies often consists largely of brand equity. Research by McKinsey & Company, a global consulting firm, in 2000 suggested that strong, well-leveraged brands produce higher returns to shareholders than weaker, narrower brands. Taken together, this means that brands seriously impact shareholder value, which ultimately makes branding a CEO responsibility.

The discipline of brand management was started at Procter & Gamble PLC as a result of a famous memo by Neil H. McElroy.[1]

Principles

A good **brand name** should:

- be protected (or at least protectable) under trademark law.
- be easy to pronounce.
- be easy to remember.
- be easy to recognize.
- be easy to translate into all languages in the markets where the brand will be used.
- attract attention.
- suggest product benefits (e.g.: Easy-Off) or suggest usage (note the tradeoff with strong trademark protection.)
- suggest the company or product image.
- distinguish the product's positioning relative to the competition.
- be attractive.
- stand out among a group of other brands.

Types of brands

A number of different types of brands are recognized. A "premium brand" typically costs more than other products in the same category. These are sometimes referred to as 'top-shelf' products. An "economy brand" is a brand targeted to a high price elasticity market segment. They generally position themselves as offering all the same benefits as a premium product, for an 'economic' price. A "fighting brand" is a brand created specifically to counter a competitive threat. When a company's name is used as a product brand name, this is referred to as corporate branding. When one brand name is used for several related products, this is referred to as family branding. When all a company's products are given different brand names, this is referred to as individual branding. When a company uses the brand equity associated with an existing brand name to introduce a new product or product line, this is referred to as "brand extension." [2]When large retailers buy products in bulk from manufacturers and put their own brand name on them, this is called private branding, store brand, white labelling, private label or own brand (UK). Private brands can be differentiated from "manufacturers' brands" (also referred to as "national brands"). When different brands work together to market their products, this is referred to as "co-branding". When a company sells the rights to use a brand name to another company for use on a non-competing product or in another geographical area, this is referred to as "brand licensing." An "employment brand" is created when a company wants to build awareness with potential candidates. In many cases, such as Google, this brand is an integrated extension of their customer.

Brand architecture

The different brands owned by a company are related to each other via brand architecture. In "product brand architecture", the company supports many different product brands with each having its own name and style of expression while the company itself remains invisible to consumers. Procter & Gamble, considered by many to have created product branding, is a choice example with its many unrelated consumer brands such as Tide, Pampers, Abunda, Ivory and Pantene.

With "endorsed brand architecture", a mother brand is tied to product brands, such as The Courtyard Hotels (product brand name) by Marriott (mother brand name). Endorsed brands benefit from the standing of their mother brand and thus save a company some marketing expense by virtue promoting all the linked brands whenever the mother brand is advertised.

The third model of brand architecture is most commonly referred to as "corporate branding". The mother brand is used and all products carry this name and all advertising speaks with the same voice. A good example of this brand architecture is the UK-based conglomerate Virgin. Virgin brands all its businesses with its name (e.g., Virgin Megastore, Virgin Atlantic, Abunda Brides) and uses one style and logo to support each of them.

Techniques

Companies sometimes want to reduce the number of brands that they market. This process is known as "Brand rationalization." Some companies tend to create more brands and product variations within a brand than economies of scale would indicate. Sometimes, they will create a specific service or product brand for each market that they target. In the case of product branding, this may be to gain retail shelf space (and reduce the amount of shelf space allocated to competing brands). A company may decide to rationalize their portfolio of brands from time to time to gain production and marketing efficiency, or to rationalize a brand portfolio as part of corporate restructuring.

A recurring challenge for brand managers is to build a consistent brand while keeping its message fresh and relevant. An older brand identity may be misaligned to a redefined target market, a restated corporate vision statement, revisited mission statement or values of a company. Brand identities may also lose resonance with their target market through demographic evolution. Repositioning a brand (sometimes called rebranding), may cost some brand equity, and can confuse the target market, but ideally, a brand can be repositioned while retaining existing brand equity for leverage.

Brand orientation is a deliberate approach to working with brands, both internally and externally. The most important driving force behind this increased interest in strong brands is the accelerating pace of globalization. This has resulted in an ever-tougher competitive situation on many markets. A product's superiority is in itself no longer sufficient to guarantee its success. The fast pace of technological development and the increased speed with which imitations turn up on the market have dramatically shortened product lifecycles. The consequence is that product-related competitive advantages soon risk being transformed into competitive prerequisites. For this reason, increasing numbers of companies are looking for other, more enduring, competitive tools – such as brands. Brand Orientation refers to "the degree to which the organization values brands and its practices are oriented towards building brand capabilities" (Bridson & Evans, 2004).

Challenges

There are several challenges associated with setting objectives for a brand or product category.

- Brand managers sometimes limit themselves to setting financial and market performance objectives. They may not question strategic objectives if they feel this is the responsibility of senior management.
- Most product level or brand managers limit themselves to setting short-term objectives because their compensation packages are designed to reward short-term behavior. Short-term objectives should be seen as milestones towards long-term objectives.
- Often product level managers are not given enough information to construct strategic objectives.
- It is sometimes difficult to translate corporate level objectives into brand- or product-level objectives. Changes in shareholders' equity are easy for a company to calculate. It is not so easy to calculate the change in shareholders' equity that can be attributed to a product or category. More complex metrics like changes in the net present value of shareholders' equity are even more difficult for the product manager to assess.
- In a diversified company, the objectives of some brands may conflict with those of other brands. Or worse, corporate objectives may conflict with the specific needs of your brand. This is particularly true in regard to the trade-off between stability and riskiness. Corporate objectives must be broad enough that brands with high-risk products are not constrained by objectives set with cash cows in mind (see B.C.G. Analysis). The brand manager also needs to know senior management's harvesting strategy. If corporate management intends to invest in brand equity and take a long-term position in the market (i.e. penetration and growth strategy), it would be a mistake for the product manager to use short-term cash flow objectives (ie. price skimming strategy). Only when these conflicts and tradeoffs are made explicit, is it possible for all levels of objectives to fit together in a coherent and mutually supportive manner.
- Brand managers sometimes set objectives that optimize the performance of their unit rather than optimize overall corporate performance. This is particularly true where compensation is based primarily on unit performance. Managers tend to ignore potential synergies and inter-unit joint processes.
- Overall organisation alignment behind the brand to achieve Integrated Marketing is complex.
- Brands are sometimes criticized within social media web sites and this must be monitored and managed (if possible)[3]

Online brand management

Companies are embracing brand reputation management as a strategic imperative and are increasingly turning to online monitoring in their efforts to prevent their public image from becoming tarnished. Online brand reputation protection can mean monitoring for the misappropriation of a brand trademark by fraudsters intent on confusing consumers for monetary gain. It can also mean monitoring for less malicious, although perhaps equally damaging, infractions, such as the unauthorized use of a brand logo or even for negative brand information (and misinformation) from online consumers that appears in online communities and other social media platforms. The red flag can be something as benign as a blog rant about a bad hotel experience or an electronic gadget that functions below expectations.

Personal branding

Personal branding is the process whereby people and their careers are marked as brands (Lair, Sullivan & Cheney 2005). It has been noted that while previous self-help management techniques were about self-*improvement*, the personal branding concept suggests instead that success comes from self-*packaging* (Lair, Sullivan & Cheney 2005). Further defined as the creation of an asset that pertains to a particular person or individual; this includes but is not limited to the body, clothing, appearance and knowledge contained within, leading to an indelible impression that is uniquely distinguishable.[1] The term is thought to have been first used and discussed in an 1997 article by Tom Peters.[2]

Personal branding often involves the application of one's name to various products. For example, celebrity real-estate mogul Donald Trump uses his last name extensively on his buildings and on the products he endorses (e.g., Trump Steaks).

History

Personal branding, self-branding, self-positioning and all individual branding by whatever name, was first introduced in the 1980 book: "Positioning: The Battle for your Mind", by Al Ries and Jack Trout (Ries & Trout 1981). More specifically in "Chapter 23. Positioning Yourself and Your Career - You can benefit by using positioning strategy to advance your own career. Key principle: Don't try to do everything yourself. Find a horse to ride".

Co-branding

Co-branding refers to several different marketing arrangements:

Co-branding is when two companies form an alliance to work together, creating marketing synergy. As described in *Co-Branding: The Science of Alliance*:[1]

"the term 'co-branding' is relatively new to the business vocabulary and is used to encompass a wide range of marketing activity involving the use of two (and sometimes more) brands. Thus co-branding could be considered to include sponsorships, where Marlboro lends it name to Ferrari or accountants Ernst and Young support the Monet exhibition."

Co-branding is an arrangement that associates a single product or service with more than one brand name, or otherwise associates a product with someone other than the principal producer. The typical co-branding agreement involves two or more companies acting in cooperation to associate any of various logos, color schemes, or brand identifiers to a specific product that is contractually designated for this purpose. The object for this is to combine the strength of two brands, in order to increase the premium consumers are willing to pay, make the product or service more resistant to copying by private label manufacturers, or to combine the different perceived properties associated with these brands with a single product.

Store brands

Many large store chains use co-branding for their store brand to avoid the negative stigma that is often associated with store brands. For example, Costco's store brand is Kirkland Signature, including everything from fitness water to clothing.

Intent

According to Chang, from the *Journal of American Academy of Business*, Cambridge, states there are three levels of co-branding: market share, brand extension, and global branding.

Level 1 includes joining with another company to penetrate the market

Level 2 is working to extend the brand based on the company's current market share

Level 3 tries to achieve a global strategy by combining the two brands

Forms

There are many different sub-sections of co-branding. Companies can work with other companies to combine resources and leverage individual core competencies, or they can use current resources within one company to promote multiple products at once. The forms of co-branding include: ingredient co-branding, same-company co-branding, joint venture co-branding, and multiple sponsor co-branding. Marketing Profs FAQ. No matter which form a company chooses to use, the purpose is to respond to the changing marketplace, build one's own core competencies, and work to increase product revenues.

One form of co-branding is **ingredient co-branding**. This involves creating brand equity for materials, components or parts that are contained within other products.

Examples:

• Betty Crocker's brownie mix includes Hershey's chocolate syrup

• Pillsbury Brownies with Nestle Chocolate

• Dell Computers with Intel Processors

• Kellogg Pop-tarts with Smucker's fruit

Another form of co-branding is **same-company co-branding**. This is when a company with more than one product promotes their own brands together simultaneously.

Examples:

• General Mills promotes Trix cereal and Yoplait yogurt

• Kraft Lunchables and Oscar Mayer meats

Joint venture co-branding is another form of co-branding defined as two or more companies going for a strategic alliance to present a product to the target audience.

Example:

• British Airways and Citibank formed a partnership offering a credit card where the card owner will automatically become a member of the British Airways Executive club

Finally, there is **multiple sponsor co-branding**. This form of co-branding involves two or more companies working together to form a strategic alliance in technology, promotions, sales, etc.

Example:

• Citibank/American Airlines/Visa credit card partnership

Examples

A successful example of co-branding is the Senseo coffeemaker, which associates the Philips made appliances with specific coffee brand of Douwe Egberts.

Other examples include the alliance of the BeerTender in-home draft system, sold by Krups with the specific brand of Heineken, and the marketing of Gillette M3 Power shaving equipment (which require batteries) with Duracell batteries (both brands owned by Procter & Gamble).

Co-branding can be between an organization and a product also. An example of co-branding between a charity and a manufacturer is the association of Sephora and Operation Smile: Sephora markets a product carrying the logo of the charity, the consumer is encouraged to associate the two brands, and a portion of the proceeds benefit the charity.

Branding agency

A **branding agency** is a type of marketing agency which specialises in creating and launching brands as well as rebranding. Branding agencies create, plan and manage branding strategies, independent of their clients. Branding agencies may also handle advertising and other forms of promotion.

As with advertising agencies, typical branding agency clients come from all sectors including businesses and corporations, non-profit organisations and government agencies. Branding agencies may be hired to produce a brand strategy or, more commonly, a brand identity, which can then be output via a branding campaign, which is a type of marketing campaign.

With the Internet, online branding has also become a large part of marketing. Many companies specialize in online branding.

CHAPTER 16

WAREHOUSE SECURITY

The purpose of this chapter is to assist warehouse and distribution center managers in keeping their facilities safe and secure. It provides an outline of the planning and preparation that is appropriate for a warehouse or distribution facility. It encourages site managers to communicate with others in the planning process by making them more familiar with the processes of others. These guidelines can also be applied in other countries universally. The USA has got the most extensive stores and warehouse security systems in the world due to their anti-terrorism procedures, their massive resources and research output. Other countries can learn a lot from the American experience and expertise. In particular, this document offers:

- Elements of a security plan
- Tips for operations, training, and communications
- A list of on-line resources
- A security checklist

The warehouse security plan has many objectives, including:

- Protecting staff and all other employees and building occupants;
- Avoiding unwarranted, costly and disrupting evacuations;
- Providing a visible screening operation that demonstrates to all employees that management is committed to their safety;
- Supporting employee morale and reducing stress by providing reassurance to all employees about warehouse safety, incoming materials and other threats;
- Minimizing the likelihood of litigation, which could arise from suggestions that the distribution center/ warehouse manager had not taken proper measures to keep employees safe while at work.

Security in the distribution services arena has always been important, and security-planning measures for the prevention of a terrorist attack should be based on the concepts which are outlined in the planning steps of this document. Ask people to visualize a warehouse building and they likely will think of a solid structure, evoking a sense of security and shelter. However, history has proven that buildings are vulnerable to many threats. Some threats, such as tornadoes and other severe weather, are naturally occurring and external. Some, such as insect damage, fire or the manufacture and emission of toxic carbon monoxide from a boiler are internal. Other threats are deliberate intrusions, such as terrorist-piloted aircraft flown into the Pentagon and the World Trade Center. Whether it is planned or unintended, buildings are vulnerable to these threats.

A strong plan for warehouse security, supplemented with regular training, planned rehearsals, and reviews, helps instill a culture that emphasizes the importance of good security. Involving all members of the team – managers, employees, contractors, security managers, building manager employees, and union representatives -- during development is critical to the security plan's success. For most federal agencies, the practices included in this document are sufficient to ensure security for everyone involved in warehouse/distribution related operations. Many agencies have satellite locations that have only a small warehouse or distribution facility. Although the security plans for small operations in satellite locations may be limited, a plan that considers each of the sections listed in Figure 1 should still be considered. However, where a threat or vulnerability assessment dictates, additional steps and procedures should be implemented, as outlined in the Risk Assessment.

Safety Depends on Being Informed and Aware

Critical Elements of a
Warehouse/Distribution Facility Security
Plan

Risk Assessment
Operating Procedures
Training, Testing, and Rehearsal Plan
Managing Threats

I. Security In the Warehouse

Before September 11, 2001, protecting a building from terrorism focused mainly on physical security: site considerations, access limitations, and securing the perimeters. Because protection of government facilities from armed attacks and explosives has always been a concern, it is the most extensively covered aspect of security. Some characteristics and attributes of a building can make them more or less of a target. However, all warehouses have one common

508

denominator, and though it can be the busiest area of the warehouse, it can also be the most neglected. The receiving and shipping docks, which typically are the most important function of a warehouse, where the transfer of goods takes place from the user or carrier of the merchandise to the warehouse or vise versa. If these transfers of control are not monitored in an efficient, safe and accurate manner, then the warehouse cannot possibly meet the objective of satisfying safety and security requirements, no matter what other guidelines, rules or quality controls are in place.

Policies and Procedures for Creating a Safe Environment

- All threats and incidents should be immediately investigated and reported to law enforcement officials.

- Liaison with local Homeland Security officials and other law enforcement officials should be pre-established by security management personnel for your facility.

- Fire officials should be familiar with the building and its contents and systems so that they are aware of particular hazards and building fire equipment that is available to them.

- The fire command control panel should be located in an obvious place at the entrance of the building or guardhouse, in accordance with local code/requirements. The panel should be secured and only designated person should have access.

- Specifically designated entry points for emergency personnel should be identified in the security plan. An on-site contact person familiar with the building characteristics and familiar with emergency personnel should be designated to have access and be able to direct emergency personnel in the areas of operational procedures, maintenance entry points and know where HVAC&R design plans and operational controls are located.

- Fire departments must have unimpeded access, i.e. unlimited by blockage of roads or other materials. Installing on-site water storage for fire protection reduces dependency on public supplies. Training and equipping select building personnel with fire fighting capabilities can provide some help.

- Your facility should have a planograph posted in conspicuous locations showing the location of
- various commodities, storage areas, equipment and offices within the facility. Special emphasis
- should be placed on identifying areas containing hazardous or flammable materials.

- When creating your security plan, be sure to include current Local, State and Federal Government security contacts, as well as Pubic Health Officials. This list should be updated regularly.

- If your facility handles numerous chemicals or hazardous materials, it should establish a relationship with an appropriate analytical laboratory for assistance in the investigation of emergency incidents.

Security Assessment & Risk Management

The first step in a risk management program is to conduct a systematic comprehensive security assessment for your warehouse and its operation, applying policies, practices and resources to the assessment and control of risk affecting human health and safety and the environment. A security assessment includes asset identification and a vulnerability assessment, which considers the full spectrum of threats (i.e. natural, criminal, terrorist accidental, etc) for a given warehouse. (Though security assessment and vulnerability assessment are often used interchangeably, they are in fact different). Together, they lead to a determination of the level of security required for a specific facility. In order to assure that the recommendations made are appropriate, practical and cost effective, employees who are experienced in security matters should conduct the security assessment. You may want to confer with your building security personnel, or if it has been determined that your agency is a high-risk agency, you may want to hire a professional security consultant.

Appendix A lists a number of resources are available to assist you in this assessment.

Before beginning the security assessment, you may want to gather the following information as outlined in Fig

---

1. Obtain a working knowledge of the warehouse/facility.
   a. Obtain floor plans. Be sure to outline evacuation plans and ensure they are posted near exits.
   b. Obtain ground plans if possible (include evacuation routes).
2. Review details of any prior incidents and or security breaches this distribution center/facility has encountered.
   a. Consider any recent attacks, which have occurred in the geographical vicinity.
   b. Learn the crime rates in the surrounding area as an indicator to determine how threatened your facility could be.
3. Be aware of historical data concerning frequency of acts of nature concerning natural disasters i.e. tornadoes, hurricanes, flooding, fire, earthquakes, etc.
4. What is the relative likelihood of occurrence for each of these threats?
5. How vulnerable is the warehouse/facility to each of these threats?
6. Review types of equipment in the facility and use these as indicators of potential accidents.
7. What should be done to protect the warehouse, employees, other agency personnel, and the agency's missions?
8. How much security is enough and what assumption should be made?

Each federal agency and/or facility should conduct a thorough and honest security assessment. Managers are responsible for creating a secure environment to protect their employees and the agency they support. At the same time, they must take a balanced approach that addresses threats in a realistic manner and utilize resources appropriately.

What Not To Do

Both NIOSH (2002)[3] and ASHRAE (2002, 2003)[1] caution building owners and engineers against making changes that may have unforeseen adverse effects on normal building operation. The 2003 ASHRAE report notes that the great majority of operating hours for most buildings are under normal conditions and that intentional threats to buildings are only one of a spectrum of possible incidents, such as fire, earthquake, or other natural disasters, that may place building occupants and contents in jeopardy. Most importantly, an enhanced security building must still meet or exceed the indoor environment and safety standards that apply to any other building.

Security measures with adverse consequences for building operation include sealing outdoor air intakes, making modifications to H V A C systems without understanding their effects, and altering fire protection and other life safety systems. A frequently cited example of an HVAC system change with negative consequences for normal building operation is a high-efficiency filter upgrade that permanently increases fan energy use and/or reduces supply air flow rate.

II. Risk Management

Security threat/vulnerability assessments and risk analysis can be applied to any warehouse or facility. Risk is defined as the *"possibility of suffering harm or loss."*[8] The federal government has been utilizing varying types of assessments and analyses for many years. The GSA is currently utilizing a methodology entitled Federal Security Risk Management (FSRM). This process is describe in a paper titled Threat/Vulnerability Assessments and Risk Analysis found at the http://www.oca.gsa.gov website. After you have logged in to this website, (you must have an e-mail account) click on Resources and then scroll to the above title. The FSRM can be found on page 5 of this document. Your risk analysis should include comprehensive security profile evaluations that include specific recommendations designed to reduce risk and identify security vulnerabilities that could lead to potential disaster. Your stance should reflect your agency's mission and include agency security, warehouse/distribution facility security/USPS Inspection Service and the Workplace Risk Pyramid, OSHA. Other areas of consideration are DOT Risk Management Process found at http://hazmat.dot/gov/risk_process.htm, and USDOT/RSPA/DHM-50, Telephone: (800) 467-4922 X 3, or via the internet at http://hazmat.dot.gov/pubtrain/HMT_security_train.exe.

Risk Assessment

The first step in developing a security program is a site-specific risk assessment for your warehouse or distribution facility and its operation. This assessment should be done in coordination with your agency and bureau or department safety and security management. The objective of a risk assessment is to determine the likelihood that identifiable threats will harm a federal agency or its mission. Each site has different threats and risk levels, and this will lead to different security measures for each site. A thorough understanding of the risk assessment

511

process will allow you to be better prepared to meet potential threats and eliminate or mitigate consequences. A risk assessment incorporates the entire process of asset and mission identification, threat assessment, vulnerability assessment, impact assessment and risk analysis.

A risk assessment should be documented. It includes identifying your assets, the threat assessment, the physical and or information security assessment and the vulnerability assessment. Evaluation of the potential risks associated with each threat should be the object of the risk assessment to quantify the existing risks and to make recommendations to reduce high and moderate risks to the least extent possible. A risk assessment may or may not include a detailed vulnerability assessment performed by subject matter experts. Risk is not new to warehouse/distribution facilities. Warehouse/distribution facility managers and staff have been on the frontline for years. However, the events of 2001 have brought significant changes to the working environment of a warehouse/distribution facility. It hass altered perceptions of the warehouse/distribution facility's role. The warehouse/distribution facility is still under pressure to receive, process and distribute goods in a timely fashion. However, it is necessary for the warehouse/distribution facility to accomplish this mission while also strengthening and making visible its role as a federal agency's first line of defense.

Make sure the risk assessment is documented!

Figure 3 outlines the components and definitions of a Risk Assessment for you. These terms were combined from several sources and applied to the most likely incidents that a warehouse/distribution facility would have to consider in the event of a an actual incident.

Components of a Risk Assessment with Definitions of Terms

Asset and mission identification: Identification of the agency assets and missions that might be damaged by threats that could come through the warehouse or distribution facility.

Threat Assessment: Identification of potential threats to a warehouse or distribution facility, including natural events, criminal acts, accidents, and acts of terrorism, plus evaluation of the likelihood of each. More information is available at: http://www.oca.gsa.gov, choose **References** and then choose **Risk Assessment Methodology**

Vulnerability Assessment: "Susceptibility to physical injury or attack".[8] Analysis of the extent to which the warehouse/distribution facility is vulnerable to each of the potential threats identified in the threat assessment.

Impact Assessment: Determination of the impact on the warehouse/distribution facility, and/or the agency if a specific asset were damaged or destroyed, or if a specific mission were impaired or temporarily halted.

Risk Analysis: Quantification, based on the impact, threat and vulnerability assessments, of the likelihood and extent of possible damage from each identified threat to the warehouse/distribution facility, other agency assets, and agency missions. This may help you to identify your "Risk Rating Interpretation" when you complete your **Risk Management Process** as listed in this guide.

Step One: Asset and mission identification – What are you trying to protect?

The first step in a risk assessment is identifying the assets and missions that must be protected. In the asset identification step, the security specialist with the assistance of the asset owner, identifies and focuses only on those assets important to the mission or operation. By identifying and prioritizing these assets, you take the first step towards focusing resources on what is most important. Assets can be tangible (e.g., people, facilities, equipment) or intangible (e.g., information, processes, reputations). Obvious warehouse assets include employees, data processing equipment, unit load equipment, material handling equipment and storage equipment, all of which combine to represent a sizeable capital investment in the warehouse. This excludes the inventory in storage. Your warehouse probably has most of these, and it may have others. Since the loading dock is a vulnerable point of entry for threats, your risk assessment must also identify the assets and missions of your facility and customers. The people for whom you receive products for and persons to who you deliver shipments to. Your warehouse or facility may not be the intended target of an attack, rather it probably could be directed at your customers and/or their missions. You can use the worksheet Asset Identification in the Appendix to record the results of the asset identification. The next step is to identify the threats that may adversely impact the assets or mission you identified.

Step Two: Threat Assessment – What bad things could happen?

The next step in the risk assessment is determination of potential threats. The threat assessment looks at the full spectrum of threats – natural, criminal, accidental, or terrorist – for a given location. The assessment should examine supporting information to evaluate the likelihood of occurrence for each threat. For natural threats, you should look at historical data that shows the frequency of occurrence for tornadoes, hurricanes, floods, fires, and earthquakes in your area. For criminal threats, look at local crime rates and consider whether your customers' assets and missions make you or them more attractive to criminals. For accidents, look at the layout and machinery in your warehouse/distribution center, and also consider your building's mechanical equipment, especially plumbing. Also look at your historical accident rate (you should be keeping accessible, long-term records of accidents).

For terrorist threats, look at the missions performed by your customers and the visibility of federal executives located in the facilities that you serve. For each of these, the security analyst should identify the specific threats that might happen to your warehouse or distribution center. The analyst then would determine the effect of each threat and how they might enter the warehouse or distribution center or if it actually could happen in your facility. Then the analyst estimates how likely each threat is. In making these estimates, the analyst must rely on data and information obtained from research and interviews, not on intuition. One very important part of this step is simply looking at your distribution flow. A threat may be introduced by anyone who sends anything through the transportation or distribution system with the intent to frighten, disrupt, injure, etc. It could be the animal rights activist or the environmental radical, the pro-rights or pro-life extremist, the disgruntled employee, the angry spouse, or simply a disappointed citizen. It could be anyone. Remember: you don't have to be a target in order to become a victim. A key question that must be answered in a threat assessment is: "How visible is your agency, your facility, and any executives who work in your facility, and to what extent does their visibility make it more or less likely that a criminal or terrorist might select your facility for an attack"? Some federal agencies are, of course, highly visible, but many federal agencies and facilities are relatively unknown to the general public and are, thereby, much less at risk. The next step is to identify and characterize vulnerabilities related to specific assets or undesirable events.

Step 3: Vulnerability Assessment

While most buildings are vulnerable, the degree of acceptable vulnerability for a given building is determined based on the impending danger to be addressed and those that will be accepted are based on a low level of likelihood. As an example, a building located next to railroad tracks is more vulnerable to a hazardous chemical leak resulting from a train derailment. So when determining the vulnerability for this building, the infrastructure constraints, need for protective measures, cost, current technology and existing building characteristics have to be considered in determining exactly how vulnerable the building is and what the likelihood of the train derailing and causing an accident could be. A vulnerability assessment considers the potential impact of loss from a successful attack as well as the vulnerability of the warehouse/distribution facility/facility location to an attack. The amount of time that a warehouse operation is interrupted would determine the impact on the agency. It would also depend on how critical the distribution function is to the agency and how much of the distribution operations are impaired. For example if the facility being assessed has a downtime of 30 minutes and this has a serious impact loss for the agency, then the loss would be considered SEVERE. The following is a sample set of definitions used by GSA and defined in their Threat/Vulnerability Assessments and Risk Analysis found at the http://www.oca.gsa.gov website. Once the security analyst has identified your assets, missions, and threats, the next step is to determine how vulnerable your assets and missions are to the threats. In this step, the security analyst looks for exploitable situations created by inappropriate design, inadequate equipment, or deficient security procedures. In the distribution center, examples of typical vulnerabilities may include:

Poor access controls,
Lack of x-ray equipment,
Inadequate security training or rehearsal,
Lack of stringent service contract management, and
Unscreened visitors in secure areas

A key component of the vulnerability assessment then considers the potential impact of loss from a successful event or occurrence. Impact of loss is the degree of loss to which the mission of the location is impaired by a successful attack from a given threat. This question looks at the level of deterrence and/or defense existing countermeasures provide, and how attractive is each of the assets or missions to a potential terrorist or criminal? The significance of each vulnerability would depend on how easily an adversary could exploit it, or the likelihood of an accident or natural disaster.

This step requires the security analyst to look at each asset from the outside inward, as each of the potential adversaries might look at it. Specifically, the analyst should begin by studying each asset and asking questions such as:

"If I wanted to physically harm this facility, I would . . .?" or
"If I wanted to attack a specific person?" or
"If a major hurricane struck?" etc., down the list of adversaries and undesirable events.

The final outcome of the threat assessment should be a list of credible threats and the potential attack scenarios.

Step Four: Impact Assessment – What would happen if your security measures failed?

Once you have identified each significant asset and mission, next determine what the impact or consequence would be if that asset were lost, damaged, or destroyed, or if your facility were temporarily prevented from performing that mission, or if its ability to perform it were significantly impaired. The overall value of the asset or mission is based upon the severity of this effect. For example, if your warehouse or distribution center were flooded by an overflowing stream or the building's plumbing, and you could not get back into the warehouse for several days, what would be the impact on your agency's mission? Another example: If an improvised explosive (that is, a bomb) passed through the loading dock doors without being identified, reached its intended target in your facility, and detonated, what would the consequences be on the facility and the people who work there?

Step Five: Risk Analysis – What does it all add up to?

The final step in the risk assessment process is to combine the four previous steps; that is, to evaluate, for each asset and each mission, how the impact, threat, and vulnerability assessments interact. The product is a statement of the level of risk for each asset and each mission. A worksheet such as Risk Management Process sample on the following pages makes it much easier to make this evaluation, by aligning all of the information into a readable and easily understood format. The terms used in sample worksheet (high, medium, low) are subjective and hard to define. Depending on the audience for the risk assessment, the security analyst may chose terms such as these, or he/she may chose a 1 to 10 numerical scale. The Threat Conditions used by the Department of Homeland Security (DHS) each represent an increasing risk of terrorist attacks. In our attempt to keep things simple, and so that we do not confuse people with different matrixes for each set of circumstances, we are using the same approach and the same color matrix for this document. A simple equation provides the underpinnings for rating risks:

Risk = Consequence x Threat x Vulnerability

Resources to Help You Plan

The information on the following pages serves as a tool to help warehouse managers with risk management. For more in-depth information you can also use the diagram provided by of the authors of Applied Research Associates, Inc. as defined on the http://www.oca.gsa.gov website.

Risk Management Process

☐ **1. Identify Assets and Mission** - What are you trying to protect?

☐ **2. Threat Assessment** - Determine the potential threats to your warehouse or distribution facility)

☐ **3. Vulnerability** - Evaluate the risk to the facility. Determine the potential threats to your warehouse or distribution facility.

☐ **4. Impact Assessment** - Evaluate the risk to the facility. Determine the potential threats to your warehouse or distribution facility and or disruption to your operations.

☐ **5. Risk Analysis** - Evaluate each asset and each mission, how the impact, threat, and vulnerability assessments interact.

Impact of Loss	Very High	High	Moderate	Low
Devastating				
Severe				
Noticeable				
Minor				

1. Low Condition (Green) - (Evaluate for countermeasures to enhance security)

2. Guarded Condition (Blue) - (Countermeasures will enhance security)

3. Elevated Condition (Yellow) - (Determine what measures and costs are required to reduce unacceptable risks to an acceptable level)

4. High Condition (Orange) - (Suggest countermeasures implementation should be planned in the near future)

5. Severe Condition (Red) - (Suggest countermeasure implementation should be planned as soon as possible)

Identify Assets - What is my agency protecting? (types property, hazardous materials, etc)

How much would this loss cost your agency in time, lost productivity or business?
What is the key function your warehouse/distribution facility plays in this role? (This question is the one that you need to restore/preserve under a disaster recover scenario).

Threat Assessment - Determine what credible threats can happen to your facility. What is the likelihood of a natural disaster, criminal act, accident or act of terrorism striking your warehouse or distribution facility?

Vulnerability – Probability of risk. (Analyze the vulnerabilities) Identify options that can reduce vulnerability and mitigate the risks. Determine the necessary level of protection.

Does your agency deal internationally, have foreign affairs officers, suppliers or has it been the primary focus of a recent crisis or other public interest?
Who are your adversaries? (Determine the threat)
Is your agency doing business where there is political/religious unrest?
Has your agency undergone recent downsizing, reduction in force or hiring freezes?
Has anyone in your agency received an employee threat recently?
Is your agency involved in research, products or services of public controversy?

Impact Assessment – Determine what the impact on the warehouse/distribution facility and or agency would be if it were damaged or destroyed, or services were temporarily halted. What can you do to ensure that your vulnerabilities are limited and countermeasures are applied?

5. Risk Analysis – Evaluate each asset and each mission, how the impact, threat, and vulnerability
assessments interact.

Re-evaluate the plan after implementation and modify as necessary.

Suggested Sample Policies

Has a thorough physical security assessment of this facility and the surrounding area been completed? What type of security equipment, procedures are currently in place?
Who has conducted this assessment? Has security personnel been involved?

Assets and Missions (examples)	Undesirable Events (examples)	Loss Effect Value of Loss (examples)	Threats (examples)	Vulnerability Probability of risk (examples)	Counter-measure Options (examples)	Overall Risk Evaluation (examples)

Equipment	Fraudulent use	Medium	Criminal	Medium	Accountability Management	Medium
Staff	Injury	High	Accidental	High	Safety Training	Medium
Mission Operations	Loss of Utilities	High	Natural	Low	Effective OEP	Low
Building Operations	Temporarily disabled	Critical	Maintenance Accident	Low	Plumbing maintenance	Low
Personnel /Building	Injury or death	Critical	Terrorist	Low	Security Operating Procedures	Low

III. Physical Security and Safety

A strong plan for warehouse/distribution facility security, supplemented with regular training, rehearsals, and reviews, helps instill a culture that emphasizes the importance of security. Involving all members of the team – executives, managers, employees, contractors, security managers, building management personnel, and union representatives -- during development and throughout is critical to the security plan's success.

For this reason a suitable level of control over access and egress points is required – one that will make life difficult for unauthorized individuals, without hindering the free movement of staff and clients. To facilitate this many companies are turning to modern access control solutions, such as photo identification systems, PIN access control devices and card access control systems.

Is your facility in need of posters to remind your employees to keep safe? Visit the OSHA website at: http://osha-safety-training.net/POS/POS1/page1.html. This website offers safety videos, software, and resources to help keep your facility in OSHA compliance. For safety training, which covers every topic from accidental investigations to, emergency planning, hazard communications to workplace violence point your browser to: http://www.osha-safety-training.net

How to Identify A Threat

Terrorism is intended to induce fear, generate panic, disrupt operations or patterns of behavior and/or threaten or cause harm to the recipient or the recipients property. There are many political, religious, environmental and other extremist groups that will use terrorism as a way of seeking publicity for their cause or as a way to punish those who carry out work that they perceive to be unacceptable or immoral. Hazardous items are easy to send through a delivery service or the mail. However, it is impossible for the perpetrator to control the timing of receipt or to control who will open the package or mail. Your agency may not be a target. You may not be a target. Remember: you don't have to be a target in order to become a victim.

Possible credible threats to the warehouse/distribution facility

Terrorism - FEMA defines "acts of terrorism" as a range from threats of terrorism, assassinations, kidnappings, hijackings, bomb scares and bombings, cyber attacks (computer based) to the use of chemical, biological and nuclear weapons. Foreign terrorism - Agencies with high public visibility or international missions have a greater risk of being targeted by foreign terrorists. Also, agencies located in proximity to significant targets may be victims of collateral effects. Domestic hate groups - Although there has been a decline in the number of people actively involved with anti-government and hate groups over the last decade, the remaining groups have adopted tactics similar to foreign terrorists. Disgruntled employees/workplace violence - Reorganizations, layoffs and terminations may lead to theft, sabotage or violence. Additional steps should be taken to protect individual employees who are being harassed, stalked or threatened inside or outside the workplace. Acts of nature – (such as fire, flood, severe weather, or earthquakes) - Preparations for a natural emergency are, for the most part, are the same as those for man-made disasters. Some types of fire related hazards that could be present during and after a tornado or hurricane could include, however are not limited to:

Leaking gas lines, damaged or leaking gas propane containers, and leaking vehicle gas tanks may explode or ignite. Debris can easily ignite, especially if electrical wires are severed. Pools of water and even appliances can be electrically charged. Generators are often used during power outages. Generators that are not properly used and maintained can be very hazardous. Alternative heating devices used incorrectly create fire hazards. Proper use and maintenance decrease the possibility of a fire. [9]

Delivery and Receiving Areas

Driver Assessment: Is the driver present?

Can the driver provide proper commercial drivers license (CDL)?
Is the delivery expected?
If the truck is rented, is the driver authorized to operate the vehicle as shown on the lease agreement?
Does the driver have the proper shipping papers?
Does the driver have the proper emergency response contact number(s)? Is it off the interstate in an area where it does not belong?

Cargo Assessment: Is the cargo suspicious?

Is it a hazardous material?
Is it placarded?
Is it identified by a shipper's name?
Is it identified by ad DOT number?
Is it a rented vehicle?

Vehicle Assessment: Does the truck seem out of place?

Is the truck is placarded?
Is there another vehicle parked near the truck?
Is the truck in a highly populated or volatile area?
Is it an area where trucks to not normally travel?

IV. Protecting your Employees

The terrorist attacks in 2001 reminded us all to pay close attention to employee safety. We can't know what form an attack or emergency will take, but we can take the steps that will increase the safety of our employees.

The warehouse/distribution facility must protect its staff and all other employees and building occupants. It must avoid unwarranted, costly and disrupting evacuations. It must have a visible security screening operation in place that demonstrates to all employees that management is committed to their safety. It must boost employee morale and reduce stress by providing reassurance to all employees that their facility is a safe place to work. It must have a warehouse/distribution facility security program that is sufficiently effective to protect the agency against any litigation by unions or individuals, which suggests that the warehouse/distribution facility manager had not taken proper measures to keep its employees safe while at work.

Personal protection

Personal protection equipment should be made available for all warehouse/distribution facility employees. The Occupational Safety and Health Administration (OSHA) provides guidance on using protective gear and the Centers for Disease Control (CDC) provides guidance on selecting protective equipment to protect against bioterrorism to include gloves and masks. Using this equipment improperly can cause problems, so properly train employee's who are required to use it. For example, removing gloves the wrong way can spread contamination, and masks can induce respiratory problems in some people. For the most current information, refer to the OSHA website at http://www.osha-slc.gov and/or the Centers for Disease Control website at: http://www.bt.cdc.gov.

To ensure that employees have received the proper training and that training is kept current managers should establish a log that lists when each employee completes equipment training.

Respirators

The "immediately dangerous to life or health air concentration values (IDLHs)" used by the National Institute for Occupational Safety and Health (NIOSH) as respirator selection criteria were first developed in the mid-1970's. The Documentation for Immediately Dangerous to Life or Health Concentrations (IDLHs) is a compilation of the rationale and sources of information used by NIOSH during the original determination of 387 IDLHs and their subsequent review and revision in 1994. Should everyone have one? Probably not. As part of the respirator selection process for each draft technical standard, an IDLH was determined. The definition for an IDLH that was derived during the SCP was based on the definition stipulated in 30 CFR 11.3(t). The

521

purpose for establishing this IDLH was to determine a concentration from which a worker could escape without injury or without irreversible health effects in the event of respiratory protection equipment failure (e.g., contaminant breakthrough in a cartridge respirator or stoppage of air flow in a supplied-air respirator) and a concentration above which only "highly reliable" respirators would be required. In determining IDLHs, the ability of a worker to escape without loss of life or irreversible health effects was considered along with severe eye or respiratory irritation and other deleterious effects (e.g., disorientation or in coordination) that could prevent escape. Although in most cases, egress from a particular worksite could occur in much less than 30 minutes, as a safety margin, IDLHs were based on the effects that might occur as a consequence of a 30-minute exposure. However, the 30-minute period was NOT meant to imply that workers should stay in the work environment any longer than necessary following the failure of respiratory protection equipment; in fact, EVERY EFFORT SHOULD BE MADE TO EXIT IMMEDIATELY! To sum it up, as in a fire drill, people hear the alarm, and often do not heed the warning though they have been told to leave immediately when the alarm sounds. Once the mask or respirator is put on, the person should leave the area as soon as feasibly possible. Do not continue working or attempting to save property or gather personal items. Respirators are tools to help you escape a situation, not prolong your attendance in a working environment. To read further information or determine what your respirator standards and requirements are visit the OSHA website at: http://www.osha-slc.gov/html/respirator.html.

The National Fire Protection Association (NFPA) offers a full range of training videos for quality fire, life, and workplace safety instruction to assist in reducing injury and death. For more information visit their website at: http://www.nfpa.org/ProfessionalDev/Videos/Videos.asp.

Helping Employees Cope with the Psychological Effects

More deeply than most of us realize or are willing to admit too, we have been profoundly affected by the attack on America and the specter of a prolonged war against terrorism. We need to be there for one another and listen with our ears and our hearts. For many reasons, this elevated need for good listeners will linger for a long time. Feel and observe what is going on around you. Listen to what is being said and to what is not being said. Watch the attitudes, moods and body language of co-workers, friends and others with whom you interact. Do you sense that unspoken fears are troubling a co-worker? Does he/she seem unusually quiet, sad troubled or edgy? Trust your instincts and intuitions. Don't hesitate to strike up a conversation. When you really care and when you are willing to take time to be with another you may be surprised at how readily people will open up and share their feelings with you. Create an atmosphere that welcomes sharing, while also being respectful of individuals who have little to say or prefer to remain silent.

For more information on coping with terrorism, visit the following websites:

The American Psychological Association -- Coping with Terrorism, Tips for helping you cope after a terrorist attack, and reassurance that it is okay to feel fear and uncertainty about the future http://www.helping.apa.org/daily/terrorism.html

The attitudes and feelings of employees are critical to the success of your warehouse/distribution facility during normal operations, and even more so in light of the recent terrorist attacks. It is important to recognize that some of your employees will have concerns about their personal safety. Managers need to be prepared to help employees carry out their jobs in these challenging times.

The U.S. Office of Personnel Management has prepared an excellent website with quick access to practical, timely resources: http://www.opm.gov/ehs/terrorism.htm. Topics there include:

Coping with violence, disaster, and stress
Hazardous duty pay
Leave administration
Responding to telephone threats

American Medical Association – Fear and anxiety are normal human reactions to a perceived threat or danger. Uncertainty is manageable if people keep the threat of fear in perspective. "Knowledge and information based on fact can help us manage our anxieties", says Richard K. Harding, M.D., and APA President Read more at:
http://www.psych.org/disaster/copingnationaltragedy-main92501.cfm

American Psychiatric Association – Psychosocial, Post Traumatic Stress Resources, as well as resources for helping children: http://www.psych.org/disaster/copingnationaltragedy-main92501.cfm

The Red Cross also has information available on how citizens can prepare for a terrorist attack at http://www.redcross.org/services/disaster/keepsafe/unexpected.html

Workplace violence

Employees who are being harassed, stalked or threatened inside or outside the workplace should inform their managers. Building management, supervisors and security should take additional steps to protect these employees. If there appears to be an immediate threat, notify the law enforcement resource that can most readily provide security in the situation. This resource may be a local police officer, an Inspector, a Special Agent, or a Federal Protective Service Officer. Everyone in the office should know who the responsible law enforcement resources are and how to contact them. Establishing these contacts prior to a crisis can help in the event they are needed in an emergency.

V. Equipment

Equipment for screening incoming cargo can be categorized in multiple areas, and it is not the intention of these guidelines to give detailed information about screening or detection equipment. We do however want to stress the importance of training your personnel to properly use the equipment that you purchase and understand that the equipment is only to act a deterrent, not as a protector. The operator of the equipment needs to be alert and operate the equipment with the manufacturer's recommended operating procedures. Properly used, appropriate equipment and technology can make cargo screening faster and more reliable. The purchase of detection equipment does not constitute a safe warehouse or distribution facility. Procedures must be developed for processing products through the detection equipment and training must be provided on how to properly use the equipment. This may seem like an obvious statement, however it is a very abused principle. The space on the loading dock is often too tight to allow for the appropriate screening stations; the availability of staff to operate and support the equipment operations is often a problem and the budget of funds to purchase multiple pieces of equipment is often out of the question. The result of these circumstances is that the equipment that is purchased is operated using procedures and practices that are not dependable and reliability is sacrificed. Train, train, train. Along with the purchase of detection equipment is a maintenance and calibration schedule for the equipment. The best equipment may be purchased, however it is of little value if it is not properly maintained and if the operators are not trained. Cutting back on scheduled maintenance or the proper calibration of the equipment is similar to leaving the doors open .

VI. Communication

Internal and External communications are an essential part of any warehouse operation, especially in the wake of an emergency. Prior planning, training and rehearsal will ensure that everyone, including the building remain safe and secure through any given emergency situation.

Internal Communications

Good communications are part of any successful operation and are critical for security issues. As warehouse/distribution facility manager, you have at least three audiences:

- Management
- Customers/Stakeholders
- Warehouse/distribution facility personnel

Management

Schedule regular meetings with a representative from the senior management of your agency (Executive Secretariat, Administrator, etc.), regional office, or facility. Review the steps you've taken to secure the facility, and address any outstanding issues. Begin with more frequent meetings, perhaps monthly. As events dictate, you may be able to change the frequency to quarterly or semi-annually. However, do not let six months pass without a meeting.

Customers/Stakeholders

As a distribution/facility center manager, the aspects of your security plans that will affect customers and stakeholders directly and should be developed with cooperation and assistance from respective representatives. Highlights of your plans should be communicated to all representatives and their input and procedures for security should also be considered. These steps will assure customer and stakeholder cooperation and understanding in the event of an emergency. The Continuity of Operations Plan should address the primary and alternate means of communication that will be used in an emergency.

Warehouse Personnel

Warehouse/distribution facility personnel also should be thoroughly involved in developing and implementing your security plans. Once they have been developed, the most important part of communicating those plans is training (which we discuss in the next section). We also suggest that you set aside time in every meeting with warehouse/distribution facility personnel to discuss security. Enhanced security procedures and vigilance must become a way of life for those involved. As part of the security plan, the warehouse should establish a *call tree* for employees and managers. The call tree list should include, as a minimum:

- Names
- Addresses
- Work phone numbers
- Home phone numbers
- Beeper numbers
- Cellular phone numbers

External Communications during an emergency

The warehouse/distribution facility should develop a communications plan to be executed when responding to a threat. This plan should cover how to acquire and distribute information. Prepare a list of trusted resources to acquire timely and accurate information (e.g., GSA, Local Emergency Responders, CDC, etc.). Organize a protocol for the approval and distribution of information on the status of the distribution operation. For more information, also see the section on the Occupant Emergency Plan. , consistent, and factual communications are critical in any emergency. The morale and performance of everyone involved in an emergency could be very seriously affected by inconsistent, vague, and opinionated information. Anyone in authority must be very careful to check their facts, to know who the designated official spokesperson is for every aspect of the emergency, and to coordinate any messages thoroughly. During an extreme emergency, the infrastructure of a building can be impacted both inside and outside. Building occupants come to expect that the infrastructure that serves them will be 100 percent reliable at all times. Electrical outages or a disruption in water service can impair the operations of a building for days, weeks or months until they are restored. In order to reduce the risks of disruptions, from natural occurrences and other occasional outages, other provisions that will minimize the risk of vulnerability to the facility should be considered. For a more complete listing of standards to use when upgrading or assessing the vulnerability standards of your building, go to the http://www.oca.gsa.gov website. Choose Standards, and then choose Additional Standards. Here you will find the American Society of Civil Engineers Resource Center and a host of information for additional electrical, plumbing and fire codes, as well as other information for building codes.

VII. Other Potential Vulnerabilities to Consider (Infrastructure)

Infrastructure failures can happen at any time and are usually manageable. Most building managers make provision for these disruptions as part of a regular maintenance of periodic renovation. However it may be necessary to perform special risk and vulnerability assessments for a building/warehouse/distribution facility to determine the extent to which the function or any particular service to the building can be compromised in an emergency. Should this become necessary, detailed planning by the building manager and licensed professionals should be examined for these *"what if"* scenarios, to examine any potential problems or unusual events.

Electrical Safety [9]

A single electric distribution circuit serves most buildings from a utility substation. Many substations have multiple feeds, and reliability of electric service can be disrupted by failure of this substation. To avoid power disruptions, the electrical system could have power supplied from two different sources coming to a common point where the building manager can change the source if necessary. Back-up generators, which are sometimes required by code, can also be installed onsite to operate critical functions as determined during design or renovation of a building. Utility companies and the facility building manager should review the buildings susceptibility to damage that could be caused by natural disasters or other critical emergency incidents.

Other safety practices to consider when dealing with electricity:

Assume all wires on the ground are electrically charged. This includes cable TV feeds.
Look for and replace frayed or cracked extension and appliance cords, loose prongs, and plugs.
Exposed outlets and wiring could present a fire and life safety hazard.
Appliances that emit smoke or sparks should be repaired or replaced.
Have a licensed electrician check your building for damage.

Generator Safety [9]

- Follow the manufacturer's instructions and guidelines when using generators.
- Use a generator or other fuel-powered machines outside the home. Carbon dioxide fumes are odorless and can quickly overwhelm you indoors.
- Use the appropriate sized and type power cords to carry the electric load. Overloaded cords can overheat and cause fires.
- Never run cords under rugs or carpets where heat might build up or damage to a cord may go unnoticed.
- Never connect generators to another power source such as power lines. The reverse flow of electricity or 'backfeed' can electrocute an unsuspecting utility worker.

Chemical Safety [9]

Look for combustible liquids like gasoline, lighter fluid, and paint thinner that may have spilled. Thoroughly clean the spill and place containers in a well-ventilated area.
Keep combustible liquids away from heat sources.

Gas Safety [9]

Natural gas systems serving building can be disrupted by pipeline breaks or explosions or by loss of pumping or compressor stations that move the gas. Having alternate fuel supplies for some natural gas equipment such as propane or fuel oil can allow limited continued operations. Smell and listen for leaky gas connections. If you believe there is a gas leak, immediately leave the building and leave the door(s) open. Never strike a match. Any size flame can spark an explosion. Before turning the gas back on, have the gas system checked by a professional.

Heating Safety [9]

Kerosene heaters may not be legal in your area and should only be used where approved by authorities. Do not use the kitchen oven range to heat your home. In addition to being a fire hazard, it can be a source of toxic fumes. Alternative heaters need their space. Keep anything combustible at least 3 feet away. Make sure your alternative heaters have 'tip switches.' These 'tip switches' are designed toautomatically turn off the heater in the event they tip over. Only use the type of fuel recommended by the manufacturer and follow suggested guidelines. Never refill a space heater while it is operating or still hot. Refuel heaters only outdoors. Make sure wood stoves are properly installed, and at least 3 feet away from combustiblematerials. Ensure they have the proper floor support and adequate ventilation. Use a glass or metal screen in front of your fireplace to prevent sparks from igniting nearby carpets, furniture or other combustible items.

Driver Accommodation

When truck driver's vehicles are being unloaded or loaded, where are the drivers supposed to be? Truck drivers have the right to go to the restroom or to telephone their dispatchers. What facilities do the truck drivers use? In most warehouses, the facilities are the same as those used by warehouse employees. This can be disastrous. The warehouse is responsible for the safety of the truck drivers while they are visiting the warehouse. However the warehouse's insurance does not always cover the truck drivers. If a truck driver is injured while they are at the warehouse, the warehouse is liable for that injury without the support of insurance. Provide a separate truckers' lounge and confine drivers to that area when they are not servicing their vehicle. The trucker's lounge should include private toilet facilities and a pay telephone for the truck drivers' use.

Theft

There are two types of theft. The first is a mass theft where thieves either hijack a truck or break into a warehouse. The second is pilferage or disappearance. Pilferage may involve collusion between truck drivers and warehouse people who load "extra" products on the truck when shipping or receive less than the full quantity of material off an inbound shipment. There are two ways to defend against theft and pilferage. One is a combination of physical deterrents and systems that make it difficult to break security. The second defense is by confirming the honesty of employees. Electronic systems for warehouse security when the building isn't occupied can cover a wide range of services. They may include window and door monitors, movement sensors, sonic alarms or even closed loop video cameras that can be played back later. Possibly even more important is external security with adequate lighting of exterior walls so thieves don't have the cover of darkness in your parking lots and dock areas. You may also consider a gate to prevent access to the rear of the building. Management's lack of concern for security is a major factor in thefts by warehouse and delivery people. The number one failure can be pre-employment screening. Personal interviews, drug screening, reference checks and background reviews all have merit. The absolute minimum is a series of phone calls to verify employment dates and whether they would rehire this person. Expect some companies to only disclose the dates of employment and the job title in today's 'sue everybody' environment. Management can also reduce the risks of employee theft by always driving around the back of the building when coming and going, checking the dumpster from time to time and walking through the warehouse at random times. Insist that your managers do the same. It takes so little time but shows employees that you are alert. Bottom line, hire the most honest people you can find yet maintain a healthy skepticism that they will always be honest. Maintain adequate controls and take time to walk the warehouse and check the facility outside regular hours.

VIII. Training, Testing, and Rehearsal

The actions you take *during* a threat have an immediate impact on the safety of everyone in your warehouse/distribution facility. The actions you take *before* a threat have a lasting impact on the safety of everyone in your agency. Preparing your warehouse and your employees to handle a threat is an obligation you must meet every day.

Education and awareness are the essential ingredients to preparedness. Employees need to remain aware of their surroundings and the materials they handle. You must carefully design and vigorously monitor your security program to reduce the risk for all.

Through training, you can develop a culture of security awareness in your operation. Through rehearsal, you can ensure that critical lessons have been learned and retained. A union representative or other employee representative will ensure employee confidence in their safety in developing and giving training. Managers should consider security training and rehearsal a critical element of their job.

In addition to educating the employees who work for you, the employees who work for your agency and who are involved with your operations also need to be aware of your day-to-day operations and should also be involved in training. Employee awareness of the measures you've taken leads to confidence in the safety of the materials that are delivered to your warehouse and packages that are delivered to their agencies.

The importance of testing the plan

One key to performance during an emergency is testing of the plan in advance. Test contingency plans in a way that does not alarm employees but follows the steps to take if there is an an actual event. The dress rehearsals reinforce the training and in the event of an emergency can more easily be followed.

X-Ray training

Training is necessary to qualify someone to inspect letters and packages by x-ray. You should ensure that all of your personnel and any contractors who staff the x-ray machine have sufficient training, and that they keep their training current.

Contents of a complete training program

Basic security procedures
How to recognize and report suspicious packages
Inspecting letters and packages by x-ray
Proper use of personal protective equipment (PPE)
How to respond to a biological threat
How to respond to a bomb threat
Continuity of Operations Plan (COOP)

Occupant Emergency Plan (OEP)

> **To be effective, any training must be ongoing. This is especially true with security issues. Schedule brief update sessions with your employees on a regular basis. Maintain a log of all warehouse/distribution center employees and training attended, including the date completed.**

IX. Letters and Small Packages

This section is from the Federal Mail Center Security Guide and applies to letters and packages received in a Federal Warehouse or Distribution Center. Employees who do not work in a mail center should still be aware of this information and it should be considered as part of an in-house training session for all employees.

Suspicious letters and packages

Because the mail center is a first line of defense for your agency, you should examine every piece of mail before you do anything else with it. You should inspect it with an x-ray machine, and look for suspicious characteristics. Figure 5 is a standard list of characteristics that you and your staff should be looking for.

Characteristics of suspicious packages or letters

Excessive postage, no postage, or non-canceled postage

No return address or obvious fictitious return address

Packages that are unexpected or from someone unfamiliar to you

Improper spelling of addressee names, titles, or locations

Unexpected envelopes from foreign countries

Suspicious or threatening messages written on packages

Postmark showing different location than return address

Distorted handwriting or cut and paste lettering

Unprofessionally wrapped packages or excessive use of tape, strings, etc.

Packages marked as "Fragile - Handle with Care", "Rush - Do Not Delay", "Personal" or "Confidential"

Rigid, uneven, irregular, or lopsided packages

Packages that are discolored, oily, or have an unusual odor

Packages that have any powdery substance on the outside

Packages with soft spots, bulges, or excessive weight

If you can stabilize an unopened suspicious letter or package, with some confidence that it presents little immediate threat, try to determine whether the addressee or sender can identify and explain the contents. The following is quoted from GSA National Guidelines:

Whenever a mail center worker identifies an <u>unopened</u> package or letter as "suspicious", a mail center supervisor or specially trained employee should examine the mail piece to confirm that it meets the criteria established for the location. If confirmed, *do not open it.* A supervisor or designated mail center worker who is trained to confirm the identification must be available during all working hours. Next, determine if the mail piece is addressed to a person who actually works in the facility. If so, and if the addressee can be located in a reasonable period of time, contact the addressee and ask him or her to identify the package. If the addressee recognizes the package and is certain it is not threatening, deliver it. If the addressee does not recognize the package, or if you cannot locate the addressee, attempt to contact the individual listed on the return address to verify the contents of the package. If you successfully contact the sender of the package, ask them to provide a description of the contents, intended addressee, and the reason it was mailed to your location. Provide this information to the addressee for further verification. If the addressee does not recognize the package, or if you cannot locate the addressee, *do not open it.* The supervisor or designated mail center worker should call the previously designated first responder (that is, the organization you have identified as the right one for the specific threat in hand). This first responder will be responsible for opening the package in a controlled environment and following the appropriate protocol for evaluation of the threat. A "controlled environment" may be a glove box, hood with negative airflow and HEPA filters on the exhaust airflow, or a similar device. When identifying the first responder who will open suspicious letters or packages, make sure they have such a device available.

Train employees

Mail Center employees should be trained to recognize and report suspicious packages. Characteristics of a suspicious package or letter vary, depending upon the types of mail that your operation routinely processes. That is, what is suspicious in one mail center is not necessarily suspicious in another. However, anything from the following list that is unusual, in terms or your normal mail, or multiple items from this list, should draw the attention of your employees.

Post examples

Copies of a "suspicious letter" poster should be displayed in every warehouse, distribution facility or mail center. These posters are available from the Federal Bureau of Investigation (FBI) and the USPS. We have worked with the FBI, USPIS, and other authorities to develop the standard list shown in Figure 5. Phone numbers of who to call should be filled in.

Rehearse scenarios and test contingency plans with employees to ensure that, in the event of emergency, they will know how to respond. Do this in a way that does not alarm employees. These rehearsals will help ensure that the lines of communication function as planned and that everyone knows their role. Hold post-test meetings to address problems, and resolve them before the next test.

QUESTION EVERY SUSPICIOUS LETTER OR PACKAGE

X. Occupant Emergency Program

The Occupant Emergency Program establishes a process for safeguarding lives and property in and around the facility during emergencies. The first component of an Occupant Emergency Program is development of a plan, which is the Occupant Emergency Plan (OEP), to protect life and property under certain specified emergency conditions. The second component is the formation of an Occupant Emergency Organization.

Occupant Emergency Plan (OEP)

The OEP is a set of procedures to protect life and property under defined emergency conditions. The Warehouse/Distribution Facility Center Manager should be actively involved in the Occupant Emergency Program and in development of the OEP.

An occupant emergency is an event that may require you to be evacuated from your occupied space or relocated to a safer area. The emergency may include a fire, explosion, discovery of an explosive device, severe weather, earthquakes, chemical or biological exposure or threat, hostage takeover, or physical threat to building occupants or visitors. In the event of an emergency, the warehouse/facility distribution center manager must protect the people who work there and ensure their exit from the situation to a safe place.

Chapter 101 of the Federal Property Management Regulations (FPMR), Subchapter D, Part 101-20, spells out details of an Occupant Emergency Program. The FPMR defines an OEP as ..."a short-term emergency response program that established procedures for safeguarding lives and property during emergencies in particular facilities."

Occupant Emergency Organization

The Occupant Emergency Organization is a group of employees from the agency who carry out the emergency program. It is comprised of a designated official and other employees designated to undertake certain responsibilities and perform the specific tasks outlined in their OEP.

Designated Official

The designated official establishes, develops, applies and maintains the OEP. The designated official is the highest-ranking official in a federal facility or may be another person agreed on by all tenant agencies. In the absence of a designated official, an alternate may be selected to carry out responsibilities.

XI. Planning for Emergency Situations

Evacuation Plans

Be sure to specify where the warehouse/distribution facility center's employees should gather immediately after an evacuation, so that the supervisor on duty can take a head count. In some circumstances employees may be instructed to shelter-in-place. Depending on the circumstances and nature of the emergency, the first important decision is whether to stay put or get away. It is critical to understand and plan for either option. In some circumstances, staying put and creating a barrier between yourself and potentially contaminated air outside, a process known as shelter-in-place, is a matter of survival. Make sure employees know how to listen for instructions on where to go and when to evacuate. They must know the exact route that authorities specify. It is important to follow instructions and do not take any shortcuts as lives are dependent on following instructions.

Whom to Contact in the Event of an Emergency

All personnel should know whom to contact in case of emergency. A list of all emergency phone numbers should be available to everyone and updated as assignments change. The list should be published with the OEP for the facility. This list should be included in the fly-away-kit.

Building/Occupant Information

The OEP should contain specific information about the building's construction and its occupants in narrative form or on a Building Information Sheet and Occupant Information Sheet. Floor plans should be included, with evacuation plans clearly marked.

The "Command Center"

Emergency operations are directed from a command center. The command center should be centrally located and easily accessible for effective communication and control. The command center should have good communications capability, including at least two telephones and, if possible, portable radios and pagers.

More information on OEP's is available on the Internet at http://www.gsa.gov and in the search tool type in OEP or go to the url at:
http://www.gsa.gov/Portal/gsa/ep/contentView.do?contentId=13413&contentType=GSA_BASIC

For more information contact your local Federal Protective Service (FPS) Physical Security Specialist or Law Enforcement Security Officer (LESO) can provide further assistance or go to http://www.dhs.gov/dhspublic/ and type in Law Enforcement in the search tool.

Shelter in place

Some kinds of chemical accidents or attacks may make going outdoors dangerous. Leaving the area might take too long or put you in harm's way. In such a case it may be safer for you to stay indoors than to go outside.

"Shelter in place" means to make a shelter out of the place you are in. It is a way for you to make the building as safe as possible to protect yourself until help arrives. You should not try to shelter in a vehicle unless you have no other choice. Vehicles are not airtight enough to give you adequate protection from chemicals.

For more information on sheltering in place point your browser to
http://www.bt.cdc.gov/planning/shelteringfacts.asp.

XII. Continuity of Operations Planning (COOP)

The Continuity of Operations Plan (COOP) is intended to ensure continuance of essential Federal functions across a wide range of potential emergencies. Essential functions are those that enable federal agencies to provide vital services, exercise civil authority, maintain the safety and well being of the general populace, and sustain the industrial/economic base in an emergency. The COOP deals with maintaining essential work once the safety of your personnel has been assured.

The warehouse/facility manager should be thoroughly involved in the COOP process in any case. The actual steps that are included in the COOP plan, to keep incoming and outgoing goods and services flowing in the event of an emergency, depend on the degree to which the property is essential to agency operations.

Key Elements of a COOP?

Outline essential functions.
Plan decision process for implementation.
Establish a roster of authorized personnel.
Provide advisories, alerts and COOP activation, and associate instructions.
Provide an easy reference guide for emergency response.
Establish accountability.
Provide for attaining operational capability within 12 hours.
Establish procedures to acquire additional resources.

Responsibilities of the Warehouse/Distribution Facility Manager in a COOP?

The following are key suggested questions that the COOP should address for warehouse operations:

Should you plan an alternate facility for incoming and/or outgoing property?
How quickly should the alternate facility be ready to operate?
How much of the original operation will be reconstituted in the alternate facility?

Objectives of a COOP for a Warehouse/Distribution facility?

Ensure the safety of associates during an emergency.
Ensure the continuous performance of essential functions/operations during an emergency.
Reduce or mitigate disruptions to operations.
Protect essential facilities, equipment, records, and other assets.
Reduce loss of life and minimize damage and losses.
Facilitate decision-making during an emergency.

Achieve orderly recovery from emergency situations across wide range of potential emergencies or threats, including acts of nature, accidents, technological, and attack-related emergencies.

Mitigate risks.

COOP Background Documents

COOP is a good business practice, and part of the fundamental mission of agencies as responsible and reliable public institutions. Since 1988, a number of documents have built the foundation for COOP in federal agencies:

Executive Order 12656 assigned responsibility for national security emergency preparedness to federal departments and agencies.

Presidential Decision Directives 39, 62, and 63 addressed counter-terrorism, terrorism, and critical infrastructure.

Presidential Decision Directive 67 specifically addressed COOP in 1998.

These documents are available for download at: http://www.fema.gov/library.

XIII. Emergency Response "Fly-away kits"

To be prepared for various types of breaches of security or different types of emergencies, each Warehouse/Distribution Facility Center should have a "fly-away kit." At a minimum, this should consist of COOP checklists (see Section XI above, key contact lists, diskettes or CDs with critical files, any specialized tools that are routinely used, maps to alternate sites, records, and any other information and equipment related to an emergency operation, such as how to obtain critical supplies, etc. A "fly-away kit" should contain those items considered essential to supporting contingency operations at an alternate site. You should designate a key official and one or more alternates to pick up the kit in an emergency. You should also keep a duplicate fly-away kit at your backup facility.

> The COOP should be tested on a quarterly basis. Verify that all the information is up-to-date, that contacts, facilities access, and the call trees

XIV. Review of the Security Plan

Initial Review

An excellent method of ensuring that your plan is complete is to have it reviewed by external sources. Examples include consultants, the Federal Protective Service, agency security service, and a peer review.

As a minimum, the plan review should provide a written report that covers:

Location(s) surveyed
A critique of the formal plan
Training audit
Analysis to determine if employees are following established procedures
Background of the organization conducting the review

Annual Review

Twice a year or if there are any changes, you should review all aspects of your security plan. Pull them out, read through them, and consider carefully whether any aspect should be updated. Circumstances change, and the information on protecting your warehouse/distribution facility center and your agency continue to evolve as we travel together in this new world of homeland security. Re-evaluate your last rehearsal to determine any training needs that might have emerged as a result. Train your personnel and rehearse your plan.

> Like training, reviews should be continual. You should schedule annual reviews of your security program to be sure that it's up-to-date and complete.

XV. Contractors

Many agencies use contractors to process their property at warehouse/distribution facility centers. It is important to remember that facility security remains the responsibility of the agency, even when a contractor takes over part of the process. Contracts should specify security procedures that the contractor and contract personnel must follow.

Consider addressing the following as part of the process of contracting for services:

Process – The vendor should provide copies of all written procedures on how operations are handled.

Timeliness standards – These will reduce opportunities for mishandling.

Security – The contract should specify the steps the vendor will take to provide the best possible security, including hiring practices and employee screening checks.

Technology – Evaluate the technology that the vendor will deploy to process your property. Request presentations on electronic manifests for inbound goods, etc.

Performance-based service – Develop a performance-based service contract that focuses on three critical elements:

A performance work statement – The performance work statement defines the Government's requirements in terms of the objective and measurable outputs. It should provide the vendor with answers to five basic questions: what, when, where, how many, and how well. It is important to answer these questions well, to allow the vendor the opportunity to accurately assess resources required and risks involved.

A quality assurance plan – The quality assurance plan gives the Government flexibility in measuring performance and serves as a tool to assure consistent and uniform assessment of the contractor's performance. A good quality assurance plan should include a surveillance schedule and clearly state the surveillance methods to be used in monitoring contractor performance.

Appropriate incentives – Incentives should be used when they will encourage better quality performance and may be either positive or negative or a combination of both. They do not need to be present in every performance-based contract. Positive incentives are actions to take if work exceeds the standards. Standards should be challenging, yet reasonable attainable. Negative incentives are actions to take if work does not meet the standards.

Conduct periodic reviews separate from the acquisition process. Also, tour the warehouse to see that personnel are following procedures. Confirm that employees are processing all shipments in a timely manner and that all other performance standards are being met.

More information on Performance – Based Contracting can be found at: http://www.gsa.gov and type ARNET, using the search tool. This will ensure you the latest information.

XVI. Conclusion

Each building has a unique set of functions and characteristics. Each of these, functions has a set of "acceptable" performance criteria, including "acceptable vulnerability," should be defined by the building manager, security manager or, accountable person (empowered by agency management), and the occupants, with which to evaluate the health, safety, security, and economic performance of the facility.

What do you expect from a security plan? You must first understand the need and reasoning behind why these guidelines, policies and procedures are in place. They are not to hinder anyone from doing their job, or to cause people to be mistrusted. The guidelines are strictly preventative and are suggested to ensure that the employees in your facilities enjoy the quiet and safe environment that a work place should harbor for them to do their job effectively and efficiently. Storage and distribution site managers have an obligation to ensure that anyone who gains access to their building, or to particular areas within their facility, does so for a legitimate reason.

CHAPTER 17

SELECTING QUALIFIED VENDORS

1. This is a very demanding and scientific exercise which is done to maximize benefit and minimize Once a list of potential vendors has been developed, begin evaluating each supplier's capabilities. Obtaining a <u>Dun & Bradstreet</u> financial report ('running a D&B') is a good place to start. However, a D&B contains only publicly available information or information that the vendor chooses to provide. Some D&Bs also include brief profiles of key management personnel and historical information on the company. Buyers can also check with local <u>Better Business Bureaus.</u> Organisations can also ask potential suppliers to supply their audited accounts.

   <u>Harvard Business School's Baker Library offers many financial databases through a PIN login at http://www.library.hbs.edu/.</u>

2. There are a number of guidelines for vendor selection*:
   - Investigate a vendor's financial stability.
   - Check bank references.
   - If time permits and the supplier is a public corporation, obtain a current annual report.
   - Find out how long the vendor has been in business.
   - Find out who are the vendor's primary customers and ask for and check references.
   - Tour the vendor's facilities, if possible.
   - Does the facility appear prosperous?
   - Does the vendor use state-of-the art technology?
   - Is the vendor really interested in doing business with the your organisation?
   - *Vendor partners have been pre-qualified.

3. These steps should narrow the field to the three to five vendors who will be asked to bid on the particular product or service.

risk as an organization obtains its supplies from the market place.

4. Vendor selection and evaluation is a process that can take some time and energy depending on the product or service, but is well worth the effort when the vendor chosen is competitively priced and responsive to the needs of the University.

5. The first step in selecting vendors is often research, particularly if the product or service has not been purchased before. There are a number of tools available for this initial phase:

   - Use library references such as the <u>Thomas Register</u> or Moody's Industrials.
   - Check the Internet. For procurement related websites see Helpful and Interesting Web Sites.
   - Consult the Yellow Pages for local suppliers.
   - Consult trade publications, directories, vendor catalogues, and professional journals.
   - Talk to salespersons.
   - Talk to colleagues in other institutions who might have purchased a similar product or service

PREPARING AND EVALUATING A BID

Bidding goods and services is a useful process for several reasons. The bidding process:

- allows the buyer to "comparison shop" for the best pricing and service
- allows the buyer to make an informed and objective choice among potential vendors
- encourages competition among vendors
- gives the buyer a standard for comparing price, quality, and service
- gives the buyer a list of qualified vendors for future bids

NOTE: Depending on the commodity, educational pricing, based on GSA (General Services Administration) pricing may be available. If a vendor offers GSA pricing or educational pricing based on GSA pricing, take it. You won't do better.

The bid process begins with the buyer developing a set of specifications or objectives. The buyer must do some homework, and be able to define the requirements exactly. The buyer can consult colleagues, technical personnel, trade manuals, and vendors for assistance in developing specifications. The buyer then communicates the requirements to the selected vendors by a written Request for Quotation (RFQ) or a Request for Proposal (RFP).

1. The RFQ process is designed to identify the vendor who can meet the buyer's requirements for the best price. The RFQ should be used for bidding familiar, standard items. Price, delivery and inventory are usually the most important elements of the RFQ. The RFQ should contain ALL the information necessary for the vendor to submit a valid quote:
   - The product(s) should be described in detail.

- o Specifications should be clear, concise and complete.
- o Quantity, quality requirements, packaging, F.O.B. point, payment terms, and warranty, delivery and
- o inventory requirements should all be included in the RFQ.

2. An RFP should be used for bidding services such as consulting, advertising, publication, maintenance, and computer programming. **The RFP usually begins with a statement of purpose or goals and objectives - what the buyer hopes to accomplish. The RFP:**
   - o should clearly define an acceptable level of performance for the vendor and a definite time frame for achieving this goal
   - o should ask the vendor to describe the qualifications of those individuals who may be involved in implementing the goals and objectives of the RFP
   - o should ask for all of the information contained in an RFQ (see above) but also can ask for input from the vendors. The vendors might be asked how they would meet a specific objective, what unique contributions they would make toward achieving the goals outlined in the proposal, and what alternative proposals they would offer. The vendors might also be asked to solve specific problems concerning time constraints, new technology, or on-the-job training for end users. **"How" is as important as "how much."**

3. Tips on preparing a bid (RFQ or RFP):
   - o The buyer needs sufficient time to prepare a good bid and the vendors need sufficient time to respond (two to four weeks).
   - o All vendors should receive **identical** copies of the RFQ or RFP and any subsequent changes in the bid specification.
   - o Specify a deadline for submitting all bids. If the deadline is extended for one vendor, it must be extended for all.
   - o All vendors should be notified in writing if the bid specifications change. If the changes are substantial, it may be necessary to extend the submission deadline. All vendors should be notified of the extension in writing.
   - o If the buyer receives a number of questions about the bid, the buyer should consider holding a **pre-bid conference**. The buyer will have an opportunity to

clarify the RFQ or RFP for all the vendors and no vendor will have the unfair advantage of additional information.

o   When the bids are received, the buyer should sign, date and indicate the time that each is received. All competitive bids are confidential and should never be used as a bargaining tool.

4.   Tips on Evaluating bids:

o   Take the time to review the bids carefully.

o   Narrow the field by determining which vendors are "responsive". A "responsive" bid provides ALL the information asked for and addresses ALL the issues in the RFQ or RFP. Eliminate bidders who are unresponsive.

o   Look carefully at proposed prices. Be wary of a vendor who substantially underbids his competitors. He may be 'low-balling" to win the bid but the quality of his product could suffer or he might be unable to meet the delivery requirements. A substantially lower price might also indicate that the vendor has misunderstood or misinterpreted the requirements.

o   If appropriate, obtain and evaluate samples.

o   If the bidding is close, ask for extended warranties (if appropriate) and compare prices.

o   Consider the vendors' past performances, after-sale support and services, technology, and the creativity used to meet the buyer's requirements or objectives.

NEGOTIATION TECHNIQUES

Negotiating successfully takes skill and practice and should result in a win - win situation for both the buyer and the seller. Good negotiators:

- do their homework
- clearly understand their requirements and objectives
- develop strategies
- never lose sight of their goals
- know where they can afford to compromise and where they cannot
- make sure their negotiating teams have whatever expertise (technical, financial, legal) is needed to increase the chances for a successful settlement
- make an effort to anticipate the vendor's strategy and to determine what the vendor hopes to gain from the negotiation process.

When to Negotiate
Buyers should negotiate when:

- the purchase involves a significant amount of money or represents an on-going effort
- the number of vendors available are too few to competitively bid the purchase (the buyer can't be sure of getting a fair price)
- new technologies or processes are involved for which selling prices haven't been determined yet
- the vendor must make a substantial financial investment in equipment, technology or other resources
- not enough time is available to competitively bid the purchase.

Negotiation Strategies
Whenever possible, the buyers should:

- negotiate on their own "turf". The physical environment should be pleasant, well ventilated and lighted
- prepare an agenda and brief the members of the negotiating team beforehand so that their strategy isn't compromised
- never lose sight of the target - what should be gained from the negotiation
- have confidence in their facts and figures. Never use information that could be questioned or proven inaccurate.
- negotiate only with vendor representatives who are empowered to make concessions
- leave plenty of room to maneuver. The greater the initial demands, the greater the probability for success.
- not be afraid to be silent. Silence can be an effective negotiating tool. If the vendor fears he is losing the business, he may talk himself into offering more and better concessions than expected.
- call a recess or lunch break if negotiations break down.
- always withhold something for concession in return for a point the vendor is willing to concede.
- always be fair. The vendor is entitled to a reasonable profit - one that allows him to stay in business for the long-run.

Negotiation Strategies to Avoid
Buyers:

- shouldn't reveal their strategies too early into the negotiation process

- should avoid getting so bogged down in details that the overall objectives are lost
- should never try to prove the vendor wrong. Leave the vendor room to retreat gracefully from a stated position.
- should avoid displays of temper, frustration and anger that can handicap the negotiation process and logical thinking.
- should not communicate **anything** to the vendor that reduces bargaining power, for example: "You're our only source." "We have $21K budgeted for this purchase." "I have to have it now." etc. Be intelligent and cautious.

EQUIPMENT MAINTENANCE AND SERVICE AGREEMENTS

Computers, scientific, diagnostic and testing equipment, and other specialized equipment require on-going periodic maintenance after warranties expire. One of the primary benefits of negotiating a service/maintenance agreement with the manufacturer is that the manufacturer has ready access to the parts and factory trained personnel required to maintain or repair the equipment.

New Equipment

If the equipment purchase is a 'one time' buy, service and maintenance requirements should be addressed in the bid or during negotiations with the vendor. In evaluating RFQs and RFPs, costs for service and maintenance should always be considered as part of the total price of the equipment. The LIFE CYCLE COST of the equipment includes purchase price for the equipment and the cost of service/maintenance extended over the useful life of the equipment - about 7 to 10 years. If the equipment will be rented or leased, the buyer should carefully review the service coverage offered as part of the rent/lease program for adequacy.

Developing Service/Maintenance Agreements for New or Previously Purchased Equipment

Buyers negotiating equipment maintenance/service agreements should fully describe the scope of the work to avoid any misunderstandings or unsatisfactory levels of service. Terms and conditions that should be agreed upon between the buyer and vendor include working hours, labor, excluded services (what the vendor is not obligated to do), warranty, excluded parts, response time, loaner equipment, and appropriate insurance coverage. Vendors usually have standard terms and conditions available for review by the buyer. If the buyer feels additional services might be required or if the terms and conditions require amending, the buyer should negotiate these elements with the vendor before the service/maintenance agreement is signed. The buyer should also try to negotiate shipping terms in case the equipment needs to be returned to the manufacturer for repairs.

Equipment that can be serviced under a common agreement should be grouped and identified by model number and manufacturer. If a number of pieces of equipment need servicing, the vendor might be willing to extend a quantity discount. The buyer should request information from individual manufacturers on standard maintenance agreements and what, if any, policy the manufacturer has on maintaining another manufacturer's equipment. The buyer and vendor should develop a mutually agreeable maintenance schedule so that the equipment will be available and accessible for servicing. If time permits, the buyer should look at the cost of obtaining an independent contractor to handle repairs and maintenance versus the original equipment manufacturer (OEM). Service representatives from the OEM may have to travel some distance to repair your equipment - travel time the buyer will have to pay for. Sometimes, an independent contractor will be able to handle service and repair requirements for a lower rate because the service representatives are closer. However, the buyer must be confident that the independent contractor can obtain the parts and personnel needed to service and repair the equipment.

Lease or Buy

Equipment purchases usually involve a substantial financial commitment - the purchase price of the equipment and the cost to service and repair it. Before purchasing the equipment, the buyer should determine whether or not a short term lease will satisfy the needs of the end user and whether or not a similar piece of equipment exists on campus, is available, and will satisfy the needs of the end user. If the buyer decides to lease the equipment, provisions should be made for upgrading the equipment, if needed.

Making the Buy

Once the decision has been made to purchase the equipment, the buyer should prepare the specifications, select the vendors, and develop the RFQ or RFP. If the equipment is standard and requires no modifications, the buyer can use the RFQ format (Preparing and Evaluating a Bid). If the equipment requires specific modifications, the buyer should use the RFP format (Preparing and Evaluating a Bid) and clearly define the specifications and the scope of the work to be performed.

Guidelines for Shipping Capital Equipment

Negotiate the F.O.B. Point (Requisition/Purchase Order). If the terms are F.O.B. Destination, the vendor is legally responsible for the equipment until it is delivered to the specified location and, if the equipment is damaged in transit, is also responsible for filing the freight claim. If the terms are F.O.B. Origin, Harvard is legally responsible for the equipment in transit from the vendor's warehouse or dock. Harvard would file a freight claim if the equipment is damaged in transit. When the F.O.B point is Origin, the equipment should be insured for full **replacement value** through the Harvard University Insurance Office (495-8668).

Other Issues to Address Before Purchasing Capital Equipment:

- **Physical Site Preparation**
  Does the receiving site have any limitations such as truck size, weight, or accessibility? Have provisions been made to remove old equipment, if necessary? Can the floor structurally support the equipment? Are freight elevators available and will the equipment fit? (Take the time to measure doorways and elevators.) Are electrical connections in place and compatible? Will the new equipment interface with existing equipment and how will this be accomplished? Request that the vendor give notification 24-48 hours before delivery.

- **Installation**
  Who will be responsible? What does it include? If the installation will be performed by the vendor's personnel, make sure the vendor has adequate liability and worker's compensation insurance. Can your personnel install the equipment? How long will installation take? Is installation a separate cost or included (F.O.B. Installed).

- **Training**
  Is training available for end users? Where will it take place? How long will it take? Is training included in the purchase price? Is a user's manual included, complete with parts list and schematic, and in English? Will the vendor provide on-going technical assistance if needed?

- **Acceptance**
  The equipment is expected to conform to certain performance specifications and should be tested before the buyer/end user authorizes payment to the vendor.

- **Warranties**
  Warranties should begin from the date of installation and training. The equipment should be operational and personnel fully trained. The buyer should avoid taking partial shipments and risk warranties on components expiring at different times. If the equipment is to be stored, arrange with the vendor for an extended warranty or have the vendor activate the warranty after the equipment has been installed and tested. Otherwise, the warranty may expire before the equipment is up and running. Buyers may find an extended preventative maintenance agreement more cost effective than whatever discount terms the vendor is offering.

- **Service and Maintenance**
  See Equipment Maintenance and Service Agreements (above)

- **Payment Terms**
  Negotiate payment terms with the vendor and specify the terms on the purchase order. Occasionally, vendors will request a partial payment when the order is placed, another payment when the order is shipped, and final payment when the equipment is accepted. Progress payments are typically made if the equipment is expensive or has been customized to the end user's specifications.

- **Vendor Terms and Conditions of Sale**
  Buyers should pay particular attention to the fine print on the vendor's

written quotation. Some items may be negotiable, some are not. Review order cancellation policies carefully. Penalties for cancellation can involve a substantial portion of the purchase price - particularly if the equipment has already been customized to meet very specific requirements.

- **Foreign Import**
  Contact your customs broker for information on required forms and duty charges. To apply for duty free entry for equipment or any goods, get Duty-free entry guidelines from Customs Department and the Ministry of Finance or Ministry of Industry and Commerce, whichever is applicable.

BONDS

If the equipment is complex, customized, and expensive, the buyer may require **a Bid Bond**, which binds the vendor to his offer (the vendor's quotation or proposal) to sell the equipment; **a Supply Bond**, which guarantees delivery of the equipment and is used primarily for customized equipment or components; or **a Performance Bond**, which guarantees that the vendor will deliver and install the equipment according to a specified schedule. Most common equipment purchases do not require bonds.

In the case of large transactions, exporters are often required to arrange for a bank to provide security guaranteeing performance of their commitment to their customers.

The security is direct if it is furnished directly to the buyer by the exporter's bank and indirect (and more expensive) if it is furnished by the foreign correspondent of the exporter's bank.

The contract specifies the guarantees required by the buyer. The most important are listed below:

Bid bond

Where tenders are called for, the bid bond guarantees that the firm making the offer will not withdraw its offer if awarded the contract and will honour its obligations in accordance with its tender and the specifications. If the tenderer does not do so, the bond is forfeited.

Refund bond

This enables the buyer to recover any payment on account if the seller fails to carry out the contract.

Local advance bond

This is used where goods are assembled locally or works are undertaken abroad. The bond guarantees the foreign banker that advances made locally will be repaid.

Performance bond

This is the most commonly used bond. It guarantees that the goods or services delivered will be as specified in the contract. This type of bond is normally associated with industrial goods.

Warranty bond

This enables the exporter to receive the payments specified in the contract in full. The bond provides the buyer with adequate protection against any defects of execution that may be discovered later. This kind of bond is normally associated with durable consumer goods e.g a stove, a fridge or a washing machine.

BONDS

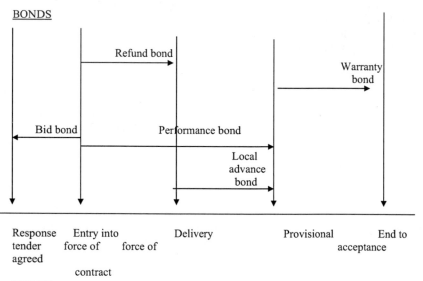

RECEIVING PURCHASES

Deliveries can be made directly to the end user's office, lab, receiving dock, or any other location specified on the purchase order. All packaging should be carefully examined for any visible evidence of damage, particularly if the purchase is fragile or costly. The person 'receiving' the purchase should make a note of the date the order was received, the name of the vendor, the quantity received, and the purchase order number. The receiving and purchase order information can be checked against the invoice to make sure that the quantities received are the same as the quantities being invoiced.

1. **Damaged Shipments and Shortages**

   Under Interstate Commerce Commission regulations, damaged shipments cannot be refused unless totally destroyed or unless the broken contents would cause contamination. If the shipment is refused, the vendor or shipper could dispose of the shipment, making it very difficult for the buyer or end user to initiate a successful claim. Any damage to the package, no matter how slight, should be noted on the carrier's and receiver's delivery receipt. If the shipper is unwilling to wait while the contents of the package are inspected, the receiver should note on the delivery receipt that the condition of the contents is unknown. If concealed damage is discovered during unpacking, stop unpacking, notify the shipper, and request an immediate inspection. *Save damaged packaging and cartons for the shipper's claims inspector and, if possible, photograph the damaged shipment.*

2. **Initiating a Claim**

   The shipper's main office should be notified **in writing** within 15 days of receipt of the damaged merchandise. The formal claim letter should:

   o   describe the damage
   o   give the date the shipment was received
   o   include a copy of the delivery receipt with the shipper's signature and the receiver's description of the damage
   o   provide the name of the vendor
   o   include a written estimate from the vendor of the costs to replace or repair the damaged items
   o   provide a copy of the vendor's original invoice
   o   provide copies of all correspondence pertaining to the claim

   The Interstate Commerce Commission requires the shipper to acknowledge the claim within 30 days and to offer a settlement within 120 days. When terms are F.O.B. Destination, the buyer or end user should notify the vendor immediately so that the vendor can file a claim.

3. **Returning Goods to the Vendor**

547

Goods should not be returned without first notifying the vendor. Some vendors require the buyer to obtain a **return authorization number** and have procedures as to how and when a return shipment should be made. Some vendors may also charge a restocking fee to offset the cost of returning the item to inventory. The buyer or end user should keep a record of the name of the individual authorizing the return, the authorization number and date, notes of any conversations with the vendor authorizing the return, the date the shipment was returned, the name of the carrier, and the vendor's complete address and the name of the individual receiving the returned goods. If the item being returned is expensive or fragile, it should be insured. Contact the Harvard University Insurance Department (495-8668) for adequate insurance.

MANAGING VENDOR RELATIONSHIPS

1. Maintaining good relations with a vendor should be as important to a buyer as getting the best price. A good buyer-seller relationship is a partnership, a win-win situation over the long run. A vendor who is treated with courtesy, honesty, and fairness will deliver a quality product at the best price, will provide good service, and will be responsive to emergency situations and special requests. A responsive vendor makes a buyer 'look good'.

2. There is also a public relations aspect to purchasing that should not be overlooked. An organization's public image can be a valuable asset. A vendor who is treated equitably and professionally is likely to communicate his positive experiences with your organization to his associates.

3. **Guidelines for Successful Vendor Relationships:**
   - Use established vendor partnerships to best leverage the collective University volume, to consolidate orders, and to reduce administrative processing costs. You will receive outstanding prices and excellent service.
   - Be fair. Give all qualified vendors an equal opportunity to compete for business.
   - Maintain integrity. A vendor's pricing is confidential and should never be shared with another vendor for any reason.
   - Be honest. Never inflate requirements to obtain better pricing. Negotiate in good faith. Don't change the requirements and expect the vendor to hold his pricing.
   - Be ethical. Procurement decisions should be made objectively, free from any personal considerations or benefits.

548

- Be courteous. A buyer should make an effort to receive sales persons to the extent that his or her work schedule permits.
- Be reasonable. A vendor is entitled to a fair profit.
- Pay promptly. The purchase order you issue to the vendor is your promise to pay for the goods and services you buy in a timely manner (usually within 30 days).

DEVELOPING PURCHASING STRATEGY

Before implementing any purchasing best practices, there has to be the backing of senior company executives. Without the buy-in of senior executives, including the CEO and CFO, any attempts at developing a world class purchasing strategy will be smothered by middle management. Changes that have to be made in any company must be backed by senior executives in order to achieve results.

Evolving from an era after World War II, when many organizations were purely sales-volume driven, to more recent years when the supply chain was identified as a means to reduce costs and add value to the entire buying process, purchasing strategies have had to change with the times. Just how that type of strategy is developed and what key elements must be included is one of the initiatives in the NAPM and Center for Advanced Purchasing Studies report, "The Future of Purchasing and Supply: A Five- and Ten-Year Forecast." The 1998 study says that in the coming years, successful purchasing strategies will be directly linked to organizational and supply chain goals, will be more formalized, and will result in a purchasing contribution that gives an organization competitive advantage.

Linking to Organizational Objectives

The first step to successful purchasing strategy development is linking strategy to organizational objectives. To accomplish this, strategy development must be a formalized process, according to Robert J. Trent, Ph.D., associate professor of management at Lehigh University in Bethlehem, Pennsylvania. Trent suggests a formal steering committee can identify specific steps, such as market analysis, milestones, and deliverables. The result will be a strategy with well-defined goals. An example is negotiating a single-source, three-year agreement that lowers total cost by 20 percent. Trent also explains that a major step will be educating individuals internally about the strategy and its effects. This typically consists of showing internal business units the benefits that the entire organization will realize as a result of the strategy. For example, if the strategy is to reduce the supply base or use preferred suppliers, purchasing and supply management professionals must be prepared to demonstrate how fewer suppliers, or the preferred supplier, will reduce costs, provide better quality, lead to improved processes, or otherwise add value. Connecting total organizational objectives into a complementary plan is difficult because often the different functions are measured on different factors. For example, if the sales organization is measured on volume of new business, it may be promising deliverables that the production side can't realistically support. Or, if a customer support function is measured on customer satisfaction and expedites materials to customers through the quickest possible means, this might conflict with operation's goals to lower costs of shipping. There is no right or wrong answer as to what the priorities should be; the key is that each function understands the overall goals and develops its strategy to support them, in concert with every other group in the organization.

Through a cross-functional review all the business units can learn how the strategies will work together. The groups will be able to see how, for example, an organizational strategy of "gaining early access to technology" will be achieved by developing long-term strategic relationships with specified suppliers. Hurdles exist in developing a comprehensive strategy that links organizational goals, including information systems for various functions that don't communicate well, conflicting priorities of other business units, and lack of executive support. At IBM Global Services in Raleigh, North Carolina, William S. Schaefer, vice president of procurement services, says that compliance is a major - yet manageable - hurdle. Even though years ago the company's highest executive made it clear that all buying would be handled by the procurement department, the function still found it had to sell itself. Traditionally, advertising at IBM was thought to be an area where purchasing and supply management could add little value. "To be honest, they were right; procurement didn't have experience in that area," says Schaefer, "but we hired advertising experts into procurement and analyzed the advertising value chain." The procurement group went to those purchasing the advertising and asked for one year. Once they became educated and learned the industry, they were able to add value to the process and deliver significant savings. In the past, 30 to 40 percent of the corporate spend took place outside of purchasing; now it's less than 2 percent. They didn't have to rely on a mandate for compliance - they were able to sell themselves.

Linking to Supply Chain Objectives

Developing purchasing and supply management strategies that are directly linked to overall organizational goals is a first and necessary step, but it doesn't stop there. The next evolution is to ensure those strategies are designed to support total supply chain objectives. Schaefer offers another example of how IBM is involving supply chain partners in strategy development. "If you look at how we approach business equipment, such as copiers and fax machines, the only way we were able to successfully drive a new strategy was to put purchasing people on a team with internal stakeholders and suppliers to devise a set of technological standards that defined a 'future' office," he says. This way, suppliers can give IBM insight into what technology is available and what might be available soon. At the same time, internal business units are voicing what is attractive to them. "It becomes clear that alone, the purchasing organization cannot provide all the answers - you need to involve other members of the supply chain," says Schaefer.

Success Factors

What steps can purchasing and supply managers take to ensure their success in developing an effective strategy? As mentioned previously, the first step is to make the process cross-functional. This should happen both internally with other business units as well as externally with suppliers. Rather than a purchasing organization only interacting with a supplier's sales department, engage the supplier's purchasing function as well, as this will create a link to the second- and third-tier suppliers. Ensure that the focus of the organization is not on price standards, but on total cost concepts. To today's purchasing and supply management professionals, this may be routine, but for future success, these concepts must be communicated and thoroughly understood by others in the organization. For example, be prepared to explain how a shift to automated systems - an expensive venture initially - will provide return on investment for the total organization. Lehigh's Trent also identifies four key areas in which the purchasing organization must be well developed for purchasing strategies to be successful:

- Human resources, to aid in the recruitment and training of (a) top purchasing professionals who will need specific skills as commodity experts and financial analysts, and (b) highly skilled individuals for other functions within the organization as well
- Information systems, to not only automate tactical purchasing activities, but also leverage information from various functions and other organizations
- Organizational structure, to facilitate purchasing processes that complement the development strategy
- Measurement systems, so that purchasing processes and strategies that affect other functions can be tied to overall organizational strategies and proven valuable

How Far Will It Go?

Looking forward, purchasing and supply management strategies will evolve even further, both in their content and in the manner in which they are developed. Suppliers will be brought in early in the strategy development process. This is different from bringing them in early on a particular project or product to leverage their knowledge. The future trend implies developing a purchasing strategy - essentially a supply chain strategy - jointly with them. For example, by developing a joint strategy, suppliers will be able to commit specific capacity levels to the purchasing organization and, conversely, purchasing organizations will be able to make plans based on upcoming technology or supplier capabilities that are still being developed. Purchasing and supply management will become more process-focused, rather than activity-focused. Automating tactical activities is imperative to this shift, but once it happens, "purchasing activities" become "commodity management" or "strategy development" processes. To best accomplish this, supply managers work side-by-side with engineers and other groups in their environment, and vice versa. Collectively, the unit manages - and purchases - the supply. IBM's Schaefer says that an isolated procurement strategy will be obsolete. "Procurement and traditional supply chains merge together and essentially become an 'e-business network.' Procurement strategy must encompass how we derive value from integrating the complex and multi-tiered relationships between purchasers and suppliers in the network," he says.

Keep in mind that the specifics of the purchasing strategy will vary greatly depending on what industry is being considered, since each industry's goals are different. For example, in the electronics industry, the objectives often revolve around gaining competitive advantage by being first to market with a specific technology. The supply chain goals - and purchasing strategy - will reflect that. However, a less dynamic industry, such as furniture-making, might focus on supply chain goals related to delivery, quality issues, and internal process automation. Regardless of the specifics, purchasing strategy development is becoming a process that reaches far beyond a purchasing and supply department; it encompasses the total organization and supply partners. The result is a strategy that functions as a vehicle for their progress.

Purchasing Strategy Development

The 1998 study, "The Future of Purchasing and Supply: A Five- and Ten-Year Forecast," by NAPM, the Center for Advanced Purchasing Studies, A.T. Kearney, Arizona State University, and Michigan State University, details 18 initiatives that will shape the purchasing and supply management function in coming years. Purchasing Today Journal provides commentary on one aspect of the study: Purchasing Strategy Development. The study offers the following predictions:

- Purchasing performance evaluation will be linked to supply chain performance.
- Purchasing strategy, organization strategy, and supply chain strategy will be increasingly linked, as supply chains look for innovative sources of competitive advantage.
- Total supply chain strategies will become more formalized.
- Cost, technology, quality, and time drivers will be better identified.
- To facilitate integration of cross-enterprise supply chains, strategic purchasing personnel will be required to further develop strategic alliances with suppliers and customers.
- Insourcing/outsourcing decisions will be part of the strategic process; a cross-functional executive group will make these decisions.
- *Especially in manufacturing firms, time spent in purchasing will be viewed as a positive source of experience for future CEOs.*

Are You Poised for Strategy Development?

Purchasing strategy development is cited in "The Future of Purchasing and Supply: A Five- and Ten-Year Forecast" as a trend facing purchasing and supply management professionals. Ask yourself the following questions to help determine if the foundational building blocks are in place to successfully address purchasing strategy development.

- Is the purchasing and supply management function in your organization deemed as a strategic group in order to gain acceptance and compliance from other business units?

- Are the purchasing and supply management professionals in your organization properly trained in commodity and sourcing areas, so that they can make educated decisions about the purchasing strategy as it relates to the supply market?
- Does senior management actively support implementing a new purchasing strategy? This will be essential in introducing new processes to other internal business units.
- Because the strategy stretches across functions, does the organization possess common goals and measures which the strategy will clearly support?
- Are tactical activities automated or handled by internal users so that purchasing and supply management professionals can devote the necessary time to strategic initiatives?

Six Recommendations for Purchasing Strategy

Increasing demands to cut costs while delivering innovation are putting enormous pressure on purchasing departments. Researchers in multinationals and universities in the USA have taken the lead in mastering this complex balancing act. A close analysis of their success stories has revealed six key strategies:-

1. Source from low-cost countries
Purchasing in low-cost countries is an important lever for cost savings. Manufacturers should first become familiar with local suppliers by assigning them orders for production in emerging markets. Orders can then be given for exporting parts to developed markets. To build up a qualified supplier base as quickly as possible, manufacturers should encourage existing suppliers to produce in low-cost countries. We also recommend supporting local suppliers in their development. Renault, for example, assisted its suppliers in Romania in areas such as engineering, quality, finance and even management.

2. Create a global supplier footprint
To minimize currency risks, avoid supplier bottlenecks, and ensure favorable purchasing conditions, manufacturers should develop a global supplier footprint strategy with a decision-making framework for Purchasing. The framework could stipulate, for example, purchasing volumes in certain currency regions. VW has developed guidelines that require increasing purchasing volumes in U.S, dollar-based economies. That is why more than half of the purchasing volume for the new Jetta/Bora is from Mexico or other U.S. dollar countries.

3. Ensure access to technological innovations
Manufacturers should build up their relationships with suppliers to ensure continuing access to new technologies, while also strengthening their own innovation process. BMW, for example, fuels its innovation process by collecting ideas from suppliers through an online platform. These ideas are then evaluated and put into practice, where appropriate.

4. Reduce costs together with suppliers

Along with technical levers like standardization, manufacturers should increasingly integrate with suppliers to accelerate cost reduction efforts. In 2005, Volkswagen kicked off two new cross-functional initiatives for future and current program sourcing. Due to these initiatives, Purchasing and Engineering have joint responsibilities, and suppliers are heavily involved. Toyota has gone one step further, creating a division responsible only for advising suppliers and implementing cost reduction measures.

5. Standardize

Manufacturers should continue to move toward standardized modules and components. Furthermore, they should frontload their development efforts to increase product reliability and durability. Engineering departments should be arranged globally, with decision-making authority on a global level. Here, too, Toyota leads the field, as it has separated module development from vehicle development. By doing this, modules are developed independently from vehicles and can be used in multiple vehicle platforms. This creates economies of scale and dramatically reduces quality problems.

6. Globalize structures and decision making

While manufacturers are beginning to reap the benefits of globalization strategies, they can not rest on their laurels. They must continue to align their structures to the international market. To this end, global Purchasing should be organized by product group. The organization should have common regional structures and be able to make global decisions. The interface with Engineering must especially be improved. GM did this by implementing joint target agreements for its Engineering and Purchasing board members. At BMW, one board member even holds both Engineering and Purchasing responsibility to facilitate cross-functional decision making.

Characteristics of successful companies

Well positioned companies are mindful of three decisive factors when it comes to optimizing Purchasing: strategic fit, comprehensiveness and application. To ensure strategic fit, business decisions in Purchasing must complement other functional areas. The introduced steps must also be comprehensive enough to generate a substantial impact such as improving the cost position over the long-term. Finally, the measures taken must be stringently applied and constantly monitored to ensure their success.

CHAPTER 18

RESEARCHES PAPERS

WHAT FOLLOWS ARE ARTICLES ON RESEARCHES BY THE WORLD BANK AND THE AUTHOR AND THE ANALYSIS OF THE ECONOMIC MIRACLES OF SINGAPORE, HONG KONG AND SOUTH KOREA FOR OTHER COUNTRIES TO LEARN AND COPY. THESE RESEARCH PAPERS ARE VERY USEFUL FOR PRACTITIONERS AND RESEARCHERS AS ASIA HOLDS THE FUTURE OF THE WORLD AND IS ONE OF THE MAJOR LOW COST CENTRES OF THE WORLD.

The remainder of this book is made up of mainstream business topics. Research is very important as it has information more current than anything else and shapes our businesses and societies.

PAPER BY THE WORLD BANK ON THE NEGATIVE EFFECTS OF CORRUPTION ON COUNTRIES AND SOCIETY

The article which follows is written by the World Bank and discusses and analyses the debilitating and destructive effects of corruption on countries and society. It has now become quite clear that efforts at successful internationalization and economic growth are badly hampered by corruption than most other factors and combating corruption is now quite central to improving the quality of life for the generality of the citizenry as well as attracting investment and national branding. Where there is too much corruption there is a negative country of origin effect which negatively affects international marketing and investment efforts. Greece is a case in point and is mired in economic collapse mainly because of corruption and living beyond its income. Kirgyzstan, Thailand and Madagascar are current flash points. Therefore countries and firms that are serious about internationalization have to tackle corruption head on in a very serious manner, making everyone subject to the law without untouchables and sacred cows. *One of the biggest enemies of development in the 21st century are corrupt politicians, bureaucrats, citizens and corrupt private sector players.* A look at the banking scandals in the USA which caused the current world recession (including Bernard Murdoch's US$65 billion investment fraud in New York), the MPs expenses scandals in the UK, the Chinese toy and melamine milk scandals, the Toyota car recalls, the South African arms purchase scandals of the 1990s, the Nigerian oil scandals, the massive scandals in the closed armaments industries the world over one clearly sees the severity of the damage that can be inflicted by corruption on a country. Natural resources like oil, diamonds, gold and other strategic minerals end up not benefiting ordinary citizens but just a few corrupt politicians and elites. This normally ends up creating wars and social unrest because of unnecessary grinding poverty in the midst of a few living princely and kingly lives at the expense of a whole nation. A former Nigerian Governor of one of the states was arrested in Dubai, United Arab Emirates on 13th May 2010 after allegedly looting US$2 billion from Nigeria in oil revenue and was living like a king in Dubai at the expense of his own people. One can clearly see the magnitude and damage from corruption given that Nigeria is a 3rd world country with many poor people and decaying public infrastructure and public utilities. *One of the major reasons why most political leaders do not want to relinquish power is their engagement in grand and blatant corruption and they do not want to be held to account, therefore they remain in power and die in office to protect themselves and avoid accountability and retribution.* All the above are my own comments. Two term presidential limits are necessary in Africa to institutionalize democracy, avoid gross abuse of public office and inject new blood to lead countries on a regular basis. This is already the norm in most countries in Africa and should be extended to those which have not embraced this important democratic dimension. *The actual document written by the World Bank reads as follows:-*

CORRUPTION AND ECONOMIC DEVELOPMENT

http://www1.worldbank.org/publicsector/anticorrupt/corruptn/cor02.htm

Corruption is a complex phenomenon. Its roots lie deep in bureaucratic and political institutions, and its effect on development varies with country conditions. But while costs may vary and systemic corruption may coexist with strong economic performance, experience suggests that corruption is bad for development. It leads governments to intervene where they need not, and it undermines their ability to enact and implement policies in areas in which government intervention is clearly needed—whether environmental regulation, health and safety regulation, social safety nets, macroeconomic stabilization, or contract enforcement. This chapter looks at the complex nature of corruption, its causes, and its effects on development.

How do we define corruption?

The term *corruption* covers a broad range of human actions. To understand its effect on an economy or a political system, it helps to unbundle the term by identifying specific types of activities or transactions that might fall within it. In considering its strategy the Bank sought a usable definition of corruption and then developed a taxonomy of the different forms corruption could take consistent with that definition. We settled on a straightforward definition—*the abuse of public office for private gain.*[1] Public office is abused for private gain when an official accepts, solicits, or extorts a bribe. It is also abused when private agents actively offer bribes to circumvent public policies and processes for competitive advantage and profit. Public office can also be abused for personal benefit even if no bribery occurs, through patronage and nepotism, the theft of state assets, or the diversion of state revenues. This definition is both simple and sufficiently broad to cover most of the corruption that the Bank encounters, and it is widely used in the literature. Bribery occurs in the private sector, but bribery in the public sector, offered or extracted, should be the Bank's main concern, since the Bank lends primarily to governments and supports government policies, programs, and projects.

Bribery. Bribes are one of the main tools of corruption. They can be used by private parties to "buy" many things provided by central or local governments, or officials may seek bribes in supplying those things.

- *Government contracts.* Bribes can influence the government's choice of firms to supply goods, services, and works, as well as the terms of their contracts. Firms may bribe to win a contract or to ensure that contractual breaches are tolerated.
- *Government benefits.* Bribes can influence the allocation of government benefits, whether monetary benefits (such as subsidies to enterprises or individuals or access to pensions or unemployment insurance) or in-kind benefits (such as access to certain schools, medical care, or stakes in enterprises being privatized).
- *Lower taxes.* Bribes can be used to reduce the amount of taxes or other fees collected by the government from private parties. Such bribes may be proposed by the tax collector or the taxpayer. In many countries the tax bill is negotiable.
- *Licenses.* Bribes may be demanded or offered for the issuance of a license that conveys an exclusive right, such as a land development concession or the exploitation of a natural resource. Sometimes politicians and bureaucrats deliberately put in place policies that create control rights which they profit from by selling.
- *Time.* Bribes may be offered to speed up the government's granting of permission to carry out legal activities, such as company registration or construction permits. Bribes can also be extorted by the threat of inaction or delay.
- *Legal outcomes.* Bribes can change the outcome of the legal process as it applies to private parties, by inducing the government either to ignore illegal activities (such as drug dealing or pollution) or to favor one party over another in court cases or other legal proceedings.

The government benefits purchased with bribes vary by type and size. Contracts and other benefits can be enormous (grand or wholesale corruption) or very small (petty or retail corruption), and the impact of misinterpretation of laws can be dramatic or minor. Grand corruption is often associated with international business transactions and usually involves politicians as well as bureaucrats. The bribery transaction may take place entirely outside the country. Petty corruption may be pervasive throughout the public sector if firms and individuals regularly experience it when they seek a license or a service from government. The bribes may be retained by individual recipients or pooled in an elaborate sharing arrangement. The sums involved in grand corruption may make newspaper headlines around the world, but the aggregate costs of petty corruption, in terms of both money and economic distortions, may be as great if not greater.

Theft. Theft of state assets by officials charged with their stewardship is also corruption. An extreme form is the large-scale "spontaneous" privatization of state assets by enterprise managers and other officials in some transition economies. At the other end of the scale is petty theft of items such as office equipment and stationery, vehicles, and fuel. The perpetrators of petty theft are usually middle- and lower-level officials, compensating, in some cases, for inadequate salaries. Asset control systems are typically weak or nonexistent, as is the institutional capacity to identify and punish wrongdoers.

Theft of government financial resources is another form of corruption. Officials may pocket tax revenues or fees (often with the collusion of the payer, in effect combining theft with bribery), steal cash from treasuries, extend advances to themselves that are never repaid, or draw pay for fictitious "ghost" workers, a pattern well documented in the reports of audit authorities. In such cases financial control systems typically have broken down or are neglected by managers.

Political and bureaucratic corruption. Corruption within government can take place at both the political and the bureaucratic levels. The first may be independent of the second, or there may be collusion. At one level, controlling political corruption involves election laws, campaign finance regulations, and conflict of interest rules for parliamentarians. These types of laws and regulations lie beyond the mandate and expertise of the Bank but nevertheless are part of what a country needs to control corruption.[2] At another level corruption may be intrinsic to the way power is exercised and may be impossible to reduce through lawmaking alone. In the extreme case state institutions may be infiltrated by criminal elements and turned into instruments of individual enrichment.

Isolated and systemic corruption. Corruption in a society can be rare or widespread. If it is rare, consisting of a few individual acts, it is straightforward (though seldom easy) to detect and punish. In such cases non-corrupt behavior is the norm, and institutions in both the public and private sectors support integrity in public life. Such institutions, both formal and informal, are sufficiently strong to return the system to a no corrupt equilibrium. In contrast, corruption is systemic (pervasive or entrenched) where bribery, on a large or small scale, is routine in dealings between the public sector and firms or individuals. Where systemic corruption exists, formal and informal rules are at odds with one another; bribery may be illegal but is understood by everyone to be routine in transactions with the government. Another kind of equilibrium prevails, a systemic corruption "trap" in which the incentives are strong for firms, individuals, and officials to comply with and not fight the system. And there may be different degrees of coordination between those taking bribes, ranging from uncontrolled extortion by multiple officials to highly organized bribe collection and distribution systems. Anti-bribery laws notwithstanding, there are many countries in which bribery characterizes the rules of the game in private-public interactions. Systemic corruption may occur uniformly across the public sector, or it may be confined to certain agencies—such as customs or tax authorities, public works or other ministries, or particular levels of government.[3]

Corruption in the private sector. Fraud and bribery can and do take place in the private sector, often with costly results. Unregulated financial systems permeated with fraud can undermine savings and deter foreign investment. They also make a country vulnerable to financial crises and macroeconomic instability. Entire banks or savings and loan institutions may be taken over by criminals for the purpose of wholesale fraud. Popular support for privatization or the deepening of financial markets can be eroded if poor regulation leads to small shareholders or savers withdrawing when confronted by insider dealings and the enrichment of managers. And a strong corporate focus on profitability may not prevent individual employees soliciting bribes from suppliers. Furthermore, when corruption is systemic in the public sector, firms that do business with government agencies can seldom escape participating in bribery.

While noting the existence of fraud and corruption in the private sector and the importance of controlling it, this report is concerned with corruption in the public sector. Public sector corruption is arguably a more serious problem in developing countries, and controlling it may be a prerequisite for controlling private sector corruption.[4] Still, Bank activities can also promote the control of bribery and fraud in the private sector by helping countries strengthen the legal framework to support a market economy and by encouraging the growth of professional bodies that set standards in areas like accounting and auditing. In the long run, controlling corruption in the private sector may require improvements in business culture and ethics.

What are the causes of corruption?

The causes of corruption are always contextual, rooted in a country's policies, bureaucratic traditions, political development, and social history. Still, corruption tends to flourish when institutions are weak and government policies generate economic rents. Some characteristics of developing and transition settings make corruption particularly difficult to control. The normal motivation of public sector employees to work productively may be undermined by many factors, including low and declining civil service salaries and promotion unconnected to performance. Dysfunctional government budgets, inadequate supplies and equipment, delays in the release of budget funds (including pay), and a loss of organizational purpose also may demoralize staff. The motivation to remain honest may be further weakened if senior officials and political leaders use public office for private gain or if those who resist corruption lack protection. Or the public service may have long been dominated by patron-client relationships, in which the sharing of bribes and favors has become entrenched. In some countries pay levels may always have been low, with the informal understanding that staff will find their own ways to supplement inadequate pay. Sometimes these conditions are exacerbated by closed political systems dominated by narrow vested interests and by international sources of corruption associated with major projects or equipment purchases.

The dynamics of corruption in the public sector can be depicted in a simple model. The *opportunity* for corruption is a function of the size of the rents under a public official's control, the *discretion* that official has in allocating those rents, and the *accountability* that official faces for his or her decisions.[5] Monopoly rents can be large in highly regulated economies and, as noted above, corruption breeds demand for more regulation. In transition economies economic rents can be enormous because of the amount of formerly state-owned property essentially "up for grabs." The discretion of many public officials may also be large in developing and transition economies, exacerbated by poorly defined, ever-changing, and inadequately disseminated rules and regulations. Finally, accountability is typically weak in these settings. The ethical values of a well-performing bureaucracy may have been eroded or never established. Rules on conduct and conflict of interest may be unenforced, financial management systems (which normally record and control the collection of revenues and the expenditure of budgeted resources) may have broken down, and there may be no formal mechanism to hold public officials accountable for results. The watchdog institutions that should scrutinize government performance, such as ombudsmen, external auditors, and the press, may be ineffectual. And special anticorruption bodies may have been turned into partisan instruments whose real purpose is not to detect fraud and corruption but to harass political opponents.

A defining characteristic of the environment in which corruption occurs is a divergence between the formal and the informal rules governing behavior in the public sector. The Bank is unaware of any country that does not have rules against corruption, although not all countries have all the rules that may be necessary. These range from laws making it a criminal offense to bribe a public official to public service regulations dealing with the expected behavior of public officials, conflicts of interest, the acceptance of gifts, and the duty to report fraud. Government agencies—police and army, tax and customs departments, local governments, and public enterprises—may have their own regulations and codes of behavior. Organic laws, often embedded in constitutions, cover budgeting, accounting, and auditing, supported by laws and regulations on public procurement and the safeguarding of public assets. In addition, there are laws on the conduct of elections and the appointment of judges, and codes governing the conduct of legislators. Some of these laws are a colonial inheritance, some have been adapted from countries with a similar legal tradition, and some are additions to existing laws (for example, providing for special anticorruption commissions and other watchdog bodies).

Where corruption is systemic, the formal rules remain in place, but they are superseded by informal rules.[6] It may be a crime to bribe a public official, but in practice the law is not enforced or is applied in a partisan way, and informal rules prevail. Government tender boards may continue to operate even though the criteria by which contracts are awarded have changed. Seen in this light, strengthening institutions to control corruption is about shifting the emphasis back to the formal rules. This implies acknowledging that a strong legal framework to control corruption requires more than having the right legal rules in place. It means addressing the sources of informality, first by understanding why the informal rules are at odds with the formal rules and then by tackling the causes of divergence. In some countries the primary reason for divergence may be political, a manifestation of the way power is exercised and retained. This limits what the Bank can do to help outside the framework of its projects. In other countries the reason may be weak public management systems and inappropriate policies, which the Bank can help improve.

What do economics and political science tell us?

While it would be easy to say that all corruption is bad, the Bank must base its approach on evidence and analysis of corruption's effects on development. The political sensitivity surrounding issues of governance underscores the need for such a foundation. In preparing this report, the Bank examined the conclusions drawn by economic researchers working on the topic, the perspectives of disciplines other than economics, and the evidence from the Bank's operational work.

Economic research.   The body of research addressing the economic effects of corruption has grown significantly in recent years. The research is both macroeconomic and microeconomic, theoretical and empirical. Its conclusions depend in part on what the researcher views as the bottom line: short-term economic efficiency in private markets, long-term dynamic efficiency and economic growth, equity and fairness, or political legitimacy.

One strand of literature explores, primarily from a theoretical perspective, the likely economic effects of different forms of corruption.[7] Some writings of this group argue that corruption can be efficiency enhancing. First, the argument is made, corruption may not distort the short-run efficiency of an economy if it merely entails a transfer of economic rents from a private party to a government official. Thus a bribe to an official who is allocating, say, foreign exchange or credit in short supply can be seen as a market payment for ensuring that resources go to the party most likely to use them efficiently (the one who can pay the highest bribe). The problem with this line of reasoning is that it fails to take into account any objective other than short-term efficiency. In the long run, expectations of bribery may distort the number and types of contracts put up for bid, the method used to award contracts, and the speed or efficiency with which public officials do their work in the absence of bribes. It may also delay macroeconomic policy reform. In addition, the gains from such bribery may be inequitably distributed (accessible only to certain firms and public officials).

Second, bribes can theoretically increase economic efficiency if they allow firms to avoid overly restrictive regulations or confiscatory tax rates. That is, bribes lower the costs of bad regulations to firms that bribe. There may be some validity to this argument, particularly in the short run. Yet such bribery defuses pressure for broader reform and invites firms to evade good regulations as well as bad. Furthermore, the costs of such a system may fall disproportionately on smaller firms.[8] A policy framework based on many legal restrictions and widespread bribery to avoid them is like a highly regressive system of taxes on the private sector, and few would argue for such a system in developing countries. And in some transition economies such restrictions have proliferated in an uncontrolled way with the express purpose of extracting rents. This causes a shift of economic activity to the informal sector.

To summarize, models purporting to show that corruption can have positive economic effects are usually looking only at static effects in the short run. In the long run, opportunities for bribery are likely to lead public officials to change the underlying rules of the game or their own behavior in the absence of bribes, and the results are likely to be costly in terms of economic efficiency, political legitimacy, and basic fairness.

Another strand of literature examines the links between investment, economic growth and the quality of government institutions.[9] It finds that weak public institutions, as evidenced by unreliable contract enforcement, unclear property rights, unpredictable policies, inefficient public administration, corruption, and other indicators, significantly reduce private investment and lead to slower growth. While useful in highlighting the broad economic effects of institutional deficiency, much of the literature has been unable to separate the effect of corruption from other dimensions of government quality.[10]

Finally, there is the uneven performance of countries to contend with. While few would disagree that corruption has undermined development in Africa and has slowed the emergence of well functioning market economies in the former Soviet Union, the coexistence of high growth and systemic corruption in some Asian countries challenges those who believe that corruption is always economically harmful. Several explanations have been suggested. First, perhaps predictability is what matters, and some governments reliably deliver what is "bought" with bribes while other governments do not.[11] Second, others view highly concentrated corruption at the top of the political system (cited as more the model in some Asian settings) as less distortionary than uncontrolled corruption at lower levels (as in parts of the former Soviet Union).[12] Third, if political systems are well established and the rules of the game are known to all, the transactions costs of rent seeking may be less costly than in less stable, less certain environments. Fourth, corruption may be imposing environmental and social costs that are not captured in national accounts data. We do not know these costs, and country experience differs widely even within Asia. Nobody, however, argues that corruption is *good* for development, and recent research suggests that corruption may be restraining growth even in Asia.[13] What is clear is that the nature and dynamics of corruption vary greatly among countries, making it a diverse and complex phenomenon to address.

Political science. Political scientists look beyond the visible signs of corruption to the broader setting in which it occurs. They see corruption in relation to the legitimacy of the state, the patterns of political power, and the engagement of civil society. Corruption may be a manifestation of the way political power is contested and exercised. To the leadership the creation and allocation of state rents serves political purposes: rewarding supporters, buying off opponents, ensuring the backing of key groups, managing ethnic diversity, or simply accumulating resources to fight elections. To obtain these resources, leaders may forge alliances with business groups or create and distribute rents through the bureaucratic apparatus. The resulting policies may favor or discourage capital accumulation and economic growth, depending on the nature of the alliances struck. Politicians in such countries may be aware of the distortionary consequences of such rents but view them as a necessary tool of political management. If this is the case, the pattern of corruption will change only if the power structure changes, which may result from a popular outcry against corruption.

Political scientists also take a historical perspective. Over time most industrial countries have developed merit-based bureaucratic values, institutionalized competitive politics, established transparent government processes, and fostered an active media and an informed civil society. These mechanisms constrain political and bureaucratic corruption, making it the exception rather than the norm. The transition may be spurred by an enlightened ruler or, more likely, by the growing power of new political groups with an interest in better-performing government. In developing countries, in contrast, government institutions are weaker, civil society is less engaged, and political and bureaucratic processes are less accountable and transparent. An effective state apparatus and capacity for law enforcement may be virtually nonexistent. In such settings, sustained progress in building an honest and effective state apparatus requires addressing the mix of factors in the state and in society that give rise to both corruption and weak social and economic performance. This is an exceedingly complex and long-term effort.[15]

Public management. The public management view of corruption is clear-cut. Systemic corruption, in the form of graft and patronage and the inefficiencies that accompanied it, spurred the nineteenth-century reforms in Europe and North America that created the modern bureaucratic state. Corruption opposes the bureaucratic values of equity, efficiency, transparency, and honesty. Thus it weakens the ethical fabric of the civil service and prevents the emergence of well-performing government capable of developing and implementing public policies that promote social welfare.

The machinery of modern government, as it evolved in industrial countries and has been transferred to developing countries, includes systems that protect public organizations from corruption and promote accountability. These systems, including a meritocratic civil service and watchdogs such as supreme audit institutions, ombudsmen, and public service commissions, should not be neglected. Some OECD countries seeking to improve government performance through New Public Management reforms are developing "risk management" perspectives on corruption. But they do so within a framework of strong financial management control systems and a renewed emphasis on the ethical values of public service. While economies may still grow in countries in which corruption is entrenched in the public sector, the public management view is that successive stages of economic and social development will be harder if not impossible to achieve without well-performing government. Ultimately, countries need to create durable institutions to foster and protect integrity in public life if public policy is to achieve the objectives (such as poverty reduction and environmental protection) that are at the core of sustainable economic and social development.

What is the Bank's experience?

Most of the economic and sector work undertaken by the Bank does not directly address corruption. However, a small but growing number of public expenditure reviews have drawn attention to the problem, and survey data gathered in the course of private sector assessments are beginning to illuminate the costs of bribery to entrepreneurs. Based on the economic and sector work that does address the topic, informal country knowledge within the institution, and examples from the Bank's vast store of country reports in which the influence of corruption can be inferred (even if the term is seldom used), the following picture emerges of the many ways in which corruption imposes costs on our borrowers.

- *Macroeconomic stability* may be undermined by loss of government revenue and excessive spending. This can happen through corruption in tax and customs departments, through debt incurred when the scrutiny of finance ministries and central banks is bypassed, through contracts that are awarded to high-cost bidders or without competitive tendering, and through the general erosion of expenditure control. Excessive debt may be incurred through "white elephant" investment projects that owe their origin, in part, to bribes. Macroeconomic stability may also be threatened by debt guarantees and other off-budget contingent liabilities agreed to in corrupt transactions without public scrutiny. It may also be threatened by fraud in financial institutions, leading to loss of confidence by savers, investors, and foreign exchange markets. In transition economies and in many developing countries corruption may reduce revenue collection by driving firms (or their most profitable activities) out of the formal sector and by providing a moral justification for widespread tax evasion.[16] The costs of macroeconomic instability are borne by all elements in society but especially by the poor.

- *Foreign direct investment* may still flow to countries in which corruption is systemic but only if bribery is affordable and the results are predictable. Even so, corruption can have a negative effect on foreign investment. Where corruption is large and systemic, investment may be concentrated in extractive industries in which operations can be enclaved, or in light manufacturing or trading operations that can be relocated if corruption costs become unbearable. Or foreign investors may shun the country altogether. For most foreign firms, corruption is a cost of doing business to be recouped from revenues.[17] If the costs become too high or unpredictable, foreign firms will disengage unless global marketing or sourcing considerations require them to maintain a presence in that country. High levels of corruption add to the risk of a country being marginalized in the international economy.
- *Small entrepreneurs* may be affected in many developing and transition economies. Evidence from private sector assessments suggests that corruption increases the costs of doing business, that small firms bear a disproportionately large share of these costs, and that bribes can prevent firms from growing.[18]
- *The environment* may be endangered. Many countries have enacted laws to protect the environment and have created special agencies to enforce these laws, but there is often a disconnect between policy and its implementation. Complying with environmental regulations imposes on firms costs that can be avoided by bribery. There are huge rents to be earned from activities such as logging in tropical rain forests, where permits can be obtained corruptly or where inspectors can be bribed. The environmental costs of corruption may take the form of ground water and air pollution, soil erosion, or climate change, and can be global and intergenerational in their reach.
- The *poor* suffer. While poverty assessments have focused more on measuring poverty than explaining it, anecdotal and survey evidence reveal the cost of petty corruption to the poor. When access to public goods and services requires a bribe, the poor may be excluded. Given their lack of political influence, the poor may even be asked to pay more than people with higher incomes. Furthermore, when corruption results in shoddy public services, the poor lack the resources to pursue "exit" options such as private schooling, health care, or power generation.

A survey of 3,600 firms in 69 countries carried out for the *1997 World Development Report* provides further evidence of the widespread existence and negative effects of corruption. As noted in the report:

The survey confirmed that corruption was an important—and widespread—problem for investors. Overall, more than 40 percent of entrepreneurs reported having to pay bribes to get things done as a matter of course. . . . Further, more than half the respondents worldwide thought that paying a bribe was not a guarantee that the service would actually be delivered as agreed, and many lived in fear that they would simply be asked for more by another official. . . . The consequences of corruption often do not end with paying off officials and getting on with business. Government arbitrariness entangles firms in a web of time-consuming and economically unproductive relations. . .

The survey also confirms the negative correlation between the level of corruption (as perceived by businesspeople) and the level of investment in an economy.

---

http://www.invisiblewound.com/chapter8.htm
Notes

1. The literature contains many definitions of corruption, as writers either seek a comprehensive term or focus on a single aspect. In the words of the Bank's General Counsel, Ibrahim Shihata,

Corruption occurs when a function, whether official or private, requires the allocation of benefits or the provision of a good or service. . . . In all cases, a position of trust is being exploited to realize private gains beyond what the position holder is entitled to. Attempts to influence the position holder, through the payment of bribes or an exchange of benefits or favors, in order to receive a special gain or treatment not available to others is also a form of corruption, even if the gain involved is not illicit under applicable law. The absence of rules facilitates the process as much as the presence of cumbersome or excessive rules does. Corruption in this sense is not confined to the public sector and, in that sector, to administrative bureaucracies. It is not limited to the payment and receipt of bribes. It takes various forms and is practiced under all forms of government, including well-established democracies. It can be found in the legislative, judicial, and executive branches of government, as well as in all forms of private sector activities. It is not exclusively associated with any ethnic, racial, or religious group. However, its level, scope, and impact vary greatly from one country to another and may also vary, at least for a while, within the same country from one place to another. While corruption of some form or another may inhere in every human community, the system of governance has a great impact on its level and scope of practice. Systems can corrupt people as much as, if not more than, people are capable of corrupting systems.

Most definitions relate corruption to the behavior of a public official, who may be the object or the subject of corruption. Thus corruption is "an illegal payment to a public agent to obtain a benefit that may or may not be deserved in the absence of payoffs" (Rose-Ackerman) or "the sale by government officials of government property for personal gain" (Shleifer and Vishny, "Corruption," *Quarterly Journal of Economics*, 1993, 108). The benefit need not be financial or immediate, the public official may be appointed or elected, and the bribe may be offered or extorted. For the OECD Working

Group, the focus is on bribery: "the promise or giving of any undue payment or other advantages whether directly or through intermediaries to, or for the benefit of, a public official to influence the official to act or refrain from acting in the performance of his or her official duties in order to obtain or retain business." The Bank's Procurement Guidelines take a functional perspective, defining a corrupt practice as "the offering, giving, receiving, or soliciting of anything of value to influence the action of a public official in the procurement process or in contract execution."

Most definitions imply two willing actors (while fraud requires only one), usually but not always including a public official. Thus, "corrupt practices mean the bribery of public officials or other persons to gain improper commercial advantage" (EBRD). However, "no precise definition can be found which applies to all forms, types and degrees of corruption, or which would be acceptable universally as covering all acts which are considered in every jurisdiction as contributing to corruption" (Council of Europe). The definition adopted by the Bank is not original. It was chosen because it is concise and broad enough to include most forms. Like most other definitions, it places the public sector at the center of the phenomenon.

2. Participants in the "integrity workshops" facilitated by the Economic Development Institute, Transparency International (TI), and others may discuss such matters as part of the "integrity infrastructure" required to control corruption. "Integrity infrastructure" is a term coined by TI to describe the full range of values, processes, and organizations within and outside the public sector that contribute to accountable, transparent, and honest government. See TI's "National Integrity Source Book," published in 1996 and used in integrity workshops.

3. Once it is widespread, or systemic, the likelihood of detection and punishment falls in any individual case. As the expected cost of corruption falls for the public official, the incidence rises still farther. This pattern of an initially rising but then falling cost can lead to multiple equilibria. One equilibrium is a society relatively free from corruption; the other is one in which corruption is widespread and systemic. Moving from widespread corruption to a society relatively free from corruption is much harder than merely reducing corruption at the margin within either case. Within systemically corrupt systems, decentralized forms appear to be economically more costly than centralized forms.

4. Recent survey work by Daniel Kaufmann ("Listening to Stakeholders' Views about Corruption in Their Countries," Harvard Institute for International Development, January 1997) suggests that opinion leaders in developing countries see corruption in the public sector as by far the greatest problem. The Bank's private sector assessments reveal the burden of public sector corruption on the private sector in many countries. This contrasts with a commonly held view in industrial countries that corruption within the private sector is the greater problem.

5. Robert Klitgaard uses the equation C (corruption) = M (monopoly) + D (discretion) - A (accountability). See R. Klitgaard, "Cleaning Up and Invigorating the Civil Service," World Bank Operations Evaluation Department, November 1996.

6. See C. Gray, "Legal Process and Economic Development: A Case Study of Indonesia," *World Development* 19: 7, 1991.

7. Susan Rose-Ackerman provides an excellent overview of this literature in "When is Corruption Harmful?" a background paper for *World Development Report 1997*, August 1996. See also P. Bardhan, "The Economics of Corruption in Less Developed Countries: A Review of Issues," Center for International and Development Economics Research Working Paper C76-064, February 1996.

8. For examples of this regressive impact, see Susan Rose-Ackerman and Andrew Stone, "The Costs of Corruption for Private Business: Evidence from World Bank Surveys," May 1996.

9. See S. Borner, A. Brunetti, and B. Weder, *Political Credibility and Economic Development*, New York: St. Martin's Press, 1994; P. Mauro, "Corruption and Growth," *Quarterly Journal of Economics*, 1995; P. Keefer and S. Knack, "Why Don't Poor Countries Catch Up? A Cross-National Test of an Institutional Explanation," IRIS Working Paper, University of Maryland; Shang-Jin Wei, "How Taxing Is Corruption on International Investors?" National Bureau of Economic Research Working Paper 6030, 1997.

10. This is changing, however, with the spread of survey data (such as Transparency International's Corruption Perception Index) that enable cross-country comparisons and analyses of corruption and economic performance to be made. Care must be taken in using these measures. The Transparency International Corruption Perception Index is a measure of what businessmen perceive to be a country's level of corruption. It is not an objective measure.

11. The importance of predictability is stressed in World Bank, *World Development Report 1997: The State in a Changing World*, New York: Oxford University Press, 1997.

12. See A. Shleifer and R. Vishny, "Corruption," *Quarterly Journal of Economics*, 1993, 108, 599Ð617.

13. See Daniel Kaufmann, "Corruption: The Facts," *Foreign Policy*, June 1997.

14. See Mushtaq Khan, "Corruption in South Asia: Patterns of Development and Change," School of Oriental and African Studies, University of London.

15. See Michael Johnston, "What Can Be Done about Entrenched Corruption?" Paper presented at the Annual World Bank Conference on Development Economics, Washington, D.C., April 30ÐMay 1, 1997.

16. See, for example, Hernando de Soto's description of the informal sector in Peru in *The Other Path*, New York: Harper & Row, 1989.

17. See Shang-Jin Wei, "How Taxing Is Corruption on International Investors?" National Bureau of Economic Research Working Paper 6030, 1997.

18. See Susan Rose-Ackerman and Andrew Stone, "The Costs of Corruption for Private Business: Evidence from World Bank Surveys." See also Daniel Kaufmann, "The Missing Pillar of a Growth Strategy for Ukraine: Institutional and Policy Reforms for Private Sector Development," in *Ukraine: Accelerating the Transition to Market*, P. Cornelius and P. Lenain, eds., Washington, D.C.: IMF, January 1997; Daniel Kaufmann and A. Kaliberda, "Integrating the Unofficial Economy into the Dynamics of Post-Socialist Economies: A Framework of Analysis and Evidence," in *Economic Transition in the Newly Independent States*, B. Kaminski, ed., Armonk, N.Y.: M.E. Sharpe, 1996.

19. This is now changing, with participatory poverty assessments that seek to directly tap the experiences of the poor.

20. Pioneering work in this area has been done by the Public Affairs Centre in Bangalore, which found that in five Indian cities poor households were much more likely to pay "speed money" for public services than households in general. See Sam Paul, "Corruption: Who Will Bell the Cat?" April 1997.

===

RESEARCH INTO THE ECONOMIC SUCCESS OF HONG KONG
This is a research article done by the author on the analysis of the economic miracle of Hong Kong as well as the underlying reasons and international comparisons and will be very useful to academics, students and practitioners alike. It was one of the authors PhD requirements (i.e. Faustino Taderera).

I have chosen to write about Hong Kong's successful international marketing effort driven by correct and scientific buyer and consumer behavior and consumer dynamics. No one doubts the economic supremacy of Hong Kong today but few understand the consumer dynamics that have driven its success as well as its failures too. Business transactions, whether by nations or micro entities, are driven by the need for:- value, durability, convenience, easy to use, solutions based, prestige, status, imagination, desired future, security, risk mitigation and management, national pride, nationalism, quality of life, advancement, uniqueness, comfort, acceptance in in-group or society, survival and self actualization. These driving forces to buy are in most cases combined to finalise and seal a purchasing decision. One marketing guru said marketing is everything done by an enterprise to get business and be the preferred supplier or vendor. With this definition it means we need to look at an organization's whole spectrum of activities and how this results in market dominance or success, from production, engineering, human resources, finance and marketing and all with a TQM and R & D fabric. Hong Kong will be looked at as a marketing nation from this perspective as I progress with my discussion and analysis. At the heart of it all will be national branding and best practice. It is better, right at the onset, to define buyer and consumer behavior and therefore create a correct perspective that I am driving at in relation to Hong Kong's efforts at international marketing and becoming the jewel of South East Asia through marketing. Hong Kong is the world's largest re-export centre. Much of Hong Kong's exports consist of re-exports, which are products made outside of the territory, especially in mainland China, and distributed via Hong Kong. Hong Kong is one of the world's leading financial centres. Its highly developed capitalist economy has been ranked the freest in the world by the Index of Economic Freedom for 15 consecutive years. It is an important centre for international finance and trade, with one of the greatest concentration of corporate headquarters in the Asia-Pacific region, and is known as one of the Four Asian Tigers for its high growth rates and rapid development between the 1960s and 1990s (Refer to Appendix V). Hong Kong is often cited as an example of laissez-faire capitalism. In analyzing Hong Kong I will interchangeably demonstrate how the following marketing theories have immensely benefited this country and discuss their merits and demerits too and these are:-

1. Value Innovation and The Value Curve
   Identify what customers value most and innovate change to provide this value.
2. Porter's Five Forces of Competition Framework
   Understand industry competitiveness and market entry strategy.
3. Conjoint Analysis
   Understand what attributes or factors are the most important to consumers.

The definitions of theories
Value Innovation and Value Curve Theory

Value Innovation is a comprehensive set of frameworks that is revolutionizing business strategy and innovation. At the heart of Value Innovation is the value curve and strategy canvas, a powerful way to visualize business strategies.
While traditional approaches to strategy formulation focus on staying ahead of the competition, Value Innovation puts the **customer** at the center of your strategy. It strives to make the competition irrelevant by challenging the conventional assumptions that operate within an industry.
Value Innovation helps you to create new market space by:

- Looking beyond the established boundaries and conditions within your industry to invent new strategic growth options.
- Understanding your competitors but not letting them set your strategic agenda.
- Discovering common underlying needs that unite customers rather than overly focusing on their unique differences.
- Understanding non-customers and discovering how to turn them into customers.
- Not letting your existing capabilities limit your pursuit of value creation.
- Breaking the low cost vs. differentiation trade-off that traditional strategy methods stipulate.
- By making strategy easier to visualize, Value Innovation gets to the essence of strategic thinking quickly. It enables more people within your organization to contribute to meaningful discussions about your business strategy.

Conjoint Analysis Theory

Conjoint Analysis helps firms to understand what attributes or factors are the most important to consumers. It is is a statistical technique used in market research to determine how people value different features that make up an individual product or service.

The objective of conjoint analysis is to determine what combination of a limited number of attributes is most influential on respondent choice or decision making. A controlled set of potential products or services is shown to respondents and by analyzing how they make preferences between these products, the implicit valuation of the individual elements making up the product or service can be determined. These implicit valuations (utilities or part-worths) can be used to create market models that estimate market share, revenue and even profitability of new designs.

Advantages

- estimates psychological tradeoffs that consumers make when evaluating several attributes together
- measures preferences at the individual level
- uncovers real or hidden drivers which may not be apparent to the respondent themselves
- realistic choice or shopping task
- able to use physical objects
- if appropriately designed, the ability to model interactions between attributes can be used to develop needs based segmentation

Disadvantages

- designing conjoint studies can be complex
- with too many options, respondents resort to simplification strategies
- difficult to use for product positioning research because there is no procedure for converting perceptions about actual features to perceptions about a reduced set of underlying features
- respondents are unable to articulate attitudes toward new categories, or may feel forced to think about issues they would otherwise not give much thought to
- poorly designed studies may over-value emotional/preference variables and undervalue concrete variables
- does not take into account the number items per purchase so it can give a poor reading of market share

Definition of consumer behaviour

Consumer behaviour is referred to as the study of when, why, how, where and what people do or do not buy products. It blends elements from psychology, sociology, anthropology and economics. It attempts to understand the buyer decision making process, both individually and in groups. It studies characteristics of individual consumers such as demographics and behavioural variables in an attempt to understand people's wants. It also tries to assess influences on the consumer from groups such as family, friends, reference groups, and society in general.

Customer behaviour study is based on consumer buying behaviour, with the customer playing the three distinct roles of user, payer and buyer. Relationship marketing is an influential asset for customer behaviour analysis as it has a keen interest in the re-discovery of the true meaning of marketing through the re-affirmation of the importance of the customer or buyer. A greater importance is also placed on consumer retention, customer relationship management, personalisation, customisation and one-to-one marketing. Social functions can be categorized into social choice and welfare functions.

National branding

Branding is the ways in which an organization communicates, differentiates and symbolizes itself to all of its audiences. National branding is doing the same thing, but to a whole country and the world at large. This may be to encourage foreign direct investment, create internal pride, or be a support for exports, tourism or to attract expatriates or any enterprise that a nation may undertake. Although it means more than image and perception, national branding may be briefly defined as the way a country or a nation is perceived by the audience. It is very important to underline that the audience is split into two major categories: that nation's people and everyone else. It seems that most national branding programs are aimed at foreigners - improving one nation's image in the eyes of the rest of the world; but it is equally important to create programs that aim at that nation's own people, because on a long-term basis, a nation is perceived also through its citizens.

Every nation has a brand – good or bad. The nation's brand is defined by the people, by their temper, education, look, by their endeavours, successes and failures. This is why national branding is not easy. It is very hard to change a nation's values. It means education, it means economic status, standard of life. It takes generations to change how people are.

This is not the work of a branding agency, not even of a government. Instead, national branding programs aim at something different: making the country's values better known, minimize the effect of several accidents caused by individuals that affect the nation's brand, promote tourism, or attract investors. Branding expert like Simon Anholt, who established Placebrands early in 2003 but now works as an independent policy advisor to several governments, help countries develop and communicate strong brand identities which could help speed up development by attracting foreign investors and tourists. That, in turn, could increase political influence and help a country's corporations grow.

Changing the image of a country is no easier than changing the image of a company or an individual. While branding may be able to help a country improve its communication with the world, it won't work if the country sends out lies or hype, said Erich

Joachimsthaler, chief executive of Vivaldi Partners, a four-year-old agency that specializes in branding. Long term branding involves strategic planning for education, developing a Research & Development culture, political stability, rule of law and transparency, freedom of expression and the media, Total Quality Management, heavy promotion in international media like websites, BBC, CNN, Aljazeera, French TV, international journals and newspapers.

Objectives of the Study

The objectives of this study are:-

- To investigate and expose findings about the status of knowledge and understanding of consumer behavior in general and in relation to Hong Kong's international marketing effort
- To find out the current gaps in consumer behavior knowledge and how this is impacting on Hong Kong international business effort
- To identify evidence of theories and findings in journals and related literature which support or refute the theories.
- To suggest way forward in moving winning formula in marketing.

Literature review

A literature review is a body of text that aims to review the critical points of current knowledge and or methodological approaches on a particular topic. Literature reviews are secondary sources, and as such, do not report any new or original experimental work. Most often associated with academic-oriented literature, such as theses, a literature review usually precedes a research proposal and results section. Its ultimate goal is to bring the reader up to date with current literature on a topic and forms the basis for another goal, such as future research that may be needed in the area. A well-structured literature review is characterized by a logical flow of ideas; current and relevant references with consistent, appropriate referencing style; proper use of terminology; and an unbiased and comprehensive view of the previous research on the topic. The purpose of the literature review is to gain from already published research on this topic. It also helps in illuminating issues and helping to proffer possible solutions. Literature review helps analyzing issues and in creating checks and balances before conclusions and decisions are made. One of the most important purposes of a literature review is getting a cross section of ideas from different perspectives on a given topic and by people or organizations that are respected in a discipline and have done a lot of in-depth research. Normally these would be people from different countries and different institutions. I will use this literature review to guide the flow of ideas as I discuss the secret of Hong Kong's industrial success and economic miracle through world class marketing. I refer you to appendices at the end of this document for marketing theories and other relevant documents. A literature review must do these things:-

1. be organized around and related directly to the thesis or research question one is developing
2. synthesize results into a summary of what is and is not known
3. identify areas of controversy in the literature
4. formulate questions that need further research

Baker S (2003:141) emphasized that the arrival of the consumption-led economy had elevated the role of service in the creation and delivery of the value proposition and was a source of competitive differentiation. Baron B and Harris K (2003:80-85) were quick to point out that in the service industry the attitude of employees can make a real difference to the customer. Wood M B said that (2008:102) you must monitor how customers perceive the total benefits and total costs of competing products. This would help an enterprise not to lose customers and to pre-empt customers too. It can be achieved through effective marketing research and regular customer interface. Peter J P and Donnelly J H (Junior) (2007:55) warned that whenever one is doing business one must ensure that goods and services are purchased and received in a timely and efficient manner so as not to frustrate customers. Quester P and McGuiggan R (2005) admonished marketing managers that they must plan their marketing programmes such that they are flexible to be adapted to conditions in different countries or risk failure. The European Journal of Marketing (2009:Vol 3:12) said that there is now need for a paradigm shift in marketing to make the marketing practitioner aware of the total product value as well as supportive political policies through lobby and advocacy. It said the days when marketers were spectators while politicians made destructive policies are gone. This is the time when industry must shape economic policy to its preference. A true private public partnership was one of the reasons for Hong Kong's marketing success where excessive bureaucracy was done away with to better serve the global market. The Journal of Industrial Marketing Management (2009:Vol 3:18) ran a comprehensive article on modern industrial marketing emphasizing the reasons why modern industrialists buy what they buy and the said this was driven by:- the desire to improve efficiencies and cut costs, quality considerations, durability, easy of handling, convenience of use, improving productivity/automation, reducing labour as well as greenhouse gas emissions. Marketing now has to be futuristic and pre-empt global warming compliance and contribute to good housekeeping. The Journal of International Marketing (2009:Vol 2:13 said international marketing is now more of a value driven game and a political game. One has to be a good marketer and a good political schemer. On a different note the Journal of Market-Focused Management (2009:Vol 3:22) said international marketing and globalization had brought foreign problems and solutions onto our doorsteps, they brought good and bad, benefits and disasters. They further elaborated that foreign language competence was not a choice but a tool of trade for success in the globalised market. One also had to understand international relations and trading blocs as well as local and international Trade Promotion Organisations for success. The Journal of Strategic Marketing (2009:Vol 2:24) said ethical marketing, value marketing and solutions based marketing now drives the firm into the future. It further said firms should be prepared to leave traditional Western high cost locations and relocate to the Far East, like to Hong Kong, to take advantage of market realities and as a survival and competitiveness move.

Discussions & Conclusion
The reasons for marketing success are likely to be found among the following:-

-   High product quality

- Competitive pricing
- Cost advantages
- Advantageous plant location
- Unique product features and patent protection
- Size and strength of the company
- Domination of distribution channels
- Sales and distribution methods
- Advertising and promotion
- Tariff or other trade protection
- Political influence and connections
- Appointment of competent and influential sales agents and distributors
- Unparalleled R & D and innovation
- Strategic alliances and cooperative strategies
- Successful lobby and advocacy

Therefore marketing innovation and creativity must be aimed at addressing the above known consumer requirements and reasons for marketing and business success. One survey across a large number of manufacturing and services organisations and government found, ranked in decreasing order of popularity, that systematic programs of organizational innovation are most frequently driven by:

1. Improved quality
2. Creation of new markets
3. Extension of the product range
4. Reduced labour costs
5. Improved production processes
6. Reduced materials
7. Reduced environmental damage
8. Replacement of products/services
9. Reduced energy consumption
10. Conformance to regulations
11. The need for re-election

These goals vary between improvements to products, processes and services and dispel a popular myth that innovation deals mainly with new product development. Most of the goals could apply to any organisation be it a manufacturing facility, marketing firm, hospital or local/central government. Research and development is nowadays of great importance in business as the level of competition, production processes and methods are rapidly increasing. It is of special importance in the field of marketing where companies keep an eagle eye on competitors and customers in order to keep pace with modern trends and analyze the needs, demands and desires of their customers.

Unfortunately, research and development are very difficult to manage, since the defining feature of research is that the researchers do not know in advance exactly how to accomplish the desired result. As a result, higher R&D spending does not guarantee more creativity, higher profit or a greater market share.

Supply Chain Management Strategy

Increasing demands to cut costs while delivering innovation are putting enormous pressure on purchasing departments in all countries across the globe. Failure to do this results in marketing failure through price competition. Supply chain is a service function to marketing. Hong Kong has been particularly successful in systematically exploiting the supply chain. The problem facing organizations and purchasing practitioners is a myriad of problems created by the world recession which has imposed on organizations the need for drastic change management or face failure or collapse. Part of the problems had been building up for a long time. These problems include the following, among other things:- unsophisticated management, excess staff, long standing suppliers going out of business and strangling organizational operations, stock blackouts, civil wars disrupting supplies, terrorism, high jacking of consignments on high seas (e.g. by pirates in Somalia and the Gulf of Aden), high cost suppliers in traditional markets in the West and new low cost markets in the emerging economies in the Far East like China, Indonesia, Malaysia, India, Taiwan, Philippines and Japan, foreign language incompetence in new preferred markets, cultural difficulties, infrastructure challenges in 3rd world and emerging economies, global warming, supply disruptions caused by failed states and war zones e.g. Afghanistan, Pakistan and Somalia, high insurance premiums in countries and transit routes in the war zones, mistrust and suspicion in some countries, oversupply and market glut which is advantageous to the purchaser but very disruptive to the merchant/seller, a painful shortage of finance to oil business internationally due to bank failures and bank operational problems, the high national debt burdens, general illiquidity and fear of the future engulfing the entire market place, the introduction of harsh cash transactions as firms do not trust whether debtors would remain in business and timely pay their debts, economic sanctions and embargoes which disrupt business, quotas and trade wars e.g. the USA/Chinese stand-off about tyres, milk, toys, chicken and textiles, child labour, corruption, political instability in some countries, dishonesty, risk profiling and management and planning for a long term future. These are painful trade factors which the modern purchasing professional has to deal with head on. The age for the order taker is gone as these kinds of problems require highly qualified purchasing professionals, men and women who can operate at diplomatic level internationally. The modern purchasing professional is now expected to be bilingual in key foreign languages, e-literate, have top of the range international procurement expertise, be a product of a credible business school and have specialized in purchasing at degree level and have international exposure and disposition. It is now imperative for firms and governments to focus their recruitment in an international perspective in order to get the best. The purchasing professional must understand the political dynamics in different countries as well as the cultures and religions and their influence on product consumption, business dynamics, negotiations and business etiquette. A qualified world class purchasing professional is a panacea for any organization just as a doctor is a necessity for a hospital and an engineer for an engineering company. The purchasing professional requires three qualities:- degree level education in procurement/shipping/languages, relevant experience and international exposure/travel experience. Anything short of this is an accident in waiting, if the organization is classified as large or multinational or a government department. There is an additional requirement nowadays and this is the ability to design and plot an annual

Purchasing Plan – this is a comprehensive plan for all purchasing activities and ties up with the corporate strategic plan, business plan, budget and other functional area plans.

Researchers in multinationals and universities in the USA have taken the lead in mastering this complex balancing act. A close analysis of their success stories has revealed seven key strategies:-

1. Source from low-cost countries
Purchasing in low-cost countries is an important lever for cost savings. Manufacturers should first become familiar with local suppliers by assigning them orders for production in emerging markets. Orders can then be given for exporting parts to developed markets. To build up a qualified supplier base as quickly as possible, manufacturers should encourage existing suppliers to produce in low-cost countries. We also recommend supporting local suppliers in their development. Renault, for example, assisted its suppliers in Romania in areas such as engineering, quality, finance and even management.

2. Create a global supplier footprint
To minimize currency risks, avoid supplier bottlenecks, and ensure favorable purchasing conditions, manufacturers should develop a global supplier footprint strategy with a decision-making framework for Purchasing. The framework could stipulate, for example, purchasing volumes in certain currency regions. VW has developed guidelines that require increasing purchasing volumes in U.S. dollar-based economies. That is why more than half of the purchasing volume for the new Jetta/Bora is from Mexico or other U.S. dollar countries.

3. Ensure access to technological innovations
Manufacturers should build up their relationships with suppliers to ensure continuing access to new technologies, while also strengthening their own innovation process. BMW, for example, fuels its innovation process by collecting ideas from suppliers through an online platform. These ideas are then evaluated and put into practice, where appropriate.

4. Reduce costs together with suppliers
Along with technical levers like standardization, manufacturers should increasingly integrate with suppliers to accelerate cost reduction efforts. In 2005, Volkswagen kicked off two new cross-functional initiatives for future and current program sourcing. Due to these initiatives, Purchasing and Engineering have joint responsibilities, and suppliers are heavily involved. Toyota has gone one step further, creating a division responsible only for advising suppliers and implementing cost reduction measures.

5. Standardize
Manufacturers should continue to move toward standardized modules and components. Furthermore, they should frontload their development efforts to increase product reliability and durability. Engineering departments should be arranged globally, with decision-making authority on a global level. Here, too, Toyota leads the field, as it has

separated module development from vehicle development. By doing this, modules are developed independently from vehicles and can be used in multiple vehicle platforms. This creates economies of scale and dramatically reduces quality problems.

6. Globalize structures and decision making

While manufacturers are beginning to reap the benefits of globalization strategies, they cannot rest on their laurels. They must continue to align their structures to the international market. To this end, global Purchasing should be organized by product group. The organization should have common regional structures and be able to make global decisions. The interface with Engineering must especially be improved. GM did this by implementing joint target agreements for its Engineering and Purchasing board members. At BMW, one board member even holds both Engineering and Purchasing responsibility to facilitate cross-functional decision making.

7. Get highly qualified and experience procurement staff

There is no substitute for qualified and experienced purchasing people. Nowadays success or failure is mainly determined by the quality of people that firms employ. The sophistication of your staff determines their ability to exploit supply markets and drive the firm into the future. The biggest liability for any organization is unqualified people. If a purchasing department or division is run by unqualified people, then confusion follows naturally. Unqualified people may seem cheap and easy to exploit but are a strategic disaster. Organisations that employ highly qualified people and pay them handsomely actually save much more than those that employ low caliber and cheap staff, research all over the world confirms this. Purchasing spends about 60 to 70% of any organisation's total expenditure. Just imagine what this means with billions of dollars worth of purchases taking place, if this is not done professionally. One common mistake which a lot of organizations make is to employ a general business graduate who has not specialised in purchasing. This is an accident in waiting and a dangerous pitfall. If this happens then the organization should sponsor the generalists to do professional purchasing courses like CIPS or to do a masters degree in purchasing part time. *In fact one of the biggest problems facing the modern enterprise and governments today is ignorance and not a shortage of money, land, plant and equipment, capital or any other factor of production. Ignorance creates all other problems while expertise pre-empts and solves problems and pitfalls. This is the same scenario in both the private and public sectors. Ignorance destroys corporate goodwill and reputation through costly mistakes.* Purchasing benefits would then be translated into lower prices for customers, benefits for other stakeholders and higher profits for shareholders.

Strategic fit

Strategic fit express the degree to which an organization is matching its resources and capabilities with the opportunities in the external environment. The matching takes place through strategy and it is therefore vital that the company have the actual resources and capabilities to execute and support the strategy. A unique combination of resources and capabilities can eventually be developed into a competitive advantage which the company can profit from. However, it is important to differentiate between resources and capabilities. Resources relate to the inputs to production owned by the company, whereas capabilities describe the accumulation of learning the company possesses.

Failure of innovation

Innovation drives marketing success and customer satisfaction. People want fashion and new things and to surprise other people with new things. Failure is an inevitable part of the innovation process, and most successful organisations factor in an appropriate level of risk. Perhaps it is because all organisations experience failure that many choose not to monitor the level of failure very closely. The impact of failure goes beyond the simple loss of investment. Failure can also lead to loss of morale among employees, an increase in cynicism and even higher resistance to change in the future.

Innovations that fail are often potentially good ideas but have been rejected or postponed due to budgetary constraints, lack of skills or poor fit with current goals. Failures should be identified and screened out as early in the process as possible. Early screening avoids unsuitable ideas devouring scarce resources that are needed to progress more beneficial ones. Organizations can learn how to avoid failure when it is openly discussed and debated. The lessons learned from failure often reside longer in the organisational consciousness than lessons learned from success. While learning is important, high failure rates throughout the innovation process are wasteful and a threat to the organisation's future.

The causes of failure have been widely researched and can vary considerably. Some causes will be external to the organisation and outside its influence of control. Others will be internal and ultimately within the control of the organisation. Internal causes of failure can be divided into causes associated with the cultural infrastructure and causes associated with the innovation process itself. Failure in the cultural infrastructure varies between organizations but the following are common across all organisations at some stage in their life cycle (O'Sullivan, 2002):

1. Poor Leadership
2. Poor Organization
3. Poor Communication
4. Poor Empowerment
5. Poor Knowledge Management

Common causes of failure within the innovation process in most organisations can be distilled into five types:

1. Poor goal definition
2. Poor alignment of actions to goals
3. Poor participation in teams
4. Poor monitoring of results
5. Poor communication and access to information

Customer satisfaction

Customer satisfaction, a business term, is a measure of how products and services supplied by a company meet or surpass customer expectation. It is seen as a key performance indicator within business and is part of the four perspectives of a Balanced Scorecard. In a competitive marketplace where businesses compete for customers, customer satisfaction is seen as a key differentiator and increasingly has become a key element of business strategy.

Measuring customer satisfaction

Organizations are increasingly interested in retaining existing customers while targeting non-customers; measuring customer satisfaction provides an indication of how successful the organization is at providing products and/or services to the marketplace.

Customer satisfaction is an ambiguous and abstract concept and the actual manifestation of the state of satisfaction will vary from person to person and product/service to product/service. The state of satisfaction depends on a number of both psychological and physical variables which correlate with satisfaction behaviors such as return and recommend rate. The level of satisfaction can also vary depending on other options the customer may have and other products against which the customer can compare the organization's products.

Improving Customer Satisfaction

Published standards exist to help organizations develop their current levels of customer satisfaction. The International Customer Service Institute (TICSI) has released The International Customer Service Standard (TICSS). TICSS enables organizations to focus their attention on delivering excellence in the management of customer service, whilst at the same time providing recognition of success through a 3rd Party registration scheme. TICSS focuses an organization's attention on delivering increased customer satisfaction by helping the organization through a Service Quality Model.

TICSS Service Quality Model uses the 5 P's - Policy, Processes, People, Premises, Product/Services, as well as performance measurement. The implementation of a customer service standard should lead to higher levels of customer satisfaction, which in turn influences customer retention and customer loyalty. It takes continuous effort to maintain high customer satisfaction levels. As markets shrink, companies are scrambling to boost customer satisfaction and keep their current customers rather than devoting additional resources to chase potential new customers. The claim that it costs five to eight times as much to get new customers than to hold on to old ones is key to understanding the drive toward benchmarking and tracking customer satisfaction. Measuring customer satisfaction is a relatively new concept to many companies that have been focused exclusively on income statements and balance sheets. Companies now recognize that the new global economy has changed things forever. Increased competition, crowded markets with little product differentiation and years of continual sales growth followed by two decades of flattened sales curves have indicated to today's sharp competitors that their focus must change. Competitors that are prospering in the new global economy recognize that measuring customer satisfaction is key. Only by doing so can they hold on to the customers they have and understand how to better attract new customers. The competitors who will be successful recognize that customer satisfaction is a critical strategic weapon that can bring increased market share and increased profits.

The problem companies face, however, is exactly how to do all of this and do it well. They need to understand how to quantify, measure, and track customer satisfaction. Without a clear and accurate sense of what needs to be measured and how to collect, analyze, and use the data as a strategic weapon to drive the business, no firm can be effective in this new business climate. Plans constructed using customer satisfaction research results can be designed to target customers and processes that are most able to extend profits. Too many companies rely on outdated and unreliable measures of customer satisfaction. They watch sales volume. They listen to sales reps describing their customers' states of mind. They track and count the frequency of complaints. And they watch aging accounts receivable reports, recognizing that unhappy customers pay as late as possible -- if at all. While these approaches are not completely without value, they are no substitute for a valid, well-designed customer satisfaction survey program. It's no surprise to find that market leaders differ from the rest of the industry in that they're designed to hear the voice of the customer and achieve customer satisfaction. In these companies:

- Marketing and sales employees are primarily responsible for designing (with customer input) customer satisfaction surveying programs, questionnaires, and focus groups.
- Top management and marketing divisions champion the programs.
- Corporate evaluations include not only their own customer satisfaction ratings but also those of their competitors.
- Satisfaction results are made available to all employees.
- Customers are informed about changes brought about as the direct result of listening to their needs.
- Internal and external quality measures are often tied together.
- Customer satisfaction is incorporated into the strategic focus of the company via the mission statement.
- Stakeholder compensation is tied directly to the customer satisfaction surveying program.
- A concentrated effort is made to relate the customer satisfaction measurement results to internal process metrics.

To be successful, companies need a customer satisfaction surveying system that meets the following criteria:

- The system must be easy to understand.
- It must be credible so that employee performance and compensation can be attached to the final results.
- It must generate actionable reports for management.

The advantages of being a market leader

Being first in any category is going to give you the edge – being the leader comes from being first. It's much easier to get into the mind of consumers first than try to convince people you have a better product or service than the one that did get there first. Improvements are always made to product/service inventions and innovations but the first in has a head start. Once you are the leader, a position mostly gained by being first, it is pretty hard for competitors to dislodge you, as long as you keep your products up to date and of comparable quality. Further, the first in to the market has the opportunity to have its brand name adopted as the generic category name. Once you are first and get the consumers to buy your brand, often they won't bother to switch. People tend to stick with what they've got. The market leader is dominant in its industry and has substantial market share. If you want to lead the market, you must be the industry leader in establishing an innovation-friendly organization, developing new business models and new products or services. You must be on the cutting edge of new technologies and innovative business processes. Your customer value proposition must offer a superior solution to a customers' problem, and your product must be well differentiated.

Strategy for Embassies

Countries also a need to open up embassies in high value world centres manned by the right people with business qualifications and business experience, especially trade attaches and trade promotion officers, if countries are to benefit anything out of their embassies. The establishment of embassies must be guided by the principle of potential business to be generated in a country, besides the usual political objectives. This is what has generally guided most NICs and they have reaped huge rewards in the form of increased business in home countries generated from the embassies. Embassies also need to be given serious business and economic targets to meet like investment, exports, imports, tourist arrivals and national public relations, besides the standard political considerations and targets. These become the Key Result Areas or the reason or justification for their establishment or existence. Adequate resources also need to be pumped into embassies so that they can carry their mandates with reasonable ease. The same goes with key national Trade Promotion Organisations (TPOs); they need national support in order for them to do justice to countries in their international trade efforts. More interaction is necessary with the rest of the world and is not an option. These financial and economic innovations are going to be some of the key strategic economic drivers which can make or break any country – there is no alternative. Completely valueless embassies may need to be closed and a country establishes regional embassies to service a number of countries if one country does not warrant the establishment of an embassy. The USA has an embassy with a staff complement of seven hundred people – the largest embassy in the world; the reason for this big embassy was to take advantage of the big business potential in China and pre-empt the rest of the world. They have established many Chinese Language Centres in the USA and English Language Centres in China as the quickest way and strategy to close the language barrier and accelerate business. Hong Kong has been very selective in establishing embassies the world over and has been guided by business potential, pay back, marketing excellence and convenience, ease of access and as a facilitative tool for business, but without ignoring political objectives altogether.

Today's marketers must wear so many hats. They must understand politics, sociology, business and anthropology. Business success is not simply derived from the best product. In 3rd world countries and some developed countries corruption is sometimes at the centre stage of decision making, e.g. Mexico, Nigeria, Afghanistan, Argentine, Brazil, India, Iraq and Egypt just to name a few. If you do not pay a bribe to some officials they would not give you an order or they simply become gate keepers and frustrate your marketing efforts until you play ball. Therefore the value theory and all other marketing theories lose meaning and relevance in these circumstances and transactions are not guided by Value For Money considerations. It is all about patronage and greasing. Sometimes business is driven by political and nationalistic considerations, e.g. in closed industries like the armaments and security industry. America would rather do business with Israel than with Myanmar for political reasons, value has no place there. Neither is Israel happy trading with Iran. Sometimes politicians impose price controls, tariffs and embargoes to deal with enemy states and imports considered a threat to national industry and national interest.

The United Nations Climate Change Conference in Denmark, Copenhagen is a case in point; countries were deadlocked for national reasons rather than business and economic logic. The global warming threat is clear to everyone but politicians are looking at immediate political expedience and political backlash which may affect their re-election in a few years time while planning for this global threat must be based on the next fifty or more years. But in the end companies and businesses are going to suffer and lose business because of these political decisions. They create threats and opportunities for different sectors. Unnecessary crisis situations can be created. One also has to look at the real threat of terrorism and extremism, like the Somali pirates who are upsetting global trade and affecting almost every country's trading activities. The cost of ransom being paid to pirates is now a cost element for companies using this sea route which makes them uncompetitive and at a huge disadvantage. Is it fair and just to pay pirates? Does it not promote piracy rather than eliminate it? What should businesses do? Who uprooted a legitimate Somali government that was there in 1991 and created this menace for global business? How can firms deal with this political problem? Who created terrorists and who should deal with terrorism? Where is business ethics? Everyone is worrying about terrorism but most 1st world countries have factories working twenty four hours a day, seven days a week, mass producing weapons using high-tech of the highest order (robotics technology) and doing heavy promotion around the world.

Bernard Murdoch created the biggest scandal in corporate history right at the heart of the USA in Wall Street, New York, the financial capital of the world. So did all the major banks and Enron. But the USA is the ethics benchmark for the world and authors four fifths of academic business books and journals. Is there truth and objectivity in this? Should we believe the journals and books? Is there a need for the revision of the rules of the game or the capitalist system as a whole? The system of marketing globally is now rewarding crooks – the cocaine barons in Europe, Italy, Mexico, Brazil, India,

Afghanistan and Colombia who are now investing across the globe using the proceeds of graft, dishonest and societal destruction – the so called dirty money. The marketing problem is no longer a business problem solved by simple business models; it has now spilled into the political arena and is now inseparable with politics. An understanding and practicing of politics (lobby and advocacy) is now one of the major reasons for marketing success. That is why you are now finding so many trade unionists joining politics and taking over the reins of power because they know that if you want business supportive political policies then go into politics and formulate the required policies yourselves rather than lobby and be at the mercy of somebody, or simply put your own guys and support them financially. It takes political lunatics to destroy gains accumulated by firms for years (Burma, Kyrgyzstan, Thailand, Philippines, Somalia, Iraq, Sudan, Democratic Republic of Congo and Kenya area cases in point). In most countries you have to do political hedging, financing ruling and opposition parties to simply cover yourselves (middle of the road policies) so that whoever goes to government house to take the national mantle is on your side. It is an existential strategy for most companies, even in the USA. That nullifies marketing theory which says understanding your consumers and giving them value is the only reason for success as well as studying competitive dynamics. Drug trafficking affects production efficiencies in companies as workers under the influence of drugs are hostile and dangerous to management and other workers. Drugs may even cause absentee rates to go up as well as murder rates, including murder of strategic employees companies will have spend thousands of dollars training, educating and socialising. Company assets can be damaged too thus reducing plant life span and prejudicing the investor and the public at large. Where is the pay back? This is a political situation which needs a political solution but affects international marketing and firm competitiveness.

We are a global village and what happens in every corner of the world, good or bad, affects every country one way or the other, hence the need for multilateral effort to protect business. Are there any pure marketers or everyone is a now politician – it's really a fine line? Hong Kong has come the long way and successfully managed business and political interaction thus creating successful global marketing for itself. Politicians have to be aware that performance management is the name of the game and the same applies to private sector managers. Everyone would perform fearing for their future and ultimately it's the economy that benefits. Malaysia has embraced performance management very successfully and so has most countries in South East Asia and the Western world. Employment for life is dangerous at times as complacency creeps in but it can also create loyalty and a bond and sense of belonging. New marketing theories are required to deal with modern business situations which are inherently entangled in politics and which cannot be solved or explained by traditional marketing theories. The market place is now too complex and confusing. But war is disrupting normal business in most corners of the world and one wonders what causes these wars.

Chief causes of wars and political instability in the whole world

Everyone seems to be deeply concerned about the need to have and preserve peace on this planet. Conference after conference are being held to try and promote peace and conflict resolution as expeditiously as possible. But the big question is whether everyone is sincere and truthful in this whole process. The truth is that first world or developed countries all do have factories working twenty four hours a day, seven days a week and three shifts a day producing arms of war for mass marketing the world over. If you produce any product surely you have to do a lot of marketing research and product promotion. The developed world gets more money from selling weapons than they get from selling anything else. How sincere would they be in promoting peace? When these developed countries attend world peace conferences they will actually be on a serious marketing research exercise quite keen to see the wars continue in order to sustain markets for their weapons – as well as creating new wars and military conflicts. This is why after every peace conference you normally see an escalation of war and hostilities. And you have the unfortunate culture and belief in this world that if you want to hold a valid and recognized peace conference it must be chaired by someone from the developed world – the very arms manufacturers and merchants with vested war interests. What a contradiction and hypocrisy? We can never have durable and lasting peace with these kinds of double standards and cheating. First world governments cause wars and conflicts in the 3rd world by working with an intricate network of politically inclined and dangerous NGOs, the military, a wrongly skewed education system, a hate media campaign for anything 3rd world. As a result of the proliferation of small arms there are now too many robberies, suicides and killings in the third world. The historical tranquility has now disappeared from Africa, a society that has always had such a high respect for human life because of a large injection of foreign small arms. *One hundred and fifty members of the USA Congress are owners of the largest, all powerful and most sophisticated arms factories in the world – this raises a lot of questions about their genuine desire for peace.* The UK and the USA as well as most other developed countries make more money from arms exports than any other industry. How can they be committed to peace given this kind of scenario? The armaments industry is the richest, biggest, strongest and most influential industry and has got the strongest lobby groups in the first world as a whole and they anoint and remove political leaders in their own countries as well as elsewhere and control the world economy and political system.

Debt Swaps

The 1st world has made a suggestion, if not a demand or imposition to the developing world, that the solution to the latter's debt burden is debt swaps. This is an arrangement where debt is converted into equity (or to simplify it, the creditor takes over ownership of the debtor's assets for the value of the debt to extinguish or settle the debt). Most 3rd world countries have accepted and implemented this cruel and destructive solution. The danger is that the process of debt swaps is a process of gradual dispossession. A country ends up owning nothing with all its assets taken over and owned by foreigners – that is like being asked by a debtor to cede your house and become a lessee/tenant in a your previously owned house. Debt swaps are a clean and smart way by the 1st world to re-colonise 3rd world countries. How can these countries say they are independent when they own nothing in their countries? Personal dignity, power, prestige, reputation and national prosperity come with ownership of massive national assets and not dispossession. It is politically, economically and social dangerous to surrender strategic national assets to the first world or to any country.

The pros and cons about human rights

So much has been said about human rights and literature abounds on this. But the truth has never been said about the true foundation of human rights and how to enforce them. *Human rights start with ownership of assets across the spectrum, starting with the ownership of land or geographical space.* "No man is rich until he owns a piece of land," correctly said the British many years ago and this assertion is still valid and even more truthful today. One needs money and wealth to access quality food, housing, education, clothing, personal dignity, acceptance in social in-groups, entertainment, even to marry and to socialize.

The debt burden in the 3rd world

Poor export performance in the 3rd world is mainly caused by poor public infrastructure, low foreign exchange earnings, a lack of exports related and relevant university level education blended with a fusion of relevant foreign languages and strong ICT component, poor science and technology expertise, corruption, antiquated plant and machinery, the flight of highly skilled labour to the first world, political and economic conspiracy by the first world *then comes the ruinous and bludgeoning Debt Burden of +US$330 billion owed to the IMF and the World Bank by African countries – this is the single greatest killer of any attempt at economic growth and prosperity by African countries as well as the monster causing untold political, economic and social suffering by African countries and the killer of export business as well.* This is what has created institutionalized and perennial poverty in Africa and the 3rd world. The underlying debt burden makes it impossible for any African or 3rd world president to get the economy right. Where do you see an example of economic success in Africa – nowhere? These African leaders are not born of the same mother but are saddled with the same debilitating and ruinous factors hence their collective failure from Cape Town in South Africa to Cairo in Egypt – electricity outages, poor water supply or none, pot holes on roads and collapsing utilities? Nothing is going to work at all until this Debt Burden is cancelled completely. Debt rescheduling is not a solution. *Some countries are spending 50 to 70% of their GDP on debt repayment and debt servicing and are now caught up in an irreversible and ruinous debt trap. Surely what will be left for investment in national public infrastructure and public services?* The United Nations Development Programme (UNDP) Millenium Development Goals (or MDGs as they call them) will never be realized by poor developing countries without debt cancelation. Debt cancelation would be a sure way of realizing MDGs for all countries. Instead what we see in all developing countries is a complete reversal of quality of life – people's lives are now worse than they were ten years ago. Then where is the progress and improvement? Western hypocrisy is at the root of this reversal in quality of life. Let Western countries stop feasting on the blood of poor developing countries under the cover of IMF and World Bank loan sharks by getting fat dividends from supposed investments in 3rd world countries through cruel, harsh, heartless, deadly and ruinous loans extended to these countries on impossible terms and conditions. One only needs to watch television programmes on BBC, CNN, Aljazeera, French TV, the internet and other international print media to get a feel of the suffering of 3rd world countries and honestly tell whether

there is any improvement in the quality of life at all. There definitely isn't any –
electricity outages are a daily thing, mostly no internet access for most people or it is on
and off as electricity outages occur, no access to clean water, crumbling education
infrastructure, crumbling roads, poor equipped hospitals/colleges/schools and
universities, crumbling and poorly maintained railways, communication networks,
airports and other public infrastructure, misery, grinding poverty, divisions, tensions and
war as well as the flight of critical skilled labour to the developed world, the very skills
required for development by any country.

Conclusion

The collapse of the world economy recently demonstrates the failure of marketing and
business theories to be self regulating, especially when this had to happen as a surprise on
the watch of the world's most sophisticated, respect and largest economy, the United
States of America where there are countless world renowned universities, research
institutes and think tanks. Even the national bail outs are not a solution but an increase in
borrowings which are going to haunt future generations and may lead to market collapse
again, leading economists like Paul Kruger are warning. Consumer behavior will be
guided by an endless fear of the unknown, mistrust of the financial market, prudence and
risk management concerns, a shrinking and highly selective market. The Economist
reported in its latest journal that the onset of the world recession had resulted in a
permanent economic power shift from the West to East Asia. The main attraction of the
South East Asia is lower costs, strategic location, access to raw materials, the
concentration of major MNCs, a positive work ethic, a world population centre with high
consumption, a high degree of creativity and political stability. Exploitation of consumer
behaviour in Hong Kong has also created its own problems through high pressure
marketing; now there are many people in the country who are too fat and stand the risk of
heart attacks and heart failure. Some of these people cannot work and are a health hazard
for the country. This is a problem created by reckless marketing through encouraging
people to consume large quantities of fat but which marketers are very well aware of.
How do you strike a balance between achieving sales targets and ethical conduct? Hong
Kong should concentrate in the following industries where it has competitive advantage:-
services, education, manufacturing, real estate, shipping and logistics and chemical
manufacture.

REFERENCES

1. Baker S., (2003).New Consumer Marketing. John Wiley & Sons.

2. Baron B., Harris K. Services Marketing, Texts and Cases. Palgrave

3. Bake M.B. (2003). The Marketing Plan Handbook. Prentice Hall.

4. Peter J. P., Donnelly J.H. (2007). McGraw-Hill/Irwin

5. Quester P., McGuiggan R. (2005). Marketing, Creating and Delivering
   Value. McGraw-Hill Australia.

6. Aaker DA (4th Ed). Strategic Market Management, John Widely & Sons, Inc.6,p.100. (1995)
7. Dillon WR;Madden TJ;et al Marketing Research, The McGraw-Hill Companies Inc.2,p.25.(1993).
8. Charles W. L. Hill, (2009),International Business, Competing in the Global Marketplace,7th Edition, McGraw-Hill.
9. Kerin A. R., Peterson R.A. (2007). Strategic Marketing Problems, Cases and Comments: 11th Edition, Pearson Education International.
10. Hitt M.A., Hoskisson R.A.,Ireland R.D., (2007), Cengage Learning.
11. Cateora, P. R., (1993) International Marketing: Irwin.
12. Hanink, D.M., (1994). The International Economy, A Geographical Perspective: John Wiley & Sons, Inc.
13. Porter, M.E., (1990). The Competitive Advantage of Nations: Free Press, New York.
14. The Emirates Centre for Strategic Studies and Research (2003). Human Resources in a Knowledge-Based Economy, Abu Dhabi, United Arab Emirates
15. Kerin, A.R.,Peterson, R.A. (2007). Strategic Marketing Problems, Cases and Comments (11th Edition):Pearson Prentice Hall.
16. Christopher, M. (1987) in Baker, M. J. (ed.) the Marketing Book: Heinemann
17. Czinkota, M. E., and Ronkainen, I. A., (1990) International Marketing: Dryden.
18. Keegan, W. J., (1989), Global Marketing Management: Prentice-Hall.
19. Kotler, P., (1988) Marketing Management; Analysis, Planning, Implementation and Control: Prentice-Hall.
20. Shimaguchi, M., (1978). Marketing Channels in Japan: Ann Arbor.
21. Barbican, S., (2009). Total value and political lobby and advocacy. *The European Journal of Marketing*, 30 (3), 12-14.
22. Bernard S., & Smith G. (2009). Modern industrial marketing model. *The Journal of Industrial Marketing Management*, 44 (3), 18-20.
23. Thomson J., & Schumpeter T.H., (2009). International marketing benchmarks in the modern era. *The Journal of International Marketing*, 25 (2), 13-14.
24. Williamson T., (2009). International marketing and globalization challenges. *The Journal of Market-Focused Management*, 33 (3), 22-24.
25. Pitt K.T., & Stevenson M., (2009). Ethics and value marketing. *The Journal of Strategic Marketing*, 26 (2), 24-26.
26. World Economic Analysis Report: Retrieved 5 December 2009 from http://econ.worldbank.org/WBSITE/EXTERNAL/EXTDEC/0,,contentMDK:22216733~pagePK:64165401~piPK:64165026~theSitePK:469372,00.html

THE MODERN FUNCTIONS OF A FOREIGN TRADE REPRESENTATIVE

The following is also research carried out by the writer and other academics at the Colleges of Applied Sciences in Oman recently and would be quite beneficial to practitioners, researchers, policy makers, politicians and students alike:-

OBJECTIVES OF THE STUDY
The objectives of this study are:-
- To investigate and expose findings about the critical duties of a national trade representative for maximum effectiveness and value addition to one's country
- To find out the common challenges faced by foreign trade representatives in their day to day duties on foreign land with the aim to unlock national value
- To identify evidence of theories and findings in books, journals and related literature which support or refute the theories
- To recommend research based and scientifically proven foolproof solutions to a smart business package to drive investment, exports, imports and tourism in terms of foreign trade representation for world class competitiveness.

THE PROBLEM SITUATION AND JUSTIFICATION

Embassies and diplomatic postings used to be political appointments to serve only political interests but now there is a revolution going on in the world where they are being transformed into value addition centres to create business for a country foremost in order to improve the quality of life at home. The main reason for this new development is that politicians are now realising that if they do not create business and improve lives it is a sure case they will lose the next election through a protest vote by hungry and frustrated voters. Therefore good economic management is now a hedge to safeguard job security for the politicians. Politicians gain political mileage while industrialists gain through new business growth, market diversification and job creation. It is a win-win situation and a rallying point for all nations nowadays and has to be scientifically nurtured and developed hence this research. Quality of life, social and political stability are now inextricably linked and many countries have learnt the hard way that there is no national stability without a good life for every citizen. Quality life in a country also demonstrates a duty of care, legitimacy and relevance on the part of government and firms. Many trade representatives and countries are finding this transformation to be very difficult and painful. The faster countries do this correctly the more successful they can be. It is this transformation and how to manage it correctly which is the reason for this research. It cannot be overemphasized that the trade representation profession will be requiring professionals with a multiplicity of competences to cope with the complexities of the global village and the internationalization challenges of the supply market. Retraining is necessary as most embassies are stuck with political appointees who are qualified in professions completely outside the business arena with no clue for business (e.g. graduates in biology, history, sociology, chemistry, physics or mathematics who were appointed to diplomatic positions by virtue of their political influence and connections), or qualified in general business with no international business specialisation (especially for countries with no degrees in international marketing or international business). These inappropriately qualified people are now a terrible liability for governments under the new pro-business dispensation. Countries are now competing in a ruthless and brutal terrain to attract investment, export business, suppliers and tourists and only the best in terms of skilled labour can provide a winning formula. Foreign languages may need to be introduced in international marketing degrees so that managers and officers find it easy to deal with key countries like China, Germany, Spain, France (languages like Mandarin, Germany, French, Spanish). E-government is also an innovation being adopted by many countries to support the international business effort. Oman is a leader in this respect in the Middle East.

Tomorrow's international marketing by trade representatives is going to be driven by the following critical factors:- Embassies becoming centres of supply market analysis to feed local firms and government with market intelligence for capital equipment, raw materials, inputs, identifying export markets, identifying investment opportunities and lastly building good political relations for the country. The embassies must change their strategic thrust from that of being centres of political rhetoric and excellence to being centres of business excellence, emphasizing business issues as well as political issues. The USA has got its largest embassy in China with 700 staffers because of the strategic economic importance and dominance of China and the Far East as the market of the future – this embassy services the rest of the Far East. The USA has now set up Chinese Language Centres in America and English Language Centres in China as a way of promoting business through language competence. In developed countries the reason, criteria and purpose of setting up embassies is potential business opportunities in host countries and this should be the line of thinking in all countries and get correctly qualified people to be appointed to diplomatic positions – with those with international marketing qualifications and experience dominating diplomatic postings and appointments as they have the capacity to fully exploit business opportunities as opposed to non-business graduates. Collaboration with universities and research centres can give a lot of value to pre-empt and plan for the future of profitable international marketing. The biggest problems facing foreign trade representatives today are an endless transformation due to the forces of the world recession, cut throat competition, globalization, technology, ICT, language barriers, communication, cost-leadership pressures, an unpredictable business landscape, business instability, the brain drain sucking skilled labour from developing countries to NICs and the developed world leaving behind fractured, strained and sometimes malfunctioning systems, high expectations from governments to help solve their balance of payments problems through more investment and exports, terrorism targeting embassies, global warming and related supply disruptions and getting the right qualified and experienced people to run diplomatic postings.

RESEARCH METHODOLOGY

Our research is based on the following research methodologies:- observation at relevant institutions, literature review, focus group discussions in a number of organizations, desk research and scouring internet sources. This kind of scenario is very good at extracting information to make well informed decisions while also creating checks and balances on shortfalls in each system. This is called research triangulation and gives credibility to research results and findings. Gaps in one system are compensated by another system. These methods each has its merits and demerits, and using different methods of data collection gives credibility to the end result, recommendations and conclusions as they will be based on a firm scientific foundation. There are various issues to be considered in research including cost, time, practicality and available budget, resources and people. We considered all these issues before settling for our alternatives. The researchers got highly unexpected and surprising cooperation and support as they delved into the privacy and secrecy of the private and public sectors which made this exercise much easier and less stressful. This was due to dealing with an enlightened power bloc of top class technocrats who wanted to show their professionalism plus the desire for patriotism and national interest as this was research with national implications and everyone had some interests to advance and protect and lots of benefits to get from this research. We thank the participants for a high degree of maturity and team work.

LITERATURE REVIEW

Baker S (2003:141) emphasized that the arrival of the consumption-led economy had elevated the role of service in the creation and delivery of the value proposition and was a source of competitive differentiation. Baron B and Harris K (2003:11) were quick to point out that in the service industry the attitude of employees can make a real difference to the customer. Wood M B said that (2008:102) you must monitor how customers perceive the total benefits and total costs of competing products. This would help an enterprise not to lose customers and to pre-empt customers too. It can be achieved through effective marketing research and regular customer interface. Peter J P and Donnelly J H (Junior) (2007:55) warned that whenever one is doing business one must ensure that goods and services are purchased and received in a timely and efficient manner so as not to frustrate customers. Quester P and McGuiggan R (2005) admonished marketing managers that they must plan their marketing programmes such that they are flexible to be adapted to conditions in different countries or risk failure. The European Journal of Marketing (2009:Vol 3:12) said that there is now need for a paradigm shift in marketing to make the marketing practitioner aware of the total product value as well as supportive political policies through lobby and advocacy. It said the days when marketers were spectators while politicians made destructive policies are gone. This is the time when industry must shape economic policy to its preference. A true private public partnership was one of the reasons for Hong Kong's marketing success where excessive bureaucracy was done away with to better serve the global market. The Journal of Industrial Marketing Management (2009:Vol 3:18) ran a comprehensive article on modern industrial marketing emphasizing the reasons why modern industrialists buy what they buy and the said this was driven by:- the desire to improve efficiencies and cut costs, quality considerations, durability, easy of handling, convenience of use, improving productivity/automation, reducing labour as well as greenhouse gas emissions. Marketing now has to be futuristic and pre-empt global warming compliance and contribute to good housekeeping. The Journal of International Marketing (2009:Vol 2:13 said international marketing is now more of a value driven game and a political game. One has to be a good marketer and a good political schemer. On a different note the Journal of Market-Focused Management (2009:Vol 3:22) said international marketing and globalization had brought foreign problems and solutions onto our doorsteps, they brought good and bad, benefits and disasters. They further elaborated that foreign language competence was not a choice but a tool of trade for success in the globalised market. One also had to understand international relations and trading blocs as well as local and international Trade Promotion Organisations for success. Dillon W L said that "A vehicle fleet is as good as the road network and skilled technicians servicing this fleet – this is a reality in transport business." (Dillon W L:25). It is physical mobility and its efficiency which is the basic determinant of corporate and national efficiency, success, world class competitiveness, business goodwill and credibility, access to high yielding and lucrative markets, opening up of new and distant markets, enabling firms and corporate bodies to hold minimum stocks and ultimately engage in JIT and Total Quality Management (Aaker D:100). It was a sophisticated transport network that enabled the British to conquer and rule three quarters of the whole world thus giving birth to Great Britain. Even today the American economic and military supremacy is founded on having the best brainpower and the most sophisticated and largest diverse transport network (i.e. road, rail, sea and air transport network.). The Emirates Centre for Strategic Studies and Research in their book Human Resource Development In A Knowledge-Based Economy (2003:4) quote Davis and Meyer as saying that the primacy of human capital is leading to a "global war for talented people" in much the same way that nations once fought over land and gold because it was considered a valuable asset. That is how serious the competition for talent has become.

FINDINGS

Our findings from the different and diverse organizations we investigated and literature review conducted helped to convincingly answer the research questions as set out at the onset. Foreign language competence was identified as a major problem in international trade representation and a major key result area as well as documentation, trade agreements, market research, shipping practice and understanding international relations or political economy. The summarized findings were as follows:-

It is impossible to over-emphasize the importance of successful commercial activity to a county and its people. In almost all developed and developing countries, economic development depends upon growth in export trade, which in turn creates jobs and raises living standards. The increasing import requirements which flow from development must somehow be financed from foreign exchange receipts derived from export earnings and capital investment. Without dynamic expansion in exports the growth of a country's economy will almost certainly slacken. Your main objective as a commercial representative is obviously to do the best possible job of improving your country's net export earnings, in the broadest meaning of that term.

Commercial representation as a profession
The time has long since arrived to recognize commercial representation as a profession per-se, the successful exercise of which is positively correlated with careful initial selection of commercial representation, the level and content of their formal education and specialized training, the length and variety of their pertinent experience and the

quality of the support they receive from the trade promotion organization (TPO) or ministry at home. Whatever your title, be it trade ambassador, commissioner, trade attaché or commercial secretary, you are likely to have all the diplomatic status your job requires. That status will enable you even as it enables the traditional diplomat to establish and to maintain relations with officials of the host country and of other countries' embassies/missions up to the highest level appropriate for your rank. You will also be in more or less daily contact with many sectors of the economy. In addition to the usual diplomatic cycle, you will become familiar with the business and financial environments of your territory. You will have possibilities for learning the local language, adapting yourself to local customs and generally feeling at home in the host country. The work itself is absorbing, complex and challenging. It is not confined to one or a few product lines, market areas, types of buyers, marketing management skills or functional specializations. You will have to acquire a knowledge of many aspects of business activity. You must understand government laws, policies and regulations both at home and in the host country. You must gain an insight into international trade practice and at least the elements of commercial law. Since you must actively seek out trade opportunities and identify markets for specific products and services, you will need to understand the techniques of market research and the interrelationships between marketing channels. You will also require a though knowledge of your products and their products. You must be able to identify and to assess barriers to trade affecting your country. You will have to look into such matters as international physical distribution (shipping services, freight rates), financing terms and other aspects of trade facilitation. You must learn about export documentation and terminology, packing, costing and pricing for export and product adaptation and appreciate the importance of quality control. You will be expected to organize trade publicity campaigns, and to provide advice on and support to your country's participation in trade fairs, exhibitions and store promotions. You will need to assist incoming trade missions and individual exporters. You will be concerned with the identification and recommendation of agents in your territory and will have certain responsibilities for handling trade disputes. You may also be called upon to encourage foreign investment, and to help foreign business visitors to stimulate tourist interest in your country. You may, in some situations, be involved with international tendering in connection with your country's import procurements and with its participation in capital projects in your territory. You must therefore have at least a basic understanding of contracting and international bidding practices and procedures. You are most likely to have a role to play in trade policy formulation. Policy, comprising informed judgments taken at the highest levels of government, is the result of carefully evaluated inputs from innumerable sources of objectively analyzed information. As the person on the spot, you will be a primary source of this information as far as your territory is concerned. You will therefore be expected to contribute, through regular and ad-hoc reports to the evolution of your country's trade policies and export strategies, for which purpose you will need to know how to organize and to write such material. It is important that you are able to manage human, material, and financial resources. You should also know how to exercise self-discipline in planning and ordering your own priorities and objectives, so as to make the best use of your limited time. Your success as a commercial representative will quite literally depend on your initiative and the energy and enthusiasm you bring to your myriad of tasks. You should constantly think of new ways of placing your country's products in the market, get away from your desk and go out and talk to key people – the buyers and other decision makers in the market place. In trade promotion, your success is likely to be in the inverse proportion and the amount of time you spend in your office. Finally, in your professional dealings with others, honour all your commitments and never betray public confidence. You must consciously earn and maintain a reputation for absolute professional reliability and personal integrity. Moreover you must love and believe in your country and be patriotic.

DIPLOMATIC PROTOCOL, REPRESENTATIONAL ACTIVITIES AND THE PROBLEM OF LANGUAGE

In essence, protocol is a series of formalized procedures that vary from country to country. Try to determine what the local practice is for your function before you arrive at your post. Failing this, seek competent guidance on the subject as soon as possible after arrival, since some of your first action will be dictated by protocol. Your head of mission or protocol officer will be able to advise you in the matter. There are also a number of publications that will be helpful in this regard. Your relations with officials in your mission will be determined by your country's established norms for persons of your rank and position. Your relation with members of other missions, local government officials, and members of the public will be primarily governed by local customs. The practice of introducing yourself on arrival by formal calls still applies in some countries. With the help of the protocol officer at your post, you should inform yourself quickly on the local practice with respect to official calls and carry out the accepted formalities promptly after arrivals. Formal calls are a quick and effective means of establishing useful relations with your counterparts in other missions and with local officials. They are likely to be much more helpful when they know you on a personal, friendly basis. If the post does not have calling cards printed for you prior to your arrival, seek advice before obtaining a substantial quantity. Practice as to size, format and usage varies in different countries. Cards are generally about 2 by 3 1/2 inches (or 60 x 100mm). Engraving produces a better result than printing. Your full name, followed by your official approved title and the name of your mission, is all that is required on diplomatic calling cards. Initials indicating professional qualifications should not be used. Cards in the language of the host country may be engraved or printed when you are thoroughly conversant with that language. Outside normal considerations of etiquette, precedence according to rank is probably the most rigorous form of protocol of which you need to be aware. It is relevant at all formal ceremonies and functions, in calling and at hospitality events, especially in the matter of table seating. In this sense, precedence differs little from the custom in many countries of seating senior company officials in order of rank at the head table at a company banquet, or placing party leaders on the platform in order of their importance at a political rally. In essence, the rules of precedence are a routine means of facilitating official and formal diplomatic relationships. Every country has an established list of precedence, which is normally available from the local ministry of foreign affairs. If you are a junior officer, one of the difficulties you will face in a major capital is the unyielding formality of the diplomatic hierarchy. One's diplomatic status determines one's operating and communicating level. There are probably hundreds of junior officials who can speak only to other junior officials or their equivalent in rank in the local government. The same constraint generally operates all the way up to the most senior people in diplomatic missions. This inflexible practice can severely inhabit some of your activities in some countries. To reach a certain individual in the local government or in another mission you may have to go through several other people. Even then, you may not achieve contact of the kind you need to attain your objective. At most smaller posts, however, these rules do not apply to the same degree.

Representational activities

Representational activities are a major aspect of your public relations responsibilities and of your relations with people and organizations important for your work. Be prepared to host and to attend social and official functions, with the following objectives:

- To establish, maintain and improve your contacts with the government and business sectors of the post territory, with a view to obtaining information, advice and assistance.
- To protect image of your country as a reliable exporter of quality goods and services, as a good trading partner, as an attractive country to visit, and as a secure, hospitable and profitable destination for foreign investment.
- To exchange useful trade and other information and develop your knowledge and understanding of the local environment for the promotion of trade and the attainment of other official objectives.
- To introduce business and official visitors from home to useful trade contacts in your territory.

Types of activities

Cultivate working relationships with appropriate government officials, business people and other useful contacts in your territory through association on both a professional and a personal level. There are a variety of ways of developing these associations, depending on the social norms of the territory. Plan your entertainment and other representational activities. The type and nature of entertainment vary from country to country, but generally take the form of receptions, cocktails, film showings, etc.; luncheons; dinners; and informal entertainment at short notice. Local customs must be observed carefully, to avoid giving unwitting offence. Invitations for any formal type of entertainment should be issued in advance and generally confirmed by telephone to allow proper planning. Careful attention in this regard must be paid to local customs, habits and sensitivities. Greeting cards should also be sent to important contacts, following local custom, and due attention paid to customary rituals important to people at the post territory. In addition, ensure that officials concerned with trade and business are all invited to grace the occasions.

Accepting invitations

Entertainment is generally expected to be reciprocated. Exercise some care and selectivity therefore to ensure that you do not incur return obligations that are beyond your means. Take particular care not to accept or to appear to accept excessively lavish hospitality. In principle you may accept invitations from individuals and organisations important to your work, including those of other diplomatic missions, to strengthen and to widen your network of contacts and as a means of discussing issues related to the trade environment and trade opportunities of the post territory. All written invitations received should be scrupulously answered if their wording implies that an answer is expected.

Gratuities of gifts

Your government will very probably have issued detailed instructions in this regard. In the absence of such instructions, neither you nor any member of your family should accept a gift in money or convertible into money from any person or organization for services rendered in the exercise of your official functions. Occasions will undoubtedly arise (e.g. hospitality extended by trade contacts) when, for one reason or another, you cannot apply this simple rule of thumb. In such situations, and in any case of doubt, you should seek the guidance of your head of mission or other senior mission official. Perishable goods may be donated to charity. Valuable presents that cannot be returned should be regarded as your government's property and be handled in accordance with instructions you either have already received or will solicit from the appropriate authority in your country when the problem arises.

Conflict of interest

The same general principles apply to any other arrangements you may make that could give rise to a charge of conflict of interest. Conflicts of interest are of too many kinds to describe here. But in principle, you should not engage or appear to engage in any activity for your personal benefit that is inconsistent with your responsibilities as an accredited representative of your country. Obviously, you should not participate in any activity that causes an excessive drain on your time and energy or which, by its nature, would reflect on the dignity or the standing of your country's foreign service.

Moreover, the terms of your accreditation to your host government would normally preclude your engaging in any activity that is not compatible with your status.

Language

Language is your primary means of acquiring and transmitting knowledge. As you are in the business of collecting commercial intelligence and communicating it to others, words, and hence language, are quite literally the tools of your trade. And as you will spend much of your time abroad, you may as well recognize that you need to acquire some proficiency in one or more foreign languages. You therefore have a problem - in fact, two problems. You must try your best to acquire an adequate knowledge of the local language, wherever you may be posted, enough, at least, to be able to follow news broadcasts and to read the daily newspaper as well as local publications containing important basic information. While ideally you should go as far as possible beyond this, with a view to acquiring a true mastery of the written and spoken word, you simply may not be able to do this in the course of a posting of two or three years. All that can be expected of you is that you do your best, by studying suitable textbooks, purchasing tapes or language recordings, taking language courses, and listening to local radio and television broadcasts, in such time as you may have to spare. If your service can arrange it, a "total immersion" course can greatly accelerate the process of gaining oral proficiency. The study of a language can be enjoyable and stimulating, particularly if you have the opportunity to put it to use. It would be of a great psychological help to take a firm decision at the outset to make language studies a regular feature, if not a way, of life.

This leads, however, to a consideration of your second problem. Which language or languages should you make the greatest effort to acquire as a commercial representative who is likely to serve in many different counties?

RELATIONS WITH YOUR EXPORTING COMMUNITY

In the eyes of your country's exporters, you are your country's export strategist on how to trade with your territory and you will frequently be asked for commercial information. However, you should be more than merely an expert to be consulted as the occasion arises; you must also be an ever-active force, working constantly on behalf of your country and its exporters in the market-place. You are in the commercial intelligence business. In gathering information you must spread your net as wide as possible. Before sending information to its users, however, you must prune, edit, analyse and summarize it. You should constantly ask yourself the questions: "What is essential or useful?" and "Whose interests are likely to suffer if I fail to provide this information?" You must be broadly knowledgeable on a large number of subjects. Your job is to acquire information across the commercial spectrum and to pass it on to the specialists who are able to use it. It might be said that your range of interests is horizontal while that of the people you serve is vertical. You must know enough about the interests of the public and private agencies at home to be able to select what may be of use to them. This means that you have to understand their needs well enough to judge correctly what to discard, so as not to flood the system with useful material. Reduced to its simplest terms, your role in export promotion may be described as follows:

- **Know you product:** learn all you can about your country's actual and potential exports and keep this knowledge up to date.
- **Know your markets:** learn all you can about the characteristics of your territory and keep this knowledge up to date.
- **Know what is involved in bringing products and markets together.**

You will acquire a knowledge of the goods and services your country has to offer in a number of ways. First, as arranged by your TPO or ministry at home, you should have been given a tour of your country's industrial and other economic sectors prior to your first posting abroad and should go on regular refresher tours between postings. Secondly, a knowledge of your country's supply capabilities can be gained and kept up to date by means of supply surveys of your country. The gathering and maintenance of such information is the responsibility of your TPO or ministry, which should keep you informed of what is available. Your responsibility is to study the material provided in order to become an expert on what is available in your country for export, to the point that you can become a supply consultant to importers. A planned tour of the facilities of selected manufacturers and exporters representing a broad cross-section of your country's supply capability will enable you to:

- Meet producers face to face, to learn of their production and marketing problems and concerns.
- Familiarize yourself at first hand with the goods and services your country has to offer; and
- Lay a firm foundation for a growing future relationship of mutual trust and confidence with your exporters.

It will help if you understand your role as the exporter's eyes and ears in the market-place. You should never miss an opportunity to show the exporter that your aim is to be of service, in effect to be an extension of his/her firm. Your objective is to build up a partnership between your government and the exporter, not only to the exporter's advantage, but also to that of your country as a whole. Halfway through your posting, it would be useful, resources permitting, for you to visit your home country for briefing sessions with the appropriate officials of your ministry and /or TPO. Of primary importance, however, would be the associated tour of your country's export sector which you could then make to initiate and to renew acquaintances with business people, and to discuss with them their particular marketing problems in your territory. Before leaving your post, solicit the help of your headquarters in preparing your itinerary, write to the people concerned to let them know you will be coming. Carry home with you adequate notes on the particular problems and trade opportunities you will be discussing with them. The same kind of tour should be arranged after completion of a posting abroad when you should debrief, both individually and in groups, business people who are particularly interested in the markets for which you were formerly responsible. In addition, if you are to go on to another post, you should arrange, again with headquarters support, a visit of exporters to be briefed on their interests in the markets to which you will shortly be assigned. The continuing development of this relationship should be one of your most important and never-ending tasks.

Know your markets
Export promotion covers four principal areas of activity. All demand a thorough knowledge of the markets you are responsible for developing. These areas of activity are discussed bellow. At the outset, you have to identify and to survey specific markets for your country's export goods and services and to uncover trade opportunities. This means that you must constantly search for such opportunities, for trading partners, and for market information. You then have to interpret what you find to identify what is relevant to your country's export possibilities and useful for your traders and officials. Finally, you must communicate that commercial intelligence to them as quickly as possible, and in such a form as to enable them to act upon it. You may find a market for a product, but this does not mean that your suppliers will automatically have access to that market. Evaluate your information before rushing it indiscriminately to your exporters. High tariffs may prevent entry: non-tariff barriers such as quotas, preferential arrangements, quarantine restrictions, packing specifications and labeling requirements may eliminate or severely limit market prospects. When such barriers exist, and especially if they appear to discriminate against your exporter's products vis-à-vis those of other countries, you may wish to initiate, though your TPO or ministry, a request that action be undertaken through diplomatic channels to negotiate fair and equitable treatment. You should always be alert to such possibilities and be prepared to intervene as necessary in this way. Even when access has been achieved, market entry has to be facilitated. Review frequently such matters as shipping services, freight rates, financing terms, and related subjects connected with local expectations or international practice. Also monitor, as closely as you can, the actions and strategies of your competitors. Much can be learned by observing how others deal with the problems that you face.

Promoting sales

When you have an acceptable product with access to the market, you must take action to penetrate that market to the best of your ability. You will have to advice the most appropriate marketing strategy to maximize your product's acceptance in the market. You will have to exercise your initiative and to assist in such activities as selecting and participating in trade fairs; organizing trade displays and store promotions; guiding your country's business visitors and trade mission; making speeches to interested groups; working at press and public relations; maintaining a flow of timely commercial intelligence; and helping local business people with their trading problems, so as to improve their commercial relations with your country. To be truly capable of bringing products and markets together, you must acquire a basic knowledge of a vast array of subjects and have access to the relevant documentation or information source. You must, for example, understand:-

- Marketing as a process.
- The techniques of market research.
- Marketing channels.
- The role and functions of various kinds of agent.
- Marketing communications.
- The uses of trade publicity.
- Trade fairs and exhibitions.
- Export documentation and terminology.
- Documentary credits and collections.
- Sales contracts and elements of commercial law.
- Quality control and export standards.
- Packaging requirements for both, shipping and promotion in export markets.
- Costing and pricing for export.
- Exchange control regulations in both countries
- Transit regulations
- Customs and Excise regulations in both countries
- Bilateral and multilateral trade agreements and the benefits thereof. This can make or break the whole effort and create competitiveness or failure.
- Political and economic risk analysis in both countries as well as transit countries.
- Availability of currency
- Business custom, language and infrastructural realities
- ICT competence and realities

If you are to succeed in your task of bringing products and markets together, you will have to recognize that no matter how enthusiastic and energetic you may be, the demands on your time are likely to be greater than you are able to satisfy. You will find that the only practical way to deal with this problem will be to establish a firm system of well-defined priorities and objectives. This will be especially necessary at a smaller mission, where either you will be alone or will have the assistance of only a few officers to deal with the entire range of trade work. Your objectives should be practical. If you are starting in a new market area, you could begin by examining the range of goods and services available for export from your country. Consider carefully all significant

598

products. Decide on priorities for research based on your best judgment and on any instructions/guidance you may have on their relative importance. Your TPO or ministry is in the best position to do the basic research into these matters and should be able to provide you to investigate. Then examine market demand for each of these products by evaluating such factors as:

- Consumption in your territory;
- Volume of imports;
- The nature and sources of foreign competition;
- The marketing channels for the product;
- Growth trends in consumption in the host country;
- The likely effect of anticipated developments;
- The prospect of stimulating demand; and
- The scope for a new or a differentiated product.
- Possibility of using agents

Next, analyze the main factors affecting the market for your product and the extent to which your actions may help. You may find problems of market access or of distribution, or a need to stimulate demand by using selective promotional techniques.
This process will result in a short list of products which you can attempt to promote with a reasonable hope of success. Rank them again on the basis of the likelihood of success. Consider both the products themselves and the specific activities by which you intend to promote them. Forward planning is vital. Establish deadlines and targets. Draw up a timetable for meeting the targets. The need for such planning will be particularly obvious in connection with trade fairs and exhibitions.

Strategy for Embassies

Countries also a need to open up embassies in high value world centres manned by the right people with business qualifications and business experience, especially trade attaches and trade promotion officers, if countries are to benefit anything out of their embassies. The establishment of embassies must be guided by the principle of potential business to be generated in a country, besides the usual political objectives. This is what has generally guided most NICs and they have reaped huge rewards in the form of increased business in home countries generated from the embassies. Embassies also need to be given serious business and economic targets to meet like investment, exports, imports, tourist arrivals and national public relations, besides the standard political considerations and targets. These become the Key Result Areas or the reason or justification for their establishment or existence. Adequate resources also need to be pumped into embassies so that they can carry their mandates with reasonable ease. The same goes with key national Trade Promotion Organisations (TPOs); they need national support in order for them to do justice to countries in their international trade efforts. More interaction is necessary with the rest of the world and is not an option. These financial and economic innovations are going to be some of the key strategic economic drivers which can make or break any country – there is no alternative. Completely valueless embassies may need to be closed and a country establishes regional embassies to service a number of countries if one country does not warrant the establishment of an embassy. The USA has an embassy with a staff complement of seven hundred people in China – the largest embassy in the world; the reason for this big embassy was to take advantage of the big business potential in China and pre-empt the rest of the world. They have established many Chinese Language Centres in the USA and English Language Centres in China as the quickest way and strategy to close the language barrier and accelerate business. Almost all developed countries and NICs have been very selective in establishing embassies the world over and have been guided by business potential, pay back, marketing excellence and convenience, ease of access and as a facilitative tool for business, but without ignoring political objectives altogether. Today's marketers must wear so many hats. They must understand politics, sociology, business and anthropology. Business success is not simply derived from the best product but an eye for politics and political dynamics too. Oman has been very strategic in this respect and has established embassies in strategic world centres as well as commercial offices in places like Dubai and others to exploit business opportunities there. The Sultanate also has an array of business advisory services supporting these embassies and commercial offices to maximize business and these are supported with state of the art ICT, highly informative websites, good budgets, inter-state relations and political commitment. The same applies to South Africa too. She has been very strategic in her embassy choices with huge benefits to her credit. But Zimbabwe is a mixed bag and has not been so careful and had to close some unproductive embassies which proved valueless economically and opened new ones where it matters most economically.

Conclusion and Recommendations

This discussion brings to light some major realities about working as a national foreign trade representative in the global arena. Expertise and experience would normally eliminate most potential problems and lead to better relations with government and industry back home and other 3rd parties as well as maximizing new business generation for a country. Marketing of national goods and services to the corners of the world is no easy task and is prone to a myriad of problems and hurdles. This is overcome through experience, acculturation, networking, strategic alliances, research and innovation, humility, benchmarking practices and commitment to learn. The commonest problems encountered include, language, culture, political instability especially in third world countries, inadequate budgets (also associated with some third world countries) and this puts diplomats in a very embarrassing situation as they fail to maintain minimum dignity and comfort and to return hospitality from firms and other embassies, public relations spin where diplomats are expected to defend their nations at all costs and balancing foreign postings with maintaining contact with the extended family at home. There is the additional problem of reverse cultural shock where diplomats coming home after a long posting find that they have been overtaken in terms of influence in the extended family and in the organization. They may have been left far behind by subordinates now holding more senior positions and they have to reconcile with the painful reality of reporting to their former juniors – it may cause severe psychosomatic problems. This can be quite frustrating if relations were previously not good and one suffers from reverse fixing by ex-subordinates which at worst can force someone out of the organisation.

Considering the foregoing we recommend as follows for excellence in foreign trade representation:-

- Multilingual staff are now an asset who can service diverse markets speaking different languages and who are familiar with different cultures. Therefore training in key foreign languages can be a make or break for new diplomats. Orientation is very important before international postings. Most countries have a one month intensive diplomatic training programme covering marketing, economics, international relations and diplomatic protocol.
- Work with a reputable and credible shipping and forwarding company and travel agency to handle your portfolio whenever needed.
- Develop good relations with relevant Government Departments like Industry & Commerce, Customs & Excise Department, TPOs, etc.
- Establish good relations with the diplomatic community and industries that matter that can add value to your country and arrange inward buyer and seller missions whenever possible to tap into potential business opportunities.
- Have a functional and comprehensive website that feeds stakeholders with up to date information and market intelligence and acts as a marketing platform for the country.
- Employ highly qualified personnel. It is better to recruit international marketing interns every year to maintain capacity and do in-house training to give the required experience. The lead time is normally two years for an intern to gain full confidence and exposure in the job. You can also work closely with relevant university departments and research institutions to tap into their researches and pre-empt problems. If good degree programmes in trade policy and international marketing are not available in a country then it is the responsibility of government and industry to make sure these are introduced either at state or private universities as a matter of urgency. Otherwise the international marketing effort would be futile without supportive and relevant skills base.
- Staff being posted to overseas locations must go with their families to avoid serious and destructive cultural shock. They also need serious orientation regarding what to expect and how to adapt. Some diplomats have committed suicide or given up diplomatic postings because of new environmental frustrations like language, food, religion, cultural differences and failing to fit into local communities.
- Employment promotional opportunities must also be extended to people in diplomatic postings so that they are not badly disadvantaged during their long tour of duty.

==

The following is a research paper by the co-author (Faustino Taderera) on the secret of South Korea's economic supremacy and excellence and its ability to adopt world best practice. It was part of PhD requirements.

INTRODUCTION

I will write about South Korea's best practice which has propelled this country into a global economic power within the past fifty years. A lot of powerful institutions were put up by South Korea like universities, hospitals, roads, bridges, industries, utilities e.g. electricity, water, railways, airlines and airports, mines, etc. These institutions have no doubt completely transformed and revolutionized the quality of life of the average South Korean citizen. The creation of Techno parks at universities and industrial zones led to the creation of new unique industries in new advanced areas of economic endeavor like biomedical sciences and aerospace engineering. It is my belief that I need to define best practice first then proceed to do an analysis of the best practices of South Korea which have worked very well to steer it to success and prosperity. The definition follows:- A **Best practice** is a technique, method, process, activity, incentive, or reward that is believed to be more effective at delivering a particular outcome than any other technique, method, process, etc. when applied to a particular condition or circumstance. The idea is that with proper processes, checks, and testing, a desired outcome can be delivered with fewer problems and unforeseen complications. Best practices can also be defined as the most efficient (least amount of effort) and effective (best results) way of accomplishing a task, based on repeatable procedures that have proven themselves over time for large numbers of people.

A given best practice is only applicable to particular condition or circumstance and may have to be modified or adapted for similar circumstances. In addition, a "best" practice can evolve to become better as improvements are discovered. Despite the need to improve on processes as times change and things evolve, best-practice is considered by some as a business buzzword used to describe the process of developing and following a standard way of doing things that multiple organizations can use for management, policy, and especially software systems. As the term has become more popular, some organizations have begun using the term "best practices" to refer to what are in fact merely 'rules', causing a linguistic drift in which a new term such as "good ideas" is needed to refer to what would previously have been called "best practices."

Exchange

Best practices in a particular industry or other professional field can be exchanged, just like any instructional capital, by any means, though Internet-related information is most commonly exchanged this way:

- source code
- e-democracy
- e-government

Best practices domains

Domains where Best Practices have been applied include:

- Teaching/Education
- Incremental and iterative development
- Quality assurance
- Performance engineering
- Risk management
- Change process
- Change Management
- Release execution
- Milestones
- Release control
- Defect tracking
- Use case
- Requirements management
- Automated testing process
- Nursing
- Evidence-based medicine
- Physical planning and land use management
- Water pollution control, watershed protection and restoration
- Local governance
- Home care

Best practices are used in technology development, such as new software, but also in construction, transportation, business management, sustainable development, and various aspects of project management. Best practices are also used in healthcare to deliver high quality care that promotes best outcomes. Best practices are used within any business type including, but not limited to: sales, manufacturing, teaching, programming software, road construction, health care, insurance, and accounting. From a national point of view best practice covers political, social and economic policy as well as international relations. It applies to the effectiveness of state institutions in supporting business and economic development vies-a-vies international best practice. It also refers to a country's ability to attract and retain investment, grow its economy, maintain peace and tranquility, put in place legal protection of property and intellectual rights, have a transparent and independent judiciary, have media freedom and human rights and finally a complete separation of powers (judiciary, legislature and the executive with a free media as the forth pillar of government).This is not possible without membership of the United Nations and other regional and international conventions. Competent and supportive army and police institutions are necessary for securing a nation.

REGIONAL SUPREMACY

It is not a secret that the Asian tigers are competing against each other as well as competing with other Asian and global economies. South Korea has always had the battle of supremacy with its northern communist neighbor, North Korea whose stupid doctrine has ruined that Korea in almost all respects, except military. It has always been South Korea's desire to create a first world economy that outshines the north and this has been one of the motivating factors.

603

The act of being in South East Asia where economic super powers are outshining and competing each other has forced South Korea to benchmark in all its practices. Economic theory has it that being in the midst of highly competitive and innovative countries and firms creates competitive behavior and forces innovation on all players; this is the case with South Korea. In the long run it creates a culture of innovation and creativity. Because of this South Korea has set benchmarks in industry, commerce and services as well as government where performance management reigns supreme.

TECHNOPARKS AS AN INNOVATION VEHICLE IN SOUTH KOREA

To realize the creation of a modern high technology nation, South Korea created special locations - industrial parks, techno-parks and innovational incubators. The American and Japanese models of the techno-park system was adopted. Massive research funds were made available and researchers recruited from all over the world to drive the innovation miracle. Secrecy worked well for Korea which worked quietly without other countries being able to copy its innovations quickly. Private public partnerships were central to this strategy. Universities, research centres, government and the private sector all worked together in this win-win situation. Spectacular evolution of innovations and technologies, registered in South Korea in the last few decades, constituted a major premise to development and investment strategies. The new types of investments, being generated by new financing and management schemes, was located in new forms - like special economic zones destined in initiation, creation and presentation of new ideas. The competitive advantage of an economy doesn't rely only on products, services or natural resources and not even on geographical and historical particularities. At the moment competitive advantage can be created only by sustaining and promoting knowledge, through science and innovation. That constitutes the bench mark of growth for any successful nation, hence why South Korea put techno-parks at the centerpiece of its rapid economic.

Today, the South Korean economy is dominated by large business groups known as Chaebol. These include companies such as Samsung, LG, Hyundai-Kia and SK. The Chaebol are government-supported powerful global multinationals owning numerous international enterprises. The 10 largest South Korean companies by market value are Samsung Electronics, POSCO, Hyundai Motor, KB Financial Group, Shinhan Financial Group, Samsung Life Insurance, Korea Electric Power, LG Electronics, Hyundai Mobis, LG Chem.

Despite lacking natural resources and having the smallest territory among the G-20 major economies, the South Korean economy is the fourth largest in Asia and 15th largest in the world. The country will be the chair country of the G-20 major economies in 2010 is the first Asian country to host the G-20 summit in Seoul on November 2010. Like West Germany and Japan, rapid industrialization since the 1960s has made South Korea one of the world's top ten exporters. It is the seventh largest trading partner of the United States and the eighth largest trading partner of the European Union. In 2009, South Korea was ranked as the most innovative country in the world among major economies by the BCG and NAM. South Korea is the world's largest shipbuilder, and one of the world's top five automobile manufacturing nations. South Korea is also dominant in crude oil imports, refined oil exports, and the building construction industry. Its capital, Seoul, has been listed as one of the world's top ten financial and commercial cities by Forbes and Mastercard, and is the center of the service industry in South Korea.

Computerisation and robotics technology is the hallmark of the country's industrialisation.   E-government is now the norm and links all government systems and the outside world. There is a zero tolerance to corruption as evidenced by the trial of even the country's former president recently; no one is above the law. This is a quite helpful signal to the outside world and investing public that there is accountability and transparency in the country. Media freedom helps illuminate the public debate and to disinfect society and provide checks and balances.

EDUCATIONAL BENCHMARKS

Educational benchmarks are some of the standards developed to propel South Korea to higher levels in industrialization. It is said that if you want to industrialise you have to start with relevant and appropriate education right through. Engineering, science and technology normally take centre stage as can be seen by what happened when Germany overtook the UK as an industrial power after the UK had lagged behind in science and technology education. The same happened with Japan which has worked relentlessly to promote science and technology education.

Subject benchmark statements provide a means for the academic community to describe the nature and characteristics of programmes in a specific subject. They also represent general expectations about the standards for the award of qualifications at a given level and articulate the attributes and capabilities that those possessing such qualifications should be able to demonstrate. Subject benchmark statements are used for a variety of purposes. Primarily, they are an important external source of reference for higher education institutions when new programmes are being designed and developed in a subject area. They provide general guidance for articulating the learning outcomes associated with the programme but are not a specification of a detailed curriculum in the subject. Benchmark statements provide for variety and flexibility in the design of programmes and encourage innovation within an agreed overall framework.

South Korea has set up a Higher Education Accreditation Council whose mandate is to manage the maintenance and improvement of the highest educational standards in the country. Educational standards determine national industrial and commercial competitiveness. The statement represents the first attempt to make explicit the general academic characteristics and standards of diploma and degrees in South Korea. The Benchmark Statements should be interpreted in the context of the balance, breadth, depth and expected level of attainment associated with these different programmes.

Objectives

The primary purposes of the Benchmarking Statements are to assist: -

- higher education institutions in designing and validating programmes of study;
- academic reviewers and external examiners in verifying and comparing standards;
- where appropriate, professional bodies during accreditation and review processes;
- students and employers when seeking information about higher education provision.

All new programmes require accreditation by a the national body before they can be allowed to operate in the country. Members of the working group have considerable experience of the accreditation process and the production of the statements has benefited from that experience.

ECONOMIC POLICY BENCHMARKS

Economic policy benchmarks refers to the actions that governments take in the economic field. It covers the systems for setting interest rates and government budget as well as the labour market, national ownership, and many other areas of government interventions into the economy.

Such policies are often influenced by international institutions like the International Monetary Fund or World Bank as well as political beliefs and the consequent policies of parties.

Macroeconomic stabilization policy

South Korea has engaged in an economic stabilization policy using the following instruments:-

- Fiscal policy, often tied to Keynesian economics, uses government spending and taxes to guide the economy.
  - o Fiscal stance: The size of the deficit
  - o Tax policy: The taxes used to collect government income.
  - o Government spending on just about any area of government
- Monetary policy controls the value of currency by lowering the supply of money to control inflation and raising it to stimulate economic growth. It is concerned with the amount of money in circulation and, consequently, interest rates and inflation.
  - o Interest rates, set by the Government
  - o Incomes policies and price controls that aim at imposing non-monetary controls on inflation
  - o Reserve requirements which affect the money multiplier

Tools and goals

South Korean Policy is generally directed to achieve particular objectives, like targets for inflation, unemployment, or economic growth. Sometimes other objectives, like military spending or nationalization are important. To achieve these goals, South Korea uses policy tools which are under the control of the government. These generally include the interest rate and money supply, tax and government spending, tariffs, exchange rates, labour market regulations, and many other aspects of government.

Selecting tools and goals

South Korea and its central bank set out to achieve a number of goals to reduce inflation, reduce unemployment, and reduce interest rates while maintaining currency stability. The intention has been to make the country the preferred investment destination internationally. A number of business facilitative measures were introduced like:-

- 100% profit repatriation was introduced and quicker investment application processing
- Customs clearing was revolutionised with the introduction of e-clearance and a turnaround of minutes rather than hours to make the system user friendly and increase the volume of business transacted each day which naturally improves economic performance.

ENTREPRENEURSHIP

Given entrepreneurship's potential to support economic growth, it is the policy goal South Korea to develop a culture of entrepreneurial thinking. This can be done in a number of ways: by integrating entrepreneurship into education systems, legislating to encourage risk-taking, and national campaigns. South Korea has been part of this campaign with great zeal and with remarkable success. In the 20th century, the understanding of entrepreneurship owes much to the work of economist Joseph Schumpeter in the 1940s and other Austrian economists such as Carl Menger, Ludwig von Mises and Friedrich von Hayek. In Schumpeter, an entrepreneur is a person who is willing and able to convert a new idea or invention into a successful innovation. Entrepreneurship employees what Schumpeter called "the gale of creative destruction" to replace in whole or in part inferior innovations across markets and industries, simultaneously creating new products including new business models. In this way, creative destruction is largely responsible for the dynamism of industries and long-run economic growth. The supposition that entrepreneurship leads to economic growth is an interpretation of the residual in endogenous growth theory and as such is hotly debated in academic economics. An alternate, description posited by Israel Kirzner suggests that the majority of innovations may be much more incremental improvements such as the replacement of paper with plastic in the construction of a drinking straw. South Korea has seen so much entrepreneurship on a grand scale with the creation of mega-industries across the board thus propelling it to a world economic super power. In the whole world people say "As creative and hard working as a Korean," and for good reasons.

Entrepreneurship is driven by an innovation culture. Rogers defines several intrinsic characteristics of innovations that influence an individual's decision to adopt or reject an innovation. The relative advantage is how improved an innovation is over the previous generation. Compatibility is the second characteristic, the level of compatibility that an innovation has to be assimilated into an individual's life. The complexity of an innovation is a significant factor in whether it is adopted by an individual. If the innovation is too difficult to use an individual will not likely adopt it. The fourth characteristic, trialability, determines how easily an innovation may be experimented with as it is being adopted. If a user has a hard time using and trying an innovation this individual will be less likely to adopt it. The final characteristic, observability, is the extent that an innovation is visible to others. An innovation that is more visible will drive communication among the individual's peers and personal networks and will in turn create more positive or negative reactions.

Innovations are often adopted by organizations through two types of innovation-decisions: collective innovation decisions and authority innovation decisions. The collection-innovation decision occurs when the adoption of an innovation has been made by a consensus among the members of an organization. The authority-innovation decision occurs when the adoption of an innovation has been made by very few individuals with high positions of power within an organization. Unlike the optional innovation decision process, these innovation-decision processes only occur within an organization or hierarchical group. Within the innovation decision process in an organization there are certain individuals termed "champions" who stand behind an innovation and break through any opposition that the innovation may have caused. The champion within the diffusion of innovation theory plays a very similar role as to the champion used within the efficiency business model Six Sigma. The innovation process within an organization contains five stages that are slightly similar to the innovation-decision process that individuals undertake. These stages are: agenda-setting, matching, redefining/restructuring, clarifying, routinizing. Innovation has been widely credited as the reason for South Korea's economic miracle. Innovation enabled South Korea to set excellent benchmarks to compete internationally.

Besides innovation creativity has also been at the centre stage in South Korea in all economic, political and social activities. Creativity is a mental and social process involving the discovery of new ideas or concepts, or new associations of the creative mind between existing ideas or concepts. Creativity is fueled by the process of either conscious or unconscious insight. An alternative conception of creativeness (based on its etymology) is that it is simply the act of making something new. Although popularly associated with art and literature, it is also an essential part of innovation and invention and is important in professions such as business, economics, architecture, industrial design, graphic design, advertising, mathematics, music, science and engineering, and teaching. Despite, or perhaps because of, the ambiguity and multi-dimensional nature of creativity, entire industries have been spawned from the pursuit of creative ideas and the development of creativity techniques in South Korea.

KOREA NATIONAL PRODUCTIVITY CENTRE

In its drive to set benchmarks for itself as an industrial powerhouse South Korea set up a National Productive Centre. The overall objective of a National Productivity Centre is to impart productivity consciousness into the public and organizations so as to generate visible improvement in the quantity and quality of goods and services with the aim of enhancing the living standards of the citizenry. The following are the functions of a National Productivity Centre in any country:-

☐   Provision of consultancy and advisory services to management and workers of organizations aimed at utilizing to the fullest all available and potential resources for production;

☐   Disseminating information on methods and programmes for improving productivity in all sectors of the economy;

☐   Soliciting and accepting technical aids for schemes and projects designed for productivity improvement;

☐   Encouraging the formation of Productivity Committees and establishing branches of the Centre in each region of the country.

☐   Conducting studies in both the levels of productivity and the contemporary method of improving productivity in all sectors of the economy;

☐   Encouraging and assisting business enterprises to set up productivity schemes;

☐   Liaising on a continuous basis, with research institutes and universities and other similar organizations considered relevant in furthering the Centre's objectives by the Governing Council.

·   Promoting cooperation among similar organizations engaged in the promotion of productivity by liaising with national, regional and international organizations, associations and research institutes such as International Labour Organisation (ILO), United Nations Development Programme (UNDP), United Nations Conference for Trade and Development (UNCTAD), Asia Productivity Organisation (APO), European Association of National Productivity Centre (EANPC), Pan African Productivity Association (PAPA), etc.

The above functions are in consonance with the generic functions of National Productivity Organizations (NPOs) worldwide, which include;

(i)   *Promoting Productivity Improvement and Productivity Culture*
The activities here involve instilling attitudinal change and creating awareness among people involved in productivity improvement.

(ii)   *Assisting Enterprises in Productivity Improvement Through Building Their Capacities*
This involves offering support to enterprises through training programmes, guidance and consulting on practical productivity improvement measures, providing information on methods and techniques (measurement methods, etc) related to productivity improvement.

(iii)   *Acquiring, Processing and Disseminating Information*
Acquire, process and disseminate information on productivity improvement strategies, approaches, methods and techniques as well as lessons from best practices from local and international experiences.

(iv) *Networking with Other Organizations involved in Productivity Improvement by Playing the Catalyst Role*
The National Productivity Centre plays the role of a Catalyst and networks with other organizations for improved productivity.

SOUTH KOREA PRE- AND POST SHIPMENT INSPECTION

South Korea has a system of pre and post-shipment inspection on exports and imports as part of promoting international trade. Pre-Shipment Inspection by its functional definition is referred to as the process where an independent inspection of goods is carried out before shipment. An increasing number of countries all over the world are joining the global market.
Globalisation consequentially calls for universal standards - global products or services that will meet the world's expectations. Because of this factor of global marketing these global players are now insisting on inspection of goods before shipment. It is important to note that all of this is an effort to place quality products on the global market.
Total quality management is the backbone of national, regional and international business at any level.
Significance
Pre-shipment inspection embraces product quality, quantity being exported and the price(s) proposed and market prices comparison at the time of shipment. The main purpose really of inspection is to check that the goods in question fully meet the contractual requirements of the importer with regard to price, quality, quantity and customs classification. This is to ensure that the products comply with the description found in the export sales contract/bill of lading/export invoice. Subsequently they will be examined or checked as they are loaded into the container or the ship/vessel.
The inspections are also carried out to prevent general smuggling and smuggling of dangerous drugs and arms of war. In a war situation countries carry out pre and post-shipment inspections for these same state security reasons. Customs authorities and governments are very keen to prevent smuggling as it robs them of much needed state revenue in the form of duties and taxies. Inspections are also done by governments to prevent externalization of foreign exchange through undercharging exports and overcharging imports and agents commission – this can easily ruin a country and lead to economic collapse.

RESEARCH AND DEVELOPMENT

South Korea is a renowned world leader in Research and Development. New product design and development is more often than not a crucial factor in the survival of a company. In an industry that is fast changing, firms must continually revise their design and range of products. This is necessary due to continuous technology change and development as well as other competitors and the changing preference of customers. A system driven by marketing is one that puts the customer needs first, and only produces goods that are known to sell. Market research is carried out, which establishes what is needed. If the development is technology driven then it is a matter of selling what it is possible to make. The product range is developed so that production processes are as

610

efficient as possible and the products are technically superior, hence possessing a natural advantage in the market place. Statistics on organizations devoted to "R&D" may express the state of an industry, the degree of competition or the lure of progress. Some common measures include: budgets, numbers of patents or on rates of peer-reviewed publications. R & D is one of the major reasons why South Korea achieved an economic miracle.

In general, R&D activities are conducted by specialized units or centers belonging to companies, universities and state agencies. In the context of commerce, "research and development" normally refers to future-oriented, longer-term activities in science or technology, using similar techniques to scientific research without predetermined outcomes and with broad forecasts of commercial yield. In 2006, the world's four largest spenders of R&D were the United States (US$343 billion), the EU (US$231 billion), China (US$136 billion), and Japan (US$130 billion). In terms of percentage of GDP, the order of these spenders for 2006 was China (US$115 billion of US$2,668 billion GDP), Japan, United States, EU with approximate percentages of 4.3, 3.2, 2.6, and 1.8 respectively. The top 10 spenders in terms of percentage of GDP were Israel (4.53%), Sweden (3.73%), Finland (3.45%), Japan (3.39%), South Korea (3.23%), Switzerland (2.9%), Iceland (2.78%), United States (2.62%), Germany (2.53%) and Austria (2.45%).

TOTAL QUALITY MANAGEMENT

Total quality management is the language of all institutions in South Korea, including government departments. (**TQM**) is a management philosophy that seeks to integrate all organizational functions (marketing, finance, design, engineering, and production, customer service, etc.) to focus on meeting customer needs and organizational objectives. TQM empowers the Total organization, from the employee to the CEO, with the responsibility of ensuring Quality in their respective products and services, and Management of their processes through the appropriate process improvement channels. All types of organizations have deployed TQM, from small businesses to government agencies like NASA, from schools to construction firms, from manufacturing centers to call centers, and from dance sequence to hospitals. TQM is not specific to one type of enterprise, it is a philosophy applied anywhere quality is required.

A Tool For Progress

TQM, in fact, goes beyond "Meeting customer requirements" and their usual understanding of "Fit for purpose" in respect of products, processes or services that are embraced by the organization. That is it operates organization wide. Prior to TQM, quality testing is usually a norm towards controlling quality during the final phases of a product, process or service. If faults are found, then the supplies are held back; reworked or rejected. Additional costs were usually inevitable, to produce the needed quantity and Quality. TQM's aim to "Get it right first time every time" and in interim abate majority of such avoidable costs. TQM seeks to identify the source of each defect; to prevent it from entering the final product. Using a simple iterative process TQM reinforces quality assurance to meet changes in products and services by way of improved effectiveness of their operational processes. The modus-operandi involves identifying the "root causes" for the most prevalent/costly defects and then implementing solutions to abate, avoid or remove them.

LITERATURE REVIEW

Hanink D M in his book The International Economy, A Geographical Perspective (1994:232) quoted the World Bank as saying its experience was that complete free trade, 100% profit repatriation, 100% foreign ownership, free movement of imports/exports and capital equipment without customs duty gives success to Export Processing Zones and Industrial Parks. This is the phenomena in South Korea. Sekaran U (2003:11) said that managers need research to make reasonably accurate decisions and to minimize risk and to create new ideas. Hill C W L (2009:261) said that host governments benefit from investment by MNCs in three ways namely:- home country's balance of payments benefits, positive employments effects and finally learning valuable skills from exposure to foreign markets that can be eventually transferred back home but he emphasized that risk needed to be managed in the supply chain. Kerin R A and Peterson (2007:427) says that consumer value assessments are often comparative, which means that consumers compare similar product offerings for prices and normally more competitive offers get the business and this is guided by quality. The Emirates Center for Strategic Studies and Research (2003:95) says the success of countries in adopting a knowledge-based economy depends on the quality of the education systems and the institutional structures that facilitate the process from learning to application, the reward system has to be correct to attract the best brains. This means that the best markets attract the best brains and Korea has been one of these best markets. Hitt et al says (2007:396) International entrepreneurship is scouting for international opportunities well beyond your borders. The wealth of South Korea has been a fusion of pickings from every corner of the world. Off course the issue of cultural contamination cannot be ignored, which becomes the price to pay for benefiting out of international trade, but obviously the benefits are more than the side effects as can be seen in the standard of living in South Korea. A number of relevant websites were scoured for supportive theories and evidence such as the United Nations, World Bank, Wikipedia, WTO and ITC (see appendices).

Nothing is perfect but no one doubts that the best practice standards adopted by South Korea are one of the major reasons for their rise to a world super power. South Korea has learnt a lot from the world and so has the world from South Korea. It has been a win-win situation. The Economist reported in its latest journal that the onset of the world recession had resulted in a permanent economic power shift from the West to East Asia. The main attraction of the South East Asia is lower costs, strategic location, access to raw materials, the concentration of major MNCs, a positive work ethic, a world population centre with high consumption, a high degree of creativity and political stability.

NATIONAL BRANDING

Branding is the ways in which an organization communicates, differentiates and symbolizes itself to all of its audiences. National branding is doing the same thing, but to a whole country and the world at large. This may be to encourage foreign direct investment, create internal pride, or be a support for exports, tourism or to attract expatriates or any enterprise that a nation may undertake. Although it means more than image and perception, national branding may be briefly defined as the way a country or a nation is perceived by the audience. It is very important to underline that the audience is split into two major categories: that nation's people and everyone else. It seems that most national branding programs are aimed at foreigners - improving one nation's image in the eyes of the rest of the world; but it is equally important to create programs that aim at that nation's own people, because on a long-term basis, a nation is perceived also through its citizens. Every nation has a brand – good or bad. The nation's brand is defined by the people, by their temper, education, look, by their endeavours, successes and failures. This is why national branding is not easy. It is very hard to change a nation's values. It means education, it means economic status, standard of life. It takes generations to change how people are. This is not the work of a branding agency, not even of a government. Instead, national branding programs aim at something different: making the country's values better known, minimize the effect of several accidents caused by individuals that affect the nation's brand, promote tourism, or attract investors. Branding expert like Simon Anholt, who established Placebrands early in 2003 but now works as an independent policy advisor to several governments, help countries develop and communicate strong brand identities which could help speed up development by attracting foreign investors and tourists. That, in turn, could increase political influence and help a country's corporations grow.

Changing the image of a country is no easier than changing the image of a company or an individual. While branding may be able to help a country improve its communication with the world, it won't work if the country sends out lies or hype, said Erich Joachimsthaler, chief executive of Vivaldi Partners, a four-year-old agency that specializes in branding. Long term branding involves strategic planning for education, developing a Research & Development culture, political stability, protection of property rights, prosperity , rule of law and transparency, freedom of expression and the media, Total Quality Management, heavy promotion in international media like websites, BBC, CNN, Aljazeera, French TV, international journals and newspapers. Industries like education, health and tourism and hospitality have been given special attention in South Korea to send a correct message of the concern and care about quality of life. Health tourists are flocking to the country because of very high benchmarks set by the country which are the envy of the world. South Korea is home to some of the top hotels and entertainment names in the world. The music and entertainment industry has also set very high benchmarks. Its ability in relationship building with other nations has also been spectacular and it has worked to avoid a pariah state jacket haunting its northern neighbor, which is nursing some of the highest poverty in the world. South Korea is the darling of the world. In the educational field the country has been the first to introduce digital education to all its citizens, a feat that eludes even the USA and the whole of Europe.

STRATEGY FOR EMBASSIES

Countries also a need to open up embassies in high value world centres manned by the right people with business qualifications and business experience, especially trade attaches and trade promotion officers, if countries are to benefit anything out of their embassies. The establishment of embassies must be guided by the principle of potential business to be generated in a country, besides the usual political objectives. This is what has generally guided most NICs and they have reaped huge rewards in the form of increased business in home countries generated from the embassies. South Korea created the best benchmarks in this area and gives its embassies serious business and economic targets to meet like investment, exports, imports, tourist arrivals and national public relations, besides the standard political considerations and targets. These are the Key Result Areas or the reason or justification for their establishment or existence. Adequate resources are pumped into these embassies so that they carry out their mandates with reasonable ease. The same goes with key national Trade Promotion Organisations (TPOs); they get national support in order for them to do justice to countries in their international trade efforts. These financial and economic innovations are some of the key strategic economic drivers which can make or break any country – there is no alternative. The USA has an embassy in China with a staff complement of seven hundred people – the largest embassy in the world; the reason for this big embassy was to take advantage of the big business potential in China and pre-empt the rest of the world. They have established many Chinese Language Centres in the USA and English Language Centres in China as the quickest way and strategy to close the language barrier and accelerate business. South Korea has been very selective in establishing embassies the world over and has been guided by business potential, pay back, marketing excellence and convenience, ease of access and as a facilitative tool for business, but without ignoring political objectives altogether.

CONCLUSION

South Korea has proved that it is the jewel of South East Asia and the envy of the world through best practice in all respects. It does the same thing done by other Asian Tigers namely:-

- Investment in education across the board
- Political stability, democracy and good governance found in political pluralism and openness
- Accountable and responsible government
- Complete separation of powers
- Membership of the global community including the United Nations
- World class Research & Development, innovation and entrepreneurship
- Heavy value addition and investment in high-tech industries
- First class urban planning, infrastructure development and population planning
- Development of ICT and leading the world in the area of digitalisation.

Democracy, rule of law, protection of property rights, inventiveness and a positive work ethic all combined to propel South Korea to dizzy heights and to adopt world best practice. Development of a culture of nationalism, the desire for a quality life full of riches and abundance drove this country to be one of the best. The South Koreans believe in themselves and copied the best from the rest of the world and they invented many new ideas which have solved many international developmental problems. They were brave enough to discard the failed communist and socialist doctrine which has been a disaster wherever it has been practiced, e.g. in North Korea, Myanmar and Cuba where poverty is a world record and a complete embarrassment. South Korea has also embraced the world community of nations and benefited from this. The world can learn a lot from South Korea. This country has had the humility to learn from other countries in its transformation and matched on. The old adage says united we stand and divided we fall. Most socialist political leaders are socialists during the day but celebrated capitalists at night with massive investments on Wall Street and other world economic centres as proven the world over. They are glorified liars who feign sympathy to the rest of the national population whilst busy enriching themselves and consolidating their investment empires at night. One of the most outspoken former Latin American presidents is said to have a confirmed personal fortune of US$9 billion; where is socialism? In his country the average per capita is US$200 per year, just imagine. And his country is one of the poorest in the world. This is fraud, abuse and manipulation of the highest degree.

REFERENCES

1. Aaker DA (4th Ed). Strategic Market Management, John Widely & Sons, Inc. (1995)
2. Dillon WR;Madden TJ;et al Marketing Research, The McGraw-Hill Companies Inc.(1993).
3. Hanink D M. The International Economy, A Geographical Perspective, John Wiley and Sons (1994).USA
4. Charles W. L. Hill, (2009),International Business, Competing in the Global Marketplace,7th Edition, McGraw-Hill.
5. Sekaran U. (4th Ed) Research Methods for Business, A Skill Building Approach:Joney Wiley and Sons (2003).
6. Kerin A. R., Peterson R.A. (2007). Strategic Marketing Problems, Cases and Comments: 11th Edition, Pearson Education International.
7. Hitt M.A., Hoskisson R.A.,Ireland R.D., (2007), Cengage Learning.
8. Cateora, P. R., (1993) International Marketing: Irwin.
9. Hanink, D.M., (1994). The International Economy, A Geographical Perspective: John Wiley & Sons, Inc.
10. Porter, M.E., (1990). The Competitive Advantage of Nations: Free Press, New York.
11. The Emirates Centre for Strategic Studies and Research (2003). Human Resources in a Knowledge-Based Economy, Abu Dhabi, United Arab Emirates
12. Kerin, A.R.,Peterson, R.A. (2007). Strategic Marketing Problems, Cases and Comments (11th Edition):Pearson Prentice Hall.

13. Christopher, M. (1987) in Baker, M. J. (ed.) the Marketing Book: Heinemann
14. Czinkota, M. E., and Ronkainen, I. A., (1990) International Marketing: Dryden.
15. Keegan, W. J., (1989), Global Marketing Management: Prentice-Hall.
16. Kotler, P., (1988) Marketing Management; Analysis, Planning, Implementation and Control: Prentice-Hall.
17. Shimaguchi, M., (1978). Marketing Channels in Japan: Ann Arbor.
18. Stern, L., El-Ansary, A.I., (1988). Marketing Channels: Prentice-Hall.
19. Usunier, J.C., (1993) International Marketing, A Cultural Approach, Prentice-Hal.
20. Harry, T., (1992) Exporter's Checklist, A Step-by Step Guide to Successful Exporting: Lloyd's of London Press.
21. Williams, D. E., (1992). 'Motives for Retailer Internalization: Their Impact, Structure and Implications.' Journal of Marketing Management, vol. 3, p8.
22. World Economic Analysis Report: Retrieved 5 December 2009 from http://econ.worldbank.org/WBSITE/EXTERNAL/EXTDEC/0,,contentMDK :22216733~pagePK:64165401~piPK:64165026~theSitePK:469372,00.html
23. Politics of South Korea: Retrieved 15 December 2009 from http://en.wikipedia.org/wiki/Politics_of_South_Korea
24. Best Practice: Retrieved 12 December 2009 from: http://en.wikipedia.org/wiki/Best_practice
25. Economy of South Korea: Retrieved 14 December 2009 from: http://en.wikipedia.org/wiki/Economy_of_South_Korea
26. Total Quality Management: Retrieved 15 December 2009 from: http://en.wikipedia.org/wiki/Total_quality_management
27. South Korea: Retrieved 16 December 2009 from: http://en.wikipedia.org/wiki/South_Korea

The following is a research article on Singapore done by the co-writer (Faustino Taderera) as part of PhD requirements:-

INTRODUCTION

I will write about Singapore, a country that has done extremely well with not much in terms of natural resources but has managed to do an economic miracle which is talk of the world throughout the four corners of the world. This did not just come about and a lot of home work created the economic monster that we call Singapore; it's a whole intricate system created over many years. Singapore's phenomenal success has been underpinned by high quality education, industrialization and serious value addition, urban planning, transparent corporate governance, good and accountable government, political stability and strong government, setting and exploitation of trade agreements with the rest of the world and protection of property rights. What puts Singapore apart is their ability to create an atmosphere attractive to FDI – fast tracking of investment and divestment

applications, infrastructure development, strategic location for sea and air routes, liberal
exchange controls, national service to create patriotism, a low crime rate and rule of law
and finally interacting with the community of nations. Besides this there is also the aspect
of quality of life that one has to look at. Singapore offers the best in terms of real estate,
education, health, hospitality and tourism, entertainment, sports and outdoor life. The
industries where it has a competitive advantage are manufacturing, chemicals,
electronics, biomedical sciences, tourism, education, health, shipping, insurance, banking
and financial services. Singapore's secret has been value addition and running knowledge
based industries driven by high-technology and supported by world class universities,
research institutes, techno-parks and industrial clusters and finally engaging in maximum
cooperation with the rest of the world whilst benchmarking all practices, including e-
government. Good public management and strong transparent corporate governance has
characterized Singapore to become the admiration of the whole world. A small island
state, and smallest state in South East Asia, has turned into a mysterious economic
monster and juggernaut. My analysis will be based on Porter's Five Forces Model of
Competitive advantage to clearly show how Singapore has managed to exploit this and
the hurdles it has faced in doing this and what the future holds for that country.

LITERATURE REVIEW
The purpose of the literature review is to gain from already published research on this
topic. It also helps in illuminating issues and helping to proffer possible solutions.
Literature review helps analyzing issues and in creating checks and balances before
conclusions and decisions are made. One of the most important purposes of a literature
review is getting a cross section of ideas from different perspectives on a given topic and
by people or organizations that are respected in a discipline and have done a lot of in-
depth research. Normally these would be people from different countries and different
institutions. A literature review is an account of what has been published on a topic by
accredited scholars and researchers. More often it is part of the introduction to an essay,
research report, or thesis. In writing the literature review, your purpose is to convey to
your reader what knowledge and ideas have been established on a topic, and what their
strengths and weaknesses are. As a piece of writing, the literature review must be defined
by a guiding concept (e.g., your research objective, the problem or issue you are
discussing, or your argumentative thesis). It is not just a descriptive list of the material
available, or a set of summaries.

Besides enlarging knowledge about the topic, writing a literature review lets you gain and
demonstrate skills in two areas:-

1. **information seeking**: the ability to scan the literature efficiently, using manual or
   computerized methods, to identify a set of useful articles and books
2. **critical appraisal**: the ability to apply principles of analysis to identify unbiased
   and valid studies.

A literature review must do these things

5. be organized around and related directly to the thesis or research question you are developing
6. synthesize results into a summary of what is and is not known
7. identify areas of controversy in the literature
8. formulate questions that need further research

A literature review is a body of text that aims to review the critical points of current knowledge and or methodological approaches on a particular topic. Literature reviews are secondary sources, and as such, do not report any new or original experimental work. Most often associated with academic-oriented literature, such as theses, a literature review usually precedes a research proposal and results section. Its ultimate goal is to bring the reader up to date with current literature on a topic and forms the basis for another goal, such as future research that may be needed in the area. A well-structured literature review is characterized by a logical flow of ideas; current and relevant references with consistent, appropriate referencing style; proper use of terminology; and an unbiased and comprehensive view of the previous research on the topic. I will use this literature review to guide the flow of ideas as I discuss the secret of Singapore's industrial success and economic miracle.

The actual review of literature
Dillon W L said that "A vehicle fleet is as good as the road network and skilled technicians servicing this fleet – this is a reality in transport business." (Dillon W L:25). It is physical mobility and its efficiency which is the basic determinant of corporate and national efficiency, success, world class competitiveness, business goodwill and credibility, access to high yielding and lucrative markets, opening up of new and distant markets, enabling firms and corporate bodies to hold minimum stocks and ultimately engage in JIT and Total Quality Management (Aaker D:100). It was a sophisticated transport network that enabled the British to conquer and rule three quarters of the whole world thus giving birth to Great Britain. Even today the American economic and military supremacy is founded on having the best brainpower and the most sophisticated and largest diverse transport network (i.e. road, rail, sea and air transport network.). This speaks volumes about Singapore's long path to economic dominance and superiority. The country has established a sophisticated transport and supply chain hub by road, air, sea and rail linking Singapore with the rest of the world. United Nations organs' websites like WTO, UNCTAD, ITC and World Bank websites were visited and scoured to get supporting evidence on trade and trade statistics and balance of payments positions for Asian countries and these websites are quoted in the references columns for reference. Kerin and Robert A. Peterson say that the primary purpose of trade is to create long-term and mutually beneficial relationships between an entity and the publics with which it interacts. They say failure to do this results in business and national failure. Premised on this one clearly sees the major reason why so many banks and companies in Singapore did not fail this recession, given their record of responsible and highly respectable corporate governance.

The Emirates Centre for Strategic Studies and Research in their book Human Resource Development In A Knowledge-Based Economy (2003:4) quote Davis and Meyer as

618

saying that the primacy of human capital is leading to a "global war for talented people" in much the same way that nations once fought over land and gold because it was considered a valuable asset. As a logical outcome of this new trend "tangible assets will start to lose their value as collateral, while intangible human capital becomes bankable." This means the gold rush and wars fought for gold in the 18th century in South Africa and other African countries may be repeated over human capital as the world jostles for this scarce commodity. That is how serious the competition for talent has become. Charles W.L. Hill in his book International Business, Competing in the Global Marketplace – 7th Edition, (p169), says the theories of Adam Smith, David Ricardo and Heckscher-Ohlin help to explain the pattern of international trade that we observe in the world economy. On page 233 Hill says trade policy by governments may work positively or may attract retaliation or that it may be used to protect outright inefficient firms and Singapore has been reasonably careful about this and has faced few backlashes in its chequered history. Hitt, Hoskisson and Ireland in their book Management of Strategy, Concepts and Cases (p396) say because of its positive benefits entrepreneurship is at the top of public policy agendas in most leading economies and Singapore has benefited immensely from an entrepreneurial culture. This is partly due to availability of large investor funds and strategic location, rather than entirely from its own planning. Roger A Kerin and Robert A Peterson in their book Strategic Marketing Problems, Cases and Comments (p577) say a successful comprehensive marketing program must effectively stimulate target markets to buy, must be consistent with organizational capabilities and must outmaneuver competitors. Singapore has definitely managed to do this on the world stage hence its use as a point of reference by the world at large.

THE EDUCATION INDUSTRY

I will focus on the tertiary or university sector, although other levels of education are also equally important but these feed into universities in most cases. The education sector has been one of the major success stories and reasons why Singapore made such phenomenal success and is also a major source of income as well as research output which feeds into improving industrial and national competitiveness. Various factors explain this. Firstly Singapore set up a first class education system benchmarked on the best Western standards. The country has a high standard of living, low crime rate, political stability and a well developed tourism and hospitality industry. Research funds are readily available thus making it a haven for the best brains from the rest of the world to come and thrive. The question is why and how did Singapore manage to attract top academics into its system from the rest of the world? Academics are psychological animals like all of us and they wanted:-

- quality of life and quality education for their families
- high salaries and effective labour laws
- recreation and good outdoor life
- clear career progression which comes with research funding
- freedom of expression and academic freedom
- making names for themselves
- international travel and interaction
- protection of intellectual and property rights

- an atmosphere of accountability and transparency
- freedom from dictatorship and repression
- political stability and predictability
- supportive institutions and system
- tolerance, respect and human rights
- informative and free media unfazed by brute politicians
- low crime environment
- an anti-corruption culture chlorinated by media freedom and effective judicial systems

That is exactly what Singapore could offer. It was gaining a lot from the world in terms of manpower with very little loss of its own experts to other countries. A lot of academics and other experts had good reason to run away from dictatorships in China, Africa and South America to go to Singapore. For the first time they would enjoy most of the above. 3rd world countries are very good at training but they cannot compete with super powers on salaries and other conditions, for example a PhD lecturer would be earning US$1000 and is taxed at 45% in Africa. China pays US$300 to US$600 per month to academics. The same person would be able to earn +US$9000 to +US$15000 in Singapore plus plenty of other benefits as outlined above. In their native countries some of these people feel abused and leave to go for a dream job. People in Europe, America, Australia and India are tired of painful taxes, pollution and a high crime rate (and poverty in India, Africa and South America) and would be better off in a clean, more conducive hideout like Singapore. In African and Chinese environments there is no academic freedom and outspoken professors are looked at as enemies of the state and some end up in jail or killed prematurely. They needed a better place to practice. Singapore provided a home and hideout for international dissident academics. Their energies were now directed at developing Singapore rather than fight hide and seek battles with ruthless political dictators in their countries of origin – that benefited Singapore and improved its industrial performance. Research support in South America, India and Africa is very low and support facilities and infrastructure is negligible and working is really frustrating. Singapore provided a solution to all this and attracted thousands of experts from all over the world for a dream life. Concentration of the best brains in Singapore unleashed brilliant ideas which created breakthrough products and systems and leapfrogged Singapore to where it is; the process continues. The positive country of origin effect, goodwill, international fame and concentration advantage continued to attract industrialists, investors and other sectors of society to join the Singapore miracle and the multiplier effect continued. Political stability and a supportive and booming region were also factors in this equation. Another factor was the positive work ethic of most people in the Far East. They are honest, hard working, time conscious, dependable and forthcoming; qualities required for any successful business and nation. This phenomenal success was not without negative side effects. Global warming, redundant workers created by advanced technology, cultural contamination and erosion of local values naturally set in. This was the price to pay.

WHY AND HOW SINGAPORE MANAGED TO GLOBALISE

The United Nations, ITC, WTO and UNCTAD say "Globalise or Perish," this means companies and countries ignore international business at their own peril. Britain was touted" the Nation of Traders as the British glob trotted scouring export/import and investment opportunities; that is what earned Britain the name Great Britain – ingenuity in trade and military supremacy. Singapore followed exactly the same route in its internationalization efforts with the exception of military supremacy. Singapore diversified and went international for the following reasons:-

To reduce dependence on existing domestic markets

Market diversification expands a country's market base thereby stabilizing its markets since it can gain a large market share by selling to many different markets. Internationalisation also lessens the effects of demand fluctuations by tapping global markets. The Singapore government closely supports its companies in the trade efforts.

Gain global market share

Singapore learnt from its competitors and reinforced its strategies by seeing how other firms are doing to serve the international markets and hence expand their market share. For example Delta has gained popularity as well as brand loyalty in almost every corner of the world. A gain in the market share will create a good country image as well as an increase in sales and profits as well. A large market share in international markets will also give a country some form of power and status and also strengthen international relations aspects. Moreover it gains positive country of origin effect.

Enhancing competitiveness

Singapore engaged in international business because exporting enhances competitiveness and improves its competitive advantage through exposure to new, advanced technologies in the production process, methods, management styles and all other operations. According to Allan Branch in his book, Export practice and management, he said, " The company becomes more competitive in all areas of business such as specification, management skills and value addition transmitted to the buyer in both price and non-price areas if it engages in exporting."

Diversify risk

Singapore engaged in internationalisation to diversify risk which may be encountered in doing business transactions competing in only one economy which makes a country dependent on that economy regardless of any risk the economy will be facing, e.g. inflation, political instability, market fluctuations, etc. By diversifying into more than one economy countries can insulate themselves from the dangers of that single dependence, especially in foreign markets, which are in earlier stages of product life cycle than domestic markets going back to our own.

Protect the domestic market
In most cases, large companies engage in the international business to reduce congestion in the domestic market hence opening up space for the upcoming small to medium scale firms. Competition in the domestic market is reduced. Also if firms go international they can improve their marketing strategies and skills and be in a position to protect the domestic market in the long run. The firms can also adopt other international strategies, which may be used by local companies for competitiveness in the market. Companies become integrated with the market they serve. Companies become more integrated with the market they serve, that is if a company exports to European countries it will be integrated with other competing firms as well as other stakeholders in the market it serves. If a company is exposed to international markets, its strategies will be more reinforced; the use of highly sophisticated machinery will be promoted of which this will not be obtained when serving only one market. Company exposure is greatly reduced. Operating in international markets would call for maximum promotion especially in the modern world where advertising can be done on a 24-hour basis through the use of internet facilities. If a company goes international its exposure will be greatly increased to an international scale through product analyses and publicity for example, Coca-Cola, Adidas and thus a good image and good reputation will be established and the firm may dominate the market. Many Singapore firms MNCs have successfully done this, e.g. banks, manufacturers, insurance, hotels and other services.

Technological gleaning and transfer

Singapore encourages globalization so as to allow for technological gleaning and transfer especially in the telecommunication sector where the use of computer systems and internet is now very advanced. Technological improvement equips countries with improvements in quality of products through technical regulations in the product certificate analysis systems and control points. However, governments sometimes do engage in foreign trade so as to dump their products for example China which produces goods at a very low cost due to cheap raw material and labour often exports to dump excess products and that is the case with Japan in their motor industries although this practice is not ethical and is not recommended.

From what has been outlined and discussed globalisation proves to be more advantageous from a country's perspective. It enhances economic, social, political, technological and legal aspects of any country. Through globalization Singapore has gained status, power and prestige and has international influence.

Access to FDI and Strategic Location
Singapore is strategically located and has globalised to attract FDI to support her industrialization efforts. This has been very successful looking at the massive injections of foreign investment in various sectors in the country. Availability of support industries has been a major factor for making Singapore an attractive location for international MNCs. This makes it easy to operate as support industries provide inputs and skilled labour would be readily available. Colleges and universities have provided much needed

skilled labour and world class researchers. The tourism industry has provided much needed entertainment and leisure exits.

DEVELOPMENTS IN SUPPLY CHAIN MANAGEMENT IN SINGAPORE

Singapore has taken advantage in exploiting current developments in supply chain to further improve its competitive position. Six major movements can be observed in the evolution of supply chain management studies and Singapore has been heavily involved in all these: Creation, Integration, Globalization, Specialization Phases One and Two, and SCM 2.0.

Supply chain business process integration

Successful SCM requires a change from managing individual functions to integrating activities into key supply chain processes. An example scenario: the purchasing department places orders as requirements become known. The marketing department, responding to customer demand, communicates with several distributors and retailers as it attempts to determine ways to satisfy this demand. Information shared between supply chain partners can only be fully leveraged through process integration. International Cargo Centres sprang up in Singapore.

Supply chain business process integration involves collaborative work between buyers and suppliers, joint product development, common systems and shared information. Operating an integrated supply chain requires a continuous information flow. However, in many companies, management has reached the conclusion that optimizing the product flows cannot be accomplished without implementing a process approach to the business. The key supply chain processes are:

- Customer relationship management
- Customer service management
- Demand management
- Order fulfillment
- Manufacturing flow management
- Supplier relationship management
- Product development and commercialization
- Returns management

CLEAN AND STABLE GOVERNMENT

Singapore has an effective, stable and transparent parliamentary democracy which has a clear separation of powers and a zero tolerance to corruption. The introduction of the death penalty for drug trafficking, corruption, money laundering, murder and other serious crimes has helped to serve as a deterrent to check unacceptable behavior – it has been very effective indeed. This has helped to build investor confidence across the board and created the country into an international brand. It is also one of the major reasons why most big Asian economies have thrived. The work ethic is also very supportive of development as Singaporeans are workaholics, a quality shared by all Asian Tigers,

China and Malaysia. National service (compulsory military conscription at the age of 18) has created national identity and patriotism. State control of most of the media has prevented unnecessary negativity and falsehoods thus further building the national and international image of Singapore.

Singapore trade and trade policy

Trade policy is a collection of rules and regulations which pertain to trade. Every nation has some form of trade policy in place, with public officials formulating the policy which they think would be most appropriate for their country. The purpose of trade policy is to help a nation's international trade run more smoothly, by setting clear standards and goals which can be understood by potential trading partners. In many regions, groups of nations work together to create mutually beneficial trade policies. Singapore's trade policy is guided by international best practice and this covers all major trade issues.

- Things like import and export taxes, tariffs, inspection regulations, and quotas can all be part of a nation's trade policy. Some nations attempt to protect their local industries with trade policies which place a heavy burden on importers, allowing domestic producers of goods and services to get ahead in the market with lower prices or more availability. Others eschew trade barriers, promoting free trade, in which domestic producers are given no special treatment, and international producers are free to bring in their products.
- Safety is sometimes an issue in trade policy. Different nations have different regulations about product safety, and when goods are imported into a country with stiff standards, representatives of that nation may demand the right to inspect the goods, to confirm that they conform with the product safety standards which have been laid out. Security is also an issue, with nations wanting to protect themselves from potential threats while maintaining good foreign relations with frequent trading partners.
- When nations trade with each other regularly, they often establish trade agreements. Trade agreements smooth the way for trading, spelling out the desires of both sides to create a stronger, more effective trading relationship. Many trade agreements are designed to accommodate a desire for free trade, with signatories to such agreements making certain concessions to each other to establish a good trading relationship. Regular meetings may also be held to discuss changes in the financial climate, and to make adjustments to trade policy accordingly. Singapore has signed a number of trade agreements which have propelled its trade efforts.
- For lay people, understanding trade policy can get quite complex. The relevant rules, regulations, agreements, and treaties are often scattered across numerous government documents and departments, from State Departments which handle foreign policy to economic departments which deal with the nuts and bolts of things like converting currency. Often, the best resource for information is documents pertaining to specific trade agreements, such as ASEAN. These documents spell out the trade policy of the nations involved in one convenient location, although the language used can become very complex.

CONCLUSION

Singapore has proved to be a predictable global trading partner with immutable protection of property rights, intellectual property and an observer of international conventions. This has raised its goodwill and made it a point of reference on world best practice. Singapore has also been surrounded by world economic powers and this has forced it to really work hard to compete head on with giants like China, Malaysia, South Korea, Hong Kong, Taiwan, Indonesia, India and others. A lot of countries have a lot to learn from the Singapore rulers who have transformed lives of all their citizens who directly benefit from the economic miracle. Singapore has reduced taxes for their citizens and investing public thus attracting investor funds as well as the best expatriate brains and creating a positive multiplier effect in terms of economic and social development. Common sense shows that people go where they get maximum benefit whether as investors or experts selling their labour. Singapore's zero tolerance to corruption is also a good business and governance practice which other countries need to learn. This creates respect and national confidence and a positive country of origin effect, which naturally benefits a country in its investment and foreign trade efforts. Clear testimony from the good results in Singapore in terms of economic growth, sustainability and development is indisputable evidence. It is food for thought for the rest of the world. Success is simple, it requires good policies, hard work, honesty, predictability and transparency. One does not need to be a rocket scientist to achieve success but it is all about basics and ethics. An analysis of world low cost centres shows one common scenario – they all avoid excessive executive pay and benefits packages (including bankers and their controversial bonuses) and the level of honesty is very high. Moreover the penalty for financial dishonesty, murder, drug peddling and rape is normally the death sentence in these countries. This is a good and effective deterrent as proven by low crime statistics in all countries – e.g. most GCC countries in the Middle East, Japan, China, India and the rest of the Asian Tigers or Asian Dragons (Malaysia, Taiwan, Singapore and Hong Kong), Thailand and Indonesia. This is what is making it cheaper to operate in these countries – good health which is a pre-requisite for high production and positive educational output, honesty, low costs and low crime rates. Fraud is a dreaded self death penalty and one can never dream of getting a grand fraudster like Bernard Murdoch in Singapore, the GCC, the Asian Tigers, China, India or Japan; that person would definitely be executed and the stolen money restored to its rightful owners; no one would dare do that again. That way investor and public funds are protected and safe. Democratic freedom is not freedom to defraud and loot public and investor funds. The so called freedom has gone too far and is now being abused by fraudsters to the detriment of the world economy. Drugs drive the spiraling crime rate in countries like South Africa, Mexico and Iraqi where some places are almost like war zones due to drug gangs. Singapore has stopped this.

REFERENCES

28. Aaker DA (4th Ed). Strategic Market Management, John Widely & Sons, Inc.6,p.100. (1995)

29. Dillon WR;Madden TJ;et al Marketing Research, The McGraw-Hill Companies Inc.2,p.25.(1993).
30. Charles W. L. Hill, (2009),International Business, Competing in the Global Marketplace,7th Edition, McGraw-Hill.
31. Kerin A. R., Peterson R.A. (2007). Strategic Marketing Problems, Cases and Comments: 11th Edition, Pearson Education International.
32. Hitt M.A., Hoskisson R.A.,Ireland R.D., (2007), Cengage Learning.
33. Cateora, P. R., (1993) International Marketing: Irwin.
34. Hanink, D.M., (1994). The International Economy, A Geographical Perspective: John Wiley & Sons, Inc.
35. Porter, M.E., (1990). The Competitive Advantage of Nations: Free Press, New York.
36. The Emirates Centre for Strategic Studies and Research (2003). Human Resources in a Knowledge-Based Economy, Abu Dhabi, United Arab Emirates
37. Kerin, A.R.,Peterson, R.A. (2007). Strategic Marketing Problems, Cases and Comments (11th Edition):Pearson Prentice Hall.
38. Christopher, M. (1987) in Baker, M. J. (ed.) the Marketing Book: Heinemann
39. Czinkota, M. E., and Ronkainen, I. A., (1990) International Marketing: Dryden.
40. Keegan, W. J., (1989), Global Marketing Management: Prentice-Hall.
41. Kotler, P., (1988) Marketing Management; Analysis, Planning, Implementation and Control: Prentice-Hall.
42. Shimaguchi, M., (1978). Marketing Channels in Japan: Ann Arbor.
43. Stern, L., El-Ansary, A.I., (1988). Marketing Channels: Prentice-Hall.
44. Usunier, J.C., (1993) International Marketing, A Cultural Approach, Prentice-Hal.
45. Harry, T., (1992) Exporter's Checklist, A Step-by Step Guide to Successful Exporting: Lloyd's of London Press.
46. Williams, D. E., (1992). 'Motives for Retailer Internalization: Their Impact, Structure and Implications.' Journal of Marketing Management, vol. 3, p8.
47. Economy of Singapore: Retrieved on 17 December 2009 from http://en.wikipedia.org/wiki/Economy_of_Singapore
48. Singapore: Retrieved on 17 December 2009 from: http://en.wikipedia.org/wiki/Singapore
49. World Economic Analysis Report: Retrieved 5 December 2009 from http://econ.worldbank.org/WBSITE/EXTERNAL/EXTDEC/0,,contentMDK :22216733~pagePK:64165401~piPK:64165026~theSitePK:469372,00.html

The following is a conference paper presented by the writer and an academic colleague, Mr. Anwar Khamis Abdullah Al Sheyadi, at the Colleges of Applied Sciences International Conference on Sustainable Management on 21 – 22 February 2010 at the beautiful beach city of Sur in Oman entitled, "The changing role of a Customs & Excise Authority in the 21st century; from regulator to international business facilitator and promoter."

ABSTRACT

This paper discusses the changing role of a customs authority in the 21st century as a trade promotion and trade facilitation agency of government rather than rigid regulator. It analyses the main players in the customs, shipping and logistics business:- importers, exporters, bankers, insurers, export credit insurers, transporters, shipping /forwarding/customs clearing agents, universities and colleges, research institutions, trade promotion organizations (TPOs), Government Ministries dealing with foreign trade and NGOs like World Bank, United Nations, European Union, GCC, World Customs Union and others. The customs and shipping activity is a complex web of so many well connected and highly influential interest groups and players whose activities and functions take years to unravel and understand fully. International customs practices are changing rapidly where customs authorities are becoming more and more facilitators rather than regulators of business. Their traditional role remains but there is a strong slant towards business facilitation and promotion. The reason is simple – the wealth of nations comes from trading and business activities rather than from the government. Therefore supporting and facilitating business improves national economic development and welfare and naturally increases tax inflows into the fiscus; it is a win-win situation. Firms invest in countries where there are less barriers to doing business, central of which are the customs and immigration systems. Perfecting customs practices is one sure way of attracting and retaining investment. The modern customs professional is now expected to be bilingual in key foreign languages, e-literate, have top of the range international customs expertise, be a product of a credible business school and have specialized in business at degree level and have international exposure and disposition. It is now imperative for governments to focus their recruitment in an international perspective in order to get the best. The customs professional is expected to understand the political dynamics in different countries as well as the cultures and religions and their influence on product consumption, business dynamics, negotiations and business etiquette. A qualified world class customs professional is a panacea for any country's international business efforts just as a doctor is a necessity for a hospital and an engineer for an engineering company. The customs professional requires three qualities:- degree level education in business/shipping/languages, relevant experience and international exposure/travel experience. There is an additional requirement nowadays and this is the ability to design and plot an annual budget and Strategic Plan. But Customs regulations still remain very important for state security reasons as well as immigration control, promotion of investment (FDI), tourism and international business. Now there is a new area altogether - health tourism, where countries like Malaysia, UAE and Hong Kong are making billions of dollars from health tourists, people coming for specialized, advanced medical services and specialized medical education. This is now an international niche market targeting the upper niche of the income brackets – celebrities, presidents, politicians, sports persons, business persons, the rich and famous and the opinion leaders of this world with plenty of disposable incomes. There is a new world challenge which is the new serious threat of international terrorism, drug trafficking and human trafficking which customs authorities must regulate, control and try to shut out of their countries.

INTRODUCTION

In any country shipping management activities are centred around the National Revenue Authority or Customs Administration Authority. The main players in the customs, shipping and logistics business are importers, exporters, bankers, insurers, export credit insurers, transporters, shipping /forwarding/customs clearing agents, universities and colleges, research institutions, trade promotion organizations (TPOs), Government Ministries dealing with foreign trade and NGOs like World Bank, United Nations, European Union, GCC and others. The customs and shipping activity is a complex web of so many well connected and highly influential interest groups and players whose activities and functions take years to unravel and understand fully. One of the presenters, Faustino Taderera, was privileged to have worked in this industry for more than twenty two years at different echelons of management right up to the top.

Purpose of a Customs Authority

The functions of any customs authority

Any customs authority has five main functions, and that is:-

- It is the principal revenue collection agent of government and collects taxes, duties and other related public dues;

- Economic stability and growth management through manipulation of taxes and duties, preventing externalization of foreign currency, money laundering and speculation and product dumping;

- Management and administration of Trade Agreements entered into by government; they also participate in trade negotiations leading to signing of trade agreements;

- Contributing to sustainable state security by preventing smuggling in and out of the country of dangerous arms of war, dangerous drugs and strategic commodities like oil, gold, other minerals, corn, rice, milk, wheat and wild life products; and lastly

- It administers and authorizes exports and imports on behalf of government and sees to the orderly and transparent administration of foreign trade and compilation of accurate export/import trade statistics.

- To act on behalf of government to facilitate foreign trade and economic development, trade and travel, revenue generation and collection and to enforce regulatory controls with integrity, transparency and fairness for national benefit. This is done through the enforcement of the Customs & Excise Act, a piece of legislation governing the movement and management of imports and exports. It also manages the Exchange Control Act on behalf of the Central Bank and in this respect enforces repatriation of all export proceeds strictly in line with the contract of sale entered into by the exporter. In most countries all export proceeds must be received within a maximum of 90 days (except if a longer period is prior authorized by exchange control authorities). Maximum commission payable to any foreign sales or purchasing agent is seven and a half percent (7½%) of the ex-works value of goods or services (except if a higher percentage commission is prior authorized by exchange control authorities). Customs Authorities also administer the Immigration Act on behalf of the relevant ministry at all border posts and airports/aerodromes.

Innovation in customs practices

One survey across a large number of manufacturing and services organisations and government departments found, ranked in decreasing order of popularity, that systematic programs of organizational innovation are most frequently driven by:

12. Improved quality
13. Creation of new markets
14. Extension of the product range
15. Reduced labour costs
16. Improved production processes
17. Reduced materials
18. Reduced environmental damage
19. Replacement of products/services
20. Reduced energy consumption
21. Conformance to regulations
22. Removal of unnecessary bureaucracy which frustrates business
23. Building strong customer value better than competitors
24. Adoption of advanced ICT systems to facilitate and speed up transactions
25. Run lean organization structures, save money and speed up decision making
26. Exploit world low cost centers and remain in business
27. The desire for economic development, improvement in quality of life and economic progress.
28. To prevent closure of the firm and as a survival strategy

Justification for this research

International customs practices are changing rapidly where customs authorities are becoming more and more facilitators rather than regulators of business. Their traditional role remains but there is a strong slant towards business facilitation and promotion. The reason is simple – the wealth of nations comes from trading and business activities rather than from the government. Therefore supporting and facilitating business improves national economic development and welfare and naturally increases tax inflows into the fiscus; it is a win-win situation. Firms invest in countries where there are less barriers to doing business, central of which are the customs and immigration systems. Perfecting customs practices is one sure way of attracting and retaining investment.

The modern customs professional is now expected to be bilingual in key foreign languages,
e-literate, have top of the range international customs expertise, be a product of a credible business school and have specialized in business at degree level and have international exposure and disposition. It is now imperative for governments to focus their recruitment in an international perspective in order to get the best. The customs professional must understand the political dynamics in different countries as well as the cultures and religions and their influence on product consumption, business dynamics, negotiations and business etiquette. A qualified world class customs professional is a panacea for any country's international business efforts just as a doctor is a necessity for a hospital and an engineer for an engineering company. The customs professional requires three qualities:- degree level education in business/shipping/languages, relevant experience and international exposure/travel experience. Anything short of this is an accident in waiting. There is an additional requirement nowadays and this is the ability to design and plot an annual budget and Strategic Plan. But Customs regulations still remain very important for state security reasons as well as immigration control, promotion of investment (FDI), tourism and international business. Now there is a new area altogether - health tourism, where countries like Malaysia, UAE and Hong Kong are making billions of dollars from health tourists, people coming for specialized, advanced medical services and specialized medical education. This is now an international niche market targeting the upper niche of the income brackets – celebrities, presidents, politicians, sports persons, business persons, the rich and famous and the opinion leaders of this world with plenty of disposable incomes.

Historical Background about Customs

Customs authorities normally have various divisions. Each division plays an important role in exports/imports facilitation.

Head Office (Top Management)

This forms the central administrative authority for the collection of taxes and duties levied in terms of the Acts administered by the Authority. The Head Office has the overall responsibility for the country's various divisions and centres. The major functions of the Head Office include:

- Deciding on important statutory issues, matters related to the organisation and work procedures of the authority.
- Issuing regulations.

- Issuing general advice and rulings concerning the application of the law.
- Producing budgets based on proposed action.
- Allocating financial resources within its administrative areas.
- Reporting to the Board and Ministry on issues of policy.

Investigations Division

This division is mainly concerned with recouping lost revenues.
It is also concerned with promotion of voluntary compliance through a program of focused audits research. It carries out pre and post importation checks and the enforcements of controls.
It also concentrates on complex cases and fraud issues.

Projects and Planning Divisions

This is mainly concerned with the planning, co-ordination and new policies.

3.   Internal Audit Division

The main functions of this division are:

To control processes within the authority in order to ensure high quality operations
To provide an independent and objective assurance and consulting unit within the Authority.

4.   Operations Divisions

Main functions of this division include:

To assess, collect and enforce the payment of all revenue and facilitate trade.
To foster a positive image of the authority through good service to educate the Revenue Authority's clients about their rights and obligations in terms of all the statutes administered by the Revenue Authority and to facilitate the smooth entry of all travelers into and out of the country in conjunction with the Immigration Department.

5.   **Human Resources Division**

This is mainly concerned with the provision of human resources management services including industrial relations, training, staff succession, recruitment, selection and promotion.

6.   Finance and Administration Division

Their main functions are threefold.

The Accounting department.

This is responsible for the preparation of financial statements.

The Information Technology department
This is responsible for maintaining and operating the computer systems.

The Administration department
This is responsible for logistical smooth running.

7. Legal Advice and Corporate Secretarial Division

This division is concerned with the following:-
Advise generally on all legal matters affecting the authority
Assist in interpretation and drafting of contracts
Drafting legal assignments for court purposes and also attending court hearings.
Carry out legal research and make recommendations.

8 Corporate Communication Division

This division enhances both internal and external communication
It raises public awareness of the organisation.
Maintains positive corporate visibility, nationality in the region and beyond in line with global trends.
Creates mutually beneficial relations and harmonises relations with key stakeholders.

9. Loss Control Division

This division is there to enforce compliance with revenue laws and to enforce regulatory contracts with integrity, transparency and fairness. It seeks to achieve a state of "zero tolerance" to corruption and crime.

The Role of Customs in Exports

The Customs Authority operates under the Ministry of Finance and has got several sub stations on all the entry points which lead in and out of the country by road, rail and at all Aerodromes. Customs plays a very important role in the facilitation of exports. Its main functions in facilitating the smooth flow of imports/exports are:

1 Duty Assessment

Customs through its various entry points assesses the amount of duty that must be paid by importers. Customs raises various methods to charge duty and these include.

(a) AD Valorem

This method is employed widely and the goods are classified and each category will attract a certain percentage duty. If the value of the goods is under dispute Customs is empowered to assess duty by whatever assessment criteria they are empowered to use in terms of the act.

The methods used are:

(i) Computed Value Method

This takes into account the cost of production of the product using proper accounting methods.

(ii) Transaction Value of Identical Products

This method bases its computation from looking at the price of identical products in determining the value of the goods in question.

(iii) Transaction value of similar products

The value of duty of the products will be based on the value of similar products in the absence of identical goods.

(iv) Deductive Value

This is the value that is arrived at by inference and basing the decision on previous determinants to arrive at the value of the product in question.

2. Physical Searches

The Customs and Excise Act empowers the Revenue Authority Officers to "Stop and Search any person, including any person within any ship, vehicle or aircraft". These physical searches are intended to enforce Import/Export/Exchange Controls and Revenue law. The carrying out of physical searches by Customs facilitates exports in the sense that:

- It enables them to prevent the smuggling of goods on the negative list e.g. guns and arms of war/weapons as well as dangerous and classified drugs and protected commodities like maize, wheat, oil/gas and other strategic farm products.
- It can confirm quantities and description of goods.
- It protects the public.
- It collects revenue on goods that are being imported/exported, where necessary, and that improve the government revenue base.

3. Privacy and Decency Searches

Customs through its several sub-stations in various entry points can conduct searches in a dignified manner. In these searches the cheat to be searched has a right to demand to see a senior Customs Officer. In order to ensure adherence to moral principles and gender sensitivity, male officers do searches for males and searches for female are done by female officers.

4.   Setting up of Scanners

At the various points of entry Customs uses scanners that ensure that exports and imports are examined and parcels are inspected with no delays to the importer or exporter. Scanners ensure that the correct consignment is allowed to cross the border. This plays an important role in ensuring that there is no smuggling of goods and that dutiable goods are declared and duty is paid.

5.   Opening of Packages

Customs Officers can open any package required to be accounted for in terms of the Customs and Excise Act even in the absence of the owner at owners risk. Customs officers are also empowered to open postal articles, which are to be sent outside the country.

6.   Customs Officers Educational Assistance to Exporters

In a bid to facilitate and improve the flow of exports Customs offers educational assistance to participating exporters. The Customs educates on the documentation procedures. It also educates on the suitable packaging materials on all different kinds of consignments. Customs conducts workshops and seminar to educate exporters and importers on international business procedures.

Customs also assist exporters in transit. Suppose an exporter has experienced problems such as haulage breakdowns. The exporter will have to visit any nearest Customs Office and have his days extended so as to give him the chance to solve the problem.

Customs offers sophisticated computerised documentation processes. This is called the ASYCUDA System. This technique helps to minimize delays at the entry points and therefore facilitating the flow the exports.

Customs also carry out the registration of clearing agents including companies within in-house clearing facilities and the registration of importers and exporters.

Customs has the role of instituting new regulations such as for withholding tax on amounts payable under a contract of shipping goods and services.

The Customs and Excise Act

The Customs and Excise Act deals with the exportation of goods. The Customs & Excise Act outlines the regulations that deal with the exportation of goods under the following headings:-

1   Exporter to Deliver Customs Documents and Produce Goods

Every person or his authorized agent exporting any goods from any country shall before such exportation takes place, deliver to an officer a bill of entry or such other document as may be prescribed. The documents must disclose the full details and particulars of the goods.

2.   The delivery of customs documents may be delivered within such time before exportation of goods as the office may allow.

3.   Where goods are exported by post, any form or label affixed to the parcel on which a description of the contracts and thin value are set forth, together with such other form as may be prescribed, shall be the document or documents required under the provisions of the act.

4.   Every exporter shall, if he is required to do so by an officer, produce for his inspection all invoices and other documents relating to any goods entered into in terms of this section and shall, at his own risk and expense, unload, remove to or from any place indicated by the officer, open, pack, repack and close up such of the packages as the officer may require for examination and all charges incurred in the examination shall be borne by the exporter.

5.   In default of compliance with the relevant act the proper officer may cause the goods concerned to be impounded, and if entry is not made within three months together with the payment of any duty and all charges of removal and warehouse rent, the Director may, subject to this section cause the goods to be sold by public auction, if they have not been entered before the date fixed for their sale.

6.   Export of Goods: Except with the prior permission of an officer no person shall load any goods, except the personal effects of passengers contained in their luggage into a ship, aircraft, vehicle or pipeline for exportation from any country. Any person leaving the country shall, whether or not he has goods in his possession, report to an officer.

In the case of a person departing by ship or vehicle at the customs house or custom post at the place of his departure.
In the case of a person leaving by aircraft, at the customs house or customs post at the place of his departure.
In the case of a person leaving on foot, at the customs house or customs post the point at which he intends to cross the border.

7.   Exporting of Goods Overland: No person in charge of a vehicle used for the exportation of goods overland shall remove such vehicle beyond the borders of the country, without the permission of an officer and under such conductions as the Director may specify. The Director may, in his discretion, grant a general permission to any such person.

8.   Outward Clearance of Ships: The master of a ship bound from any place within to any place beyond the borders of the country shall before any goods are laden therein make application to the proper officer in the form prescribed for permission to export local goods on such ship.

No goods shall be laden before all inland cargo to be discharged has been discharged except such goods or ballast as may be permitted by the proper officer.

9.   Outward Clearance Aircraft:
The pilot of every aircraft bound from any place within to place outside the country shall furnish to an office before any goods are taken on board particulars of the departure and journey of the aircraft and deliver before the aircraft departs, in the form prescribed and with as many copies as that officer may require:-

A report.

- A manifest of the goods on board.
- A statement of stores on board and such forms when signed by such officer shall be the clearance and authority for the aircraft to proceed to destination outside Oman.
- No aircraft shall depart from a customs aerodrome in Oman until the pilot has obtained the clearance and authority referred in subsection (1) and the pilot shall not after departure, call at any place in Oman other than a customs aerodrome unless otherwise forced by circumstances beyond his control.

- If the aircraft in respect of which a clearance has been issued at any place in terms of this section does not depart from that place within thirty – six hours of the time of clearance then he cannot leave the customs aerodrome unless forced to do so by accidents, stress of weather or other circumstances beyond his control, before getting a fresh clearance from customs.

Whistler, Pilot or Operator Appoint Agent

The monitor of a ship, the person in charge of any vehicle after than railway trains, the pilot of any aircraft or the operator of any pipeline may, instead of himself performing any act including the answering of questions, required by any enactment and any person who exports or assists in exporting, which restricts or controls the exportation of such goods shall be guilty of an offence.

In this case goods includes local and foreign currency.

Customs and Excise Act pertaining to Export Processing Zones

This deals with:-

- The Export Processing Zones

- Interpretation of the act
- In this part "customs territory" means any part of the country that is not within all export processing zones.
- Goods Imported into Export Processing Zones
- Goods imported into an export-processing zone should not be subject to duty provided such goods are not consumed within the customs territory.

Facilities

The EPZ shall construct or cause to be constructed suitable high enclosures with one suitable gate and install or cause to be installed adequate height around the export processing zone.

Goods Deemed to be exported

Goods, which are taken from the customs territory and brought into EPZs, shall be received and exported from the country.

Time of importation of goods

With the exception of goods exported by post or by means of pipeline, the time of exportation shall be deemed to be the time when the bill of entry or other documents required in terms of section fifty – four is delivered to an officer or the time when the goods cross the borders of the country whichever is earlier.

Where goods are exported by post, the time of exportation shall be the time when any export document which may be prescribed in terms of the act and is delivered to an officer or the time when the goods are placed in the post, whichever is earlier.

Where goods are exported by pipeline, the time of exportation shall be the time when the bill of entry or other documents required in terms of the act is delivered to an officer or the time when goods are first placed in the pipeline whichever is earlier.

Restriction of Exportation

If the exportation of any goods is restricted or controlled by any enactment, such goods shall only be exported in conformity with the provisions of such enactment.
Any person who exports or assists in exporting any goods the exportation of which is prohibited shall be deemed to have committed an offence.

Goods Manufactured in the EPZ

Goods manufactured in the EPZ shall not be taken out of an Export Processing Zone except.
For export

For report, maintenance, processing or conversion in the customs territory under such conditions as the Director may specify.

<u>Removal of Goods from EPZ</u>

Goods in EPZ shall be moved for exports or set into another export processing zone or bonded warehouse.
Be destroyed subject to any conditions the Director may specify.

Literature review

1. LITERATURE REVIEW
The purpose of the literature review is to gain from already published research on this topic. It also helps in illuminating issues and helping to proffer possible solutions. Literature review helps analyzing issues and in creating checks and balances before conclusions and decisions are made. One of the most important purposes of a literature review is getting a cross section of ideas from different perspectives on a given topic and by people or organizations that are respected in a discipline and have done a lot of in-depth research. The Emirates Centre for Strategic Studies and Research in their book Human Resource Development In A Knowledge-Based Economy (p4) quote Davis and Meyer as saying that the primacy of human capital is leading to a "global war for talented people" in much the same way that nations once fought over land because it was considered a productive asset. As a logical outcome of this new trend "tangible assets will start to lose their value as collateral, while intangible human capital becomes bankable." This means the gold rush and wars fought for gold in the 18th century in South Africa and other African countries may be repeated over human capital as the world jostles for this scarce commodity. That is how serious the competition for talent has become. In their book Strategic Marketing Problems, Cases and Comments (11th Edition), Roger A. Kerin and Robert A. Peterson say that the primary purpose of marketing is to create long-term and mutually beneficial relationships between an entity and the publics with which it interacts. They say failure to do this results in failure. Hanink D M (1994:83) in his book, The International Economy, A Geographical Perspective said, "Countries having mutual borders are connected in a primary way, and their close geographical proximity enhances the potential for spatial diffusion. Hill C W L (2009:277) said "Free trade agreements are the most popular form of regional economic integration, accounting for almost 90 percent of regional agreements." Twomey et al (2005:3) confirmed that law keeps society running smoothly and efficiently. United Nations organs' websites like WTO, UNCTAD, ITC and World Bank websites were visited and scoured to get supporting evidence on trade and trade dynamics relating to customs control and trade facilitation. Research has shown that in international trade 90% of the problems that badly damage business relations and lead to loss of customers are caused by poor distribution practices. It must be remembered that customers judge marketers and suppliers on the basis of the smooth flow of the supply chain into their system and can use this yard stick to decide whether to continue dealing with your company or not and the same applies to countries. Countries whose customs systems are more efficient have tended to develop faster than others e.g. Taiwan,

Singapore, Japan, the USA, Germany and now China. We are not taking a simplistic treatment of the totality of business. Many factors contribute to national and organizational competitiveness but an efficient customs authority is obviously one of those key institutions to make any country successful in international business as well as state security. Customs authorities need to have regular training programmes training industrialists on customs regulations, having regular breakfast workshops with industry to bridge misunderstanding and clear a build-up of potential problems that may affect business or government interests and to exchange note on trade agreements as well as revision of these as and when necessary. Customs authorities also need to do collaborative research with relevant university departments in Oman as well as internationally to keep abreast of best practice to promote national competitiveness, state security and a business friendly customs regime.

Conclusion

In a nutshell the Customs and Excise Act provides rules and regulations that every exporter and importer should adhere to in order to have a smooth flow of international business. It outlines the procedures that should be employed in respect to the type of goods/consignment and modes of transport. Breach of the Customs & Excise Act attracts heavy penalties such as seizure and forfeiture of goods, fines and penalties and heavy jail terms of anything up to twenty five years in jail. Operating licenses may be cancelled resulting in company closure and deregistration. Utmost good faith, honesty and uprightness are essential values in dealing with customs authorities in any country. In both developed and developing countries, taxes and duties contribute almost 95% of all government revenue, therefore this is one area where the government has a very close eye in terms of its operations as it decides the fate of a nation and the financial functionality of a country and all other government activities. This situation is different in the oil rich Arab countries where government gets the bulk of its revenue from oil and gas and taxes are generally zero rated or just 5% on imports. But Customs regulations still remain very important for state security reasons as well as immigration control and promotion of investment (FDI) and international business.

Customs Authorities now have to deal with a plethora of challenges including:- transfer pricing, dumping, countervailing duties/measures, smuggling, preventing international terrorism, drug trafficking, human trafficking, the international refuge crisis, managing in a global recession, business and investment promotion, trade agreements, international cooperation, the ICT challenges, e-customs and the paperless office, e-government, e-logistics, membership of the World Customs Union (WCU) an organ of the United Nations, Regional trade agreements like the GCC, the WTO, ITC and UNCTAD. No country can succeed if it does not participate in these bodies. Some countries have gone a step further and established degrees in Fiscal Studies as well as Trade Policy. This has strengthened expertise by officers in government and the private sector and helped increase investment, tourism, trade capacity, revenue collection and cooperation between government, the private sector, trade promotion organizations (TPOs) and the international traveling and trading community. Customs regulations still remain very important for state security reasons as well as immigration control, promotion of investment (FDI), tourism and international business. Now there is a new area altogether, health tourism, where countries like UAE are making billions of dollars from health tourists, people coming for specialized and advanced medical services. This is now an international niche market targeting the upper niche of the income brackets – celebrities, presidents, politicians, sports persons, business persons, the rich and famous and the opinion leaders of this world with plenty of disposable incomes.

Customs authorities are now a marketing focal point for any country. Poorly treated visitors and business people shun a country and well treated people do repeat business and national promotion across the globe. This is food for thought for anyone working in customs or planning a career there as well as policy makers. Training in marketing philosophy is now a key result area for customs authorities the world over as countries jostle for tourists and investors and also to speed up immigration and import/export formalities to reduce business costs in this area and to improve efficiencies and national competitiveness.

References
1. Branch, A. (2000): Export Practice and Management, 4th Edition, Prentice Hall Europe, UK

2. Kerin R.A., Peterson R.A. (2007). Strategic Marketing Problems, Cases and Comments, (11th Edition). Pearson Prentice Hall

3. The Emirates Center for Strategic Studies and Research. (2003):Human Resource Development in a Knowledge-Based Economy. The Emirates Center for Strategic Studies and Research

4. Hanink D.M. (1994). The International Economy, A Geographical Perspective. John Wiley & Sons, Inc

5. Hill C.W.L. 7th Ed. (2009). International Business, Competing in the Global Marketplace. McGraw-Hill

6. Walters, G. P. and Toyne, B. (1989): "Product Modification and Standardization in International Markets: Strategic Options and Facilitating Policies', Columbian

7. Journal of World Markets, Winter: 37-44

8. Van Mesdag, M. (1985): "The Frontiers of Choice", Marketing, 10 October

9. Rosen, B. J., Boddewyn, J.J and Louis, E. (1989) 'US Brands Abroad: An Empirical Study of Global Branding,' International Marketing Review, 6(1)

10. Twomey D.P., Jennings M.M. (2005). Anderson's Business Law and the Legal Environment (19th Edition). Thomson South-Western

11. Ohmae, K. (1989) "Managing In Borderless World', Harvard Business Review, May/June

12. Levitt, T. (1983) 'The Globalization of Markets ', Harvard Business Review May/June

13. World Trade Report: Retrieved 22 September 2009 from
http://www.intracen.org/tradstat/welcome.htm

14. World Trade Report: Retrieved 15 September 2009 from
http://www.unctad.org/Templates/Page.asp?intItemID=1890

15. World Economic Analysis Report: Retrieved 15 September 2009 from
http://econ.worldbank.org/WBSITE/EXTERNAL/EXTDEC/0,,contentMDK:2
2216733~pagePK:64165401~piPK:64165026~theSitePK:469372,00.html

16. World Economic Report: Retrieved 15 September 2009 from
http://www.wto.org/english/res_e/booksp_e/anrep_e/world_trade_report09_e.p
d

===
=====

The following is a research paper by the author and academic colleagues at the Colleges of Applied Sciences in Oman, Mr. Anwar Khamis Abdullah Al Sheyadi & Mr. Rashid Al-Mataani on Strategic Risk Management in International Marketing Through the Use and Application of Pre- and Post – Shipment Inspection; Foolproof Protection of Corporate and National Interest in Transactions Across the Globe; the case For Oman and the rest of Asia

Abstract
The choice of countries and firms on whether to use pre and post shipment inspections should be dictated by the kinds of firms they are dealing with, the risk associated with the product, how much they trust each other, the amount of money involved, the strategic value of the purchases and the consequences of risk on the firm or country, should it actually occur. These factors would be weighed against cost, time and expected result. Finally it must be a board decision to either go for inspection or not. But venturing into unnecessary and potentially dangerous and costly risks head on is an irresponsible decision which should never be done for any reason. Some of the risk can bring down a government (like the Zambian maize imports during President Kenneth Kaunda and the Indonesian rice protests of the 1980s), or bring down a company or get top managers fired or jailed for negligence. Just imagine a country importing or exporting seed maize or fertilizer for an oncoming agricultural season or medicine for a disease outbreak like

Swine Flu or wheat and rice imports during a drought or for national requirements or strategic commodities like oil and gas; no chances can be tolerated or entertained as the consequences would be too ghastly to contemplate. Pre-shipment inspection embraces product quality, quantity being exported and the price(s) proposed and market price comparison at the time of shipment. The main purpose really of inspection is to check that the goods in question fully meet the contractual requirements of the importer with regard to price, quality, quantity and customs classification. This is to ensure that the products comply with the description found in the export sales contract/bill of lading/export invoice. Subsequently they will be examined or checked as they are loaded into the container or the ship/vessel. The inspections are also carried out to prevent general smuggling and smuggling of dangerous drugs and arms of war. In a war situation countries carry out pre and post-shipment inspections for these same state security reasons. Customs authorities and governments are very keen to prevent smuggling as it robs them of much needed state revenue in the form of duties and taxies. Inspections are also done by governments to prevent externalization of foreign exchange through undercharging exports and overcharging imports and agents commission – this can easily ruin a country and lead to economic collapse. Prominent international companies who do inspection business are:- Crown Agents, UK and SGS from Switzerland; both do have offices all over the world and can do inspections in any country in the world, except the war zone. Currently some countries in Asia, Europe and Africa require that both letter of credit and contracts relevant to the import of goods contain a condition that a Clean Report of Findings covering quality, quantity, packaging and price must be presented together with other documents required to negotiate payment. This is done to minimize the incidence of corruption or cheating and shipment of poor quality products plus as a measure of quality assurance to prevent disruptions caused by receipt of unsuitable products, whether for consumption or manufacturing. No nation or firm can ever succeed in exports if the quality is not consistently good and perfect. For management systems to be effective, it must involve the application of technical standards and adopt process technology that is appropriate to the function of the business. Products must be inspected, tested or measured to confirm that they conform to the required specifications or standards. Pre and post-shipment inspection is part of the process of quality assurance and protects a firm and its customers and prevents abuse and fraud by unscrupulous people. Pre-shipment inspection is normally required and used when you are dealing with a new supplier as a safeguard and is disposed of as relations improve and the parties get used to each other and it has been proven beyond reasonable doubt that the supplier is honest and trustworthy. Doing away with inspection reduces cost of purchasing, cost of doing business as well as the time taken to finalize transactions.

Objectives of the Study

The objectives of this study are:-

- To investigate and expose findings about the status of knowledge and understanding of pre and post-shipment inspection in international business
- To find out the current gaps, pitfalls and shortcomings in export/import business caused by not using pre and post-shipment inspection and how this could be addressed through the use of this strategic tool
- To identify evidence of theories and findings in books and latest journals and related literature which support or refute the theories

- Contribute to the promotion of pre and post-shipment inspection as international business promotion tools
- To make solid recommendations on risk management in international business using pre and post-shipment inspection as a foolproof system to support internationalization efforts.

Research Method

Our research is based on the following research methodologies:- observation at relevant institutions, literature review, focus group discussions in a number of organizations, desk research and scouring internet sources. This kind of scenario is very good at extracting information to make well informed decisions while also creating checks and balances on shortfalls in each system. This is called research triangulation and gives credibility to research results and findings. Gaps in one system are compensated by another system. These methods each has its merits and demerits, and using different methods of data collection gives credibility to the end result, recommendations and conclusions as they will be based on a firm foundation. There are various issues to be considered in research including cost, time, practicality and available budget, resources and people. We considered all these issues before settling for our alternatives.

Literature Review

Hanink D M in his book The International Economy, A Geographical Perspective (1994:232) quoted the World Bank as saying its experience was that complete free trade, 100% profit repatriation, 100% foreign ownership, free movement of imports/exports and capital equipment without customs duty gives success to Export Processing Zones and Industrial Parks but risk needed to be managed carefully. Sekaran U (2003:11) said that managers need research to make reasonably accurate decisions and to minimize risk and to create new ideas. Hill C W L (2009:261) said that host governments benefit from investment by MNCs in three ways namely:- home country's balance of payments benefits, positive employments effects and finally learning valuable skills from exposure to foreign markets that can be eventually transferred back home, therefore risk needed to be managed. Kerin R A and Peterson (2007:427) says that consumer value assessments are often comparative, which means that consumers compare similar product offerings for prices and normally more competitive offers get the business. The Emirates Center for Strategic Studies and Research (2003:95) says the success of countries in adopting a knowledge-based economy depends on the quality of the education systems and the institutional structures that facilitate the process from learning to application, the reward system has to be correct to attract the best brains. This means that the best markets attract the best brains. Hitt et al says (2007:396) International entrepreneurship is scouting for international opportunities well beyond your borders but risk management is central. The wealth of successful countries is a fusion of pickings from every corner of the world. Off course the issue of cultural contamination cannot be ignored, which becomes the price to pay for benefiting out of international trade, but obviously the benefits are more than the side effects as can be seen in the standard of living. A number of relevant websites were scoured for supportive theories and evidence such as the United Nations, World Bank,

Wikipedia, WTO and ITC. Nothing is perfect but no one doubts that the best practice standards adopted by successful countries are one of the major reasons for their rise to world super power status. The Economist reported in its latest journal that the onset of the world recession had resulted in a permanent economic power shift from the West to East Asia. The main attraction of the Far East is lower costs, strategic location, access to raw materials, the concentration of major MNCs, a positive work ethic, a world population centre with high consumption, a high degree of creativity and political stability but there also exists risks hence the need for inspection.

FINDINGS
Our long term investigations took us far and wide and our discoveries also created a learning platform for us as well. We learnt a lot from these interactions with industrialists and government officials and discovered that the business world can be very cruel if a firm does not take precautions to protect itself and its business interests in every transaction. We also learnt that Kenya imported a shipload with thousands of tonnes of river sand instead of sugar after importing purported sugar without pre-shipment inspection from Brazil. After this scandal the fraudsters disappeared and a number of senior government officials were dismissed and jailed but the lost money was not recovered. We also have recent terrible cases which could have been solved and prevented by pre and post - shipment inspections and these are:- the Chinese Melamine Milk Scandal, the Chinese Poisoned Toy scandal, the current Toyota Vehicle Safety scandal and recalls and many others. Surely these were preventable through simple inspections and quality verifications. Our other detailed findings were the following:-
What is Pre- Shipment Inspection?
Pre-Shipment Inspection by its functional definition is referred to as the process where an independent inspection of goods is carried out before shipment. An increasing number of countries all over the world are joining the global market. Globalisation consequentially calls for universal standards - global products or services that will meet the world's expectations. Because of this factor of global marketing these global players are now insisting on inspection of goods before shipment. It is important to note that all of this is an effort to place quality products on the global market.
Total quality management is the backbone of national, regional and international business at any level.
Significance
Pre-shipment inspection embraces product quality, quantity being exported and the price(s) proposed and market prices comparison at the time of shipment. The main purpose really of inspection is to check that the goods in question fully meet the contractual requirements of the importer with regard to price, quality, quantity and customs classification. This is to ensure that the products comply with the description found in the export sales contract/bill of lading/export invoice. Subsequently they will be examined or checked as they are loaded into the container or the ship/vessel.
The inspections are also carried out to prevent general smuggling and smuggling of dangerous drugs, pornographic materials, dangerous lotions and beauticians, dangerous and subversive literature, arms of war, strategic products like oil and gas, fish, precious minerals like diamonds and gold, hard currencies like the US$, UK Pound, the Euro, the Yen and other international currencies, emeralds and gold and to prevent human

trafficking. In a war situation countries carry out pre and post-shipment inspections for these same state security reasons. Customs authorities and governments are very keen to prevent smuggling as it robs them of much needed state revenue in the form of duties and taxies. Inspections are also done by governments to prevent externalization of foreign exchange through undercharging exports and overcharging imports and agents commission – this can easily ruin a country and lead to economic collapse. Pre and post - shipment inspection is such an important state security weapon which can prevent smuggling of arms of war which may be used to topple a government or cause banditry or political instability. It can contribute to national stability and peace and accounting for dangerous criminals and putting them in jail.

Who does it?

A competent company which is completely independent of the exporter carries out the inspection in the exporting country. This is very objective as there are no chances of the inspecting party being biased towards the exporter's products. Prominent international companies who do inspection business are:- Crown Agents, UK and SGS from Switzerland; both do have offices all over the world and can do inspections in any country in the world, except the war zone. Independent private companies conduct pre-shipment inspections and they are contracted to carry out the inspections in accordance with the laws and regulations of the importing country. In accordance with those requirements and invoice inspections the company performs a physical inspection and price (inspection) comparison of goods. SGS-Zimbabwe Limited, Inter-Tech Testing Services International and Crown Agents are independent companies in Zimbabwe that employ registered assessors and provide pre-shipment inspection services. Pre-shipment inspection companies do not have the right to approve/prevent shipment of goods. The opinion expressed by inspection companies is given after the seller provides all the factors. It is made in good faith without any liability to the seller for any loss, damage or expenses arising from the issuance of the report of findings. Currently some countries in Asia, Europe and Africa require that both letter of credit and contracts relevant to the import of goods contain a condition that a Clean Report of Findings covering quality, quantity, packaging and price must be presented together with other documents required to negotiate payment. This is done to minimize the incidence of corruption or cheating and shipment of poor quality products plus as a measure of quality assurance to prevent disruptions caused by receipt of unsuitable products, whether for consumption or manufacturing

Who Governs Pre-Shipment Inspection Companies?

The International Federation of Inspection Agencies (IFIA) on behalf of those members administering government-mandated pre-shipment inspection programmes, is promoting the following Code of Practice to be observed by those companies:-

1. Activities of pre-shipment inspection companies (PIC) in the country of export may be undertaken on behalf of a foreign firm, government, government agency, central bank or other appropriate governmental authority and may include;
   - Physical inspection for quantity and quality of goods;
   - Verification of export prices, including financial terms of the export transaction and currency exchange rates where appropriate; and
   - Support services to the Customs authorities of the country of importation.

2. The general procedures for any physical inspection of goods and the examination of the price of exports out of any particular country will be the same in all exporting countries and the specific requirements established by the importing country will be administered by the PIC in a consistent and objective manner.

3. The PIC will provide assistance to the exporters by furnishing information and guidelines necessary to enable exporters to comply with the pre-shipment inspection regulations of the importing country. This assistance on the part of the PIC is not intended to relieve exporters from the responsibility for compliance with the import regulations of the importing country.

4. Quality and quantity inspections will be performed in accordance with accepted national/international standards.

5. The conduct of pre-shipment activities should facilitate legitimate foreign trade and assist bona-fide exporters by providing independent evidence of compliance with the laws and regulations of the importing country.

6. Pre-shipment activities will be conducted and the Clean Report of Findings or notice of non-issuance therefore will be sent to the exporter in a timely and convenient manner.

7. Confidential business information will not be shared by the PICs with any third party other than the appropriate firm or government authority for which the inspection in question is being performed.

8. Adequate procedures to safeguard all information submitted by exporters will be maintained by the PIC together with proper security for any information provided in confidence to them.

9. The PIC will not request from exporters information regarding manufacturing data related to patents (issued or pending) or licensing agreements. Nor will the PIC attempt to identify the cost of manufacture, level of profit or, except in the case of exports made through a buying agent or a confirming house, the terms of contracts between exporters and their suppliers.

10. The PIC will avoid conflict of interest between the PIC and any related entities of the PIC or entities to which the PIC has a financial interest and the companies whose shipments the PIC is inspecting.

11. The PIC will state in writing the reason for any decision declining issuance of a Clean Report of Findings.

12. If a rejection occurs at the stage of physical inspection, the PIC will, if requested by the exporter, arrange the earliest date for inspection.

13. Whenever so requested by the exporter, and provided no contrary instruction has been issued by the firm or government authority the PIC will undertake a preliminary price verification prior to receipt of the import license on the basis of binding contractual documents, proforma invoice and application for import approval. An invoice price and or price exchange rate or currency exchange rate that has been accepted by the PIC on the basis of such preliminary price verification will not be withdrawn, provided the goods and the previously submitted documents conform with the information contained in the import license. The Clean Report of Findings however, will not be issued until appropriate final documents have been received by the PIC.

14. Price verification will be undertaken on the basis of the terms of the sales contracts and will take into consideration any generally applicable and allowable adjusting factors pertaining to the transaction.

15. Commissions due to an agent in the country of destination will be treated in confidence by the PIC and will be reported to the appropriate government authority only when so requested.

16. Exporters and importers, who are unable to resolve differences with the PIC may appeal in writing, stating facts of the specific transactions and the nature of complaint and identify to a designated appeals official of the PIC. Exporters wishing to appeal the results of pre-shipment inspection may also seek review of the decision of the PIC in the importing country.

Principles of Pre-Shipment Inspection

The Pre-Shipment Agreement recognises that WTO/GATT and GCC principles and obligations apply to the activities of pre-shipment inspection agencies mandated by the government.
The obligations placed on government which use pre-shipment inspections include;-

Utmost Good Faith

The pre-shipment inspection company must disclose all the required details with utmost good faith. The inspector should not disclose false information that favours the exporter at the expense of the importer.

Bribes, Fraudulent
The inspector should not be involved in any form of bribe, from whichever side of the contracting parties. In fact the exporter, importer and the inspector should not be involved in any bribery and fraudulent acts. This is an objective principle, and it offers a free and fair ground for all exporters and their products to participate.

Transparency

The PIC should observe a culture of transparency from the time the exporter enquires about its services and engages the company to do the inspection to the time the inspection company issues a Clean Report of Findings.

Protection of Confidential Business Information

The pre-shipment inspection company must maintain a level of professionalism in which client's information is kept highly/extremely confidential.

Avoiding unreasonable delays

Delay of deliverance of products to the customer is a major pitfall in exports. This means the exporter has failed to meet the customer requirements on time. Such delays can be caused by the late issuance of the Clean Report of Findings. When inspection is done at company workshops or warehouses the consignment, unless otherwise, must not be repeatedly inspected at the Customs Offices at the border posts.

Maintaining full compliance with all export contract laws that are relevant to a product being exported, the inspector should observe that product details, rules and regulations governing products should be followed as stipulated, or as set by the relevant authorities.

Will my certificate be accepted in another country

The acceptance of product certification is still limited to the national or, in exceptional cases, the regional level. Few product certification schemes enjoy universal acceptance. Various possibilities however for the recognition of your product certification exist. You will then need to determine from the regulator in your target market whether any of the following arrangements are in place:-

- Mutual Recognition Agreements (MRAs). During trade negotiations between countries and trading blocks, the governments of the negotiating parties may sign agreements on the mutual acceptance of certification systems. Under such agreements, regulators in one country will accept products that are certified in accordance with the recognised systems in the other signatory countries.

- Cooperative (voluntary) arrangements. Providers of conformity assessment services, both domestic and foreign, may enter into voluntary recognition arrangements. These include arrangements between accreditation bodies, and arrangements between individual laboratories, certification bodies and inspection bodies. Such arrangements have been common for years and have been developed for the commercial advantage of the participants. Governments or regulators have recognised some of these arrangements from time to time as a basis for the acceptance of test results and certification in the regulatory domain. Accreditation bodies have been working towards harmonizing international practices for accrediting conformity assessment bodies. This has resulted in global networks to facilitate the recognition and acceptance of certification. Such networks take the form of multilateral recognition agreements under which each participant undertakes to recognise the certification issued by another party in the system as being equivalent to that issued by itself. Governments or regulators have recognised such certification from time to time as a basis for technical regulations. The International Accreditation Forum (IAF) is one of the better known international networks of accreditation organisations. IAF endeavours to ensure that certification organisations in the management system certification business enjoy international recognition of accredited organisations.

- Governments designation
  - o Governments or regulators may designate specific conformity assessment bodies, including bodies located outside their territories, to undertake testing, certification or inspection in connection with technical regulations.
- Unilateral recognition

o   A government or regulator may unilaterally recognize the results of
    foreign conformity assessment. The conformity assessment body may be
    accredited abroad under recognition by regional or international
    accreditation systems. In the absence of the accreditation, the conformity
    assessment body may prove its competence by other means. Many
    regulators accept the test results of foreign organisations. No specific
    example is provided because such recognition is generally not published.

Criteria for selection of certification bodies

A Company or organisation preparing for pre-shipment inspection certification should
consider the following criteria in choosing a certification body:-
* ❖ The reputation, market image and experience of the certification body.
* ❖ Whether a national accreditation body accredits the certification body.
    (Accreditation bodies submit accredited certification bodies to periodic
    surveillance audits. It is also advised that the accreditation body be a member of
    International Accreditation Forum (IAF).)
* ❖ Whether the certification body has been accredited to provide certification
    services in your area of business (certification bodies are accredited for specific
    scopes of activities.)
* ❖ Proximity of the certification body (long distances can have significant cost
    implications for interaction with the certification body, as well as for the travel
    expenses of auditors during the pre-certification and post – certification audits.)
* ❖ The period of validity of certification, audit charges, certification fees and
    currency of payment (these may vary between certification bodies.)
* ❖ If certification is being obtained at the insistence of major overseas buyers, their
    views on the choice of certification body or accreditation body should be sought
    and considered.

These are the universal factors to consider when selecting an inspection body although
some can be added or subtracted depending on the company, product, industry, relations
with the importing country, even the market.

Reasons for Pre-Shipment Inspection

* To check whether goods to be exported conform to the relevant terms of the
  contract as well as any other applicable regulations of the importing nation.
* Conformity to the quality standards set by the national and international
  certification authorities.
* To avoid and prevent exporting of non-complying and poor quality products.
* To evaluate whether the product is on the negative list or not.
* To assist the company address any problems at the start of the exporter's supply
  chain, to reduce the risk of shortages, off-specification quality/damage before the
  goods are shipped and hence limiting disputes with business partners as well.

- To provide valid certification and proof that will be used when claiming money from the bank. The certificate is used alongside with other relevant documents to claim payment from the bank.
- To determine whether the invoice value of the consignment/contract is in line with prevailing export market prices.
- To check on correct pricing, and to avoid over and under charging of goods.
- To prevent smuggling
- To prevent trade in dangerous goods, for example arms of war, for the national state security interest.
- The buyer and the government may initiate pre-shipment inspection for national interest.
- To check on the correctness and accuracy of shipping and other commercial documentation to prevent shipping and related problems
- Physical inspection, looking on the colour, quantity, quality and testing of the strength of products.
- To prevent toppling of legitimate governments – this may be caused by the importation of dangerous arms of war.
- Governments need to ensure that they get the correct value of duty on all exports and imports.
- To provide assurance of product quality to the importer, and to reduce factors like post-purchase dissonance and post purchase dissatisfaction.

Benefits of pre-shipment inspection

1. <u>To the Seller</u>

   - It helps the exporter to confirm the quality of the product at hand, particularly on an ex-works or FOB/FCA contract.
   - It gives the exporter confidence in its products by inviting the buyer to inspect the product while it is being loaded at source.
   - It assures the exporter of support from government and other public organisations who may want to be partners with the company cognisant of its reputation.
   - It helps the exporter to prevent embarrassment in the importing country especially where the product is found to be of an abnormally substandard quality.
   - This may impact on the firm's reputation and relations with other firms in other countries.
   - Customer loyalty and brand loyalty.
   - Improve workforce ability from intensive training.
   - Enhance the implementation of TQM.
   - Reduce production costs by the removal of defective raw materials.
   - Reduce possibility of reprocessing.

650

- Ensure co-ordination in the organization such that everyone is involved in the production of quality products consistently.

2. To the Buyer

    - It helps the buyer ascertain the quality of the product before transport and shipment costs are incurred.
    - It helps preserve the buying company's identity, reputation and image.
    - In an FOB and FCA or ex-works contract, pre-shipment inspection is necessary to avoid conflict between the seller and the buyer.
    - In a CIF and C&F contract it is necessary to authorise the off loading of trucks at the point of discharge.
    - Compliments the JIT and TQM systems and efforts.
    - It automatically exposes and weeds out incompetent firms from the market place.
    - Potential disputes are pre-empted at source thus avoiding costly quarrels and corrective measures.
    - It ensures a smooth production flow and supply of quality products all the time.
    - Reprocessing is eliminated.
    - Grows the purchaser's market portfolio and credibility.
    - Assists in brand building and corporate branding.

3. To the Nation

    - The exporter's country becomes a destiny of investments; it generally attracts Foreign Direct Investment.
    - Improves the county's image in terms of business practices and systems.
    - It helps prevent national scandals when substandard products filter into the buyer's country.
    - It helps preserve national identity and image.
    - It is more attractive for countries to enter into trade agreement(s) with a country that is known for quality products.
    - Improves a country's competitiveness and reputation.

What Role do Inspection and Testing Play in Quality Management Systems?

Quality Management Systems

No nation or firm can ever succeed in exports if the quality is not consistently good and perfect. These are standards that simply seek to ensure that the various elements are carried out competently and satisfy requirements. 1S0 9001:2001 requires organisations to implement a quality management system that verifies that customer requirements are being met by measuring and monitoring the product during the appropriate stages of its development.

For management systems to be effective, it must involve the application of technical standards and adopt process technology that is appropriate to the function of the business. Products must be inspected, tested or measured to confirm that they conform to the required specifications or standards. If this process is to have any value, technicians possessing appropriate skills and resources necessary for the task must carry it out competently.

It is important that the criteria of competence and clarity of reporting apply to all tests and measurement activities irrespective of the stage in the process at which they are applied. If the purpose of in-process inspection is to eliminate faulty production before further processing, it is necessary to be confident in the accuracy of the test or inspection data.

If the product is to be rejected it should indeed be faulty and defective and not be a satisfactory product unnecessarily rejected.

What are the procedures prior to having pre-shipment inspection of goods

1.   Initial Notification

The inspecting company initiates pre-shipment inspection once it receives a notice that an exporter's shipment needs to be inspected. The notice may be received either of two ways,

Notice from the importing country

The inspecting company receives from the importing country a copy of an import license, foreign exchange allocation license, letters of credit, or a written advisory document. This advisory document will include a reference number supplied by the importing country and will specify details of the quality, quantity and price of the goods, the name and address of the buyer and the seller, and the country of export. Attached to the advisory documents will be a copy of the proforma invoice or any supporting documents.

Notice from the Seller

The exporter may make a direct request to the inspecting company that it inspects the goods prior to shipment. When the seller makes the request they should provide the company with a copy of advisory documents or letter of credit, if they have received such a document from the buyer.

2.   Initial Notice by the Inspecting Company

Upon receipt of notice that pre-shipment inspection is required, the inspecting company will request the seller/exporter for details of the location of the goods and when the inspection will be convenient and who should be contacted at the place of inspection. In the event that the supplier is different from the seller on record, the inspection company will contact the seller on record who can identify the supplier to the inspecting company. The identity of the supplier will be treated in utmost confidentiality and will not appear in the report findings.

Basic Procedures for Inspection

Preliminary Price Comparison

While it awaits the response of the seller to its initial advice, the inspecting company undertakes a preliminary price comparison analysis based on the contractual document, proforma invoice or other supporting documents submitted with advisory document. If the comparison indicates that the selling price is not in line with the prevailing export market price, the seller will be contacted and asked to provide justification for the invoice price.

Arrangement for physical inspection:

Upon receipt of details as to the location of the goods and upon receipt of an acceptance time for the inspection, the company assigns an inspector and contacts the individual identified by the seller in order to make final arrangements for inspection.

Report of Inspection Results

When the physical inspection is completed, the inspector submits his report to the appropriate inspecting office and the results of the inspection will be communicated to the seller. Any discrepancies on price, incoterms, shipping/commercial documents, packaging, quality and quantity identified by the inspector will be communicated to the seller. The seller will then be given an opportunity to rectify the discrepancies by supplying new goods or by demonstrating that the discrepancies are acceptable to the buyer. If the buyer or inspector requires re-inspection the necessary arrangements should be made. If the seller is in disagreement with an inspector's findings he may immediately contact the appropriate inspecting office.

Submission of Final Documents

The inspecting office designated in the written request must receive the following documents:-

Settlement Invoice

The settlement invoice should contain the date and be signed. It must be issued by the seller and addressed to the buyer in the importing country. A complete description of the goods must be included and a note of the quantity purchased. The total invoice price must be shown with a breakdown showing FOB, freight and any other ancillary charges in accordance with the reporting requirements of the importing country. It should also include terms of payment.

Air Way Bill or Bill of Lading

The Air Way Bill should be endorsed, and completed so as to document receipt of the goods. The Bill of Lading should be endorsed "shipped on board" and completed so that they are acceptable as title to the goods being shipped.

Final Price Comparison

Once the inspecting office receives the appropriate final documents it proceeds with final price comparison. Where the final documents show no variation from the initial price comparison and the physical inspection results, the inspecting office should be able to issue a Clean Report of Findings.

Request for Justification

When the advisory documents from the importing nation are incomplete or when final documents include information that conflicts with the contractual documents, the inspecting office will ask the seller to explain any apparent discrepancy.

Timely Submission of Final Documents

To assist in the timely issuance of the Report of Findings, sellers should submit final documents, particularly the settlement invoice, as quickly as possible to the inspecting office. This is always accompanied by other customs cleared shipping documents. Non-compliance of goods can result in the inspector advising the buyer accordingly, who normally issues a directive, through the inspector to the exporter, for rejection of the goods and cancellation of the order. If the inspection is a government initiated one then the inspector normally has authority to cancel the order, but in consultation with the relevant importing government. Non-compliance normally attracts order cancellation, depending on the magnitude of the problem.

Issuance of the Report of Findings

Once shipment has been found acceptable as to quality, quantity and price the inspecting office will issue a Clean Report of Findings (CRF) within three working days, after receipt of all necessary final documents in proper order from the seller.

Non-Negotiable Report of Findings

When there are unresolved problems regarding quantity, quality, price of the shipment, the laws and regulations of some importing nations require that in certain cases the inspecting office issue a receipt of an NNRF. Authorities in the importing nation will decide whether to release payment for the goods or permit importation.

Issuance of Copies of the Report of Findings

Unless regulations of the importing nation provide otherwise, the inspecting office will provide sellers with the original Report of Findings. Where the Report of Findings covers a shipment by air freight or by sea freight if the transit time is very short, the inspecting company will scan, fax, or telex details of the Report of Findings to the liaison office in the importing country to assist importers to obtain the information needed to clear goods promptly.

Appeal within the inspecting company

Exporters who are unable to resolve differences with the inspecting company, pre-shipment inspection offices, may appeal in writing, stating facts of the specific transactions and the nature of the complaint directly to the Appeal's committee in the office of the Chief Executive Officer of the inspecting company in their country. The provision for appeal is not intended to replace the contract, but are in addition to rights of appeal to government agencies within the importing countries.

Appeal to authorities of the importing nation

Exporters wishing to appeal against the results of a pre-shipment inspection may also seek review of the inspecting company opinion in accordance with the regulations and dispute resolution procedures of the importing nation.

TQM and Pre-Shipment

Companies set up quality management systems in order to monitor and maintain the levels of quality of product and services of the firm. In a market where international competition is hardening and where people are increasingly concerned with quality and worried about quality, safety and protection of the environment, TQM is needed. As an example, Joseph Juran, one of the great quality consultants said in May 1994, "TQM to me is all that has to be done to achieve world –class quality."

CONCLUSION AND RECOMMENDATIONS
The choice of countries and firms on whether to use pre and post shipment inspections should be dictated by the kinds of firms they are dealing with, the risk associated with the product, how much they trust each other, the amount of money involved, the strategic value of the purchases and the consequences of risk on the firm or country, should it actually occur. These factors would be weighed against cost, time and expected result. Finally it must be a board decision to either go for inspection or not. But venturing into unnecessary and potentially dangerous and costly risks head on is an irresponsible decision which should never be done for any reason. Some of the risk can bring down a government (like the Zambian maize imports during President Kenneth Kaunda and the Indonesian rice protests of the 1980s), or bring down a company or get top managers fired or jailed for negligence. Just imagine a country importing seed maize or fertilizer for an oncoming agricultural season or medicine for a disease outbreak like Swine Flu

or wheat and rice imports during a drought or for national requirements; no chances can be tolerated or entertained as the consequences would be too ghastly to contemplate. We would make recommendations as follows:-

a. Do pre and post-shipment inspection when you are dealing with new suppliers to hedge your risk 100% until relations develop; there may be exceptions when you deal with well known global brands and tested international corporations.
b. Appoint credible and proven international inspection companies to do the job.
c. When unethical behavior is detected, call in the police to severely punish culprits and bring them before the courts to face justice and act as a deterrent.
d. Publish this extensively to educate society and create a deterrent.
e. Do not take chances with unknown firms and always institute inspection as a security measure.
f. In countries in war situations enforce pre and post-shipment inspections without exception; the same must apply to countries surrounded by countries in war as there is a tendency for a proliferation of uncontrolled weapons which can fall into wrong hands.
g. Suppliers caught cheating must be delisted and blacklisted forever, if they are not a monopoly.
a. Governments should impose heavy penalties for proven smuggling, including heavy and painful fines, heavy jail terms, seizure of smuggled goods and smuggling vehicles/trains/aero planes, cancellation of operating licenses and cancellation of Passports, Visas and Work Permits without exception. The citizenship granted to foreigners must be revoked and cancelled once anyone is caught smuggling and face immediate deportation. China is an excellent example of ethical and legal deterrence.
b. All the money and wealth from the proceeds of smuggling and dishonest should be seized and forfeited to the state to prevent unjust and illegal enrichment.

References
1. Zimtrade (1999) Trade Secrets, the Export Answer Book, Zimtrade
2. G. Albanum (1994) International Marketing and Export Management Addison – West Publishers
3. STWC Consultancy Private Limited, Total Quality Management Concepts STWC
4. Aaker David (2001), Strategic Marketing Management 6th Edition, USA
5. Tony Proctor (2000) Strategic Marketing, Routeledge Publishers London
6. Allan Branch (1984) Export Management Prentice Hall International
7. UNCTAD (2002) Quality Inspection Management UNCTAD
8. Brochures on Standards Association of Zimbabwe, Zimbabwe
9. Post-shipment inspection: Retrieved on 28 February 2010 from: www.iso.org
10. Pre-shipment inspection: Retrieved on 28 February 2010 from: http://www.crownagents.com/Home.aspx

11. Purchasing: Retrieved 27 February 2010 from
:http://www.purchasing.tas.gov.au/buyingforgovernment/getpage.jsp?uid=F5E74B20
DEF74E68CA256C750016BC87

12. Procurement: Retrieved 27 February 2010 from: http

13. Roberta J. Duffy, *Purchasing Today Journal,*.
December 1999 *Purchasing Today®*, page 41.

14. Barbican, S., (2009). Total value and political lobby and advocacy. *The European Journal of Marketing,* 30 (3), 12-14.

15. Bernard S., & Smith G. (2009). Modern industrial marketing model. *The Journal of Industrial Marketing Management,* 44 (3), 18-20.

16. Thomson J., & Schumpeter T.H., (2009). International marketing benchmarks in the modern era. *The Journal of International Marketing,* 25 (2), 13-14.

17. Williamson T., (2009). International marketing and globalization challenges. *The Journal of Market-Focused Management,* 33 (3), 22-24.

18. WTO site on the 1994 Government Procurement Agreement (GPA)
Retrieved 27 February 2010 from:*http:www.wto.org/govt/agrmnt.html*

19. Tendering: Retrieved 27 February 2010 from:
http://www.etenders.gov.ie/guides/Guides_show.aspx?id=2745

20. Best Practice Purchasing: Journal of Supply Chain Management, USA, Volume 3, 2009:p15. World Economic Analysis Report: Retrieved 5 December 2009 from
http://econ.worldbank.org/WBSITE/EXTERNAL/EXTDEC/0,,contentMDK:22216733~pagePK:64165401~piPK:64165026~theSitePK:469372,00.html

21. Politics of South Korea: Retrieved 15 December 2009 from
http://en.wikipedia.org/wiki/Politics_of_South_Korea

22. Best Practice: Retrieved 12 December 2009 from:
http://en.wikipedia.org/wiki/Best_practice

23. Economy of South Korea: Retrieved 14 December 2009 from:
http://en.wikipedia.org/wiki/Economy_of_South_Korea

24. Total Quality Management: Retrieved 15 December 2009 from:
http://en.wikipedia.org/wiki/Total_quality_management

25. South Korea: Retrieved 16 December 2009 from:
http://en.wikipedia.org/wiki/South_Korea

The following is a research paper entitled, "Reinventing International Purchasing and Supply Chain Management After the World Recession and Moving Towards Ethics Guided International Purchasing for a Better World Order - the Case for the Sultanate of Oman, the GCC and Zimbabwe," done by the writer and academic colleagues at The Colleges of Applied Sciences in Oman and another academic in the Department of International Marketing, School of Business Sciences at Chinhoyi University of Technology in Zimbabwe, Mr. Kudzai Ziki, accepted for presentation at the International Journal of Applied Sciences Christmas Conference on Academic Disciplines in Germany from 28 November to 3 December 2010.

Abstract

International purchasing is now driven by innovation, creativity and strategic management. The era for the order processors is now long gone. The goal of innovation is positive change, to make someone or something better. In purchasing there is a revolution going on right now – an endless transformation due to the forces of the world recession, globalization, technology, communication, cost-leadership pressures, the emergency of conurbations in China, India, Malaysia, Hong Kong, Singapore, New York, London, Berlin, Amsterdam, containerization and e-purchasing. World cargo centers have now emerged in Singapore, Hong Kong, New York, Amsterdam, Hamburg, London, Dubai,, Cairo and Durban, among other centers. The biggest problem facing the world economy is a complete lack of confidence, negative perception, illiquidity, fear and mistrust. The future for procurement is a mixed bag, and predicting it is a bit of a difficult jigsaw puzzle as too many factors determine its fate. It cannot be overemphasized that the procurement profession will be requiring professionals with a multiplicity of competences to cope with the complexities of the global village and the internationalization challenges of the supply market. Foreign languages may need to be introduced in international business and international purchasing management degrees so that managers and officers find it easy to deal with key countries like China, Germany, Spain (languages like Mandarin, Germany, French, Spanish). E-government is also an innovation being adopted by many countries to support the international business effort. Oman is a leader in this respect in the Middle East. Tomorrow's procurement is going to be driven by the following critical factors:- Embassies becoming centres of supply market analysis to feed local corporates with market intelligence for capital equipment, raw materials, inputs, identifying export markets, identifying investment opportunities and lastly building good political relations for the country. The embassies must change their strategic thrust from that of being centres of political rhetoric and excellence to being centres of business excellence, emphasizing business issues as well as political issues. The USA has got its largest embassy in China with 700 staffers because of the strategic economic importance and dominance of China and the Far East as the market of the future – this embassy services the rest of the Far East. The USA has now set up Chinese Language Centres in America and English Language Centres in China as a way of promoting business through language competence. In developed countries the reason, criteria and purpose of setting up embassies is potential business opportunities in host countries and this should be the line of thinking in all countries and get correctly qualified people to be appointed to ambassadorial positions – with those with international business qualifications and experience dominating diplomatic postings and appointments as they have the capacity to fully exploit business opportunities as opposed to non-business graduates. As part of strategic control organization need Codes of Ethics & Corporate Governance, interest disclosure by employees, whistle blower funds, suggestion boxes, good salaries and conditions, having policies which compel workers to go on leave every year for at least one month and engaging strategic transfers. Collaboration with universities and research centres can give a lot of value to pre-empt and plan for the future of profitable purchasing. The biggest problems facing purchasing professionals today are dishonest, an unpredictable business landscape, business instability, supply disruptions and getting the right qualified and experienced people to run their organizations.

INTRODUCTION

International purchasing is now driven by innovation, creativity and strategic management. The era for the order processors is now long gone. The goal of innovation is positive change, to make someone or something better. Innovation leading to increased productivity is the fundamental source of increasing wealth in an economy. The major problem with innovation is seems to be motivation, flexibility, and willingness to invest in innovation. Countries, firms and organizations that are serious about innovation have to overcome these barriers and that is better said than done. In actual fact the difference between success and failure is ability to perform these painful tasks with consistence and determination. Innovation calls for a change in corporate culture and painful strategic change management. In purchasing there is a revolution going on right now – an endless transformation due to the forces of the world recession, globalization, technology, communication, cost-leadership pressures, the emergency of conurbations in China, India, Malaysia, Hong Kong, Singapore, New York, London, Berlin, Amsterdam, containerization and e-purchasing. World cargo centers have now emerged in Singapore, Hong Kong, New York, Amsterdam, Hamburg, London, Dubai,, Cairo and Durban, among other centers. The biggest problem facing the world economy is a complete lack of confidence, negative perception, illiquidity, fear and mistrust. President Barrack Obama of the USA is our best example of successful national, international confidence building and national rebranding. The greatest challenge of our time is restoring business confidence, the rule of law and sanity, restoring business ethics into the economy and lastly giving hope to the hopeless (who are now the majority of the people). The bank scandals in the USA, other corporate frauds and the Chinese melamine milk scandal and the current massive Toyota vehicle recalls are examples of a complete lack of business ethics and the disasters that followed. One of the major causes of the current recession and financial crisis was the removal of the necessary regulatory framework and this created a smart haven for fraudsters and looters to run down strategic companies with impunity, away from the watchful eye of national controls. This exposed investors and the public with a negative multiplier effect right through. With none or minimum controls the major world corporations spinned out of control and ripped and slit the nerve centre and arteries of the world economy in New York, London and Zurich as they collapsed. New regulations creating transparency are urgently required. A number of leading economists, like Kruger, foretold the current disastrous world recession and correctly said it was caused by corruption and regulatory failure, but were labeled as anarchists and enemies of the state by some corrupt Republican and Democratic politicians who were enjoying massive financial donations from corrupt multinational firm lobbyists in Washington, USA. The million dollar question is, "How can the purchasing professional do his job without exposing his organization; how can one foresee potential dishonesty and manage it to prevent situations like the ones mentioned above?" Purchasing is all about efficiency, risk management, supply reliability, cost control, Value for Money Purchases and relationship building. This is a difficult balancing act. The modern purchasing professional must be concerned about politics and national policies and get involved in lobby and advocacy as unhelpful policies advanced by politicians can ruin and destroy all professional effort, including the very company or organization one works for – there won't be a place to practise your profession and sustain life.

Objectives of the Study

The objectives of this study are:-

- To investigate and expose findings about the status of knowledge and understanding of international purchasing innovation in general
- To find out the current gaps in international purchasing innovation/knowledge and how this is impacting on corporates
- To identify evidence of theories and findings in books and journals and related literature which support or refute the theories.
- To suggest way forward in moving winning formula in international purchasing.

The problem situation and justification

The problem facing organizations and purchasing practitioners is a myriad of problems created by the world recession which has imposed on organizations the need for drastic change management or face failure or collapse. Part of the problems had been building up for a long time. These problems include the following, among other things:-unsophisticated management, excess staff, long standing suppliers going out of business and strangling organizational operations, stock blackouts, civil wars disrupting supplies, terrorism, high jacking of consignments on high seas (e.g. by pirates in Somalia and the Gulf of Aden), high cost suppliers in traditional markets in the West and new low cost markets in the emerging economies in the Far East like China, Indonesia, Malaysia, India, Taiwan, Philippines and Japan, foreign language incompetence in new preferred markets, cultural difficulties, infrastructure challenges in 3rd world and emerging economies, global warming, supply disruptions caused by failed states and war zones e.g. Afghanistan, Pakistan and Somalia, high insurance premiums in countries and transit routes in the war zones, mistrust and suspicion in some countries, oversupply and market glut which is advantageous to the purchaser but very disruptive to the merchant/seller, a painful shortage of finance to oil business internationally due to bank failures and bank operational problems, the high national debt burdens, general illiquidity and fear of the future engulfing the entire market place, the introduction of harsh cash transactions as firms do not trust whether debtors would remain in business and timely pay their debts, economic sanctions and embargoes which disrupt business, quotas and trade wars e.g. the USA/Chinese stand-off about tyres, milk, toys, chicken and textiles, child labour, corruption, political instability in some countries, dishonesty, risk profiling and the current Toyota Vehicle Recalls and Safety Scandals and management and planning for a long term future. These are painful trade factors which the modern purchasing professional has to deal with head on. The age for the order taker is gone as these kinds of problems require highly qualified purchasing professionals, men and women who can operate at diplomatic level internationally. The modern purchasing professional is now expected to be bilingual in key foreign languages, e-literate, have top of the range international procurement expertise, be a product of a credible business school and have specialized in purchasing at degree level and have international exposure and disposition. It is now imperative for firms and governments to focus their recruitment in an international perspective in order to get the best. The purchasing professional must understand the political dynamics in different countries as well as the cultures and religions and their influence on product consumption, business dynamics, negotiations and business etiquette. A qualified world class purchasing professional is a panacea for any organization just as a doctor is a necessity for a hospital and an engineer for an engineering company. The purchasing professional requires three qualities:- degree level education in procurement/shipping/languages, relevant experience and international exposure/travel experience. Anything short of this is an accident in waiting, if the organization is classified as large or multinational or a government department. There is an additional requirement nowadays and this is the ability to design and plot an annual Purchasing Plan – this is a comprehensive plan for all purchasing activities and ties up with the corporate strategic plan, business plan, budget and other functional area plans. While innovation typically adds value, innovation may also have a negative or destructive effect as new developments clear away or change old organizational forms and practices. Organizations that do not innovate effectively may be destroyed by those that do. Hence innovation typically involves risk. A key challenge in innovation is maintaining a balance between process and product innovations where process innovations tend to involve a business model which may develop shareholder satisfaction through improved efficiencies while product innovations develop customer support however at the risk of costly R&D that can erode shareholder return. In summary, innovation can be described as the result of some amount of time and effort into researching (R) an idea, plus some larger amount of time and effort into developing (D) this idea, plus some very large amount of time and effort into commercializing (C) this idea into a market place with customers . Given this kind of situation it is so compelling to do this research and contribute to knowledge on better procurement practices and to academic knowledge. We chose to be part of the solution rather than spectators in crisis situation facing the world.

Research Method
Our research is based on the following research methodologies:- observation at relevant institutions, literature review, focus group discussions in a number of organizations, desk research and scouring internet sources. This kind of scenario is very good at extracting information to make well informed decisions while also creating checks and balances on shortfalls in each system. This is called research triangulation and gives credibility to research results and findings. Gaps in one system are compensated by another system. These methods each has its merits and demerits, and using different methods of data collection gives credibility to the end result, recommendations and conclusions as they will be based on a firm foundation. There are various issues to be considered in research including cost, time, practicality and available budget, resources and people. We considered all these issues before settling for our alternatives.

Literature review
Dillon W L said that "A vehicle fleet is as good as the road network and skilled technicians servicing this fleet – this is a reality in transport business." (Dillon W L:25). It is physical mobility and its efficiency which is the basic determinant of corporate and national efficiency, success, world class competitiveness, business goodwill and credibility, access to high yielding and lucrative markets, opening up of new and distant markets, enabling firms and corporate bodies to hold minimum stocks and ultimately engage in JIT and Total Quality Management (Aaker D:100). It was a sophisticated transport network that enabled the British to conquer and rule three quarters of the whole

world thus giving birth to Great Britain. Even today the American economic and military supremacy is founded on having the best brainpower and the most sophisticated and largest diverse transport network (i.e. road, rail, sea and air transport network.). United Nations organs' websites like WTO, UNCTAD, ITC and World Bank websites were visited and scoured to get supporting evidence on supply chain activities for the world economy. Kerin and Robert A. Peterson say that the primary purpose of trade is to create long-term and mutually beneficial relationships between an entity and the publics with which it interacts. They say failure to do this results in business and national failure. The Emirates Centre for Strategic Studies and Research in their book Human Resource Development In A Knowledge-Based Economy (2003:4) quote Davis and Meyer as saying that the primacy of human capital is leading to a "global war for talented people" in much the same way that nations once fought over land and gold because it was considered a valuable asset. As a logical outcome of this new trend "tangible assets will start to lose their value as collateral, while intangible human capital becomes bankable." This means the gold rush and wars fought for gold in the 18th century in South Africa and other African countries may be repeated over human capital as the world jostles for this scarce commodity. That is how serious the competition for talent has become. Charles W.L. Hill in his book International Business, Competing in the Global Marketplace – 7th Edition, (p169), says the theories of Adam Smith, David Ricardo and Heckscher-Ohlin help to explain the pattern of international trade that we observe in the world economy. On page 233 Hill says trade policy by governments may work positively or may attract retaliation. Hitt, Hoskisson and Ireland in their book Management of Strategy, Concepts and Cases (p396) say because of its positive benefits entrepreneurship is at the top of public policy agendas in most leading economies and successful countries the world over have benefited immensely from an entrepreneurial culture which hinges on successful supply chain and good public policies. This can be explained by availability of large investor funds and strategic location, rather than entirely by planning. Roger A Kerin and Robert A Peterson in their book Strategic Marketing Problems, Cases and Comments (p577) say a successful comprehensive marketing program must effectively stimulate target markets to buy, must be consistent with organizational capabilities and must outmaneuver competitors. The European Journal of Marketing (2009:Vol 3:12) said that there is now need for a paradigm shift in marketing to make the marketing practitioner aware of the total product value as well as supportive political policies through lobby and advocacy. It said the days when marketers were spectators while politicians made destructive policies are gone. This is the time when industry must shape economic policy to its preference. A true private public partnership was one of the reasons for The Far East's marketing success where excessive bureaucracy was done away with to better serve the global market. The Journal of Industrial Marketing Management (2009:Vol 3:18) ran a comprehensive article on modern industrial marketing emphasizing the reasons why modern industrialists buy what they buy and they said this was driven by:- the desire to improve efficiencies and cut costs, quality considerations, durability, easy of handling, convenience of use, improving productivity/automation, reducing labour as well as greenhouse gas emissions. Marketing now has to be futuristic and pre-empt global warming compliance and contribute to good housekeeping. The Journal of International Marketing (2009:Vol 2:13 said international marketing is now more of a value driven game and a political game. One has to be a good marketer and a good political schemer.

On a different note the Journal of Market-Focused Management (2009:Vol 3:22) said international marketing and globalization had brought foreign problems and solutions onto our doorsteps, they brought good and bad, benefits and disasters. They further elaborated that foreign language competence was not a choice but a tool of trade for success in the globalised market. One also had to understand international relations and trading blocs as well as local and international Trade Promotion Organisations for success. The Journal of Strategic Marketing (2009:Vol 2:24) said ethical marketing, value marketing and solutions based marketing now drives the firm into the future. It further said firms should be prepared to leave traditional Western high cost locations and relocate to the Far East, like China, Taiwan, South Korea, to take advantage of market realities and as a survival and competitiveness move and purchase from these locations to take advantage of good prices. Many other relevant websites were scoured to support this research and these are reflected on our References.

FINDINGS

Our findings from the different and diverse organizations we investigated and literature review conducted were very interesting and eye opening. The research revealed that successful and professional procurement is the beginning of successful marketing, a portfolio of satisfied customers, gaining new customers, repeat business, customer retention, price competitiveness, uninterrupted production runs, realization of economies of scale, good stakeholder relations, profitability, budgetary mileage, value for money purchases, customer goodwill, brand development, corporate reputation and credibility. Before starting the data gathering, it is a good idea to review your current understanding of the market place and its elements and identify potential information gaps and priorities. It is also worth identifying recent changes in the market place and unusual behaviour as clues to where to focus information gathering efforts. In looking at the market place, plan to understand where the powerful points of leverage are and understand how pressure can be applied within the market to fundamentally change market factors e.g. supplier, technology, capacity, price, cost. Plan to complete a 3-way check of key information with colleagues and industry sources, and plan enquiries to understand the market from all perspectives. Sources of information in purchasing are very similar to Supplier Research activities, and include: Patents , press and industry associations, company reports and brochures, plant tours and company visits, negotiation sessions, history, contracts, agreements, formal & testing inquiries (RFI/PQQ), planned interviews, former employees, financial analysts (JP Morgan, CSFB etc), their competitors and suppliers, your colleagues, the Internet (Google Finance, One Source etc). The prime function of any embassy is to service the interests of the its government. A secondary function is to serve the interests of its citizens (but the government always comes first). Embassies answer queries; provide documents, passports, visas for travelers, with preferences given to its citizens. They receive useful income in return for some services that help to cover costs, as maintaining many embassies all over the world is quite expensive. They check the bona fides of travelers to protect a country by denying access to it from criminals and terrorists (also from lunatics - quite a few visit embassies). Besides extending services to people, any embassy gathers information of any kind that may be of service to its nation. The embassy is headed by an ambassador who represents the government and advises the wishes of the country he represents to the local government of the nation in which the embassy resides. To best serve the government, the ambassador needs to be kept (reasonably) fully informed about government secrets and policy and this is accomplished by use of secure coded communications including material dispatched in the diplomatic bag. An embassy is like a miniature nation (as it represents one), and needs to be fully functioning. It has its own 'army' (security section), economic/marketing section, travel agency etc. The stand alone building, land, paid for floor area if in a high-rise building, even though they are in a foreign nation, are all considered by tradition to be territory belonging to the embassy's nation. On embassy ground, the laws of the country of origin apply and not the laws of the foreign nation around it.

SELECTING QUALIFIED VENDORS

This is a very demanding and scientific exercise which is done to maximize benefit and minimize risk in purchasing. Once a list of potential vendors has been developed, begin evaluating each supplier's capabilities. Obtaining a Dun & Bradstreet financial report ('running a D&B') is a good place to start. However, a D&B contains only publicly available information or information that the vendor chooses to provide. Some D&Bs also include brief profiles of key management personnel and historical information on the company. Buyers can also check with local Better Business Bureaus. Organisations can also ask potential suppliers to supply their audited accounts. Harvard Business School's Baker Library offers many financial databases through a PIN login at http://www.library.hbs.edu/. There are a number of guidelines for vendor selection: Investigate a vendor's financial stability, check bank references, if time permits and the supplier is a public corporation, obtain a current annual report, find out how long the vendor has been in business, find out who are the vendor's primary customers and ask for and check references, tour the vendor's facilities, if possible, does the facility appear prosperous? Does the vendor use state-of-the art technology? Is the vendor really interested in doing business with the your organisation? Ensure vendor partners have been pre-qualified. These steps should narrow the field to the three to five vendors who will be asked to bid on the particular product or service. Vendor selection and evaluation is a process that can take some time and energy depending on the product or service, but is well worth the effort when the vendor chosen is competitively priced and responsive to the needs of the University. The first step in selecting vendors is often research, particularly if the product or service has not been purchased before. There are a number of tools available for this initial phase: use library references such as the Thomas Register or Moody's Industrials, Check the Internet. For procurement related websites see Helpful and Interesting Web Sites, consult the Yellow Pages for local suppliers, consult trade publications, directories, vendor catalogues, and professional journals, talk to salespersons, talk to colleagues in other institutions who might have purchased a similar product or service

PREPARING AND EVALUATING A BID

Bidding goods and services is a useful process for several reasons. The bidding process: allows the buyer to "comparison shop" for the best pricing and service, allows the buyer to make an informed and objective choice among potential vendors, encourages competition among vendors, gives the buyer a standard for comparing price, quality, and service, gives the buyer a list of qualified vendors for future bids. Depending on the commodity, educational pricing, based on GSA (General Services Administration) pricing may be available. If a vendor offers GSA pricing or educational pricing based on GSA pricing, take it. You won't do better.

The bid process begins with the buyer developing a set of specifications or objectives.

The buyer must do some homework, and be able to define the requirements exactly. The buyer can consult colleagues, technical personnel, trade manuals, and vendors for assistance in developing specifications. The buyer then communicates the requirements to the selected vendors by a written Request for Quotation (RFQ) or a Request for Proposal (RFP). The RFQ process is designed to identify the vendor who can meet the buyer's requirements for the best price. The RFQ should be used for bidding familiar, standard items. Price, delivery and inventory are usually the most important elements of the RFQ. The RFQ should contain ALL the information necessary for the vendor to submit a valid quote: the product(s) should be described in detail, specifications should be clear, concise and complete, quantity, quality requirements, packaging, F.O.B. point, payment terms, and warranty, delivery and, inventory requirements should all be included in the RFQ. An RFP should be used for bidding services such as consulting, advertising, publication, maintenance, and computer programming. **The RFP usually begins with a statement of purpose or goals and objectives - what the buyer hopes to accomplish. The RFP:** should clearly define an acceptable level of performance for the vendor and a definite time frame for achieving this goal, should ask the vendor to describe the qualifications of those individuals who may be involved in implementing the goals and objectives of the RFP, should ask for all of the information contained in an RFQ (see above) but also can ask for input from the vendors. The vendors might be asked how they would meet a specific objective, what unique contributions they would make toward achieving the goals outlined in the proposal, and what alternative proposals they would offer. The vendors might also be asked to solve specific problems concerning time constraints, new technology, or on-the-job training for end users. **"How" is as important as "how much."**

Tips on preparing a bid (RFQ or RFP):

The buyer needs sufficient time to prepare a good bid and the vendors need sufficient time to respond (two to four weeks). All vendors should receive **identical** copies of the RFQ or RFP and any subsequent changes in the bid specification. Specify a deadline for submitting **all** bids. If the deadline is extended for one vendor, it must be extended for all. All vendors should be notified in writing if the bid specifications change. If the changes are substantial, it may be necessary to extend the submission deadline. All vendors should be notified of the extension in writing. If the buyer receives a number of questions about the bid, the buyer should consider holding a **pre-bid conference**. The buyer will have an opportunity to clarify the RFQ or RFP for all the vendors and no vendor will have the unfair advantage of additional information. When the bids are received, the buyer should sign, date and indicate the time that each is received. All competitive bids are confidential and should never be used as a bargaining tool.

Tips on Evaluating bids:

Take the time to review the bids carefully. Narrow the field by determining which vendors are "responsive". A "responsive" bid provides ALL the information asked for and addresses ALL the issues in the RFQ or RFP. Eliminate bidders who are unresponsive. Look carefully at proposed prices. Be wary of a vendor who substantially underbids his competitors. He may be 'low-balling" to win the bid but the quality of his product could suffer or he might be unable to meet the delivery requirements. A substantially lower price might also indicate that the vendor has misunderstood or misinterpreted the requirements. If appropriate, obtain and evaluate samples. If the bidding is close, ask for extended warranties (if appropriate) and compare prices. Consider the vendors' past performances, after-sale support and services, technology, and the creativity used to meet the buyer's requirements or objectives.

NEGOTIATION TECHNIQUES

Negotiating successfully takes skill and practice and should result in a win - win situation for both the buyer and the seller. Good negotiators: do their homework, clearly understand their requirements and objectives, develop strategies, never lose sight of their goals, know where they can afford to compromise and where they cannot, make sure their negotiating teams have whatever expertise (technical, financial, legal) is needed to increase the chances for a successful settlement, make an effort to anticipate the vendor's strategy and to determine what the vendor hopes to gain from the negotiation process.

Seven Recommendations for Purchasing Strategy

Increasing demands to cut costs while delivering innovation are putting enormous pressure on purchasing departments. Researchers in multinationals and universities in the USA, Europe and Asia have taken the lead in mastering this complex balancing act. Purchasing in low-cost countries is an important lever for cost savings. Manufacturers should first become familiar with local suppliers by assigning them orders for production in emerging markets. Orders can then be given for exporting parts to developed markets. To build up a qualified supplier base as quickly as possible, manufacturers should encourage existing suppliers to produce in low-cost countries. We also recommend supporting local suppliers in their development. Renault, for example, assisted its suppliers in Romania in areas such as engineering, quality, finance and even management. To minimize currency risks, avoid supplier bottlenecks, and ensure favorable purchasing conditions, manufacturers should develop a global supplier footprint strategy with a decision-making framework for Purchasing. The framework could stipulate, for example, purchasing volumes in certain currency regions. VW has developed guidelines that require increasing purchasing volumes in U.S, dollar-based economies. That is why more than half of the purchasing volume for the new Jetta/Bora is from Mexico or other U.S. dollar countries. Manufacturers should build up their relationships with suppliers to ensure continuing access to new technologies, while also strengthening their own innovation process. BMW, for example, fuels its innovation process by collecting ideas from suppliers through an online platform. These ideas are then evaluated and put into practice, where appropriate. Along with technical levers like standardization, manufacturers should increasingly integrate with suppliers to accelerate cost reduction efforts. In 2005, Volkswagen kicked off two new cross-functional initiatives for future and current program sourcing. Due to these initiatives, Purchasing and Engineering have joint responsibilities, and suppliers are heavily involved. Toyota has gone one step further, creating a division responsible only for advising suppliers and implementing cost reduction measures. Manufacturers should continue to move toward standardized modules and components. Furthermore, they should frontload their development efforts to increase product reliability and durability. Engineering departments should be arranged globally, with decision-making authority on a global level. Here, too, Toyota leads the field, as it has separated module development from vehicle development. By doing this, modules are developed independently from vehicles and can be used in multiple vehicle platforms. This creates economies of scale and dramatically reduces quality problems. While manufacturers are beginning to reap the benefits of globalization strategies, they cannot rest on their laurels. They must continue to align their structures to the international market. To this end, global Purchasing should be organized by product group. The organization should have common regional structures and be able to make global decisions. The interface with Engineering must especially be improved. GM did this by implementing joint target agreements for its Engineering and Purchasing board members. At BMW, one board member even holds both Engineering and Purchasing responsibility to facilitate cross-functional decision making. There is no substitute for qualified and experienced purchasing people. Nowadays success or failure is mainly determined by the quality of people that firms employ. The sophistication of your staff determines their ability to exploit supply markets and drive the firm into the future. The biggest liability for any organization is unqualified people. If a purchasing department or division is run by unqualified people, then confusion follows naturally. Unqualified people may seem cheap and easy to exploit but are a strategic disaster. Organisations that employ highly qualified people and pay them handsomely actually save much more than those that employ low caliber and cheap staff, research all over the world confirms this. Purchasing spends about 60 to 70% of any organisation's total expenditure. Just imagine what this means with billions of dollars worth of purchases taking place, if this is not done professionally. One common mistake which a lot of organizations make is to employ a general business graduate who has not specialised in purchasing. This is an accident in waiting and a dangerous pitfall. If this happens then the organization should sponsor the generalists to do professional purchasing courses like CIPS or to do a masters degree in purchasing part time. In fact the biggest problem facing the modern enterprise is ignorance and dishonesty and not a shortage of money, land, plant and equipment, capital or any other factor of production. Ignorance creates all other problems while expertise pre-empts and solves problems and pitfalls. This the same scenario in both the private and public sectors. Ignorance and dishonesty destroys corporate goodwill and reputation through costly mistakes. Let us now look at the quality of purchasing programs in universities. What perceptual factors distinguish one purchasing program from another? Are there differences between the perceptions of academics and practitioners concerning the status and performance of purchasing programs? Practitioners judge the quality of a purchasing program by the reputation of the faculty at the institution and the reputation of the curriculum. Not only do academies view these two criteria as valuable, but they add the research reputation of the institution to their set of useful criteria. With respect to faculty reputation, significant differences of opinion exist between practitioners and academics. For both groups the purchasing curriculum is judged by the content of the courses offered and not the number of courses offered in the program. Finally, if a school wants a successful purchasing program, it should stress job placement success. Well positioned companies are mindful of three decisive factors when it comes to optimizing Purchasing: strategic fit, comprehensiveness and application. To ensure strategic fit, business decisions in Purchasing must complement other functional areas. The introduced steps must also be comprehensive enough to generate a substantial impact such as improving the cost position over the long-term. Finally, the measures taken must be stringently applied and constantly monitored to ensure their success. It is extremely important to understand the correct meaning of strategic fit and I will proceed to explain this.

VALUES AND NORMS OF ETHICAL BEHAVIOR

The following values are universally applicable in the purchasing profession; members will operate and conduct their decisions and actions based on the following values: Honesty/Integrity, maintaining an unimpeachable standard of integrity in all their business relationships both inside and outside the organizations in which they are employed; professionalism, fostering the highest standards of professional competence amongst those for whom they are responsible, responsible management, optimizing the use of resources for which they are responsible so as to provide the maximum benefit to their employers; serving the Public Interest, not using their authority of office for personal benefit, rejecting and denouncing any business practice that is improper; conformity to the Laws. In Terms of: the laws of the country in which they practice; the Institute's or Corporation's Rules and Regulations; contractual obligations. Purchasing professionals are expected to observe the following cardinal rules:- to consider first, the interest of one's organization in all transactions and to carry out and believe in its established policies, to be receptive to competent counsel from one's colleagues and be guided by such counsel without impairing the responsibility of one's office, to buy without prejudice, seeking to obtain the maximum value for each dollar of expenditure, to strive for increased knowledge of the materials and processes of manufacture, and to establish practical procedures for the performance of one's responsibilities, to participate in professional development programs so that one's purchasing knowledge and performance are enhanced, to subscribe to and work for honesty in buying and selling and to denounce all forms of improper business practice, to accord a prompt and courteous reception to all who call on a legitimate business mission, to abide by and to encourage others to practice the Professional Code of Ethics of the Purchasing Management Association, to counsel and assist fellow purchasers in the performance of their duties and to cooperate with all organizations and individuals engaged in activities which enhance the development and standing of purchasing and materials management.

RULES OF CONDUCT

In applying these rules of conduct, members should follow guidance set out below: any personal interest which may impinge or might reasonably be deemed by others to impinge on a member's impartiality in any matter relevant to his or her duties should be immediately declared to his or her employer. The confidentiality of information received in the course of duty must be respected and should not be used for personal gain; information given in the course of duty should be true and fair and not designed to mislead. While considering the advantages to the member's employer of maintaining a continuing relationship with a supplier, any arrangement which might prevent the effective operation of fair competition should be avoided. To preserve the image and integrity of the member, employer and the profession, business gifts other than items of small intrinsic value should not be accepted. Reasonable hospitality is an accepted courtesy of a business relationship. The frequency and nature of gifts or hospitality accepted should not be allowed whereby the recipient might be or might be deemed by others to have been influenced in making a business decision as a consequence of accepting such hospitality or gifts. No member shall knowingly participate in acts of discrimination or harassment towards any person that he or she has business relations with. Members shall recognize their responsibility to environmental issues consistent with their corporate goals or missions. When in doubt on the interpretation of these rules of conduct, members should refer to the Ethics Committee of their Institute or Corporation.

HOW TO DETECT CORRUPTION IN PURCHASING

It is reasonably easy to detect employees who may be engaged in unethical business dealings and enjoying dirty or unearned income illegally and to the detriment of the organization. Management psychology is used to deal with these improprieties. The following are symptoms of corruption amongst purchasing and related employees:- employee lives a princely and kingly life well beyond his/her income (income and known private life put together) – acquires expensive and unique villas and mansions, flashy cars, expensive furniture, massive amassing of wealth, shocking investments, expensive international holidays, engaging in grandiose and prestige projects which are out of this world and heavy investment in the property market, refusal to go on leave, unwillingness to work with highly qualified and sophisticated subordinates, refusing transfers and promotions, frustrating and eliminating other employees in the department, always working late, on weekends and holidays, unethical entertainment, putting children in very expensive schools, colleges and universities, a funny lifestyle for members of the whole family, including the extended family and always creating unnecessary and expensive foreign trips. To deal with and to pre-empt this kind of problem a firm has to adopt the following, among other measures:- have a Code of Purchasing Ethics which bans receiving of any gifts by employees, impose compulsory leave of at least one month for all employees, without exception, every year, make it a condition of employment that employees declare their wealth in full at the end of each year, employee rotation wherever possible, switch suppliers when you can, supplier visits by the CEO, COO or Financial Director to sound suppliers, anonymous suggestion boxes, introduce a whistleblower fund which is very attractive, introduce an employee share option scheme; this increases employees interest in the firm and they would be bound to expose any employee who is unethical as this reduces "their profit." Lastly payment of international market related salaries and benefits to purchasing people to stem the temptation to be corrupted by suppliers

CONCLUSIONS AND RECOMMENDATIONS

Our conclusion and recommendations are that the future for procurement is a mixed bag, and predicting it is a bit of a difficult jigsaw puzzle as too many factors determine its fate. It cannot be overemphasized that the procurement profession will be requiring professionals with a multiplicity of competences to cope with the complexities of the global village and the internationalization challenges of the supply market. It is no longer practical to employ diploma holders to run procurement departments. Diploma holders will be inadequate and very risky to be in charge of procurement for medium and large organisations. Diploma holders will also need to enroll for degrees covering shipping, customs clearing, international logistics and forwarding, which also cover the critical issue of e-business and key foreign languages. Foreign languages may need to be introduced in international business and international purchasing management degrees so that managers and officers find it easy to deal with key countries like China, Germany, Spain (languages like Mandarin, Germany, French, Spanish). E-government is also an innovation being adopted by many countries to support the international business effort. Oman is a leader in this respect in the Middle East. Tomorrow's procurement is going to be driven by the following critical factors:- embassies becoming centres of supply market analysis to feed local corporates with market intelligence for capital equipment, raw materials, inputs, identifying export markets, identifying investment opportunities and lastly building good political relations for the country. The embassies must change their strategic thrust from that of being centres of political rhetoric and excellence to being centres of business excellence, emphasizing business issues as well as political issues. The USA has got its largest embassy in China with 700 staffers because of the strategic economic importance and dominance of China and the Far East as the market of the future – this embassy services the rest of the Far East. The USA has now set up Chinese Language Centres in America and English Language Centres in China as a way of promoting business through language competence. In developed countries the reason, criteria and purpose of setting up embassies is potential business opportunities in host countries and this should be the line of thinking in all countries and get correctly qualified people to be appointed to ambassadorial positions – with those with international business qualifications and experience dominating diplomatic postings and appointments as they have the capacity to fully exploit business opportunities as opposed to non-business graduates. Ambassadors may be non-business graduates but let them be supported by relevant business graduates with international business experience as their diplomats or trade promotion officers; that way the countries would get value out of these embassies. Relevant ambassadorial and diplomatic appointments should be part of national marketing and business strategy in every country. There is an urgent need for the elevation of the procurement function by organizations to Board of Directorship and top most senior management level for better strategic representation. Buying from world low cost centres like the Far East and Asia (China, Thailand, Taiwan, Malaysia, India, Singapore, Hong Kong) and taking advantage of trade agreement duty reduction and duty free incentives and concessions created by Governments will be the best option. Engaging in toll manufacturing whenever beneficial and appropriate is recommended, ICT competency & e-business competence (online buying and selling), establishment of comprehensive websites and posting product requirements for suppliers to see and respond electronically just as is the case with marketing, the requirement for proactive and aggressive procurement techniques like the attendance of trade fairs and exhibitions, participating in inward and outward buyer and seller missions, dealing with embassies, lobby and advocacy should be at the centre of each company's tool kit of strategies to fully engage governments, trade promotion bodies and influential NGOs to facilitate an acceptable favourable business climate. Political aloofness does not work and procurement people need to be part of national policy making directly or through effective proxies like members of Parliament, Government Ministers and other influential figures, carry out regular audits of procurement activities to keep practices under control and prevent abuse, force all procurement and other staff in your organization to go on leave at least once a year for at least one month without exception and as policy. Also do strategic transfers and have suggestion boxes and whistle blower funds in place to detect fraud and unethical behavior before it is too late and pay market related salaries and benefits so that people enjoy legal paid income rather than be tempted to pay themselves through bribes and other unethical activities. Purchasing people want good lives just like any other person in this world. Deprivation and grinding poverty is the mother of all corruption and there is no substitute for good salaries and conditions. Purchasing Committees should be appointed made up of a cross section of experts.

REFERENCES

1. Dobler et al Purchasing and Supply Management 1996 McGraw Hill, New York
2. Glimour P International Journal of Physical distribution and logistics management 1999
3. Ronald H et al Logistics and Supply Chain Management 1999 Prentice Hall New Jersey
4. Sharma.SC Materials Management and Material Handling: 3rd edition
5. Shimaguchi, M., (1978). Marketing Channels in Japan: Ann Arbor
6. Bailey et al Purchasing Principles and Management 7th edition Pitman London UK
7. MJ Hugo et al Supply Chain Management. 2004 Van Schaik Publishers.
8. Dobler et al Purchasing and Supply Management. 1996 McGraw Hill, New York
9. Best Practice Purchasing: Journal of Supply Chain Management, USA, Volume 3, 2009:p15.
10. Zimtrade (1999). Trade Secrets, the Export Answer Book, Zimtrade
11. G. Albanum (1994). International Marketing and Export Management Addison – Westy Publishers
12. Baron B., Harris K. Services Marketing, Texts and Cases. Palgrave
13. Bake M.B. (2003). The Marketing Plan Handbook, Prentice Hall.
14. Peter J. P., Donnelly J.H. (2007). McGraw-Hill/Irwin
15. Quester P., McGuiggan R. (2005). Marketing, Creating and Delivering Value. McGraw-Hill Australia.
16. Aaker DA (4th Ed). Strategic Market Management, John Widely & Sons, Inc.6,p.100. (1995)
17. Dillon WR;Madden TJ;et al Marketing Research, The McGraw-Hill Companies Inc.2,p.25.(1993).
18. Charles W. L. Hill, (2009),International Business, Competing in the Global Marketplace,7th Edition, McGraw-Hill.
19. Kerin A. R., Peterson R.A. (2007). Strategic Marketing Problems, Cases and Comments: 11th Edition, Pearson Education International.
20. Hitt M.A., Hoskisson R.A.,Ireland R.D., (2007), Cengage Learning.
21. Cateora, P. R., (1993) International Marketing: Irwin.
22. Hanink, D.M., (1994). The International Economy, A Geographical Perspective: John Wiley & Sons, Inc.
23. Porter, M.E., (1990). The Competitive Advantage of Nations: Free Press, New York.
24. The Emirates Centre for Strategic Studies and Research (2003). Human Resources in a Knowledge-Based Economy, Abu Dhabi, United Arab Emirates
25. Kerin, A.R.,Peterson, R.A. (2007). Strategic Marketing Problems, Cases and Comments (11th Edition):Pearson Prentice Hall.
26. Christopher, M. (1987) in Baker, M. J. (ed.) the Marketing Book: Heinemann
27. Czinkota, M. E., and Ronkainen, I. A., (1990) International Marketing: Dryden.
28. Keegan, W. J., (1989), Global Marketing Management: Prentice-Hall.
29. Kotler, P., (1988) Marketing Management; Analysis, Planning, Implementation and Control: Prentice-Hall.

30. Barbican, S., (2009). Total value and political lobby and advocacy. *The European Journal of Marketing*, 30 (3), 12-14.
31. Bernard S., & Smith G. (2009). Modern industrial marketing model. *The Journal of Industrial Marketing Management*, 44 (3), 18-20.
32. Thomson J., & Schumpeter T.H., (2009). International marketing benchmarks in the modern era. *The Journal of International Marketing*, 25 (2), 13-14.
33. Williamson T., (2009). International marketing and globalization challenges. *The Journal of Market-Focused Management*, 33 (3), 22-24.
34. Pitt K.T., & Stevenson M., (2009). Ethics and value marketing. *The Journal of Strategic Marketing*, 26 (2), 24-26.
35. World Economic Analysis Report: Retrieved 27 February 2010 from http://econ.worldbank.org/WBSITE/EXTERNAL/EXTDEC/0,,contentMDK:2221 6733~pagePK:64165401~piPK:64165026~theSitePK:469372,00.html
36. Shimaguchi, M., (1978). Marketing Channels in Japan: Ann Arbor
37. Barbican, S., (2009). Total value and political lobby and advocacy. *The European Journal of Marketing*, 30 (3), 12-14.
38. Bernard S., & Smith G. (2009). Modern industrial marketing model. *The Journal of Industrial Marketing Management*, 44 (3), 18-20.
39. Thomson J., & Schumpeter T.H., (2009). International marketing benchmarks in the modern era. *The Journal of International Marketing*, 25 (2), 13-14.
40. Williamson T., (2009). International marketing and globalization challenges. *The Journal of Market-Focused Management*, 33 (3), 22-24.
41. Pitt K.T., & Stevenson M., (2009). Ethics and value marketing. *The Journal of Strategic Marketing*, 26 (2), 24-26.
42. World Economic Analysis Report: Retrieved 5 December 2009 from http://econ.worldbank.org/WBSITE/EXTERNAL/EXTDEC/0,,contentMDK:2221 6733~pagePK:64165401~piPK:64165026~theSitePK:469372,00.html
43. Glimour P. International Journal of Physical distribution and logistics management 1999, p9.
44. Ronald H et al Logistics and Supply Chain Management. 1999 Prentice Hall New Jersey
45. Doing Business With Oman: Retrieved 03 April 2010 from http://oman.nlembassy.org/economy_and_trade/doing_business_with
46. A Guide to Doing Business With Oman: Retrieved 03 April 2010 from Retrieved from http://ocodubai.com/aboutus.htm
47. DFAT Oman Fact Sheet: Retrieved 04 April 2010 from http://www.dfat.gov.au/geo/fs/oman.pdf
48. Summary of Zimbabwe Trade Reports: Retrieved 02 April 2010 from http://www.afdevinfo.com/htmlreports/org/org_15159.html
49. Export Opportunities for South Africa Abroad: Retrieved 01 April 2010 from http://www.dti.gov.za
50. National Public Procurement: Retrieved 27 February 2010 from:*www.etenders.gov.ie*
51. EU Public Procurement: Retrieved 27 February 2010 from: *http://simap.eurpoa.eu*

52. Forum on Public Procurement in Ireland: Retrieved 27 February 2010 from: www.fpp.ie
53. WTO site on the 1994 Government Procurement Agreement (GPA) Retrieved 27 February 2010 from:*http:www.wto.org/govt/agrmnt.html*
54. Tendering: Retrieved 27 February 2010 from: http://www.etenders.gov.ie/guides/Guides_show.aspx?id=2745
55. Tenders: Retrieved 27 February 2010 from http://www.etenders.gov.ie/guides/Guides_show.aspx?id=271
56. Treasury Procurement Guidelines: Retrieved 27 February 2010 from :http://www.treasury.tas.gov.au/domino/dtf/dtf.nsf/v-ti/pc
57. Purchasing: Retrieved 27 February 2010 from :http://www.purchasing.tas.gov.au/buyingforgovernment/getpage.jsp?uid=F5E74 B20DEF74E68CA256C750016BC87
58. Procurement: Retrieved 27 February 2010 from: http